Empire and Revolution

*The publisher gratefully acknowledges the generous
contribution to this book provided by the
General Endowment Fund of the Associates
of the University of California Press.*

Empire and Revolution

The Americans in Mexico since the Civil War

JOHN MASON HART

University of California Press

BERKELEY   LOS ANGELES   LONDON

University of California Press
Berkeley and Los Angeles, California

University of California Press, Ltd.
London, England

© 2002 by the Regents of the University of California

Library of Congress Cataloging-in-Publication Data

Hart, John M. (John Mason), 1935–

    Empire and revolution : the Americans in Mexico since the Civil
War / John Mason Hart.
      p. cm.
    Includes bibliographical references and index.
    ISBN 0-520-22324-1 (cloth : alk. paper)
    1. Americans—Mexico—History.   2. United States—Relations—
Mexico. 3. Mexico—Relations—United States. 4. Investments,
American—Mexico. 5. Nationalism—Mexico—History. I. Title.
F1392.A5 H37   2001
972'00413—dc21   2001027815

Manufactured in the United States of America

10 09 08 07 06 05 04 03 02 01

10 9 8 7 6 5 4 3 2 1

To the Mexican widows of Veracruz and Chihuahua,
and the American widows of World War I

Do you think that after doing all that you have done, you still have a right to love? That life's law can be changed now so that with everything else you will have love too? You lost your innocence in one world, you can't reclaim it in another. Maybe you had your garden. I had mine, too, my little paradise. Now we have both lost. Try to remember, for you can't find in me what you have lost forever and by your own action. I don't know where you came from, or what you did. I only know that your life lost before I knew you what you made mine lose later: the dream, the innocence. We will neither of us ever be the same again.

Carlos Fuentes, *The Death of Artemio Cruz*

Contents

Illustrations follow pages 212 and 436

Acknowledgments

Many people merit my thanks for making this book possible, especially the archivists upon whose expertise I depended. There are also many institutions and personal associates whose assistance helped to shape this book. They include the National Endowment for the Humanities, for a senior research fellowship; the Shelby Cullom Davis Center for Historical Studies at Princeton University, for a Davis research fellowship; the U.S.-Mexico Center at the University of California, San Diego, for a visiting research fellowship; and the University of Houston, for multiple grants, including more than one faculty development leave.

Professors Tom O'Brien of the University of Houston history department and Paul B. Hart of the history department of Southwest Texas State University read the manuscript and offered critical input, while Lisa Stross of the Texas State Historical Commission offered important research assistance. Rebecca Frazier, Rose Anne White, Sheila Levine, Kristen Cashman, and Juliane Brand of the University of California Press applied their professionalism to the manuscript, seeing it through the complicated publication process. Pauline Warren contributed ideas and indexing, while Mark Saka, Norman Caulfield, Cristina Rivera, and Terry Rugeley added the inspiration and complexity of their deeds and thoughts, as did many of my graduate students. The input of companions and friends are almost intangible, but Mary Hart, Colin MacLachlan, Bill Beezley, Joseph Glatthaar, Andrew Chesnut, and Sue Kellogg contributed in myriad ways.

Mexico.

Introduction
Imperial Ambition

In 1883 a group of the most prominent capitalists and politicians of the United States gathered with their Mexican counterparts in the banquet hall of the Waldorf Astoria Hotel in New York. The cabinet members and financiers took their seats at the long dining table. Facing each other at the left and the right of the head chair were General Porfirio Díaz and Ulysses S. Grant, both former presidents. Collis P. Huntington, one of the leading railroad industrialists and financiers of his time, took the head chair. In the meeting that ensued, the Mexican officials presented their case for pervasive American participation in the development of their economy, and the American investors bargained for access to Mexico's abundant natural resources. The program of free trade, foreign investment, and privatization of the Mexican countryside that they agreed upon that evening continues to resonate. The benefits and detriments of the agreements that they struck have influenced the relationship between the peoples and governments of the United States and Mexico to this day. It was the Americans' first step in a progression that has determined the relations between the United States and the nations of the Third World in the twenty-first century.

The story of the American experience in Mexico is one of intense interaction between two peoples and the relationship that developed between two nations as a result. Mexico was the first of the many legally recognized but economically and militarily weak nations that Americans encountered after the Civil War. Between 1865 and 2000, when this narrative concludes, the contacts and connections between Americans and Mexicans were marked not only by intervention and revolution, but by accommodation and cooperation as well. The history that unfolded during those 135 years offers critical insights into how the United States became a global empire, the impulses behind neo-liberalism, the growth of American culture in Latin America, Asia, and Africa, and the process of globalization.

Americans entered Mexico well before they developed the capacity to exercise a powerful influence in the farther reaches of the world, but the most powerful among them already had a vision of world leadership. From the beginnings of the nineteenth century until the present era, the citizens of the United States attempted to export their unique "American dream" to Mexico. Their vision incorporated social mobility, Protestant values, a capitalist free market, a consumer culture, and a democracy of elected representation.

The first stage of American involvement in Mexico began just after the Civil War. The economic and political leaders of the United States, led by an elite group of financiers and industrialists, envisioned a greater American nation—in some cases one that included Mexico and western Canada—that would have cultural, economic, and political hegemony over the peoples of the Caribbean, the Pacific, and Central and South America while offering an example of cultural, economic, and political success to the rest of the world. Sensing the opportunities for wealth and power that their southern neighbor offered, U.S. elites sought to extend their interests into Mexico by employing the strategies that were so successful for them in the American West. Following the establishment of initial mercantile and financial relations, they began by developing Mexico's infrastructure. The start of Porfirio Díaz's regime marked the second stage of U.S. involvement in Mexico— the active construction of railroads. The railroads allowed these men to gain access to Mexico's rich resources and encouraged other Americans to settle there. The participatory nature of American society soon added tens of thousands of immigrants to the U.S. presence in Mexico, deepening and broadening the influence of American culture.

During the Porfiriato the Americans sought ownership of Mexico's natural resources, and they also began to settle there as colonists. After the Mexican Revolution began in 1910, these Americans found themselves at the mercy of rebels and nationalists who destroyed property and appropriated land. The seizures continued after the revolution ended in 1920, and by 1940 Americans, both residents and absentee investors, had lost most of their material assets in Mexico. As the twentieth century progressed, the ambitions of U.S. citizens in Mexico changed. The economic pressures of World War II prompted Americans not only to seek cheap and efficient immigrant labor but also to reinvest in Mexico itself. After the war they increasingly accepted partnerships with their Mexican neighbors that at least provided access to the resources in Mexico that they had once owned. New contingents of students, teachers, artists, and retirees replaced the businesspeople and the "boomers" who had formed colonies before the revolution.

The evolving patterns of American behavior in Mexico have reflected and usually anticipated the interactions of U.S. citizens in other Latin American and Third World societies. By the end of the twentieth century, U.S. interests had stretched to Eastern Europe and Russia, and the business and technological juggernaut envisioned by the American elite in the 1860s had tied Mexico to their interests through fiber optics and international electrical power grids.

Despite this long history of interaction, the vast majority of Americans maintained a remarkable indifference to their neighbor. In consequence, elite interests in the United States disproportionately influenced U.S. foreign policy toward Mexico. A pervasive American belief in their personal superiority over Mexicans and an entrenched economic insularity created that sense of distance and continued to prevail in the last decade of the twentieth century despite the development of closer business and political ties. In spite of the intense and long-standing relationship between Mexico and the United States, the domestic "War on Drugs" and working-class Mexican immigration, documented and undocumented, dominated public awareness of Mexico. The indifference of the great majority of Americans has left bilateral affairs in the hands of economic and political elites who are less than representative of American diversity, especially in the development of democratic institutions and respect for Mexican sovereignty.

This book addresses the nature of U.S. involvement in foreign countries for American readers and the nature of U.S. influence in Mexico for Mexican readers. It does so by explaining the activities of individuals and businesspeople who as a collectivity constituted much of the American influence in Mexico. The Mexican reader is all too familiar with the loss of Texas, the causes and outcome of their war with the United States, the American filibustering raids of the nineteenth century, and the invasions of Veracruz and Chihuahua in the twentieth century. Indeed, the overwhelming evidence points to a compulsion on the part of the American elites toward external wealth, global power, and deeper personal contacts with other peoples, often in order to "save" them. This compulsion was first expressed internationally in Mexico.

This book will note political and military events after 1865, but with less emphasis than traditional diplomatic and political histories offer. Here I will concentrate on the more hidden but history-making interactions between Americans and Mexicans in Mexico. As a part of this project I personally visited the rural areas of every state in Mexico and virtually all of the pueblos and estates mentioned in the text. The research and writing of this work was a twelve-year process, and the reader should be advised that I have resisted accepting as absolutes the unsettling similarities that have emerged in recent years between the strategies of the contemporary American and Mexican regimes and those of the period before the revolution of 1910. The emphasis is still the search for money and power, but it focuses on industrial production for export to the United States, and it is no longer a one-way street. Today the Mexicans exert an enormous and growing cultural and economic influence in the United States.

Because Mexico provided the first setting for an American encounter outside the territory that now comprises the forty-eight contiguous states, the American experience in that country offers a unique opportunity to gain insight into the nature of U.S. power. Because Mexico is still intimately associated with the United States, our involvement there allows us to assess new events and measure long-term effects. Manifest Destiny, World Wars I and II, and the ratification of NAFTA are all part of the story, but the depth of the American commitment to Mexico transcends moments of economic and political drama. Throughout the 135 years between 1865 and 2000, immigrants from the United States persisted in maintaining their interests and lives in Mexico. They faced hardships on the cold, windswept lands of the north, disease in the tropics, and revolutionary nationalism. The continued presence of the Americans, almost one million strong in 2000, and that of their even more numerous descendants, who are native citizens of Mexico, remains impressive.

When the Americans began their search for opportunities in Mexico, the Mexicans were in the throes of their own civil war, which had turned into a struggle against an invading foreign power. It began as a fight between the Liberal and Conservative Parties but turned into a popular effort to expel a powerful French army and defeat Louis Napoleon's effort to establish a European-controlled monarchy in the Americas. The victorious Liberal leadership that emerged sought new economic and political vitality for their destitute country through foreign investment and immigration. Their neighbors to the north became logical, if unequal, partners in that quest.

The dramatic history of the interactions that ensued between the two peoples, including the great Mexican Revolution of 1910 and its aftermath, is now possible to tell because of declassified materials in the archives of the United States and the rich diversity of materials found in the public libraries and private collections of both countries. The period after 1947 is still shrouded by government security classifications, and therefore information is incomplete, but the historical knowledge of the previous eighty years provides us with sufficient insight to see the directions of the immediate past and the possibilities for the present and near future.

In a poignant observation, historian William Appleman Williams called Latin America the laboratory for American foreign policy.[1] In Mexico, particularly, the American elites tested a variety of approaches they have since used to extend their power and influence around the globe. Those ventures include partnerships with local elites, cooperative arrangements among multinationals, particularly in the area of finance, and interventions ranging from covert operations such as funding and equipping Díaz's overthrow of President Sebastian Lerdo de Tejada and the "equip and train" operation at Veracruz, to outright invasions such as General John Pershing's foray into Mexico. In short, the study of the Americans in Mexico explains much about the origins of globalization. What follows is the complicated story of the Americans in Mexico as a precursor of world events. Much of it has not been revealed before.

Part I

THE RISE OF AMERICAN
INFLUENCE, 1865–1876

1 Arms and Capital

During the winter and spring of 1866 we continued covertly
supplying arms and ammunition to the Liberals—sending as
many as 30,000 muskets.
General P. H. Sheridan, *Personal Memoirs*

[Juárez] was joined at El Paso by another 300 soldiers, and he
acquired ten more cannons from the United States.
Jasper Ridley, *Maximilian and Juárez*

At the end of the American Civil War, as the expanding American population began to move west in search of land and opportunity, the Mexican government was engaged in a struggle to expel the occupation forces of Napoleon III. The Liberals had gained control of Mexico in 1860, after two years of fighting the Conservative army in the Wars of the Reform. The following year France occupied Mexico in an attempt to establish an overseas empire that would not only provide markets and raw materials but also check the expansion of the United States. In 1863 the French troops, aided by the Mexican Conservative Party, reached Mexico City and proclaimed Archduke Maximilian of Austria the emperor of Mexico. The U.S. government, wary of Napoleon's ambition, was pressuring the French through diplomatic channels to leave Mexico. The Liberal government, led by President Benito Juárez, was resisting French aggression with a widespread guerrilla war. Mexico looked north, hoping for help. At the same time, the United States was looking south.

ARMS FOR MEXICO

In 1864, American observer John Austin Stevens described an interest in northern Mexico that was shared by many of his more powerful countrymen:

> A railroad from Point Isabel to Brownsville and from Matamoros . . .
> to Monterrey would turn the whole of the supply of the rich and fertile
> country into American hands. . . . The northeastern states of Mexico,
> encouraged by our sympathy, would put forth new efforts and inspired
> by the noble example of the patriots of the Rio Grande districts, would
> throw off the yoke of the [French] invaders and reassert their ancient
> liberties.
> With the rebellion [of the Confederacy] vanquished, the Union

9

reestablished, never again to be assailed, and Mexico once more a free and vigorous republic, what power or combination of powers would dare to stop the western course of Empire?[1]

This growing interest of American elites in Mexico coincided with a rapidly escalating need for aid on the part of the Mexican government. The Liberal leaders were desperate for funds, whether public or private. They realized that the Union victory in the Civil War offered them a chance to procure munitions from America, and they began their efforts to acquire military supplies by selling Mexican bonds to American investors. Mexican agents for President Juárez carried out their efforts in Boston, Hartford, Philadelphia, New York, San Francisco, Washington, D.C., and other cities with the approval of high officials in the United States government.

Primary among those who worked with American political leaders and financiers was Matías Romero, the Juárez government's minister to the United States. Romero did an exemplary job of creating sympathy for the Mexican republican cause, not only with Presidents Abraham Lincoln and Andrew Johnson but also with the business establishment of the Northeast, especially the elite merchants, bankers, and industrialists of New York City. In 1865 Hiram Barney, the port captain of New York and a merchant, attorney, and banker in the city, along with Thomas E. Stillman of the National City Bank and other leading New York financiers, agreed to consult with Romero.

> We are ready to carefully listen to your proposal to offer the people and capitalists of the United States an opportunity to loan the Mexican Republic the funds necessary to vindicate their rights and govern themselves.[2]

Some American businessmen and politicians openly anticipated the advantages that might be gained by obtaining the gratitude of the Mexican government, then in exile at Paso del Norte (now Ciudad Juárez). These leading "capitalists-merchants, shipbuilders, and manufacturers" of New York composed a core group of wealthy Americans "who furnished material to Juárez during the late war in Mexico."[3] Financiers James W. Beekman, a real estate developer, banker, and merchant, William E. Dodge and Anson Phelps of the Phelps Dodge Corporation, John Jacob Astor of the National City Bank, and Secretary of State William Henry Seward held Romero in high regard, and his endorsement of the bonds gave them salability in the rarefied air of the New York financial market and in Washington. At the same time, most American investors were willing to assume the high risks incurred with the purchase of the Mexican Liberal bonds only in return for large discounts. Some of the bonds guaranteed land and other concessions in case of default, a proviso that became highly significant. The Mexican agents immediately used the funds obtained through the bond sales to purchase arms and supplies for their military struggle. Sometimes they used the bonds to pay directly for weapons.

Dodge, who envisioned a "Young America" that would extend from the Arctic Circle to Panama, pledged his support to Romero and recommended the John W. Corlies brokerage house to Romero for the sale of bonds: "They have some resources, a good reputation, and are respectable."[4] Romero was aware of the ambition and the power of Americans like Dodge, but he needed their resources to oust the French, and he hoped for their support in rebuilding Mexico. Other powerful New York investors dealt with Romero. Among the most prominent were Ed Morgan, a cousin and business partner of J. P. Morgan, who was the heir to the Anglo-American banking empire of his father, Junius Morgan; John S. Kennedy, a correspondent banker for Morgan and a railroad financier; and William Aspinwall, the head of the Pacific Mail Steamship Company. Aspinwall was a close associate of Moses Taylor, the head of National City Bank, and one of the nation's leading sugar importers.

The group also included Beekman, David Hoadly, a son-in-law of Dodge who succeeded Aspinwall as president of the Panama Railroad, John Jacob Astor, investment banker and railroad backer Henry Clews, and New York newspaper publisher William C. Bryant. Many of these men had helped finance the Union effort against the Confederacy during the Civil War. Indeed, Romero often met with them at the Union Club, an organization dedicated to the support of President Lincoln and the Northern war effort. With Taylor, Morgan, and Kennedy leading the way, they had developed a formidable network of financiers and industrialists, who, through their competitiveness and ability to come together and cooperate, would pioneer American investments in Mexico during the 1870s.[5]

Juan Bustamante, another of Juárez's agents, enjoyed some success, especially in New York, but he fell far short of meeting the government's goals for material support. Bustamante came to New York in search of 36,000 muskets and rifles, 4,000 swords, 1,000 pistols, 18,000,000 cartridges, and 500 barrels of gunpowder. After "extensive efforts" and the assistance of port captain Barney, Bustamante sent back 8,200 muskets, 4,000 rifles, 2,500 swords, and 500 pistols—far fewer than the Liberals needed.[6]

Juárez also sent the well-connected José María Carbajal, governor of the Mexican state of Tamaulipas, to New York to raise private donations and forward munitions. Educated at Bethany College in Pennsylvania, Carbajal spoke English with fluency and knew at least a few of New York's most prominent capitalists, including Charles Stillman, the brother of Thomas E. Stillman and a leading investor in the National City Bank, and William Woodward, head of the Hanover Bank. Stillman and Woodward's New York importing firm, Woodward and Stillman, was the largest American business interest in Tamaulipas. Carbajal took advantage of the goodwill developed in the American business and political communities by Romero. He played up the idea that Mexico represented opportunity to American businessmen as they looked toward the Pacific Ocean and the future.

Carbajal granted remarkably one-sided terms to his American clients. Initially he offered some $50,000,000 in bonds that were discounted some 60 percent and backed by guarantees of 106,000 acres of agricultural, oil, and mining lands in Tamaulipas and San Luis Potosí. He authorized New York broker Daniel Woodhouse to sell the bonds without the prior approval of the Mexican authorities. General Lew Wallace, President Johnson's first emissary to Mexico, also endorsed Carbajal's efforts, giving the bonds more legitimacy. When Romero learned of the giveaway, he canceled the arrangement and attempted a recall, but he achieved only partial success. Carbajal's brief foray as head of the Mexican fund-raising effort in New York led to many of the conflicts that later became acute.

The firm of John W. Corlies continued to sell bonds for Romero throughout the financial community, using the Central Trust Company of New York, where Edmund Corlies and Kennedy served together on the executive committee of the board, for more leverage. In less than two years Jonathan N. Tifft, a member of the Corlies firm, sold a minimum of $3,000,000 in Mexican bonds at a 30 percent discount. He was authorized to sell up to $30,000,000 in bonds, and later complaints to Romero indicate that Tifft sold far more than the declared $3,000,000. Kennedy purchased a sizeable bloc of the securities.[7]

The Mexican Liberals engaged General Herman Sturm, the former quartermaster of the Indiana militia, to acquire weapons. He operated independently of the Corlies firm. Although Tifft appears to have acted in accordance with the tact and propriety of the business community at that time, Sturm was much more aggressive and often exceeded his authority in promising payment to American arms manufacturers in Mexican currency and bonds. Acting as a middleman, Sturm procured weapons and logistics and arranged their delivery to entrepôts in Mexico. Sturm bought the munitions from merchants and manufacturers with bonds and cash, whereas Tifft tended entirely to financial matters, selling bonds to members of the New York financial community. Sturm filled orders directly from Mexican generals in the field, including Porfirio Díaz in southern Mexico, who received 1,300 carbines, 1,020 small barrels of powder, and 1,700 sabers and belts in one shipment.[8] Sturm praised Díaz to his American clients and expressed his growing desire for the general to become president of Mexico. Sturm admired Díaz because he demonstrated personal strength, and he believed that Díaz shared the American ideals of political freedom, economic development, and industrial initiative more than did Juárez and Sebastián Lerdo de Tejada, who was chief justice of the Mexican Supreme Court and the de facto vice president. Both Juárez and Lerdo temporized with breaking up rural community properties and allowing foreign ownership of Mexico's communication and transportation infrastructure.

Ulysses S. Grant and his personal friends Rufus Ingalls, quartermaster general of the Army of the Potomac, and Orville E. Babcock, a civil engineer and Grant's former aide-de-camp, assisted Sturm in the acquisition of war materials for the Mexicans. Grant, Ingalls, and General John M. Scofield were close friends who shared another Mexican connection—they belonged to the Aztec Club for veterans of the Mexican War. During 1866 and early 1867 General Philip Henry Sheridan, commander of the U.S. Army units in Louisiana and Texas, and General William T. Sherman, who was in charge of the U.S. Army, allowed General Wallace to visit the border and look into the need to raise a force of Civil War veterans to help the Liberal forces. The Liberals gained quick victories against the French and the Conservatives, and Wallace's assistance was no longer needed. During the early 1870s all of the officers who worked with Sturm sought compensation from Mexico by applying for land and commercial fishing concessions.[9]

On the other side of the continent, Placido Vega, a descendant of a prestigious family of Californios, behaved just as naively—or incompetently, or dishonestly—as Carbajal and Bustamante. Juárez sent Vega, the governor of the state of Sinaloa, to San Francisco. He contracted with M. T. Vallejo, a former general in the Mexican army, and Agustín Alviso and Victor Castro, both prominent Californian landowners, for some 20,000 rifles, promising to pay $250,000 for the weapons and $10,000 in expenses. He promised them that if the contract fell through they could file a claim against the Mexican government for $600,000. The deal failed. Some 5,000 rifles were impounded at the San Francisco Customs House and the others were stored elsewhere. Meanwhile, already owing $600,000, Vega continued to seek the resources he needed.

> General Vega . . . sold lands in Mexico, purchased on credit, contracted on behalf of the Mexican government to pay interest at 2.5 percent per month, and this compounded every six months, and even entered into certain cattle transactions.[10]

The properties Vega sold consisted of "a strip of land two leagues wide [seven miles], on the eastern side of the Gulf of California, and another strip of the same width on the western side." Vega's deal violated the Mexican constitutional rule against foreign ownership of the shoreline. The property to the west extended from the Bajia San Felipe in Baja California to the American border, and to the east it reached from the Gulf north across Sonora from the twenty-ninth parallel to the international boundary. A group from San Francisco owned the eastern strip, and the western area was taken up by a consortium from Los Angeles. The quantities of arms obtained by Vega and their disposition has not been uncovered.[11]

The successful diplomatic efforts of Romero and Juárez provided a protective shield of American troops along the border between Mexico and the United States. The Americans transferred enormous quantities of arms and ammunition to the Juárez administration, which was located at El Paso del Norte. The American military personnel at nearby Fort Bliss and local businessmen received the Mexican president with open arms. Juárez "acquired ten more cannons from the United States" upon his arrival, and three hundred American men joined the Liberal forces.[12] General Sheridan described the extent of American support:

> During the winter and spring of 1866 we continued covertly supplying arms and ammunition to the Liberals—sending as many as 30,000 muskets from Baton Rouge Arsenal alone—and by mid-summer Juárez, having organized a pretty good sized army, was in possession of the whole line of the Rio Grande.[13]

The American leadership sometimes found it difficult to contain grassroots enthusiasm for the Liberals along the border. At Bagdad, Stillman's privately owned port located at the mouth of the Rio Grande, a contingent of U.S. troops crossed into Mexico and attacked the royalist garrison. They stayed on to sack the town. Secretary of State William Henry Seward convinced the president to order General Sheridan to dismiss the officer leading the troops that had gotten out of control.[14]

The amount of financial power supplied by the American supporters of the Mexican Liberal cause testifies to the combined success of Romero in stimulating their interest and of Sturm and Tifft in persuading them to convert that support into arms. The Mexican agents developed an impressive list of investors and suppliers, whom they often repaid with concessions. Arms merchants and financiers composed the widest network of American elites involved in Mexican affairs. Banker Eugene Kelly, of Kelly and Company, held one of the largest blocs, some $500,000 of the Mexican issue. The amounts recruited by Tifft and the expenditures made by Sturm indicate that there were other purchasers as well, but only a few of Sturm's arms transactions have been uncovered. In one case he enlisted Henry Du Pont, the president of E. I. Du Pont de Nemours and Company, who supplied 800 barrels of gunpowder and other explosives for bonds valued at $32,487. Perhaps looking for future advantages, Du Pont insisted on the bonds rather than cash. In another case Sturm bought military supplies valued between $471,000 and $1,709,735 from arms dealers Dewhurst and Emerson and Merritt, Walcott, and Company. Dewhurst and Emerson held at least $294,375 in bonds. The prominent arms dealers and manufacturing firm of Schuyler, Hartley, and Graham accepted bonds valued at $598,046. Munitions worth $563,700 were obtained from financier Henry Simons.[15]

Other agents for the Liberals also incurred large debts with arms providers. In 1862 Francis W. Latham, William Sprague, and Bertram H. Howell of P. P. Howell and Company agreed to a "contract for supplying arms of war" to Bustamante. The deal called for an initial $500,000 to be deposited in Matamoros, while $1,800,000 in bonds was to be sent to Howell in London, where he would exchange them for arms. The arrangement collapsed after more than a year of work and Howell's purchase of thousands of weapons because the deposit and the bonds were never forwarded.[16]

The arms merchants probably held less than $1,000,000 each in the Mexican certificates, given the 40 to 60 percent discount rate on the bonds, although the transactions that are still hidden would increase this amount considerably. Whatever the size of the debts, the merchants were not men to trifle with: their influence exceeded the mere sale of weapons. Marcellus Hartley, part owner of Schuyler, Hartley, and Graham, served as the president of the Union Metallic Cartridge Company and as a director of Remington Arms. As a director of the Equitable Life Assurance Society of the United States he was also connected to the highest levels of finance. Using his access to large amounts of capital, he eventually assumed control of Remington and merged it with Union Cartridge. He was a close associate of Stillman, Dodge, Beekman, and Taylor. All of them avidly supported Romero and the Mexican Liberals against the French.

Others who supported the Mexicans included Herman Funke, a director of the St. Nicholas Bank and the Germania Fire Insurance Company of New York. He was also the founding director and principal force for the German-American Insurance Company and the head of Herman Boker and Company, New York's leading hardware and cutlery concern and an exporter of arms including rifles, pistols, knives, and bayonets. Funke owned $274,500 in bonds. Sturm and Tifft also gained funds from New York financier C. W.

Brink, who already owned 1,776,000 acres of property in Mexico, port captain Barney, and General Benjamin Franklin Butler, Barney's law partner and a future governor of Massachusetts. They committed large but unknown amounts to the bonds.[17]

Other Wall Street brokers also took part in the sales. Samuel Fowler and John Boynton each earned $5,000 in commissions for the sale of the securities to their clients, a figure that indicates another million dollars in gross sales. Henry Clews was perhaps even more effective in raising funds for the Liberals than were Corlies, Tifft, and Sturm, but the details are undocumented. Romero and Clews became friends during Romero's stay in New York and Washington during the early 1860s. The records allude to their close association but provide no details. Clews gained his reputation during the American Civil War as head of the firm of Livermore, Clews, and Mason, one of the two leading government bond brokers of the era. He was a mainstay of the Union bond drives carried out by Treasury Secretary Salmon P. Chase, and he helped Romero as well.

Sometimes the financiers helped the Mexicans in other ways. Dodge's son-in-law Hoadly used his Panama Railroad to transport Mexican officers across the isthmus from one ocean to the other at cost, and in 1864 Barney, as port captain, authorized the shipment of 5,000 rifles. Many of the financiers who helped Romero during his desperate search for arms and cash gained increasing power in Cornelius Vanderbilt's New York Central Railroad. Among them were J. P. Morgan, Ed Morgan, Moses Taylor, Auguste Belmont, Levi P. Morton of Morton, Bliss, and Company, Cyrus W. Field, Russell Sage of the Union Pacific Railroad and the Pacific Mail Steamship Company, railroad tycoon Jay Gould, and Winslow, Lanier, and Company.

The initial sale of Mexican bonds, those sold between 1865 and 1867, totaled in excess of $30,000,000 in face value. These are the sales for which transaction records are available. The actual total was probably between $16,000,000 and $18,000,000. The contemporary sale of what is known as the Ochoa bond issue added another $3,500,000, drawn from the pockets of investors in New York and San Francisco. The Mexicans claimed that they had received a mere $3,425,000 in cash and materials from the American financiers and industrialists with whom they struck their deals. The ensuing conflicts regarding the high fees and discounts that characterized the bond sales, disagreements regarding their value, the worth of the supplies sent to Mexico—some of which did not arrive—and the interest payments due became a complicated, intractable problem between the two nations for a decade.[18]

The exchange of arms for bonds was an extraordinarily risky venture for a mere return of interest and discount margins. The powerful Americans who invested in the Liberal cause believed that the transaction presented an opportunity for great profit and power, an ambition that was coupled with sympathy toward their southern neighbor's struggle with a European invader. A Liberal victory would restore a potentially rich and subordinate republican trading partner.

Neither the American arms merchants nor the U.S. government could have expected the Mexicans to pay back the bonds. The Liberals had suspended payment on Mexico's foreign debt in 1861, before the French invasion, and they were far poorer by the mid 1860s. The expansionists among the Americans, however, found the land concessions offered by the Mexican agents attractive. These cutting-edge American expansionists measured the situation from the standpoint of business opportunities, land acquisitions, and influence over the Mexican government.

PLANS FOR A CAPITALIST ECONOMY

Immediately before the massive intervention of American capital into the Mexican economy that marked the end of the American Civil War, the Liberals began draconian land privatization measures that deeply affected the traditional lifestyle of the peasantry and the long-established power of the Church. In 1854 they inaugurated La Reforma, a movement to commercialize agriculture, create democracy, unfetter internal trade, and universalize private property. The struggle for control of rural landholding had been going on since the Spanish invasion, but the rise of commercialized agriculture as an early phase of modern capitalism placed the countryside in a state of unprecedented transformation.[19]

The Liberals estimated that the Church held about 48 percent of the arable land in tax-exempt status and that the cooperative and communally governed pueblos—the smallest legally incorporated rural settlements—possessed an additional 25 percent. In 1856 the Liberal congress enacted the Ley Lerdo, which outlawed all communal and corporate holdings. In 1857 the constitution adopted by the Liberal-controlled Constitutional Convention included the reform laws as crucial provisions and provided a process by which land could be denounced and sold. The Liberals had supported earlier agricultural privatization laws enacted by the state legislatures from the late 1820s through the 1840s as well as the Ley Lerdo. Powerful members of the Conservative Party had accepted them all. Both saw the validity of change in local political power and property ownership.

Liberal leaders believed that privatization would lead to the commercialization of agriculture, which could then become the basis of greater national wealth. The abolition of pueblo communes would remove the barriers to horizontal and vertical mobility and create a more individualistic and entrepreneurial citizenry. Moreover, because real estate held by the Church and pueblos had been exempt from taxation, privatization would increase the tax base. The additional revenue would ensure success in the modernization project.

The Liberals also believed that privatizing agriculture would end Mexico's chronic undercapitalization. Under the traditional regime, the great landowners had mortgaged their holdings to the Church because it was the principal lending institution in the country. The clerics used a considerable part of the interest earned for charitable activities instead of economic investment. The economic system of the pueblos was based on a system of community property and cooperative labor. The pueblos sold agricultural surplus on the free market, as did the Church, but most of their crops were used for food. Lacking cash, the pueblos generated little of the consumer demand needed for a flourishing free market. The Liberals saw these agricultural practices as a brake on the economy.

The privatization laws, which cost the government nothing, stripped the Church and the pueblos of their rights to hold community farmlands in perpetuity and required them to divest themselves of their holdings over an ambiguous period of time. The Church was compelled to sell its lands to private individuals. The lands were to be sold intact, however, and only the rich could afford such a purchase. Pueblo lands were to be divided among the local citizenry, but this plan also backfired. When the peasantry refused—or were confused—and did not comply, as was frequently the case, the land was denounced by local elites as "unclaimed," allowing them to buy it at a bargain price. The laws resulted in the creation of immense tracts of private property. They constituted the ultimate threat to the survival of the pueblos as relatively independent self-governing and self-sufficient entities, and they created a new group of elite Mexican landowners.

The peasants resisted these laws by means of the courts, their most effective instrument. An intricate body of law had developed pertaining to agricultural disputes and litigation in the Mexican countryside over the previous three centuries, and judicial decisions frequently favored the pueblos. In one such decision in 1825 the Mexican government recognized the validity of the property titles originally issued by Spain in 1767. In its petition the pueblo of Santa María Ozumbilla relied on tradition and Mexican law.

> [T]he ancient legal code protects Santa María . . . and now the indigenous people are free and equal[;] . . . however, despite that fact, many pueblos remain in misery, ignorance, and incapable of supporting

themselves. For that reason [the government] should grant common holdings to all of its citizens.[20]

In submitting their case, the pueblo citizens demonstrated a sense of citizenship and of belonging and participating in juridical and political processes. On the basis of a long record of legal successes for pueblos in such disputes, they expected the state to serve their interests, despite the fact that their opponents included the most powerful individuals in rural society—the hacendados (the owners of large estates) and provincial politicians. In the adjudication of this case, the court not only saw to it that Santa María received property; it also included the adjoining pueblo of San Pedro Atrompán in its dispensation. San Pedro had also petitioned for lost property. The state officials issued the grant to San Pedro to satisfy the peasants' demand for the opportunity to conduct "commerce, industry, and agriculture." Rulings such as these constantly frustrated those who wished to promote the development of free enterprise in the countryside.[21]

The traditional self-sufficiency of rural society presented an eloquent ideological and legal obstacle to the Liberal project. From its beginnings, the rapid development of private enterprise in the Mexican countryside engendered resistance among townspeople, the peasantry, and those rural agricultural workers imbued with the idea that as citizens they held an entitlement to the land they needed to produce their own sustenance. The evolution of land tenure toward private holdings and individual accumulation provoked passive everyday resistance and sometimes even revolt. Sporadic violence usually resulted from sudden changes in land ownership in which the pueblos lost out. By the 1860s rival juntas in the pueblos of central Mexico affiliated with the Maximilian government, or surreptitiously with the Liberals, struggled for control of local polity and property.

The Maximilian administration held power in central Mexico, where traditionalist leaderships were still the most powerful forces in the vicinity. Maximilian sought to gain wider public support in the largely rural nation by soliciting the grievances of dispossessed peasantry and promising them redress. Maximilian established the Committee for the Protection of the Poor and appointed Faustino Chimalpopoca as its head. Chimalpopoca went into the countryside to hold town meetings with the people and hear their complaints. The peasantry shocked the Maximilian administration with its eloquent appeals, knowledge of the law, command of local land tenure histories and disputes, and virtual worship of Chimalpopoca.

The density of settlement in central Mexico provided for rapid communications, a sense of cohesion, and the basis for concerted action. Leaders in pueblos from Ixtapalapa to the west and Chalco to the east made applications to the Committee for the Protection of the Poor. Each pueblo learned of the successes and failures of the appeals made by their neighbors. That intimacy, and proximity to Mexico City, also heightened their awareness of the rapid breakdown of their way of life. Land developers were already draining the water from the shallow but extensive Lake Chalco, which had provided their sustenance since *tiempos inmemorables.*[22]

In the spring of 1866 the leaders of Cocotitlán, a pueblo in the district of Chalco, asked for the "restoration" of their *fundo legal,* the basic property of the pueblo. In Cocotitlán and other Mexican pueblos the *fundo legal* comprised an urban living area, a zone set aside for a central plaza and civic buildings, a *huerta,* or garden, and adjacent fields sufficient to adequately support the citizenry. The Spanish Crown had donated these properties to the pueblo's population in the sixteenth through the eighteenth centuries. Expressing the trauma of a people undergoing the privatization of their communal lands, the pueblo of Cocotitlán asked for

> the restoration of the town hall and coeducational school, because under the [Liberal] laws of desamortization these buildings have fallen into private hands. . . . All the pueblos of our many times violated country have suffered horribly . . . especially since the last war brought us the Constitution of 1857. An evil administration of justice both locally and overall has caused the destruction of government in Cocotitlán. As a result of the Law of June 25, 1856, one finds not one resource in the community directed to the public good . . . [such as] a school, infirmary or orphanage. . . . We need property dedicated to the general benefit in addition to that intended for private use.[23]

The leaders of Cocotitlán were divided, however, and their differences underscored the political conflicts that had started to split rural Mexico. An important group of leading citizens, who had abandoned tradition and were benefiting from privatization, opposed the appeal to the Maximilian government. The Liberals enjoyed the support of many of the most aggressive and individualistic villagers. Maximilian and his Conservative supporters rallied traditionalists, communalists, and those citizens who stood to lose from privatization.

On 15 May 1866 the imperial government offered Cocotitlán a property called Teopanixtal to satisfy the pueblo's grievance. The favorable response to the desperate plea of the villagers was motivated by concerns other than the social welfare of the aggrieved workers, peasants, and elites. The Maximilian administration sought to exploit the widely different interests that existed between the peasantry and the leaders of the Mexican Liberal Party, and they saw land reform as an opportunity to gain popular favor among those who had been dispossessed in the countryside.[24]

The peasants' resistance to private investment provoked impatience among national and regional elites who feared their country and its people were failing to advance toward prosperous modernity. In contrast to the majority in many pueblos, the Mexican elites desired the introduction of "money" crops, raised by commercially oriented farmers, and the reduction of peasant holdings focused on traditional crops intended for local consumption. By the late 1860s and 1870s the continuous litigation conducted by sympathetic lawyers on behalf of the pueblos against private interests, and the receptiveness of some judges and statesmen to the grievances of the pueblos, spread frustration among those who favored privatization of landownership. They complained that

> outside agitators and troublemakers are helping the pueblos in these legal actions . . . because the pueblos in general lack the capacity to carry them out on their own. . . . We demand that the said pueblos pay the legal costs incurred.[25]

The Liberals led most of the Mexican elites—local, provincial, and metropolitan—to a consensus that rapid economic change and a wider base of political participation were necessary if the nation was going to survive and prosper. The elites saw Mexico falling ever further behind the United States, and they grew desperate in their quest to bring about modernization and profits. The successes of the pueblos in defense of their properties hardened the stereotypes held by the elites, who thought the indigenous population to be racially inferior and criticized the rural populace as "stubborn" and unwilling to change. An ever stronger consensus emerged that the communal properties had to go.

President Juárez advocated the commercialization of agriculture to provide a basis for this economic development, but he planned for land to be privatized in a manner consistent with Mexican legal traditions and the varied cultures and aspirations of the rural populace. His vision of privatized architecture included respect for community land rights. Lerdo also supported gradual privatization, in which the rural masses would suffer minimally. He established a reputation as a nationalist in the 1850s, when, as secretary of the treasury, he blocked the sale of Baja California. Working through Edward Lee Plumb, the first secretary of the U.S. legation in Mexico City, Taylor offered the liberals $15,000,000 for Baja at a moment when they were desperately seeking loans to assist them in their fight against the conservatives. Lerdo handled the matter as gracefully as possible. Instead of rejecting the proposal outright he demanded $30,000,000—more than twice the amount settled upon by his fellow cabinet members. President Juárez used Lerdo's opposition to the deal and skillfully denied the American bid without earning their personal enmity.

The Liberal elites seeking to modernize Mexico believed that the higher wages and earnings offered in highly capitalized zones of commercial export agriculture, such as the sugar producing areas of Morelos, or in the mining, timber, and textile industries offered the nation the chance to stimulate the beginnings of an internal marketplace. The high degree of capitalization required to achieve the economy of scale that made these enterprises profitable, the risks, and the need for railroads to provide market access combined to create a sense of urgency in the recruitment of foreign monies. It was natural for the Mexicans who sought such economic change to seek closer ties with their increasingly wealthy neighbor to the north.

Privatization proceeded slowly throughout Juárez's presidency. Juárez believed in the "bonds of fraternity linking democratic countries," and in that context he supported American economic cooperation with Mexico. He promoted an association marked by mutual respect and juridical equality. Lerdo also believed foreign investment to be essential, and he facilitated the process of privatization and foreign investment through executive acts after he became president in 1872. Lerdo was an economic nationalist, however—he feared that the issuance of overly large land concessions would lead to national dismemberment and that American ownership of Mexico's railroads would give the foreigners too much control.

THE RICHEST MAN IN TEXAS

Charles Stillman came to prominence in southern Texas during the Mexican-American war, when he landed a contract to take supplies up the Rio Grande from the Gulf of Mexico and deliver them to the army of General Zachary Taylor during the campaign that resulted in the capture of Monterrey. Stillman's dealings in Mexico in 1848, at the end of the war, reflected a ruthless character that American entrepreneurs exhibited all too often in the late nineteenth and early twentieth centuries.

After the war the Americans controlled the north bank of the Rio Grande. Before the war, however, the city government of Metamoros had exercised its power of eminent domain by denouncing farm land on the north side of the river in order to enlarge on the communal properties needed by its citizens. The denunciation procedure was commonplace for growing cities and towns, and the land was annexed despite the protests of the original owners of the land in question, the Cavazos family of Texas, members of the Matamoros elite who supported the Americans during the war. Following the American victory Stillman purchased the *ejido*, or village farmlands, of Matamoros from Sabos Cavazos. Spanish and Mexican law held community properties as inalienable, and the purchase was legally invalid, but the land was on the north side of the Rio Grande and therefore subject to the judgments of the Texas courts. Those decisions went against the Mexicans.

Stillman created the Brownsville Town Company and began selling city lots for as much as $1,500 each. He quickly attracted some 2,000 settlers. Stillman and Samuel Belden, his associate, sold the bulk of the properties and then quickly sold the remainder of the site to E. Basse and Robert H. Hord for a handsome profit of $35,000. In doing so Stillman escaped complex and expensive battles in the Texas courts over who legally owned Brownsville.

Basse and Hord moved rapidly to gain the support of the Texas state government for their Brownsville claim. In January 1850 the state legislature incorporated the City of Brownsville and recorded its opinion of any Mexican claims to the property, regardless of law:

> [A]ll the right, title and interest of the State of Texas in and to all the land included within said tract, that was owned by the town of Matamoras, on the 19th day of December, 1836, shall be and is hereby relinquished to the corporation of Brownsville, and their successors in office, in trust for the use and benefit of said city, provided this act shall not impair private rights.[26]

Stillman also bought vast properties north of the river for himself and his associates, Richard King and Mifflin Kenedy. Each man gained title to hundreds of thousands of acres of hotly disputed lands. Portions of these purchases became the famous Kenedy and King ranches. Stillman, King, and Kenedy fought to validate their ranchland acquisitions. From the 1850s to the mid 1870s their controversial claims to these properties were backed up by the Texas Rangers, the U.S. Army, and their own private armies. For years their militias fought the Mexicans who confiscated cattle and burned ranches in retaliation for their displacement. The titles were still in dispute in Texas courtrooms at the end of the twentieth century.[27]

By the 1850s Stillman was easily the richest man in Texas and the most important American capitalist in Mexico. He enjoyed close contacts with the leading capitalists of New York. James Woodward, the brother of Stillman's partner William, provided financial support for Stillman's projects from the Hanover National Bank, which he headed. Taylor, Stillman's best friend, con-

tributed to the rearing of Stillman's son James, who later took over as head
of the National City Bank. Stillman used his connections to win the lucrative contract for provisioning Taylor's army.

Stillman developed a trade and manufacturing nexus in northeastern
Mexico which was anchored in Monterrey and the Brownsville-Matamoros
area. It reached the docks of New York and the markets of Guadalajara. During the 1850s Stillman, King, and their associates amassed ever larger real
estate holdings in Texas. They paid extremely low prices, usually no more
than ten cents an acre, frequently to sellers like the Cavazos family, who
had dubious rights to the land. Mexican claimants contested the land grab-
bing, but they rarely won because court officers such as Judge Stephen Powers of Brownsville functioned as virtual employees of the powerful ranchers. In 1854 Stillman probably joined his junior partner Joseph Morell in
the formation of La Fama de Nuevo León, the first large textile mill in Monterrey.[28] He also purchased iron, lead, silver, and copper mines in the states
of Nuevo León and Tamaulipas.[29] By the late 1850s Stillman, King, Kenedy,
and a few others dominated large-scale trade, finance, and landholding in
the Rio Grande Valley.

Stillman and King looked beyond mere investment. In 1851 through 1852
they supported an invasion of Mexico led by General Carbajal, an ill-fated
effort to topple the Conservative government in Tamaulipas. Stillman and
King provided arms and ammunition to Carbajal's army, which was composed of Texans, U.S. Army deserters, and Mexicans. The purpose of the attack was to establish the "Republic of the Sierra Madre" from the states of
Tamaulipas, San Luis Potosí, and Nuevo León. Had the invasion been successful, Carbajal, Stillman, and King would have gained control over northeastern Mexico. Most of the Mexican populace, however, regarded Carbajal's invasion as a filibustering raid and refused to support it. For Stillman,
the formation of the Republic of the Sierra Madre had promised a chance
for a personal empire.[30]

When the Union naval blockade cut off reliable cotton exports during
the Civil War, the Confederate government sought relief by way of Mexico. From 1862 until the end of the struggle, Stillman, King, and Kenedy
bought cotton from growers in western Louisiana, Arkansas, and Texas and
shipped it to Alleyton, Texas, the terminus of the Galveston, Harrisburg,
and San Antonio Railroad. From there the cotton was hauled on *carretas*,
large Mexican two-wheeled carts, to Stillman's storage facilities in Matamoros and to other points in Mexico. The wagons returning from the border area carried textiles, uniforms, medicine, and military supplies for the
Confederacy. Stillman, King, and Kenedy received a commission of 2.5 per-

cent of the value of the merchandise that successfully reached its destination, and they received an additional 2.5 percent for storage and marketing services in Matamoros. Payment was in gold, not Confederate currency. The partners averaged $60,000 each per month during 1862, 1863, and 1864. George Brackenridge, a native Texan, served as Stillman's principal cotton buyer, ranging far and wide to make purchases. Brackenridge was actually a treasury agent who was spying for the Union, a role noted by Francis Jay Herron, a Union general.[31]

King and Kenedy focused their activities on Texas. Stillman, however, had wider horizons. He seized the opportunities available through his mercantile connections to ship cotton to New York, Liverpool, and Manchester while manufacturing textiles in Monterrey. The Fama de Nuevo León mill produced cloth and, probably, confederate uniforms. Morell assisted in the export of cotton from the Mexican port of Bagdad, the Stillman-owned enclave at the mouth of the Rio Grande east of Matamoros. Some sales netted large profit margins. In one case Stillman netted $18,851 profit on a mere $21,504 gross.[32] Stillman sold his cotton for equally large profits in Liverpool and Manchester. He grossed $500,000 in New York sales between May 1861 and January 1863.

Stillman's volume and profits increased in 1863 after the Union naval blockade reduced trade from American ports. He sold cotton shipped from Mexico at over four times its cost for an average profit of some $14,500 per shipment. Hides garnered even greater gains—one shipment in 1864 netted $26,070. At this time Stillman broadened his already established business relationship with T. W. House, the leading cotton broker in Houston, the head of the largest private bank in Texas, and key developer of the Houston Ship Channel. House's son, Colonel Edward Mandell House, would play a key role in formulating American policy during the Mexican Revolution of 1910. There is no doubt that the War Department of the United States government purchased massive quantities of southern cotton through Stillman. Despite their known operation of a supply system that provided materials to the Confederacy from Mexico, much of the cotton that they shipped the other way ended up in Union Army uniforms. The American authorities dropped treason and other charges against both King and Stillman soon after the war ended.[33]

Charles Stillman had amassed a fortune by the end of the Civil War. His interests in the Mexican northeast included warehouses in Matamoros and Monterrey, a port, and mines. He joined his friend Taylor as a leading stockholder in the National City Bank. He was the largest American import-export merchant and railroad investor in southern Texas. Later, Stillman and

Woodward purchased Mexican Liberal bonds, and they may have helped Carbajal sell them. Their powerful connections would have assisted an old friend who represented a bankrupt and exiled government, one in which Stillman and Woodward had compelling interests.[34]

DISTRUST AND ANIMOSITY

A deep distrust developed between the Liberal leaders and their American supporters as the war between the Mexican and the French neared its end in 1867. Storms, fires, and interdictions carried out by French forces had taken a high toll on the number of weapons that were actually received by the Liberal army. In some cases partial shipments had arrived, but the Americans presented bills for larger quantities of arms and supplies than had been delivered. Some of the Liberals suspected that arms for which they were held responsible had never been sent. A series of disputes developed between the bondholders and the Mexican government over the latter's failure to redeem its debts.

The American bondholders and other American creditors, especially Sturm and Funke, began pressing the Mexicans for payment of the interest on their securities. Two of Sturm's claims alone totaled $600,000. Merchant L. S. Hargous claimed almost $1,500,000 for Mexican bonds issued in payment for two vessels and miscellaneous arms. The Mexicans objected, pointing out that they never received the ships or shipments. Charles Butterfield, the freight line owner of New York, claimed that the Mexican government owed him $202,743 for two ships, the *Iturbide* and the *Santa Ana*. The officials of E. I. Du Pont de Nemours claimed the Mexicans owed the company principal and interest for $3,000,000 in Liberal bonds. When they produced their evidence, it included the bonds and a contract signed by General Carbajal that promised land as insurance.[35] Others in the New York economic elite held Mexican obligations not necessarily tied to the purchase of bonds. Charles H. Wheeler lost $217,700 when troops seized his brigantine at Tampico, Charles Stillman $55,960 in a similar seizure at Matamoros, banker Albert Speyer $635,000 in 1872, Henry Hyde, who served with Hartley as a director of the Equitable, $344,000 in merchandise at Mazatlán, and J. H. Phelps $200,000 in confiscated military cargo. Interestingly, Morgan's Lower California Company claimed damages totaling $12,500,000 because of canceled land grants.[36]

In 1868 the American creditors, bankers, arms manufacturers, and arms merchants stepped forward and demanded payment of their large equities. Some of the larger American creditors demanded the assistance of their government. James T. Ames of the Sharps Rifle Company of Massachusetts complained about his unsuccessful search for compensation. Charles H. Pond of the firm of Cooper and Pond in New York indicated that he had sent arms for which "bonds or corresponding orders were forwarded to the creditors" but were then not honored. Banker Herman Funke sought payment for an arms shipment arranged by broker Lewis Schumaker. Augustus Morrill, a financier, demanded compensation for a shipment of weapons he sent the Liberals in 1860, and W. S. Hutchinson, another financier, sought reimbursement for a loan.[37] By the early 1870s arms providers Latham, Sprague, and Howell were using the services of prominent Washington attorney Edward Landes to sue the Mexican government for $3,500,000 in losses. E. Peshire Smith of the State Bank of Hartford demanded payment from the Mexican government for a shipment of arms made in 1860. He cited a summary written by Secretary of State Seward to the U.S. ambassador to Mexico, Arthur Corwin.

> In April 1861, Mr. Seward wrote to Mr. Corwin, the U.S. Minister at Mexico, that he found his archives full of complaints against the Mexican government *for violation of contracts* and spoilations and cruelties practiced upon American citizens.[38]

The situation that had started when the Liberals seized power in the mid-1850s grew worse until General Díaz seized the presidency in 1876. In each case the Mexicans replied that the goods had been overpriced, damaged, or lost through French seizures or shipwrecks or were simply unrecorded disbursements. The Liberals continued to refuse to accept responsibility for the goods unless someone in authority had already done so. The Liberals also refused other claims, including a $21,000 forced loan suffered by Edward, Francis, and George MacManus, Pennsylvania and Camden Steel magnates who had bought the state mint of Chihuahua. The bankrupt Mexican politicians held to their position in the face of American threats to deny them international credit.[39]

The tension between the Mexican Liberals and their American supporters continued to intensify. Following the French evacuation of Mexico in 1867, the government of Maximilian and his supporters in the Conservative Party quickly collapsed. By the end of the year the Liberals had gained effective control of the nation, with Juárez at its head. By 1868 the American investors had lost confidence in the honesty of the Juárez government. As the disputes grew, other Americans who had not necessarily helped the Liberals entered the fray. They believed they had legitimate claims against the Mexican government. Charles Stillman and his partner Samuel Belden filed a suit for the seizure of a shipment of 445 bales of goods in transit from their mercantile outlets in Matamoros and Monterrey. Cornelius Stillman, brother of Charles, filed a complaint for $104,538 for the loss of cattle in Mexican border raids that struck his Laureles Ranch in the Lower Rio Grande Valley. Richard King and Mifflin Kenedy filed a $570,000 claim against the Mexican government for their cattle losses and the seizure of a ship at Tampico.

Others claiming compensation from the Mexican government were Americans involved in land development, mining, and railroad projects. J. B. G. Isham, Charles P. Stone, an individual named Calhoun, and Swiss bankers Jecker, Torre, and Company each claimed a one-fourth interest in an 1850s concession to colonize and survey *terrenos baldios,* or uncharted lands, in Sonora, Sinaloa, and Baja California. The project became a filibustering expedition. These armed efforts to seize territory infuriated the Mexican leaders. In 1859 the Mexican government and the governor of Sonora jointly canceled the grant, which included the "uninhabited lands" of the Yaquis and other groups. During the late 1860s the Lower California Company asserted a claim to the Baja portion of the concession. The Juárez administration rejected repeated pleas for restoration of the land grants or suitable compensation, and Lerdo did so with finality in 1875. The filibustering activity played a major part in the Mexican government's reading of the situation.[40]

American shipping interests, which sought port and adjacent land concessions, also challenged the Mexican government. Aspinwall filed a complaint with the U.S. government on behalf of the Pacific Mail Steamship Company, claiming a debt of $43,607 and complaining that the Mexicans had used excessive violence in ousting a group of eighty-five American filibusters who were attempting to seize Baja California. Lerdo rejected the claim several times, and in 1875 he rejected it finally with contempt. In doing so he angered some of the most powerful men in New York, including Taylor, who, with Aspinwall's cousin and partner William E. Howland, was heading the consortium that was developing the Mexican National Railroad. Taylor and Aspinwall had worked side by side throughout their careers. They began together as clerks in the Gardiner Green Howland mercantile house of New York, which Aspinwall and Howland later inherited. The Howland firm "was without a rival in the Pacific trade" and held a "virtual monopoly with Venezuela." As a result, Aspinwall became "one of the richest men in New York." Lerdo then compounded the crisis by rejecting a complaint lodged by Alfred Phipps, who was financially connected to Taylor, Morgan, and Stillman through his ties to the New York Trust Company and the Hanover Bank. Phipps conducted trade between the United States and Baja, and he asserted that since 1855 the Mexicans had refused claims totaling $280,000.

Edgar Conkling of New York, the owner of Mackinaw Island in Michigan, complained that he had lost a large and legitimate land grant in Sonora given to him by Maximilian. Juárez refused to recognize the legality of the land grant despite the fact that the new administration was obliged by law to accept Maximilian's reckless decisions. Jonas P. Levy of New York, another concessionaire favored by Maximilian, filed a $5,000,000 claim after Juárez abrogated his grant to build a canal across the Isthmus of Tehuantepec.[41] The U.S. government failed to support Levy, but his voice joined the growing chorus of protests emanating from the New York financial community. The Americans and Mexicans expressed mutual distrust as the disputes went on.

During the late 1860s and early 1870s Lerdo demanded full documentation for each claim. When the Americans submitted their receipts and other papers, Lerdo and his supporters rejected them outright or recognized the validity of some petitions but turned them down on the grounds that Carbajal, Sturm, Tifft, and others had undervalued the discounted bonds. Lerdo claimed that these agents had given their friends "insider" trading advantages. The Mexicans pointed to the large commissions claimed by Kelly, Tifft, and Sturm as evidence of fraud. Lerdo and his supporters also complained that the arms, in addition to being overpriced and frequently undelivered, were often faulty.

During the controversy Romero wrote Clews more than once, calling the banker his "dear friend" and expressing his desire to reach a satisfactory settlement with the New York creditors once conditions improved in Mexico. Clews, whose reputation as an investment banker was one of conservative avoidance of speculation and the protection of his clients, must have been chagrined. He did not reply, but at the height of the dispute he published one letter from Romero in a New York newspaper without comment. A sense of betrayal pervaded the Wall Street banking community.[42]

In May 1868 Mexico's most powerful American creditors formed the New York Bondholders Committee to represent their interests in Washington and to pressure the Mexicans. They confronted what they saw as financial deceit in Mexico City. After several meetings they resolved

> [t]hat a committee be appointed to confer with Gen. Sturm and urge the prosecution of our claims before the Mexican Government, or the Government of the United States, and to take such other steps as may be necessary in pursuance of the plan proposed and to secure the cooperation of all American claimants.[43]

Sturm served as the committee chairperson. Funke, Hartley, Taylor, Edward A. Quintard of Quintard, Ward, and Company, and David C. Dodd, representing the P. P. Howell arms exporting interests, served as the executive board.

Many of these men had established their business relationships during the Civil War. The Quintards were no exception. During that struggle and the postwar years George W. Quintard, Edward's brother, developed close ties to Clews, Morgan, and other Union fund-raisers. He ran the Morgan Iron Works, one of the nation's major shipbuilding concerns, and he participated in the construction of the Union steel-clad monitors. The Quintard interest in Mexico was profound. George Quintard acquired a major holding in the Batopilas Mining Company of Chihuahua, where he, his fellow investors from the Park National and Wells Fargo Banks, and operating manager Alexander Shepherd extracted $1,000,000 annually for twenty years during the 1880s and 1890s.[44]

Funke began the bondholders' campaign against the Mexican government by denouncing Lerdo for his refusal to recognize the validity of the bonds. Sturm then printed a pamphlet attacking the Mexicans. Funke, Sturm, Barney, and Brink lobbied cabinet officers in the administrations of Andrew Johnson and Ulysses S. Grant to pressure the Mexicans for payment. Clews, a bondholder himself, reported a change of character on the part of Romero after he became the Mexican secretary of the treasury. Once he held a post in Juárez's cabinet, Romero no longer seemed to be the optimist that he had been when he served as the Liberal government's representative in New York and made promises to American supporters.[45] Funke and his associates understood the impossible financial situation of the Mexican government, but its refusal to recognize the validity of most of their claims and its delaying tactics in the consideration of their proposals for concessions in lieu of cash angered them. Many considered themselves the victims of fraud perpetrated by Lerdo's partisans.

The *New York Times* editors agreed with the creditor-critics of the Mexican government and declared that the debts

> are in the hands of many of our most prominent merchants and
> manufacturers, and several meetings have been held here recently
> to take action as to the best manner of collecting them. The question
> of the rights of Americans in Mexico is of national importance.

The editors focused on northwestern Mexico.

> The Territory, rich in minerals and agricultural resources, lies between
> us and the Pacific Coast; and it is requisite for our own prosperity that

we should be permitted, when so inclined, to conduct commercial and other pursuits there in undisturbed tranquility.[46]

Finally, the *Times* ran an unsigned report that supported the expansionists.

> The northern Mexican States are a source of weakness instead of strength to the central government. The United States Government needs those states. . . . Mexico, freed from her load of indebtedness and rid of a territory notorious for breeding civil commotions, may then be able to establish a Republican Government on a firm basis; while without such a settlement, she will sink deeper and deeper into the gulf of anarchy. . . . A strong centralized government is an imperative necessity to the restoration of order.[47]

POWER OF THE PLENIPOTENTIARY

In 1868 President Johnson chose General William Stark Rosecrans as the U.S. minister plenipotentiary to Mexico. Rosecrans, from a prominent Ohio family and a graduate of the U.S. Military Academy at West Point, was driven by the desire to redeem the military disgrace he had suffered during his ill-fated appointment as commanding general of the 1863 Tennessee campaign. He had been removed from his command by General Grant, ending any important role for him in the war, and in 1867 he had resigned his army commission. He sought a leadership role in the emerging American West and Mexico, and he intended to achieve that goal through railroad and real estate development.[48] Rosecrans temporarily replaced Edward Lee Plumb, the departing first secretary of the American legation at Mexico City, as the principal promoter of investments and business in Mexico. Part of the job was to advance American claims and railroad interests in Mexico.

In the mid 1860s Plumb had worked with Taylor, Aspinwall, Samuel Phelps of the Pacific Mail Steamship Company, and Francis Skiddy, the leading figure at the National Bank of the Republic and a partner in Skiddy, Minford, and Company, one of the nation's largest importers of Cuban sugar, in their efforts to construct ports and a railroad from Guaymas, a port on the Gulf of California, to El Paso. The leaders of Pacific Mail anticipated American expansion and actively pursued their vision of American hegemony over an area transcending Mexico and encompassing what they called the Pacific Basin. The concession for the railway, which they called the Mexican Pacific Railroad, was still being negotiated when Plumb left for government service in Cuba.[49]

Rosecrans and Plumb shared a vision of a United States that dominated the Pacific and North America, but the two men contrasted starkly. Both understood the implications of American growth, but Rosecrans sought to be at the forefront, whereas Plumb hoped to reap rewards for his service as an intermediary. Rosecrans's short-lived appointment was an important turning point in the history of American-Mexican relations. Before leaving for Mexico he recruited the American entrepreneurial and political combinations that spearheaded a new era of intense economic, cultural, and political interactions between the two nations. Unfortunately for him, he failed to unite the factions representing the Pennsylvania Railroad with those based in New York, but he succeeded in organizing the support needed for a railroad network among a cross-section of Mexicans. Rosecrans's greatest success would come later, in California real estate and as a director of the Central Pacific Railroad.

In 1868 Rosecrans mobilized business associates in Philadelphia, Boston, and New York who foresaw an American empire in the making. Unlike his wealthy retainers, Rosecrans did not favor territorial gains at Mexico's expense, and that attitude favorably impressed his Mexican hosts. Taylor and his partners believed that Mexico would inevitably lose territories to the United States in addition to those ceded at the end of the Mexican-American War in 1848 and through the Gadsden Purchase in 1853. They justified that ambition with the belief that a smaller Mexico, with an economy that was integrated with that of the United States, would emerge as a more prosperous nation. The betterment would come when Mexicans worked for American capitalists in the construction of utilities and transportation and communications services, in the extraction of minerals and timber, and in the production of agricultural and livestock exports. The United States in turn would gain a new market. These capitalists believed that American emigration into Mexico would lead to the absorption of the Mexican northern states. As a corollary to this expectation, Hubert Howe Bancroft, in a volume of his classic series on Mexican history, devoted volume eighteen to a detailed examination of the people and resources of the far north. In a few cases the American leaders, including the politicians, envisioned the outright annexation of virtually all of northern Mexico and western Canada by purchase or military means.[50]

Rosecrans widened the presence of American capital in Mexico and established long-term ties between leading American investors and Mexican politicians. By actively representing the American bondholders, he was able to combine their economic power with investors interested in other areas of economic activity, thus increasing their influence on the Mexican and U.S. governments. Rosecrans interested both groups because he proposed the payment of Mexican debts through land and railroad grants rather than cash payments, which the bankrupt Mexican government could not afford.

Before leaving for Mexico Rosecrans met with the "Railroad Parties" of the United States, including Colonel Thomas A. Scott, head of the Pennsylvania Railroad, and J. Edgar Thomson, Scott's immediate predecessor. Rosecrans's railroad project also attracted interest and promises of support from men affiliated with the El Paso–Guaymas route proposed by Pacific Mail. They included Dodge, Astor, merchant capitalist George Updyke, Morris Ketchum of Rogers, Ketchum, and Grosvenor (a railroad developer), banker Morris Ketchum Jesup of M. K. Jesup and Company, architect Antonio Jaime Dovale, and others in New York, Philadelphia, and Boston.[51]

In 1868, when Rosecrans arrived in Mexico City, he carried their endorsement to gain concessions for the establishment of a national railroad system. The railroad would link Mexico City with New York and the East Coast of the United States by way of El Paso. It would also cross Mexico from the small port of Tuxpan, which was on the Gulf north of European-dominated Veracruz, through Mexico City to Guadalajara, and to Acapulco and Mazatlán on the Pacific. The plan included harbor easements, telegraphic services for the Mexican interior, and smaller railroad lines to timber mills, mines, smelters, and processing centers for other raw materials.[52]

The American investors also wanted to establish a Mexican national bank, which they would control. In the short run the idea of a national bank encouraged investor confidence by complementing their commitment to industrial, communications, and transportation infrastructure with the reorganization of Mexico's chaotic finances. They understood that control of a national bank would enable them to strongly influence state policy and specific decisions. Rosecrans began to organize American land and mine owners already present in Mexico. His intention was to link their investments and his own to the shipping and railroad network that would result from the concessions issued by the Mexican government.

Rosecrans also recruited Mexican partners. His plan to relieve the Mexican debt through economic growth and the sale of concessions attracted the support of Romero, Juan Fermin Huarte, a member of the family of Agustín de Iturbide, the corrupt Mexican emperor who was deposed in the 1820s, and a number of Mexican congressmen. Rosecrans established a long-term working relationship with Romero, who considered the United States a role model for Mexican development. The allied American businessmen and Mexican politicians regarded railroads and their related agricultural, livestock, and timber enterprises as the key to personal profit and Mexico's prosperity. In 1868 they selectively began purchasing potentially profitable rural properties from local landowners. The properties were close to the proposed rail routes.[53] Rosecrans and Robert Symon, a financier with interests in Boston and New York and later a leading force in the Santa Fe and Mexican Central Railroads, bought properties inland from Tuxpan, the planned eastern terminus.

Rosecrans and his principal associates in Mexican real estate—Brink, Symon, and railroad and real estate developer William Mackintosh— anticipated the onrush of American land purchases that would nearly overwhelm Mexico twenty-five years later when they bought the Yrriate family's rights to the Hacienda Estaca, a large estate between Mazatlán and Durango. They promised Juárez a colonization project, but they intended to cut timber and develop silver and gold mines in the Sierra Madre highlands, of which the Estaca was a part. The estate comprised several hundred thousand acres. President Juárez and Mexican minister of the interior Blas Barcarcel conferred the property on the Americans because it represented an infusion of capital, railroad service, and mines. The government gave the Americans "two years of unlimited power to form the [colonization] company." As part of the inducement, Rosecrans received 54 percent of the mineral rights and lands of the concession as personal property. Predictably, Lerdo opposed the concession as a "give away." Rosecrans gained at least part of the grant, and years later he sold part of the lands to other financiers in San Francisco, who established timber enterprises and mines.[54]

Rosecrans also accepted an offer from William Winder of Los Angeles, California, for a 50 percent interest in twenty-two square leagues in Baja California. Winder's title was insecure, and his offer depended on Rosecrans's ability to convince President Juárez to reconfirm the grant. Despite his many successful real estate ventures in Mexico and California, this effort appears to have ended in failure.[55]

THE CONCESSIONAIRES

In 1867 Lerdo repudiated the debt incurred by the government of Maximilian, which included the claims of American investors. Although the importance of the Americans who supported the emperor was marginal, the New York financial community viewed the cancellation of any international debt with alarm. Lerdo then rallied opposition in the Mexican Congress and the Mexico City press to the American demands for payment on the national debt. Unfortunately for Rosecrans and his associates, opposition was also directed toward their proposed railroad plan. Lerdo viewed the plan for an extensive railroad network with outlets on both coasts as a threat to Mexico's independence. The Mexican public and the Mexican press were divided between those who wanted economic development in concert with the Americans and those who feared the loss of national independence.

The opposition blocked congressional approval of the plan during 1868 and 1870. Nationalists in the Mexico City press denounced the debt and railroad proposal as a "filibustering expedition." The Americans suspected that Lerdo was the source of most of their problems and, indeed, Juárez's second-in-command spoke out against each modified proposal as quickly as Romero supported it.[56] He rebuffed the New York Bondholders Committee and the imperious Rosecrans. He delayed the long-term debt holders by claiming, truthfully, that Mexico could not yet meet her international debt obligations. His response to the blandishments of those who had funded the Liberal effort against the French was seen as ingratitude and made him many enemies in American financial circles.[57] Although he opposed Rosecrans's railroad plans, Lerdo supported the earlier proposal made by Plumb for the Mexican Pacific's single rail line from Guaymas. The Mexican Pacific group had gained Lerdo's goodwill through its attempt in 1862 to obtain American funds to help the Juárez government fight the French invaders.[58]

In 1869 the bondholders and railroad men lobbied the U.S. government for help in gaining their concessions and collecting on the Mexican debts. Brink, a disgruntled bondholder and a supporter of the more ambitious railway project promoted by Rosecrans, met with President Grant, Secretary of State Hamilton Fish, and Chase, who was now the chief justice. As a result, Grant invested in the enterprise himself. Chase was interested but withdrew because of "old age." Fish agreed with the objectives of the American capitalists although there is no evidence of his participation as an investor. Carlos Merighi, one of the men backing the Rosecrans proposal, interviewed Grant and Secretary of War John A. Rawlins. Merighi warned Rawlins "that Vice-President Lerdo, being a bad man, dislikes [Rosecrans]" and reported that he was generally opposed to the Americans. Rawlins endorsed the efforts of the railroaders and bondholders.[59]

American landholders already residing in Mexico welcomed the new railroad initiatives enthusiastically. Stephen Auld typified their position. He owned a pulque hacienda called Sochihuacán and a mercantile establishment at a crossroads fourteen miles from Pachuca, a provincial capital northwest of Mexico City. Auld had 70,000 maguey plants. He paid his one hundred workers the usual low wages that prevailed on pulque haciendas—twenty-five centavos per day—and shipped the beverage by cart to Mexico City and Pachuca over rough roads. This part of his enterprise netted him some fifty to sixty pesos per week. Local and carriage trade brought in a net sum of eighty to one hundred pesos per month. Many of the goods offered for sale were brought in over the same primitive roads. Auld believed that railroad service would heighten output and economic activity in the region and multiply his income.

In February 1869 Rosecrans, acting on behalf of a powerful American consortium, petitioned the Mexican government for a railroad concession from El Paso to Guaymas. The line would be called the Mexican National Railroad. The proposed route, which had first been sought by the Mexican Pacific Company, offered a 1,000-mile shortcut for cargo moving to the eastern or midwestern United States from points south. The syndicate offered the array of strengths that typified the successful American railroads of the time. In New York, Francis Darr of A. Gross and Company recruited participants, and bankers William R. Travers, Auguste Belmont, who represented the London Rothschilds in the United States, William K. Fargo of Wells Fargo, and merchant and financier James Logan composed the financial strength of the consortium.

John A. Griswold, the steel manufacturer, joined the group and supplemented the financiers' capital by offering access to the metal at the lowest possible rates. Griswold was a lifelong business associate of Taylor. He had worked with George Quintard in the construction of the ironclad Monitors during the Civil War. Fargo joined Quintard as a major investor in the Batopilas Mining Company, which was located south of the proposed railroad route. Attorney General Caleb Cushing and law partners Barney and Butler provided the group with all the international legal expertise needed and strong connections in Washington. Symon joined Rosecrans in purchasing real estate in anticipation of the completion of the line. Symon stimulated the interest of Grant and Congressman Rutherford B. Hayes. All remained interested in the project over the following fifteen years.[60]

The strategies of the group planning the Guaymas railroad characterized the American railway industry in the western United States and Mexico in that era. The proposed Guaymas line would tie into Tom Scott's transcontinental Texas and Pacific Railroad at El Paso. Most of the consortium in the Guaymas to El Paso concession was already connected to Scott through his presidency of the Pennsylvania Railroad, and this connection would give the Guaymas line special status. The consortium then lined up political support in both countries, securing the backing of congressmen, cabinet officers, and future presidents. Darr anticipated success for both the Mexican trunk line concession and the Guaymas line, Rosecrans's "favorite railroad," when their man Joe Reynolds won election to the U.S. Senate from Texas. Meanwhile, Rosecrans, Conkling, and other members of the group purchased a tract of land adjacent to the proposed railroad, in which they projected an investment of $200,000 in improvements.[61]

Farther south, on the west coast of Mexico near Puerto Angel, in the state of Oaxaca, Oliver Eldridge of the Pacific Mail Steamship Company and Rosecrans purchased lands that the company directors believed might have large oil reserves. The directors of Pacific Mail had considerable experience in foreign trade. Skiddy and Taylor were major figures in the Cuban sugar market in New York. Skiddy later bought a vast tract of land in Chiapas along the Guatemalan border. The Bank of the Republic, in which Skiddy was an important director, would play an active role in urban development in Mexico City a bit later in the nineteenth century, while Taylor used his resources and those of his National City Bank clients to establish a transatlantic cable and then extended it to Veracruz.

The complexity of the developing American presence in Mexico during the late 1860s and 1870s included important entrepreneurs and enterprises that were separate, even geographically removed, from the railroad machine that would soon envelop the country. Joseph Headley Dulles, a great grandfather of John Foster Dulles and related by marriage to John Foster, the American ambassador to Mexico during the 1870s, operated the Triunfo Silver Mining and Commercial Company in Baja California. Headquartered in Philadelphia, the Triunfo was connected to the firm of Junius Morgan of that city and London, which later served as the basis for J. P. Morgan's British banking business. The Triunfo owned "a tract eighteen miles square in the southern part of the peninsula." The properties sprawled over 208,000 acres, and Dulles claimed to have expended $500,000 in acquisition and development. The mines produced $20,000 in silver monthly, but he considered the 33 percent annual return on the investment to be inadequate. Dulles felt that Mexican taxes were too high, and he wanted Rosecrans as minister plenipotentiary to assist in having Baja California "transferred to the United States." Dulles's interests were separate from those of Taylor, Morgan, and their associates, and he may even have competed with them, but he shared their desire to annex Baja.[62]

John MacManus of Senfert, MacManus, and Company helped pioneer the development of industrial and financial links between Mexico and the United States. He also shared the hope of annexation. MacManus, a close associate of Scott and Thomson, controlled the Reading Iron Works, the Gibraltar Iron Works, the Scott Foundry, the Steam Forge Company, the Camden Tube Works, and Sheet Mill Companies with plants in Pennsylvania and Camden. He invested heavily in the development of the ill-fated Texas and Pacific Railroad from Fort Worth to El Paso and speculated in Mexican mining, timber, and real estate with Rosecrans. Two of his sons took up residence in Mexico as a result of their father's commitment. One became a businessman in Chihuahua with interests in the mint located in the capital city, and the other resided in the American-owned housing development of Chapultepec Heights in Mexico City, where he was killed during the Mexican Revolution. Zapatistas were blamed for his death, which occurred when he opened fire on them after they entered the neighborhood.

During the late 1860s and 1870s General Thomas Sedgwick and Cincinnati industrialist Ephraim Morse joined those American business leaders with ambitions to extend their operations to Mexico with the expectation that annexations would follow. A pending resolution in the Mexican Congress endorsing American investments and railroads in Mexico provided what they thought was the security needed for "the full development of Mexico and the true school to educate and prepare them for annexation." Sedgwick and Morse extended their Kansas and Pacific Railroad, also known as the Union Pacific Southern Route, toward the southwest in order to merge with Scott's Texas and Pacific line. They, too, envisioned a rail network that would extend from the American heartland to Mexico via El Paso and Chihuahua, and to California via Yuma and San Diego, and they tied the annexation of the Mexican northwest to those ambitions. Like the Pennsylvania and New York groups, Sedgwick and Morse obtained support from influential American politicians, including J. D. Cox of Ohio, secretary of the interior, and A. J. Stewart of New York, secretary of the treasury. William Rockefeller, president of Standard Oil and a director of the National City Bank, and James Stillman later gained control of the line. In 1892, as a new owner, Stillman agreed with Sedgwick and Morse and predicted the annexation of Sonora.[63]

In the late summer of 1869 Rosecrans returned to New York in an effort to reconcile the New York railroad group, which sought concessions for the El Paso–Guaymas line, and the Pennsylvania group, which was pursuing concessions for the Tuxpan line. William A. Hegemon, an investment banker and close associate of J. P. Morgan, helped Rosecrans line up American financiers for the Mexican projects. The Hegemon banking house represented the continuity between the financiers of the 1860s and those who came later. It continued its efforts in Mexico through the next two decades, taking part in the creation of the Santa Fe, the Southern Pacific, and the Mexican Central Railroads. Later, it joined in the International Banking Corporation, which was headed by a cross-section of American financiers including Edward H. Harriman, Marcellus Hartley Dodge, and William Salomon. Dodge was the grandson of arms merchant Marcellus Hartley, who had acquired Mexican bonds during the 1860s.[64]

In Mexico City Mexican supporters continued to fight for the Tuxpan railroad concession against a tide of nationalist opposition in the Juárez cabinet, the congress, and the capitoline press. Rosecrans recruited politicians to pave the way for the approval of the concession, just as other railroad promoters did. The Mexican advocates for the Tuxpan line included some of the country's foremost figures from the oligarchy and government. Romero, members of the Solorzano family, and Vicente Pontones, among others, backed up their words with economic commitments.

Lerdo and Romero were still warring, with Lerdo opposing the impending concessions and Romero supporting them. Romero barely escaped dismissal from the cabinet. Amid the tension, his American confederates questioned the integrity of President Juárez and other Mexican leaders. They doubted Juárez's commitment to the railroad projects despite their centrality to any hopes for Mexican economic success. The American businessmen quickly came to the conclusion that the president and his advisers were corrupt. Dr. J. A. Skelton, one of the Pennsylvania Railroad men in Mexico City, contemptuously called Juárez and his cabinet "the big injun and his satalites [sic]." Sturm continued to praise Díaz "as our kind of man."[65]

Above all other considerations the Tuxpan railroad promoters wanted political stability. The governors of the states of San Luis Potosí, Zacatecas, Jalisco, and Michoacán, located to the north alongside the proposed lines, demoralized the investors by staging a revolt that was rooted in the struggle for states' rights versus centralized authority. The dispute was related to railroad development and involved a fight over the control of tax revenues and local resources. The central government needed a wider tax base to pay construction costs, but the provincials did not cooperate. In 1868, before the fighting began, the local and state authorities sought to raise emergency funds by imposing forced levies on businessmen, including foreigners, confiscating their assets when they resisted, and, in San Luis Potosí, even imprisoning them. The rebellion thwarted the effort to recruit more investors in New York, Philadelphia, and Boston. Astor and Taylor, who had supported the Guaymas line, and Royal Phelps of Phelps Dodge, as well as less interested members of the financial community, backed away from investing because of "Mexican conditions during the last few days." The *New York Times* and the *New York Herald* compounded the problem with "damaging articles" on the Mexican strife, which demoralized the syndicate managers. Some of the new partners decided to wait until Mexico could sort out its affairs before making new investments, but others, including William Dodge, John MacManus, Rosecrans, Scott, Seward, Symon, and General William Jackson Palmer, the head of the Denver and Rio Grande Railroad, continued their support.[66]

Palmer enjoyed the support of not only the Pennsylvania Railroad men but also New York and Boston financier George Foster Peabody and Thomas Jefferson Coolidge of the Old Colony Trust Bank in Boston.[67] Scott and Mac-Manus proceeded to "line up the construction men" and decided "to drive a hard bargain" with the Mexican government.[68] They demanded 20,000 acres of land per mile of track laid. The demand was unrealistic but was consistent with the territorial ambitions of the American railroad pioneers. American business and public leaders recognized the potential for power over Mexico that was inherent in the railroad plan. In 1872 the *New York Journal of Commerce* commented on Rosecrans's plan for a banking, communications, and transportation network:

> [T]o establish a national bank and railway company in Mexico, [and] accepting . . . any concessions Mexico may grant . . . would encourage investments in transportation lines that would control the trade of Mexico.[69]

The railroad men garnered strong political backing in the United States. In addition to Seward's support, congressmen and future presidents James A. Garfield and Rutherford B. Hayes requested that the Mexican railroad bill be introduced to the U.S. House of Representatives under their auspices. John T. Hoffman, the governor of New York, offered to help "in any way in my power."[70] Chief Justice Chase reiterated his support, and Elisha Dyer, the speaker of the lower house, invited Rosecrans to address the Rhode Island legislature. Senator Matthew Hale Carpenter went even further than the railroad men when he endorsed Mexican "annexation . . . because the United States is destined to supplant all other governments on this continent." His scenario seemed peaceful. It was to be achieved "by leading Mexico to a higher plane of civilization," presumably through a process of colonization that would follow the model established in Texas and Hawaii.[71] Others, like Governor Horace Austin of Minnesota, endorsed using armed force to establish and maintain American banks and railroads in Mexico. The Mexican government could

> guarantee no protection to property; which would of course leave everything that might be *taken* there, or developed or acquired there, by our citizens, at the will of the wild and reckless barbarians and semi-savages. . . . Must we not first take the government of Mexico in hand, Either to Establish a Protectorate Over the Country, or by undertaking to give the President, or the person in power there, a *Military Support* that will insure domestic tranquility and a due regard for the rights of foreigners?[72]

POLITICS OF SUBJUGATION

An American ideology necessary to support the Mexican project, but ultimately more far-reaching and more enduring, had emerged. The expansionist attitudes toward Mexico expressed by the remarkably military post–Civil War political leadership of the United States reflected the increasing assertiveness of the American people. Their attitude was encouraged by their victory in that great struggle, their gains against the "savages" on the frontier, and the effects of rapid economic and technological development. They discounted Mexican jurisprudence as "corrupt" and hence inferior to American courts. Assertions that Mexicans were "barbarians" and "semi-savage," that "they couldn't rule themselves," and that their government had to be "taken in hand" not only gained acceptance, but validated American ambitions. The men associated with the railroad effort constituted an important interplay between the American government and the business community. While they were divided over the issue of annexation, they agreed that it was the duty of the United States to redeem Mexico by transforming it to a "higher plane of civilization."

Ironically, at the moment that key Americans repudiated the legitimacy of Mexico's government, Mexican law was enjoying a golden age. The complexities of the legal treatises of supreme court justices Ignacio Ramírez, Jesús González Ortega, and José María Iglesias, and general and governor Trinidad García de la Cadena equaled or excelled the erudition of those written by their American counterparts, but they passed unnoticed by Mexico's American critics. Ramírez, for example, wrote some of the most poignant defenses of individual liberty ever expressed on the American continent.[73]

The Americans framed their objectives in Mexico by mixing ideas of progress with theories of Mexican racial inferiority. Some, like Rosecrans, wanted to uplift the Mexicans, their economy, and their "civilization." Others articulated their racial bias and linked racial inferiority to Mexico's underdeveloped economy and its standard of living, which was lower than that of the United States. One of those interested in the Mexican project was Nahun Capen, a Boston capitalist, publisher, and phrenologist. Capen linked racial theory to financial risk and a need for a high rate of return on investments, most likely his own.

> [I]n view of the real character of the Mexican people, it will be necessary to enlist large numbers of the superior race. To save that nation, you want a solid foundation of character, and what you cannot find there, it will be necessary to carry with you. . . . Businessmen will not readily venture where governmental protection is doubtful. If they

incur large risks they demand large profits, and if you promise these
you cannot easily advance or strengthen the nation you desire to
develop or aid.[74]

New York import-export merchant and financier James William Simonton complemented Capen's view of racial inferiority, favoring an "American Protectorate" because of political "chaos." The protectorate would insure American investors against confiscation and was the duty of the U.S.
government. Fellow merchant banker William Burwell of New Orleans also
advocated annexation in view of the importance of the vast acreage that he
assumed would be gained via the railroad concessions.

The American racial pronouncements and territorial ambitions outraged
Mexican nationalists and helped fuel the opposition to the Tuxpan railroad
concession led by Lerdo. The explicit racism toward Mexicans issued by a
variety of American politicians derived from the deep-seated prejudices that
turned Caucasian Americans against those of African, Asian, and Native
American derivation and facilitated the ongoing liquidation of indigenous
groups in the southwestern United States. The racial stereotypes of Mexicans offered by governors and senators from all regions of the United States
in the late 1860s constituted a major step in the transition of racism from
a domestic setting to one of international relations.[75]

Whatever their differences, those who favored closer economic ties and
those who favored annexation agreed that Mexico's failure to develop its
resources justified American exploitation of those opportunities even if "development" meant merely the extraction of Mexico's valuable natural resources. American businessmen and politicians contrasted the "hard working and independent" virtues of the Anglo–Saxons with the "laziness and
docility" of the Mexicans. In their eyes the political confrontation was between American "democracy and honesty" and Mexican "dictatorship and
corruption." The mental image of "chaos in Mexico" reduced the possibility of a legitimized Mexican state and jurisprudence in the minds of "law-
abiding Americans." The image of "undeveloped resources" was being used
contemporaneously in the struggle between Native Americans and American settlers in the western part of the United States and their backers in the
U.S government.[76]

For the extremists—and there were many of them in the Eastern business community and on the frontier—the Americans and the Mexicans were
absolute representations of the "civilized World" and the world of "semi-
savages." The early members of the Pennsylvania Railroad consortium in
Mexico directed their scorn indiscriminately toward Mexican leaders, in-

cluding ex-emperor Iturbide and ex-presidents Antonio López de Santa Anna and Ignacio Comonfort, as well as Juárez and Lerdo. At the same time, during the late 1860s and the early 1870s, the Pennsylvania group accepted the descendants of Iturbide, then the owners of Dumbarton Oaks in Washington, D.C., as worthwhile business partners in their Mexican venture, presumably to facilitate support from the oligarchy.

CULTURE JOINS CAPITAL

By the early 1870s a considerable number of America's most powerful businessmen had made direct investments in Mexico. A much larger group that included most of the nation's greatest capitalists, military officers, and politicians had an increasing stake in that nation. Their commitments to the transcontinental railroads being built across the Southwest to border points and their vision of dominating the Pacific Basin made success in Mexico imperative.

This infusion of capital was accompanied by American culture as a visible element in expansion. Following the war between Mexico and the United States, religious missionaries arrived in the more populated area of the border region, just south of the Lower Rio Grande Valley, endeavoring to convert "Papists" into Protestants. In 1852 Melinda Rankin went to Monterrey as a missionary for the American Biblical Society. She revealed the feelings of many immigrants about such ventures through a chapter title in her book, "Looking over into Mexico—A Dark Prospect." During Rankin's twenty years of combating "Romanism" in the region between Monterrey and the border, she received support from capitalists and theologians in New York, New Haven, and Boston. Among her individual backers were William Dodge and Deacon Charles Stoddard of Boston. The American and Foreign Christian Union in New York, of which Dodge was a leading member, supported her in the construction of a mission at Monterrey. The American Tract Society of Texas and a variety of Methodists and Presbyterians also contributed to the Rankin mission.

Rankin reflected a more generalized American opinion. She found that "the Mexicans are a simple, inoffensive people," but she viewed the Mexican nationalists who were raiding American holdings in the border region as "ruffians." The American missionary effort in Mexico grew alongside economic, ideological, and political involvement. In 1860 Rankin's Baptist counterparts, led by James Hickey, founded a school "for Bible, English, and arithmetic" in Matamoros. In 1864 Hickey and Thomas Westrup started the Primera Iglesia in Monterrey, "the first Spanish-speaking evangelical church in Latin America." Hickey and Westrup offered Rankin important moral support until Hickey's premature death in 1866. Since the Civil War the American missionary effort in Mexico had included introducing the Bible written in indigenous languages and the residency of hundreds of lay preachers and ministers in cities and even remote areas.[77]

Following the Civil War, issues of economic power and political authority pushed the American missionary effort into the background. American cultural influences reached Mexico City and, along with other foreign and metropolitan contributions, spread into the countryside. The work experience, pastimes, and sports of the rural and urban masses began to change. The introduction and partial adoption of Cinco de Mayo celebrations across the country, in honor of President Díaz's role in the historic 1862 victory at Puebla against the French, signaled a new era of state intervention in popular culture and symbolized the onset of changes that altered the habits of virtually everyone. Rodeos and fairs that encouraged mass attendance grew in frequency, and the new sports of bicycling and baseball, both popular in the United States, were introduced.

During the 1860s the central valley of Mexico, dominated by the national capital, experienced the most intensive changes in the nation. Economic, social, and cultural exposure to the outside world, especially through the trade nexus with and lifestyle offered by Mexico City, encouraged the growth of commercial agriculture, the rapid adoption of Spanish over "Mexican," as Nahuatl was called, changing culinary and clothing tastes, greater secularism, and even industrial labor for some. To the northeast of the capital, the citizens of San Salvador Tisayuca in the state of Pachuca pointed out the depth of the cultural crisis and hinted at its psychologically damaging effects:

> The undersigned are the children and native born citizens of San Salvador Tisayuca, . . . although our pueblo has its incorporation and property titles, nonetheless, . . . today we cannot read them easily . . . [because] these titles contain maps, signs, paintings, hieroglyphs, and figures that . . . none other than persons trained and dedicated to the study of this form of Mexican antiquity can understand, explain, or indicate their meaning.[78]

Despite its rapidity, the pace of change seemed slow to an increasingly powerful and impatient sector of the Mexican elites who sought immediate personal gain via the universal opportunities associated with the Industrial Revolution. They considered the indigenous population "simple," "backward," "stubborn," and "barbaric." Their sense of frustration inured them to the plight of even the most desperate pueblos. Mexican leaders were divided. They all wanted a national railroad system and recognized that cost effectiveness and technological considerations required that the lines be built by foreign entrepreneurs. Many hoped for quick and efficient ties to the U.S. marketplace; others feared American domination and stalled the process.

The American entry into Mexico was prompted by the growing economic strength, technological sophistication, and population of the United States, combined with a political need to create a national ideology that stressed freedom and non-intervention by European nations in the affairs of the "American Republics." As the American elite began to invest in the resources of their southern neighbor, a new relationship between the two countries began to form. The nations shared a 2,000-mile border, and the Americans, while competing with the Mexicans for control of resources and territory, began to interact in a manner unprecedented for peoples not in a formalized colonial relationship. This interaction, which was promoted by local commerce and industry, the sharing of food, music, and clothing, and the merging of families through marriage, became extensive and profound.

During the 1870s the New York and the Pennsylvania Railroad–Boston syndicates were on the cutting edge of American development and expansion. They began in the eastern United States and moved through the rest of the nation, first penetrating the Midwest and the South, then the western part of the country. Next was Mexico. After Mexico came Latin America, the Pacific Basin, Asia, and Africa.[79]

2   Rival Concessionaires

Must we not first take the government of Mexico in hand, Either
to Establish a Protectorate Over the Country, or by undertaking
to give . . . the person in power there, a *Military Support* that will
insure domestic tranquility and a due regard for the rights of
foreigners?

Horace Austin, governor of Minnesota, 1870

During the last third of the nineteenth century, as the United States grew
ever more powerful, it asserted a more forceful role in Mexico and in the
global competition for empire that preoccupied the Western powers. American concerns, spearheaded by financiers, industrialists, and politicians,
quickly deepened in Mexico and the Caribbean and then spread to the Pacific
Basin and to Asia. The purchase of Alaska presaged the later occupation of
Hawaii and the Philippines. By the end of the century the Americans had
consolidated control over the western reaches of North America and dominated trade in the Pacific.

During the 1860s and 1870s, given the roughhouse nature of westward
expansion and international relations, it was to be expected that those who
promoted and profited from America's growth toward the Southwest would
seek economic and territorial gains in Mexico. They also sought any political advantage that would facilitate those aims. Mexico attracted the immediate interest of the powerful owners of the largest financial and industrial
institutions in the United States. The first to arrive were the owners of the
American railroads.

CONCESSIONS GAINED

In January 1870, in a letter to Rosecrans, Juárez quietly affirmed his support of an American project that he believed would benefit the country.

> I will be greatly pleased if the venture capitalists you have referred to
> would come here and invest part of their wealth in industrial enterprise,
> extending by that means the bonds of fraternity between the two re-
> publics and linking their identities by means of the same democratic
> institutions.[1]

Soon afterward Juárez and the Mexican Congress approved two Pennsylvania Railroad projects, granting the Tuxpan and the Tehuantepec concessions. The first provided for a comprehensive nationwide rail system, and the second reestablished the route for a line across the Isthmus of Tehuantepec, connecting the Pacific and Atlantic Oceans. The Pennsylvania Railroad group quickly sold the Tehuantepec grant to a British syndicate in order to raise cash for the construction of the national system. The system would link American cities with their Mexican counterparts and ports on the Mexican Pacific Coast, and it would exclude European competitors, who were considering constructing a canal that would ease their access to the Pacific.[2]

The negotiations on the conditions of the grants were difficult because the interests of the Americans and the Mexicans differed on two principal issues. The Mexicans wanted an internal communications and transportation network that would span their two great mountain ranges, which ran north and south on the nation's east and west sides, breaking the nation into three distinct zones. They gave equal importance to the routes running east and west and those running north and south. The Americans, however, emphasized the north-south line from El Paso to Mexico City. In addition, the Mexicans conceded less than 10,000 acres of land per kilometer of railway constructed, less than one-half what the American railroad men claimed was the bare minimum needed to pay their construction costs. Another telling problem plagued Rosecrans and the Pennsylvania group: although they needed capital to build the El Paso–Mexico City line, the American investors could not sell their tracts of land in the desolate stretch between Fort Worth and El Paso. That land was needed to complete the Texas and Pacific line, which would link the Mexican system with markets in the eastern United States.

The Tehuantepec concession encompassed extensive tracts along the Pacific coast of Tehuantepec that extended to the Guatemalan border. It included about 1,500,000 acres of lands that were traditionally claimed by the Tzeltal, Tzotzil, Lacandon, Zope, Tehuana, and other indigenous groups. Mexican officials specified the acreage as "unused" public lands. The Liberal government used the designation "national lands" as the basis for including them in the railroad grant. Romero acquired large estates adjacent to the right-of-way. At the same time the government used the "public lands" label in other areas such as the Sierra Madre Oriental and the Sierra Madre Occidental in San Luis Potosí, Hidalgo, Veracruz, Chihuahua, Durango, and Sinaloa to encourage Mexicans to develop their own private commercial agricultural enterprises. The privatization of so-called national lands there provoked unrest in Huastecan, Otomí, Nahuatl, Mayo, Tarahumara, Yaqui, and mestizo pueblos, and peasant uprisings broke out soon afterward.

During the ensuing twenty-five years the lands of the Tehuantepec concession were sold several times before important American settlements developed at Medina, Oaxaca, and Pijijiapan in Chiapas. Despite the revenues from the Tehuantepec sale, the failure to complete the Texas and Pacific line to El Paso in a timely fashion stalled the Mexican project. The delay, however, did not lead to a cessation of private acquisitions of land and resources. Mackintosh, John MacManus, Rosecrans, and Symon, all associated with the Tuxpan enterprise, bought the Tapia estate, which covered a vast territory between the cities of Mazatlán and Durango, a region of mountains and valleys rich in "virgin timber and silver mines." To develop the hacienda's mineral resources, they joined with Arthur Curtiss James of Phelps Dodge and Henry Hyde, the founder and president of the Equitable, and created the Durango Mining Company. The Estaca and Tapia property acquisitions opened the way for later American investments in southwestern Durango. Rosecrans and his associates also bought large tracts of land in Sonora in anticipation of the railroad from El Paso to Guaymas. They made the purchases despite a history of land disputes between private holders and Yaqui communities along the route and anti-Americanism among other Sonorenses.[3]

Once the American financiers had committed their resources to build lines to the frontier, delays endangered their fortunes. The cancellation of the grants to build in Mexico would mean disaster and require political intervention. By 1875, as a result of the Carabajal bond sales, some thirty-one claims had been filed with the U.S. government by American businessmen, financiers, and arms merchants, seeking redress from cancellations and non-payment by the Mexican government. Eight smaller claims resulted from the arms transactions of General Vega in San Francisco. Meanwhile, many of the most important investors shunned the United States–Mexico Claims Commissions and worked with Romero to achieve satisfaction. The claims, however, provided the immediate motivation for the actions of the arms merchants who railed against the Mexican government. Texans and others saw the extension of American interests in the border regions as essential to American progress. Charles Butterfield, a freight line owner in New York, anticipated a "similar effect to be produced by the silver of Mexico as has been produced by the gold of California."[4]

THE RACE TO MEXICO CITY

In the early 1870s Moses Taylor, as the head of National City Bank, joined Anson Phelps, Francis Skiddy, and fellow bank directors Percy Pyne and John Jacob Astor in a project for a railroad system that would cross the southwestern United States and continue to Mexico City. Taylor was an established leader in American expansion, with investments in transoceanic shipping on the Pacific and the Atlantic, telegraph cables to Mexico, South America, and Europe, railroads in the United States, and real estate in California, Cuba, Oregon, Texas, and Mexico. Taylor and Skiddy were also competitors, each operating one of the nation's two leading sugar importers. Pyne, Astor, and Phelps participated in many of Taylor's enterprises, in addition to the National City Bank and their own banking, trading, and mining companies.

The syndicate members saw investment in Mexico as an essential element in the development of American hegemony over all of North America and, eventually, the Pacific Basin. At the same time, they exercised cool judgment on what would succeed or fail. They correctly viewed Scott's Texas and Pacific project as a poor investment. They were "indisposed to consider any land speculations in Texas," according to canal and railroad developer Henry Stebbins, because of the low value of the land to be traversed between Fort Worth and El Paso. Instead, they focused on a route that would reach Mexico by crossing eastern and central Texas and enlisted Plumb as their agent to the Mexican government. Plumb had recently returned to Mexico City from Cuba, and he used his friendship with Lerdo to gain support for the project.[5]

This new group of New York financiers from the National City Bank and the Phelps Dodge Corporation turned down proposals of unity issued by the Pennsylvania and Boston group of directors. Anson Phelps and William Dodge shifted their support to the new consortium but let Scott and Rosecrans down as easily as possible, saying only that the "timing" was bad.[6] Actually these New Yorkers already had a line to the West Coast—the Union Pacific. For Mexico, they preferred a direct route originating in Cairo, Illinois, crossing Arkansas and Texas by passing through Fulton, Texarkana, Austin, San Antonio, and Laredo, and running to Monterrey and Mexico City. Compared to the Tuxpan route, this line would reduce the distance to Mexico City by a thousand miles. They were "uniting in turn with the St. Louis and Iron Mountain Railroad, under the same control." That meant that one company would own railroad access from coast to coast in the United States and into Mexico, linking St. Louis, Chicago, Philadelphia, and New York to Mexico City. The syndicate called their new company the International Railroad.[7] Their plans included a 200-mile spur from Laredo to the port at Corpus Christi, Texas, to serve the eastern United States and to supplement the lines running into the American heartland.

The array of American capitalists that had suddenly burst on the scene awed the Mexican leaders.[8] Ignacio Mariscal, the Mexican minister in

Washington, researched and reported on the American capitalists involved. He judged them to be "[m]en whose names give strength to any railroad plan."[9] The executive committee of the International Railroad included Taylor, Dodge, John S. Kennedy, and William Walter Phelps. Kennedy, chief of J. S. Kennedy Bankers on Wall Street and correspondent banker for Junius Morgan and his son J. P., represented their interests as an incorporator of the Union Pacific. Phelps was a leader of Phelps Dodge, already one of the nation's leading mining firms. David Parish Barhydt played a useful role as a politically connected past treasurer of Texas who had "laid out the central city streets" of Austin and served as treasurer of the Erie and Kalamazoo Railroad. His family had been prominent importers of Latin American precious metals since the late eighteenth century. James Pearsall, a construction engineer and financier, directed several northeastern railroads. Paul N. Spofford, the chief engineer of the State of New York, played a political role as well. He was also financially powerful, serving as a partner in the financial firm of Spofford, Tileson and Company and as a director of multiple banks, railroads, and insurance companies.

The other principal investors in the International were all important New York financiers. Henry Gurdon Marquant led the Wall Street securities firm H. S. Marquant and Dimrock and was the president of the Iron Mountain Railroad and a director of the Equitable Life Assurance and Mercantile Trust Companies. Gardiner Greene Howland led one of the oldest and most venerable mercantile houses in New York and had given Taylor and William Aspinwall their first jobs. They served him as clerks. He was a director of the Old Bank of New York and of the Hudson River Railway Company. James A. Griswold, a Bessemer steel heir, entered railroading as a natural enlargement of his role as one of the nation's wealthy steel and steel ship manufacturers. James A. Roosevelt was a prominent banker, venture capitalist, and uncle of future president Theodore Roosevelt.[10]

Among the investors were some of the leading New York bondholders of the Mexican debt, including J. P. Morgan. The firm of Duncan, Sherman, and Company, with which Morgan was closely associated, was also involved. Emlen Roosevelt, who represented "old money," sat as a director of the Chemical Bank and the New York Bank and Trust. J. Edgar Thompson was the chairman of the Pennsylvania Railroad, the largest industrial enterprise and the largest rail system in the United States. William A. Hegemon was an investment banker and a close ally of Morgan, whose interests he often represented. Robert Symon held a major share of the Atcheson, Topeka, and Santa Fe.

The New York syndicate also sought a concession for the construction of a national telegraph system in Mexico, and members of the group worked diligently on its development as well. They simultaneously sought to extend their telegraphic capacity to South America and Asia. Aspinwall, president of the telegraph firm, and directors Astor and Pyne envisioned Mexico as the first segment of a trade, communications, and transportation nexus that would span the Pacific. Morgan, who held a directorship with the telegraphic firm, saw the enterprise as a step in the development of an American-controlled communications system for the Americas and the Pacific and Atlantic Oceans.

These New Yorkers had worked with the Pennsylvania Railroad men and their allies from Boston in the past, and Plumb had tried to reconcile the rival groups in Mexico. But the terms could not be agreed upon. Although both groups were still years from actual construction in Mexico, they vied to be the first to gain Mexican government concessions and to finish their lines to the Mexican border. Plumb and Rosecrans, who acted as their agents in Mexico, developed a mutual dislike.[11]

The New Yorkers appointed James Sanford Barnes to act as president of the Texas branch of the International Railroad—the Texas International. He was a member of the Kennedy firm, a Morgan Bank correspondent, and the head of the Saint Paul and Pacific Railroad. He consolidated several railroads in Texas, creating a viable system. Barnes had worked on naval armaments during the Civil War in conjunction with members of the Pennsylvania Railroad group, including Griswold, Secretary of War Simon Cameron, and Undersecretary of War Thomas Scott. Barnes also helped Herman Sturm acquire "armored" warships for the Mexicans, although these were small and did not amount to much. When illness forced him to take a leave of absence, Kennedy served as interim president. Kennedy's role indicates that Morgan probably participated in the financing of the Texas railroads.

The Texas members of the new company represented the interconnectedness of American expansion on the frontier. They were concerned primarily with the extension of their operations into the nearly vacant adjacent areas of Mexico. They included rancher Richard King and bankers George Brackenridge and T. W. House. King had purchased the world's largest ranch, located in the Rio Grande Valley, from Charles Stillman. Mexican border residents had long contested King and Stillman's ill-gotten landholdings in the region. Brackenridge held real estate and business investments in Monterrey.[12] After the war Stillman had advanced him $200,000 to establish the San Antonio National Bank, which became the most important financial institution in central Texas. Brackenridge facilitated the development of ties between the National City Bank and Texas landholders by brokering the sale by of Arthur James Balfour's XIT Ranch in western Texas to a National City Bank board member.[13] House was the largest private banker in the state and founder of the Houston Cotton Exchange. In the 1840s he had commissioned an exploratory expedition of northern Tamaulipas in a search for exploitable resources.[14]

Confronted by such formidable competition, the Pennsylvania-Boston group attempted to appease Juárez and Lerdo with a $200,000 bond. Ulysses S. Grant, Thomas Jefferson Coolidge of the Old Colony Trust of Boston, George Foster Peabody, and Pennsylvania Railroad directors J. Edgar Thomson, Samuel M. Felton, and L. H. Meyer each contributed at least $25,000. While not as strong as the New York group, these men commanded respect. Grant's participation was important not only because of his political prominence but also because he was the most visible figure among a group of officers who were involved in the Mexican struggle against the French. To further advance the Pennsylvania-Boston position Coolidge, Felton, Grant, Meyer, Peabody, Scott, and Thomson gave Rosecrans "full power as Executive Director for Mexico in representations with the Mexican government on behalf of the North American Railroad."

To win the race to Mexico City, Scott decided to enlarge the Tuxpan rail network. A new line would begin at the port of Acapulco and run across the sugar producing region of Morelos to Mexico City, where it would intersect with the other lines of the system. Scott based his decision on a study of sugar production in Morelos and the level of traffic between the valley of Morelos and Mexico City. From the capital the trunk road would run due north to El Paso and Denver, then turn east toward Chicago and the eastern seaboard. Proud of their strength, and suspicious of the Mexicans, the Pennsylvania Railroad men were confident that "[b]ankers would recognize that the U.S. Government would never allow such a company to be stripped of all their rights." Just in case, both groups of competing American entrepreneurs placed part of their companies' holdings in the United States in order to better ensure government support in negotiations with Mexican officials.[15]

Juárez was ambivalent and cautious about the proposed rail projects. He wanted American capital and technology, but the power and assertiveness of the United States concerned him. He died in 1872 without granting any of the railroad concessions. President Lerdo, who succeeded Juárez, was also concerned about the power of Mexico's northern neighbor. Mariscal was less worried about the Americans, and he wanted their railroads because he believed that they would spur Mexican development. He investigated the Pennsylvania Railroad–Boston concessionaires and reported that the Union

Contract Company, the railroad's construction firm, had an impressive roster: "I have seen the official documents of incorporation of the Union Contract Company of Pennsylvania . . . and it is composed of many very rich, experienced American railroad men."[16]

The project alarmed wary nationalists in Mexico City. The publishers of the important newspaper *El Federalista* complained that, through the proposed concessions, the American railroad men would receive 219,908,730 acres of land, or more than 40 percent of the nation's surface area. This, they said, was far more than they had received for their investments in the United States. They complained that the Americans "want too much." Indeed, William Mackintosh, who was acting for Rosecrans as the representative in Mexico of the Union Contract Company, the construction firm of the Pennsylvania Railroad, had demanded 12,500 acres of land for each mile of track.

Lerdo resorted to granting concessions to save the Liberal government's standing in the face of complaints by the New York bondholders. In 1872 he granted the New Yorkers the concession for the construction of the Mexican National Railroad, which would extend their International Railroad from Laredo to Mexico City and to the Pacific Ocean at San Blas and Mazatlán. This time the Mexican government offered 9,500 pesos per kilometer of completed road and one hundred yards of right-of-way on each side of the tracks for the entire length of the line rather than acreage. Lerdo also immediately renegotiated the Pennsylvania-Boston group's proposal, replacing the land proviso with a subvention of 10,000 pesos per kilometer of track completed. He expressed reservations about the overwhelming size of the Tuxpan network with its multiple lines and ports, but he finally approved the plan. The New York syndicate and the Pennsylvania Railroad and Boston interests were now in direct competition, even though the Pennsylvania Railroad–Boston group was still waiting for the completion of either the slow-moving Texas and Pacific route or its alternative, which would run through Denver. Plumb, who represented the New Yorkers, continued to lobby Lerdo, and later that year he almost convinced the Mexican government to cancel the Tuxpan concession.[17]

The subvention that Lerdo offered the Tuxpan railroad men actually exceeded by 500 pesos the offer of 9,500 pesos per kilometer accepted by the New Yorkers, but Rosecrans was furious. Above all other considerations, he and his associates wanted land so that they could control the country's natural resources and have additional acreage for real estate development. In reaction Rosecrans published an ominous newspaper article in Mexico City in which he announced his resignation as executive director of the National

Railroad. He denounced Lerdo and claimed that his administration would have to be replaced before "progress" could occur.[18]

The Lerdo government's opposition toward American investments in Mexico also worried the American ranchers and merchants of the Lower Rio Grande Valley. Like the bondholders, financiers, and railroaders, these Americans also had critical interests in Mexico. In the aftermath of the war between the United States and Mexico they had acquired private and public properties that enabled the creation of vast landholdings on Mexican soil. The Mexicans violently contested American ownership of their despoiled lands, and they fought back with cattle raids and banditry. The attacks by aggrieved Mexican nationals against the Rio Grande Valley landholders had abated during Mexico's war with its French invaders, but in the late 1860s the fighting renewed, and it continued during the early 1870s. General Juan Cortina, an officer honored by the Mexican government for battlefield heroism, a former governor of Tamaulipas, and mayor of Matamoros, led the efforts. Cortina was to inherit some of the tracts of land acquired by the Texans, including those sold to Stillman and King by his alienated half-brother Sabas Cavazos.

The entrepreneurial landowners of southern Texas promoted trade with Mexico, the exploitation of its minerals, and even the occupation of its lands. At the same time, these new American elites demanded the Mexican government's protection from the raids. The violence at the border, coupled with Lerdo's hostile attitude toward their troubles, frustrated their plans for the development and expansion of mining and ranching ventures in northeastern Mexico. The oncoming railroads would provide access to Mexican "treasures" and increase American control in the area.[19]

The New Yorkers, Philadelphians, Bostonians, and Texans reflected the complexity of the cultural geography of the United States. If the northeasterners tended to be bankers, civil engineers, industrialists, merchants, and ex-military officers backed by the U.S. government, the Texans were bankers, merchants, and ranchers with private cavalries. All, however, aspired to mining empires, personal profit, and national aggrandizement. Diverse in their professions as well as their personal and local loyalties, these men could transcend competition and unite when they were faced with external rivals. They manifested those unities whenever the American or Mexican government attempted to regulate their industries or modify or reject their proposals.

On 12 December 1874 the Mexican Ministry of Public Works gave its final approval for the Mexican National Railroad, the Mexican branch of the New York syndicate's railroad system. The concession provided railroad rights-of-way from the Rio Grande at Nuevo Laredo—and, later, from Matamoros—to Monterrey, where the two lines would merge and run on to León in central Mexico. It also stimulated an unprecedented flow of investment capital from new financiers into the coffers of the directors of the Texas International, who were extending their lines toward Laredo. Everything seemed to be going well. The Mexicans gave the American builders the discretionary power to select the most apt routes. The trunk line from the border to Mexico City would cover some 800 miles. The construction fees, to be paid by the Mexican government, were $9,500 per kilometer, or $15,288 per mile. The funds were to be generated by a 25 percent deduction from the customs revenues generated at Laredo and, later, Matamoros.

In February the New York railroad consortium in charge of Texas International sold $3,500,000 worth of company bonds for the construction of the lines between Jefferson and San Antonio. The directors came up short of liquid assets, however, when the government of Texas issued them 2,560,000 acres of land instead of the cash they had expected. That action created a serious debt problem, with $1,038,846 in unsatisfied obligations. By the end of March 1875 the combined Texas and Mexican railroads under the control of the New York consortium held 4,367,000 acres in two accounts, but the bankers lacked the cash to pay their bills.

A LEGACY OF CONFLICT

When the American financiers, railroad men, and politicians entered Mexico they became enmeshed in land disputes and class hostilities that predated their arrival. The American entrepreneurs were decisive and had a clear understanding of political processes at the national level, and their ignorance of the subtle tapestry and workings of Mexican rural society was irrelevant to them. At that time they were fighting myriad wars against Native American "savages" in what became the western United States. The Americans had little feeling for the Mexican rural masses, whom they called "semi-savages," or the politicians who sympathized with them.

The laws of La Reforma began to shift the balance of power in rural Mexico, and the great changes that started in the 1850s continued during the Juárez administration. Although the many social groups that composed the predominantly rural Mexican society between 1865 and 1876 shared a sense of social cohesion demonstrated by language, religion, work, and legal rights and continued to cooperate in production, celebrations, and pastimes, they increasingly competed for political power and control over resources. They usually adjudicated their disputes in the courts, but when unfair legal decisions became intolerable, one group or another sometimes resorted to violence.

At Chalco, in the southeastern corner of the Valley of Mexico, a strong system of pueblo-based agriculture operated alongside the elite-owned haciendas, producing corn, beans, chiles, wheat, sugar, olives, and other crops. The hacendados had long complained of labor shortages and high salaries, the result of the peasants' self-sufficiency and their option to not work. Between May 1836 and November 1838 the owner of San Diego Aculco, General Gabriel Duran, grossed 23,045.7 pesos and paid out 8,120 pesos to his employees. In 1838 the eleven peons who worked the corn, beans, and chiles grown in the hacienda's fields earned 24 centavos daily while working a six-day week. The captain, or crew chief, received 34 centavos per day. The *mayordomo*, who supervised the overall operation of the estate and its complete complement of thirty-one workers, earned 80 centavos daily.

Duran's labor outlay exceeded 34 percent of his gross revenues, reflecting the complaint of the region's hacendados that labor costs were too high for profitable operations and economic growth. The share of revenues that went to the workers exceeded by nine points the ideal figure of 25 percent of gross profits cited by nineteenth-century economists as satisfactory for adequate capital accumulation. Since the data do not include his total investment or even the value of the hacienda, his rate of return on capital outlay cannot be calculated. Based on hacienda income alone, however, he was clearly not in a position to introduce new technology or expensive improvements to increase production. Labor shortages forced him to pay four times the wages offered by hacendados a mere thirty miles to the northwest.[20]

Between 1856 and 1872 individual owners claimed former communal parcels while Mexico City land developer Inigo Noriega drained Lake Chalco for settlement and farming with government authorization. The reduction of water supplies ruined fishermen, small farmers, and orchard operators. By 1868 significant numbers of peasants and local elites, including some who had initially welcomed privatization, had been deprived of their sustenance and felt betrayed. Some of the losers had participated in the guerrilla war against the French and they knew how to fight. They responded favorably to anarchist organizers from Mexico City, and agrarian uprisings erupted.

Between 1868 and 1870, 1,500 campesinos in the Chalco area followed the leadership of revolutionary anarchist Julio Chávez López and rose up against the government, attacking the authorities and raiding haciendas. They demanded the overthrow of the Liberal government of Juárez in Mexico City and the restoration of "usurped" lands. It is unclear whether Chávez López was a hacienda employee, as his anarchist supporters in Mexico City claimed, or a dispossessed orchard operator or ranchero (a small-scale farmer or rancher) displaced by the drainage of the lake.[21] The uprising grew rapidly, with some 1,500 fighting in its main force. The government suppressed it vigorously, preventing what it called a "caste war." The prefect at nearby Texcoco reported the underlying social tensions when he warned the government that the "men of reason were surrounded by a sea of Indians." Chávez López was executed in the town plaza at Chalco, where the local citizens could clearly witness his death, thereby preventing the development of legends that he still "rode."

In Morelos the pueblo collectives had suffered serious land depredations following national independence in 1821. The pueblos around Ticayan are a case in point.

> To the citizen mayors of the pueblo republics listed on this document be it known: that citizen José Miguel Ortega, the agent of Señor Don Manuel José de Araos, owner of the hacienda of Buena Vista has obtained a judgment giving him possession of lands to begin from the year before last; these lands of which he takes possession are known as Camotin-chan, Llanos de Merino and San Andres, purchased from the *cacique* [town leader] of Amusgos.[22]

The integral role of these properties in village life transcended economic considerations. Land titles defended properties that had special meanings to the peasantry and rural working class. They identified with religious symbols, language, and rituals associated with the Nahuatl past that survived through syncretic processes. Venerated ancestors and loved or feared spirits inhabited these places. The generalized transformation of the countryside under way in Mexico by the 1850s and 1860s inevitably violated sacred properties while replacing pre-Columbian rituals and beliefs with more modern ones regarding authority and land possession.

> [O]n the 18th of April 1836, I, the judge indicated, accompanied by my attendants and representatives of the republics [towns] of Sayultepeque, Ixpatapa, and Zacatepeque and all other persons mentioned in the documents herein, leave this point at 7 A.M. Delineating and taking possession from this point onward.[23]

With the proceedings duly noted by a secretary and legitimated by a notary, Judge Santos de Vera, joined by an agent representing the hacendado and the carefully chosen delegates of the nearby pueblos of Sayultepeque, Ixpatapa, and Zacatepeque, trekked the outer boundary of the new property, agreeing on its location and marking it with duly authorized monuments. Then they held a closing ceremony in which the judge asked the representatives of the republics present if they oppose the taking of possession by the duly authorized, or if they feel that some part of the boundary is incorrect, in the name of justice let us hear them speak to the contrary now.[24]

Despite the deep anguish of the pueblo citizenry and prolonged litigation preceding the ceremony, none of those present protested. The presence of armed guards encouraged silence.

The hacienda of Buena Vista produced sugar. Its mill operated at Zacatepeque, later Mexico's largest sugar *ingenio,* which presented the local working class with a lucrative source of employment. By bringing at least some of the pueblo elites into agreement with the transaction that enabled Buena Vista to enlarge its holdings, the hacendado and local authorities were able to marginalize the claims made by the leadership of Ticayan and its citizens. The leaders of Ticayan and their supporters, who seemed to be out of line and holding back progress, realized their political position was now hopeless. They resorted to the federal appeals courts. Eventually, rural opposition was reduced to posting fliers on doorways in the dead of night while social banditry grew. That practice grew in frequency in late-nineteenth-century Morelos and in the mountainous Huasteca region during the 1880s.[25]

During the late 1860s and early 1870s the process of pueblo farmland displacement continued and, as usual, involved the collusion of local, state, and higher authorities with the intruding private interests. The mode of production and the manner in which people related to their jobs was changing from the less formal, more intimate procedures of the villages and small producers to the more industrialized and more regimented style of modern capitalism. Absentee ownership, company supervision, and more direct political contact with Mexico City were replacing the older decentralized systems of work and politics. The state played the role of peacekeeper and demonstrated its power by moderating disputes between communities, individuals, and agricultural companies. The balance of political influence shifted away from the pueblos and local authorities in the countryside to the impresarios and state building elites in Cuernavaca and Mexico City.

The political and economic inequality that resulted from the privatization program led to endemic civil unrest. That situation forestalled the development of a more modern agricultural economy until General Porfirio Díaz imposed order in the area. In 1863 the war with the French had disrupted the operations of the Acamilpa hacienda, and the absentee owner, Dolores Noriega de Sayago, could not pay the 6 percent mortgage fee due her creditors. Forced to sell the property, Noriega de Sayago received 242,750 pesos. The price of the property reflected the high value placed on it by investors if only peace could be achieved. Prior to its sale profits had been nil. The purchaser, Bernabe Reyes, could not succeed where Noriega de Sayago had failed. The seasonal needs of sugar production and commercial agriculture were exacerbated by continuous friction and litigation with the neighboring pueblo citizenry. Much of Reyes's workforce came from the pueblos. Reyes could not find a buyer for the property and, facing bankruptcy in the mid 1870s, he subdivided and sold it to smaller farmers and renters. The division of private lands multiplied the number of owners and greatly increased their political strength. The strategy worked in the state of Michoacán as well. Had it been implemented on a national scale the revolution of 1910 might have been limited to a movement for political democracy.[26]

The uprisings continued throughout the early 1870s. In 1872 the Mexican government enacted and enforced a law that strengthened the property rights of peasants and rural municipalities subject to land denunciations under the La Reforma laws. Mexican jurisprudence once again found a provisional balance between the contending forces of tradition and change in the countryside.

DÍAZ'S REVOLUTION

Late in 1875, after waging a victorious presidential campaign against General Díaz in which he assured the Mexican public that he welcomed the railroads and modernity, President Lerdo canceled all of the American railroad concessions in Mexico except that for the New Yorkers' Mexican National Railroad. Lerdo probably recognized the need for one line, and his longtime friend Plumb had done an excellent job in representing the New York interests. The Pennsylvania Railroad group lost out. Lerdo's exception, however, was not good enough for the businessmen of the Empire State. He had infuriated key members of the New York syndicate with actions that affected their interests. One was the cancellation of the Tehuantepec railroad concession because Taylor, the leaders of the Pacific Mail Steamship Company, and other New Yorkers saw it as the equivalent of a transoceanic canal that would connect with the New Yorkers' northern shipping companies in the Atlantic and the Pacific. Lerdo also continued to reject the claims of New Yorkers who held Mexican bonds, and most of the Mexican National men held at least some of these bonds. Importantly, unilateral decisions by politicians, especially foreign leaders, against a group of American businessmen were seen as an attack on the rights of all. In this case Lerdo's cancellation aggrieved the Pennsylvania Railroad people because it negated their primary contract, but it was also seen as threatening all American interests in Mexico.[27]

In February 1876 President Lerdo followed up his railroad contract cancellations by rejecting a bilateral trade exchange pact between the United States and Mexico. The action seriously undermined the daily cartage of the cash-starved Texas International directors. It was the last straw. The trade agreement, negotiated in conjunction with a rescheduling of the payment of the Mexican national debt, was also the last hope of the New York Bondholders Committee. The Americans had expected the Mexicans to begin payments on their obligations in the near future, but Lerdo dashed their hopes. Lerdo acted from a sense of Mexican nationalism. He feared that adoption of a special trade arrangement would isolate Mexico from its European trading partners and lead to American hegemony. The Mexican president had alienated all of the American interest groups involved in his country at the very moment in which the American railroads, at great expense and risk to their owners, were approaching the Mexican border.

Lerdo's American and Mexican critics labeled him an "obstructionist" and called him "treacherous" and "double dealing." In contrast, the Americans saw in General Díaz a strong, decisive military leader capable of disciplining a fractious nation. A paraphrase of Franklin Delano Roosevelt captures the prevailing hope of Americans with interests in Mexico: "Díaz was a Son of a Bitch, but he was our Son of a Bitch." This was a critical juncture, the most critical yet for American enterprise in Mexico. Leading financiers and industrialists from the eastern United States joined elites from southern Texas to influence the course of Mexico's history. They participated in the overthrow of the Lerdo government by providing financial assistance to General Díaz and his band of rebels.

Porfirio Díaz was the son of a provincial elite family in the southern state of Oaxaca. He chose a career as an officer in the Mexican army and distinguished himself as a leader of the Liberal forces during the Wars of the Reform (1858–1860). His popular reputation reached almost mythical proportions when in 1862, as a young general, he helped lead a cavalry flanking movement during the battle of Cinco de Mayo that forced an already retreating French army to break in disarray and suffer the humiliation of near total defeat. Later that month the government of President Juárez and the populace of Mexico City celebrated the result and the select handful of heroic generals that had led their forces to victory. Díaz never forgot Cinco de Mayo or the celebration. He honored the generals of that battle for the rest of his life.

Díaz, who owned a hacienda in the area of Tuxtepec in eastern Oaxaca, became an avid advocate of Mexican modernization. He believed that privatization, modern communications, and transportation had to be achieved as quickly as possible if Mexico was to achieve its potential. He also understood the great profits that could be realized if hacendados could extend their markets to the nation and the world. Modernization could make the nation more powerful economically while enriching his own class of great estate owners. Unlike Juárez and Lerdo, he did not intend to temporize with those people living in the pueblos who insisted on self-sufficient, minimally commercial peasant agriculture. In 1868 he rallied troops in an unsuccessful attempt to overthrow the Juárez government. In 1871 he attempted to win the presidential election. Failing that, in 1872 he enlisted conservative officers and tried a second futile *golpe de estado*. Juárez allowed him to survive, only to die himself later that year.

When Lerdo defeated him in the 1875 presidential race, General Díaz and his military office corps once again attempted to overthrow the democratically elected Mexican government. They were known as "the railroaders," a sobriquet taken from the rallying cry used by Díaz's supporters during his presidential campaign. The railroaders believed that American capital and technology would modernize and transform their nation. In 1876 Díaz and his followers succeeded, with important American help. Díaz had been a principal recipient of American arms shipments procured from the bondholders during the war against the French, and he used those connections to obtain weapons, which reached him through the port of Coatzacoalcos. He deposed Lerdo and seized control of the Mexican government.

In 1872 Díaz had informed Rosecrans, who represented the Pennsylvania Railroad and New York banking interests in Mexico, that if he were president he would sell Americans coastal properties in order to develop them. Three years later, in December 1875, Díaz visited New York in search of support. He met with National City Bank leaders and the young James Stillman, heir to the Charles Stillman estate and protégé of Taylor. When he returned to Brownsville he was escorted by Charles Sterling, the famed lawyer of the law firm of Spearman and Sterling. Sterling accompanied Díaz to the Rio Grande Valley "in order to represent" Stillman's interests. In addition to handling Stillman's affairs, the firm of Spearman and Sterling handled many of the legal needs of Taylor and the National City Bank. The Lerdo government immediately protested Díaz's presence in Brownsville to the U.S. government, claiming that he was a revolutionist and filibusterer.

Meanwhile, on 15 January 1876 General Fidencio Hernández proclaimed the Revolution of Tuxtepec from the small town of that name in the southern state of Oaxaca and identified Díaz as the leader of the revolution. Tuxtepec was symbolically important. Díaz had been born in Oaxaca, and he claimed Tuxtepec, where he owned a hacienda, as his home. Proclaiming the revolution from Tuxtepec gave it legitimacy since a revolution staged from Texas might be seen as a filibustering raid, risking public rejection. Díaz began to mount attacks on Mexican forces from the Texas side of the Rio Grande. Sterling remained in Brownsville until the fighting was well under way in the spring of 1876.[28] The Texas ranchers and financiers avidly wanted to recover their position in Mexico, and Díaz evoked their sympathy, high praise, and expectations.

> General Díaz one of the bravest and most distinguished soldiers of the Republic has, in order to defend himself from arrest, been forced to quit the country and is now a refugee in Brownsville where he is awaiting the expected outbreak.[29]

At first Díaz attracted only minimal support in Mexico, especially around Matamoros. When his force of 1,600 men, including 800 Americans, seized the city, only one soldier in the entire Mexican garrison accepted his appeal to join him in the struggle to "liberate" the country. But after Díaz's forces showed that they could stay in the field for several months, he began to gain enlistments from army officers, generals, state governors, congressional deputies, jurists, and intellectuals, all of whom favored the most rapid and widespread introduction of railroads possible. The key to Díaz's success was his ability to maintain his military campaigns for the first half-year—and his ability to enlist sufficient American support to feed and arm his soldiers. His tenacity demonstrated Lerdo's inability to suppress the revolt. Lerdo tried and failed to raise emergency loans in New York and elsewhere to sustain his bankrupt government.[30]

Besides Stillman, the Americans who supported Díaz included Rosecrans, Taylor, leading members of the New York Bondholders Committee, the Union Contract Company, and the Central and Southern Pacific Railroads. They came together at the most critical juncture in the history of their enterprises. Díaz was also supported by a variety of Texas ranch owners, among whom Richard King was the most prominent, and local military and police officials in Texas. Colonel John Salmon Ford, the leader of the Texas Rangers in the Lower Rio Grande Valley, and General E. O. C. Ord, commander of Fort Sam Houston and an accomplished engineer who had prepared the designs for what became central Los Angeles, stood out in importance.

Lerdo enjoyed only isolated support in the U.S. Congress. Plumb complained of the partisan actions of U.S. Army officers at Fort Brown in Brownsville who ignored the arms traffic to Díaz and the hit-and-run raids across the border. Plumb urged Secretary of State Hamilton Fish to order a halt to the open violations of the neutrality acts of the United States and to officially announce

> that the government of the United States will not in any instance . . .
> permit the weight of its official influence . . . to be used or given in any
> manner in favor of any revolt, . . . that it condemns and looks with
> disfavor upon all such appeals to force and violence, and that its official
> recognition will be extended . . . only to the legitimate representative
> of the Constitutional order . . . even if such representation be driven . . .
> to a foreign land.[31]

Playing for support from the Texans, Díaz promised to put an end to the incessant border fighting. He assured Rosecrans and other American railroad men that he would restore their concessions immediately. Francisco Z. Mena, General Díaz's personal aide and later his secretary for public works, the official who approved railroad concessions and other public works contracts on behalf of the Mexican government, went to San Francisco. He sent a wire to Rosecrans

> in the name of Porfirio Díaz with regard to an important issue. . . . If
> convenient for you, it would be better if you went to Brownsville to
> meet with General Díaz and negotiate the issues I was bringing to put
> before you.[32]

Rosecrans, whose U.S. transcontinental railroad projects took precedence, failed to respond immediately. Mena followed up with a more direct plea for support, asking Rosecrans to confirm statements he had made several years earlier about the need to replace the Lerdo government with one more sympathetic to railroad construction.

> The General wants to know if you are of the same disposition that you
> expressed in your letters of 20 February and 19 September 1873, and
> in case you are, if you could demonstrate this by giving whatever you
> can; because the time has finally arrived in which the caudillo [military
> strongman] you predicted in those letters is taking an active part in
> Mexican politics, . . .
> I assume that upon realizing the object of my mission you will want
> to write the general directly, but place your letters in doubled envelopes
> and direct them in care of Mr. Don Miguel de la Pena in Brownsville.
> This person is trusted—you can be sure that the letters you send will
> reach the General.[33]

Rosecrans almost certainly became involved at that point because, as the fighting intensified, Juan Fermin Huarte gave him progress reports on the revolution. Huarte, a descendant of Agustín de Iturbide, was one of the Pennsylvania Railroad's agents in Mexico and a business partner of Rosecrans. He explained why Rosecrans should support Díaz.

> General Porfirio Díaz went to Brownsville in December. It seems that he has reached an agreement with some Mexican army leaders, and as a result *we* [emphasis mine] are releasing the telegram from the city of Lagos proclaiming that General Donato Guerra has adhered to the Plan [of Tuxtepec] proclaimed by Porfirio Díaz. You understand that this plan has vast ramifications and that the revolution is sweeping the country. . . . Mr. Lerdo de Tejada will be responsible because he has placed the *interests* of the *Nation* secondary to his own. . . . [A] president is obligated to provide work and wellbeing to the poor, those who have no other resources than their personal labor—the personal manipulations of a false and tricky man have earned him the general disgust of his fellow citizens. . . . His vacillations were due to ill will, it is late and his bad conduct weighs heavily, he and he alone is responsible for the innocent blood that will be spilled because if he had accepted the propositions of the "Union Contract Company" of Philadelphia there would be a railroad in Guadalajara by now, there would be no thoughts of revolution, there would be a great deal of money in circulation, and more than anything else, a source of support for the working class. . . . He lost the favorable moment in which you presented yourself in the good faith that marked the "Union Contract Company," and today it is no secret that said company is charging the Mexican government twenty million pesos for expenses, damages, and penalties, because Mr. Lerdo de Tejada did not comply with the concession issued by the government of the distinguished Mr. Juárez, who with a grand vision of the future, granted the concession, but in the view of this President, it is not good that the "Union Contract Company" should have the concession. He carried his arguments forward lacking all reason or justice; because he wanted the English company to have a railroad *monopoly* in Mexico. This individual has discredited the government and the entire country to the extent of drying up all sources of foreign finance, he has canceled all of the concessions, including that of Mr Edward Lee Plumb in Oaxaca [the Isthmus of Tehuantepec line], and, without money it is impossible to build railroads *anywhere*.
>
> I am sure that with the impending fall of Mr. Lerdo de Tejada, the American companies will be called upon and they will build the viaducts without so much discussion; . . . the reopening of relations with the construction companies through honorable arrangements, with indemnities, and other areas of agreement with respect to the construction of railroads, will commercialize relations between the two nations.[34]

Díaz worked, however, with all American interest groups. In February 1876 a group of railroad financiers representing the New York syndicates joined with some of the southern Texas land barons at Kingsbury, Texas. That town, located forty miles east of San Antonio, was the railhead of the Galveston, Harrisburg, and San Antonio Railroad (GH&SA). The men in attendance represented powerful forces in America's westward expansion. Among those present were Thomas Wentworth Peirce, president of the GH&SA, who was building his "Sunset Line" from east to west across Texas.[35] Peirce, a cousin of President Benjamin Franklin Pierce, was well connected in Washington and New York. The Brazoria Tap branch line of the GH&SA, which ran to the rich cotton estate of T. W. House, was entirely financed by Taylor. Peirce's ambitions complemented the political power of his cousin, who envisioned a United States that would stretch from Panama to the Arctic. Peirce wanted to direct the construction of the Pan American Railroad, which would run from Mexico's northern border to Panama. In 1883 Peirce participated in the organizing of the company in Tennessee, but it languished for several years before a short section was built from Salina Cruz, a seaport on the Isthmus of Tehuantepec, down the Pacific shoreline to Tapachula on the Guatemala-Mexico border.

Thomas Wentworth Peirce's brother Andrew also attended the Kingsbury meeting. Andrew, the new president of Texas International, was directing the railroad's construction from the Texas-Arkansas border to Laredo. He also served as president of the Atlantic and Pacific Railroad, which provided connecting lines from the north and east. James Griswold was also in attendance. The manufacture of steel was an important cog in the infrastructure needed for railroad building, and Griswold wanted to secure the El Paso to Guaymas concession from Díaz when he came to power. Another New Yorker, Thomas T. Buckley of Brooklyn, a vice president of the Bank of the Republic of New York, served as treasurer of the Cleveland, Youngstown, and Pittsburgh Railroad of New York and as a director of the Atlantic and Pacific Railroad, the Metropolitan Gas Company of New York, and the Home Insurance Company. Well connected financially, he was a founding director of the New York syndicate that created the Tehuantepec Inter-Oceanic Railroad. Buckley's presence at the Kingsbury meeting with Díaz no doubt helped the New York syndicate gain a later railroad concession, issued by President Díaz in 1879, that included 200,000 acres of land running from ocean to ocean.[36]

Ford reported years later on the negotiations that occurred between the "prominent Americans" and Díaz. He noted that during the meeting King, who purchased $30,000 in Mexican National Railroad stock, promised the Mexican leader financial aid if he would rid southern Texas of the troublesome Cortina.

Díaz asked if the Americans would loan him cash. He was told "you are no doubt fully aware of the trouble that General Cortina is causing on this frontier. . . . If you will give your word that, if successful in the revolution you are about to inaugurate, you will order Cortina to be removed from this frontier, Americans will loan you money." General Díaz gave his word. He obtained money from American citizens. . . . General Cortina has been under surveillance for nearly twenty years. Can any gentleman dare say President Díaz has not fully redeemed his pledge?"[37]

Díaz received $40,000 in American contributions in February, soon followed by separate grants of $14,000, $20,000, $30,000, $50,000, $60,000, and $320,000, forwarded to him by King, Cavazos, Juan Bustamante, and Alberto Castillo. In order "to hide their identity" the New York Bondholders Committee sent the $320,000 contribution to Díaz via Castillo; Castillo then sent it to Bustamante. Castillo, a business agent who bought sugar for Taylor in Havana, was not a newcomer to insurrectionary activities in foreign countries. He was serving as a middleman between Taylor and the Cuban insurrectionists during the Ten Years' War, which was supported by Taylor and the other New York industrialists, merchants, and financiers. Díaz kept his part of the bargain with King. He held Cortina in a military prison and under house arrest at Mexico City until 1892.[38]

Using Stillman's Civil War facility at Bagdad and American cash contributions of at least $500,000, Díaz established a flow of supplies during the winter and spring of 1876. In March arms from New York began to arrive. Ordinance provided to Díaz through the merchants in Brownsville included 500 rifles, 250,000 rounds of ammunition, and 2,000,000 recharging cartridges from the Remington Arms Company of Marcellus Dodge Hartley, a long-aggrieved Mexican bondholder. After a prolonged siege made possible by military supplies shipped by the Whitney Arms Company and the Wexel and De Gress Arms Company of New York, Díaz's forces seized Matamoros in April. The owners of these companies were also Mexican bondholders. The arms, ammunition, horses, and provisions continued to flow in from American suppliers during the spring.[39]

Secretary of State Fish responded to complaints from Congress and Plumb and ordered the American armed forces to halt rebel troop movements north of the border. At San Antonio, General Ord, a drinking buddy of King, refused to comply despite the fact that the order was forwarded to him by his immediate superiors Generals Philip Sheridan and William Sherman. Ord, risking reprimand and even court martial, cynically argued that enforcing the command would "violate the civil liberties of Mexicans."

The problem with Ord's claim was that his troops frequently committed excesses, violating the international boundary and killing "suspicious"-looking Mexicans on both sides of the border during their conflicts with Mexican raiders. In addition, in that region of Texas, Mexicans suspected of minor crimes frequently suffered summary execution at the hands of Texas Rangers and local authorities. The men who supported Díaz later praised Ord for his "protection" and "for helping the forces that altered the public order in Mexico."[40] Ord narrowly escaped military punishment for his open support for the rebels and his failure to comply with direct orders to suppress them.

Díaz exhausted Lerdo's financial resources by prolonging the fighting. Unable to secure loans, Lerdo could not replenish his army. By the spring of 1876 the rebels' persistence gave ambitious Mexican army officers the encouragement they needed to accept impressive promotions offered by Díaz as inducements to join him. By changing sides and bringing their troops with them, these officers moved up, skipping grades in rank.[41] The leaders of provincial elite families such as the Balli family of Tamaulipas, the Treviños of Nuevo León, and the Maderos of Coahuila also mobilized their resources in support of Díaz. In November 1876 Díaz seized power after defeating Lerdo's troops at the battle of Texoac, and six months later, in May 1877, he was formally elected to the presidency.

Rosecrans had anticipated the course of the Americans' conflict with Lerdo, including the Mexican president's failure to pay the debt. He also recognized the growth of a powerful coalition in the Mexican military that saw the railroads as the beginning of the solution to Mexico's economic underdevelopment. Some very important Mexican generals and politicians had been listening when Rosecrans declared that Lerdo's government stood in the way of progress and appealed to the opposition to seize power. His reading of the balance of forces and interests at work in the Revolution of Tuxtepec goes far in explaining the ultimate outcome.

> [I]t was obvious that the foreign debt was a weapon which might be used [to mobilize Americans and deny Lerdo sources of credit]. . . .
> [It] seemed wise for the United States to take care to control all the elements of opposition to Lerdo. . . . From these elements of opposition . . . could be obtained all that was necessary for the development of the country as required by its own best interests and that of the United States.[42]

Rosecrans, like some other early investors in Mexico, lost his enthusiasm for such ventures and by 1876 was committed to equally profitable and less troublesome ventures in California. He teamed up with Collis Huntington, Tom Scott's railroad rival in the American West, moving from the beleaguered Texas and Pacific project to a board membership with the more dynamic Central Pacific–Southern Pacific Railroad, which was constructing a trunk line from San Diego to Yuma. In doing so he transcended the personal distrust and enmity that had existed between him and Huntington. Huntington wanted access to San Diego and Yuma, and Rosecrans controlled the land. It was good business. Rosecrans simultaneously bought large tracts of real estate in and around the rail viaducts approaching San Francisco, Los Angeles, and San Diego, following the practice he had established in Mexico. Although some early players, like Rosecrans, stepped out of the picture, more stayed, and an even greater number rushed in.

In the first decade of the twentieth century President Theodore Roosevelt declared that the United States would regard any European intervention in the Americas as an act of aggression and oppose it with force. The American elite believed that Latin America, especially Mexico, the Caribbean, Central America, and northern South America, should be directly within their sphere of influence. The American military, political, and business leaders backed Díaz, and it was their support that enabled the overthrow of President Lerdo. This was the first engagement in which the American elite mustered itself against a duly constituted, elected, and internationally recognized government in what is now called the developing world. The drama had begun with the arrival of U.S. power in a foreign nation, and it now included considerations of American economic hegemony, colonization, and the outright annexation of Mexico.[43]

The charges of corruption that were asserted by American business leaders against Juárez and Lerdo in the aftermath of the Civil War served as a source of empowerment. Americans could justify violent acts against a government that was corrupt. In the modern world "corruption" has become a legitimizing instrument for American military intervention in less developed countries. The continued use of this discrediting terminology against the political elites of the Third World, including the recent use of the sobriquet *warlord* in Somalia, has grown in accordance with recent and expanding American involvement in global affairs. In the last part of the nineteenth century the use of the word *corruption* against Mexico ignored that nation's rich juridical culture and offered a one-sided view that ignored the participation of politically and financially powerful Americans in illegal activities.

In Mexico the stage was set for an even deeper engagement that would test the character of the Americans and the enduring quality of Mexican civilization. It would reveal the depth of American idealism and pragmatism. It would also expose the fatal flaw of that republic conceived in liberty—a deep and abiding racism that still underscores its assertiveness toward underdeveloped nations.

Part II

THE DÍAZ REGIME, 1876–1910

3   Ubiquitous Financiers

[The National City Company represented] a union of power in the same hands over industry, commerce, and finance, with a resulting power over public affairs.

    Frederich Lehmann, solicitor general of the United States, 1911

Díaz and his followers were determined to modernize what they believed was a poor and backward country, but the Mexican government was deeply in debt and had few cash reserves. Díaz viewed the Americans as essential to the task of creating a prosperous and growing nation. He believed that only American involvement in all aspects of the Mexican economy could transform the country. The changes would be spearheaded by the development of railroads and communication systems and the privatization of agriculture. The Americans who had been frustrated by the cautious Lerdo were optimistic about American opportunities under the new regime.

Aggressive American capitalists began to move forward with commitments to banking, railroads, technology, resource exploitation, and land ownership in Mexico. The bankers gave direction and coordination to this increasing flow of U.S. investment, which deepened the intermixing of American and Mexican businessmen. Leading U.S. bank directors established personal and institutional operations in Mexico. They also began to enlarge their sphere of operations in Europe, Latin America, Asia, and Africa, and they increased their economic and political power at home.

RECOGNIZING THE NEW REGIME

Formal recognition by the United States was essential for the success of Mexico's new administration. The U.S. government had continued to deal with the Mexican president in a positive manner despite Plumb's success in creating tension between the two countries by lodging complaints against Díaz with President Rutherford B. Hayes, who had taken office in 1877. Two issues were of primary concern to the Americans. They wanted to strengthen their control of trade along the border, and they wanted to stop the raids across the Rio Grande that had tormented Texas ranchers since 1848. The administration's approach was benign rather than confrontational. Secretary of State Hamilton Fish directed John Foster, the American minister to Mexico, to

> leave an impression that the United States, prior to deciding in favor of that step, would expect . . . the repeal of the law creating the "Zona Libre" . . . and efficient measures towards checking inroads into the States and Territories adjacent to Mexico. Though these measures might not in the end be deemed indispensable to a formal recognition of that government, they are deemed so important to the preservation of friendly relations between the two countries, that our earnestness upon the subject must not be left in doubt.[1]

The *zona libre* was an area in which customs duties and oversight were not imposed. It stretched along the border, extending from the Gulf Coast inland beyond Laredo. European goods could enter Mexico via Bagdad and Matamoros and then pass over the border into the United States duty-free. German, Irish, and Spanish merchants had long dominated this trade from Matamoros, which, because of its location near the mouth of the Rio Grande, controlled some two-thirds of all such imports into northern Mexico. Among the most important merchants in this trade were Irishman Patrick Mullins (also known as Patricio Milmo) and Spaniard José San Roman, who had been close associates of the now-deceased Charles Stillman.

The Stillman holdings in northeastern Mexico and the Lower Rio Grande Valley included the Brownsville Ferry Company, which controlled most of the shipping that moved from the coast at Port Isabel and Bagdad to Brownsville and Matamoros and the transmittal of goods between Brownsville and Matamoros. Also under Stillman control was the largest overland cartage company, which carried goods from Brownsville and Matamoros to Mier, Monterrey, and the interior. Stillman's Brownsville Town Company continued to own and sell urban lots. Stillman's son James, who had replaced Taylor as head of the National City Bank in 1892, was busily divesting himself of this overwhelming commitment. He and his father's partner, Richard King, were now interested in the construction of a branch of the Mexican National Railroad that would run from Corpus Christi, where Stillman held large sections of land, to Laredo and Mexico City.

Foster enthusiastically performed the tasks that Secretary Fish had given him. A maternal ancestor of John Foster Dulles and the son of an American secretary of state, Foster was Levi P. Morton's "man in Mexico." He had developed close ties to the New York banking and mercantile firm owned by Morton and George T. Bliss, and Morton had retained him to represent his interests in Mexico. Morton and Bliss was one of the most important investment banking concerns in the United States. The partners had been members of the Rosecrans railroad syndicate. Morton invested widely in Mexico during the Porfiriato, taking a major interest in the railroads and Corralitos hacienda and Candelaria silver mine in Chihuahua. He eventually merged his Morton Trust Company with the Guarantee Trust Bank of New York. Morton was also a prominent politician. He was a future governor of New York and a future vice president of the United States, and he lost the Republican presidential nomination in 1900 to William McKinley by only one vote.

In June 1877 the Hayes administration directed General William Sherman to seek "cooperation" with the Mexican authorities in the suppression of the bands of Mexican raiders. It had become the most pressing political issue on the Texas frontier.

> The President desires that the utmost vigilance on the part of the military forces in Texas be exercised for the suppression of these raids. It is very desirable that efforts to this end . . . be made with the co-operation of the Mexican authorities; and you will instruct General Ord commanding in Texas, to invite such co-operation on the part of the local Mexican authorities, and to inform them that while the President is anxious to avoid giving offense to Mexico, he is nevertheless convinced that the invasion of our territory by armed and organized bodies of thieves and robbers to prey upon our citizens should no longer be endured. . . .
>
> At the same time he will inform those authorities that if the Government of Mexico shall continue to neglect the duty of suppressing these outrages, that duty will devolve on this government, and will be performed, even if its performance should render necessary the occasional crossing of the border by our troops.[2]

General Ord was commanded to pursue the "bandits" led by General Juan Cortina across the border. General Ord enjoyed close ties with the new Mexican government, especially the state administrations appointed by Díaz in northern Mexico. Geronimo Treviño, the new governor of Nuevo León, Evaristo Madero, the new governor of Coahuila, and Manuel González, now the most powerful man in Tamaulipas, had benefited from Ord's refusal to aid federal troops during the Revolution of Tuxtepec—Díaz had been quick to reward his friends. Ord was also tied to General Treviño also in a more personal way: Ord's daughter Lucy married Treviño shortly after Díaz seized the presidency.[3]

Ord complied zealously with his new orders. This time he assisted Treviño by pursuing the raiders after they crossed the border back into Mexico. In doing so he denied them sanctuary, committing what some regarded as an act of war. This conduct provoked public outrage in both countries, and the two presidents quickly distanced themselves from his actions. U.S. Army officers arrested Ord and placed him before a military court, but he was cleared of all charges. After the trial Ord retired to the Monterrey residence of his daughter and son-in-law and accepted their gift of 90,000 acres, a portion of the 880,000-acre land grant that Treviño had obtained from Díaz.[4]

Under pressure from the U.S. government, Díaz moved to crush the raiders. He exiled Cortina from the border area and this, combined with Ord's actions and cooperation from the Mexican army, put a stop to the raids on American properties in the Lower Rio Grande Valley. They would not begin again until the early years of the Mexican Revolution. Colonel John Salmon Ford of the Texas Rangers reported decades later that after Díaz removed Cortina from the border he kept him away for twenty years. In fact, Cortina's fate was grimmer—he remained under at least house arrest in the Mexico City area until the early 1890s.[5]

A NEW ERA OF AMERICAN INFLUENCE

The end of border disorders, the removal of the recalcitrant Lerdo, the assertiveness of the new chief executive in the suppression of anti-American sentiment, and U.S. recognition of the new government opened up Mexico to a new period of American influence. While not as visible as their French counterparts, the American bankers in Mexico assumed an increasingly important role.[6] They served as leaders and intermediaries in business, channeling American investments toward the exploitation of natural resources as well as infrastructure projects. Most of the bankers who decided to do business in Mexico had begun by investing in commerce and real estate along the border between Texas and Mexico in the wake of the Mexican-American War or by purchasing Liberal bonds during the 1860s.

John S. Kennedy, one of the earliest investors in northern Mexico and a correspondent banker for the firm of J. P. Morgan and Company, participated in the 1860s sale and purchase of Mexican government bonds. During the Porfiriato he acquired Mexican railroad bonds. Moses Taylor also bought government and railroad bonds. An early investor in the transatlantic cable, he then financed the underwater connection that reached Matamoros, Tampico, and Veracruz. The Stillmans led in the development of the Texas-Mexican borderland and American trade in northern Mexico, and they committed the National City Bank, the largest financial institution in the United States by the 1890s, to the Mexican railroad system. In 1906 James

Stillman, William Rockefeller, and Henry Rogers, the heads of the Amalgamated Copper Company, took over the Cananea copper mines of Sonora. James A. Stillman, the third generation of the family to become involved in Mexico and later the chief executive of the National City Bank, invested heavily in the Candelaria silver mines of Durango and continued the bank's commitment to the railroads.

Jay, George Jay, and Edwin Gould began with Mexican railroad, telegraph, and telephone investments, and Edwin added to them with the purchase of the Sainapuchic hacienda in Chihuahua. Bostonians George Abbott and Thomas Jefferson Coolidge of Old Colony Trust began their involvement in Mexico with investments in the Mexican Central Railroad. They also sought to develop routes to the ports of Guaymas, Topolobampo, and Tampico. Those routes would have transported goods moving north through the Pacific Ocean to El Paso as quickly as they could reach Los Angeles or San Francisco.

George Brackenridge, the owner of the San Antonio National Bank, became active in Mexican investments in the 1870s. An investor in the International Railroad, the Great Northern Railroad of Texas, the Mexican National Railroad, and the National City Bank, he anticipated the other American bankers in Mexico by twenty years. Other prominent New York financiers with early interests in Mexico included J. P. Morgan of J. P. Morgan and Company, George Baker of the First National Bank, Jacob Schiff of Kuhn Loeb, and investment banker William Salomon. After them came the smaller-scale financiers, who represented a second generation of American investment. They came from dozens of cities in the northeastern, midwestern, and western United States. They entered Mexico in search of fortunes associated with mining in the north and tropical export agriculture in the south and along the coasts. Several of them created or participated in financial institutions in Mexico City, Chihuahua, Durango, Saltillo, Monclova, and elsewhere. They mainly used these facilities to concentrate and allocate capital for their endeavors.

These financiers followed the lead of their predecessors Kennedy and Taylor, who had invested in the bonds of the Mexican Liberal government in the 1860s and supported the earliest railroad endeavors. They agreed on Mexico's potential for profits in shipping, railroads, telegraphs, and resource development. By 1910 their experience dictated that a diversified American presence should bear the burden of development. Stillman's liquidation of his father's real estate, manufacturing, and mining assets in northern Mexico reflected this philosophy and allowed him to move into the control of infrastructure.

The American bankers in Mexico first operated on an individual rather than a collective basis in most industrial and commercial endeavors because in the early years they merely extended their operations from the United States to their geographical neighbor. The first broadly cooperative ventures came with the formation of the New York Bondholders Committee and the syndication of Mexico bond issues. The Speyer Bank of New York became a significant long-term holder of Mexican bonds, while J. P. Morgan and Company, which was larger and less specialized, served as the most important American bank in the sales of Mexican government securities. Speyer's ties to Collis Huntington, who owned the International Railroad of Mexico and was associated with industrial enterprises in Coahuila and Durango, caused him to be more intimately tied to Mexican enterprise than Morgan was.

PREEMINENT FINANCIER

J. P. Morgan's father, Junius, established the house of Junius S. Morgan and Company in London during the 1850s. He favored the Union cause in the Civil War and began selling U.S. Government securities to British investors. He achieved such success that "a large portion of all British investments made in America went through this banking firm, which naturally worked closely with Drexel, Morgan, and Company in New York."[7]

Morgan enlarged on that beginning. He used Junius S. Morgan and Company and his partnership in the house of Morgan Grenfell and Company in London as an operating base. Morgan focused on loans to foreign governments and the development of railroads, telegraph, cables, shipping, and mining. These firms presented him with influential British partners, including his brother-in-law Walter H. Burns, Robert Gordon, and Frederick W. Lawrence. For dealings with French capitalists Morgan formed a partnership with Joseph William Drexel that they dubbed Drexel, Morgan, and Company. The new firm had offices in Paris, New York, and Philadelphia. That move also gained him Drexel Hartjes of Paris and Philadelphia, run by Joseph Drexel's brother. Thereafter, Morgan brought French participants into his domestic and foreign undertakings.

From the 1890s on, Morgan's financial ties included the leaders of the largest institutions in Britain and France. In London, Barclay and Company, Baring Brothers, Morgan Grenfell, Junius S. Morgan and Company, Peabody and Company, N. M. Rothschild, and the Bank of England headed the list. In France, Morgan and his associate Stillman dealt with all of the largest banks and maintained somewhat less extensive ties with German capitalists. The French banks were the Banque Française pour le Commerce et l'In-

dustrie, the Banque de Paris et des Pays-Bas, Credit Moblier, Rothschild
Frères, the Société Générale de Crédit Industriel et Commerciel, Drexel, the
Bank of France, the Banque de l'Union Parisienne, the Comptois National
d'Escomptes de Paris, Crédit Lyonnais, and Emile Erlanger.[8]

Morgan's interest in Mexico dated from the original financing of the
Mexican National Railroad in the 1870s, when the firm played a decidedly
minor role. In the late 1870s Morgan joined Emlen Roosevelt, Taylor, and
other New York bankers to finance the Mexican Telegraph Company, which
was closely related to the railroad. The firm, which was headed by James
Scrymser, was part of a larger communications conglomerate that included
the Central and South American Cable and Telegraph Company and the
Pacific Cable Company. Morgan then backed Scrymser in an unsuccessful
effort to lay a transpacific cable through Hawaii to China.

During the 1880s two of Morgan's more notable commitments were to
the International Company of Mexico and to the Mexican Telephone Company. In 1886 Morgan accepted a position on the board of directors of the
telephone firm. The effort to control Baja California through the International Company commanded even more of his attention. In 1887 Morgan
took the lead in floating a $3,000,000 bond issue for the firm, forming a syn-
dicate of American buyers, and loaning it $500,000. Morgan already recog-
nized the arid climate on the peninsula and lack of water as liabilities for
development, but the military potential of the long peninsula was enormous.
He directed the managers of the company to promote its activities with the
proviso that they make "no sales or arrangements without our knowledge
that might prejudice the security of our claims." Unfortunately, the military leadership of the United States saw nothing but problems associated
with the dearth of protected harbors on the Pacific side, the aridity, and Mexican sovereignty.[9]

Morgan placed the company headquarters in his hometown of Hartford
and named Edgar Welles president. Welles, an old friend, was the son of Secretary of the Navy Gideon Welles, who had worked closely with Junius Morgan in financing the buildup of the Union armed forces during the Civil War.
The company actively held 3,500,000 million acres of Baja California real
estate and held Mexican government concessions for as much as or more
than 17,500,000 additional acres. Morgan hoped to exploit the mineral, salt,
and fishing resources of the peninsula and unsuccessfully tried to settle
Americans in its more desirable locales.[10]

Morgan followed his initial investment with a $200,000 loan in return
for $800,000 in the bonds of the International Company's mining subsid-
iary, the Mexican Phosphate and Sulphur Company. He then sold the bonds

through Drexel Morgan in London and Philadelphia in order to finance the construction of the Peninsula Railway from the United States border to La Paz. The successful Probst Development Company of New York took charge of the project, but it could not be completed without collateral development in Baja. The Probst house later became the proprietor of several hundred thousand acres in Campeche. By the end of 1887 Morgan was looking for a way out of what had become a failed stab at empire. Welles signed over $750,000 in International Company debenture bonds for Morgan "to do with as he wishes" and an additional $550,000 of the phosphate subsidiary's paper. In 1888 the International Company paid Morgan $100,000 "with interest" from its revenues from stock sales. Morgan got out, avoiding serious damage, and the company went into receivership.[11] Then the firm reportedly passed from American to British ownership.

The peninsula's desert climate, sandy soil, and paucity of natural resources, combined with the apathy of the military and political leadership of the United States, were too much for even Morgan to overcome. The International Company's land and mining claims remained valid in law and the Mexican government respected many of the concessions for two more decades. Some of the British bondholders held their investments past World War I. Welles continued to work for the firm in Baja and southern California for years after its transfer to British registry. In the 1890s Welles resigned from the International and took directorships with two of Morgan's railroads, the Wabash and the Baltimore and Ohio. He continued in that capacity into the 1920s.

Despite the official change in national ownership, which was probably facilitated through the sale of International Company stocks by Junius S. Morgan and Company in London, the American banker retained contact and probably controlled the firm. Drexel, the financier's brokerage in Philadelphia, served as the International's fiscal agent. J. P. Morgan and Company continued to function as the firm's principal bank in the United States, while Morgan's frequent syndicate partner Glyn, Mills, Currie, and Company served as its European representative. Glyn, Mills, Currie, and Company also represented the financial interests of the Mexican government in London.

Morgan's project of the 1880s represented a continuation of American efforts begun in 1858 by Taylor, Aspinwall, Skiddy, and Plumb to purchase Baja California for the Pacific Mail Steamship Company. Morgan, like Taylor, regarded Baja California from an economic standpoint as strategically important for American interests in the Pacific. Unfortunately for him, military men did not see it that way. The Baja California venture reflected the far-ranging vision of America's financial leaders as they reached out for "the

Pacific Basin." At the same time they were moving directly south toward central Mexico and "South America," which meant the Western Hemisphere south of Mexico. The evidence indicates that Morgan remained an interested participant in the International because of U.S. strategic interest in the region, but, as he usually did, the banker had successfully interested others in the ownership of the firm itself. He profited through the banking services and stock offerings associated with it. After 1910 the growing nationalism of the Mexican Revolution obviated the strategic possibilities of acquiring Baja as a U.S. territory and left the enterprise moribund. The revolutionary government later revoked the land concessions.[12]

Morgan's bank widened its influence abroad by establishing investment pools with the leading British banks and branches of the National City and First National Banks in Africa and Asia. Each of the American banks gained a 5 percent share in the foreign enterprises. The same arrangement held in Mexico and South America, except that Kuhn Loeb joined the consortium. In Mexico the ratio was reversed, with the British and the Europeans accepting a 15 percent share.

During the 1880s and 1890s Morgan was favorably impressed by Díaz's achievement of political order and therefore security for investors in Mexico. Morgan took a special interest in the development of a railroad system owned by Americans and tied directly to the American transcontinental trunk lines. The London *Daily Mail* reported that Morgan's Mexican strategy was "to get into close contact with the Government . . . [in order] to have the inside track when railroad or other concessions are going."[13] Morgan's decision to underwrite and sell the Mexican government bond issue of 1898 spearheaded the willingness on the part of the larger American banks to take part in foreign ventures. The involvement of Morgan, Stillman, and Baker (Morgan's "Trio") in the British Empire and Morgan's actions in Mexico constituted major turning points in the history of American banking and financial arrangements in other nations.[14]

The *Daily Mail* proved visionary in its assertion that Morgan sought an inside position with President Díaz. In 1901 Morgan's London firm gained a $150,000 share in a loan to the Mexican National Railroad. During the stock market panic in 1907 J. P. Morgan and Company defended besieged Mexican securities by forming buying syndicates in London and New York. In 1908 Morgan cosponsored stock issues of the Interoceanic Railroad of Mexico with the Dresdener Bank, but he kept power and control over Mexico in mind.[15] During the Porfiriato he supported governmental infrastructure projects, including railroads and telephone and telegraph systems. Morgan's firm took few risks in American-owned Mexican agricultural, mining, and industrial projects, unlike other banks. The Knickerbocker invested in sugar, the Empire National had investments in the Northwestern Railroad and in timber, and the Wells Fargo directors had holdings in the silver mines at Batopilas.

In 1900 Morgan created the International Mercantile Marine (IMM), which consolidated Anglo-American shipping interests. This was a major step toward taking control of communications and transportation infrastructure in the Americas. The creation of IMM strengthened the already powerful position of the United States in transoceanic cable and telegraph services. The American investors included Morgan at $14,000,000, New York Life Insurance Company at $4,000,000, John D. Rockefeller with $3,671,000, Baker at $2,000,000, and the National City and First National Banks at $1,000,000 each. The British capitalists included Sir Clinton Dawkins, J. B. Ismay, Viscount R. J. Pirrie, and Harold Sanderson, who served on the board of directors.[16]

Morgan believed in Anglo-Saxon hegemony over the rest of the world and in the future of the banking elites of the United States as partners in the economic ambitions of the British Empire. The Civil War had taught Morgan that strong men were needed to forge a union out of blood and steel. Those men—the bankers and industrialists of the Northeast, primarily New York—could transcend the inefficiencies and weaknesses of small businesses and regionalism. Behemoth corporations reaching across national boundaries to incorporate undeveloped resources and develop larger markets were the answer, but that required special men like himself. He believed that concentrated wealth and expertise, with political power working on behalf of that wealth and expertise, would benefit everyone.[17]

A GREAT GAME

In the first decade of the twentieth century the "trusts" created by American bankers dominated the American economy, and although that achievement deepened the animosities toward them on the part of domestic rivals and sectors of the public, including the Progressives, it reflected their vision and ability to act. As America's financiers extended their domestic and foreign economic holdings and influence, they increased their political power with the inner councils of the U.S. government. From 1892 until the end of World War I successive American presidents appointed Stillman's choices as secretaries of the treasury, much as they would accept the recommendations for secretary of state from David Rockefeller and the Council on Foreign Relations following World War II.[18]

As the American bankers entered the arena of foreign investments, they solved the problem of European competition with the cooperative approach used at home. Morgan, Stillman, and Baker formed a partnership. Dubbed the "Trio" by Morgan, the three financiers were the most powerful of the growing number of American bankers and business executives seeking investments abroad, especially in Mexico. Morgan, Baker, and Stillman saw finance, industry, and politics as part of an integrated world system. Each headed financial syndicates devoted to creating global financial, shipping, telegraphic, railroad, and industrial integration. Their cooperative relationship allowed the Trio to successfully deal with events such as the consolidation of the steel, rubber, and maritime industries, the merger of the rival Mexican railroads into a national system in 1905, and the financial panic of 1907. It also allowed them to control the Northern Pacific Railroad.

The Trio's partnership for global investments transcended the often fierce competition they practiced in the United States. At home, during the late 1880s and 1890s, Morgan and Baker, the National Bank of Commerce, and New York Life often rivaled the combination of William Rockefeller, the president of Standard Oil, Stillman of National City, and Schiff of Kuhn Loeb. During the 1890s and the first decade of the twentieth century the contending groups developed interlocking directorates over the nation's largest industries and banks, which they ran with limited government regulation.

At the beginning of the twentieth century, American capitalists deepened their role in Mexico by dramatically increasing the financial support for the government along with their influence over business and industry. The shift began in 1899 when Morgan became the co-manager of a foreign loan for the first time. Until the late 1890s the German bank of Bleichroder & Company had enjoyed a monopoly as the leader of multinational Mexican securities syndicates. After complicated negotiations the firm of Junius S. Morgan in London accepted, on behalf of the Trio, a 15 percent share of the Mexican government's 1898 bond issue, joining the Deutsche Bank and Bleichroder as one of the three leading firms in the loan.[19] The following year Morgan sold bonds worth £2,200,00 in New York, while the National City Bank, this time a member of the second tier of participants, easily placed its share of £2,500,000 with its New York clients. Stillman was intensely interested in the Mexican issue. In Great Britain, Morgan Grenfell received requests for Mexican paper worth over £16,000,000, exceeding their supply.

Eleven years later, on 2 July 1910, the Trio reached an agreement with French and German bankers in Paris who were attempting to sell bonds worth £11,100,000 of a £22,000,000 loan to the Mexican government. In the process they froze out the smaller New York banking house of James Speyer, which, because of its connections in Europe, had previously taken part in Mexican bond issues. On 1 April 1911, however, the Trio abandoned Díaz and canceled the agreement, citing political unrest. They had sold only £808,000 of the bond issue in New York.[20]

The Trio spearheaded partnerships with the leading financiers of Europe for investments in Asia, Africa, South America, and Europe itself by developing the special ties formed by Morgan's father during the Civil War and by Stillman in France and Britain during the 1880s. Between 1890 and 1914 the Trio maintained a constant relationship with their West European associates, usually dividing their 15 percent participation in Asian, African, and South American investment into three equal parts. They worked primarily with the same British partners who participated with them in American railroad and real estate development ventures, but French bankers were also important. In Mexico the balance was reversed, with the Trio offering their European associates, usually British, minority participation.

In the late 1890s Schiff joined the consortium for ventures in Latin America, and in that geographic region he and the members of the Trio were known as "the South American Group," a misnomer referring to the Western Hemisphere south of the United States. The Group divided a 15 to 20 percent participation in predominantly British syndicates. While Baker quietly financed the development of the Paseo de la Reforma in Mexico City and the Lomas de Chapultepec subdivision, he joined Morgan and Schiff in more discreet uses of investment capital. In these cases they controlled the destinies of companies yet remained out of public scrutiny.[21] The opportunities were usually in Argentina, Brazil, Chile, and Mexico, but they occasionally occurred on other continents when the Europeans needed Schiff's clients.[22]

Between 1890 and 1917 the Trio led the global expansion of American interests through the Anglo-American alliance by joining in the control of transportation and communications in South America—focusing on Argentina, Brazil, and Chile—followed by China, South Africa, and other places with special resources. They regarded China as the most important future market in the world. In 1902, in order to gain entry into that country, they joined the British-dominated Chinese Development Company.[23] The Trio organized their power by following the pattern they had established in the domestic economy and in Mexico. They began with the conduct of trade, and then extended loans to the governments, following that with railroad concessions and then the development of natural resources and industries.

Between 1892 and 1910 Stillman turned the National City Bank into the nation's foremost financial combine dedicated to the development of transportation, communications, industry, and national resources in the United States and Mexico. His board of directors integrated high-level interests. Among the board members were Henry Clay Frick, a director of the International Banking Corporation, J. Ogden Armour, who held ranches in southern Chihuahua, Cleveland Dodge of the firm of Phelps Dodge, who led one of the two principal mining interests in Sonora, Cyrus McCormick of International Harvester and the Yucatán henequen trade, Peter Grace of W. R. Grace and Company, and J. P. Morgan Jr. By 1910 Rockefeller, Schiff, and E. H. Harriman, all National City directors, controlled the Union Pacific and the Southern Pacific Railroads. Together with Morgan and Baker, they dominated the Mexican National Railroad.[24]

Step by step, Stillman had been reducing his involvement with the daily workings of the National City Bank as he pursued ever greater things. In 1909 he resigned from the presidency of the bank, surrendering everyday management to vice president Frank Vanderlip, and took the position of bank chairman. He then moved to Paris and began to recruit European capital for U.S. economic development. He immediately went to work developing closer business ties with financiers in France. Prince and Princess Poniatowski, the Count de Montsaulnin, and the Baron Von Andre all increased their large blocks of stock in Standard Oil, Union Pacific, and Southern Pacific, firms controlled by Stillman, the Rockefellers, and the directors of the National City Bank.

In 1911 Stillman, William Rockefeller, and Vanderlip created the National City Company as a holding company designed to dominate the U.S. economy. It thus avoided the laws that prevented banks from investing money abroad and would use National City directors and allies in varied combinations. Frederick Lehmann, the solicitor general of the United States, described their success. The National City Company

> made investments in . . . sixteen banks and trust companies and [had] $3,200,000 in other companies of different character, . . . a holding company of banks, with added power to hold whatever else it may find to be to its advantage . . . . [It represented] a union of power in the same hands over industry, commerce and finance, with a resulting *power over public affairs,* which was the gravamen of objection to the United States Bank.[25]

Lehmann's emphasis on power derived from his intimate knowledge of the Trio. Money was only part of their motivation, as Stillman noted while lying on his death bed: "'Twasn't the money we were after, 'twas the power. We were all playing for power. It was a great game."[26]

FINANCIAL BONDS WITH BRITAIN

Stillman's role in Britain had begun in the 1880s when he started his long service as secretary and later president of the American Advisory Committee for the United States Trust and Guarantee Company (UST) of London, managing the firm's investments in the United States and Mexico. Edward Charles Baring (Lord Revelstoke), Sir Ernest Cassel, and Arthur James Balfour led the UST in London. Baring was a director of the Bank of England and the senior partner of the Baring Brothers Bank. Cassel, "one of the wealthiest and most powerful financiers in the city of London," enjoyed a "close friendship with King Edward VII" and sat on the Privy Council. He advised the government on the financial crisis arising from the onset of world war and arranged the "Anglo French Loan in America" with Morgan. An intimate friend of the American tycoons, he joined them in buying up the bond issues of the New York Central, Pennsylvania, and Baltimore and Ohio Railroads, and in reorganizing the Louisville and Nashville line. Cassel deepened his ties to Mexico in 1893 when he "issued the Mexican government a 6 percent loan" and to American financial elites in 1899 when he formed the Mexican Central Railroad Securities Company, acquiring "a preponderate holding" of that railway's bonds.

Balfour's early ties with the United States came by way of his participation in the UST and in his investments in the rapidly growing American economy. Stillman gained Balfour's favor in the 1880s by combining success with the avoidance of danger. Stillman warned him to sell all of his stocks in the Mexican Southern Railroad, "even at a loss" if necessary. Shortly thereafter the line went bankrupt, ruining former American president Grant, who had assumed the leadership of the company and staked his fortune and prestige on its success. Stillman also gave Balfour and his associates timely warning to quit the uncompetitive Inter-Oceanic Railway of Mexico by pointing out that "these companies will eventually have to be reorganized before they are upon a paying basis and that basis will be at a price considerably less than the actual cost of the Railways." Stillman placed most of the British money in American railroads, banks, mines, and real estate, and in the sugar trust. One of his more successful ventures on their behalf was the Century Realty Company, which the British owned and he directed. It became an American giant. In Mexico the British financiers faithfully joined Stillman in investments in railroads serving Monterrey.

Stillman used information gained from Brackenridge, who had large investments in Monterrey. He placed Balfour's money in Texas, in western frontier enterprises, and in the Mexican National, the Monterrey Belt, and the Monterrey and Mexican Gulf Railroads. Stillman anticipated the development of Tampico and advised Balfour to buy into those railroads because impending improvements and the oil boom promised to "make Tampico the best harbor on the Mexican Gulf." He believed that the Monterrey and Mexican Gulf Railroad would become "a very large business as it can be operated successfully at a rate that, I think, would ruin the Mexican Central Railway." Stillman and William Rockefeller, plus John Stewart of the UST, controlled the Monterrey Belt Railroad, which encircled the steel manufacturing and commercial center of northeastern Mexico. Monterrey interested Rockefeller because Standard Oil was attempting to develop fields on the nearby Gulf Coast and the city provided connections with the Mexican National Railroad and the United States. Stillman, Balfour, Baring, and Cassel became partners in a number of other ventures, including holdings on Corpus Christi Bay in Texas.

The men of UST continued to rely on Stillman even after he turned over his active role in the company to Vanderlip and Edwin S. Marston, a director of the bank and president of the Farmers Loan and Trust of New York, which later merged with National City. Stillman remained the head of UST and advised Balfour, Baring, and Cassel to emphasize investments in the United States over those in Mexico because they offered more economic and political stability. He chose only carefully selected Mexican investments, including the Mexican Central Railroad and government bonds, for his British partners.[27]

Stillman oversaw the top-level integration of American and British capital in real estate development, railroads, and steel manufacturing in the United States for a group of American financiers who were known as the "Big Four" because of their domination of the railroad industry in much of the midwestern, southern, and southwestern United States. In addition to Stillman, the members of the Big Four were E. H. Harriman, William Rockefeller, and George Jay Gould, a National City Bank director and a leader of the American Surety Company of New York. Harriman, the member in charge of railroad operations, died in 1909. Noting the concern of his British partners, Stillman assured Baring Brothers that two other members of the Big Four would take over:

> There will be no material change in the executive officers of the several roads in which we are all interested. . . . I regard the organization as very

strong as it is. Mr. William Rockefeller and Mr. Schiff have gone on the Board of Directors of these properties [the UP, SP, and International Railroad of Mexico], and they will have careful and able attention.[28]

The British leaders' successes in American and Mexican business encouraged warm friendships and the notion of unity between the two countries. Balfour strove to achieve that unity as prime minister, as first lord of the admiralty during World War I (when he sat on the Committee of Imperial Defense—the "Inner Cabinet" that met at 10 Downing Street), and then as the head of the Foreign Office. In the latter post he headed the diplomatic mission of April 1917 that met with President Wilson and arranged the conditions for American entry into the war. He was well suited for the task given his fervent advocacy of a close relationship "between the two Anglo-Saxon peoples." The Anglo-American military alliance of World War I depended on the British gaining U.S. credits and supplies. As a result, the American banking community, led by the Trio, acquired British holdings in Canada, South America, Asia, and Africa.[29]

The early ties between the American and British financiers were strengthened by British participation in IMM. The British IMM participants were politically important, complemented the American financiers' experience in global shipping, had extensive contacts in Western Europe and the world, and shared the South American Group's vision of an Anglo-American economic alliance. In 1889 Dawkins served as private secretary of the Exchequer and in 1899 as the financial member for the Council of the Governor General of India. He also served as undersecretary for finance in Egypt. In 1900 Dawkins became a partner in J. S. Morgan and Company of London, where he represented the British interests in the Peruvian Development Company and in Peru's great copper mining complex of Cerro de Pasco. During World War I he took the chairmanship of the Committee on War Office Reorganization.

In 1901 Morgan acquired the Hamburg American Packet Company for IMM, paying $77,000,000. The Hamburg American fleet included the steamship *Ypiranga*, the ship that provided the pretext for the intervention at Veracruz in 1914. Morgan advised his American IMM directors Peter A. B. Widener, Clement Grissom, and Bernard N. Baker to "avoid publicity" regarding the acquisition of the Hamburg American because of the rising public concern about his monopolies. IMM subsidiaries also operated the *Titanic*.[30]

Ismay, as the senior partner in the White Star Line, negotiated the IMM deal with Morgan. He assumed the presidency of the firm from 1904 until

1912, when partner Sanderson replaced him. Sanderson had run a shipping firm in New York during the 1890s and specialized in transatlantic shipping and marine insurance. The IMM would not have been a vertically integrated trust without a shipbuilding division, and Pirrie provided that dimension. He headed the great shipbuilding company of Harland and Wolff, which at one point employed 50,000 workers in its yards at Belfast, Liverpool, and Clyde. Deeply interested in "port development in South America," he served as a privy councilor to the king after 1897 and ran a major defense industry during World War I. Together, the American and British participants financed a shipping trust with $120,000,000. By 1909 Morgan had gained control of the Holland American Line and transferred it to IMM for $50,000,000, again specifying that it remain seemingly independent to allay U.S. political concerns about trusts and monopolies.[31]

Following the creation of IMM, the South American Group joined British financiers in lending to the Argentine, Chilean, and Peruvian governments. Then they helped finance the Argentine and Chilean Transandean Railroads. In 1912 the South American Group gained a 10 percent share of a £15,000,000 issue of Argentine rail stock and then purchased an interest in the Chilean portion of the Transandean Railroad. Those investments fit with their share in Anglo-American development projects before 1914 at Cerro de Pasco in Peru, and in the Braden, Kennicut, and Penyon copper mines in Chile. The Trio recruited the veterans of Mexico and the Comstock, James Ben Ali Haggin and William Randolph Hearst, into the Cerro de Pasco and Chile. The Trio was also interested in the Brazilian interior. In 1911 it took one-third of a £600,000 loan to the Southern Brazil Lumber and Colonization Company for the construction of a railroad and then invested £300,000 in a £1,500,000 South American development loan to a consortium including the Société Générale and the Banque de Paris et des Pays-Bas. During World War I the Trio purchased many British interests in southern South America, including virtually all of their mining resources in Chile and Peru.[32]

THE PANAMA PROJECT

By the turn of the century the Trio was extending its power far beyond Mexico. Morgan and his clients had joined the British in China, began independent ventures in southern South America and Africa, and brought the Englishmen into minority participation in seaborne transportation. In 1902 Morgan arranged a $10,000,000 refinancing of the Cerro de Pasco mines using American money. He bought 11 percent, Haggin 34 percent, Frick 11 percent, and Phoebe Hearst 11 percent. At the same time the South American Group bought and sold stocks and bonds in New York for Haggin's Jalapa Railroad and Power Company of Mexico.[33]

The acquisition of the rights to the Panama Canal in 1904 demonstrated the growing influence of the American financial elite. The financiers had centralized in New York, developed close ties to the U.S. government, and continued their success in the systematization of financial, economic, and political power. Morgan coordinated the canal effort and Schiff assisted in the deliberations. On 28 April, Morgan, Schiff, and their representatives concluded negotiations with the French interests for the rights to the canal on behalf of their New York financial partners. The French received a check for $25,000,000, written to the Banque de France. The contributors included Stillman and the National City Bank ($8,000,000), Morgan, Kennedy, and the National Bank of Commerce ($5,500,000), Baker and the First National Bank ($3,600,000), and James Woodward and the Hanover Bank ($2,000,000), as well as others.[34] The U.S. treasurer then forwarded $40,000,000 to Morgan, who disbursed the profits. Morgan, who grossed $15,000,000, realized a net profit of only 296,076 francs. Kuhn Loeb grossed $5,000,000, and First National $5,000,000. Richard W. Thompson became the head of the Panama Canal Company and passed on his directorship of the Mexican Telephone Company, which was controlled by the South American Group, to Morgan.[35]

The Mexicans were surrounded by manifestations of American power, from the Panama Canal project, to the increasingly frequent U.S. military incursions in Central America and the Caribbean, to the growing magnitude of American control of Mexican exports. When Morgan financed and organized the acquisition of the Deering Harvester Company by International Harvester in 1902, he brought an important cross-section of the American elite together in Yucatán. American railroad interests gained a role in henequen exports from Yucatán. Although Cyrus McCormick of Harvester and George Foster Peabody continued to exercise direct control of the henequen market, Morgan bought $3,000,000 in new shares, John D. Rockefeller invested $5,000,000, Stillman and Rodgers took $500,000 each, and E. H. Harriman purchased shares worth $100,000.[36]

Morgan's Panama Canal project, the consolidations of IMM, International Harvester, U.S. Rubber, General Electric, the U.S. Steel Corporation, American Telephone and Telegraph (AT&T), and the New York Central Railroad, and the refinancing of the Pennsylvania and Santa Fe Railroads found many of the same leaders and investors as did ventures in Mexico, South America, Asia, and Africa. The growth and centralization of American financial power marked an emergent plutocracy, one with increasing influence over the Mexican economy and ambitions beyond that.

THE FIRST GLOBAL BANK

The International Banking Corporation, or the IBC, emerged in Mexico in 1902 as a conduit for U.S. investments in government bonds and securities, mining, oil companies, agriculture, timber, and ranching. As individual financiers, the directors of the IBC were essential to the survival of the Díaz regime. As a result, these capitalists usually got what they wanted in the way of business and resource concessions. The IBC was the first American multinational bank. It began in New York and Mexico City, and then, once established in capital-poor Mexico, it expanded to Shanghai. By 1910 the financiers had IBC branches in London, San Francisco, Washington, D.C., Manila, Hong Kong, Yokohama, Shanghai, Singapore, Bombay, Calcutta, Canton, Cebu, Kobe, Panama City, and Colón. As a source of support for the development of American-owned enterprises, especially larger multinational concerns, the IBC directors provided venture capital, institutional investments, and services such as insurance on capital goods.[37]

The IBC directors reflected the concentration of financial power in New York. In the nineteenth century banks and insurance companies with vanguard investment strategies, such as the National City Bank and Equitable Life, invested heavily in real estate on the frontier. Employing specialized knowledge, the directors of these institutions realized much higher profits than their more conservative counterparts and had more liquid capital for investment. In 1899, in an example of this managerial know-how, Morgan refinanced the Mexican national debt using passive European capital. He controlled the issue and therefore could determine who would participate. When the IBC opened in Mexico City, its National City and Morgan bank directors became the official fiscal agents for the United States. They also took over that crucial function and others in China, India, Japan, Panama, the Philippines, and Santo Domingo.

Almost all of the IBC's directors figured prominently in the American insurance industry, and several had close ties to the National City Bank, the Western National Bank, and J. P. Morgan and Company. The insurance companies had higher profit margins than other types of financial institutions, so their directors were able to commit a higher percentage of their capital to projects in Mexico and the western United States. They made initial outlays in areas for railroad building, followed by investments in resource extraction, ranching, farming, and urban development. They sought areas with potential for population growth or concentrations of raw materials, or ranchlands and croplands that promised above-average profits. In addition, the insurance men used their experience in risk management and their underwriting services to handle the tricky problems inherent in the transportation, communications, mining, and petroleum industries.

The directors of the Equitable joined the IBC to further the development of their interests in Mexico and other parts of the world. Eight of them served on the IBC board, including Colonel Edwin Mandell House of Houston. House had close ties with the San Antonio and Aransas Pass Railroad and the Texas Oil Company, which had acquired about 4,000,000 acres of land in northeastern Mexico. His presence on the board underscored the intermediate role of the southwestern capitalists. The New Yorkers had more money and controlled more votes, but the Texans were leading financiers, and they had also extended their holdings into Mexico. The colonel's brother John House later served as a director of seven Mexican mining concerns that were controlled by New York financiers.

Thomas H. Hubbard, a leader of the law firm of Butler, Stillman, and Hubbard, served as the chairman of the IBC. In addition to family ties to the National City Bank, Hubbard had business relations with Morgan, and his law firm had long experience in Mexican affairs dating back to dealings with Matías Romero in the 1860s. Hubbard and law partner Thomas E. Stillman, brother of James Stillman, controlled a major portion of Southern Pacific stock through their administration of the estate of Mrs. E. F. Searles, who had inherited an interest in the railroad following the death of Mark Hopkins, her husband. Hubbard was a member of the board. During the first decade of the twentieth century the directors of Southern Pacific operated a Pacific route that extended from Nogales to Mexico City and the Mexican International, controlled by Huntington, which ran from Eagle Pass–Piedras Negras to Durango. Hubbard and Stillman were instrumental in consolidating the International into the Southern Pacific system.

Hubbard also sat on the boards of several other railroads originally organized by Moses Taylor—the Guatemala Central, the Wabash, the Central Texas, and the Northwestern—and he assisted in restructuring the Wabash Railroad as a holding company for Morgan's railways in the Great Lakes region. His participation in these projects epitomized the importance of the IBC directors in American expansion. Hubbard reflected the intimate nature of American and Mexican railroad ownership: like several of his colleagues, he served as a director of the Western National Bank, which focused on railroad and frontier investments. His leadership also linked the IBC directors to the U.S. government, which chose the bank for the collection of the indemnity China owed to American investors because of damages inflicted during the Boxer Rebellion.

In 1903 IBC president William L. Moyer served on the boards of the Butte Copper and Zinc Company and the Butte Central and Boston Copper Corporation, copper mining companies capitalized in New York with operations in Montana. The Amalgamated directors bought both firms in 1904. At that point Moyer was already working in tandem with Henry Rogers, the president of Amalgamated and a director of IBC, in furthering the interests of the "copper trust" in the United States and Mexico. The combination underscored the strong position in IBC held by Stillman, William Rockefeller, Harriman, and George Gould through their intermediaries.

Jules Bache, another board member, represented a complex of New York banking, insurance, railroad, and petroleum interests, plus the National Bank of Cuba and the Houston Oil Company in Texas. His role as a director of the Empire Trust Bank of New York placed him in an important position in Mexican railroading. The Empire Trust owned stocks and the first mortgages for the properties of the Northwestern Railroad of Chihuahua. The international activities of another IBC director, Juan M. Ceballos, focused on politics and law relating to the communications and transportation infrastructure of his native Cuba. He presided over the Development Company of Cuba, the Rosario Sugar Company, and the Iron Steamboat Company of New Jersey, where he worked with John B. Jackson, a fellow IBC director and state department official. Jackson provided the bankers with direct influence in foreign policy decisions.

Ceballos interacted with a large group of American industrialists interested in the Caribbean and Mexico. He and other IBC leaders presided over the sugar export business from the fields in the Caribbean and Gulf Coast of Mexico to the distilleries in the United States. As a director of Tuinucu Sugar Cane Manufacturing, Hooper Drying Machine, New York and Porto Rico Steamship, and the India Wharf Brewing Companies, all involved in sugar manufacturing and transportation, Ceballos did business with the Mexican National Sugar Company and its directors Moses Taylor Jr., Charles W. Gould, and Charles T. Barney. All were New York financiers whose fathers had pioneered economic relations between the United States and Mexico. Like other IBC directors, Ceballos served on the board of the Western National Bank, a firm noted for its commitment to the development of new agricultural and ranching lands. The New Yorkers, however, did not have complete control of the American sugar industry. The directors of the Canal Bank of New Orleans enjoyed a monopoly over sugar production in San Luis Potosí and Tamaulipas through the ownership of the Rascon hacienda.

IBC director George Crocker, a former director of the Southern Pacific, shared Ceballos's interest in the sugar industry. He served on the boards of the Cuba and Federal Sugar Refining Companies. As a financier of the Kansas City, Mexico, and Orient Railroad, he encouraged the support of political leaders, including President Hayes, who invested in the project. His foreign railroad interests included the Cuba and the Guatemala Central Railroads. Eugene Delano, like Crocker, was deeply involved in Mexico and the Caribbean Basin. He was a partner in Brown Brothers, an old-line private Wall Street banking firm with offices in Baltimore and London. The firm held a sizeable minority interest and took an active management role in the Tlahualilo Estates, an agricultural complex centered in the rich La Laguna basin of Coahuila. In 1912 Brown Brothers purchased the national debt of Nicaragua. Delano and Crocker tied Mexico into a financial network that included New York, Philadelphia, Wilmington, and San Francisco, where they led major banks and insurance and railroad companies.

The IBC directors enjoyed a base of economic support almost as wide as the United States. Specifically, their connections linked them with the founding elements of the American military-industrial complex. The New York financial community became inextricably merged with that complex when it financed the logistical needs of the Union Army. As the United States began its rapid westward expansion the New York bankers and insurance industry leaders continued their high level of cooperation with the U.S. government and military. Those linkages proved important during the first years of their engagement in Mexico.

IBC director Marcellus Hartley Dodge, an intimate of James Stillman and William Rockefeller, presided over the Remington Arms Company, the Bridgeport Gun Implement Company, and the Union Metallic Cartridge Company. The directors of those firms represented a cross-section of the New York financial community. Many of them intermarried. Dodge's uncles Percy and William Rockefeller Jr. married Isabel and Elsie Stillman, Charles's daughters. Like his grandfathers William Dodge and Marcellus Hartley, Dodge combined his financial, insurance, and arms resources with a sense of Christian mission often found among those involved in American expansion. He sponsored American Christian universities abroad and the American Missionary Society. The combination of banking, arms dealing, warfare, and Christian mission may seem contradictory to some observers, but they have been an American characteristic from the Pequot Wars to the war in Vietnam.[38]

Dodge, as a director of the Equitable, was one of the pioneers of insurance in Mexico. He was also a leader of American Surety and the Western National Bank. His service on these boards coincided with the appointments of seven other IBC directors. The roles of those companies in manufacturing, finance, firearms, communications, and transportation reflected essential elements in the process of American expansion. Dodge, as a director of the American District Telegraph Company and the Westinghouse Electrical and Manufacturing Company, added Mexican infrastructure control to his already impressive role in arms sales and mining. Dodge sold financial, insurance, and communications services in Mexico while the family mining firm of Phelps Dodge gained concessions of land and mineral resources from Díaz. Dodge also sold Díaz armaments needed to maintain domestic tranquility. In later years the Phelps Dodge leadership, in tandem with international banking organizations, continued its expansion to other parts of Latin America and the Third World.

IBC director Henry Clay Frick ran the Carnegie Brothers Steel Company with Grant B. Schley, Carnegie's son-in-law, and Charles M. Schwab. Their roles in insurance, railroads, and industry brought them into close contact with the American capitalists interested in Mexico. Schley and Schwab pioneered Chihuahua railroads in the 1880s and 1890s. They began the lines that Bostonian Frederick Stark Pearson later consolidated as the Mexican Northwestern. While still serving under Frick's tutelage, Schwab joined Bache as a member of the board of directors of the Empire Trust. The bank bought Pearson's mortgages. Later, while Schwab was president of Bethlehem Steel, his experience in Mexico enabled Bethlehem to purchase and exploit the Las Truchas hacienda and its iron deposits in Michoacán.

Frick's diverse interests reflected IBC's role with the giants of American finance and industry. He sat on the boards of the Mellon National Bank, the Pennsylvania Railroad, the Union Pacific Railroad, the Chicago and Northwestern Railroad, the Philadelphia and Reading Railroad, and the U.S. Steel Corporation. The Mellon interests controlled the Gulf Oil Company, a major player in the state of Tamaulipas. Through these positions Frick participated in the oversight of the consolidated lines of the Mexican National Railroad. He was a part of the action in 1898 when Morgan spearheaded American sales of Mexican railroad bonds. In 1901 Frick worked closely with Morgan and Baker, now head of the Paseo de la Reforma Development Company in Mexico City as well as the First National Bank, in creating the U.S. Steel Corporation. Charles Schwab had followed Schley as president of Carnegie Steel and accepted the merger, led by Morgan, that created U.S. Steel. The controlling syndicate of U.S. Steel included John D. Rockefeller of the Standard Oil Company, the principal provider of lighting oil in Mexico. In 1901 these financiers bought the Iron Mountain Company of Durango, originally modernized during the 1880s by Huntington, who also owned the International Railroad of Mexico.

Edwin Gould represented the far-flung banking, railroad, and land development interests of his family on the IBC board. Those interests included the Mexican National Railroad and the International Railroad of Mexico, the Texas International Railroad, which ran southwesterly across Texas to Laredo, and ranch holdings in Chihuahua and Durango. The other Gould interests that were directly engaged with Mexico included the Missouri Pacific, the Saint Louis Southwestern, and the Texas and Pacific Railroads, which Tom Scott had pioneered. The railroads all traversed Texas and tied Mexico to the United States.

The IBC patriarchs brought their sons into the Mexican nexus. Until 1901 Edwin's cousin Emerson W. Gould Jr. owned the large Hacienda de Sainapuchic in western Chihuahua. The estate comprised "some of the finest ranch land in northern Mexico." Gould's obligations grew rapidly, and he found it inconvenient to take the time and trouble to run a mere hacienda. In 1901 he sold the estate to F. G. Oxsheer, a cattleman from Fort Worth. Gould's interests in Mexico assumed a higher level as he accepted the presidency of the Atlantic and Mexican Gulf Steamship Company. His ships hauled the products of the Tezuitlan Copper Company and the Tezuitlan Copper Mining and Smelting Company in Puebla, which he also directed.[39]

Edwin Gould operated at an even higher level among the Mexican and American financial elites than did his cousin Emerson. In addition to those of the IBC, other banks, and railroads including the Wabash, he served on the boards of communications companies that dominated the industry in the United States and Mexico. They included the Western Union Telegraph, the American Telegraph and Cable, the American Speaking Telephone, and the International Ocean Telegraph Companies. He was one of the eight directors of the Equitable Trust Company that participated in the leadership of the IBC. Emerson, Edwin, and the IBC played an important role in American financial, transportation, and communications operations in Mexico.

IBC director Isaac Guggenheim, the financial genius of his family, headed the family's vast investments and operations in Mexico. One of Simon Guggenheim's seven sons, Isaac worked through the investment bank of Kuhn, Loeb, and Schiff (formerly Kuhn Loeb), and to a lesser degree with Stillman at the National City Bank, to arrange loans, consolidations, and the issuance of stocks and bonds for the Guggenheim-controlled American Smelting and Refining Company (ASARCO). Besides Schiff and Stillman, the smaller IBC provided additional capital reserves for his Mexican operations. Amplifying his role with ASARCO, Isaac sat on the boards of directors of Guggenheim Exploration and American Smelters Securities and served as president of the Mexican Union Railroad.

Harriman brought his experience with global finance, insurance, railroads, shipping, and communications to the board of the IBC. He served as the chairman of the Wells Fargo Bank. He also chaired Union Pacific and served as president of Southern Pacific and its Mexican subsidiaries, including the Sur Pacifico and Mexican International. During his tenure the Pacific Coast Company, a subsidiary of Southern Pacific, bought a large land tract near Atoyac, north of Acapulco, as a timber investment. He buttressed his vision of Mexico as a stepping-stone to the Pacific Rim by heading the Portland and Asiatic Steamship Company and serving as a director of Pacific Mail. Back home, he joined other Equitable directors on the IBC board. His high-level directorships in the United States tied the IBC to the leaders of the National City Bank and the New York Central, the Union Pacific, and the Baltimore and Ohio Railroads.

IBC director Sylvester C. Dunham served as the president of the Travelers Indemnity Company and a variety of secondary East Coast banks and insurance companies. An associate of Morgan and a director of American Surety, Dunham committed his and the IBC's resources to the Mexican National Railroad. IBC directors Hegemon and Haley Fiske, Hegemon's protégé, ran the Metropolitan Life Insurance Company as president and vice president of financial services. Metropolitan Life was another of the first insurance companies to open in Mexico. Hegemon's experience with Mexico went back to his participation in the 1860s bond sales. Hegemon and Fiske also integrated Mexican livestock imports with American finance through the former's directorship of the National Shoe and Leather Bank. Hegemon served with Crocker and Edwin Gould as a director of the Mexico Mining Company. IBC director Henry Hyde controlled Equitable Insurance and directed the Durango Mining Company of Mexico. Insurance man Henry S. Manning was another IBC director supporting Arthur E. Stilwell's Kansas City, Mexico, and Orient Railroad.

Episcopal clergyman John James McCook of Hartford served as a key member of the IBC board. He was an outspoken supporter of American expansion and vehemently opposed European "empire" in the Americas. In the early 1890s he joined fellow IBC director Robert Alexander C. Smith in an attempt to purchase Cuba from the bankrupt Spanish government. McCook, who sometimes delivered Sunday sermons to Morgan and Welles, advocated the worldwide dissemination of American Protestant beliefs. He believed that Protestantism, thrift, hard work, and punctuality would create better people in Mexico and in the Caribbean and Pacific Basin as well. He joined the Mallet Prevost and Dodge families in that project. Prominent attorney Sergio Mallet Prevost represented the Anglo-American owners of the most important cotton production complex in Mexico, the Tlahualilo Estates of Durango, for many years. McCook was a member of the board of Wells Fargo and that ubiquitous Mexican insurer, the Equitable.

IBC director W. H. McIntyre owned timber tracts in Durango and Chihuahua, which were linked to the outside world by the Mexican International and the Mexican National Railroads, lines controlled by fellow IBC directors. Like other IBC board members, he held a directorship on the board of the Western National Bank. In 1910 he served on the board of the San Antonio and Aransas Pass Railroad, founded by House, financed by the National City Bank, and now controlled by Southern Pacific. The line connected the most important city in Texas with the Gulf Coast—the New York railroad men considered San Antonio the gateway to Mexico and its resources.

Paul Morton, one of IBC's most influential directors, reflected the far-reaching importance of the IBC in Mexico. He was the son of Levi P. Morton, an owner of the Corralitos hacienda in Chihuahua, who had been vice president of the United States, governor of New York, and head of the Guarantee Trust Bank of New York. Paul maintained extensive connections in the New York financial community with directorships in banks and railroads including the Santa Fe, the parent of the Mexican Central. As a result, he held a large stake in the Mexican national system after the consolidation of the major Mexican lines in 1905. His leadership of Western Union gave IBC yet another tie to Mexican communications and transportation infrastructure. Morton also served as a director of the Continental Rubber Company, which dominated the Mexican guayule rubber industry with its nearly 3,000,000 acres in Zacatecas, factories at Torreón, and harvesting contracts in Coahuila and Chihuahua. The Mexican Central Railroad and the International Railroad of Mexico served those factories and fields. Inevitably, Morton was also a director of Equitable Life.[40]

Director Henry Clay Pierce tied IBC to a large part of the Mexican economy, and he had a greater percentage of his worth committed to Mexico than any other member of the bank. He served as head of the Mexican Central Railroad and on the boards of the American-Mexican Steamship and the Mexican and Northern Steamship Companies, the Mexican Pacific Company and the Mexican National Railroad, the Waters Pierce Oil Company of Mexico, the Tampico Harbor Company, the Mexican National Construction Company (Constructora Nacional), and the Bank of Commerce and Industry of Mexico City. His financial base in New York included the Title Guarantee Trust Company.

The interests of William Salomon and the IBC reached as far as Asia, but he focused his initial foreign investments in Mexico. He began with the finance, railroad, and oil industries. In one stroke he invested $2,000,000 in Edward Doheny's Mexican Petroleum Company, giving that firm the ability to expand its operations in northern Veracruz and southern Tamaulipas and compete with Weetman Dickenson Pearson's British operations to the south. Salomon's railroad ventures included the Mexican National, and he served on the board of the Empire Trust Bank, which held the first mortgages of the Mexican Northwestern. Salomon quickly expanded into Asia, took part in establishing an IBC branch in Manila, and chaired the board of directors of the Philippine Railroad Company. In New York, Salomon concentrated his interests in trust companies, ensuring his access to a wide financial base and low-cost technology.

IBC director Alfred Gwynne Vanderbilt was one of three Vanderbilts remaining as major players in the ownership of American railroads in the early 1900s. Alfred, a grandson of Commodore Vanderbilt, served on the IBC board for several years, from its inception in 1902 until the liquidation of many family assets in the years that followed. In 1902 Vanderbilt and his siblings William Kissam Vanderbilt and Frederick W. Vanderbilt possessed large holdings in the Pennsylvania and New York Central Railroads and thus, after 1905, institutional interest in the consolidated Ferrocarriles Nacionales de Mexcio. They sold their New York Central shares to a combination headed by Morgan and William Rockefeller. Vanderbilt was yet another Equitable director in the IBC leadership.

The IBC sometimes represented American interests in large transactions with the Mexican government. In one such case H. C. Smith, representing an unnamed syndicate of New Yorkers, "acquired about 500,000 acres of pine timberland in what is known as the García [Teruel] tract, in the western part of the state of Chihuahua." The purchasers planned to build an electric power plant, a sawmill, and a railroad. The IBC directors also provided the large amounts of capital needed for expensive technology on a personal basis. William Salomon anticipated IBC's global operations when he provided funds to Doheny that allowed him to extend pipelines and enlarge the refineries and storage facilities of the Mexican Petroleum Company near Tampico.[41]

The IBC constituted the first institution formed by American bankers to develop a wider investor base in the process of global economic expansion. By working with the Mexican government and its officials, the directors of

IBC attempted to link economic growth in Mexico with the United States and themselves. In that sense the IBC directors anticipated the strategies of such multinational institutions as the Import-Export Bank, the World Bank, and the International Monetary Fund. Their operations in Mexico preceded expansion to Latin America, Asia, and the Middle East at the beginning of the twentieth century and revealed the depth of their vision.

INTERLINKING OPERATIONS

During the last years of the nineteenth century America's most powerful bankers, most of them tied to IBC, literally created the Mexican insurance industry. They remained in New York, where they concentrated their assets and channeled their profits. They used the IBC to provide a broader base of financial support for their Mexican insurance operations, but they did not shrink from competing with one another for their share of the market.

The New York Life Insurance Company, the largest American insurance company in Mexico, was intimately associated with the Trio. Its trustees included Kennedy, who was closely associated with Morgan. Five New York Life leaders—Charles S. Fairchild, William R. Grace, IBC director John A. McCall, George W. Perkins, and Stillman—were directors of the National City Bank. Fairchild, a former treasurer of the United States, connected the Trio and the American insurance and railroad leadership politically to the highest councils of the U.S. government. The board of the First National Bank, which included Morgan, James A. Blair, and McCall, also held a strong position at New York Life. Blair, a shareholder in the National Railroad, took a special interest in Mexico. The leaders of New York Life and their insurance industry counterparts appointed managers to handle matters in Mexico City, where they often became longtime residents and leaders in the American colony there.[42]

By the end of the century the Mutual Life Insurance Company of New York had overtaken New York Life, the Equitable, and Metropolitan and sold the greatest number of policies in Mexico. Several of its directors had other important Mexican investments. William Rockefeller and Henry Rogers had interests in Amalgamated Copper, which owned the mining complex at Cananea, the Standard Oil Company, and the National City Bank. Baker, of the First National Bank, was associated with the Mexican National Railroad, the development of Chapultepec Heights, and the Paseo de la Reforma. Cornelius Vanderbilt held shares of the New York Central and the Mexican National Railroads. Speyer was an important source for Mexican bond sales. He also had investments in petroleum and the development of other natural resources. Hamilton McK. Twombley was a Morgan man with the U.S. Steel Corporation and a director of many railroads, including the New York Central.

The directors of the Equitable included a powerful assemblage of financiers in Mexican railroad, banking, petroleum, ranching, and mining enterprises. Bliss, Harriman, Chauncey M. Depew, the president of the New York Central Railroad and a director of nearly fifty other railroads and financial firms, and Auguste Belmont, an agent for Rothschild, all held Mexican railroad stocks and bonds. Marcellus Hartley Dodge of Remington Arms provisioned the Mexican government. Schiff helped finance Mexican railroad bonds and Coolidge, a grandson of the author of the Declaration of Independence, had railroad and mining investments.

The directors of the American Surety Company of New York made up another important American insurance group in Mexico. American Surety leader George Jay Gould inherited the role of his father, Jay Gould, as a railroad tycoon. He served as a member of the Big Four, who consolidated control over the Mexican National Railroad and many American lines. Gould's family interests in Chihuahua paralleled those of steel magnate Schley, another Surety director, who pioneered railroading in that state. Stillman and Gould linked the National City, New York Life, and American Surety operations in Mexico through their directorships. Other financiers who controlled American Surety included Bliss, Depew, Stuyvesant Fish, and Elihu Root, the latter two having combined banking careers with tenures as secretary of state. Fairchild, Coolidge, Morton, Fish, and Root wielded a high level of political influence. This connection to political power among American investors in Mexico has been represented in the contemporary era by Secretary of State George Shultz, of the Bechtel Corporation, and Treasury Secretary Robert Rubin, from Goldman Sachs, who became the chief executive of Citigroup when he returned to the private sector.

Root, an admirer of President Díaz, had served Levi P. Morton as the legal counsel of the Morton Trust before becoming first the secretary of war and later the secretary of state under President Taft. Root represented Morton's interests in Mexico, including those of the Corralitos hacienda, the Candelaria silver mine, and the Mexican National Railroad. His legal and political career joined key American financial interests, including the Guarantee and Morton Trusts, the National City Bank, J. P. Morgan and Company, the First National Bank, and other American banks that were tied to Guarantee Trust, plus the Mexican National Railroad. Root verbally championed a broader-based democracy in Mexico, as did the magnates of the financial firms and the directors of large American industrial interests. Unfortunately, their business practices and their support of the Díaz dictatorship belied their words.

These men, the eight directors of the IBC who were also on the board of the Equitable, and other financiers with similar linkages throughout the financial and insurance industry made the American insurers a power to be reckoned with in Mexico. The American elites wove together banking, insurance, industry, and politics in New York and Washington. They used the unity that resulted to advance their activities in Mexico. The directorship of the Guarantee Trust Bank was typical in that it represented the remarkable integration that the highest levels of American financial capital achieved in Mexico and, later, in other countries of the Third World. Its directors included Levi P. Morton of the Corralitos hacienda and Candelaria silver mine, Harriman of the Big Four and the National City Bank and the chief executive of the Southern Pacific and the Union Pacific Railroads, Baker, the chief executive of the First National Bank and a member of the Trio, Speyer, and Charles A. Peabody. Each owned interests in Mexican mineral companies, railroads, government bonds, real estate, and trade concessions. That unity gave them a strong policy-making influence in Washington.[43]

Many small and sometimes undependable banks and development companies operated by American citizens opened in Mexico at the turn of the century. Many of the smaller American bankers preferred Mexico City because communications, transportation, and political power emanated from that point. Most of the available investment funds also passed through or originated in the capital. The establishment of these institutions paralleled a pattern that occurred in the American West, although their long-term importance was far greater in the United States, where they became crucial elements in the development of civil society.

In 1897 Parker H. Sercombe helped organize the American Surety Bank in Mexico City. The bank was not connected to its namesake in New York and lacked capitalization. It nearly failed at the outset despite the needs of the increasing number of Americans in the capital, in other urban areas, and in virtually every part of the rural economy. In 1910 the American population in Mexico City exceeded 10,000, more than double what it had been in 1900. Sercombe met the challenge through a combination of personal acumen and the recruitment of aggressive and talented men. They included mining engineer John Hays Hammond of the Guggenheim's ASARCO, Robert Gorsuch, who had served with Rosecrans and others in surveying early railroad routes including the Tuxpan concession and routes associated with the Mexican National Railroad, and well-connected if not rich individuals such as John R. Davis, the general manager of the Waters Pierce Oil Company.

The founding of American Surety fused the financial interests of elite Americans and Mexicans. Joaquin Casasus, a future Mexican ambassador to Washington, led the Mexican financiers who participated. In a related endeavor, Davis helped form the Mexican Building and Loan Company, a capitoline banking institution that integrated Mexican and American resources for real estate development. Davis served as a director along with E. N. Brown and W. O. Staples. Brown was well connected with the large New York banks and served as a director of the Mexican National Railroad. The less influential Staples worked as a vice president of the Mexico, Cuernavaca, and Pacific Railroad. In 1902 Julio Limantour, a brother of José Ives Limantour, the powerful secretary of the treasury, joined the Surety directorate.

In 1900 Sercombe left Mexico, seeking to enlarge the company's financial resources in the Chicago and eastern financial communities. Initially he was able to attract some interest from directors of the North American Trust Company of New York and the Continental Bank of Chicago. The directors of the first institution included longtime Mexican investors and leading New York financiers, among them Auguste Belmont, C. T. Barney, John J. Riker, and P. A. B. Widener. Eventually the negotiations broke down.

Sercombe then helped create a group which formed the International Bank and Trust Company of Mexico City, serving as its Mexican general manager. The president was William H. Hunt of Chicago, but most of the directors were marginal figures in the American financial world. The IBC directors noted grandiose claims by Sercombe regarding his new bank and warned their associates and patrons that the International Bank and Trust was not to be confused with the IBC. To their credit, the directors of the International Bank fired Sercombe, but Hunt was caught playing the New York stock market with bank funds. He scandalized Mexico City by fleeing prosecution in New York with some $60,000 in redeemable notes.

Despite its failure to attract major American figures, the International Bank demonstrated that a growing number of American investors in Mexico City wanted to take part in the development of new enterprises and territories. Sercombe recruited Díaz's railroad development adviser, General John B. Frisbie, and arms dealer W. J. DeGress, one of the major importers of Remington Arms on behalf of the Mexican government. Mexicans who joined the enterprise included congressman Emerterio de la Garza, the publisher of the newspaper *La Patria* and president of the New York, Mobile, and Mexico Steamship Company. For several years the bank directors engaged in scandalous operations in Mexico and the United States. In Mexico they worked with fraudulent tropical rubber plantation developers on the Isthmus of Tehuantepec and Chiapas who cheated investors by selling them shares in estates that they stated would be developed into fabulously profitable enterprises.[44]

Other banks successfully brought about Mexican and American business interactions. For example, in the far north, the Bank of Chihuahua joined the Creel family of New York and Chihuahua City with the MacManus family of Philadelphia, Camden, and Chihuahua City. During the late 1860s and early 1870s John MacManus had helped Rosecrans in his efforts to obtain the Tuxpan railroad concession. Later the MacManuses developed relations with the Chihuahua elites—among them was the Terrazas family—through various enterprises, including silver and iron mines and the state mint. Enrique Creel, the son of New Yorker financier Rueben Creel, the American consul in Chihuahua, married a daughter of Luis Terrazas, the wealthiest member of the state's elite. Enrique joined the Bank of Chihuahua, a joint Mexican and American enterprise, before entering government service and becoming the Mexican minister of foreign relations. In the far south, the Bank of Chiapas also integrated American financiers with their Mexican counterparts. Ambassador David E. Thompson and investors in Los Angeles, Omaha, and New York joined Creel, Romero, and Carlos Pacheco, the Mexican secretary of development, in land ventures and another ill-fated attempt to complete the Pan American railroad across the Isthmus of Tehuantepec and extend the line to the capital of Guatemala.[45]

As the layered, coordinated, but competitive American economic leadership consolidated its power, Mexico was a significant part of the larger process. It was the country where the American financiers first took the lead in the syndicates they established with their European—primarily British—partners. The trusts these powerful men formed at home had logical corollaries abroad. The South American Group led investment in foreign countries. They were accompanied by a phalanx of other entrepreneurs. The Steel Trust, led by Morgan and Schiff, reached out to Liberia and Mexico, and the rivals for a Copper Trust, controlled by Stillman, William Rockefeller, and Rogers on the one hand and by Morgan with Guggenheim on the other, extended to Mexico, Chile, and Peru. Morgan, while leading the Shipping Trust, successfully concluded the negotiations for the Panama Canal concession. He joined Baker, Schiff, and Stillman to organize twenty-five banking institutions in the United States and the IBC in Mexico.

The Rubber Trust, which comprised Morgan, Bernard Baruch, John Rockefeller, and others, extended U.S. Rubber operations via Intercontinental Rubber to Mexico, the Belgian Congo, Sumatra, and eventually Liberia. The railroad Big Four reached the American West Coast and every major city in Mexico, while Morgan and Baker extended their Northern Pacific Railroad the length of the Canadian border. Baker, Stillman, and Morgan served as leaders in Western Union and AT&T at home, and they reached into Mexico, Central America, and South America with the Mexican Telegraph Company, the Pacific and Atlantic Cable Company, and the South American Telephone and Telegraph Companies. James and W. Emlen Roosevelt, lesser bankers but politically important, served with Morgan as directors of the communications companies.[46]

When the South American Group—Morgan, Stillman, George Baker, and Jacob Schiff—reversed the ratio of financial participation with their British partners in Mexico from that which prevailed elsewhere, they anticipated that they would gradually gain strength within the relationships that would evolve. The Anglo-American financial relationship was established during the Civil War as Britain's leading financiers purchased Union bonds and helped lay the economic basis for the American military-industrial complex that coalesced during that conflict. The Anglo-American partnership, which included the same elements of competition between oil and other companies that existed within their respective economies, then expanded into Mexico and, to a lesser extent, Cuba. Mexico and Cuba were the first foreign economies to come under American control. In Cuba the British played a minor role, and U.S. strength was augmented with outright political authority. Mexico was different, although the same financiers were involved. It lay adjacent to the southern transcontinental railroad line and offered opportunities for the development of transportation, communications, trade, and resources combined with inexpensive labor.

United States bankers and financiers laid the basis for the entry of American industry into Mexico during the Porfiriato. They made the American-Mexican frontier profitable for explorers and traders who brought back hides, silver, and other raw materials after the Civil War. They financed the Mexican government's struggle against the French and organized railroads. Those steps paved the way for miners, ranchers, and farmers. Town companies and real estate settlements followed. In the late 1890s and first decade of the twentieth century, banking infrastructure took on new importance as thousands of small operators and colonists yearly began to move into Mexico from the recently settled states of Oklahoma, Texas, New Mexico, Arizona, and California. By 1900 the American financiers dominated the Mexican economy.

4 Building the Railroads

We maintain that it is a right of humanity . . . that this vast
territory be inhabited by an industrious people.

> Atlantic Pacific Railroad,
> on the displacement of Native Americans

In late 1876 Díaz inaugurated an ambitious program of reform that would
continue for a generation, undoing much of what had existed in Mexico for
centuries and changing the trajectory of the nation until the end of the century. Díaz and his alter ego, General Manuel González, who served as president from 1880 to 1884, radically altered the previously irregular balance
of power between contending collectivist-owned pueblos and private landowners in the Mexican countryside. Their policies sealed the fate of the communities that had been trying to save their collective properties from private interests.

The leading American capitalists recognized that the establishment of a
railway system was the first step toward a modern, multidimensional infrastructure in Mexico. To encourage foreign interest Díaz reduced the chances
of insurgency by taming troublesome radicals among the peasantry and in
the organized labor movement, and he approved legislation that sped up the
privatization of agriculture. Most important for the Americans, he constructed a network of roads and approved railroad concessions that ultimately
totaled 8,200,000 acres in rights-of-way and operational zones. Díaz was
pragmatic in his dealings with Americans, but he was also opportunistic—
and he demonstrated a considerable lack of ethics.

NEW CONCESSIONS

During the first months of his administration Díaz promoted an anti-American campaign in order to consolidate his political position in Mexico. One
of his first public acts as provisional president was to cancel Lerdo's remaining concession, the one negotiated by Plumb for the Mexican National Railroad. At the same time he quietly worked to improve relations with his

northern neighbors by negotiating concessions of the most profound sort with American investors. He also consolidated his support among Mexican economic elites.

Most observers assumed that his acceptance of Lerdo's cancellations was an anti-American gesture, but Díaz was not acting against Mexico's northern neighbor. In 1876, when Lerdo canceled the major railroad grants, he exempted the Barron-Forbes contract for a major trunk line. The Barron-Forbes consortium was British, not American, and it was headquartered in London. William Barron, an opponent of American interests and an avid Lerdo supporter, told Plumb in 1873 that he "did not think the government ought to make a concession to American companies, that they ought to be made to Mexican capitalists, who could get their funds from Europe." Barron added that he "held no confidence in the American government or people."[1] Plumb felt the rivalry too—he noted that Barron put forward "a feeling of dislike for the United States and . . . Americans."[2]

Díaz canceled the concession and fined the Barron-Forbes syndicate $150,000. He claimed that they had failed to meet the terms of their contract. This claim was literally true, but railroad construction projects regularly fell behind schedule and were modified simply as a matter of routine. The accusation was more serious than the fine because it jeopardized Barron-Forbes's extensive investments in Mexico. The proviso forced Barron-Forbes onto the defensive, creating the need for continuous appeals. It also forestalled additional pressure from the British concessionaires in their competition with American interests for new contracts.[3] His public posturing notwithstanding, Díaz began to reissue the American concessions shortly after taking office.

During the 1870s and 1880s the major American railroad financiers formed alliances in New York, Boston, and Philadelphia that consolidated control over the railroads of the United States and Mexico. In the United States several competing yet overlapping consortiums evolved. The Southern Pacific, the Northern Pacific, the Santa Fe, and other railroad holding companies competed for market shares across the United States. The owners even tried to wrest control from each other. Yet they also presented considerable cohesion. Virtually all of the leading owners held interests in other trunk lines, and although they competed for concessions in Mexico, they also merged their interests when needed. When Lerdo had jeopardized the entire program in the mid 1870s, they had united behind Díaz to protect their interests.

The American financiers who supported the Mexican National Railroad all enjoyed Díaz's goodwill. They included those who were on the New York

Bondholders Committee and those who were members of the New York and Pennsylvania Railroad groups. These men received the first railroad concessions issued by Díaz, and the new concessions placed the competing American syndicates on an even footing in Mexico. Díaz made it clear to the New Yorkers that Plumb was out. Lerdo's American friend ended his diplomatic career broke, protesting his fate to the U.S. Department of State to no avail. The groups originally represented in Mexico by William Rosecrans, and enlarged since, continued to enjoy the direct services of John Foster, the American minister to Mexico.

In August 1877, three months after Díaz was formally elected to the presidency, Caesar Cousin, a longtime Rosecrans intermediary with the Juárez and Lerdo governments, received the "Interoceanic Concession" for the construction of a second railroad running west from Veracruz to Mexico City and northwest through Morelia, Guadalajara, Tepic, and San Blas to the Pacific Coast. Díaz wrote out the contract by hand. As part of the deal the recipients were to loan Díaz $2,000,000 in gold. The repayment schedule would be based on customs duties: "This reimbursement to the lenders shall be made via the Maritime Customs House at Veracruz, which shall be expressly and preferentially mortgaged for the said amount."[4]

Rosecrans received assurances from George F. Henderson, a representative of the Pennsylvania Railroad in Mexico, that his new Pacific Coast route was safe from competition.

> [N]o other concession of a similar character over the route will be given until sufficient time be given (say up to September next) for Cousins to make his arrangements. Although other projects may be presented, I have good reason to know they will not even be entertained by the President Porfirio Díaz.[5]

At the same time, Díaz reissued a concession made by Lerdo in 1874 to Robert Symon, Rosecrans's former partner. In late 1875 Lerdo had canceled the concession following his electoral victory over Díaz in the presidential race. The line, called the Mexican Central Railroad, would run from El Paso to Mexico City. Symon was a major figure in the Santa Fe Railroad, which a group of Boston capitalists and John S. Kennedy were then organizing. The Mexican Central would be a Santa Fe subsidiary, giving the Santa Fe investors a powerful position in the Mexican north. This agreement demonstrated the president's sympathy for the early Boston partners of the Pennsylvania group who now controlled the American railroad.

Díaz also renewed a Lerdo railroad grant to investment banker David Boyle Blair for another Sonoran railway. As usual, the Americans sought real estate. The concession called for 13,913.51 acres of land per kilometer of track completed to be given to Blair and his partners, Rosecrans and Collis Huntington. This line had two branches, one from Nogales to Hermosillo, Guaymas, and Alamos, and the other from the state capital of Hermosillo to the copper mines at Cananea. Blair had close ties to Rosecrans through his interest in the Southern Pacific Railroad, in which Rosecrans was now a major player. The copper mines at Cananea were another mutual interest; Rosecrans and Symon had investigated their development in the late 1860s.[6]

Díaz reached another accord in 1877, this time with William Jackson Palmer and James Sullivan. Sullivan had replaced Rosecrans as the representative of the Pennsylvania Railroad and Plumb as the negotiator for the New York group in Mexico City. That group included Rosecrans, James Stillman, Moses Taylor, Richard King, Thomas Scott, and others, with Taylor in the lead. The new concession merged parts of the original Tuxpan route, on which Robert Gorsuch had already surveyed sections and had completed some construction work. This concession, for the Mexican National Railroad, called "for the construction and exploitation of a railroad and corresponding telegraph line, extending from the City of Mexico to the Pacific Ocean and the Rio Bravo del Norte," and terminating at Laredo.[7]

At first the nationalists in the Mexican Congress and press opposed the Palmer-Sullivan project, which was the first Díaz proposal for a trunk line. They viewed it as an "annexationist plot" on the part of the United States, and the lower house rejected the concession. Díaz, playing both sides, whipped up public protest. His partisans organized anti-American protests and staged demonstrations at which women in Mexico City reportedly donated their jewelry and even wedding rings to raise monies to be used to equip the army against potential U.S. invaders. While this was happening, the American railroaders and their supporters were negotiating the approval of their concessions. Foster, in a report to the Manufacturers Association of the Northwest, complained that Díaz lacked resolve, suggesting that he should do something about the opposition to the railroad concessions in the Mexican Congress.[8]

The Mexican Congress soon went more than halfway to settle the crisis. Imbued with the ideals of federalism and under pressure from a president who had seized power by military force, it conceded to the state governors the right, with Díaz's approval, to make concessions in their jurisdictions. This was the opening that the American railroad men and Díaz needed. Survey teams from American construction companies were already developing the plans for the lines that would later be approved by the Mexican president. In the course of Díaz's first presidency, between 1876 and 1880, the governors of at least twenty-two states joined him in piecemeal approvals for the construction of railways. With that decentered approach, Díaz avoided a crisis with congress and the state governments, while the legislators avoided confronting the new president.[9]

The amalgam of American financial interests had to mobilize more capital and political support to reach the Mexican border with trunk lines, which would connect the Mexican railroads to the major American cities. When the penetration of the underdeveloped country began, the railroad men were backed by the concentrated force of the political and economic leaders of the United States. When they reached Mexico these "pioneers for profit" brought with them the beginnings of a new social order. Many of the American financiers joined the Hayes administration in favoring the peaceful acquisition of Mexico's northern states. The railroads were the key in this scenario. Completion of the trunk lines would allow construction of secondary lines. Settlement and economic development would follow, aided by negotiated concessions, particularly for colonization companies. Finally, the railroad men and some politicians anticipated that the settlers would petition for statehood.

Rutherford B. Hayes, whose presidential term began in 1877, had personal interests in Mexico. In general, the serious tensions caused not only by the long-standing turmoil along the border but also by political unrest within the United States encouraged the president to apply public pressure on his new Mexican counterpart. Hayes, his intimate friend Senator Stanley Matthews, the president's personal secretary William King Rogers, and other Ohio businessmen and friends were interested in Mexican railroads. Condemned by congressional Democrats for his confrontational policies toward Díaz, Hayes in turn blamed Secretary of State William Maxwell Evarts, who was "willing to grant recognition but demanded concessions as a price [resulting in] a series of haggling negotiations that settled little."[10]

Two projected lines especially concerned the Hayes group. One, the International Mexican Railway Company, included as its principal incorporators Senator Matthews, who later became a Supreme Court justice, Thomas Scott, railroad tycoon Jay Gould, Pacific Mail Steamship Company director Russell Sage, and Governor John C. Brown of Tennessee. Matthews was a friend of long standing and a confidant of Hayes. He corresponded with Hayes about the project.[11] The plan was a reasonable one. The route would run from El Paso to Guaymas (or Topolobampo), saving some 600 miles in the transportation of goods moving from the South Pacific and the west coast of South America to the American Midwest and East Coast. Like the other Civil War generals who took the helm of America's postwar railroad building project, Hayes was a graduate of the Military Academy at West Point and held a degree in civil engineering. He probably gave more than moral support to the project, but his records only indicate the enthusiasm of his associates and their investments.

The projected line from El Paso to Guaymas also attracted Rogers, Rosecrans, Symon, and William Windom, President Garfield's secretary of the treasury, who served as president of the line. Another consortium that invested money in the project included John C. Frémont, who purchased 95,000 acres of land just south of the Arizona border, including territory adjacent to Agua Prieta. Matthews recruited many of the investors for this line.[12] Unfortunately for the consortium, the Yaquis opposed the construction of the line, and their attacks on surveyors and construction crews forced the partners into receivership.

The other project that interested the consortium was one proposed by the San Antonio and Border Railroad Company. In 1881 its directors, mainly Texans, contracted to buy 1,018,440 acres of land east of Santa Rosalía, Chihuahua, and 1,107,000 acres of land south of Santa Rosalía for twenty-five cents per acre. One plan would have run the line from Chihuahua toward Presidio, Texas. A lack of funds dampened their enthusiasm. Meanwhile, Symon continued to seek funding for a railroad that would traverse the properties he and Rosecrans had bought between Mazatlán and Durango.[13]

William K. Vanderbilt inadvertently enabled the eventual consolidation of American railroad ownership in Mexico when he ended his control over the New York Central Railroad in 1879. He broadened participation in the rail company by selling $35,000,000 in voting shares to Morton, Bliss and Company, Auguste Belmont, Taylor, Stillman, Sage, Gould, L. Von Hoffman and Company, Cyrus Field, Ed Morgan, J. S. Morgan and Company of London, Drexel, Morgan, and Company, and Winslow, Lanier and Company. The Morgan men, through their control of the Wabash Railroad, a holding company that dominated transportation in the states surrounding the Great Lakes, provided the directors of the New York Central with a service area that covered the industrialized North of the United States.[14]

A network of competitive but overlapping interests developed after Vanderbilt sold his majority holding. The investment strategy of Charles F. Woerishoffer, a leading American investment banker during the 1870s and 1880s and a Wall Street bear, was typical of the New York Central group. Woerishoffer often went in the opposite direction of associates such as Gould and Sage. He joined Stillman, Taylor, and J. P. Morgan in the Mexican National Railroad, Morgan in the Northern Pacific Railroad, Stillman and

William Rockefeller in the Kansas Pacific Railroad, and Philadelphia and Boston interests in offering early support for the Denver and Rio Grande Railroad and, later, the Santa Fe Railroad. The competitive Woerishoffer cooperated in backing all of these properties until they showed weakness. At that point "loyalties" became secondary and he sold off enormous holdings, driving their market values down and costing his partners, or competitors, large sums of money. Sage and Gould joined him in some ventures, but he made $1,000,000 in fighting them off during their bid to gain control of the Kansas Pacific. This was characteristic of the railroad men who invested in the Mexican lines.[15]

THE LIMITS OF PRIVATE CAPITAL

Albert Kinsey Owen, the son of famed American utopian socialist Robert Owen, took over the promotion of the San Antonio and Border Railroad Company. His records contain the evidence needed to reconstruct many of the tactics used by the American railroad entrepreneurs to extend their control into Mexico. Owen called the proposed line the Texas, Topolobampo, and Pacific Railroad and Telegraph Company (TT&PR). It would extend from Ojinaga-Presidio southwest to Chihuahua City, cross the Sierra Madre, and end at the Pacific port of Topolobampo. The route was designed to compete with the other trunk lines that connected Mexico's cities and material resources with the United States. It would provide the shortest route linking the markets of the American East Coast with Mexico and the southern Pacific Coast, and in doing so it would compete with the Southern Pacific Railroad, the southernmost transcontinental trunk line traversing North America from east to west. Motivated by a promising business opportunity, Owen began looking for poor workers and wealthy American investors. He used his father's reputation as a utopian socialist to attract a workforce of idealistic Americans who were willing to become colonists and able to build a port on the steaming coastline of Sinaloa at Topolobampo. In that way Owen minimized labor costs while the colonization company acquired vast real estate holdings from the Mexican government. The company was based on the workforce of colonists, but the property titles went to Owen.

Owen initiated the project in the early 1870s, employing Fred G. Fitch to survey the bay and the surrounding lands. Fitch found that the bay measured between three and four fathoms in two of its channels, a depth that encouraged all of the potential participants. Owen then used the report and his father's good name to obtain financial backing in the United States and land concessions from the Mexican government. He forwarded Fitch's report to capitalists in Boston with a prospectus describing the region's potential in optimistic terms and explaining what they could expect from a Mexican government concession. One of the men who received the report was B. R. Carman, the U.S. consul at Mazatlán. Carman had bought land at Topolobampo in 1862. Owen convinced Carman to join the project, and in 1881 Carman conceded his properties at Topolobampo to Owen in return for shares in the railroad. C. S. Retes, Blas Ybarra, and L. Ybarra, members of the Sinaloa elite, also joined the project as partners.

Owen recruited presidential secretary Rogers to serve as the legal counsel for the Texas, Topolobampo, and Pacific Railroad and Telegraph Company, as the firm was called. Everyone knew that Rogers handled President Hayes's business affairs and most of his correspondence. In the TT&PR undertaking Rogers represented himself and, given the context of his letters, probably President Hayes. To acquire capital and a wider base of leadership, Owen and Rogers recruited some of the same Boston and New York financiers who had organized the Santa Fe and the Mexican Central Railroads. During the 1880s and 1890s the TT&PR syndicate grew even stronger. In 1880 and 1881 "the Boston Blind Pool" for the Topolobampo railroad consisted of the honorable Frederick O. Prince, the mayor of Boston and the secretary of the National Committee of the Democratic Party, General Benjamin Franklin Butler, who was Hiram Barney's old partner and now the governor of Massachusetts, Ulysses S. Grant Jr. and several other bankers with interests in Mexico and South America.[16]

The officers of the TT&PR—Windom, who was now a senator from Minnesota, and Grant—personally delivered $100,000 in earnest money to Díaz in Mexico City. In 1882 President Díaz responded by issuing to Owen a colonization grant of 400,000 acres, located between the Fuerte and Sinaloa Rivers, that included Sierra Madre timberlands. The Mexican Congress had enacted a colonization law in 1875 that allowed the president to approve grants and concessions of government-owned land to commercial entities, including foreign firms, to promote immigration. Díaz supported colonization projects with these grants quite often, offering the incentive of land to promoters and colonists alike. In this case much of the land was intended for the 138 "integral cooperators," or American colonists. The utopian settlers proceeded to build a community at Topolobampo. They constructed dwellings, a rough network of wagon roads, canals, water ditches, a dam, and a port, plus a customs house, a storehouse, a stone pier, and a railroad terminal. By the early 1880s they were even publishing a newspaper, the *Credit Financier of Sinaloa*.[17]

The project attracted Boston capitalists John Abbott and Levi C. Wade of the Old Colony Trust Bank. The potential of a Pacific entrepôt overcame fears that focused on the certain challenge of crossing the rugged Sierra Madre and a probable challenge from the Yaquis, whose territories were north of the line. The financiers hoped to meet the challenge of the mountains with support from the U.S. and Mexican governments. To help buttress their political strength the directors brought in Judge Joshua G. Abbot, Stephen Elkins, the secretary of war under President William Henry Harrison, Judge Solon Humphries, who was a partner in the mercantile firm of E. D. Morgan and Company, and former president Grant and his sons Jesse and Ulysses Jr. In 1884 Baron Reinache of Paris joined the railroad syndicate.[18] The involvement of some investors dated back to connections forged in the New York Bondholders Committee of the 1860s and early 1870s. They included Butler, Grant, John S. Kennedy, and Matías Romero. A. Foster Higgins, another syndicate member, served as the director of a subsidiary, the Sierra Madre Construction Company, and was in charge of the most difficult engineering tasks in building the TT&PR.[19]

The Topolobampo project was unusual in that its supporters came from a cross-section of American life, ranging from utopian colonists to elite Boston patriarchs. This wide range of support did not prevent difficulties, however. The project constantly encountered new problems. During the 1880s, after the colonists had nearly completed the town site, they discovered that shifting beds of silt and a sandbar made constant dredging necessary. The region was beset with alternating droughts and floods.[20] In addition, the mountains provided more of an obstacle to railroad construction from the west than the investors had anticipated. Construction was costly, and other railroad men, especially those committed to the rival lines in Mexico, opposed the syndicate's efforts to gain funding from the U.S. Congress.[21]

As the cost of constructing the railroad over the Sierra Madre became evident, the flow of funds from investors in the eastern United States dried up. In 1885 James Campbell, the general manager of the Mexican-American Construction Company on Nassau Street in New York City reported that it would cost at least $12,000 per mile to lay rails over a tortuous sixty miles. Even the forty miles of foothills on the western side of the mountains would cost $10,000 per mile. These expenses were extraordinary considering that "Indian" labor in the area cost only "twenty-five cents per day." The calculation was more than double the monies needed for rail construction on level terrain.

Since construction estimates were invariably low in order to encourage investors, Campbell's figures were a serious blow to the project. Campbell, however, noted the richness of the area and recommended continuing onward with American funds only, despite the waning enthusiasm of the Mexican government. Without help from the U.S. Congress, the effort was doomed. President Díaz recognized that the success of the project depended on enormous outside financing, in contrast to the railroad network being constructed to connect central Mexico with the border of the United States. In 1890 Díaz renewed the colonization grant, but he then rejected further subsidies until Owen could show some progress in obtaining more funds.[22]

By 1890 the consortium had spent $100,000 on the project without a return. But they would not give up. At this point the Boston financiers recognized that the land values would rise dramatically once the Southern Pacific line running along the Mexican coast was built, even if their mountain route failed. They began purchasing properties around Los Mochis and Topolobampo. Meanwhile, they joined Owen in seeking to refinance the mountain route through British participation. In 1890 Owen brought in a group of investors led by W. J. Sutherland, a director of the Globe and Industrial Trust in London and president of the Holmes Mining Company of Nevada. They provided enough new financing to keep the construction project alive while the effort to procure still larger sums from other bankers or the U.S. government continued. By 1892 the British investors had realized the depth of the problem, and they withdrew.[23]

Faced with reorganization, the Topolobampo promoters followed the usual practice of acquiring enormous tracts of land. They made these purchases as individuals and as the directors of land companies legally separate from the railroad. Members of the railroad syndicate set out to gain control of the Pacific coastline north and south of Topolobampo. In 1893 Humphries, Higgins, Windom, and A. J. Streeter of Chicago, operating under the name of the Kansas Sinaloa Investment Company, purchased the Retes land near Los Mochis and Topolobampo in separate transactions of 10,000, 11,000, and 7,000 acres and then bought 69,480 acres from the Ybarra family.

The Topolobampo concessionaires had even greater riches at stake in the Mexican interior. The Díaz government, recognizing the difficulties of building a railroad over the Sierra Madre, made 14,000,000 acres of mountainous terrain in Chihuahua, Coahuila, Durango, and Sonora available to the Kansas Sinaloa Investment Company through script redemptions valued at $3,000 per kilometer of road completed. The Mexican government hoped that the grant would help Owen and his early supporters attract more investors and ensure that the work would begin by the stipulated year of 1895. The directors claimed the lands as they completed kilometers of road in northeastern Chihuahua, just as they had around Topolobampo. The concession brought more capital to the project, but its value was only 25 percent of the actual cost of construction. Without more support from the U.S. government the company would not have enough money to complete the railroad. Other powerful railroad interests opposed government subsidies to Owen's project— they did not want to see their routes undercut by a shorter line.[24]

In 1895 Windom, the president of the Topolobampo line, died. At that point most of the prominent Americans who had joined the project in its early stages were still connected with it. Owen was still promoting the railroad and serving as the principal agent in Mexico. Among the political luminaries still involved were Elkins, the Grant brothers, nine U.S. senators, governors Brown and H. C. Warmouth of Louisiana, Blair of New Hampshire, Henry Cabot Lodge of Massachusetts, presidential secretary Rogers, Humphries, and Charles Foster, the U.S. secretary of the treasury. James Stillman had recommended Foster to the president for the job, demonstrating the Topolobampo leaders' direct ties to the leadership of the United States.

Humphries, who also had direct ties to the core interests on Wall Street, invited the owners of the 890,000-acre Corralitos hacienda to join the Topolobampo rail project. The Corralitos was southwest of El Paso in Chihuahua. The hacienda's owners included Ed Morgan, a Humphries partner and cousin of J. P. Morgan, Levi P. Morton, vice president of the United States, and Edward Shearson, the founder of the New York banking house bearing his name. The costs of crossing the Sierra Madre intimidated them. In 1896 a badly needed $300,000 in new investments almost came from some German friends of Higgins in Berlin, but the arrangement fell through.

Díaz, recognizing that the line could not be completed for decades, canceled the agreement of land in payment for miles of rail laid, leaving only the colonization grant for the promoters. They could reap reward from the Mexican government only by finding American settlers. The owners of the Mexican Central Railroad had not received a concession comparable to the Topolobampo grant, and Díaz noted that they disliked the competition. Huntington, meanwhile, had completed his International Railroad of Mexico, running from Durango to Eagle Pass, Texas, without subsidies.[25]

In 1896, when the Texas, Topolobampo, and Pacific Railroad and Telegraph Company failed, the Topolobampo colonists discovered that all the land titles were in Owen's name and that he had set aside only 6,000 to 10,000 acres for them. Internal disputes between the settlers favoring communal property and the newcomers who wanted private parcels caused the colony to break up. The promoters, led by Humphries and Higgins, claimed most of the 400,000-acre coastal grant in a purchase of "468,000 acres" originally issued by the government to land surveyor Telesforo García. The majority of the colonists left. Owen asserted his rights to 79,188 acres at the nearby town of Los Mochis, an additional 175,000 acres of "agriculture, beaches and mountains" from the original grant of 400,000 acres, and 21,760 acres at the Topolobampo town site in the name of his Pacific Colonization Company, a firm over which he held full control after the colonists abandoned their efforts. The promoters influenced local authorities and won out over the remaining colonists in bitter court battles in which the bribery of court officials was alleged. The remaining small property holders lost all of their larger claims.[26] American domination of the northern Sinaloa coastal region continued for the next several decades in the midst of endless legal disputes over land titles.

In 1897 Owen talked Díaz into a new colonization grant, probably as an incentive to buyers of the railroad concession. In 1899 the line's importance to the state of Chihuahua caused Enrique Creel to meet with Owen. Creel, now a member of the Chihuahua oligarchy by virtue of his marriage, had been born in Mexico and had opted for Mexican citizenship. He was a major principal in the Bank of Chihuahua and vice president of the Chihuahua and Pacific Railroad Company, which still held a concession to traverse the Sierra Madre from Chihuahua. His wife was an heiress to the state's largest latifundio, complexes of haciendas that characterized the largest landholdings of the Mexican elite. Creel, the Empire Trust Company of New York, Grant B. Schley, Charles M. Schwab, and Alfred Spendlove of the Chihuahua Mining Company were the largest interests in the Chihuahua and Pacific Railroad. Creel and Owen reached a tentative agreement in which Owen would merge his interests with the railroad under the latter's leadership. The arrangement fell through when the Creel consortium would not commit sufficient assets to the project.[27]

Finally, in February 1900, Owen met with Arthur E. Stilwell in Mexico City, and they reached an agreement for the sale of the railroad with Díaz's approval. Stilwell, a railroad entrepreneur from Kansas City, thought he could do the impossible. He acquired Owen's interests in the Topolobampo concession and those of the syndicate at a cost of $100,000 in Mexican 5 percent bonds, $30,000 in railroad bonds, $150,000 in 4 percent railroad bonds, and $75,000 in stock in the new railroad. The agreement placed Stilwell in charge and moved the earlier American supporters to the margin of the new company. Later that year an impressed Díaz blessed the undertaking with a concession of $5,000 per kilometer for the construction of the Kansas City, Mexico, and Orient Railway. Although the amount was still not enough, it encouraged Stilwell, who bought out the Chihuahua and Pacific interests held by Creel, Schley, and Schwab through negotiations with Creel. Stilwell's creditors from earlier railroad ventures moved against him after he announced the incorporation of his new line. His rivals included several of the biggest players in Mexico, including E. H. Harriman of the Southern Pacific, Ernest Thalmann of the investment bank of Ladenburg, Thalmann, and Company, and John "Bet a Million" Gates of the Cananea Consolidated Copper Company and the Texas Company.[28] Their claims against Stilwell prevented him from gaining the financial support in New York that he needed.[29]

The key problem with the concession remained. Construction over the Sierra Madre would cost $12,000 per mile, and the difference between the cost and the government subsidy would have to come from railroad men who preferred using the money of others. The silver mines at Batopilas, the richest site in the Sierra Madre, were in an almost impenetrable canyon and could only be reached at an estimated cost of $2,000,000. In 1902 the subsidy for the mountainous areas was increased by President Díaz to 12,000 pesos per kilometer, but by then the peso carried a value of only fifty cents. Finally, in 1905, Díaz granted subsidies ranging from 7,000 to 15,000 pesos, depending on the difficulty of the terrain. It still was not enough. The devalued pesos were worth only 20 percent more than the original concession of 5,000 pesos.[30] Stilwell described his plans and problems:

> We are building what we believe is destined to be one of the greatest trans-continental railroads in existence and the only trans-continental international railroad there is, and we feel positive that you will take pride in seeing that we have ample facilities so that we can make this railroad equal to the Southern Pacific, Northern Pacific and Canadian Pacific, and this port [Topolobampo] the equal of San Francisco or Seattle.
>
> The vital point in placing our securities is to show that we are in no wise going to be cramped and that we can handle the commerce of the Orient and Pacific equal to any other trans-continental railroad.[31]

Even Stilwell was not enough of an insider to garner the support that was needed from New York and Washington, D.C., to make the project work. Unfortunately for Stilwell and his supporters, President Díaz was a practical man who admired and closely supported the successful efforts of Harriman, the Southern Pacific, and the New York banking community, which had played the greatest role in creating the Mexican railroad system. Díaz did not want to alienate those interests in order to back a maverick. Díaz would do no more for Stilwell, and the American financiers would not increase their exposure. Stilwell's Kansas City railroad struggled until the revolution broke out in 1910 and left it in disarray. By then its lines comprised three segments. One stretched 642 miles from Wichita, Kansas, to Granada, Texas. Another ran for 287 miles from Marquez, Chihuahua, through the capital city, and on to Sanchez on the eastern edge of the Sierra Madre. The final segment ran 73 miles from Topolobampo to Hornillos in the Sierra Madre foothills. The effort was hopeless. Owen's project had been undermined not only by the 6,000-foot-deep canyons of the Sierra Madre and the shallow waters and shifting sandbars of the waters off Topolobampo but also by the opposition presented by the leaders of the Southern Pacific and Santa Fe Railroads. The Kansas City went into receivership in 1912. The Mexican government finally finished the railroad in 1961. The line climbs upward from sea level at Los Mochis to the Continental Divide, rising some 8,000 feet. Thirty-seven bridges and eighty-nine tunnels were needed to cross the Sierra Madre.

When the Topolobampo directors acquired their immense holdings in Sinaloa, they were following a well-established practice. Beginning with the first plans for an American-run rail system in Mexico, the railroad magnates bought and sold land for tidy profits. In addition to the 8,200,000 acres granted to the major railroad companies as rights-of-way and work areas, the directors bought properties that they expected to increase in value upon the arrival of the lines. In perhaps the first episode, Edgar Conkling, Rosecrans, and Symon bought the 25,000-acre Rancho San Juan del Río near the headwaters of the Yaqui River, fifty-five miles west of the Chihuahua state border and forty-one miles south of Arizona. Then, in the late 1870s, General A. S. Mansfield of Boston headed a syndicate that purchased 40,000 acres near Las Delicias, Sonora, and quickly sold it to another Boston consortium. In 1881 William Rogers, president Hayes's secretary, and his unnamed associates purchased 80,000 acres near Topolobampo for $15,000 with an option to acquire 300,000 additional acres within six months. They also bought 22,000 acres of potential sugarcane land at El Fuerte, Sinaloa. In the early 1880s Huntington purchased extensive tracts at and around the iron deposits at Durango.

Land was one area of primary concern for the railroad financiers, and another was the cost of labor. In the United States, Chinese workers saved the capitalists money. In the Topolobampo project, cheap Mexican labor was supplemented by the free work done by the utopian socialists who built the seaport needed for Pacific trade. Despite these savings and the high stakes involved, the lack of support for crossing the Sierra Madre forestalled completion of the project and demonstrated the limits of private capital.[32]

REACHING MEXICO CITY

Díaz continued to pursue his plan to develop the national economy through the construction of an American-owned railroad network that would tie

Mexico to the American market. Between 1876 and 1884 the Mexican government spent 130,000 to 270,000 pesos per year on railroad support projects, apart from the subsidies that it agreed to pay to the American companies for each kilometer of track laid. In 1879 it agreed to pay up to 32,000,000 pesos in five major railroad contracts that called for the construction of 2,500 miles of track. By 1880 sixteen concessionaires were building lines. The work continued despite an economic crisis in the United States during 1883 and 1884 that froze the availability of needed funds and caused the near collapse of the Mexican government. The González government ended in economic chaos, but Díaz quickly restored stability with new funding when he returned to the presidency in 1884.[33]

The regime stimulated railroad investments and satisfied the grievances of old bondholders by issuing land grants. Francis Skiddy dropped claims against the Mexican government and simultaneously received a large holding in southernmost Chiapas. Usually Díaz issued the grants to individuals affiliated with the banks and railroads concerned with the development program, but on occasion he issued them directly to the railroads or their controlling interests. When the Mexican National Railroad completed its line between Monterrey and Matamoros, Díaz approved a grant of 819,000 acres as compensation in lieu of payment in pesos. He issued Frederick Stark Pearson, the president of the Mexican Northwestern Railroad, the title to a 3,500,000-acre timber and colonization concession in western Chihuahua that had formerly been held by bankrupt mining impresario William C. Greene. The value of the timber and the potential for a colony depended upon, but was not legally tied to, the completion of the line. Díaz also granted Captain James Eads over 1,500,000 acres in one of several efforts to construct a railroad across Tehuantepec. During the Civil War Eads had been an associate of Secretary of War Gideon Welles, Assistant Secretary James Scott, and fund-raiser Junius Morgan.

In June and October 1878 Díaz dramatically improved Mexico's economic and investment climate by accepting the claims made by the American Bondholders Committee against the controversial Carbajal bonds and gaining the approval of the Mexican Congress for the Interoceanic Railroad concession from Veracruz to Mexico City.[34] The Isthmus of Tehuantepec had long interested the U.S. government, the leaders of the Pacific Mail Steamship Company—including Taylor, Skiddy, William Aspinwall—and the other principal financiers of New York because it promised to link the Atlantic and Pacific Oceans with a line that would run from Veracruz to Salina Cruz. The effort anticipated the construction of the Panama Canal. The project attracted well-connected New York investors during the 1850s and maverick American speculators during the reign of Maximilian. During the late 1870s the Marine National Bank and former president Grant joined a powerful array of capitalists, including Huntington, who attempted to see the Tehuantepec line, the Mexican Southern Railroad, completed. The financiers were defeated by the weak sedimentary strata in the Isthmus, which was constantly giving way. Neither the land grants nor the cash-per-kilometer given out by Presidents Díaz and González sufficed to see the project through.

Grant and the Marine National Bank committed a large part of their resources to the project. Grant went bankrupt largely because of this gamble. Officially the bank's payments to creditors of the railroad construction company fell about $500,000 short. Unofficially the Mexican Southern ran up at least $7,000,000 in unpaid and fraudulent checks. The matter clouded the former president's good name. J. P. Morgan learned from the experience, concluding that it would be wiser to get a canal contract and sell it to the government, with its greater financial resources. He did exactly that with the Panama Canal. The problems of the Isthmus of Tehuantepec, like those of the Sierra Madre, were more than private initiative could handle. The line was eventually completed by the Díaz government in the 1900s.[35]

By 1880 the Americans had laid the bulk of 1,051 kilometers of track in Mexico. In 1881 they added most of an additional 609 kilometers. At the end of 1882 the total trackage reached 3,583 kilometers. In 1883 it totaled 5,328 kilometers. In 1884 the number of concessions totaled forty-nine, controlled by some of the most important figures in American finance and railroading. The trackage laid reached 5,898 kilometers in 1885. Included in that total were over 1,100 kilometers of the rapidly growing Mexican National line and 1,970 more that completed construction of the Mexican Central route from El Paso to Mexico City.

During the rest of the 1880s, the Americans made dramatic progress as the trunk lines moved southward from the Mexican-American border toward Mexico City. The Southern Pacific's trunk line originated in Nogales; the Mexican Central, owned by Santa Fe, started in El Paso; the northernmost points for the National Railroad were Corpus Christi and Laredo and, later, Matamoros-Brownsville. Only Huntington and Owen sought a final destination other than Mexico City for their railroads. Huntington's line, the Mexican International, began at Eagle Pass. He aimed his railroad toward the coal deposits of Sabinas in Coahuila, the agriculture of La Laguna in Coahuila, and the ranching, timber, and iron deposits of Durango. He also considered a terminus at the port at Mazatlán but decided against that idea.

The Díaz-controlled Mexican Congress approved the subsidies to the Americans, which ranged from 7,500 to 15,000 pesos per kilometer. Only

Huntington chose land and resource acquisitions over cash subsidies. The banks controlled by the financiers—the National City Bank, J. P. Morgan and Company, the Brown Brothers Bank, the Empire Trust Bank, and the First National Bank, all of New York, and the Old Colony Trust of Boston—advanced the funds to the builders and loaned cash to the Díaz regime in return for bonds so that it could keep up with its payment schedules.

Between 1878 and 1883, the coming of the railroads, the privatization of land, and a road building program triggered dozens of rural working-class, peasant, and indigenous uprisings. At the same time, the burgeoning commercial market provided by steamships and railroads between Mexico, California, and Arizona supported the growing population of the Mexican northwest and the American Southwest.[36] The Yaqui struggle with the Mexicans in the northwestern state of Sonora antedated the Americans and the Iron Horse, and it would have intensified without them owing to the demand for agricultural products created by new mines and the growing towns and cities of the Mexican northwest and Pacific Coast. The Yaqui resistance, which continued until it merged with the revolutionary unrest of 1910, was more sustained in its violence and intensity than the other agrarian uprisings, and it succeeded in blocking the construction of the El Paso to Guaymas railroad. It was a rare event when Native American resistance blocked the construction of a railroad.

The most important and largest of the other upheavals swept the Huasteca highlands, or eastern Sierra Madre, from the state of Veracruz in the south to Ciudad del Maíz in the north between 1878 and 1883. The Huastecos, whose ranks included large numbers of mestizos, rose up in opposition to the privatization of former communal lands and the related road construction. Led by Juan Santiago, a pueblo *gobernador,* they followed a program conceived by Padre Mauricio Zavala, a parish priest. Contrary to the advocates of free enterprise, they demanded the creation of a new social order, the plans for which synthesized the utopia conceived by Thomas More and the social structure of the Aztec nation. It gave authority to a council of elders chosen by the electors of the four communities, who in turn were directly selected by the adult males of the constituent villages. Their plan delegated fiscal power and moral authority to the priest who served as treasurer and adviser.[37]

By 1896 the Americans had built 11,500 kilometers of railroad that tied the Mexican nation ever closer to the United States. By then a remarkable consortium of elite American stockholders owned 80 percent of Mexico's railroad stocks and bonds, worth $350,000,000. That sum amounted to some 70 percent of all American investments in the country. The railroads were the fundamental element in American power and influence. They provided the material basis that enabled the highly organized American capitalists to expand their operations into other sectors of the Mexican economy such as banking, communications, urban land development, export agriculture, ranching, mining, and petroleum production.

The motives of the participants were mixed. Although they sought wealth and power, some envisioned prosperity for both nations, while others saw Mexico as a mere pawn in a larger American-controlled nexus. The former group included Mexican leaders such as the deceased Matías Romero and the Mexican "railroaders" party. Díaz, his supporters, and Rosecrans saw the process in mixed terms. Mexico could prosper under the alliance, but there was a great risk of American hegemony. American expansionists in the financial and railroad industries and American political leaders saw Mexico as a site of great wealth and a nation that should be wrested from the backward, corrupt, and incompetent control of the Mexican government. Only then could its potential be fully realized, as James Stillman declared in 1890: "The people of Mexico will have to be supplanted by another race, which is gradually being done, before any great development can be expected there." The El Paso Bureau of Information was of the same opinion: "Commerce is the weapon . . . , the all powerful arm with which we have entered in earnest, with every prospect of success, upon our conquest of Mexico."[38]

In 1900 the Americans were approaching their goal of completing a Mexican railroad system that connected the capital and central plateau with entrepôts along the entirety of the border. The lines from El Paso and Laredo were completed, and only one major gap remained in the line between Nogales and Mexico City. The system totaled some 14,573 kilometers. The tropical croplands of southern Mexico were now connected to their ports with trunk lines. The Tehuantepec Railroad, nearing completion, connected Salina Cruz on the Pacific to Coatzacoalcos on the Gulf, fulfilling in part the earlier vision of Taylor, Skiddy, Aspinwall, and Grant. In the north and center of the nation the Americans were completing a network of secondary rail lines, or *minerales*, to areas with thick stands of timber and rich deposits of silver, coal, oil, copper, and iron.

The mining companies built their smelters adjacent to the railroads and depended on the lines for transporting ore to the site and shipping bars of silver and copper to markets in the United States. The smelter operators obtained large concessions from the railroads, discounts that independent and small-scale miners claimed were not passed on to them. The railroad discounts were the natural outcome of the many overlapping directorates in which leading railroad investors also headed mining companies. The railroads placed otherwise remote sites within the reach of mining technology, and when the last gaps of the Mexican Central were closed in 1885, mining products could reach smelters in Colorado, Kansas, Missouri, and Oklahoma. The mining companies developed large plants in Kansas City, Colorado Springs, and El Paso.

In the early 1890s the firm of Frisbie y Compañía applied for one of the more lucrative railroad concessions, a line twenty miles in length extending from Jalapa, the capital city of the state of Veracruz, to the mining center of Teocelo. The Department of Communications and Public Works issued the concession to the firm on 3 August 1895. The story of its beginning and demise a third of a century later explains in broad outline the manner in which American capitalists conducted business with the government during the Porfiriato and how things changed after the revolution. John B. Frisbie was an old friend of Porfirio Díaz. He had served as the president's personal adviser on railroad matters for many years. Frisbie accompanied Díaz on his trip in the early 1880s to New Orleans, Saint Louis, and New York in search of Mexican railroad investors. That prestigious group included Romero and the president's father-in-law, Romero Rubio. Díaz rewarded his loyal friends, and Frisbie was no exception.

Frisbie, in turn, took advantage of his position as a concessionaire to sell his property to more powerful capitalists who were capable of building the railroad and developing an auxiliary power and light company. In 1898 he sold the concession to the Jalapa Railroad and Power Company, a firm incorporated in New Jersey and controlled by financiers in New York and other cities, including James Ben Ali Haggin, a wealthy California landowner who held a part ownership of the Comstock Lode and a number of other mining concerns. Haggin's associates included Lloyd Tevis, the head of Wells Fargo Bank, and George Hearst. Morgan would later join with Haggin in ownership of the mines at Cerro del Pasco in Peru. The Americans constructed the railroad and the electrical power plant that served the city of Jalapa. The short line from Jalapa was a part of the greater Mexican railroad nexus for the remainder of the Porfiriato.

In 1888 and 1889 the Morgan, Baker, Stillman, William Rockefeller, Jacob Schiff, and Pennsylvania Railroad interests, backed by their British partners, merged around the Texas and Pacific and the Denver and Rio Grande Railroad projects. The two railways would connect California and Mexico to Denver and El Paso. Morgan loaned the Denver and Rio Grande trustees J. Edgar Thomson, Samuel M. Felton, and Louis H. Meyer, all directors of the Pennsylvania Railroad, $500,000 and accepted $1,500,000 in bonds as security. General Palmer, who had succeeded Rosecrans as the Pennsylvania

Railroad's man in Mexico, served as president of the Denver and Rio Grande. John Stewart, Rockefeller, and Stillman bought the Denver and Rio Grande mortgages through the New York Trust Company. The boom in Colorado mineral production, however, focused the attention of the directors of the Denver and Rio Grande on the Rocky Mountain region instead of Mexico and the Pacific. They left the Mexico and California project to their Texas and Pacific line, paying off New York Trust with $1,654,675 and their bond and shareholders with another $1,658,000.[39]

In the meantime the Pennsylvania directors finally found the money needed to complete the Texas and Pacific from Fort Worth to El Paso. Schiff, Morgan, George Gould, and Sage recognized the importance of American economic and political expansion to the south and helped them out. The leaders of the Texas and Pacific Railroad and the Santa Fe Railroad then combined to create the Mexican Central, which ran from El Paso to Mexico City. One of the branches ran east to the oil fields around the port of Tampico, where Stillman was urging Balfour to buy stock in two rival lines: the Mexican National Railroad and the Monterrey and Mexican Gulf Railroad. The British bought into both sides.[40]

Meanwhile, in 1880 Sullivan had acquired on behalf of Stillman the concession for the construction of the railroad from Matamoros to Monterrey. This step complemented Stillman's riparian rights—a crossing monopoly— at that point on the Rio Grande. That was Sullivan's last official act on behalf of the New York financial group that controlled the National Railroad concession. In 1886, after the National had gained the needed railroad concessions in full, the New York financiers marginalized both Palmer and Sullivan. At that point William Rockefeller and Stillman led the reorganization of the Mexican National Construction Company (Constructora Nacional), a division of the National Railroad. In the process the construction company gained the riparian rights to cross the river and the Matamoros-Monterrey concession. After the death of Huntington in 1900, the Big Four—James Stillman, George Gould, William Rockefeller, and E. H. Harriman—took over the entire Southern Pacific system, including the Sur Pacifica on Mexico's west coast and the International Railroad of Mexico.

Before 1905 the highly organized financiers associated with the National City Bank dominated most of Mexico's railroads, including all of the trunk lines, except the Mexican Central.[41] The National City group had often competed with the railroad interests organized by Morgan. The most notable confrontation was the struggle for control of the Northern Pacific. They also fought with the Santa Fe group, headed by the financiers of the Old Colony Trust, over control of routes through the Rocky Mountains to the west and for access to Los Angeles and southern California. But in the late nineteenth century the interests of the bankers, associated industrialists, and specialized railroad capitalists overlapped in myriad ways. They created trust and reserve banks in New York, collaborated in the transport and transfer of cargo, forged mutual ownerships of shipping companies, and developed railroad lines like the Harlem, the Hudson River Valley, the New York Central, and the Monterrey Belt. Morgan and James Speyer of the Speyer Bank of New York were also important leaders, along with Stillman, Rockefeller, and Schiff of the Mexican National Railroad. Speyer was not as powerful and Morgan did not have as much personal commitment to the enterprise as did the men from the National City Bank, but the participation of Speyer's clients in the National's bond and stock issues gave him participation in high-level management.

Telegraphic communications were a corollary of the railroads. During the 1880s, as the railroads approached the Mexican frontier, the New York financiers began to develop the Central and South American Telegraph Company (CSA). The Mexican Telephone Company of New York, a subsidiary of the CSA, then built a line to Brownsville and on to Tampico and Veracruz. The leaders of the parent company included James Scrymser, its president, William R. Grace, a director of the National City and mayor of New York, Jonathan Edwards, the president of the Equitable, Richard W. Thompson, a former secretary of the navy and the chairman of the American Committee of the Panama Canal Company, Alfred Pell of London, presidential relatives James and W. Emlen Roosevelt, and Cornelius Vanderbilt. Scrymser headed the Mexican Telegraph Company, which connected the border to Veracruz, Mexico's most important port, and continued on to Lima, Peru. Between 1902 and 1913 the company netted between 12 and 24 percent. Morgan chose the CSA as his first major venture in central Mexico, and Temple Bowdoin represented him on both boards. The telegraph joined the railroads as a facilitator of American business.[42]

CONSOLIDATION

Shortly after the turn of the century, the government of Mexico began buying railroad stock to reduce American control and to counter growing criticism from Mexican nationalists. The government's purchases prompted a consolidation of American railroad interests. In 1902 and 1905 Morgan organized syndicates to purchase $60,000,000 in bonds issued by Santa Fe, the line that controlled the Mexican Central. The leading financial players in the United States and their British partners each put up more than $500,000 and entered the Mexican economy yet again. The new buyers, who took over control of the unified lines with an investment of $500,000 or more, were the Trio, (J. P. Morgan, James Stillman, and George Baker), John and William Rockefeller, Morton, Guarantee Trust, Kidder Peabody, Rogers, James Speyer, Stewart, Ernest Cassel, Baring Brothers, and James Blair of the First National Bank and Kansas City Southern Industries, which controlled the Kansas City, Mexico, and Orient Railroad.[43]

At the same time, Morgan accepted Schiff's offer of a $75,000,000 share in a Southern Pacific bond issue worth $160,000,000. The monies would be used to modernize the tracks in the southwestern United States and complete the Pacific line to Guadalajara. John Rockefeller already held a $1,000,000 interest in the Guadalajara route. Now Morgan shared the risk and joined Stillman, Harriman, William Rockefeller, and George Gould—the Big Four— in financing the transcontinental trunk line that controlled the Mexican International and the Pacific Coast routes. The New York financial community then backed the Mexican Central with a $35,000,000 bond issue, allowing the railway to complete the east-west route from Tuxpan to Manzanillo that had been envisioned by Rosecrans thirty-eight years earlier. Ladenburg-Thalmann led the sale. Morgan bought a $500,000 interest, and the usual banks and individuals bought up the rest of the issue.

The bond drives came to a halt on 14 February 1906, when the Mexican government completed its $500,000,000 purchase of a 50 percent interest in Mexico's rail system, the new Ferrocarriles Nacionales de México.[44] Two boards of directors were chosen, one in the political capital of Mexico City and the other in the financial center of New York. Although the board that met in Mexico City made "suggestions" to the financiers in New York, control of the consolidated lines remained in the hands of the New Yorkers. The consortium was headed by Morgan, Stillman, Harriman, George Baker, William Rockefeller, Speyer, Gould, and Schiff. The Mexican directors took responsibility for interacting with their government, while the New Yorkers appointed the president in charge of operations and approved capital outlays. The New York board consulted regularly with Cassel, Arthur James Balfour, and Edward Charles Baring, their British partners.

The New York leaders accepted the Mexican government's demands for a buyout even though it was spurred by nationalist protests in Mexico against foreign ownership. The "nationalization" of the Mexican railroads brought the Mexican Pacific, the Tampico Harbor (an Edward Doheny enterprise), the Mexican Central, and the Mexican National Railroads into one entity controlled by the Americans, with the Mexican government gaining representation. The consolidation of the diverse lines in Mexico into a national system gave the bankers a handsome profit, unified their heretofore somewhat fragmented administrative structure, and eliminated the interference of Mexican politicians. The sale temporarily defused nationalist criticism and placed the financial burden for restoring the already decrepit rolling stock squarely on the shoulders of the Mexican government. The arrangement led to renovation and expansion of the systems on both sides of the border and allowed the American financial elite to consolidate their holdings and control of Mexican transportation and export production.[45]

The Big Four, who focused much of their railroading interests in Mexico, Morgan, and Baker welcomed the consolidations because they allowed a more narrowly focused exercise of power. Individual members of the group held controlling interests in the Kansas and Texas, the Missouri Pacific, the Southern Pacific, and the Union Pacific Southern Branch, which entered Texas from the north in the early 1880s. They exercised corresponding hegemonies over the Sur Pacifico de México, which ran along the west coast, the Mexican Northern, which extended into Sonora from Arizona, the Mexican International, which ran from Eagle Pass to Durango, and the Monterrey Belt Railway. They all served on the board of directors of the National City Bank, which they used as the base of their financial network. Their interest in the Ferrocarriles Nacionales de México dated from the concessions granted by Lerdo to the Taylor-led consortium that had created the International and Great Northern Railroad of Texas during the early 1870s.

The nature of the relations between American business interests and the Mexican government in that era was complex. By 1908 the American-controlled railroads consisted of 22,822 kilometers of track, with some 3,749 kilometers classified as *minerales*. The forty-four *minerales*, plus other specialized lines, reached out to the nation's richest mineral lodes, timber stands, and commercial croplands. Private Mexican capital controlled only the Ferrocarriles Unidos de Yucatán, a railroad network designed to bring the henequen harvests from the fields to the port city of Progreso, where buyers from International Harvester and the firm of George Foster Peabody bought it for distribution abroad. The Mexican government controlled one line, the Sur de México, which traversed the Isthmus of Tehuantepec from Puerto México on the Gulf of Mexico (now Coatzacoalcos) to Salina Cruz on the Pacific.

As the railroad nexus grew, pressures mounted on the American builders to construct east-west lines with the same dedication they showed for the north-south lines extending from the border to central Mexico. Naturally, the Americans showed less enthusiasm for the enormous outlays of cash needed to develop lines that would link Gulf Coast cities such as Tampico with their Pacific counterparts like Mazatlán. They were also reluctant to invest in the Pacific Coast route, which led toward the thinly populated American Southwest. Although the lines would have benefited the directors personally through opportunities to acquire land, the companies would not prosper as readily as would those building routes that led from Texas directly to Saint Louis, Chicago, and the Northeast. In fact, the American financiers feared that the east-west lines might even benefit the shipping of their European competitors. Railroad transportation between Mexico's state capitals and provincial localities suffered when it was not important to the export market to America.

Meanwhile, most Mexicans continued to depend on a poorly maintained system of dirt roads. Mexican politicians argued with reluctant American entrepreneurs over this issue throughout the presidencies of Lerdo, Díaz, and González. The imbalance resulted from the differing goals of the American and Mexican leaders involved in the undertaking. Immediate profitability for the American investor could be had by linking the richest resources with the largest industrial processors and consumer markets. Outlets toward the Atlantic Ocean served foreigners, whereas routes to the more provincial areas of the Mexican countryside offered costs but little remuneration, given the weak market in the country's interior.

Because of the presence of the railroads and, to a lesser degree, improvements made to the port facilities, trade between the two nations expanded at an impressive rate. In 1860 commercial exchange between Mexico and the United States totaled only $7,000,000, and in 1880 it still only amounted to $15,000,000. By 1890 the volume of commerce had reached $36,000,000. In 1900 it surpassed $63,000,000. By 1910 the effect of the railroads on the growth of the Mexican economy and the role that American entrepreneurs played in that process was evident. The total value of Mexico's foreign trade had reached $245,885,803. The value of imports was $107,061,955, and that of exports was $138,823,848. The Americans held a major share of the exchange: Mexico's imports from the United States totaled $61,029,681 and exports totaled $105,357,236, accounting for over two-thirds of Mexico's foreign commercial exchange.[46]

Railroad investments still made up 70 percent of the dollar value of the American commitment to Mexico in 1902 because of the costly machinery and the low cost of Mexican timber, mines, and land. In 1910, after the government's buyout of one-half the capital value of the American-owned trunk lines and the creation of the Ferrocarriles Nacionales de México, the Big Four and the other principal American investors in Mexican railroads still held 500,000 pesos in bonds of the new national system, controlled the voting stock, and appointed the active director of the lines in New York. The second board of directors and railroad administration in Mexico City represented the government and consulted with the board in New York, but it did not actively manage the railroads.[47]

When the Mexican Revolution began in 1910, the railroad system totaled 24,560 kilometers and provided mineral ores, timber, and agricultural products to American consumers, while American exports to the Mexicans comprised low-grade corn, finished goods, and high technology for the petroleum, mining, and construction industries. Trunk lines tied Brownsville, Laredo, Eagle Pass, El Paso, and Nogales to Mexico City. The Mexican Southern Railroad, which spanned the Isthmus of Tehuantepec, provided American and other shippers with direct access to the South Pacific, while two lines connected the port of Veracruz with Mexico City and another ran between the Pacific port of Acapulco and the Mexican capital. North of Acapulco the railroads helped link the ports of Manzanillo and Mazatlán with San Francisco, Los Angeles, and the Mexican interior.

The nationwide process of railroad construction had begun with surveying teams, the acquisition of rights-of-way, and the requisitioning of men and materials. The employment of 50,000 laborers and the purchase by the Americans of materials to construct the railroad system had provided the nation with an infusion of cash and a sense of hope. The Americans had launched an era of economic growth which benefited the elites.

The growth of foreign investment and the introduction of modern communications spurred popularity for the Díaz regime during the mid and late 1880s, but the period of optimism proved fleeting. The American railroads failed to prolong prosperity. The railroads, which had been the leading American industry in Mexico since 1876, lost their momentum in the final years of the Porfiriato. In the two years between 1908 and the onset of the Mexican Revolution, railroad construction slowed to a snail's pace of only 869 kilometers per year. Foreign railroad builders had reached most of their goals by then, capital was more expensive, and the market offered by Mexican cities in the interior never developed.

5   Silver, Copper, Gold, and Oil

The Standard and Waters Pierce oil companies are fighting the
oil business hard. . . . This is why I am trying to get a start in old
Mexico, before they get it all, as they will soon control the whole
thing.

Walter B. Sharp, oil entrepreneur, 1901

The heads of the American mining companies were among the first industrialists to understand the richness of Mexico's resources. The nation contained major deposits of essential metals and one of the world's largest petroleum fields. The completion of the Mexican Central Railroad coincided with
congressional approval of the 1884 mining code, which was written specifically to attract foreign investment. The legislation reversed the colonial-era
law that declared that Mexico's subsoil resources were owned by the government. The new legislation provoked public protests, but it worked. American mining companies began to arrive in earnest, searching for silver, copper,
oil, lead, zinc, gold, and coal. Miners, encouraged by the new opportunities,
led the first surge of American immigration into Mexico.

Many American miners failed to appreciate the enduring nature of or-
ganic law in this case, but they understood intent and got what they wanted—
a minimum of government interference and lower taxes. In 1887 the Mexican government added more inducements for oilmen to the ever growing
number of concessions to American miners by abolishing state restrictions
on mining practices and replacing state taxes on the industry with one administered uniformly by the national government. The position of the
American mining and oil interests was strengthened in 1892, when the Mexican government bequeathed "unquestioned title to whatever subsoil deposits there might be" to property buyers.

THE MEXICAN COMSTOCK

Govenor Alexander Robey Shepherd exemplified the successful American
silver mine operators in Mexico. He used vast amounts of capital provided
by New York financiers, applied high technology, and employed American

engineers and supervisors and Mexican workers to make the Batopilas mines of the Sierra Madre the "Mexican Comstock." His methods combined financial strength and solid business management strategies.

Shepherd was the last governor of Washington, D.C. In 1879 he left the American capital in the wake of a congressional investigation into his misuse of funds during an intense city building program. Traveling by way of Panama, he visited the legendary Batopilas mine, which had been started by a Spanish nobleman in the 1600s and was operated by John R. Robinson, a Wells Fargo Bank executive who lived in Ohio. Robinson's principal backers since 1860 had been William K. Fargo, the head of the bank, and directors Ashbel H. and Danford N. Barney. Batopilas was famous for the "native" (pure) silver that had been extracted in bulk and transported by ship to the San Francisco mint during the 1860s and 1870s. Three centuries of exploitation had depleted the deposits of native silver that had made the mine a commercial success. The mines were still rich, but the silver was located in pockets deep inside the mountain. The deposits included ornate herringbone silver, as well as spiky and wire silver, all in fissure veins. Everyone realized that recapitalization and high technology could make the mines profitable again, although enormous amounts of capital would need to be invested in exploratory digging.

Shepherd liked what he saw. He returned briefly to the United States, where he interested investors and bought a share in the ownership of the largely idle mines. The new owners included George Pullman of the National City Bank and Lloyd Tevis of Wells Fargo. Pullman invested in the mine as an individual, while the Wells Fargo involvement may have been institutional, since bank directors Ashbel and Danford Barney continued as major backers of the enterprise. Shepherd returned to Washington, D.C., for his spouse and children and then transported them to San Antonio by railroad and to Chihuahua by stagecoach. On the last leg of the journey, from Chihuahua City, they crossed the rugged Tarahumara zone of the Sierra Madre and descended into the 6,200-foot-deep Batopilas *barranca* (canyon). It is still one of the most remote places in North America.

Successful operations at Batopilas required an enormous amount of money, the latest technology, and engineering brilliance. The financiers provided the first two, and Shepherd selected and supervised the engineers. The mine was a bargain at any price for Shepherd, Pullman, and Tevis. It was the center of the richest silver mining district in North America and perhaps the world, as noted in 1876 by the *San Antonio Express:* "The big bonanzas of the Comstock Lode are said to be inferior in yield to the possibilities of the silver mines of the north Sierra Madre." Geologists referred to it as an epithermal precious metal province. The three American financiers and engineers were a combination that the Mexican miners, who knew Batopilas and its riches all too well, could not rival.

The early years presented a challenge to the financial strength and resolve of the directors. During the early 1880s the original technology and some rich strikes provided the incentive for further exploration and development. Between 1880 and 1886, while Shepherd was purchasing machinery and developing the site, the mines produced silver valued at 600,000 pesos, only partially offsetting some 2,000,000 pesos in expenditures. Shepherd purchased the nearby San Miguel tunnel in 1880 for $600,000, and he continued to expand the holdings during the next decade. In the late 1880s the company owned 125,000 acres and had full mineral rights over sixty-one square miles. The firm was capitalized at $5,175,000, and it employed 1,500 workers, including a detachment of 70 armed horsemen. Shepherd's men had surveyed "over 500 profitable veins in the sixty-four square mile area surrounding Batopilas." The profits began to roll in.[1]

At that point Shepherd sought new sources of financial support. Reorganized as the Batopilas Consolidated Mining Company in 1887, the Batopilas enterprise produced world-class profits that were indeed comparable to those taken from the Comstock Lode in Nevada. Its directors were men who were prepared to take a chance on a remote site far beyond easy reach. The proprietors who joined Shepherd included Charles T. Barney, president of the New York Loan and Improvement Company and a director of the Knickerbocker Trust, Juan M. Ceballos, a director of IBC and the Western National Bank, and George W. Quintard, a director of a dozen New York railroads and financial and insurance institutions. Among Quintard's connections in Chihuahua were Charles M. Schwab, a fellow director of the Atlantic Mutual Life Insurance Company. Schwab was the founder of the Chihuahua, Sierra Madre, and Pacific Railroad, chairman of Bethlehem Steel, and a director of the Empire Bank of New York, which held the mortgages on Pearson's Mexican Northwestern Railroad of Chihuahua.[2]

Shepherd introduced cost-cutting technology that made the mines profitable and their expansion not only possible but necessary. His system depended upon enormous capitalization, an economy of scale, and astute management. He husbanded resources and simultaneously explored for new deposits, striving to make the output of the mines as constant as possible and avoid boom-and-bust cycles. He maintained the professional supervision of labor and employed a strict wage system rather than *gambusino*, or profit sharing. *Gambusino* was eliminated, despite the resistance of the miners, because of the enormous value of the ore extracted.

The profits produced by the Batopilas mines allowed for an ever greater economy of scale. When completed, the industrial complex, known as the Hacienda San Miguel, contained the latest technology in the industry. Shepherd imported one of the first modern ore crushers to operate in Mexico. Shipped in from San Francisco and carried in pieces from Mazatlán, the processor finished forty tons daily. The miners continued to extend the Porfirio Díaz Tunnel until the company closed in 1921. The tunnel entered the mountain at its base and ran for more than two kilometers. Despite Brazilian claims to the contrary, it was the longest excavation of its type in the world. It enabled the workers to excavate the ore from the rich silver deposits above and then move it down to the tunnel, where carts powered by a turbine hauled it out on rails. Between 1880 and 1 January 1909, the mines produced silver valued at $21,664,467.89.

After the refining and smelting of the ore into *barras* (ingots), the men loaded the silver on mules—the company owned some five hundred—and carried it out of the *barranca* to Chihuahua under the protection of an armed escort that Shepherd retained as a private security force. The mule trains took a week to reach Chihuahua City. The ore was then shipped north on the Mexican Central Railroad to El Paso. The monthly bullion trains, known as the *conducta*, carried between fifty and two hundred bars of silver valued in their aggregate from $60,000 to $240,000, although shipments of the lower and higher amounts were rare. The Batopilas company superintendent sometimes ordered the silver shipped directly to the National Park Bank in New York City, which included among its directors John Jacob Astor of the National City Bank and a major investor in the mining industry, Auguste Belmont, Isaac Guggenheim of ASARCO, Cornelius Vanderbilt Jr., and Stuyvesant Fish, the son of the secretary of state who had failed to embargo Díaz during his insurrection in 1876. The directors of the Batopilas Mining Company held directorships in other companies with all these men. Even in Chihuahua, Shepherd's accounts with the Banco Minero placed him in direct contact with Enrique Creel, the future Mexican minister of foreign affairs and son of U.S. consul Rueben Creel. Shepherd used the bank, which was controlled by Creel and associates, as his depository.[3]

The headquarters complex at Batopilas included some twenty buildings. Located across the Batopilas River from the town, it had a barracks that housed more than fifty troops, a foundry, a warehouse, a stable, an arsenal, a smelter, and guard towers. The river served as a moat between the complex and the settlement where his workers lived. Shepherd's comfortable office building, dubbed "Shepherd's Castle," was situated next to his residence. The castle dominated the five-acre complex, which included a number of guest houses. The castle had three stories. Its first two levels were constructed of quarried stone, and the upper floor was finished in adobe covered with white stucco. The veranda faced a tropical garden. The castle was "a beautiful example of American Gothic Revival," which was in vogue during the construction boom on the East Coast of the United States during the 1870s. The stone work was "possibly carried out by Italian and Spanish stonemasons." Artisans lined the doors and windows with wood and red bricks. Shepherd chose a design, building materials, and color that strikingly resembled those used for the Smithsonian Institution building, which had been under construction in Washington, D.C., during his term as governor.[4]

Across the river, on the upstream edge of town, Shepherd constructed a hospital of considerable size. Three Americans, a doctor and two nurses, directed a staff of Mexican nurses' aides and clerical personnel. The miners often suffered disabling injuries and illnesses from mishandling dynamite and exposure to cyanide and silica dust. Crushed limbs were common, and amputations were frequently necessary. The hospital lacked certain amenities such as ether, but it was better than nothing. One scholar has asserted that the Mexican government required the facility. A more likely explanation is that the hospital was needed to induce several dozen American mining engineers and other skilled personnel to remain on the scene. The presence of medical services at the site reduced downtime for experienced miners who were costly to replace, it served as an inducement to attract and retain workers, and it was humanitarian. The facilities also included a school and recreation center.[5]

The high level of capitalization introduced by the Americans at Batopilas paralleled their efforts at other mines, in the timber and oil industries, and in industrial-agricultural centers such as the 1,400,000-acre Rascon sugar hacienda complex extending from San Luis Potosí into Tamaulipas. It resulted in an economy of scale that made previously tenuous businesses not only reliably profitable but sometimes extraordinarily so. The introduction of well-paid technicians and high technology was invariably the first result of capitalization. The managers and supervisors at Batopilas received salaries ranging from $18,000 per year for the superintendent to $1,500 per year for an assistant electrician. The hundreds of miners earned about $1.50 per week. If they were employed the entire year, they could hope to gain little more than $75, despite the enormous wealth that they produced.[6]

The captains of American industry and finance applied their prior experience in the southwestern United States to their endeavors in Mexico. Shepherd's strategies for maximizing profits and maintaining segregated living facilities at Batopilas reproduced the contemporary practices of his coun-

terparts in the New York financial community who maintained racially segregated mines in Arizona. Rather than instituting the salary ratio of 2.5 to
1 between managers and their employees that was common in the United
States at the time, however, mine owners adapted the existing wage dispar-
ities they encountered in Mexico. The standard ratio of managers' salaries
to workers' wages was 20 to 1. This practice was one of many that reinforced
the vast cultural differences that existed between the formally educated
Americans, some of them engineers, and the Mexican mine laborers.[7]

Owners and supervisors commonly lived in "big houses" and ordered
the construction of *chozas,* or shacks, nearby for the Mexican workforce.
They placed the shacks, normally made of thatch with dirt floors, in neat
rows within view of the big house, which had long porches that often reached
around all four sides of the building. At Batopilas the owners built the workers' housing only at outlying mining sites so that the workers would not
lose time traveling to the mines. Many Americans who headed mines and
plantations lived like an aristocracy and considered their Mexican employees as a racially inferior rabble that they were bringing, ever so slowly, toward civility.[8]

The Americans suspended operations at Batopilas several times during
the revolution. In 1911 and 1912 the *conducta* could not be undertaken for
prolonged periods. The stockpiles of bullion at Batopilas were so large that
they attracted rival bands of revolutionaries, who occupied the town and
"taxed" the mines. After years of enduring depredations, the Batopilas Consolidated Mining Company finally shut down in 1921 as a result of the decline of silver values in the global market and depletion of its financial reserves, which were necessary to maintain exploration and steady silver
output.[9]

MINING IMPRESARIOS

After the American, and some European, miners had surveyed the Mexican countryside, staked claims, and bought out operating and defunct mines,
they proceeded to build *minerales,* the lines that connected their sites to the
trunk lines of the Mexican Central, Mexican International, and Mexican
National Railroads. These lines connected remote areas of northern Mexico with El Paso, Eagle Pass, and Laredo. From there the Southern Pacific
and other lines carried ore to smelters in Colorado, Kansas, Missouri, and
Oklahoma. The railroads placed mineral deposits in Sonora, Chihuahua,
Coahuila, Durango, Zacatecas, San Luis Potosí, Guanajuato, México, and
other states in direct contact with smelters in the United States. Many of

the foreign mining investors believed that Mexico had joined the world of laissez-faire nations.[10]

During the late 1870s and 1880s highly capitalized American mining impresarios introduced high technology and came to dominate three important silver-producing areas. The centers were in San Luis Potosí and Coahuila; Chihuahua, Sonora, and Durango; and Guanajuato. In 1878 high prices and the discovery of ores at the Sierra Mojada in Coahuila brought an onrush of miners to the virtually abandoned and desolate site. By 1885 the miners were shipping 1,000 tons of ore per week. It contained 25 percent lead and yielded 20 ounces of silver per ton.[11]

The McKinley Tariff Act of 1890 and the subsequent Sherman Silver Purchase Act stimulated American interest in the ownership of Mexican mines. The new tariff called for a higher duty to be paid on lead content in ores, while the silver legislation required the U.S. government to purchase an increased amount of silver bullion every month. In some areas, however, water supplies and local agriculture were extremely limited, and labor had to be imported from other regions. Transporting the ore by mule was slow and costly. Only modern capital could solve these problems, and highly capitalized American investors bested smaller-scale American and Mexican miners who could not afford the expenses. The largest mining capitalists constructed smelters in northern Mexico, exported the silver, and avoided the duty on lead.

Monterrey, the capital of Nuevo León, was emerging as an industrial city. Here Italian, Irish, British, and Mexican industrialists competed with their American counterparts as both sides built smelters. British businessman William Purcell built a smelter in Saltillo, a site close to the mines, which held down the high shipping costs of ore. Robert S. Towne of New York and the Kansas City Smelting and Refining Company supervised the construction of the Mexican Northern Railroad, which connected the Sierra Mojada mining area with the Kansas City company's smelter at El Paso. Towne, working with capital provided by George Foster Peabody and others, purchased several mining companies, quickly displaced Purcell as the major economic presence at Sierra Mojada, and put the Americans in a dominant position.[12]

During the 1890s Towne recruited the support of a formidable array of New York capitalists who gave him the ability to widen his base of operations. In 1890 he organized the Compañía Metalúrgica Mexicana (Mexican Metals Company), backed by Peabody and financiers Henry O. Havemeyer, A. Foster Higgins of the Kansas City, Mexico, and Orient Railroad, Henry L. Higginson, F. B. Tilghman, Spencer Trask, and Nathaniel Wetherell. Towne's principal investors were well connected in the New York financial community. Havemeyer had extensive experience in foreign operations. He served as the president of the American Sugar Company and as a director of the American Coffee Company, and he acted as a director of the Colonial Trust Company of New York. Higgins served with Mexican railroad and sugar entrepreneurs Moses Taylor and Charles T. Barney as a director of the Knickerbocker Trust Company and as a director of the chamber of commerce of New York City. Higginson's tenure as a director of General Electric, which had extensive operations throughout Latin America, and his leadership of the Manhattan Trust Company provided Towne with even more diversity.

Peabody acted as a director of the Mexican National Railroad and its affiliate in charge of maintenance and expansion, the Mexican National Construction Company. In addition, Peabody directed the State Trust Company of New York, served on the boards of General Electric and various American railroads, and played a major role in Yucatán henequen exports. Tilghman, a partner in the investment firm of Tilghman, Rowland, and Company and a director of the Kansas City Smelting and Refining Company, served with Towne on the board of the Mexican Northern. As a director of the Chihuahua, Sierra Madre, and Pacific Railway Company, Tilghman offered support in the form of Mexican expertise, financial sources, and railroading experience. Trask, the president of Edison Electric Illuminating Company, complemented the skills and know-how of his colleagues as a director of the Mexican National Construction Company. Wetherell, a financier, held a directorship with Kansas City Smelting along with Towne and Tilghman. The consortium provided financial strength, vertical integration for mining operations, the capacity to provide communications and transportation, and the political influence with Díaz and the U.S. Congress that was needed for the success of large-scale business in Mexico.[13]

Towne purchased mines at Sierra Mojada and in San Luis Potosí and organized the Sombrerete Mining, the Mexican Lead, and the Montezuma Lead Companies. He also secured five concessions from Díaz for the construction of smelters. The one at San Luis Potosí proved timely when the U.S. Congress established the lead tariff. His exports were now refined metals instead of silver ore, which carried extra charges because of its lead content. Towne connected his mines with the Mexican Mineral and the Potosí and Río Verde Railroads. He further developed his mining operations through horizontal integration, creating the Alvarez Land and Timber Company, which provided railroad ties and trestles, housing materials, and the wood used to reinforce the mine tunnels.

Mining in Mexico on that scale required a secure market, one that did not fluctuate wildly. The American Metals Company of New York bought all of Towne's shipments, paying in advance on a prorated basis. The financial and business connections of the company leaders in New York and Towne's on-the-spot ingenuity formed a highly successful combination. In San Francisco, D. Percy Morgan, another Towne investor, exported silver to Asia. Morgan was also well connected in New York, serving on the board of the National Surety Company with Edwin Gould, John Hegemon, and Henry Huntington of the IBC. The companies that operated in Mexico under Towne's name had varying degrees of success, but all were professionally managed and profitable. They prospered until the onset of the revolution in 1910, when production and profits peaked and then declined.

In the late nineteenth and early twentieth centuries silver was the largest sector of the Mexican mining industry, and the Guggenheim family controlled the largest complex of mines, smelters, and mineral railroads in the country. Daniel and Isaac Guggenheim, both IBC directors, mined copper, iron, gold, and zinc. The family placed the majority of its holdings under the aegis of ASARCO, but they also controlled properties in their own names. M. Guggenheim's Sons, Aguascalientes Metal Company, Mexican Ore Company, American Smelters' Security Company, Guggenheim Exploration Company, and the Mexican Exploration Company represented a complex of transportation, resource development, and processing enterprises that had no equal.

On 9 October 1890 Daniel and Isaac Guggenheim received a concession from Díaz to build three smelters. In 1891 and 1892 they obtained state construction permits from the governor of Nuevo León, Bernardo Reyes. Once again, local practices merged with business opportunity. The concessions were issued to Daniel because he was the family patriarch, although Isaac conceived the idea. The approval gave the Guggenheims the green light to move ahead from mineral extraction to the processing of ore inside Mexico. They built the Gran Fundición Nacional Mexicana at Monterrey, the largest smelter in Mexico. Farther south, at Aguascalientes, they constructed the Gran Fundición Central Mexicana. Aguascalientes was an important railroad junction, and the southern smelter handled the output of copper ore from their mines at nearby Tepezala.

The Guggenheim operations were not a simple family affair. They successfully integrated an array of New York financiers into their operations, including Grant B. Schley, the brother-in-law of George Baker, the head of the First National Bank of New York, and William C. Whitney, his son Harry Payne Whitney, and Henry Rogers, all of Standard Oil. The Guggenheims were also closely associated with Levi Morton while he served as vice president of the United States and as governor of New York, and during his later appointments in the Morton Trust Company, the Guarantee Trust Bank, the National Bank of Commerce, the National Park Bank, and the Plaza Bank. The Guggenheims had access to large amounts of development capital whenever they needed it.

The Guggenheims' social life reflected the financial strength of the American elites in Mexico. In Manhattan their neighbors and social partners included John D. Rockefeller Jr., Mrs. John Jacob Astor, and Chauncey M. Depew, president of the New York Central railroad and a director of the Equitable, which took part in the pioneering of American investments in Mexico. Other leading industrialists and bankers who attended their social events were James Speyer, Andrew Carnegie, the Seligmans, and the Rothschilds. In 1899 Schley announced that ASARCO enjoyed a capitalization of $65,000,000. As their wealth and power grew, the Guggenheims came to dominate Mexican mineral production. Ultimately, only the Whitneys and Thomas F. Ryan of the Equitable would share real authority inside the company with them.[14]

The Guggenheims bought mines throughout northern Mexico and undertook explorations as far south as the state of Oaxaca. Working through John Hays Hammond, they also purchased the rich Esperanza gold mine at El Oro. In a six-month period between 1902 and 1903, they paid $16,000,000 for six mines in Michoacán, Aguascalientes, San Luis Potosí, Coahuila, Chihuahua, and Durango to ensure a steady flow of ore to their smelters.

The purchase of the Esperanza mine gave the Guggenheims a chance to outshine their neighbor James Ben Ali Haggin. The mine was already highly profitable, and they paid over $2,000,000 for it. In 1903 they used the good offices of famed British oilman Weetman Pearson to sell 51 percent of the Esperanza's shares in London at a total capitalization of £450,000, far more than the purchase price. The Guggenheims then imported advanced machinery and created an economy of scale. Once again the wise use of capital and technology was the recipe for success. They constructed a 120-stamp mill and cyanide plant and used the newly available electrical power generated by the Nexcaca Dam. They also carried out intensive explorations. New discoveries and the increased refining capacity resulted in a surge of profits. The Guggenheims turned the Esperanza into a mining bonanza. Between 1904 and 1910 the company paid out an average yearly dividend of 68.8 percent, peaking in 1906 when the shares paid 160 percent of their value. In 1905 the mine produced refined ores valued at 10,292,530 pesos. In that year the Guggenheims merged all of their holdings into ASARCO except the Esperanza, which they found more profitable to operate as a separate venture. A year later the total value of the mine's output had increased by

50 percent, to 15,357,690 pesos. By that year, 1906, the value of a share of the mine's common stock had increased 50 percent in three years, from £200 to £300. The profits continued to roll in for several more years.[15]

Isaac and Daniel invested over $1,500,000 to upgrade and enlarge their smelters. They constructed copper and lead smelters at Monterrey, Aguascalientes, Chihuahua, Durango, and El Paso to complement their earlier installations in Colorado. Daniel and Isaac also worked to prevent others from building competing smelters. Their holding company, Guggenex, created a subsidiary, the National Metallurgical Company of Mexico, that controlled most of the large mines and the *minerales* that connected them to the trunk lines and smelters. By 1907 the Guggenheims held a virtual smelting monopoly in north-central and northeast Mexico. The only exceptions were Towne's plants, a small installation at Torreón owned by the Maderos, and the Fundidora in Monterrey. Only the Amalgamated Copper Company and Phelps Dodge, producers of copper in Sonora, rivaled the Guggenheim operations.[16]

The Phelps Dodge Corporation concentrated its efforts at Moctezuma, at a mining site known as the Pilares de Nacozari. It was located some seventy-five miles east of Cananea. The Guggenheims had pioneered modernization at Nacozari during the 1890s, but problems with Native American resistance and geographic remoteness had rendered transportation too difficult and expensive. The Guggenheims and their partner, A. H. Danforth, had lost interest in the enterprise because of these problems and the fact that the copper industry was an entity apart from their undertakings in iron, steel, gold, zinc, lead, and silver mining. In addition, Daniel and Isaac were probably not anxious to compete with their powerful friends in the financial market— William Rockefeller, Henry Rogers, John D. Ryan, and James Stillman—who were creating the kind of dominance over copper production that ASARCO had established elsewhere in metallurgy. In 1897 the Guggenheims sold Nacozari to Phelps Dodge. Directors James Douglas and Cleveland Dodge agreed to pay the Guggenheims in full for their investment.

Phelps Dodge created the Moctezuma Copper Company as a Mexican subsidiary and placed James Douglas in charge. Douglas began by acquiring tracts of timberland, dry rolling hills, and mining claims that eventually totaled 350,000 acres in northeastern Sonora. His first purchase was in 1897, when he paid only sixty centavos per acre for the 12,500- and 16,600-acre Juárez and San Nicolas Ranches in nearby Cumpas and Arizpe. Douglas continued to buy land near Nacozari as the company's need for cattle and timber grew. In 1910 he concluded the last purchase before the revolution intruded, buying 124,000 acres of the ranch originally owned by

George F. Wheeler of the Wheeler Land and the Sinaloa Land and Water Companies.[17]

Following the pattern of American mining enterprises in Mexico, the Phelps Dodge leaders established an economy of scale to realize a profit from marginal ore. With a capitalization of $3,000,000, the Moctezuma Copper Company installed a coal-fired power plant, two 5-ton Bessemer converters, two 150-ton furnaces, and two 200-ton mills. The company planners were led by Douglas and Louis D. Ricketts, a noted mining engineer who later worked for Greene at Cananea. They designed a carefully conceived American-style town, which they built on an older site known as Nacozari de García. The company headquarters, which faced a beautiful fountain, dominated the plaza, which was surrounded by less imposing civic and commercial buildings. Cobblestone streets and impressive houses filled the center of the town. The more modest structures for skilled American employees were located on nearby streets. Douglas and Ricketts relegated the housing for two concentrations of Mexican workers beyond the end of the pavement. One was located over the hill to the north of town, in the direction of the mines, and the other was farther down the hill, below the town. The latter location required a rigorous climb to visit the shopping center and an even longer, more difficult hike to the mines.

As always, transportation costs had to be controlled to convert a money-losing operation into a bonanza. Phelps Dodge built a seventy-five-mile-long *mineral* from Agua Prieta–Douglas at the Arizona border to Nacozari. At the border the branch line intersected with the company's El Paso and Southwestern Railroad. That improvement and the addition of a giant smelter near Bisbee, which processed the ore coming out of Phelps Dodge's Copper Queen mines, gave the operation at Nacozari access to the most sophisticated and cost-efficient technology of the time. The company closed the Nacozari smelter in 1904 because of obsolescence and replaced it with a 1,500-ton concentrator, reducing excess materials and the cost of shipping even more. By 1910 the Moctezuma mining company had 5,000 head of cattle to supply meat for its labor force. This guaranteed the steady supply of high-quality provisions needed for the morale of the skilled workers, and it extended the company's control over local affairs from the workplace to the dinner table. If Phelps Dodge paid the Mexican workers at the wage rates that prevailed elsewhere in the mining industry—and the segregated living areas indicate that the company probably did—then meat would have been a luxury.[18]

Although the leading businessmen in Monterrey, headed by the Italian Ferrara family, united to establish the successful and ultimately more enduring Fundidora smelter in the city, successes similar to those of the Guggenheims and Phelps Dodge gave the highly capitalized Americans a dominant position in northeastern metallurgical production. The concentration of power led to complaints by independent American miners that a few large interests controlled them through arbitrary pricing strategies. The imbalance of power between American and Mexican capitalists contributed to the enmity between Governor Reyes, who was closely tied to the Americans, and the Madero family. The Maderos, who operated a smelter at Torreón with relatively low capitalization, welcomed concessions to Americans and their investments if the Porfirian politicians took the family's interests into account when making them. For example, they welcomed John Brittingham when he established "a big dynamite factory at Gomez Palacios," which was on the Mexican Central line. Brittingham went on to forge a vast industrial complex around agricultural processing, ceramics manufacturing, and explosives.[19]

HIGH TECHNOLOGY AND DANGER PAY

Profitable production in the American mines and adjacent mills required cheap labor and the incorporation of high technology. Teams of Mexican workers performed dangerous tasks while the owners employed their own countrymen as foremen and engineers. One of the more irresponsible labor practices involved the use of cyanide during refining. In 1894 Haggin, who held a partnership in the Comstock Lode with Tevis, George Hearst, and Marcus Daly, introduced the use of cyanide in the processing of gold at El Oro, seventy miles northwest of Mexico City. Since higher efficiency in extracting gold from the ore led to greater profits, El Oro became one of the most prosperous gold fields in the world. In 1898 his firm paid out $1,000,000 in dividends. Although the chemical and technical expertise employed by the Americans in Mexico enabled the profitable reopening of many mines, the employment of cyanide meant countless agonizing deaths to Mexican mine workers.

The owners of the silver complexes in the state of Guanajuato exceeded even Haggin in the use of cyanide. The ratio of earnings between the American foremen and Mexican laborers in Guanajuato mines was probably the same as the ratio that prevailed at Batopilas and the Towne mines—about 20 to 1, or $1,500 per year to $75. The American companies in Guanajuato included the Guanajuato Development Company, La Luz Mines, the Mexican Milling and Transportation Company, the Peregrina Mining and Milling Company, and the Pinguico Mining Company. They all depended on cyanide to process the tailings that had been ignored for centuries because no one could extract the silver efficiently. John H. House, Colonel T. W. House's older brother, served as an officer and director of all but Guanajuato Development. He and his associates created the Refugio Syndicate and the Securities Corporation Limited, both of New York, to generate the investment support required to apply the technology.[20]

Potter Palmer, the noted financier and hotel operator in Chicago, employed cyanide refining to regenerate the long-exhausted Cubo Mining and Milling Company in Guanajuato. Irving Herr, the foreman at the mine, described the process: Cars pulled by cables brought the ore, via a vertical shaft, to the mouth of the mine. Workers then dumped it down an incline and placed it in more cars, which carried it to the mill, where steel rock crushers broke it into smaller pieces. Stamping machines then mashed the ore into pulp, using

> hollow steel cylinders . . . half full of steel balls. That reduced the ore
> to virtual dust. Then they added a solution of potassium cyanide and
> agitated the mix for hours . . . until virtually all of the silver and gold
> was dissolved in the solution.

The process was extremely dangerous. The Mexican miners repeatedly immersed their arms in the cyanide mix. After working in this manner for several hours they washed off their arms and ate lunch. Next the material went to the "zinc room," where zinc shavings precipitated the gold and silver in the form of a black powder that the workers packed for shipment on the *minerales*. The workers would simply wash the zinc off their hands and arms at the conclusion of their labors, and the trains carried the ore away to smelters. There is no available estimate of the workers' life expectancy.

The Cubo mines were supervised by H. L. Hollis, a mining engineer, metallurgist, and administrator of the Palmer estate. Hollis applied his labor system at other mines as well. He ran a number of mining operations, including the Cusi mines in Chihuahua, for at least two decades. In January 1910 Hollis hired mining engineer Herr to run the Cubo operation. Herr was attracted to the job by the salary, which was based on Hollis's six-day work regimen. Each of the three daily work shifts at the mine consisted of two overseers, twenty-two specialized workers doing tasks such as loading, timbering, running the machinery, and sharpening tools, and twenty muckers, or laborers. This latter group suffered the greatest exposure to cyanide. Another forty-six men worked as drillers, pumpmen, and muckers in the exploration for and development of new bodies of ore. In addition to the constant struggle to find new deposits and keep the work moving, the mine manager faced the task of maintaining acceptable relations with the "highly organized workers," the *jefe politico* (the local political boss), and the priest. The latter individuals all resided in the "village."[21] A number of workers' unions were being formed at this time in the mines of central Mexico, and it is certainly possible that unions were recruiting members at Cubo as well.

The Cubo was isolated in rugged terrain some thirty miles northwest of Dolores de Hidalgo, the birthplace of Mexican independence and eighty miles from the city of Guanajuato. It provided the basis of support for a sizeable population. When running at full capacity the Cubo employed 672 persons. The workers and their direct dependents totaled 1,992. In 1910 the mine produced 150 tons of ore per day, each ton holding 360 grams of silver and 6.5 grams of gold. Over ninety days the operation yielded $85,000 in silver and another $54,000 in gold, for a yearly gross of $556,000. After deducting 10 percent for taxes and $260,000 for wages and operating expenses, $240,000 remained as net profit. The muckers, drillers, and other laborers received considerably less than $1 per day, a wage that was much higher than documented wages elsewhere.

Rich mines such as the Cubo maintained the economy of the state capital. The city of Guanajuato consisted of some 35,000 souls supported by tax revenues from the mines and provisioning businesses. The mine owners and engineers, merchants, lawyers, and the clergy prospered, as did the few bankers. Apart from the mint and the state capital, Guanajuato contained a college, an opera house, and religious institutions, which provided a picturesque social and cultural ambience that could be tolerated by the American engineers and supervisors. Because of the advantages offered by the city, which could not be found in other largely rural Mexican settings, about 225 Americans clustered there in a colony. The colony included Englishmen and "northern Europeans." Insulated from their Mexican neighbors, the Americans probably agreed with mining engineer Herr that the workers were usually docile, but volatile, susceptible to agitators, and in need of a dictatorial government before they could have democracy.[22]

The labor system used in the mines created an economic gulf between the American and Mexican personnel, who were already divided by social and cultural differences such as language, work habits, cuisine, and custom. The differences between the two groups put the Americans in a distinct position that meshed with the onset of nationalist turmoil. At the Towne mines the eruption of the Mexican Revolution included attacks on the mills and railroads and caused metals shipments and gross earnings to fall by 50 percent in 1914 and then another 50 percent in 1915.[23] William C. "Colonel" Greene, who achieved short-term success at the Cananea Consolidated Copper Company in Sonora, created the classic enclave economy. He exploited a Mexican resource using Mexican workers, but the capitalization, technology, and daily supplies for his operations came from the United States, and he exported the entire product there. Much of Greene's story has been misunderstood. He cultivated the image of the rugged individualist who rediscovered and single-handedly developed the Cananea copper deposit, when in fact he worked closely with the most powerful mining speculators on Wall Street. Greene, looking to the future, also purchased a vast tract of timber in the Sierra Madre for building materials and exports.

Inaccurate legend held that Greene realized the value of Cananea and outsmarted the boys on Wall Street. In fact, the largest American mining investors already knew about the Cananea site but considered it uneconomical because of the Yaquis and Apaches and the troubles they had experienced in the failed effort to build a railroad line from El Paso to Guaymas. The consortiums headed by William Rosecrans and Robert Symon had considered the acquisition of Cananea beginning in the late 1860s, when Rosecrans obtained a sixteen-page report on the site filed by Robert L. D'Amuaile, the assayer for the state of Sonora. D'Amuaile detailed the nature and exact locations of the rich deposits. Rosecrans's first representative in the area, a man named Greene, could well have been William's father. The persistent threat of Indian depredations, however, made Cananea a high-risk investment in a country that yielded Rosecrans and other American investors many possibilities for safer and equally lucrative investments in railroad, timber, and mining ventures.[24]

In 1898 the younger Greene obtained a concession from the widow of Sonoran governor Ignacio Pesqueira for $47,000 and set about capitalizing the Cobre Grande Copper Company in New York and Pennsylvania. In September of the next year Greene reorganized his assets following two hostile takeover attempts and called his new firm the Cananea Consolidated Copper Company. Steel magnate John W. Gates, who also backed the Texas Company's endeavors in Mexico, recognized a potential bonanza and provided the financial backing Greene needed to survive the corporate raiders. Cananea, the largest copper mine in Mexico, had all the necessities for success: a rich deposit of copper, cheap but capable labor, nearby railroad transportation, access to technology, strong financial support, market demand, and competent management. The initial application of technology at Cananea came in the form of a 200-ton smelter, a 600-ton ore concentrator, six furnaces, and a *mineral*, built in 1901 by the Southern Pacific Railroad.

The previous Mexican owners, despite being from the Sonoran oligarchy, had never owned the resources necessary to successfully operate the mines. They could not establish the economy of scale set up by the Americans. The new technology and the Southern Pacific's service line, which tied into the transcontinental railroad in southern Arizona, furnished what was needed to generate a bonanza. Ricketts guided the mining operations. Ricketts and Greene stabilized output by working poorer ores in balance with richer ones to minimize the fits and starts inherent to the mining industry. Greene was a strict taskmaster and struggled to keep wages and costs under control.

The owners' desire to keep labor costs down reinforced the customary practice of discriminatory wages. Mexican workers at Cananea received about one-half the pay of their American counterparts and then had to make their purchases in company stores or those of immigrant Chinese merchants who, the Mexican workers complained, overcharged. Greene aggravated the situation at Cananea by imposing inferior living and working conditions on the Mexican workers. In Arizona mining camps such as Bisbee, which was just twenty miles away, Mexican workers were paid low wages, were denied promotions, endured segregated, inferior housing, and were forbidden to use public facilities designated for "whites," including bathrooms. Greene maintained those practices at Cananea while paying the Mexicans in silver and scrip and the Americans in gold dollars.

In 1904 Cananea became integrated into the highest echelons of American capitalism. In that year three Southern Pacific and three Wells Fargo directors, including Henry Huntington, who served as a director of the railroad, the bank, and the IBC, joined the Cananea board. The directors of Wells Fargo, who backed the Southern Pacific financially, had long experience with the Mexican mining industry. Bank president Lloyd Tevis had invested in the Batopilas mines decades earlier. That same year Greene's company merged its interests with those of ASARCO through Anton Eilers, who served as a director of that company as well as Wells Fargo and Southern Pacific. After the merger, the bank and railroad directors had de facto control of the Cananea mines, and Greene was left with on-site management responsibilities. When Harriman, Rogers, Stillman, and Harrington moved in, however, they were determined to take over all of Greene's holdings. In 1906, although Greene retained an active role in his companies, his debts gave control to the directors of Amalgamated, who then reorganized his holdings. The Guarantee Trust Bank of New York, led by Harriman, Rogers, Morton, Belmont, and Baker, among others, served as the depository of the Greene Gold Company. This specialized company was directed by Emil Berlzheimer of the Rio Grande, Sierra Madre, and Pacific Railroad and the Eagle Pencil Company until it was merged with Cananea Consolidated under the leadership of Amalgamated's directors. Their strength dwarfed that of Wells Fargo and ASARCO.

The enormous resources of the Cananea leaders made the application of modern technology possible and helped turn the mines into producers of major wealth. The company obtained a concession of 900 square kilometers for an outlay of $49,273.35 for Mexican government bonds, probably paying a modest 5 to 8 percent. The bonds were purchased to secure the mining concessions and 380,573 acres of land in the immediate area. The company paid dividends of $432,000 in 1903, $259,000 in 1904, and $1,900,800 in 1905. During the 1905 fiscal year the copper mines produced 64,211,895 pounds of bullion. By then the total investment in the firm totaled $15,213,873.58, and the return exceeded 13 percent on the capital invested.[25]

The growth of mining profits was not matched by improvements in the mining camps at Cananea, or in those in Arizona and other southwestern states. The camps seethed with unrest. Radical American labor organizers, some of them anarchists, circulated among the mines. At Cananea, the American radicals found their Mexican counterparts. Some of the Mexican workers formed anarchist cells dedicated to sabotaging the mines, while others backed the revolutionary Mexican Liberal Party (PLM), headed in Los Angeles by anarchist Ricardo Flores Magón. The PLM operated under the banner cry of "Mexico for the Mexicans."

On 1 June 1906 the workers at Cananea went on strike, sabotaged mine shafts, broke machinery, and paralyzed the mines. An angry Greene invited intervention from the territorial governor of Arizona. Vigilantes led by a captain of the Arizona Rangers crossed the border carrying rifles and shotguns. They blustered onto the scene, menaced the workers, and infuriated the Mexican press, who inflamed public opinion. That blunder provoked nationwide patriotic criticism of the Díaz government for failing to protect Mexico's sovereignty. The Cananea workers had directly challenged some of the most powerful capitalists in the world. The radicals knew that Greene represented the evil capitalists portrayed in Flores Magón's propaganda, but they never realized how close he was to the American elite.

The rebellion, combined with Greene's overcommitment to new projects, exhausted his wealth. He ran out of money almost immediately after the strike. He had no time to develop his other properties in Sonora and Chihuahua. A few years later he went bankrupt and lost those undeveloped timber and mining investments.[26] Greene has been criticized as an incompetent manager because he kept in responsible positions many Americans who were loyal, but not necessarily skilled. It is clear that he lacked the genius of Towne, but it is equally clear that his labor practices coincided with the prevailing mode of operation in the southwestern United States and northwestern Mexico. Much of the criticism directed toward him emanated from his financial associates, who saw him as "common." These more powerful partners wanted to control the entire operation, and the strike justified their efforts to undermine his authority. Here again Greene was no Towne, who maneuvered himself from a manager's position into one of company president and owner while maintaining a successful relationship with the directors of the American Metals Company of New York. Greene and Towne, however, eventually shared the same fate. Undercapitalized compared with Phelps Dodge, ASARCO, and the Amalgamated Copper Company, and lacking the wherewithal to launch multicontinental operations, Greene lacked the diversity to survive in an industry that required ever more technology and an ever widening range of resources.

FORMING A COPPER TRUST

In 1899 the Big Four of the American railroad industry—Stillman, Rockefeller, E. H. Harriman, and George Gould—chose Henry Rogers, a director of the IBC, to forge a copper trust "with the intention of controlling the copper industry of the world."[27] Rockefeller, Stillman, and Harriman, with Jacob Schiff, financed the creation of the trust, the Amalgamated Copper Company, as a copper securities firm, or holding company. Their goal was to control copper supplies and prices in the United States and as much of the rest of the world as possible. They used William L. Moyer, the president of the IBC, to influence Díaz in Mexico City, and they placed Rogers at the head of the company, giving him the charge to defeat ASARCO and Phelps Dodge and to dominate the marketing of copper in North America.

The assignment was perfect for Rogers. He believed in monopoly. He served on the boards of Amalgamated, Union Pacific, Standard Oil, and the International Navigation Company as well as the IBC. His leadership roles tied together the interests of the Big Four and the Trio—Stillman, Baker, and J. P. Morgan, the three major American bankers of the era. Rogers played a key role in the efforts of the Big Four to consolidate control of the major railroad lines in the United States. Logically, Henry Rogers Jr. later sat as a director of the National Copper Bank of New York.

The network of banking, transportation, and industrial interests in which Rogers participated illustrates the capacity for unity that the otherwise competitive groups of capitalists, headed by Baker and Morgan on one side and the Big Four on the other, could achieve when necessary. They demonstrated the capacity to settle their differences when it was mutually profitable, as they would with the formation of the Ferrocarriles Nacionales de México.[28] In 1899 the Amalgamated directors brought IBC chief Moyer into the trust when they took over his Butte Copper and Zinc Company and the Butte Central and Boston Copper Corporation. Moyer ran Amalgamated's Montana operations and consolidated control over the richest mines in the state.

In 1901 the Amalgamated directors purchased the fabulously rich Anaconda Copper Company to complement their activities in the spheres of railroads, banking, and petroleum. The Anaconda had originally been developed by Haggin, Daly, and Hearst. These three had begun to divest their Anaconda holdings in 1891 by issuing the company's stock for public sale. This allowed them to expand Anaconda's operations and to create cash liquidity for other investments. Daly sold his shares to Haggin, who had retired as the president of the firm in 1899. Haggin then sold 978,000 shares to Amalgamated for $15,000,000. Amalgamated paid $79,609,150 for a total of 78,959,150 of the firm's 150,000,000 outstanding shares.

The Amalgamated directors reorganized Anaconda, placing William Rockefeller on the board and keeping Moyer as the key leader of the Butte and Boston firms. The Amalgamated leaders were now the largest producers of copper in the United States, and Moyer, as the president of the IBC and with Rogers and Gould at his side, was well positioned to move investment capital into new mining undertakings in Mexico and the world. Haggin, who had interests in the Santa Anita and Churchill Downs Racetracks, was highly capitalized and held a strong position in American industry through his position as a director of the American Car and Foundry Company. Haggin turned his attention to Mexico and the Pacific Rim. The sale of Anaconda freed him for the development of monumental ranches, plantations, and mines in Campeche, Chihuahua, and Durango. Hearst and Tevis, the president of the Wells Fargo Bank and one of the original leaders of the Anaconda, joined him in a number of these ventures. Haggin also joined Rockefeller and Morgan in the Cerro de Pasco Mines in Peru, Morgan in the Oriental Consolidated Mining Company in China, and other Americans in the ownership of the El Oro gold mine.

In 1902 Amalgamated acquired 30,800 shares of the Cananea Consolidated Copper Company. Rogers orchestrated the purchase of the Cananea stock. The Amalgamated directors understood that with adequate capital Cananea, located in the extreme north of Sonora, could become the greatest copper producer in North America, exceeding even their Anaconda complex. The acquisition of the property was essential if they were to achieve their goal of controlling the price of the commodity. In August 1906, immediately after the strike, Amalgamated bought out the Greene companies in Sonora. The shares were purchased by the Cananea Central Copper Company of Duluth, a division of Anaconda Copper. Cananea Central was headed by Thomas F. Cole, Charles A. Duncan, and John D. Ryan. In December 1906 Rogers, Rockefeller, Stillman, and Ryan, the leaders of Amalgamated, formed the Greene Cananea Company, a securities holding company, and openly took over the remainder of Greene's operations at Cananea. More powerful American capitalists had replaced a weaker one.

The leaders of Amalgamated sought to control copper production and marketing in the United States, Mexico, and eventually the entire Western Hemisphere. Unlike Haggin and Hearst, who ran businesses and industries with Tevis as their financier, the men of Amalgamated were bankers first and foremost who used Rogers and Moyer as their industrial operators. The Amalgamated controlled productive facilities through stock ownership but left the mining to experts. The Wall Street panic in 1907 and 1908 and the decline of the copper and silver markets combined to cause enormous losses for the company. Once again Mexico mirrored global patterns. Although Cananea was the largest copper deposit in Mexico, the Amalgamated directors recognized that they could not defeat ASARCO or Phelps Dodge. In 1910 they reorganized as the new Anaconda Corporation. The Amalgamated directors "sold" their holdings in Montana and Mexico to the new corporation in exchange for over 2,000,000 shares in the enterprise. This was probably done to escape Amalgamated's terrible reputation as an "octopus"—a rapacious organization with many far-reaching branches. Rockefeller and Moyer continued to control their holdings, this time as directors of the new corporation.

The directors of Amalgamated had been able to gain control of Cananea, but they had failed to eliminate Phelps Dodge, ASARCO, and Towne. Morgan had initially remained aloof from the contest between Amalgamated and the Guggenheim interests, and in 1909 he correctly judged that Amalgamated would not be able to establish the monopoly over copper that its backers sought. ASARCO was already the largest mining company in Mexico. At that point Morgan helped finance the Guggenheim's American Smelters Securities Company and a Guggenheim-Braden mining operation in Chile that guaranteed failure to the trust. Schiff also raised monies for Daniel Guggenheim.[29]

In 1911, after everyone realized that the trust would not succeed, Morgan helped the Amalgamated directors save face and money and modernize Cananea at the same time. That year he joined Rockefeller, Stillman, Harriman, and Rogers in financing the enlargement of Amalgamated Copper and its operations at Cananea with $12,500,000 in 5 percent bonds.[30] He took $2,000,000 in Cananea stock, sold it to the Guarantee Trust Bank, and proved that he was a stalwart partner despite their differences.[31] Stillman, Rockefeller, and Rogers never controlled more than 15 percent of world copper production.

THE STRENGTH OF FOREIGN INTERESTS

In 1884 American mining concerns worked only 40 sites in Mexico. The completion of the railroad trunk lines, their connecting *minerales,* and the application of capital and high technology brought the total number of active properties to 2,382 by 1892. In that year the Mexican government bequeathed "unquestioned title to whatever subsoil deposits there might be" to property buyers. By 1896 the American operators, aided by the incentives offered by the two governments, controlled the great majority of Mexico's burgeoning total of 6,939 mines. In 1904 the number of active mines in Mexico reached 13,696 and involved over 550,000 acres in concessions and many acres more that had been directly purchased.[32]

Late in the Porfiriato, American capitalists held 81 percent of the capital in the Mexican mining industry and owned seventeen of the thirty-one largest mining enterprises. British mining investors held 14.5 percent of the total capital and ran ten of the remaining fourteen companies. Mexican capitalists owned very little of the nation's principal export industry. Evaristo Madero, the father of future president Francisco Madero, owned the Torreón Metallurgical Company. At that time the Maderos were the only Mexican entrepreneurs who owned a vertically integrated mine-to-smelter complex. Using the rails of the Mexican Central and International, they transported products to the United States, to ports on the Mexican Pacific, and to Mexico City. Later, after Francisco assumed the presidency, the Madero family would own the only petroleum company controlled by Mexicans.

Before the onset of the revolution, in 1910, a handful of American industrialists dominated the mining industry. By that year, because the government had partially bought out the railroads for $500,000,000, ASARCO had become the largest privately owned business in Mexico. In 1910 ASARCO reported a worth of 100,000,000 pesos, while Anaconda, which controlled Greene Cananea, held an assessed value of 60,000,000 pesos. Phelps Dodge continued to control the rich Nacozari deposit but did not reveal its value to the U.S. government. A few Mexican national and state government officials held directorships in the American mining companies. By engaging these congenial and cooperative individuals the American entrepreneurs consolidated their ties with the Porfirian elites. From the point of view of the participating Mexicans, these arrangements offered them technology, access to markets, investment security, and profits. In return they offered important services to the Americans, including the recruitment of government concessions. Both groups regarded these practices as ethical and legal. The American entrepreneurs and the Mexican elites understood the strategy and applied it in most industries.

Mexico became a major source of raw materials production. In the 1870s the value of silver output averaged about 26,500,000 pesos per year. During the 1880s it increased to 39,840,000 pesos. Following the enactment of the 1892 mining code, the yields increased dramatically. Between 1890 and 1893 the value of silver output reached 45,840,000 pesos. In the late 1890s it shot upward to 70,000,000 pesos per year. Between 1902 and 1905 output value reached its zenith, totaling 80,055,000 pesos annually. The deepening financial crisis that began in 1906 was related to worldwide overproduction, and it lowered demand for Mexico's principal export and source of foreign exchange revenue. The value of Mexico's silver exports declined from 72,420,883 pesos to 65,523,646 pesos between fiscal years 1902 and 1905, a decrease of 9.5 percent, and continued to slide thereafter. Between 1905 and 1908, two years before the onset of the revolution, Mexican silver production, measured by weight, dropped 6 percent and the market value of silver diminished 20 percent.[33]

The mine closings in Colorado that resulted from the crisis caused a depression in the state's silver industry, and a wave of laid-off Mexican miners were forced to return to Chihuahua and Sonora from their employment in the Rocky Mountains. In Mexico they joined a large semi-employed and migrant work force. Employers welcomed experienced surplus labor, but many of the citizenry of Chihuahua and Sonora came to regard the unemployed miners as a source of trouble. These men had witnessed, and some had taken part in, the labor struggles at Cripple Creek, Colorado, and in Arizona, where the copper industry had also suffered layoffs. Relatively sophisticated in contrast to those who were less traveled, the returning miners brought with them the values and political perspectives of their American protagonists who were forming unions that led to the creation of the Western Federation of Miners and the even more combative Industrial Workers of the World.

The output of copper, lead, and other nonferrous ore stagnated and then declined along with that of silver. The mining industry went through one of the many downturns that characterize its topsy-turvy history. The expansion of the highly capitalized copper industry in Mexico between 1890 and 1905 rivaled the success of silver and involved Phelps Dodge, Anaconda and Amalgamated, and ASARCO. Output grew from 5,650 to 65,449 metric tons annually. By 1908, however, production had slid disastrously, to only

38,173 metric tons. The workers at the Anaconda-Amalgamated complex at Cananea and throughout Mexico's mining districts were in dire straits, as the *Commercial and Financial Chronicle* of New York reported:

> Of course Mexico could not escape being affected by business depression in the United States. . . . An even more serious matter for Mexico was the drop in the price of silver and of other metals, more particularly copper. . . . The low prices are still affecting adversely many of the mines and some of the smelting plants along the lines of the National Railroad.[34]

Without an adequately developed internal market, Mexico's dependence on foreign consumption of its raw materials left it unduly vulnerable.

THE OILMEN

The American petroleum industry entered Mexico at a relatively early date. In 1876 a group of Boston capitalists invested in explorations around Tuxpan, where Rosecrans and Gorsuch had completed route and resource surveys for Thomas Scott and the Pennsylvania Railroad group. The early effort achieved modest results, but the limited size of the domestic kerosene market curtailed the scope of their operations. After the Americans abandoned the project Weetman Pearson and Cecil Rhoades of Great Britain spent hundreds of thousands of dollars in their own unprofitable effort to find and develop an oil field.

It was not until 1900 that California oilman Edward L. Doheny and his partners pioneered the first breakthrough in Mexico. That year A. A. Robertson, the head of the Mexican Central Railroad, signed an accord with Doheny that formed the Mexican Petroleum Company. Robertson was looking for cheap fuel and cargo, and he suggested that Doheny explore the tropical Gulf Coast. The venture was backed by investors in earlier oil discoveries in California. The maps that Doheny used had been developed by Mexican cartographers. The Mexicans knew about the potential richness of their petroleum reserves, but they lacked the resources, technology, and marketing infrastructure needed to make the industry viable. A Mexican guide led Doheny and his companions to the Cerro de la Pez, some thirty-five miles west of Tampico and a mere five miles south of the Mexican Central station at Auza, "where bubbled a spring of oil, the sight of which caused us to forget all about the dreaded climate."[35]

Doheny, Pearson, and Joseph Cullinan of the Texas Company had good reason for their push to find more oil. European and American demand for black gold had exploded at the end of the century, just as the output of American petroleum fields began to decline. Innovations in metallurgy and technology produced ever more useful and powerful steam-powered engines. In 1895 Rudolph Diesel had made his contribution to the process with the introduction of a more powerful internal combustion engine. These great machines, using oil as fuel, brought on a new phase of industrial growth. The American and European economies were growing at an impressive rate, and the oilmen were competing for markets and resources. In 1900 the American oil pioneers in Mexico, led by Doheny, Cullinan, and their respective brain trusts, including drilling genius Walter B. Sharp, began to explore the fields near the Gulf Coast. The directors of Standard Oil and other risk-taking fortune seekers soon followed. Standard already dominated the Mexican lighting business. They purchased land, oil drilling leases, pipeline rights-of-way, and harbor facilities from local landowners and governments.

Early reports of oil, followed up by observations of seepage and surface deposits, encouraged the Americans in their search for petroleum on the Gulf Coast. Demand was growing, output from the petroleum fields in the United States was declining, and competition among the oilmen was fierce. The Mexican Gulf afforded immediate access to the resource and to the United States market. The terrain was level and ports could be easily developed, affording ample opportunity for storage and transport. As a secondary consideration, the San Luis Potosí branch of the Mexican Central Railway offered access to the limited, yet still profitable, Mexican market. The railroad made the transportation of asphalt and kerosene to the more densely populated Mexican plateau a simple and economical exercise.

Robertson's arrangement with Doheny included the use of fuel by the railroad in return for the transportation of petroleum by train inland from Tampico. They retained the prominent attorney Pablo Martínez del Río to represent their interests in Mexico City. In return for a membership on the board of Mexican Petroleum, Martínez del Río obtained concessions from President Díaz, taking advantage of incentives in the laws designed to attract "new industry." The grants included tax exemptions, land grants, and mineral rights. The most important advantages derived from the ordinances of 1884 that revised the rules of ownership over subsoil resources. In contradiction to precedents in Spanish and Mexican law, the 1884 code "guaranteed" the ownership of subsoil resources to private purchasers. Foreigners in coastal and frontier areas could now claim "inalienable rights." In 1905 Doheny signed a new contract with the Mexican Central to deliver 6,000 barrels daily for fifteen years.[36]

Doheny made his first big land purchase, 450,000 acres, at El Ebano, which was located west and south of Tampico. The rush of oilmen to Mexico began when he struck a gusher at El Ebano on 14 May 1901. He followed up that success with additional purchases of land. He later claimed that the Mexican Petroleum Company owned 600,000 acres outright.[37] In 1910 Doheny's wells at the El Ebano field greatly surpassed the output of their counterparts in the United States, but it was his field in the Juan Casiano Basin, sixty-five miles south of Tampico near the Tuxpan River, that proved to be the greatest success. On 11 September 1910 Doheny's Casiano Number 7 came in with a roar. Initially it produced 60,000 barrels of oil daily, with the black gold spewing out of control. Efforts to cap Casiano Number 7 failed, so Doheny ordered the construction of a reservoir with a volume of 750,000 barrels, storage tanks, and a pipeline to Tampico. These measures reduced evaporation, which could turn the oil into tar in a relatively short period. It was not a short-lived bonanza. By 1918, when the Casiano field's output began to slow, Number 7 had produced 85,000,000 barrels of oil. According to Doheny, its production did not fall below 20,000 barrels a day "until November 1919."[38]

Doheny and his associates continued to expand their efforts. In 1905, 1906, and 1907 they bought new lands in the area and formed two new companies, the Huasteca Petroleum Company and the Mexican Petroleum Company Ltd. of Delaware. The latter concern claimed 1,400,000 acres in its domain. The steady growth in oil output assured the companies of continued financial support. By 1910 Huasteca Petroleum was building a new 55,000-barrel retaining tank every four and one-half days. The development of the company's rich El Ebano field had to be suspended in 1910 because of rich finds on the Huasteca Company's properties and because Casiano Number 7 continued to produce as much as the pipeline and refinery could handle.[39]

The rapid expansion of their operations required new capitalization. Doheny and A. C. Canfield, a Mexican Petroleum partner, had already reached their limits, having contributed $3,000,000 to the project, and they felt that they needed to bring in additional investors. Doheny recruited $500,000 from Michael Benedum and Joseph C. Trees of Pittsburgh by selling them 5,000 shares of common and 2,500 shares of preferred stock. Benedum and Trees controlled the South Penn Oil Company. More important, in 1910 William Salomon, a leader in the IBC, invested $5,000,000 in Mexican Petroleum Company bonds in return for a mortgage on the firm's properties. The IBC financiers were interlocking their wide variety of interests in Mexico, as they were in Cuba, Guatemala, Chile, and China. Doheny used the funds to complete the Tampico pipeline. On the eve of World War I, the United States depended on the Mexican Petroleum Company "to procure petroleum for its military forces."[40]

British construction and oil magnate Pearson offered the Americans stiff competition. He entered the Mexican oil business in 1901. Pearson earned an international reputation in construction before he went to Mexico. His firm, headquartered in London, upgraded ports in Egypt and helped save the Hudson Tunnel project in New York. In Mexico he successfully finished the failed American effort to build the Grand Canal, which furnished drainage for the Valley of Anahuac around Mexico City. In 1907 his engineering skills enabled the completion of a dependable rail line across the Isthmus of Tehuantepec—the Sur de México—which the Mexican government owned and operated.

Pearson initially held exploration grants around Tuxpan, where he leased properties owned by the parents of Manuel Peláez, a renegade Mexican general who took up arms on behalf of the oil men during the revolution. By 1905 he owned 600,000 acres and held another 300,000 in oil leases, largely in the area south of Veracruz and the northern portion of the Isthmus. He had a refinery constructed at Minatitlán, twenty-five miles inland from Coatzacoalcos on the Gulf Coast. In 1906 a grateful Díaz conferred on Pearson a grant that included "all national lands lakes and lagoons in the state of Veracruz." The Americans resented what they regarded as Díaz's favored treatment of the Englishman.

Pearson's concession allowed him to move his efforts inland. He struck it rich in 1908, when he found oil at Dos Bocas. Crude oil spurted out of the well at the rate of 100,000 barrels a day. By 1909 Pearson was ready to challenge American sales supremacy in Mexico, if not in the United States. Pearson retained Willard Hayes, director of the United States Geological Survey, to oversee the exploration and development of his fields. Hayes's assistant, geologist C. Everitt DeGolyer, was a man of exceptional talent. He played a central role in developing the gushers that followed. His successes on behalf of Pearson in the Potrero del Llano oil fields near Tampico helped bring Mexico to the forefront in world oil production. DeGolyer then moved from Mexico City to pioneer the development of petroleum resources in the Middle East. Pearson's Mexican Eagle Petroleum Company began to export oil products to Europe.[41]

Doheny and his partners and the men of the Texas Company and the Standard Oil Company made Mexico the first Third World oil producer to be bonded to the American economy. Even before the formal creation of the Texas Company in 1902, the future directors—president Joseph Cullinan, Richard E. Brooks, Edwin Jessop Marshall, and Will Hogg—were already planning oil ventures in Mexico. Cullinan had long experience in the Pennsylvania oil fields and the Standard Oil Company before he developed the rich oil reserves at Spindletop, Texas. He knew the petroleum business from exploration to field development, pipeline construction, refining, distribution, marketing, and financing. His acumen attracted leading American capitalists, including John "Bet a Million" Gates, a conservative man with money. He had opposed J. P. Morgan's early efforts to consolidate U.S. Steel, causing that magnate to coin Gates's uncomplimentary sobriquet. Cullinan garnered repeated successes in Texas with the financial backing of Gates. Brooks, Marshall, Hogg, and Cullinan, the leader, created the largest oil company in Texas and made Houston an important hub for the oil business. As oil production declined at the Texas Company's base of operations at Spindletop, Cullinan and his associates began to seek alternative sources of production in Mexico, Louisiana, and Oklahoma.

Cullinan and the directors of the Texas Company needed to find new sources of oil immediately in order to maintain the support given them by Gates, Chicago bankers John A. Drake and John F. Harris, New York investors Lewis Henry Lapham, James Hopkins, and John Lamber, and Boston financiers Thomas Jefferson Coolidge Jr. and George Abbott of Old Colony Trust. Gates recognized Mexico as a source of wealth and backed Cullinan in his decision to compete for Mexican fields. Gates was already there, having invested in the copper mines at Cananea and in land development projects along the Mexican border in the Rio Grande Valley. Gates expected high returns on his investments, and he had always gotten them with Cullinan.

Lapham was a financier with wide-ranging interests in the West, Mexico, and the Pacific Basin. He held directorships in the Central Leather and the American-Hawaiian Steamship Companies and wanted control of the Texas Company. Ranching and oil products interested him, and in that respect Mexico constituted an extension of his endeavors as head of Central Leather. He had close ties with Stillman, Taylor Jr., Morton, and Edward Shearson through his directorships, and with Central Leather investor P. A. Valentine at the National City Bank. In 1886 Lapham, his brother John J. Lapham, and F. H. Rockwell bought the 110,000-acre San Rafael de la Noria hacienda in the Moctezuma district of northeast Sonora, only 138 miles from the Southern Pacific's line in Arizona and much closer to the branch lines that later ran to the copper mines at Bisbee and Nacozari. The partners paid only $25,000 for the hacienda because it had been virtually abandoned during the previous forty years owing to Apache raids. Over the next twenty-five years the Laphams and Rockwell invested another $85,000 in its development, and the hacienda became part of the dense network of American interests in northwestern Mexico.[42]

Lapham gave lawyer Arnold Schlaet his power of attorney for matters affecting the Texas Company. Lapham welcomed the expansion of American railroad, ranching, and oil interests into Mexico, but he used Schlaet to remind the company's other investors of the high costs, high risks, and short-term profitability of ventures in Mexico. Schlaet watched Cullinan's actions closely and critically. For the time being Cullinan enjoyed the support of Gates and thus a majority of the voting shares. In the long term, however, Cullinan had to deliver healthy dividends to meet Lapham's demands. He had to protect his retail market by maintaining a virtual monopoly in Texas against the challenges from Standard Oil and find and quickly develop new fields.[43]

Cullinan's interest in Mexican oil fields grew out of this perpetual pressure. He did some exploration in the last two years of the nineteenth century, but his successes in Texas distracted him until 1901. In that year he chose Richard Brooks, a Texas Company director and the mayor of Houston, to guide the company's operations in Mexico. Brooks was a good organizer and a wise judge of men. He selected Sharp, already a friend of Cullinan and a fellow Houstonian, to explore and make purchases of oil and land concessions in Mexico. Sharp was a technical genius who had helped Cullinan at Spindletop by introducing newly designed drills. His successive achievements and the income from his patents enabled him to cofound the Hughes Tool Company. Sharp explained his reasons for entering Mexico to the directors of the Texas Company:

> I will go to the City of Mexico soon to look into some deals. The Standard and Waters Pierce oil companies are fighting the oil business hard and it will take every energy and good business plans or they will own it all, this is why I am trying to get a start in old Mexico, before they get it all, as they will soon control the whole thing.[44]

Walter and his son and assistant John B. Sharp were well received by General Treviño and the Mexican elites at Monterrey. They explored the area encompassed by a line running south from Laredo to Monterrey to Veracruz and north along the Gulf Coast to the border. Arriving in 1902, after Doheny and Pearson, the Sharps were unsuccessful in purchasing properties capable of delivering the output of their competitors. They had to buy and lease property that mostly was north of the highest-bearing soils. They worked tirelessly during the next decade, however, and succeeded in obtaining 4,500,000 acres along the Gulf Coast of Tamaulipas at a cost of $1,000,000. The prices varied, and sometimes leases cost less than nearby purchases. Sharp developed producing wells along the Pánuco River west of Tampico and on the Chapacao Plantation near Ozulama. By the time of the

revolution in 1910, as a result of Sharp's efforts, the Tampico region had become the Texas Company's principal source of oil.

As Sharp began his explorations in Mexico, Cullinan faced a crisis in
Texas. Field production in the state was in decline and his exploratory efforts in the neighboring regions of Louisiana and Oklahoma had not yet
been rewarded. Between 1904 and 1909 the percentage of American oil produced in Texas fell from 21.52 to 5.94. Between 1902 and 1905 output at
Spindletop fell from 17,420,949 to 1,652,780 barrels per year. Cullinan,
Hogg, Brooks, and Sharp anticipated the American dependence on foreign
oil sources, as noted by Sharp:

> There have been no new discoveries of crude oil in South Texas in
> the past few years, and the supply has become quite low. The larger
> refineries have been compelled to go elsewhere for their crude supply.
> The United States government, three years ago, took the tariff off crude
> oil and put it on the free list, since which time the oil companies in Texas
> have found it necessary to go into Mexico to obtain their supplies of
> crude. They have encountered all sorts of difficulties with the Mexican
> government, and it has almost become necessary for them to organize
> separate companies in this republic, not being able to take out permits
> for the main company, as would be possible in this state.[45]

Cullinan sought new petroleum sources in Mexico as production at
Spindletop fell off, and he merged the Heywood-Jennings oil group of
Louisiana with the Texas Company. William Henry Jennings and partner
Alba Heywood joined the board and joined in their new colleagues' real es-
tate speculations along both sides of the Rio Grande. Jennings, along with
Democratic leader John Rufus Blocker of San Antonio, the U.S. consul to
Parral during the revolution, bought the 1,237,000-acre Piedra Blanca ha-
cienda in Coahuila. The merger greatly enhanced the Texas Company's
financial resources, lessened the threat of control from East Coast capital,
and made it easier to access new fields in Mexico as well as Louisiana and
Oklahoma.[46]

Between 1900 and 1910 production at the Texas Company's oil fields in
the southwestern United States fell to an average daily output of between
100 and 600 barrels per well. At the same time Doheny's Casiano Number 7
delivered 60,000 barrels every twenty-four hours. The survival of the Texas
Company required that they move into Mexico quickly. The entry of the
Texas Company into Mexican exploration and field development critically
affected the company and future relations between Mexico and the United
States. It deepened the involvement of the Texas state political leaders and,
later, officials of the U.S. government in Mexican affairs. The Texans had

been in the forefront of relations between the United States and Mexico since the independence dispute of the 1830s and 1840s, taking major roles in the ensuing war between the two countries, the border fighting of the 1850s, 1860s, and 1870s, and the advent of the Díaz regime. Now their focus was on the oil boom. The Texans gained unprecedented national political influence during the Wilson Administration and the Mexican Revolution.[47]

Cullinan, Brooks, and Sharp, as the active leaders of the Texas Company's operations in Mexico, created a series of subsidiary companies to forestall two problems. First, they sought to blunt what they saw as mistreatment by Díaz. They thought he was "sandbagging" them and favoring Pearson. They also recognized Díaz's concern that large American companies might overwhelm Mexican interests. Second, they needed a strategy to escape the increasingly critical and assertive intervention against their control of the company that was being led by Arnold Schlaet, who was generating dissent among his fellow New York investors.

The Texans acquired land and created six new companies: Producers Oil, Tamesi, Pánuco, Tampico, Mexican Fuel Oil, and Mexico Companies. The Mexico Company specialized in landholding through purchase and lease. Under Brooks's leadership it later offered to broker the sale of over 2,000,000 acres of land in northern Tamaulipas to American buyers for agriculture and colonization. The Texas Company directors let go of the Mexico Company when the revolution began and sales collapsed. The Producers Oil Company held far-flung interests in the northern Gulf region and involved the active participation of Cullinan, Brooks, Sharp, Henry House (the cousin and life-long friend of Colonel House), and William F. Buckley Sr., who served as the legal counsel of the Texas Company in Mexico. The formation of the subsidiaries worked to some extent. Sharp obtained Mexican government approvals for pipelines, storage tanks, retaining pools, and refineries for Producers Oil and its subsidiaries at the same time that proposals submitted in the name of the Texas Company faced delays and refusals, which damaged the directors' standing with the ever vigilant New York stockholders. Because of the Mexican government's delays, reports to New York on expenditures in Mexico often had to be sent forward before revenues could mitigate criticism.

The directors of the Texas Company established more of a personal presence in Mexico than did Doheny or the British. Texans had a long-standing interest in ranching, agriculture, and colonization projects in their own state and Mexico. Marshall, the founding treasurer of the Texas Company, and Hogg, the founding secretary of the firm, reflected the abiding interest that the company leaders had in economic opportunities in Mexico and the south-

western United States. Hogg later bought the 350,000-acre Rodrigo Ranch
in Coahuila. Marshall resigned his position in 1902, when his colleagues
found a large sum of money missing. When he left the company he purchased the 2,500,000-acre Las Palomas hacienda in Chihuahua. The Palomas estate, located immediately south of New Mexico, extended from Ciudad Juárez to the border of Arizona. It was the largest ranching establishment
in Mexico. Marshall also purchased an estimated 2,500,000 acres in Sinaloa
for sugar cultivation and American colonization projects and in Chiapas for
coffee plantations. His commitments in the Southwest included oil and timber ventures in Arizona and oil exploration and real estate development in
southern California. He purchased Chino Hills, which at that time lay just
outside Los Angeles, and three enormous expanses that he later "donated"
or sold to the U.S. government: Vandenberg Air Force Base, Goleta Oil Reserve, and the land along the north rim of the Grand Canyon.

The Texas Company leaders were part of a regional elite that used its
wealth and political power in Texas to reach into Mexico. Colonel House,
their close ally and friend and a stockholder in the company, ran the Texas
Democratic Party machine that obtained the election of Will's father, James
Hogg, as governor of the state. House, the principal adviser to President
Woodrow Wilson, was a key figure in American financial expansion into
Mexico. He served as a director of the Equitable, a position that connected
him with the eight board members who ran the IBC. His brother John di-
rected several American mining companies in Guanajuato.

The close relations between the Texas Company directors and the state's
political elite were revealed during the antitrust decisions against Standard
Oil in 1908, which kept that company from operating in Texas and protected
the interests of the Texas Company. State judge Victor L. Brooks decided
the case against Standard Oil. Judge Brooks was a cousin of Texas Company
director Richard Brooks. The judge was an ally of House and Texas congressman Albert Sidney Burleson, who later was the postmaster general of
the United States. Brooks also held a partnership in the Rio Grande Land
Company with Frank Andrews, a Houston attorney who represented the
Southern Pacific and directed one of its subsidiary lines, and Thomas Watt
Gregory, the attorney general of Texas and later the solicitor general of the
United States.

Hogg and House interacted with the leaders of the Texas Democratic
Party in the development of the legislation against Standard Oil, and House,
Gregory, and Cullinan filed suit against the company. House's political con-
federates in the state included Governor Hogg, Attorney General Gregory,
Houston attorney Andrews, Congressman Burleson, John Henry Kirby,

who held 1,000,000 acres of mining claims in the Mexican state of Guerrero and a silver mine in Jalisco, John Sharp, who headed the Texas Company program in Mexico, Duval West, an attorney in San Antonio who later represented President Wilson in Mexico, and attorney James B. Wells of Brownsville, who represented the Stillman and King Ranch interests against the Mexicans in border land disputes.[48] House, Gregory, Burleson, and David S. Houston, the secretary of agriculture, later joined President Wilson in determining U.S. policy toward Mexico during the Mexican Revolution.

TRANSITORY BENEFITS

The American oil companies transformed life in and around Tampico. The population of the towns and ports of the Tampico-Tuxpan area grew rapidly. In 1900 Tampico counted 17,500 residents and Tuxpan 13,000. By 1910 Tampico had grown to roughly 25,000 souls and the population of Tuxpan had also expanded. Considering the inflationary spiral, the wages of common workers remained extremely low. Teams of American and European supervisors and technicians lived in segregated colonies, although in Tampico at least some Americans lived alongside Mexican neighbors. The complex process of urbanization and racial and economic segregation dominated settlement patterns, however, and replicated American life back home. Segregated work crews toiled to develop the new oil fields. Typically the filthy Mexican workers who hauled pipes across muddy fields to the rigs were not allowed on the drilling platforms with the skilled American workmen who handled the machinery. By 1918, as a result of the development of the oil fields, the population of Tampico had increased to 75,000.

In a very short time a concentration of Mexican industrial and transport personnel working in a newly technological and capitalized economy had replaced communities of traders and artisans in the towns and the previously pastoral order in the surrounding countryside. Around Ozulama, just south of Tampico, a population of 4,000 Huasteco-speaking campesinos confronted a new world comprising 75,000 mostly Spanish-speaking workers, a smaller number of English-speaking technicians, and the world of capitalist industrialism. Tampico and its environs became overcrowded and terribly polluted. Life in the region was less healthy in terms of physical well-being and spirit than it had been before the gushers and the bonanzas. Mexican critics pointed to the proliferation of prostitution, bars, and public disturbances, and they blamed them on the Americans. From the standpoint of traditionalists, the new industries and urbanism had transformed Mexican lifestyles for the worse.

Since the censuses in that era did not accurately record indigenous groups, we have no idea how many Native Americans still lived in the oil producing zone. Many among the nearby rural population survived through small-scale ranching, providing the urban population with meat. Others were probably forced out through enclosure proceedings made possible by the Ley Lerdo of 1856 and its amplifications. Sixty-five miles further south, the region around Tuxpan experienced a significant change in land tenure because of the growth of the petroleum industry and commercial agriculture.[49]

Despite the growth of government income that resulted from increased petroleum output, the successes of the oil industry offered Mexicans limited benefits and considerable hardship. The cities of the Mexican plateau gained asphalt paving and a greater and more economical supply of lighting fuel and lubricants. Mexican workers found new forms of employment in the oil fields and Tampico, but they made lower wages than those holding jobs requiring higher skills—and Mexicans were not given those jobs. The foreign capitalists who invested the money, provided the technology, accessed the markets, and repatriated the profits that were not directed toward field development. Compounding these problems, the owners of the oil companies enjoyed the support of the Mexican and American governments whenever their interests were challenged.

Díaz supported the American ventures in metals and petroleum production. He and other leading Mexican statesmen such as Romero remembered the vast wealth produced by mining and its supporting industries during the colonial era, and they imagined how a new golden age of mining would benefit them in the form of profits, the state in the form of tax revenues, and the economy through the vast infusion of capital. The administration's adversaries, however, recognized another aspect of foreign investment. How much would Mexicans benefit if the profits were expatriated and the mines or the oil fields stopped producing? Those who followed the American development of the mines at Vallecillo, one hundred miles north of Monterrey in Nuevo León, discovered that the benefits were transitory and peripheral.

Charles Stillman had purchased the Jesús María, Dolores, and Teresa mines at Vallecillo shortly after the conclusion of the Mexican War. When he decided to develop the mines the people living there were in deplorable shape. Established in 1778, the mines and town had survived tolerably well until the surface deposits ran out in 1816. The population languished between 1816, when there were 483 residents almost equally divided between men and women, and 1825, when only 4 miners continued to ply their trade. In 1833 the community reached its nadir when 53 persons died during a cholera epidemic.[50] As the economy slowed, people sank into misery and fled. The secretary of state of Nuevo León declared that "a generalized poverty dominates the people who are entirely lacking in basic resources."[51]

When Stillman entered the scene, only one mine, the Jesús María, was operative. He immediately poured an unprecedented amount of capital into the site in order to make it pay, and he put people to work, including eight recently arrived foreigners. As mining output grew, the population changed. By 1856 Vallecillo had 448 single men, 320 single women, 166 married men, and 199 married women, plus uncounted children. The number of employees at the mines totaled 198, including 46 miners, 144 day laborers, and 8 mule skinners. The number of residents doubled again in less than ten years. By 1880 the population totaled 2,195. The number of single men was still high relative to the rest of the population, a common characteristic of mining towns. A crude way of life that included prostitution dominated the scene, but the people were materially better off than they had been before.[52]

In 1881 the mine laborers received between four reales and one peso per day. The base pay of four reales, or one-half peso, was substantially more than workers on the haciendas of central Mexico could expect. The town also had a small group of businessmen who sold supplies to satisfy the needs of the mines and miners. Some local producers could compete with importers because transportation from Matamoros and Monterrey by mule was slow, unreliable, and expensive. In 1856 the mines used 40,000 candles, many of them locally produced, at a price of 1,100 pesos. The wealth of the community increased, and, as a result, Vallecillo displayed new elements of refinement. In 1882 a public school claimed thirty-seven students, and the increasingly diverse population included artisans, mining specialists, storekeepers, and a teacher.[53]

The wages of the workers at Vallecillo, however, were actually quite low in comparison with the wealth they produced. During the 1850s the mines of the Real de San Carlos de Vallecillo complex produced more than $4,000,000 in silver and lead. In 1881 the entire work force earned a maximum of 44,300 pesos, or only slightly more than 1 percent of the value that they had produced annually twenty-five years before. Stillman marketed shares in the Vallecillo mines on the New York Stock Exchange. He took advantage of the prevailing wage rates, with labor costs constituting a mere 10 percent of his gross revenues. (The prevailing economic wisdom of capitalists at that time held that labor costs should constitute no more than 25 percent of income.) There is some evidence that Stillman reinvested some of his profits in the development of the Monterrey textile industry, yet, from the perspective of Mexican development, Vallecillo was a failure. In the mid

1880s silver discoveries slowed and the town went into decline. By the end of the decade only one mine, the Dolores, continued to operate.[54]

Mexicans who supported the notion of foreign investment could point to the increased salaries and population of Vallecillo and its prosperity during the 1850s, 1860s, and early 1870s as a model of successful development. Nationalists and skeptics could indicate the discrepancies between value produced and wages, the transitory nature of mining and oil production, and the vulgarization of society and culture that they had brought about, and blame the foreigners for not caring.

The ruthless tactics of the American capitalists and the lack of lasting benefits from mining combined to frustrate the plans of the Díaz administration. The American business leaders and company employees largely failed to accept their hosts as equals and remained too remote for assimilation and acceptance. Elitism and cultural isolation on the part of American mining industrialists, engineers, and oilmen paralleled the attitudes and practices of American landowners, colonists, and settlers. Their segregationist beliefs and all too frequently haughty manners antagonized the Mexicans. These American attitudes became an important factor in 1910, when the Mexican revolutionaries rejected many of their employers and neighbors and forced them from the country.

6   Absentee Landlords

Surrounding the hacienda . . . were buildings that not only housed
the hundreds of hired laborers but . . . factories where practically all
they ate, wore, and used was manufactured. There were warehouses
and stores selling imported goods.

Nelle Spilsbury Hatch

As Díaz anticipated, inexpensive land, cheap labor, and valuable products
caused wealthy and powerful Americans seeking profit to rush in and buy
up properties. The most powerful among them constituted a new elite class
of absentee landowners. By the late 1890s businessmen from across the
United States were investing in sugar and henequen plantations, sawmills,
and cattle ranches. As American capitalists arrived, they extended into Mexico the strategies of land development that they had carried out in the western United States. They also adopted the labor practices that were prevalent
in the Mexican countryside. The ease with which American entrepreneurs
were able to gain control of Mexican property led William Randolph Hearst
to comment, "I really don't see what is to prevent us from owning all of
Mexico and running it to suit ourselves."

DENOUNCING THE LAND

Díaz's plans to privatize agriculture were intended to modernize the Mexican economy by attracting more capital investment, encouraging European
and American immigration, and creating a middle class of Mexican farmers. The Ley Lerdo of 1856 had allowed considerable latitude in the denunciation of properties, but new land surveys were not required, a feature that
accommodated Mexico's rugged topography as well as a frequent lack of
funds on the part of individual claimants. Díaz made land surveys obligatory after 1876. The survey companies that appeared served as a crucial link
in attracting foreign investments for the growth of individual landholding,
capitalizing commercial agriculture, and infrastructure and industrial development. Survey companies bid for government contracts to demarcate

the countryside, and then, after the survey was completed and the properties were ready for sale, the companies received one-third of the land they
had surveyed from the government. They could then sell the parcel on the
open market. The survey companies also could buy the other land that they
had surveyed at a bargain rate, often enjoying an "insider advantage" over
other interested parties.

Díaz also used the reform laws to ensure the continued loyalty of the
provincial elites who had supported him during the 1876 Revolution of Tuxtepec. The system of patronage over which Díaz presided and the ambitions
of his associates ensured the failure of any plan for a balanced result from
the agrarian reform program. The landholding elites, including his friends
and members of his family, used the laws to enhance their positions from
the U.S. border to that of Guatemala. State leaders such as Geronimo Treviño, Luis Terrazas, and the Madero, González, and Pesqueria families, in
Nuevo León, Chihuahua, Coahuila, Tamaulipas, and Sonora, profited greatly
from the president's efforts to ensure their loyalty.

Mexican elites carried out widespread land seizures. Those who benefited
the most from the agrarian reform program were some of Díaz's closest
associates. They included finance minister José Ives Limantour in Chihuahua; his nephew Felix Díaz in Tamaulipas; his father-in-law, Manuel
Romero Rubio, and cabinet officers Matías Romero and Carlos Pacheco on
the Isthmus of Tehuantepec; and Olegario Molina, Díaz's minister of development, in Yucatán. The president's friend Luis García Teruel garnered
several million acres concentrated in Campeche and Chihuahua. Romero
Rubio, Romero, and Pacheco became the most important land concessionaires on the Isthmus of Tehuantepec, while Molina enjoyed that status in
Yucatán. They all sought and obtained properties near prospective railroad
lines.

The beginnings of privatization brought quick gains for commercial
Mexican landowners and extreme hardships to the peasantry. The well-
established pueblo communities between Mexico City and San Luis Potosí tried to defend their lands by forming "communal leagues." They sued
in the courts and made political appeals. Hundreds of years of precedent
in individual court rulings favored or partially favored the Church and the
pueblos, and each of those decisions provided loopholes and new arguments.
The appeals of the communal leagues were futile, however, and between
1878 and 1882 these occupants of "unoccupied lands" rose up in rebellion.
The army defeated them in brutal campaigns over a wide area extending
north, west, and east from Mexico City to Monterrey, Guadalajara, and
Veracruz.[1]

During the 1860s the *vecinos,* or citizens, of the pueblo of San Andrés Apaseo el Alto, located in the drought-prone yet densely populated state of Guanajuato, had lost much of their land and were unable to maintain a level of income sufficient to support their traditional, self-sufficient way of life. Further losses of land to local landowners occurred, and by 1878 the peasants were insolvent. Reduced to the level of day laborers, the citizenry of San Andrés could not afford to send someone to look for the pueblo's land records in the Ramo de Tierras of the National Archives in Mexico City. They were unable to recoup their communal properties.

By 1890, well after privatization was complete and American mining companies had gained a prominent position in Guanajuato, infant mortality rates in the state were 84 percent. In San Andrés the death rate may have been higher. These conditions were duplicated in many localities. In 1867 the pueblo of Santa María Mazatla, in the central valley of Mexico, suffered a nearly complete lack of water because the stream had been diverted by the Mexican owner of a nearby hacienda.[2]

In 1884 the Porfirian government modified the Ley Lerdo, further weakening appeals against privatization. The legislation limited the size of individual parcels that a survey company could claim to 6,200 acres, but the vast expanses of northern and southern Mexico were exempted from the limitation. Even though the new law reflected the government's growing awareness of rampant abuses, the ordinance greatly strengthened the powers of individuals denouncing communal or public lands. During the 1890s Díaz sought to create ever larger rural estates, probably in the belief that the better-financed haciendas would increase agricultural output more than the smaller holdings would. In 1893 he removed the limit on the amount of land a survey company could acquire. In 1894 he eliminated the population requirement for new grants of government properties and even permitted the acquisition of lands not fully mapped out. The prices for these tracts often averaged less than ten cents per acre.

During the 1890s the denunciation of pueblo communal charters reached its peak. By the end of the century the remaining Church lands were negligible and the peasantry retained no more than 2 percent of the arable properties, down from 25 percent a half-century earlier. By 1901 the social tragedy of displaced peasants, debt peons, and impoverished workers was obvious to everyone. Díaz finally acceded to the pleas of the villagers and the rising demands of his critics. He approved a new law permitting the creation and assuring the survival of communal properties. The law, however, could not be applied retroactively, and private individuals already held the better lands. The damage was done. Public protests and unrest began that would not cease until well after the revolution of 1910.

SURVEYING RURAL MEXICO

The importance of the Ley Lerdo and the survey companies as a mechanism that enabled nationwide, large-scale, and immediate secularization and the rapid increase of American ownership was evident in the state of Durango, which possessed a strongly individualistic mestizo population, the rugged Sierra Madre, and reclusive indigenous groups. Shortly after the Mexican government promulgated the Ley Lerdo, Francisco Valenzuela denounced eighteen *sitios de ganado mayor* (a *sitio de ganado mayor* consisted of approximately 3,500 acres devoted to cattle) in the Sierra Madre of Durango, while the patriarch of the Sáenz de Ontiveros family denounced thirty additional *sitios*. These properties had for the most part been nominal Church holdings worked extralegally by independent small-scale timber men. The foresters lived in myriad small settlements in the mountains. Most of these sites had informal status and had not been recognized by the government as pueblos with municipal rights, including the privilege of common lands.

Díaz issued survey contracts for the Valenzuela and Sáenz de Ontiveros holdings in 1876. The owners had not previously tried to sell the Sierra Madre properties, but with the promise of secure titles for tracts of land that in some cases exceeded 100,000 acres, it became possible to interest buyers on the open market. Those who bought the land needed large amounts of capital, business relationships, and know-how to make a profitable return on their investment. The advantages of volume encouraged the consolidation of large holdings. Hence, when Daniel Murphy, who represented financier Thomas Fisher of San Francisco, bought out the Valenzuela and Sáenz de Ontiveros interests, the sellers made a handsome profit of about 50,000 pesos, but the expectations of the American buyers made the price seem like a bargain. Murphy and Fisher were two of the first Americans on the scene.

American buyers frequently purchased former *terrenos baldios* (unoccupied lands) directly from land surveyors. That is how Fisher acquired three additional timber stands in 1876 from Valenzuela. The Aguinaldo and Soldado haciendas and adjacent forestlands totaled 85,000 acres. Fisher, through Murphy, his Durango agent, paid 7,500 pesos for the tracts. In the neighboring state of Sinaloa, Edwin Jessop Marshall profited from the use of survey companies, taking personal advantage of the legal option to buy one-third of the lands that his Sinaloa survey company mapped. Usually, however, the survey company denounced a property and sold it on the free market. The absentee American buyers acquired some of their properties in that manner, but they acquired even more land from private Mexican sellers. The Mexicans involved in these transactions sometimes operated as brokers, sometimes as middlemen, but they were usually private owners looking for a profit in a booming real estate market.

Sometimes the survey companies operated as mere fronts for powerful American interests. William Randolph Hearst and his mother, Phoebe Hearst, used "Verger," their representative, to gain survey grants for parts of western Chihuahua, northern Durango, northeastern Sinaloa, and eastern Sonora. Earlier, Phoebe, the most dynamic American businesswoman in Mexico, had attempted to make direct purchases in the border areas with presidential approvals. To her chagrin she found that the procedures took time and had no certainty of success. Verger purchased control of a land survey concession originally issued by the government to José Valenzuela, giving Verger one-third of all of the state-owned properties that his company surveyed, with an option to purchase another one-third of those lands at 10 percent of their estimated value. Valenzuela functioned as an intermediary who brought Verger and Hearst in contact with the government. The government cooperated with Valenzuela, Verger, and the Hearsts.[3]

The greatest expenses incurred by the survey company were the "kickbacks" paid to General Pacheco, the minister of development, who approved the concession and who could have intervened to block the transfer of rights. Sometimes the government assisted in changing the ownership of survey grants. The parties called such transactions "transfers." Verger's private transaction with Valenzuela on behalf of Hearst was not a transfer. This sale, made with the government's approval but not its involvement, reliably demonstrates how American investors gained control of vast territories in Mexico without even being recorded as property owners by the Díaz regime. Valenzuela operated the largest surveying company in northwestern Mexico and was essential to the process. Hearst assessed Valenzuela's intermediary role and the potential for American interests in their neighbor to the south, noting that Valenzuela was a "very powerful man in this section [and] must be conciliated."[4]

Mexicans and foreigners other than Americans seemed to own or control a significant number of the survey companies, but Americans actually owned some of them and worked well with others. The companies served as intermediaries in the president's program to capitalize and privatize agriculture. It was a simple matter for the Americans to acquire the concessions made by the Díaz government to Mexican companies and in this way to gain control of a great deal of land. This procedure was especially important along Mexico's borders and coasts.

Ultimately, through the survey companies and private purchases, Americans came to own the majority of land along Mexico's entire periphery. They accomplished this goal by making innumerable individual petitions to Díaz for exemptions to the rule that foreigners could not own land within two hundred miles of Mexico's borders or fifty miles of its shorelines. Sometimes successful and sometimes not, the petition process involved the government. That took time, and the outcome was not always predictable. The Americans soon learned that Mexican survey companies already had contractual relationships with the government and that the use of their good offices speeded up the process and increased their chances. The survey companies then sold land to Americans and other foreigners at handsome profits.

In Sonora, Manuel Teniche assumed the nominal leadership of the Sonora Land Company in the 1880s. In October 1887 he obtained a concession from the Mexican government for 1,320,000 acres in the districts of Arizpe, Moctezuma, and Sahauripa in northern Sonora. On 30 November 1894 Teniche sold the entire property and some additional tracts acquired during the interlude, which together totaled over 1,610,000 acres, to Los Angeles banker and real estate developer Francis T. Wheeler. These lands were adjacent to the enormous holdings of Plutarcho and R. C. Elías, the patriarchs of the family of future Mexican president Plutarcho Elías Calles. Years later the U.S. government learned that Teniche had merely represented the Sonora Land Company in Mexico. The actual head of the firm was "a Mr. McIntyre of Chicago." Financier William H. McIntyre, a key director of the IBC in Mexico, based his operations in Chicago and New York. In addition to speculating about land and railroad development in Sonora, McIntyre served as the president of the San Antonio and Aransas Pass Railway of southwest Texas. The railroad directors, who once included Colonel Edward Mandell House, sought to develop Aransas Pass as San Antonio's principal port on the Gulf of Mexico. At various times the San Antonio Chamber of Commerce and the local press proclaimed the city as the "Gateway to Mexico." Meanwhile, the leading bankers and industrialists of the city actively invested in Mexican ranching and mining, especially in Coahuila and Sonora.[5]

Henry Muller, a survey company operator and rancher, was one of the earliest and most active investors in Mexican real estate. He serves as an excellent example of a seeming non-American who commonly passed as a foreigner but never denied or even disguised U.S. citizenship. Muller, a German who had been naturalized as an American citizen at Saint Louis in 1856, acquired and sold numerous properties in northern Mexico to Americans. He also retained a number of properties that he left to his nine heirs, all U.S. citizens. His estates in Chihuahua—the Haciendas Santa Ana del Torreón, Santa Clara y Anexos, El Tintero, and Carmen de Namiquipa, and the Rancho de Aransas—covered 1,250,000 acres. El Tintero supported 5,000 cattle. Following Henry's death in 1899, his son-in-law George C. Douglas actively managed the estate, exporting cattle via the Mexican Northwestern and the Mexican Central Railroads to the stockyards in El Paso for distribution throughout the United States.

Many American investors purchased properties in Durango after Díaz took power. A thinly populated state, Durango experienced all three modes of acquisition: private sales, survey company sales, and denunciations. In 1877 Marcos Tyson denounced 18,000 acres immediately south of the state capital, which later became part of the real estate empire of John McCaughan, a resident American hacendado. The Mexican foresters, ranchers, and farmers, who depended on small-scale operations in and around the pine forests, protested the sales. Despite their prior tenancy, the local citizens lacked municipal incorporation papers, had minimal legal standing, and wielded no influence with the authorities, who ignored their appeals.[6]

After American realtors gained control of a large property, they usually directed their marketing efforts toward buyers in the United States, and land values skyrocketed. Given their experience with railroads in their own country, the Americans knew what a tremendous increase in value the mining, timber, agricultural, and livestock properties would undergo because of market accessibility. Murphy and Fisher anticipated the arrival of the railroads. In 1875 they bought the Cerro del Mercado iron deposit at Durango for a modest price. They had to wait only seven years. In 1882 Murphy sold Fisher's half of the concession to the Iron Mountain Company of Philadelphia. This concern included John MacManus, who had worked with William Rosecrans in the 1860s. By the mid 1880s Collis Huntington had purchased the company, and the mine became the terminus of his International Railroad of Mexico. He sold it to the Iowa Loan and Trust Company for 900,000 pesos in 1890. The price of the property had leaped upward with each transaction, leaving the original Mexican sellers, who were not experienced with such a rapidly growing and volatile economy, gasping at the increases in value. In 1892 Daniel and Isaac Guggenheim bought two hectares of land at the Cerro del Mercado on behalf of ASARCO, further driving up prices.[7]

In 1895 Murphy found an American purchaser for his half and paid 8,524 pesos in service fees to obtain a clear title from the Mexican government and Díaz personally. The fee was a small expenditure for the security of ownership that it bought. He then sold the land for a healthy profit. That same year Lazard León of San Jose, California, bought the consolidated Fisher properties through Murphy for $125,000—a profit of $121,250 in nineteen years. The combined tracts now totaled 501,080 acres, of which about 442,000 had been obtained from the government through denunciation as *terrenos baldios*. During the 1890s new American companies moved in. The Mexican Highlands Company bought the nearby 109,000-acre San Ignacio timber tract, while the U.S. and Mexican Realty Company of Minnesota acquired the 35,000-acre Rancho San Blas from its "denouncer," Luis G. Avila.

CORRUPTION AND CHICANERY

Corruption was inherent in the process of American expansion in Mexico. In 1906 William Wallace Cargill, the head of the Cargill grain transportation and marketing empire, joined with railroad magnate George Gould and others and bought 542,000 acres of land in the Sierra Madre of Chihuahua from Limantour. Cargill and his partners paid 642,772.45 pesos, or about $321,000, for the tract, which contained large forests of virgin pine. The events leading up to the purchase linked the history of the American occupation of California in the 1840s, the further growth of U.S. interests into Mexico, and the abuses of power in the Díaz regime.

In 1888 Fernandez Leal, the secretary of agriculture, acted for the Díaz government and deeded the property to José and Julio Limantour in exchange for lands in Baja California and Sinaloa. The Limantours claimed that in 1843 and 1844 the governor of the Californias, General Manuel Micheltorena, had made four land grants in Baja and Sinaloa to their father, José Ives Limantour, "in recognition of his services to the nation." They added that the protocol had been approved by the appropriate cabinet officer. The Baja lands included several million acres of coastal properties. The four grants each reached inland for thirty-five miles, and the north-to-south extensions were even greater. The concessions included the islands of Cedros, Santa Margarita, and San Juan Nepomuceno. The Limantours also claimed that Micheltorena had granted their father the island of Creston Grande in the bay of Mazatlán in Sinaloa. The Díaz government accepted these assertions and even arranged for American surveyor Luis (Louis) Huller to delineate them in order to facilitate the transfer.

There were several problems with the Limantour grants, however, that should have prevented the government actions and alarmed Cargill had he

known about them. In the 1850s Jose Ives Limantour Sr. presented land
claims to the American authorities at San Francisco that were identical to
those asserted by his sons thirty-five years later. The originals included a
"three-fourths part of the City of San Francisco." Limantour also demanded the "islands in the bay, upon which the American government had
constructed lighthouses, buildings, and other works" and land totaling "134
square leagues." The federal judge at San Francisco found that the land titles supposedly issued by Micheltorena to Limantour and countersigned by
a Mexican cabinet officer were forgeries.

> (1) Many titles in blank, signed by Micheltorena and Bocanegra, or
> supposedly signed by them, on paper of the Mexican Government,
> circulated in California after the ratification of the treaty and served
> for the fabrication of supposed titles; (2) Limantour and Jouan [one of
> his associates] had brought a great number of these papers to California
> in 1852; and (3) There had been an association of falsifiers of land.[8]

After being "condemned to prison and freed on a bond of $35,000," Li-
mantour and his associates "fled to Mexico in 1856." Upon his return to
Mexico, José and his spouse, Adela N. de Limantour, acted to develop their
pretensions in Baja. They requested that an officer of the department of agriculture validate their land claims there. The "Chief of the Fourth Section"
of that ministry investigated and expressed his doubts by "pointing out . . .
the serious defects in the titles . . . and attesting to the lavishness of the gift."
In 1861 the government of Benito Juárez, soon to be fighting a war with the
French army of occupation, rejected the Limantour claims.

> No political or military authority in the Territory of Lower California
> can transfer or alienate, without the consent of the General Government,
> the uncultivated public lands located in that part of the Republic; con-
> sequently the transfers lacking this requisite are null and void.[9]

The political position of the Limantours improved immensely under Díaz.
In 1887 José and Julio requested that an official survey be conducted by Huller
under the authority of General Pacheco. In 1888, using the Huller survey
results for precise delineations, Pacheco and Leal authorized the trade of the
Baja tracts for "unoccupied public lands" in Chihuahua and Tehuantepec.
These properties had people living on them, but the government deemed
communal claims to the lands to be invalid. The pueblo of Tomochic, located
in Chihuahua, lay in the center of the Cargill tract. Tomochic was populated
by mestizos and Tarahumaras, of which the former were in the majority.
The pueblo's rejected claims to community property were being litigated in
the courts. At the same time that it rejected the pueblo's claims, the gov-

ernment gave relief to several private property owners situated in the midst of the Limantour tract.

> The gentlemen favored by this gift took possession of the lands situated in Guerrero and Abasolo with the exception of 19,491 hectares which was excluded because they were found to be occupied by other individual owners. It is to be noted that at the time when the measurement and fixing of boundaries of the lands selected in Chihuahua by the interested parties was done the Indians of the Pueblo of Tomochic rebelled in consequence of the discontent which this produced.[10]

In lieu of the 50,000 acres already held by individuals on the property claimed by the Limantours, Leal and Pacheco authorized a grant of 50,000 acres of similarly "unoccupied lands" on the Isthmus of Tehuantepec. It should be noted that the two tracts were in line with the projected routes of the Kansas City, Mexico, and Orient Railroad in Chihuahua, and the Mexican Southern Railroad in Oaxaca.

In 1906 Cargill bought the land for 642,772 pesos. It is unlikely that he knew of the Limantours' chicanery, but his probable knowledge of the Tomochic peasant uprising of 1892 is another matter. It became a cause célèbre in the Mexican press, and Heriberto Frías created a best-selling novel and literary classic, Tomochic, out of the story. That novel, which was gobbled up by the Mexican public, showed good, hardworking, and humble Mexicans fighting for their rights against corrupt businessmen and evil politicians and being destroyed for their efforts. Tomochic served as the forerunner of a genre of protest literature that soon featured greedy American impresarios in the role of villains. Cargill knew of the unrest just as surely as the railroad men of his generation knew of the some 200 rural uprisings in Mexico and the Native American displacements in the American West that were generated by their activities. They had armed guards for their construction crews in Mexico and in parts of the American West for precisely that reason. But for Cargill the lands surrounding Tomochic were a good buy from a business point of view. They held fine stands of pine forest, and the railroad surveys indicated that the right-of-way would cross his property.[11]

By 1907 Cargill, Gould, and their associates were complaining that they could not develop the tract because of, as their Mexican supervisor reported, "outbreaks . . . instigated by a class seeking chances to rob and plunder." Cargill and Gould ignored the claims of the local populace and depended on Díaz for protection. During the decade of revolution that began in 1910, F. G. Oxshear of Fort Worth, who had bought the nearby 60,000-acre Sainapuchic hacienda from Emerson Gould in 1901, was able to maintain stability on his estate through the personal protection of his friend Francisco Villa. Oxshear found that the protection afforded by Villa could not be maintained from afar. Cargill and Gould remained absentee owners. They did not use or "develop" the properties from the time of prerevolutionary unrest in 1907 until after the violence had passed. Gould surrendered his share of the property to Cargill.[12]

CONTROL FROM AFAR

The holdings of the absentee American landowners extended across the nation. In the south, for example, 990,950 acres were acquired by New York financier Edward Shearson and his Pennsylvania lawyer, Severo Mallett Prevost, for their Guerrero Iron and Timber Company. In the north, Shearson had another set of partners. Levi P. Morton, Ed Morgan, and Thomas Wentworth Peirce joined Shearson as heads of a syndicate that acquired the 890,000-acre Corralitos hacienda in Chihuahua. That property was carved from the common lands of the pueblos of Casa Grandes Viejo and Janos, causing deep resentments among the citizens of those towns. The Mexican government facilitated both purchases by approving the survey grants and the denunciations.

The American owners purchased the Corralitos in 1883 and began developing the property after 1900, when Mexican Northwestern began providing railroad service. Before 1900 the company held some 2,000 horses, many of them wild, 3,000 unbranded bulls—"the worst of scrubs"—15,000 sheep, and 38,000 cattle. The Corralitos and San Pedro Rivers provided an undependable supply of water, the latter being dry eight to nine months every year. Water shortages, the lack of fencing, and long cattle drives caused enormous losses. An unpredictable labor supply and a lack of trained horses forced the company to employ Mexicans with their own horses at the exorbitant salary of $3 per day during roundups. Some laborers came cheaper, accepting sharecropping plots near the river. After the herds were driven to Fort Hancock in New Mexico, the Kansas City Livestock Commission Company sold the cattle for about $8 a head and the horses for $7.50 a head in return for part of the gross profit.[13]

In 1900 the owners in New York decided that the Corralitos could be highly profitable because the Mexican Northwestern Railroad now ran across the estate from El Paso. Announcing that news, they sold well over $200,000 in bonds yielding 8 and 10 percent and used the proceeds to construct an elegant big house, warehouses, stores, barns, corrals, wells, pipelines, irrigation channels, and fences. They dammed and channeled the river on the south side of the estate, which also supplied the pueblo of Casas Grandes

Viejo, so that they had access to as much of the river's water as possible. The workers drilled 24 water wells and strung 434 miles of four-strand barbed-wire fence while the Glasgow Brothers, under contract, eliminated prairie dogs from an expanse of 100,000 acres. The owners imported blooded breeding stock. In 1911 the company sold 5,500 cattle at $21 each, with another 3,200 head contracted as future sales. The railroad picked up the cattle at corrals immediately adjacent to the right-of-way. Around the Corralitos big house was "a city in miniature" with housing for the laborers, as well as "factories where practically all they ate, wore, and used was manufactured." Warehouses and stores offered "imported goods."[14] The buyers of Corralitos cattle included Swift and Company. Meanwhile, Edward Morris, the head of another packing house giant, married one of the Swift heirs. They owned the even larger T. O. Riverside Ranch, which was located along the border in northeastern Chihuahua.

Edwin Jessop Marshall was representative of the individual American entrepreneurs who built up absentee real estate and ranching empires in Mexico. Marshall, like Hearst, visited his properties and understood them, but he maintained his principal residence in the United States. He demonstrated great skill and know-how in managing his enterprises from California and committed an enormous amount of capital to his projects. Born in 1860 in Baltimore County, Marshall served as the first treasurer of the Texas Company. He resigned the position after his colleagues found a large sum of money missing. The other directors bought up his shares, giving him a considerable fortune. Marshall moved to California and established his headquarters at Casmalia, near the Goleta oil field in Santa Barbara County. In addition to buying and selling real estate, he bought into and participated in the development of oil production at Goleta and at Signal Hill, near Long Beach.[15]

Marshall's ventures in Mexico included the creation of the Palomas Land and Cattle Company of California. Initially Marshall owned 90 percent of the company and the cofounder, H. S. Stephenson, held the remaining 10 percent. In 1908 Marshall bought out Stephenson and became sole owner. Through the company he controlled the 2,500,000-acre Las Palomas hacienda in Chihuahua, which extended from the area of Ciudad Juárez–El Paso along the southern side of the New Mexico border to the border of Sonora and southeastern Arizona. Marshall proclaimed it the "largest fenced ranch in the world" after installing 650 miles of barbed wire. His construction crews built ranch houses, barns, stables, corrals, wells, dams, reservoirs, and windmills at strategic locations throughout the ranch. Then he imported breeding stock: "Hereford bulls, high grade beef cattle, horses, mules, jacks, donkeys, and similar ranch animals."[16]

Marshall, ably assisted by his vice president, Nelson Rhoades Jr., of Cleveland, also developed the Sinaloa Land Company, which became a survey company serving itself. Marshall and Rhoades conducted their own "surveys" of unmapped lands in the state. By 1908 these *deslindes* had given Marshall ownership of 331,000 acres. The "concessions" cost him 75,000 pesos. He spent an additional 579,000 pesos on the purchase of private lands covering another 1,276,000 acres in Sinaloa. In 1908 Marshall held 1,607,000 acres in the state and his total expenditures, including development costs, totaled 3,600,000 pesos. He also enjoyed a concession from President Díaz for the waters of the Culiacán River sufficient to irrigate an enormous tract. Marshall retained a large property adjacent to the state capital of Culiacán, and after completing the construction of a canal he planned to sell outlying small tracts to "the Mexican people themselves." Marshall also bought lands and plantations on the Pacific Coast of Chiapas, Mexico's southernmost state, which he subdivided and sold to private investors. Marshall created "Mexican companies" in Mexico City for his Sinaloa and Chihuahua enterprises, but they were "subsidiaries" controlled by the Marshall Corporation of Los Angeles. The parent company, capitalized at $2,500,000, controlled his entire operation in Mexico. The Title Insurance and Trust Company of Los Angeles handled his many banking needs, including the sale of securities and title transfers.[17]

James Ben Ali Haggin, Lloyd Tevis, and George Hearst were also active in Mexican ranching. Their interests south of the U.S. border were a logical extension of their long-standing partnership in real estate development in the United States. Haggin and Tevis had worked together in a series of enormous California land transactions that concluded in 1890 when they merged their separate properties and created the Kern County Land Company, the largest property holder in the state. The Kern Company, the equivalent of a Mexican latifundio complex, dominated the San Joaquin Valley. After Hearst's death Haggin and Tevis welcomed his son William into their undertakings. Haggin and the younger Hearst became partners in the acquisition of vast tracts of property in Mexico as a continuation of earlier acquisitions in California, Montana, Nevada, and New Mexico. Haggin, Tevis, and, probably, George Hearst, followed by his son William, enjoyed the support of Wells Fargo in their Mexican ventures.

William Randolph Hearst acted on the speculative assumption that the United States was about to absorb most of northern Mexico and to dominate the Isthmus of Tehuantepec. For those reasons he joined Haggin and bought a vast tract of land extending from Deming, New Mexico, almost fifty miles to the border. He also convinced his mother, Phoebe, to join him in a series of Mexican land acquisitions. He hoped for rapid increases in real estate value and profits from agriculture, mining, and ranching in Chihuahua, Durango, and Sonora. In the south, mother and son sought control of hardwood forests in Campeche and the transportation corridor across the Isthmus of Tehuantepec. They hoped to profit from the planned rail and canal viaduct connecting the seas.[18]

Hearst and Haggin, buying separately, each acquired enormous tracts of land in Chihuahua. Hearst bought the 1,192,000-acre Babícora hacienda in Chihuahua, while Haggin established the Victoria Land and Cattle Company on 199,000 acres located halfway between the Babícora and the New Mexico border. In the south, Hearst acquired 389,120 acres on the Gulf Coast side of the Isthmus of Tehuantepec. A few years later Haggin became the major shareholder in the Jalapa Railway and Power Company, located in the state of Veracruz not far to the north of the Hearst Tehuantepec holdings. The Jalapa firm was the potential source of power for central Mexico and, specifically, for sawmill operations immediately to the south in Tehuantepec. Haggin and Hearst's tract of land between Deming and the border lay alongside Marshall's Las Palomas hacienda, and Marshall's enormous properties in southern California lay adjacent to Hearst and Tevis's Kern County Land Company holdings. The New Mexico property did not contain minerals in commercial quantities. It had agricultural and livestock potential in a few limited areas, but for the most part it was arid desert. Haggin and Hearst bought it believing that northern Mexico would be absorbed by the United States, which would give them control of rail access to the rich fields of western Chihuahua from the Southern Pacific terminal at Deming.[19]

IGNORANCE AND ARROGANCE

Survey companies and prominent Mexicans made a practice of claiming controversial properties and selling them to Americans. Absentee investors such as Cargill, Hearst, and Marshall stepped into the middle of the Mexican land seizure process and either wittingly or unwittingly encouraged it by purchasing tracts of land from individuals who the Mexican villagers felt had violently usurped or defrauded them in order to obtain them. When the Americans bought these properties they entered the intense fights that were under way among the Mexicans and became new objects of resentment.

The International Land and Livestock Company, headed by Chicago financiers H. E. Bullock, James D. Sheahan, Palmer A. Montgomery, and Morgan F. Edwards, serves as an example of the traditional method of land seizure and eventual American ownership. In this case hacendados in the vicinity of Jimenez, Chihuahua, denounced a large extension of the community property of a village and then sold it for a profit to Juan H. Faudoa and his spouse. In 1906 American financiers bought part of the land from Faudoa, the 362,000-acre Hacienda de Corrales. The Corrales was a magnificent estate, with the Río Florida running through the middle of it. The new owners immediately capitalized the ranch, erecting barbed-wire fences, barns, silos, and corrals and importing blooded breeding stock. They began exporting cattle to El Paso by way of the Mexican Central Railroad. Almost defensively, they pointedly emphasized that they had built a schoolhouse and housing for tenant farmers and employees. It was a sparsely populated region, however, and the owners hoped for friendly neighbors. The partners urged other Americans to buy land and settle there, but there was, of course, a catch.

The objections of the citizens of the nearby Atotonilco Villa López constituted a continuing problem for the American hacienda owners. In 1639 the Spanish Crown had approved the incorporation of a settlement that came to be known as Villa López. The viceroy granted the citizenry of the town an extensive and, at that time, largely uninhabited expanse. Over the next two centuries, however, private landholders came into competition with Villa López. By 1853 the owners of the Hacienda de Corrales had gained authority over much land that was still claimed by Villa López, reducing its area of control to only 20,500 acres. In the same year Juan N. de Urquidi, the owner of another neighboring hacienda, the Santa María, seized 14,000 acres of the land that remained of the Villa López holdings. The protests of the leaders of Villa López, as the *vecinos* now called it, were made in vain, but the citizens did not forget. During the revolution insurrectionists and "bandits" repeatedly sacked the Haciendas de Corrales and Santa María, and after the revolution the citizens of Villa López quickly formed agrarian committees and began legal proceedings for the recovery of their lands. Before, during, and after the revolution, the American hacienda owners never indicated knowledge of or interest in the long-standing land claims of the rural populace centered at Villa López. When the litigation began they remained completely skeptical of the validity of their neighbors' claims.[20]

In 1897, in a similar case of conflict with local communities, investors Alfred Shapleigh, Charles H. Peck, and John J. O'Fallon of Saint Louis and Charles Davis from El Paso bought the Santísima, San Antonio, Vado de Piedra, and El Comedor tracts in Chihuahua. The properties totaled some 220,000 acres, extending east from El Paso and south from the Rio Grande. The investors paid a stipulated amount of "10 pesos" and other considerations to an unnamed survey company for the properties. During the revolution the American owners were surprised and outraged when the citizenry of the neighboring rural settlements of San Antonio and Vado de Piedra claimed the land as their own. The local citizenry came to view the resistant owners as enemies, and the competition between the two sides continued for decades.[21]

Americans sometimes bought strategic properties in the prohibited border zones for specific purposes and sold them for enormous profits. In the 1870s Robert Symon, Rosecrans's early real estate partner in the purchase of haciendas in Durango and Sinaloa and a director of the Santa Fe Railroad, made his most successful acquisition when he purchased the San Marcos y Pinos hacienda in northeastern Mexico. The San Marcos y Pinos covered 1,300,000 acres, but, as with so many of its American-owned counterparts, its importance transcended mere size. The hacienda encompassed the broad pass between the cities of Monterrey and Saltillo—the only direct railroad route to the central plateau from Mexico's most important city near the United States.

The ancestors of a Spanish nobleman, the Marqués de San Miguel de Aguayo, originally acquired the property by virtue of a viceregal mandate in the sixteenth century. The Sanchez Navarro family of Coahuila, the largest landowners in Mexico during the 1860s, held the property until the French were defeated. Since they had supported the foreign invaders, Juárez declared them traitors, confiscated the property, and sold it to magnates Jean B. La Coste, the owner of the San Antonio Water Company in Texas, and J. F. Crosby, a merchant and southwestern railroad financier of Boston and Galveston. Symon, also of Boston, and his partner William Broderick Cloete of San Antonio purchased the estate from La Coste and Crosby, thereby gaining control of the only feasible railroad route between Laredo and Monterrey and the Mexican interior.

The Mexican National Construction Company, headed by chief engineer James Converse, chose the pass for the route of the Mexican National Railroad, which was controlled by the New York financiers. Symon and Cloete sold the right-of-way for an undisclosed profit. The new line benefited Cloete in another way. He owned mines that the railroad would access in Coahuila. On 9 July 1886, after the railroad had determined its route, Symon sold his share of the estate for $60,000. The buyers were a group of British investors headquartered in London and long active in American enterprises. They incorporated as the San Marcos and Pinos Company. Cloete remained as the majordomo of the estate and became a director of the new company. The British held the property until 1913, when revolutionary disturbances encouraged their decision to sell 1,000,000 acres to Mexican capitalists from Monterrey.[22]

Many of the Mexican landholding elites were financially weak. A number of them faced bankruptcy brought on by war, increased freight rates, and the rising costs of industrial goods, while the market for agricultural products remained relatively low. That crisis continued until the end of the nineteenth century. Some broke up their estates to create more efficient units and sold sections to raise the capital needed to modernize their remaining operations. Pressed by economic exigencies, many sold their properties to Americans for what initially seemed to be handsome prices. The La Coste–Crosby acquisition of the strategic pass between Saltillo and Monterrey presaged similar transactions along both coasts and borders. By 1910 these land divisions and sales combined with the privatizations of the government to multiply the numbers of Mexican landholders to some 7,000 hacendados and 45,000 rancheros. They also created hundreds of American owners of large haciendas and plantations and some 15,000 smaller ranch owners, farmers, and colonists.

The growing American presence in Mexican landholding represented several interrelated problems brought to the fore by Mexico's increasing exposure to the dynamic and expanding U.S. economy. Those factors included the increasing strength of the gold dollar versus the weakening silver peso, the extreme inequality between American and Mexican landowners in gaining access to the American market, and the Mexican operators' need to buy manufactured goods such as barbed wire and mill machinery at relatively high prices. The American consortiums that bought Mexican lands often included manufacturers of the technologies that were essential for developing their farms, railroads, and mines.

COFFEE, SUGAR, AND RUBBER

We possess considerable knowledge regarding the Americans who conducted the trade in agricultural products, largely from Veracruz and Yucatán, New Orleans and New York. The Intercontinental Rubber Company of New York came to dominate the production of natural rubber from guayule, which it shipped to the U.S. market. The Intercontinental directors exercised an even more pervasive role in the Mexican rubber industry than George Foster Peabody and Cyrus McCormack did in the growth of the Yucatán henequen industry. Peabody, the railroad financier and merchant of Boston and New York, and McCormack, a key figure on the board of directors of the National

City Bank, the head of International Harvester, and a leading merchant of Chicago, financed growers in Yucatán and shipped, warehoused, and distributed goods in the United States. Unlike the Intercontinental directors, however, they did not own the industry at its source.[23]

In 1904 Bernard Baruch, of the Baruch Brothers investment bank of New York, went to Mexico and founded Intercontinental. His partners were Senator Nelson Aldrich, Daniel Guggenheim, John D. Regan of Standard Oil, John D. Rockefeller Jr., H. P. Whitney, Levi P. Morton, and "some of their relatives and friends."[24] They purchased the 1,800,000-acre Cedros hacienda and the 680,000-acre Grunidora hacienda in Zacatecas for the purpose of extracting latex from the guayule shrubs that covered those vast expanses. The presence of financiers, chemical experts, and manufacturers characterized the sophisticated strategies of American businessmen as they advanced into the Third World. The directors of Intercontinental included Aldrich, Paul Morton, president of the Equitable, Bernard's brother Herman, also of Baruch Brothers, and Charles H. Sabin, vice president of the Guarantee Trust Bank and president and director of the National Copper Bank of New York and the Colima Lumber Company.[25]

Once again Mexico figured as the prototype of American business and economic expansion into the underdeveloped world. The Intercontinental directors planned to create a rubber trust to control the harvest and production of the raw material used in raincoats, galoshes, and paints. A few years after their Mexican investment they purchased vast properties in the Belgian Congo and in Dutch-controlled Sumatra. The directors focused, however, on their Mexican venture. They built the largest guayule processing plant in the world at Torreón, which far exceeded their other sites in terms of capital outlays and improvements. Their other factories, at Ocampo and Cedral, employed the latest technologies. Rural northern Mexico offered them an abundance of raw material, inexpensive labor, and direct access to the U.S. market via the Mexican Central to El Paso and the Mexican International to Eagle Pass. The company entered into direct competition with local guayule producers, including the wealthy Madero family of Coahuila, and soon overwhelmed them.[26]

American agribusiness reached into every facet of Mexican production. In Veracruz it was coffee. The Arbuckle Brothers Company of New York dominated the coffee trade between the two countries, and Veracruz was the largest center of Mexican production. During the first decade of the twentieth century John Arbuckle, a director of the Importers and Traders National Bank and other firms, led the Arbuckle Brothers Company to primacy as the leading importer of Mexican coffee in the United States. Between 1900 and 1914 the company was also the leading coffee *aviador,* or moneylender, in Veracruz, extending mortgage loans to the leading plantation owners. The principal on the debts grew through yearly extensions of credit and loans for improvements. As a result, Arbuckle Brothers gained control of most of the coffee exports in the state.

> [F]or many years prior to and until . . . 1914, Arbuckle Brothers' business in Mexico consisted in buying and selling coffees, exporting the same, habilitating, supplying and furnishing coffee growers with money and capital for the fomenting, development and cultivation of their coffee plantations; . . . for the increase of their holdings and the purchasing of coffee trees, and . . . for the acquisition and development of land suitable for the cultivation and production of coffee . . . through contracts of *avio* . . . guaranteed by real estate mortgages.[27]

Arbuckle had little trouble gaining funds for his operations in Mexico and Latin America through his connection with Lawyers Title and Insurance. The board of directors included powerful colleagues in international trade. James Stillman, Richard Babbage, G. F. Butterworth, and Henry Rogers Winthrop all had long-standing family commitments to railroads and trade in Mexico. At the Importers and Traders National Bank, directors Adolph Lewisohn of the National Copper Bank and Edward C. Rice of the Produce Exchange Bank and Cananea Consolidated Copper Company specialized in the art of financing import industries. They shared Arbuckle's interest in Mexico. Arbuckle also worked with National City Bank board member, Latin American investor, and fellow *aviador* Joseph P. Grace as a director of the Kings County Trust Company.[28]

When Arbuckle died, his grandson William Arbuckle Jamison became the head of Arbuckle Brothers. Jamison continued and even built upon his grandfather's ties to the financial community in New York. He served as a trustee of the Brooklyn Trust Company and as a director of the Mechanics National Bank, the Orange National Bank, the United States Mortgage and Trust Company, and the U.S. Safe Deposit Company. The boards of all of these institutions included members with immediate ties to Mexico. One of the most impressive consortiums sat on the board of the Mechanics, where Jamison worked with Thomas Hubbard of IBC, Edgar Marston of the National City Bank, Percy Rockefeller of Standard Oil, and George W. Quintard of the Batopilas Consolidated Mining Company. Quintard later became a trustee at the Atlantic Mutual Life Insurance Company, where he served with Gustav Schwab, a director of the United States Trust Company who also had investments in Chihuahua. Jamison's network of associates also included Schwab.

The United States Trust Company, ably headed by John Stewart, was one of the most important New York financial institutions where Mexico was concerned. Its board included Stillman, William Rockefeller, and representatives from the other financial houses. It owned, principally through Rockefeller and Stillman, the Monterrey Belt Railroad, which circled the city of Monterrey. In addition to its terminal sites, train yards, and rights-of-way, the line owned and controlled large plats of land set aside for industrial development. Schwab's Mexican interests reached even further. His brother Charles M. Schwab, the president of Bethlehem Steel, maintained large tracts of iron-bearing lands in Michoacán and had been the principal owner of the Chihuahua, Sierra Madre, and Pacific Railroad before selling it to Frederick Stark Pearson of Boston. That sale placed the mortgage of the consolidated Mexican Northwestern Railroad line of Chihuahua in the hands of the Empire Trust Bank of New York, where Charles Schwab was one of the leading directors and a power to be reckoned with.[29] Jamison also developed ties with Moses Taylor Pyne of the National City Bank, Mortimer Schiff of Kuhn, Loeb, and Schiff (formerly Kuhn Loeb), and Cornelius Vanderbilt of the New York Central and Mexican National Railroads.

Jamison and the other financiers came together as directors at the United States Mortgage and Trust, which specialized in *aviador* loans and contracts exactly like those issued by Arbuckle Brothers Company to the plantation owners in Mexico. These men all had deep commitments in Mexico, with investments in natural resources, mercantile trade, railroads, and telegraph and telephone companies. As the representative of Arbuckle Brothers, Jamison worked with the most experienced and powerful Mexican entrepreneurs in the New York financial community. It is no wonder that he found the resources to extend over $1,500,000 in mortgage loans to Veracruz growers.[30]

At the time of the revolution, the Arbuckle Brothers Company dominated Veracruz coffee production with mortgage loans to the growers totaling some 3,048,056 pesos, or about $1,500,000. Between 1907 and 1912 the firm claimed to have paid its Mexican and American growers an average of $31.11 per hundred kilograms of coffee. The firm, however, not only held liens on the crops; it held "actual title thereto." By law, the Mexican owners were in fact making payments on Arbuckle properties.

In filing later damage claims against the Mexican government, the attorneys for the firm undoubtedly exaggerated the amount paid to the growers for the coffee so that they could bargain for a higher compromise settlement. The production data, however, are more reliable. In its peak year, 1912–13, the Arbuckle Brothers Company collected some 1,123,664.42 kilograms of coffee from its Veracruz growers. Arbuckle Brothers paid the growers about $350,000 in that year. It is clear that the growers were not realizing an income sufficient to relieve their debt. Considerable tension developed between the growers and the merchant bankers to whom they were bound by indebtedness. When the revolution came to Veracruz, the owners of Arbuckle Brothers found that they had very few friends in the state.[31]

During the last few years of the Díaz regime, American investors, led by Charles T. Barney, A. Foster Higgins, Moses Taylor Jr., Charles Gould, and other directors of the Knickerbocker Trust Company of New York, entered the Mexican sugar industry in the state of Veracruz. The Knickerbocker consortium's ties with Mexico reached back half a century, when members' fathers had first invested in the country. The matrix of American sugar refinery holdings included the Tabasco, Cuatotolapam, and Motzorongo Plantation Companies in the south, complemented by the United Sugar Company in Sinaloa, the Miller plantation in Guerrero, and other plantations in Sinaloa, Tamaulipas, and San Luis Potosí. Spanish and Mexican owners held the largest plantations and refineries in the states of Morelos and Puebla, which ranked first and third respectively in Mexican sugar production. Veracruz ranked second, however, among the Mexican states in total output and first in exports. The Americans were very important there. Among several American companies, the Mexican National Sugar Company invested heavily in Veracruz. In 1905 it purchased the rich 10,000-acre El Potrero hacienda near Córdoba and its sugar refinery. During 1905 and 1906 the New Yorkers invested heavily in plant expansion and improvement, including the development of the first factory with the ability to produce high-grade refined sugar. They also built a railroad spur to connect the fields and factory to the Mexico City–Veracruz trunk line. In conjunction with the technical improvements, they enlarged the area of cane production at El Potrero to 2,500 acres.[32]

The ability to market their product in New York enabled the American investors to make those improvements. Mexican operators would have been reckless to attempt these projects because of their tenuous access to an unpredictable market. The Knickerbocker men enjoyed easy access to the New York market, and, unlike the Mexicans, they had the ability to purchase high technology at factory prices. For reliable and skilled labor the company recruited colonists to work the land cooperatively. In 1908, however, during their first harvest, disaster struck. A fire of unknown origin destroyed half the crop, compounding the problems created by depressed prices in the United States and the high interest payment due on the mortgage for the refinery and the land. The weak U.S. market, engendered by surplus sugar production in Cuba and Hawaii, affected all foreign sugar exports. The combination of ills left Mexican National Sugar in a state of hopeless insolvency.

The directors chose bankruptcy, and the overcommitted Knickerbocker Trust collapsed, creating a sensational scandal in New York. The embarrassment of men like Barney and Higgins required the intervention of the Trio—J. P. Morgan, James Stillman, and George Baker—to assure their fellow Wall Street investors of financial stability in both Mexico and the United States. Morgan and Stillman still held enormous investments in Mexican railroads and oil, while Baker shared those interests and required a constant flow of cash for his Mexico City development projects.[33]

CONTESTED PROFITS

During the Díaz regime, American landowners gained hegemony along most of Mexico's Pacific coastline, from Chiapas to Sonora. That situation initiated local protests and unrest during the last years of the Porfiriato and led to the nationalization of the properties, or their seizure by other means, in the decades between the revolution and World War II. In the early phases of unrest, the Mexicans challenged the Americans on the issues of community and water rights. The protests from the villages carried a dangerous nationalist undertone, predicated on the belief that as Mexicans who made their livelihoods from the land, they had an inviolable right to it. The disputes between the Americans and Mexican private landowners were different: they centered on generally agreed-upon principles of law.

The potential for profits in the cultivation of sugar, palm oil, rubber, coffee, and henequen attracted several thousand American settlers and entrepreneurs to southern Mexico and both coasts. Benjamin Francis "the Captain" Johnston proved to be one of the most ruthless and successful among the American entrepreneurs. Ignoring the claims of villagers, he created the United Sugar Company in the fertile Río Fuerte valley of northern Sinaloa. By 1910 his Los Mochis mill at the town of the same name was the most productive in the nation, processing some 5,000 tons of Sinaloa's yearly sugar output of 10,462 tons.[34]

Johnston gained economic control over the area when he won a struggle with private farmers over control of the waters of the Río Fuerte. Johnston's sugar refinery was upstream from the small sugar farms operated by Mexicans and the American colonists at Topolobampo. The Americans had been recruited by Albert Kinsey Owen to construct port facilities at Topolobampo.[35] The Mexicans asserted points of law that supported their rights to water; the colonists claimed to have oral promises and contracts that granted them ownership of the estuaries and bottomlands. The settlers, however, had been misled—they did not have title to the land. The titles had been held by Owen and the Boston financiers, associated largely with the Old Colony Trust, who had joined the effort to create the Topolobampo railroad. After giving up on the railroad project they had sold their rights to Johnston.

A combination of political influence and money enabled Johnston to buy judges at the local level, and he also won the appeals at the federal level. When Johnston decided to move against the colonists, the judges quickly negated their claims despite the fact that they and their predecessors had dredged out a port, dug canals, built warehouses and piers, and prepared the earth for farming. Johnston and a few Mexican allies, most of whose lands he later acquired, diverted the river and seized the contested properties. His actions left the settlers without irrigation water or assets. Just as important, they lost ownership of the Los Mochis Canal, which connected the town to the Gulf of California, and the modest amount of commercial exchange that it provided. Most of the colonists returned in defeat to the United States. Some of those who left Mexico did not give up, however. For decades they demanded compensation for their losses through the U.S. Department of State and the various postrevolutionary United States–Mexican claims commissions.[36]

Meanwhile, Johnston developed a deep and eventually fatal rift with neighboring Mexican plantation owners, whom he gradually forced out, buying their bankrupt enterprises at bargain prices. He fought longest and hardest with Zacarias Ochoa, the owner of the El Aguila Sugar Plantation. In 1893 Ochoa contracted to deliver increasing quantities of sugar cane each year to Johnston's mill in Los Mochis for processing in return for discounts. Ochoa believed that he would obtain cost-effective refining that would prepare his sugar for export. He was unable to meet the quotas to which he had agreed, and that failure made him liable to penalties. After years of acrimonious litigation, Ochoa declared bankruptcy and Johnston gained ownership of his estate. In 1905 Johnston merged the three sugar plantations that he had acquired—the El Aguila, the La Victoria, and Sinaloa Sugar— into the United Sugar Company. In 1908 he demonstrated one of the advantages enjoyed by American capitalists over their Mexican neighbors. Unable to survive the general depression in sugar prices, he mortgaged his properties in Chicago for $300,000. He survived despite the deep depression in the sugar market. His profits returned when market conditions improved, just in time for him use subterfuge to turn the anti-Americanism of the Mexican Revolution to personal advantage.[37]

The conflict between the American owners and Mexican interests in and around the port of Acapulco began in 1900. William Stephens had already established Acapulco's first modern cottonseed and soap factories and, based on that experience, he felt capable of entering the tropical and livestock export business there. Trouble started almost immediately after Stephens and his two brothers formed the Stephens Brothers Company and purchased the 8,800-acre El Potrero hacienda. The hacienda included the terrain and the terminal of the present-day Acapulco airport and extended to the town of Puerto Márquez. Situated in the prime area south of Acapulco and west of the coastal road, it dominated the coast south of Mexico's most important Pacific port. Stephens immediately hired Mexican laborers to plant coconut palms and clear the forested land. Unfortunately for the Americans, the agrarian workers and villagers in the vicinity felt that they held a vested right to work the land, gather firewood, and exercise other privileges inconsistent with the erection of fences.

The Stephens brothers expanded their holdings on 28 November 1908, when they bought the 50,000-acre Hacienda de Cacalutla in the Costa Grande north of Acapulco for 20,000 pesos. They noted the apprehension of local and state officials regarding the growing concentration of American power and "monopoly" along the coastline and sought to dilute those concerns by forming Stephens Brothers and C. L. Vucanovich and Company. The firm's owners included Cris Vucanovich, who claimed to be a Slovenian, his spouse, and one Mexican partner, thereby giving the firm an international character. On 10 July 1909, the new company took formal possession of the Cacalutla.

The unnamed Mexican lent credence to the claim that a national firm controlled the Cacalutla estate. There is no evidence that Vucanovich, his spouse, or the Mexican ever exercised power in the concern. Vucanovich, a man of limited means, left Mexico during the revolution and became a stevedore working at the Southern Pacific docks in Galveston. The Stephens brothers designed the partnership to deceive local and state authorities as to American control of the estate. Commonly in such arrangements the uncapitalized partners signed an associated agreement, or codicil, declaring the original proprietors to be the owners in fact. Agents representing American landowners used this strategy quite often. At any rate, the Stephens brothers continued to operate the El Potrero independently of their partners.

Despite the threats of local authorities regarding their ownership of lands along the coast, the brothers developed a mix of cattle raising and *coquito* (coconut) farming on both estates. By 1910 the Cacalutla featured several hundred "fine cattle" and enough cleared and planted land to have 10,000 *coquito* palms in production. The *coquito* palms provided a "valuable" oil, which was processed in the Stephens brothers' Acapulco plant and was sold in Mexico and the United States. The rural populace in and around Cacalutla felt a deep sense of deprivation and rights denied.

> We cleared hundreds of acres of land in the dense forest, introduced modern machinery, made miles of fences, and brought blooded stock from the U.S. In short, we turned this comparatively worthless land into highly productive property. On this tract of land we had 10,000 Cocoanut Palms just beginning to bear when Madero's revolution broke out and the natives cut them all down.[38]

Immediately south of the *casco* (big house) of the El Potrero, which today is the Acapulco airport terminal, large American-owned estates extended southward to the border of the neighboring state of Oaxaca. In 1904 the Guerrero Trading Company gained possession of the largest of these properties, the Hacienda San Marcos, which covered some 485,000 acres. The neighboring American-owned estates south of Acapulco ranged in size from 7,700 to 50,000 acres. Some eight Mexican settlements were within the perimeters of the San Marcos properties, but their claims of communal land rights had long since been declared without merit by the national government. The San Marcos estate produced sugar, coconuts, and salt along the coastal lowlands, and cattle and a variety of crops on the hills of the interior.[39]

To the south of the Costa Chica (the coastline extending south from Acapulco), the Americans were less concentrated, but equally powerful. The Parraga brothers—Charles, Frederick and Rafael, all of New York—controlled "two hundred miles of salt beds and adjoining territories" known as the Salinas de Tehuantepec, that is, the salt beds of Tehuantepec. They built canals, giant ovens, and warehouses, harvested the salt on their privately owned beaches, and marketed it in the United States and Mexico. "Private individuals and local authorities" constantly harassed the operations of their coastal hacienda. The Parraga brothers found their most important allies to be the Mexican judges who issued rulings that thwarted the challenges mounted by the citizenry of Juchitán and Tehuantepec.[40]

Near the operations of the Parraga brothers, the Gulf Hardwoods Company owned the 125,000-acre Chivela hacienda in the district of Juchitán, a site in the middle of the projected canal route across the Isthmus of Tehuantepec. The firm harvested hardwoods for export to the United States. Romero had for many years bought land in and around Chivela and promoted to his American friends the potential for profits from tropical agriculture in southern Mexico. He helped to set in motion an almost frantic buying spree in the region. As a result, American investors came to own most of the Isthmus.[41]

The Mexico Land Securities Company, headed by George G. Wright, was the largest landholder on the Isthmus. It controlled 1,500,000 acres in outright titles and in representation of other sellers. It acquired parts if not all of its property from Pacheco, Romero, and Romero Rubio. All three men had been among the original promoters of the Mexican Southern Railroad, which would span the Isthmus, and had accompanied Díaz in 1883 when he toured the United States in search of investors. After 1905 the Land Securities Company sold 58,000 acres to the Mexican Agricultural Land Company and 20,000 acres to the Fortuna Development Company, which combined land sales and development. The investors in the Fortuna Development and the Mexican Agricultural Land Companies came from Missouri and Louisiana, but some of the capital in these firms was probably still held by the original operators of the Land Securities Company. The investors in the Agricultural and Fortuna firms hired salesmen who recruited the purchasers of smaller parcels by inviting them as guests. The men who formed the Fortuna Development Company apparently paid some $75,000 for the land and hoped to garner some $410,000 from the American colonists.[42]

Entrepreneurs and settlers came to the Isthmus from all over the United States. Citizens from Portland, Tacoma, and Seattle formed investors groups and perhaps even sent immigrant parties. In 1902 four of the leading businessmen of Portland, J. J. Bowen, David W. Dunne, Frank C. Barnes, and Charles V. Cooper, formed the Mexican Rubber Culture Company. In May, Cooper visited the site and nearby properties around Palenque. After testing the trees for the quality of the latex, he chose the Chullipa Plantation tract as the most desirable. The buyers from Portland had bought into an area, known as the "rubber belt," that was rife with plantations owned by absentee American owners. In 1903 the Portland businessmen paid the already disreputable U.S. Banking Corporation of Mexico City the high sum of $45,000 and "other good and valuable consideration" for the 10,000-acre plantation.

The new owners immediately employed Mexican work crews and set about clearing the land and planting *castilloa* trees. *Castilloa* (now known as *castilla*) produced the highest grade of latex then available. The Portland businessmen financed the ongoing work by selling futures, known as Harvest Certificates, on their rubber production. In 1906 Barnes, Bowen, Dunne, and Lemeul Young of Pittsburgh organized the Castilloa Rubber Plantation Company. In 1907 they acquired 5,000 acres adjacent to the

Chullipa from the Chacamax Land Company, which had bought the land from the U.S. Banking Corporation. The men from the Castilloa company paid $40,000 for the addition to their holdings, a price to be met through mortgage payments. By 1910 their work crews had planted some 400,000 *castilloa* trees on 2,500 acres of cleared land. Another 500 acres were cleared for cattle pastures. Two thousand acres were left uncleared. The owners complemented these achievements with the usual assortment of houses and storage buildings.

Young also joined with other western U.S. businessmen, including a group from Greeley, Colorado, in the purchase of other estates. The men from Greeley acquired a 5,000-acre tract that they called the Montecristo Rubber Plantation. Some twenty absentee American consortiums bought 5,000-acre tracts from the Chacamax Land Company, which had acquired the 135,000-acre Dorantes Survey, or "Chacamax Lands," from U.S. Banking. Chacamax promised to clear and develop the land and make quick fortunes for the investors. By 1911 most of the buyers had gone broke.[43] The Chullipa Plantation was an exception. By 1911, 2,221 cleared acres had been planted in rubber trees. In addition, the estate boasted wood frame houses for the administrator and foremen, thatched huts for the workers, roads, bridges, storage facilities, processing equipment, one hundred acres of fruit trees, and other lands set aside for beans and corn to support the workers. The estate still held 2,670 acres of mahogany and other hardwoods.[44]

The Guerrero Iron and Timber Company, located on the Pacific Coast north of Acapulco, dominated the Balsas River Basin. The firm was headed by Shearson and Mallet Prevost, his Pennsylvania lawyer, who also held an interest in the Tlahualilo Estates of Durango. Their 990,950 acres included some 123,5000 inland acres near the Guerrero state capital of Chilpancingo. These lands included the *ejidos* (community properties) of the village of Coronilla and the settlement of San Vicente. Unfortunately, the Americans inherited preexisting land disputes when they bought the properties from a survey company that had been given clearance by the Díaz government. The Mexican authorities had glossed over the deeper problems by declaring Coronilla *extinguida* and deeming that San Vicente lacked legal claims to the disputed lands because it was not incorporated, being a mere *ranchería*. These disputes led to violent attacks and invasions of the land by the local Mexican populace during the revolution.[45]

Farther north, in the state of Jalisco, Alfred Geist owned the 100,000-acre Hacienda Union en Cuale. The property line started at the coast, where it surrounded the "mosquito ridden fishing hamlet of Las Penas," later renamed Puerto Vallarta, and extended across the Sierra Madre. In 1856 and

1858 President Juárez had granted the land to unknown private interests, perhaps American, for colonization; Juárez had issued several grants to Americans at this time in Sonora and Baja California. During the years that followed, the rural citizenry in the area also obtained land grants from the government. During the rule of Porfirio Díaz, however, the Mexican state refused to recognize the validity of the claim submitted by the citizens of Puerto Vallarta. The *vecinos* had appealed for government recognition of a grant approved by Juárez that gave them some of the land claimed by Geist. Since Geist owned all of the land bordering Puerto Vallarta, the local citizenry considered the matter a question of survival. After Díaz turned them down, they continued to dispute the Geist claims during and after the revolution, arguing that Mexican law provided every municipality the right to land needed for survival.[46]

To the north, from the borderlands of Chihuahua to southwestern Durango, American purchasers acquired vast estates of Sierra Madre timberlands, ranchos, and haciendas from land "denouncers" and sellers like García Teruel and the survey companies such as the Valenzuela Company. In Chihuahua these estates included the vast Babicora, Palomas, and Corralitos haciendas. In 1884 the government issued new survey company grants for Durango, Sinaloa, Zacatecas, and Jalisco. One example of the process, which Díaz repeated innumerable times, suffices to explain how a revolution in land tenure took place. In 1885 the president approved the denunciations made by Epitacio Ríos on 11 July 1882 of large sections of the Mazquerotes and Guajolotes land tracts in the Sierra Madre of Durango. Díaz officially designated the properties as *terrenos baldios* despite the fact that lumbermen and timbering settlements already derived their living from the bounty of those lands. Immediately upon receiving the president's approval, Ríos sold the land to William O. Wood of Springdale, California, for 3,750 pesos. The tracts contained about 60,000 acres.

In 1888 the president awarded Rafael García Martínez 18,000 acres at Pinos Altos and an undetermined amount of land at San Francisco del Mezquital in Durango for a mere processing fee. García Martínez held the tract for fifteen years without working it and then sold his holdings to Hubert Warner in 1903 for 23,400 pesos. In a like manner, Ignacio Ortega obtained the Quebrada de San Francisco, a small tract of 15,000 acres near Pueblo Nuevo, Durango. He sold the property to Mexicans, and then Edward Hartman bought it. In 1892 Hartman acquired an additional 32,000 acres at nearby Pinos Altos from the Compañía Mexicana Deslindadora de Terrenos, a survey company commissioned by the Mexican president. In 1896 Hartman bought 81,627 previously denounced acres from land speculator Luis Vazquez. Hartman rapidly expanded his holdings by means of other purchases as American land buyers gained the vast majority of acreage in southwestern Durango.[47]

DEFRAUDING AMERICAN INVESTORS

Some firms sold land to small American investors with the promise that they would develop the land and pass big profits on to the titleholders. Colonel J. M. Bain and J. H. Henderson of Pittsburgh organized the Jantha Plantation Company. In May of 1907 they bought 27,000 acres adjacent to the Castilloa Rubber Plantation Company estates, paying forty cents per acre. The property lay in the district of Tuxtepec, in the state of Oaxaca. The seller, the Huasteca Development Company of Mexico City, specialized in promoting land sales to American investors who had never been to Mexico. The company was also involved in the myriad land promotions being conducted around the Rascon hacienda in San Luis Potosí. Bain and Henderson called the property El Porvenir (the future) and began selling plots to Americans largely from western Pennsylvania. Bain built a large two-story house at Macieniso, a nearby settlement with a sizeable concentration of Americans. They maintained the company's headquarters in Pittsburgh's "Empire Building."

The Pennsylvania buyers typically did not venture into southern Mexico. They bought titles to land to be cleared and developed by Bain and Henderson through the Alvarado Construction Company. The procedure began with a private sale between the Jantha Plantation and the buyer. The broker and the buyer negotiated the price of each parcel, and then they signed a separate agreement for land development. By 1909 Americans held numerous small plots that had been cleared of jungle vegetation by the Alvarado Company and planted with 200 banana trees to the acre. In 1913 some 8,705 acres had been planted. The sellers promised the small owners enormous profits once the trees reached maturity. The land cost the Alvarado Construction Company about eighty dollars to clear, plant, and maintain for two years. The Alvarado officials charged considerably more for their services. Their customers, in addition to the purchase price, paid $200 per acre for clearing, planting, and maintenance. By 1913 over 600 American investors had bought land at El Porvenir from Jantha. The buyers of these properties in faraway places may have been naive, but these ventures were often promoted by leading citizens in Mexico and the United States.[48]

Most of the rubber plantations in the tropical lowlands of southern Mexico resulted in failure, often bankrupting the Americans who invested in them. Unscrupulous promoters exaggerated profit opportunities and failed to mention the onerous problems associated with clearing the jungle, planting and nurturing the trees, and transporting produce from remote locations. In many places only the construction of the railroads made the plantations imaginable. The promoters victimized investors, colonists, and suppliers.

Some promoters had an additional agenda—American control. The recruitment of small-scale rubber and tropical fruit growers to new towns and colonies like Medina in Oaxaca were part of an effort to make certain areas "thick with Americans." Frederick Stark Pearson, the Boston impresario, controlled Medina. By 1910, some 160 American residents occupied lots in a carefully laid-out town site that contained over 500 residential sites. The promoters of Medina in Oaxaca, and the slightly smaller Pijijiapan in Chiapas, wildly exaggerated the topographic charms, profits, and climate in their promotional literature. In all cases the American settlers encountered difficult and primitive conditions. They often suffered from disease and a lack of sanitation in addition to other disappointments. To compound matters, sometimes their land titles were not forthcoming after full payment had been made for the properties concerned.[49]

The southern coffee, banana, and rubber plantations meant losses not only for small-time settlers and naive investors but also for the financiers. James A. Stillman and Percy Pyne invested in Tehuantepec plantations. Ambassador David E. Thompson, Hearst, Cargill, Treasury Secretary Charles Foster, and Thomas Alva Edison lent their names to rubber enterprises in the Mexican jungle. Their investments continued the long-term commitment of leading U.S. citizens in Mexican railroads, mines, petroleum, and ranches that began in the 1860s and encouraged the participation of others. The presence of prominent names on the letterheads of promotional mail enticed businessmen from Davenport, Houston, Kansas City, New Orleans, Pittsburgh, Portland, Tacoma, Spokane, Los Angeles, San Diego, Saint Louis, Tulsa, and dozens of other American cities and sent them to the Isthmus of Tehuantepec in search of properties to develop. Thousands of innocent investors and occupational groups such as schoolteachers' unions joined them. The promise of high returns encouraged the participation of these "suckers."

Of the many frauds two examples suffice. The Ubero Plantation Company, which was registered in Boston and headed by W. D. Owen, a citizen of India, claimed to be a prospering coffee producer with established plantations on the Isthmus. The company's officers included E. H. Nebeker, secretary of the U.S. Treasury, Jonathon H. Blackwell, state treasurer of New

Jersey, and H. H. Ward, attorney general of Delaware. The company claimed a capitalization of $1,000,000 and identified George A. Alden and Company of Boston, with annual imports of $16,000,000, as their associate for distribution and sales. The International Trust Company of Boston served as the Ubero trustee, while the Massachusetts National Bank and the American-owned United States Bank, controlled by George Ham in Mexico City, provided financial services in their respective countries. The directors expended a great deal of the company's capitalization to develop the Ubero holdings on the Isthmus, but an auditor periodically verified the company's expenditures and capital goods on the Isthmus, and nothing seemed amiss.

In 1905 U.S. authorities caught the firm buying coffee in New York. Owen and his partners had been reselling the coffee in the United States under the pretense that it was part of the firm's Mexican crop. An investigation revealed that the $1,000,000 in capitalization was gone, if it ever existed, and that the cost of improvements on the Ubero property on the Isthmus could not have exceeded $70,000. The American press sensationalized the story, and in a short time the Ubero and more than a dozen other plantation companies in proximity to the railroad collapsed.

The organizers of some of the "colonization" companies joined the Tehuantepec plantation "boomers" in taking advantage of those back home who wanted to make higher returns on their money. The crooks relied on their ability to find naive investors who were willing to buy into land development projects on faith alone. These men found naive buyers among the general public and investors who had less experience than did the financiers and businessmen who established independent operations. The frauds were most frequent in the development of plantations in Chiapas and the Isthmus of Tehuantepec, but they took place throughout Mexico. The watchword for buyers was "beware."

The frauds followed a similar pattern and sometimes went much further than simply overcharging for the lands. The perpetrators duped small investors into buying "shares" in their companies. These "shares" were actually development contracts for small tracts at onerous rates or for outright purchase of the plots. The new "owners" could then contract with the company for development. By clearing the lands for hundreds of absentee buyers, the company ostensibly could carry out the preparation of the land, planting, and harvesting at reduced costs. The unequal combination of firms in Mexico and absentee small owners living in the United States yielded a situation in which the small investors were often duped.

William N. Smith, D. C. Eldridge, and William J. Robinson, the managers of the San Luis Land and Cattle Company of Nebraska, promoted a fraudulent land development project in the sugar growing zone of eastern San Luis Potosí. Although many American immigrants did settle there, the investors in this firm chose not to colonize. They remained at home in the United States and awaited their profits. The directors incorporated the company with the declared intent of obtaining an option to buy the Hacienda San Rafael de Minas Viejas near the Ciudad del Maíz. Announcing their possession of the option to buy the estate, and describing the ongoing settlement of the region by American "pioneers," they created the illusion that the San Luis Land and Cattle Company was in the middle of a region with an exploding American population. They sold stock through brokers, mailers, and promotional advertising, greatly exaggerating the profit potential.

The available San Luis stock soon sold out, but the public shareholders never received a dividend, or a balance statement, or anything that rendered information on the status of their investment. Once the first stock issue had been sold, Smith, Eldridge, and Robinson merged the firm with another that was incorporated in Maine and had double the previously claimed capitalization. They gave the firm a new name, the El Maíz Sugar Plantation Company. They then sent the investors a false report of "bumper crops" and massive forthcoming profits, which stalled objections to the merger long enough for it to be consummated. Smith, Eldridge, and Robinson again controlled more than half the shares and resumed the sale of stock to the public. Each share entitled the holder to one acre of the hacienda land. The sellers, however, did not own the property in question.

After the dividends failed to materialize for the original San Luis Land and Cattle Company, George D. Ayers, a Chicago financier who had bought stock in the venture, began an investigation. To the surprise of the public buyers, he revealed that the stocks of both the Nebraska and Maine companies were only land use rights and development contracts. The stock buyers in the El Maíz stage of the promotion acquired one acre of land for 400 pesos, but they did not obtain voting representation in the management of the company, and the price was at least one hundred times the actual value of the property.

As the scandal broke, Smith, Eldridge, and Robinson rushed to buy 500 acres of the Hacienda San Rafael and to bring the Mexican owner into the El Maíz firm as a full partner. They could now claim that they did own the land. The stock sales had made the acquisition possible. The Mexican hacendado apparently did not know of the legal problems. The El Maíz company then took over the planting, cultivation, and harvesting of *cana dulce.* The sugarcane was to be grown by the company on a minimum of two-thirds of each lot. The stockholders were to pay the firm a fee of 10 percent of the gross value of the harvest. The U.S. Postal Service determined that Smith and his accomplices had committed mail fraud, and a court in the United States ordered them to dissolve the Maine company and to give up the shares they had obtained through the phony stock split. In an attempt to stall the prosecutors and reassure the public, Smith and his allies surrendered all their rights in the Maine company and, in accordance with a court order, turned the land "titles" over to the Western Trust and Savings Bank of Chicago. These gestures changed nothing.

Smith, facing prosecution, moved to incorporate a new Mexican firm to which he transferred the title of the hacienda and its assets. He then moved to Mexico, took up residence on the estate, and claimed it as company president over the objections of the former owner, a Mexican. He cultivated the friendship of the local authorities in order to solidify his position. When Ayers asked President Díaz to intervene, he pointed out that the hoax had scandalized the public in both countries and that the courts in the United States and Mexico already had issued rulings against Smith. He added that the investors in the Hacienda San Rafael came from the United States, Canada, and Great Britain. They had paid out 300,000 pesos and had lost another 160,000 pesos in assets. By 1910 there were 21,000 shares in circulation and a court-appointed referee controlled 1,920 of them. Ayers reported that the shareholders had elected him as the new overseer of the hacienda company.

The president's feelings about the case are unknown, but the local authorities that Smith had befriended rejected the claims of the former owner and the court orders from the United States and Mexico City. Smith then liquidated his assets. He mortgaged the crops and sold the equipment and shares in the new Mexican company in San Luis Potosí and Mexico City. Finally, after prolonged litigation, the American shareholders forced an audit of the hacienda, but it no longer had enough assets to compensate them. In 1910 Smith still occupied the hacienda as his primary residence, which was legally unassailable, and Ayers and the shareholders held several unenforced court orders.[50] Their investors lost everything. The losers were mostly small investors searching for high returns. The more powerful American businessmen survived the debacle because of their diverse investments, financial reserves, and marketing connections. The problems stemmed not just from the corrupt promotion but from much higher costs than had been anticipated and the competing exports from Cuba and Hawaii. Between 1900 and 1910 the price of bananas, sugar, coffee, and rubber fell. Profits were rare and small, and most of the promotions became moribund after a few years. Some small operators hung on, unable to sell their land but unwilling to accept defeat.

The American business and Mexican political leadership believed that the land enclosure process that took place between 1875 and 1910 was a necessary step in Mexico's capitalist transformation. During the late 1870s, 1880s, and 1890s the Mexican peasantry lost most of its land, largely to Mexican real estate investors, but with a significant level of American participation. American entrepreneurs gained control of a large part of rural Mexico. Local populaces contested many of the purchases, but the highest Mexican authorities approved the transactions and denied the complaints. In economic terms, the result for the displaced campesinos was largely the same—they had to choose between performing labor in estate agriculture or emigrating in search of employment.

The widespread participation of powerful, unacculturated, and even anonymous foreigners in the land transactions exacerbated the tensions between rich and poor, landed and landless. The wealthiest Americans created great landholdings in Mexico and alienated large parts of the Mexican public in the process, while naive smaller investors committed their resources to poorly researched land development ventures, hoping to get rich but often losing everything.

7 Resident American Elite

I passed by his garden, and marked, with one eye,
How the Owl and a Panther were sharing a pie;
The Panther took the pie-crust, and gravy, and meat,
While the Owl had the dish as its share of the treat.
   Lewis Carroll, *Alice's Adventures in Wonderland*

In the late 1890s and the early 1900s an impressive number of Americans bought great estates in Mexico and took up residence on them. These buyers were no longer a select group of New York financiers or railroad men. Now they came from every state in the Union, eager to join the Mexican experience. Sometimes they fled legal or other problems in their homeland; sometimes the threat of prosecution impelled them to immigrate south, particularly along the border, where activities that were illegal in the United States flourished. The relatively low cost of land and houses allowed them to live in high style and to operate much larger businesses than would have been possible in the United States. Many of them formed partnerships with Mexican elites.

Modern railroad transportation and telegraphic communications made it possible for them to purchase the cheap land, take advantage of the inexpensive labor, and use the rich timber, mining, petroleum, agriculture, and ranching resources that the country offered. Some lived in the northern border region or in the cities. Others started life over in remote or rugged areas. They established colonies, ranches, farms, banks, mines, bars, brothels, and casinos. The new on-site landowning capitalists, like their absentee and corporate counterparts, exacerbated the tensions that had long existed in Mexican society over land seizures and labor practices.

THE MCCAUGHAN INVESTMENT COMPANY

Knowledgeable American land buyers knew a great deal about ongoing Mexican land disputes, yet most remained undeterred. John Sheppard McCaughan was such a man, one who went to Mexico and, without a great amount of capital, built up a real estate and ranching empire largely on the basis of skill and know-how, but who dismissed the growing indications of discontent among his Mexican neighbors toward him, the local American community, and local Mexican elites.

McCaughan became the most successful American real estate and hacienda operator in Durango. He seized every good opportunity for profits from land sales in the state, purchasing from individuals and survey companies alike. McCaughan was born in 1843 in Sidney, Ohio. In December of 1888 McCaughan, a minister and skilled businessman, left Des Moines to take a position in Durango City as the manager of Collis Huntington's Iron Mountain Company. The company, which took its name from a mountain on the eastern edge of the capital city that was literally composed of iron ore, controlled Durango Iron Works. Huntington had purchased the company in the 1880s as a part of a complex of holdings rich in natural resources, including timber and silver, and grazing land for cattle. He intended to export the products to the United States. Huntington's enterprise was so important to the state that the governor donated the land needed for the 150-mile railroad right-of-way between Torreón and Durango City.[1]

McCaughan traveled on Huntington's International Railroad of Mexico from Eagle Pass, at the border, to Torreón, a new city growing up at the junction of the International and the Mexican Central line from El Paso to Mexico City. Because the International was not completed, he covered the last twenty-five miles to Durango in a crowded carriage, traversing a badly rutted road. Upon arrival he discovered that fifty to sixty Americans lived in the city and that the Methodist and Presbyterian Churches were already developing missionary programs. McCaughan, a self-described missionary, joined his fellow Methodists in the decision to construct a church without negotiating with the unhappy local Catholics. The unrest led to a small riot on 5 July 1891, when rock-throwing protesters disturbed the cornerstone-laying ceremony. The governor wrote an apology to McCaughan, who, as manager of the Iron Mountain Company, the largest enterprise in the state, employed five hundred workers.

Labor relations at the Iron Mountain Company constituted one of McCaughan's challenges, and he handled it better than the religious issue. In 1891, shortly after his arrival, he faced the only strike that occurred during his short tenure as head of the company. He was stunned to learn that the workers' grievances were not related primarily to their rate of pay, which was 6 reales, or 75 cents, per day. That salary contrasted favorably with the 3 reales, or 37.5 cents, offered at the neighboring ranches. Rather, the workers wanted free time so that they could return to their fields and plant corn and beans, for "if the people did not plant, then there would not by anything to eat next year." Demonstrating uncommon flexibility, Mc-Caughan not only yielded to the workers' demands but also agreed with their desire to maintain their ties to the land, calling it a "pretty good philosophy." He also liked the code of honor under which the Mexican businessmen made their agreements. McCaughan decided to settle in Durango, and he brought his family from Des Moines.[2] The marriage of his daughter reflected the growing sophistication of the American community in Durango. She chose the minister of the Methodist Episcopal Church, who was a graduate of Duke University. McCaughan's children were educated in American schools—they attended Grinnel, Stanford, and the University of Michigan—and a daughter married Princeton graduate Charles R. Hanna.

McCaughan began the development of his personal business interests in Durango with the purchase of a mine that seemed no longer workable to the Mexican operators. He noted that "the chemical nature of the ore had materially changed with depth and a new process of treatment was required." McCaughan bought and renovated the mine for $80,000. Its net earnings averaged $36,500 yearly for the next two decades. His real estate speculations began on 15 April 1899, when he acquired the first 13,000 acres of the San Juan de Michis hacienda in southeastern Durango. The initial acquisition cost only $8,700, and he was able to triple the value of that property in a short time. The big house of the estate was located only twenty-one miles from the Mexican Central Railroad stations at Suchil and Vicente Guerrero. Those outlets and his connections with Huntington gave McCaughan access to the markets of Mexico City and the United States. He then bought up the rest of the 180,000-acre estate for $128,895. By 1910 McCaughan and his sons Frank and Steven had developed a herd on the San Juan de Michis of some 2,500 to 3,000 Durhams and Herefords, using imported bulls. The ranch ran 400 to 500 horses, many sired by stallions and mares from Kentucky and Kansas, and thirty to forty mules. That year the value of the family's buildings and livestock exceeded $200,000.[3]

On 8 August 1902 McCaughan and sons formed the Compañía de San Juan de Michis, named after their largest and most valuable hacienda, and began buying and selling land, keeping some for themselves. Their business increased steadily, and in 1906 they changed their name to the McCaughan Investment Company. Their real estate ventures began with the purchase of the 120,000-acre Atotonilco hacienda from its Mexican owners, which they quickly sold to Raymond Bell, McCaughan's nephew, for a handsome profit. Next, they paid 26,080 pesos for the 351-acre Rancho Santa Cruz, which was immediately south of Durango City, and then acquired the adjacent Rancho Revueltas for $18,000. On each of the ranches their Mexican work crews constructed "a large residence, quarters for laborers, storerooms, stables, fences, orchards, and an irrigation plant." A telephone line, owned by the McCaughan Investment Company, "connected the Santa Cruz Ranch with the City of Durango." The McCaughans raised fine horses at Santa Cruz. Their leading stallion, The General, won an award as "the finest horse in the state of Durango." Frank settled down to raise his family on the combined estates. The Revueltas and Santa Cruz estates were taken over by state elites after 1910, and they eventually became the site of the Durango Country Club.[4]

During the years from 1902 to 1911 the McCaughans brokered the sales of a large number of Durango properties, most of them by Mexicans to Americans. They also bought properties and later sold them for profits that angered Mexican observers. In 1904 they paid 10,274 pesos for the Hacienda Santa Isabel, also known as the Cienega de Batres, located in the Sierra Madre, northwest of the capital. In 1910 William Vann, the president of the Creek Durango Land Company, paid the McCaughans 100,000 pesos for the Santa Isabel. Vann sold smaller tracts of the estate to buyers in Oklahoma for even greater profits. He planned to create a relatively dense community of American small farmers relative to the dispersed Mexican population. The Santa Isabel, with 55,000 acres and a river, was a feasible site.

Perhaps the McCaughans' most profitable and controversial venture came in 1907 when they purchased the Llano Grande property, located in the Sierra Madre about twenty-five miles southwest of Durango City. McCaughan paid the owner, the elderly widow Señora Matilde Ceballos, 7,875 pesos for 8,700 acres. Her late husband had acquired and consolidated Llano Grande after denouncing community lands in the area. McCaughan resold the property almost immediately for 84,188 pesos to Robert Chasteen, who represented the International Mexico Land, Lumber, and Stock Development Company of Lawton, Oklahoma.

Christian religious commitments did not deter the McCaughans from taking advantage of naive Mexican landholders, even widows. The reaction of local businessmen to such excesses must have been mixed and probably sometimes extreme. To minimize resentment, American land dealers like McCaughan commonly held the property for a discreet period of time before reselling it or used Mexican middlemen as presumed buyers, with the actual owners coming to the fore only during court proceedings and title disputes. In 1907, after the death of Rodrigo Gainey, the supposed owner of the 17,000-acre Pilares estate in Durango, John Davis of Chicago revealed that he was the actual owner. Davis stated that "in 1899 Licenciado Rodrigo Gainey had only loaned his name to the title."[5]

The properties that the McCaughans sold between 1902 and 1912 ranged in size from 10,000 to 500,000 acres. Even when the first violence of the revolution scared other American investors away, the McCaughans continued operating like Wall Street bulls. John tried to overcome their initial losses by using the crisis as an opportunity to buy land cheaply. Most of the family moved to Texas, where they became urban developers in Brownsville and Corpus Christi. Some went to California, but McCaughan senior stayed in Durango. In 1912, as revolutionary violence increased, he bought the valuable Hacienda Animas de Cerro Verde from frightened Charles and Anna Lorimar of Kansas for only $10,000. The selling price for the 11,000-acre estate was a giveaway. The Lorimars had paid $30,000 for the Cerro Verde property in 1893 and had developed it for twenty years.[6]

During the years before the revolution the McCaughans chose to keep some haciendas as their own, developing them for cattle and timber exports. Among them was a parcel that totaled 10 percent, or 47,000 acres, of the vast Hacienda Pelayo y Cadena in northeastern Durango. The McCaughans bought the land for $18,000. Other Americans owned the remaining 423,000 acres of the estate. The owners used both the Mexican International and the Mexican Central railways to ship their cattle. The McCaughans also selected two timber tracts totaling 87,626 acres in the western Sierra Madre, at the other end of the state. In this case they paid only $40,445 for properties covered by dense pine forests. The largest estate they decided to retain, the Hacienda La Montaña, totaled 285,000 acres. Their 25 percent share of the Rancho Miravalles in north-central Durango cost $40,000, but its 83,394 acres included some of the best grazing land in the state.

The McCaughans' partners in joint ranching ventures were all Americans. Presumably, their American associates valued the McCaughans because of their knowledge and their contacts. The family had a long-standing relationship with the management of the Mexican International, which transported virtually all of the American exports from central and western Durango to the U.S. market, and the Mexican Central, which handled products from eastern Durango. The McCaughans also enjoyed friendships with the highest officials of the state government and the respect of at least some in the local Mexican business establishment. As their businesses developed, they became associates of the Cudahy Meatpacking Company and established offices for their Durango operations in Corpus Christi, Texas. Frank later served as mayor of that city.[7]

COMMERCE AND INDUSTRY

Land and industrial ownership intertwined in most entrepreneurial undertakings. Land titles served as the basic element in the emerging capitalist economy, and the associated industrial plants dwarfed anything the Mexicans had ever seen. Natural resources and industry provided goods to be sold, railroads provided transportation to the markets, and American financiers provided the capital that made the system possible and kept it running.

The Iowa Loan and Trust Company was one of the dominant forces in the state of Durango by the end of the 1890s. It controlled the Compañía Maderera de la Sierra de Durango and the Durango Iron and Steel Company. In 1890 Durango Iron and Steel bought the 37,000-acre Rancho de Morga, which extended fifteen miles from Durango City past Chupaderos. The landscape that American cinema audiences later associated with the "Old West" was actually an area of Durango that extended north from the Rancho de Morga to the John Wayne ranch, which was north of Chupaderos. Chupaderos was the filming location for many of John Wayne's movies.

Durango Iron and Steel also acquired several other estates. The total cash outlay for the ranchos and haciendas acquired, estates comparable in size to the Rancho de Morga, totaled only 200,000 pesos. This was just a small fraction of the capital investment made by the Americans. The timber company spent $811,000 developing a lumber mill on the Morga property, while Durango Iron and Steel expended $900,000 on the steel plant in the same year. Capitalizing the land resources drove property values up rapidly. The cost of developing the land quickly outran the wherewithal of Mexican competitors. Few of them possessed cash resources. They did not have cheap access to industrial technology, and they lacked marketing goodwill in the United States.[8]

The demands of the industrializing American economy reached deep into the Mexican heartland, touching every form of rural endeavor. Near the town of Papantla, midway between Tampico and Veracruz, William Vernon Backus pioneered higher levels of capitalization in the *castilloa* rubber industry. His estates were about 30 miles southeast of Tuxpan and 175 miles southeast of the American colony of San Dieguito. Once again, access to the U.S. market made the effort feasible.

Born in 1860 in Cleveland, Backus went to Mexico in 1899 and bought tracts of land that included the Santiago de la Peña hacienda in the "rubber belt." Three of his most important tracts combined to total 12,600 acres and were situated close to the new railroad that ran from Tuxpan to Mexico City, which gave Backus access to Gulf Coast shipping. To reduce his risk and obtain capital, Backus created a maze of companies: the Tuxpan Valley Rubber Estates, the Imperial Plantation Company, the Mexican Investment and Manufacturing Company, the Federal Plantation Company, and the William V. Backus Company. The last firm was a holding company that controlled the others. Through this arrangement Backus could approach the American investment market with the image of a public company and at the same time minimize his personal risk. By 1903 the Imperial Plantation Company stockholders had provided him with $87,235, and other investors had committed some hundreds of thousands. At the beginning of the year Backus had already spent $31,728 on plantings and construction.

Unlike some of his counterparts, who earned dark reputations by overcharging their stockholders and not assuming risk, Backus strove to develop the properties. By 1906 he had invested $135,000 of his own monies in the development of the estates. His crews planted some 470,000 *castilloa* trees between 1900 and 1904, as well as tobacco plants and vanilla vines. The planting of 97,500 rubber trees during nine months in 1903 cost $52,475. Backus also tended and harvested chicle from native trees. By 1904 his men had also planted between 18,250 and 27,200 vanilla vines on at least seventy-seven acres. Within six years the crews had built a large plantation house, several dozen *chozas* (palm thatch shacks), barns, and other structures. By 1910 the Backus companies had planted 400,000 rubber trees, some with ten years' maturity and already bearing latex.

Backus succeeded because he diversified, had access to American produce markets, and found ways to generate profits while his trees were still growing. In 1902 and 1903 he sold the mineral subsoil rights to Lemeul Young of Pittsburgh for oil exploration and development. In 1909, while that work was under way, he sold 1,000 acres of the Hacienda Santiago de la Peña to the Santa Teresa Banana Company for $100,000. In 1910 a group of British investors, headed by Clarence Weston, attested to the value of high-quality Mexican rubber to the U.S. market when they offered Backus £250,000 for his entire 11,600-acre operation. The outbreak of the Mexican Revolution disrupted the sale.[9]

During the 1880s and 1890s, as American businessmen began to buy up vast tracts holding Mexico's natural resources, Americans who were developing technology for agricultural, construction, electrical, mining, and other industries joined in the creation of an avant-garde sector within the Mexican economy. Charles Brush, Thomas Alva Edison, Elihu Thomson, and

Edwin J. Houston all established outlets in Mexico City to market electrical products bearing their patents. As the American presence grew, Mexican businessmen became the first outside members of what would become a global marketing network. In 1890 Western Electric of New York, in a notable example of this process, retained W. Loizano and Company of Mexico City as their "exclusive agent."[10]

Mexico also presented commercial opportunities to Americans who were well placed near the border and who possessed technical knowledge, access to markets via railroads, adequate capitalization, and connections with the leaders of the new American mining companies. The needs of miners in Coahuila, Guanajuato, and San Luis Potosí presented Edwin Chamberlain with the opportunity of a lifetime. A man of some means, he was born in Brownsville, Texas, in 1857. He lived in San Antonio and knew the leading businessmen in the state. In 1901 Chamberlain and some Texas associates started the San Luis Lumber and Fuel Company to provide charcoal and timber to the burgeoning American mining industry in Mexico. In 1905 Chamberlain bought the timber-rich Hacienda La Labor de San Diego from San Antonio National Bank chief George Brackenridge. Brackenridge had purchased the estate, also known as Nietos, from José Nuñez in 1902. The estate was located about thirty-two miles east of the city of San Luis Potosí. The property was part of Brackenridge's Mexican real estate investment operations, which primarily focused on the states of Coahuila and Nuevo León. By 1905 Brackenridge was making tidy profits selling timber for railroad ties, but he felt he had grown too old to undertake the vexing problems associated with foreign enterprise.

Both parties to the contract recognized that the miners needed timber, and Chamberlain paid the enormous price of 95,000 pesos for 27,000 acres. The price almost equaled the amount paid to Nuñez four years earlier, when the estate had abundant stands of old-growth trees. Chamberlain immediately converted the hacienda into a source of fuel for the smelters and tunnel timbers for the mining companies. His workers constructed "large furnaces . . . in order to start a charcoal industry so that mines, smelters, electric and other companies could be supplied with fuel." Graded livestock supplemented the business. By 1909 the company showed a net profit of 10,334 pesos for the year, and its lumber was valued at 147,547 pesos. The enlarged market had created assets from what previously had been considered scrap timber. Brackenridge and Chamberlain had each made sizeable profits by adapting their resources to needs that were created by changing conditions and taking advantage of their connections with railroad and mining entrepreneurs.[11]

Sometimes local landowners made handsome profits when American businesses expanded. In the 1890s Santiago Lavin, a Spaniard, owned the strategically located 120,000-acre Hacienda Noe near Torreón in northeastern Durango. When Walter S. Moore, representing the Mexican Central Railroad, offered to buy a right-of-way across the Noe, Lavin rejected the bid. After lengthy negotiations the hacienda owner relented in return for the development of a town site that would include warehouses, a soap factory, planted trees, and housing construction. Lavin named the new city Gómez Palacio after an illustrious son of the state of Durango. In 1898 national, state, and railroad officials ceremoniously inaugurated the new city as a major railroad center.[12]

OPPORTUNITY AND ANTAGONISM

Mexico offered opportunities even to American capitalists with only limited assets. One was Lewis Booker of El Paso. Booker headed the Booker Lumber Company of Chihuahua and El Paso and became one of the most dynamic of the American landowners in Mexico. His timber holdings, which he bought in the early 1900s for about twenty cents an acre, included a 165,000-acre tract of pine forest in the Sierra Madre, twelve miles west of Pearson, Chihuahua. From that point it extended to the southwest for about thirty-four miles. Booker's ability to market his lumber in the United States provided the incentive for capital investment, an asset his Mexican counterparts could not match. In 1910 the lumber mill on the property had a daily capacity of 20,000 board feet, and the milled lumber on hand had a retail value of $6,500. Booker's combined labor costs constituted a negligible percentage of the value produced. He employed between twenty and thirty men as lumberjacks, mill workers, and mule drivers, but his administrative costs averaged only about $1,000 a month. Booker marketed most of his output in the United States for a high profit.

Transportation was Booker's overriding concern. As was the case for most of the American mining and timber companies and agricultural estates, the remoteness of his holdings dictated the construction of a railroad. He could use Frederick Stark Pearson's Mexican Northwestern Railroad to transport his lumber from Pearson to El Paso, over two hundred miles away. His most difficult task was getting his cuttings from the forest to the mill and the lumber from the mill to the Northwestern station at Pearson. The logs had to be cut to a size that could be transported by carts pulled by mules and workhorses.

By 1909 Booker had amassed enough wealth to plan the construction of a *mineral* from Pearson to Colonia Pacheco, a Mormon settlement, where he intended to develop a storage facility and station, eliminating the need for mule carts. In 1912 Booker's civil engineer, Levi P. Atwood of El Paso, began directing the construction of the line. He used a crew of between 250 and 400 men. Levi ordered an inventory of Booker's holdings at the site, which along with another report gives us a good idea of how well the lumber entrepreneur had prospered. According to the most conservative estimate, Booker at that point had some 520,000 board feet of timber at his mill awaiting shipment. The cut timber was valued at an estimated $15 per thousand board feet, or $7,800,000.

Booker had four lumber yards and fully equipped mills, and sixteen framed buildings, including a general store, a mess hall, and houses for the workers. The store's inventory had a value of approximately 5,000 pesos. In addition, Booker had 28 wagons, 25 workhorses, 102 mules, and the gear, barns, sheds, silos, and corrals needed for their support. Booker had a great deal to lose when the revolution began, but he showed no interest in nor concern for the growing agrarian, nationalist, and labor unrest at Casas Grandes, Naco, and other neighboring towns until it enveloped him.[13]

Antagonism and conflict were frequently the result of the opportunities that Mexico offered. The Mexicans and Americans who purchased Sierra Madre lands in private transactions obtained most of them from survey companies, including George and William Randolph Hearst's favorite, the Valenzuela Survey Company, run by brothers Jesús and José, the largest such company in Mexico during the Porfiriato. The complaints of Mexican foresters, who had harvested the forests without formal titles for years, and sometimes generations, found that their claims were not even registered by the Porfirian bureaucrats and that their land had been declared uninhabited. The employment opportunities offered by the new owners mitigated the dispossessions suffered by the campesinos and foresters of the Sierra Madre. Other dispossessions were felt more severely. The government declared the inhabitants of the Balsas River Basin, where Edward Shearson and Severo Mallet Prevost bought almost 1,000,000 acres, to be legally nonexistent.

Ingebricht Ole Brictson, of Deerfield, Wisconsin, stands out as a dynamic and ambitious American small businessman who committed both his fortune and his life to Mexican real estate investments and disastrously antagonized local elites. Brictson's troubles were brought on by a combination of bad luck and his own ignorance of the tensions that were developing among the Mexicans over foreign ownership of property. He was plagued by rival land claimants and the local authorities rather than working-class agrarians.

Born in 1850, Brictson emigrated with his parents from Norway to the United States in 1861. He graduated from Albion Academy in Wisconsin in 1873. He became a citizen, married, and entered into tobacco farming and real estate. In 1888 the staunchly Lutheran family moved to its new home on a farm near Deerfield that had been inherited by his wife. By 1897 Brictson owned the western side of the main street of Deerfield, including the drug store, a doctor's office, a tobacco warehouse, and a store. Brictson served as a director of the Deerfield Bank and, like so many of his contemporaries, was an aggressive investor. A Progressive, he established good relations with the political leadership of Wisconsin, including Senator Robert La Follette, and conducted business with bankers in Chicago.

In the early 1900s some members of the Doukhobor religious sect, anxious to escape what they considered to be political oppression in Canada, sought to purchase land in Mexico. They wanted the 1,200,000-acre San José de las Rusias hacienda in Tamaulipas, with its ninety miles of coastline. In 1905 or 1906, John Joice, the cashier of the nearby Dane County Bank in Stoughton, Wisconsin, and W. F. Olson of Chicago convinced Brictson that acting as the middleman in the transaction would bring him a handsome profit. Brictson went to Texas, where he met with Doctor Samuel W. Scott of San Antonio and Cuero, Texas, and his partner Otto Koehler, the president of the San Antonio Brewing Company and the operator of a new brewery in Monterrey. Scott and Koehler represented Ramon and Nicholas López, brothers living in Soto la Marina, the town nearest the hacienda. The López brothers wished to sell their rights to the San José de las Rusias. Scott and Koehler also had personal motives for promoting the sale—they held both state and national government "concessions" on 75,000 acres of the property. The original price of the estate appears to have been $400,000.[14]

In 1906 or 1907 Brictson met with Doukhobor representatives in Saint Louis, where they agreed to the sale arrangements. Brictson then returned to Deerfield. He convinced the leaders of the Stoughton State Bank and the Stoughton Bank and Trust to loan him the additional funds he needed to buy the estate prior to selling it to the religious sect. He also recruited additional support among his friends in Deerfield, Stoughton, and Madison. The investors included local businessmen, politicians, and even Rasmus B. Anderson, the head of the Scandinavian Languages program at the University of Wisconsin.

Following the common practice of the time, Scott represented Brictson before the notaries public in Texas, where the sale was recorded, and assisted him in Mexico, where they employed the legal and estate title services of Patricio Milmo and Sons of Monterrey. Milmo, formerly Patrick Mullins, was of Irish extraction and unknown citizenship. He was also well connected in Mexico City, having access to President Díaz. The Americans retained Milmo because Koehler already enjoyed a friendship with him. Brictson seems to have temporarily satisfied Scott and Koehler, but the López brothers balked, demanding more than the 600,000-peso asking price for their share if they were going to sell to the Doukhobors. In 1907 Brictson closed the sale with Koehler, Scott, and the López brothers at a higher price, and he returned to Saint Louis. The Doukhobor representatives refused to pay the extra amounts, and Brictson suddenly owned a hacienda in Mexico. He also had a 600,000-peso debt, lenders in Wisconsin he could not pay, and sellers in Mexico and San Antonio who were expecting more cash.

Brictson's legal troubles started immediately. Wisconsin authorities arrested Joice for embezzlement at the Dane County Bank and closed the institution. That event shattered the confidence of Brictson's investors. Then the escalation of costs associated with the sale caused many to want out of the enterprise. In 1907, when Brictson took possession of the hacienda, the cash expenditure was much higher than the original price. He estimated the eventual cost at "almost 1 million dollars" because of the expenses incurred while trying to satisfy claims made by the López brothers, Scott, Koehler, Milmo, and Olson and his associates. Brictson's persistence in completing the purchase is understandable. The hacienda was an impressive piece of property. It reached thirty-five miles inland from the Gulf of Mexico and stretched ninety miles to the south from its northwestern corner near Soto la Marina. It included ranges of hills on its east and west sides and enjoyed the benefits of the Soto la Marina River, which served as its northern boundary. At the heart of the San José estate was a fertile valley with a stream running its entire length.[15]

The higher purchase price was only the beginning of Brictson's troubles. When he arrived at the estate, he discovered with dismay that the López brothers had harvested the sugar cane and were confiscating the cattle. He immediately enjoined them from completing the latter action and arranged to sell the herd to R. M. Bennet and T. M. and W. A. Bates, local men residing at San José, for $92,035. Brictson was able to negotiate an additional $7,000 above their initial offer, which was a good thing because his supporters back in Wisconsin, including H. B. Fargo, the cashier of the bank in Deerfield, wanted out of what they considered a nightmarish entanglement. In addition to these pressures, the American Trust and Savings Bank of Chicago wanted the $27,322 it had extended to Brictson as a sixty-day loan. Brictson lacked the necessary cash and liquidated his assets in the United States. To his credit, when Brictson sold the properties, including his share

President Benito Juárez, no date. (Culver Pictures)

Railroad bridge over the Metlac ravine in Veracruz state, c. 1880s. (Library, Getty Research Institute, Los Angeles. Acc. no. 96.R.143–2)

Indigenous Mexicans in a studio photo, c. 1890–1900. (Photo: Lorenzo Becerral/Library, Getty Research Institute, Los Angeles. Acc. no. 99.R.17)

Thanksgiving in Tampico, c. 1910. (Photo courtesy Tom Hale)

A hacienda, typical of the residences of wealthy American and Mexican landholders, no date. (Brown Brothers)

American ranch, c. 1910. (U.S.-Mexican Claims Commission, National Archives and Records Administration/NARA).

Parraga Brothers Company salt mines near Salinas Cruz, Oaxaca, c. 1910.
(U.S.-Mexican Claims Commission, National Archives and Records
Administration /NARA).

Oilfield in Tampico, no date. (Photo courtesy Tom Hale)

American rubber plantation, no date. (U.S.-Mexican Claims Commission, National Archives and Records Administration /NARA).

Cíudad Juárez in 1911. (Library, Getty Research Institute, Los Angeles Acc no. 89.R.46–22)

Home of A. W. Ivens, c. 1910. The veranda and neat lawns were typical of affluent American residences in western Chihuahua.

President Díaz, c. 1911. (Library of Congress. LC-USZ62–100275)

Leaders of the rebellion in a photo taken 30 April 1911. Back row, from left: Francisco (Pancho) Villa, Gustavo Madero, Francisco Madero, Sr., Giuseppi Garibaldi, F. Garza, Lucio Blanco; front row, from left: Venustiano Carranza, Emilio Vasquez Gómez, Francisco Idalencio Madero, Abraham González, José Maytorena, Pascual Orozco. (Library, Getty Research Institute, Los Angeles. Acc. no. 89.R.46–32)

Pancho Villa and aides, c. 1910–11. (Photo courtesy Otis A. Aultman Collection, El Paso Public Library)

Group of American Villistas, c. 1911.(Photo courtesy Otis A. Aultman Collection, El Paso Public Library).

The three leading figures of the Convention government seated at a banquet, ca. 1911; starting with the third figure from the left: Francisco Villa, Eulalio Gutiérrez, and Emiliano Zapata. (Harry Ransom Humanities Research Center, University of Texas, Austin)

AMERICANS AND INSSURECTOS AT RIO GRANDE

Americans and insurrectionists at the Rio Grande, 1911. (Library, Getty Research Institute. Acc. no. 89.R.46–18)

Native Mexican Americans with Madero's army, c. 1911. (Photo: D. W. Hoffmann, El Paso, Texas/Library, Getty Research Institute. Acc. no. 89.R.46–27)

José María Pino Suárez, Emilio Vasquez Gómez, Francisco Idalencio Madero, and Francisco S. Carbajal, c. 1911. (Library of Congress. LC-USZ62–118311)

President Francisco I. Madero on his way to the presidential palace, 9 February 1913. (Library, Getty Research Institute, Los Angeles. Acc no. 2000.R.15)

Victoriano Huerta and Guillermo Rubio Navarrete, 1913. (Library, Getty Research Institute, Los Angeles. Acc. no. 89.R.46–11)

of downtown Deerfield, he used the proceeds to pay back his friends and former partners.

The Hacienda San José de las Rusias held great potential. It had attracted the attention of potential buyers in New York as well as Brictson and the Doukhobors. The estate offered vast and inexpensive grazing lands immediately adjacent to the border and ready access to a railroad and international ports at Brownsville and Tampico. An underwater cable connected Brownsville to New Orleans and New York. The estate also offered mineral deposits for mining and smelting. In 1908 Captain Charles E. Phelps visited the tract. Phelps was a member of Kean, Van Courtland, and Company, realtors connected to Lackawanna Steel, and a director of the Santa Juliana Mining Company of Mexico and New York. Phelps noted that Brictson had capitalized his enterprise at $5,000,000, and that the estate held 18,000 head of cattle, 3,000 mares, 150 stallions, 3,000 sheep, 7,500 goats, and 1,000 hogs. He also observed banana, coconut, orange, and lemon groves, but he did not include an estimate of the estate's iron resources. He and Brictson discussed the sale and purchase of the hacienda in the context of the assets and a colonization project: "Land sales to colonists at advanced prices are . . . a most important consideration." In addition, Phelps estimated that the estate would require some $777,000 in improvements to place it at the production levels that his company expected.

Brictson's troubles with the López brothers spelled doom to his efforts to sell the estate for a quick profit. Later that year W. H. Ellis, representing an investment firm located in the Drexel Building on Wall Street, with branches on Broad Street and Avenida Balderas in Mexico City, attempted to take advantage of Brictson's difficult situation. He offered Brictson $150,000 in "Nebraska (Omaha) and Kansas City stock for the López Ranch" with its "10,000 head of marketable cattle, and about 5,000 head of stock." Ellis informed Brictson, "I am fixing to go into the cattle business in Cuba and Texas." Ellis later became a vice president of the New York Water Company. A man of less determination might have accepted his losses and sold the property. Instead, Brictson arranged jaguar hunting tours to raise cash. He refused to sell, but his problems were just beginning.[16]

> The López brothers and Scott filed separate lawsuits against Brictson.
> Scott's case caused some concern, but his demand for "$35,000 in gold
> for [the] concession of the state or the federal one" could be negotiated.
> A deeper set of tensions underlay the López brothers' suit. They insisted
> that they were entitled to reoccupy the property since Brictson had
> broken his contract by forcibly preventing them from selling the cattle.
> From their point of view the sale of the estate had nothing to do with

the moveable assets, a point not clarified in the contracts drawn up by Scott and Milmo. The Americans questioned the López brothers' sincerity in this regard, but according to Mexican law transactions could include the removal of certain assets unless they were specifically mentioned in the contract. In addition, the valuation of the estate in 1904 estimated its market value at $1,750,000, indicating that the López brothers might indeed have assumed that they were keeping the cattle. It is clear that Brictson and his associates believed from the outset that the livestock were part of the sale.

The López brothers won their suits against Brictson in front of the local judge in Soto la Marina and followed that victory by defeating Brictson in the appeals court at Ciudad Victoria. In a short time the American owners held the López brothers and local Mexican authorities in deep distrust.

> First López in plain words is a raskal [sic] as all Mexicans are when you learn to know them[.] [T]hey are sweat [sic] and pat your shoulders so long as they can get any thing out of you and in fact will do anything for money.[17]

Milmo appealed to the Mexican Supreme Court on Brictson's behalf, and over a period of years wrote personal letters to President Díaz, explaining the situation. The supreme court and the president supported Brictson, but the López brothers renewed their challenge with favorable court decisions at the local and state levels. Brictson found it necessary to employ armed men and periodically to take unreliable recourse with the local army commander to protect his property from the hostile incursions of his neighbors in Soto la Marina.

Presidential and supreme court interventions on behalf of foreign newcomers and against local Mexican elites exacerbated the tensions between Mexicans and their government, divided the lower courts and higher courts, and turned important groups of Mexicans against the American entrepreneurs. Differences of culture and language, compounded by mutual distrust, led to hostility and complicated the lives of Americans and Mexicans across the nation.

DISCREPANCIES OF WEALTH AND POWER

The vast discrepancies of wealth and power between the great landowners and Mexican pueblos led to unequal representation in the courts and blatant miscarriages of justice. In 1898 oilman William Jennings of Louisiana and Mississippi joined with Texas ranchers John Blocker and John T. and George N. Lytle to purchase the first portion of what later became the

1,237,000-acre Piedra Blanca hacienda. They established its headquarters in Coahuila, one mile east of Del Rio, Texas. Blocker and the Lytles were leading figures in San Antonio. They established the Compañía Vacuna de Piedra Blanca, S.A., to run the property. The tracts that they combined to enlarge the Piedra Blanca centered on the Burro Mountains and included rivers, vast expanses of grazing land, and the *casco,* or big house, called Piedra Blanca.

The tract that held the *casco* was purchased from some of Mexico's leading citizens: Evaristo Madero, the father of the future president, Ernesto Madero, the future president's uncle, and Lorenzo González Treviño, a relative of the former governor of Nuevo León, Geronimo Treviño. The American ranchers then paid an additional $150,000 for a neighboring tract of more than 970,000 acres to augment the property that contained the *casco.*

The owners of Piedra Blanca and the neighboring La Babia hacienda had ignored the charges of "usurpation" set forth against them by the Kickapoos, Pottawatomies, and Seminoles and the "Muscogee Negroes" of the surrounding pueblos. In 1876 the newly elected Díaz had ignored the claims of these people when he gave La Babia to Treviño's father as a reward for assistance during the Revolution of Tuxtepec. Treviño ignored them in turn when he gave the hacienda to General Ord. The American general repeated the oversight in transmitting the property to Lucy, his heiress. Lucy Treviño sometimes resided at La Babia.

The Piedra Blanca contracts signed by the Madero, Treviño, and American interests likewise made no mention of the claims of the people living on the estate. These people practiced communal land ownership and defended it fiercely. President Juárez had given them land entitlement in return for military duties against raiding parties of Comanches and Apaches and incursions by Texans. Their land claims carried the authority of the former president and postdated the Ley Lerdo. The Native Americans and "Negroes" had already united and lodged claims for the land against the Mexican interlopers before the American investors arrived. The Americans set about improving the property with "windmills, pipelines, water tanks, fencing, houses, quarters, corrals, stables, farming implements, 25,000 head of high-grade Hereford cattle, and 1,400 head of horses and mules." The appeals of the rural folk, accompanied by their manifest antagonisms, continued until the revolution of 1910, when the American owners were forced to evacuate the region after losing most of their cattle.[18]

The wealthy ranchers A. E. and John W. Noble of Victoria, Texas, owned the nearby Nacimiento hacienda and had the same conflict with the Kickapoo, Seminole, Pottawatomie, and Muscogee communities over land occupancy. The Nobles used the 70,000-acre Nacimiento as a supplement to their extensive ranching operations in southern Texas. They bought it as the Texas International Railroad reached south toward Laredo and the Southern Pacific–owned "Sunset Line" extended west toward nearby Del Rio. The Nobles seized the opportunity to buy productive land that would soon be accessible. They imported cattle from Texas and planted pecan orchards on land that they had bought in 1883 for one-tenth the price of comparable acreage in Texas. The Nobles, however, were fully cognizant of the Kickapoo, Pottawatomie, Seminole, and Muscogee claims, which they regarded with contempt. The Native and African Americans, who had been relegated to the status of criminals and outcasts in the United States, claimed 17,600 acres of the Nacimiento. In 1883 the Mexican courts had not yet resolved the land disputes, but court decisions after 1883 satisfied the aspirations of the Nobles and later American buyers.

Another dispute involving great estate owners arose between the Nobles and José M. Garza Galan. The Mexican, who served as the political chief of the district, owned the Cavillo hacienda. The estate adjoined the Nacimiento, and the Nobles had fenced the property. Their cowboys had at least one armed encounter with Garza Galan's men. The two sides fought over boundaries and water rights until the revolution of 1910 ended federal authority and the Nobles fled.[19]

Given the unreliable status of the land surveys in the area, these disputes seem to have been inevitable. The connections enjoyed by the Texas investors with cabinet officers in Mexico City enabled them to override local objections from above and below. The Mexican claimants demonstrated their tenacity in Coahuila as they did elsewhere. In 1904 A. E. Noble complained that "Indians" originally from Oklahoma were cutting down his pecan trees. He hoped to invalidate the campesinos' claim to the lands by pointing out that they, as a people, were natives of the United States and not Mexican in origin. The Mexican government had originally granted the land to these groups in 1852, and it had validated the titles during the 1860s in return for their service against Comanche raiders. The campesinos' legal dispute faded prior to the revolution because they lacked the resources to litigate in the Porfirian courts, but afterward they began to press their claims again. Unduly impressed by their own strong political connections in Mexico City, the American owners of large estates generally underestimated the strength of resentful local elites and citizenries.[20]

Jennings and Blocker, the Lytles, Brictson, Marshall, Ord, and the Nobles typified the Americans who held enormous estates on the northern Mexican frontier. They used sound business reasoning in the economic development of their haciendas. With the exception of Brictson, they were members of the financial elite of the southwestern United States. When they found that land cost only a fraction of the price of property in Texas, they bought vast expanses. The Southern Pacific and the Mexican Northwestern Railroads provided Marshall with immediate market access to El Paso. The International Railroad of Mexico serviced the Piedra Blanca, joining the American rail network at Eagle Pass, while the Mexican National Railroad, running between Matamoros and Monterrey, carried Brictson's cattle to Texas stockyards.

Another Texan, Edward Morris, paid only $525,000 for the T. O. Riverside hacienda. Morris, the president of Morris and Company, one of the largest packinghouses in the United States and the first large operator in the Union Stockyards at Chicago, married an heiress to the Swift Packing Company. Morris duplicated the improvements of the Piedra Blanca owners. Brictson oversaw the construction of over two hundred miles of fencing, but Marshall doubled that figure, creating the largest fenced property in the world. Although Morris only had two years to develop his holdings before the revolutionary disturbances began, he and Marshall each ordered the construction of over one hundred water wells, built dams and corrals, and developed herds that numbered in the tens of thousands. Morris bought blooded Angus stock and sent it to his ranches in the Dakotas, Texas, and Chihuahua. Morris had just begun shipping the progeny to his slaughterhouses in Kansas City, East St. Louis, St. Joseph, and Chicago via the Southern Pacific and the El Paso Southeastern Railroads when the revolution broke out.[21]

Sometimes American property acquisitions caused friction among competing Americans. In 1884 the Mexican government approved the sale of "enormous expanses of land to Joaquin Gurrola in the district of San Dimas," located in the Sierra Madre of western Durango. The transfer of survey lands led to a dispute with the local citizenry. Meanwhile, Gurrola sold the land to the Durango Development Company of New Jersey. Less than a decade later the company, which included James Stillman among its leaders, had to defend its title to the property against the claims of the prior tenants, who protested that the survey company had made errors. The Candelaria silver mine, one of the richest in the world, was the prize. The preferred stockholders included Auguste Belmont, members of the Harriman, Morgan, and Morton families, and Francis R. Appelton, a director of the National Park Bank. Thomas H. Watkins, of the Inde Gold Mining Company of New York and a director of various railroads and timber companies in New York and Pennsylvania, served as president.

A drawn-out and intense struggle for control of the silver lode com-

menced between the New Yorkers and another group that claimed ownership of the mine, Colonel Daniel Burns and some unknown San Francisco
"interests." Burns served as the Democratic court clerk of Alameda County
at the time, and he lacked the financial resources to conduct the vicious fight.
William Randolph Hearst, a fellow resident of the San Francisco area, a mine
owner at San Dimas, and a Democratic Party activist, was a political ally of
Burns. It is possible that he was a silent partner in the enterprise.

In 1900 Mark Birmingham, a director of Inde Gold, obtained the support
of John Hay, the U.S. secretary of state, who intervened with Díaz on behalf of the New Yorkers. But the Candelaria was located in the Sierra Madre,
remote from centralized authority. The local Mexican officials, including the
judges and the army officers, favored Burns, whom the New Yorkers accused
of using wholesale bribery. Burns and his San Francisco associates won the
battle after almost two decades of litigation and even armed confrontations
at the mine, despite presidential orders and decisions by the Mexican
Supreme Court that favored the East Coast investors. The mine rewarded
Burns and his associates with 70,000,000 pesos in output in just twenty-
five years.[22]

Although the Mexican elite increasingly resented the American acquisition of land through concessions, whether direct or indirect, acquiring an
estate through marriage was a different matter. The marriage of Americans
into the Mexican elite served as an important mechanism by which the foreigners came to hold large properties. The practice had facilitated the transformation of land ownership in California and the southwestern United
States. While not as important as an agent of change in Mexico, these relationships helped develop a sense of intimacy among neighbors and to create extended families, which meant many cousins.

The marriages of George Reeder and Charles Dickman to the heiresses
of the Milmo family of Monterrey and the Valenzuela clan of Durango and
Chihuahua placed Americans in control of large properties. Reeder became
one of the largest landowners in northeastern Mexico. The most notable
wedding and ensuing divorce was that of Joséfa Valenzuela and Charles Dickman. Joséfa, an heiress to the fortune of surveyor José Valenzuela, inherited a number of valuable properties and haciendas. Dickman's divorce settlement included the rich Hacienda la Estación in northeastern Durango and
several other estates. The marriage of American women to Mexican elites
also played a significant, if not a principal, role in advancing American landholding in Chihuahua, Coahuila, Durango, Nuevo León, San Luis Potosí,
and Tamaulipas. Lucy Ord, the daughter of General E. O. C. Ord, married
General Geronimo Treviño, the owner of one of the largest latifundia com-

plexes in Coahuila and Nuevo León. Cora Townsend married the largest landowner in San Luis Potosí.

A WOMAN'S PERSPECTIVE

Cora Townsend provides a perspective on the special status of the few American women on their own in Mexico. Unlike Phoebe Hearst, who bought extensive properties for exploitation of natural resources but preferred to reside in metropolitan centers in the United States, Townsend came as the bride of José Rascon, a prominent Mexican industrialist and landowner, and took up long-term residence on the Rascon hacienda, a sugar estate that stretched across eastern San Luis Potosí and western Tamaulipas. She later inherited her deceased husband's uncontested estate. Her mother, Mary Ashley, and father, Gideon Townsend, a "capitalist" of Fishkill, New York, married in 1853. Her mother's side of the family had long played a leading role in the ownership and direction of the Canal Bank of New Orleans. They were good friends of the Whitney family, which owned the Whitney Bank of New Orleans, and financier-publisher Charles A. Dana of New York, who had supported Matías Romero's efforts to enlist American help during the Liberal government's struggle against the French. Among their other friends were the well-connected Mellon and Woodward families of New Orleans.

One of Cora's sisters, Adele, married Lewis H. Stanton, the son of President Abraham Lincoln's secretary of war. Her other sister, Daisey, married one of the nation's leading gynecologists, George H. Lee of the University of Texas Medical Branch at Galveston. Cora chose an older man, Mexican tycoon José Martín Rascon.[23] Rascon came from one of Mexico's oldest and richest families. He counted a complex of factories and haciendas in the states of San Luis Potosí and Tamaulipas among his many assets. In conjunction with those interests and his commitment to modernization, Rascon supported and invested in the American-financed national railway system. One of the proposed lines, from Tampico to San Luis Potosí, held special interest for him, since it would cross his properties at Micos.

Townsend and Rascon were married in 1883, shortly after Rascon visited New Orleans as a member of a Mexican delegation to the United States. In the delegation's itinerary were New Orleans, Saint Louis, Washington, D.C., and New York. Díaz headed the delegation and addressed a group of New Orleans financiers in that city on 17 March 1883. He was serving as the minister of development before reassuming the presidency in 1884. Díaz immediately identified the raising of funds for a railroad to be built across the Isthmus of Tehuantepec as one of the principal objectives of his trip. He chose a topic sure to stimulate the interest of the merchants of New Orleans, which was America's most important port on the Gulf of Mexico. After extolling the economic possibilities of the line, Díaz asserted that the railway "would yoke the two oceans together."

The Mexican party included Díaz, Rascon, Manuel Romero Rubio, Matías Romero, and General J. B. Frisbie, formerly of California and Díaz's adviser on railroad affairs. The Díaz family, Romero, Romero Rubio, and various officers in the Mexican government including Governor Carlos Pacheco were already large landholders along the planned route of the Tehuantepec railroad.

The highlight of the trip for all concerned—with the exception of Rascon, who had met Cora Townsend—was a banquet featuring the leading figures of the Mexican railroad construction program. The numbered seating arrangements revealed the pecking order in the new world of Mexican railroads. Huntington of Southern Pacific sat at the head of the table, while former presidents Díaz and Grant sat at his right and left, respectively. The seating for the railroad financiers reflected their wealth, interests, and influence. Leland Stanford of Southern Pacific sat in seat seven, Roscoe Conkling of the Pennsylvania Railroad took chair eight, Jay Gould of United Pacific occupied place nine, Thomas Wentworth Peirce of the Sunset Line number eleven, Rascon seat thirteen, George Hammeken of the Tacubaya and Pennsylvania Railroads chair fourteen, Henry Sanford place sixteen, diplomat Edward Lee Plumb number seventeen, financier John Gates seat twenty-one, and Frisbie place twenty-two. The financing of Mexico's railroad construction projects was the principal topic of discussion.[24]

Immediately after her marriage to Rascon, Cora left for a memorable trip to Mexico. She described her experiences in Mexico in a seventy-seven-page diary and a rich and informative, if uneven, manuscript of several hundred pages. The record of her journey documents the extent of American influence in the country. In the summer of 1883 she sailed on a Morgan liner to Veracruz. From Veracruz she traveled by train to Mexico City and then north to Querétaro. At Querétaro she visited the Hacienda de Hercules and the better-known textile factory of the same name, both owned by Romero Rubio. Cora Townsend de Rascon described what she saw, unconsciously reflecting the economic and security concerns of the American investors who went to Mexico:

> The property belongs to the Rubio family. . . . A guard of twenty-five soldiers is kept on the premises, but their services have never been called into request. Only one strike has ever occurred and on that occasion the strikers were allowed to depart and never allowed to

return. . . . English superintendents are paid $150 [pesos] per month. It employs nearly 1500 indian [*sic*] men and women, who are paid at the rate of three reales a day or thirty-seven and a half cents. They produce seven thousand pieces of cotton, 32 *varas* to the piece, weekly.[25]

The presence of the military and the low salaries of the workers relative to the value they produced were familiar to Townsend, since they resembled the labor regimes of her family's estates in Louisiana. She also noted that the Romero Rubio family represented old money. They dominated Querétaro, lived in a grand manner, and exercised considerable influence.

> Maximilian was brought from the prison in Senor Rubio's carriage under a guard of twenty-five soldiers, and accompanied by some of his own captured officers, to hold an interview with General Escobedo.[26]

Townsend left behind the elegance of her lifestyle in New Orleans, but she found power at the Rascon estate. By the time she reached the hacienda that bore her husband's name, she was becoming versed in the rules that defined her status.

> The old established rule for a hacienda was that it should contain 21,690 English acres of ground, and have upon it good store buildings. . . . A hacienda in agriculture was called a *hacienda de labor*. A hacienda in stock raising was called a *hacienda de ganado*. These distinctions [however] are no longer adhered to.[27]

The estate, which included several haciendas, had supposedly been owned by the "Jesuits" until the secularization of church holdings in the 1830s. While possible, that claim is weakened by the fact that the Jesuits had lost much of their property well before that date because of their expulsion from Mexico in 1767. "The Federal Government" probably confiscated it from the Franciscans in 1833 and sold it in 1842 to Felipe Neri del Barrio of "the tobacco company." In 1865 José Domingo Rascon, the father of Townsend's husband, purchased the hacienda from Neri del Barrio.

When her husband died in 1896, Cora Townsend, *viuda de Rascon*, inherited the entire hacienda complex of irrigated fields, mills, warehouses, and power plants, which were situated on a domain of 1,400,000 acres. Staying on at the hacienda as an active administrator, Townsend sent her daughter, Cora Ann Rascon, to live with her sister in Galveston, where she could experience a more genteel society. The mother delegated the responsibility of "tutor" for her daughter to her brother-in-law, Dr. George Lee. Townsend administered the hacienda for nearly ten years.

The task of running a sugar hacienda was not insurmountable for an

American woman with Townsend's education, experience, determination, and connections. Her family in New Orleans made technological, administrative, financial, and marketing expertise available through its impressive resources. In addition, she paid civil engineer L. M. Barlow an annual salary of $1,500 to continue as superintendent. Townsend proved herself more than equal to the challenge, using her resources and those of others to the utmost. In 1905 she initiated the construction of a branch railroad from the Mexican Central line, which ran by her estate, to her principal concentration of mills and warehouses. She had fulfilled her husband's vision of ready access to the world marketplace.[28]

The Mexican workforce at Rascon was immense. The estate was home to 14,000 Mexicans. Some women worked in the main house under her supervision, while the men toiled full-time in the fields, mills, and power plant. An undetermined number of the residents were sharecroppers. During the cane harvest and when the land was prepared for planting, the resident work force was supplemented by hundreds of part-time workers. Townsend upheld the same discriminatory salary differentials that she had noted twenty years earlier in Querétaro. She paid superintendent Barlow and the American manager of her largest sugar mill $1,500 yearly. Yet the Mexican common laborers earned only 30 centavos per day, or less than $50 per year, a ratio of 30 to 1. The workers' wages were even less after deductions were made for purchases in the *tienda de raya* and other services. Townsend underscored this discrimination in June 1903 when she expended $288.35 for the "purchase of negroes." The extreme inequality of earnings between American supervisors and Mexican laborers created vastly different cultural, economic, and social conditions for the two populations and created a separation between the Mexicans and Americans rather than the merger of peoples that might have been expected or desired.

Townsend continued to direct and develop her properties until her death in 1906. At that point the Rascon operations were taken over by impresarios intent on increasing its value, extracting a maximum of wealth, and then selling to selected buyers at attractive rates. The transition, which was influenced by the gender relationships that prevailed in American society at that time, began when Cora's sister Daisey and her daughter Cora Ann inherited the bulk of the estate. The American family, headed by Dr. Lee, and the bankers in New Orleans reorganized the properties. They formed the Rascon Manufacturing and Development Company and established its administrative headquarters at New Orleans. One of their first acts was an estate inventory in 1907 that confirmed Townsend's impressive entrepreneurial acumen.[29]

The results showed that the largest segment of the estate, the Hacienda de Papagallos, covered over 1,000,000 acres. The *ingenio*—the sugar mill— and the cane fields claimed 25,000 acres. Among the other properties, the annexed Sabinito hacienda, also known as the Hacienda del Salto, held 40,000 acres. The accounts receivable for the *ingenio* showed $19,000 in payments due. The sugar ready for harvest totaled 180,000,000 pounds, with a value of 6.5 cents per pound, and the milled sugar in storage was worth $19,476.75. The mansion, mill, warehouses, *tienda de raya,* and other facilities on the estate were valued at $250,000. Two of the company stores, which sold their goods to the workers and their families, produced a yearly net profit of $3,000. The nine-mile-long railroad was worth $30,000.

The total assets of the enterprise in real estate, improvements, equipment, sugarcane, and other commodities were approximately $5,000,000. In addition to sugarcane, the estate produced timber, marble, tobacco, mescal, palms, corn, and istle, a fibrous plant used to make cordage. The inventory justified the directors' decision to gain control of the Rascon Company through the purchase of stocks rated at over $1,000,000 and bonds valued at $5,000,000. The twelve directors of the U.S.-based company were all men. Cora Ann Rascon and Lillie Lee did not participate in the management of the enterprise.[30]

George Lee's professional commitments left little time for managing a sugar estate, and competition from sugar growers in Cuba and Hawaii resulted in a weak U.S. market and low profits for Mexican sugar. Lee and the New Orleans bankers decided to sell the Rascon operations if they could get the price they wanted. The sophistication of the buyers varied widely. Lee preferred the hundreds of "square" Americans at the Agua Buena colony, "who paid the highest price ever for their land." He noted that a real estate promoter named Spillane was "still booming the country and the values are still going up." In 1906 he negotiated the sale of the hacienda complex with G. E. Patton of Kansas City. Lee wanted $1,000,000 for the entire Rascon estate. Patton countered with an offer of $525,000 for the San Luis Potosí portion only. It was a losing proposition for Lee and his associates because the Tamaulipas section would have been denied control of the railroad and power plant and the crops needed to support the nutritional needs of the workforce.[31]

Unable to sell at the price they wanted, Lee and the directors moved quickly to further capitalize, streamline, and expand their operations. The Mexican government wanted the area developed to its full potential, so it assisted in the granting of clearances for the movement of goods and land titles. The Rascon management purchased new milling equipment with the funds derived from a bond issue and installed a power plant at Salto, where the river fell 600 feet in five miles and at one point had a sheer drop of 200 feet. The power plant solved the persistent problem of fuel shortages. Lee then offered "to furnish" A. A. Robertson of the Mexican Central Railroad with enough "electrical energy to haul at least 1,000,000 gross metric tons per annum up grade from Tamasosopo to Cárdenas and as much tonnage as may be desired in the opposite direction." Robertson did not act on the offer. Seeking to rationalize their resources further, Lee and the directors sold marginal and excess lands. Between 1905 and 1910 he succeeded in "booming" property in the Micos–San Dieguito area to 160 American colonists while ignoring Saint Louis capitalists who wanted to lease lands at an annual rate of 5 cents per acre.[32]

A TRADITION OF INEQUITY

The labor regime at Rascon was not exceptional. In adjacent Tamaulipas the oil field crews worked separately, with the Americans on the platforms and the Mexican "muckers" working in the oil-inundated earth around the derricks. In other locales the discrepancies could be even more extreme despite the high degree of value that the workers produced and the wealth they generated for the owners and management of foreign concerns. These inequitable labor practices did not originate with the arrival of the American entrepreneurs. Taking advantage of the rural population was a long-established practice of the Mexican elite.

The Mexican elites who owned commercial agricultural estates depended on the residents of the neighboring pueblos to supply the labor they needed to work their property. The hacendados faced two problems wherever the pueblo citizenries were well off, such as in the well-watered and rich soil of the Chalco area in central Mexico. First, since the pueblo residents supported themselves, they offered no sales opportunities to commercial crop growers. Second, since their self-support activities occupied much of their time, they had little time for wage labor. That situation forced the hacendados into a complex situation. They either had to pay wages higher than the level justified by worker output to overcome the resistance to outside employment, or they had to recruit workers from considerable distances. In the latter case the hacendados had to advance the workers monies for the purchase of goods, including alcohol, in the *tienda de raya*, offer them food allotments in lieu of cash, and establish sharecropping arrangements.

The results were negative. The labor shortages and high costs led many hacendados to use the privatization program to acquire the land worked by the peasants, driving them into the full-time rural labor market. They then used their money and power to impose legal entailment or debt peonage. The strategy worked quite effectively among the less sophisticated laborers. However, it reduced commercial exchange, restricted local markets, and circumscribed working-class mobility and experience, and the impoverishment led to reduced social services, including education. Meanwhile, the hacendados had to transport their produce farther to urban markets. The expenses of transportation, combined with their misguided efforts to control labor costs, lowered the rate of capital accumulation and, therefore, of economic growth.

Debt peonage set back any hope for a growing economy, as evidenced at the San Antonio Acolman hacienda, in a region less prosperous than Chalco. The hacienda paid its "unskilled" workers 1.6 pesos per month—about $1.60—and a ration of maize. The entire unskilled workforce at the hacienda incurred debts totaling 4 pesos per person, the upper limit permitted by the hacendado.[33] The hacendado advanced the more skilled workers even greater loans relative to their wages. Teamsters received credit lines of 17 pesos on salaries of 2 pesos monthly and the basic allotment of maize. Clerks and mill machinery operators received credits of 64 and 72 pesos, respectively, against salaries of 5 pesos per month. The food allotments restricted the workers' ability to achieve the liquidity necessary to pay off the debt. Food credits, indebtedness, and the company stores combined to remove the workers' salaries from outside circulation, effectively eliminating the potential development of small businesses and economic diversity in the region.[34]

Forced labor also prevailed at the pulque hacienda of San José Buenavista, situated in the semiarid zone north of Mexico City, near the town of Cuautitlán. The estate produced pulque, corn, beans, and chiles for the market in Mexico City—crops that were far less profitable than those grown at Chalco or the sugar produced at estates farther south in Morelos. Operation of the hacienda required a lower capitalization and a workforce that was less skilled and complex than that needed in the orchards and at the sugar haciendas. Debt peonage and miserable working and living conditions for the workers resulted from the hacendado's drive to keep costs down in order to show enough profit to justify his business. The depressed wages and profits created few opportunities for other businesses to prosper.

During a typical six-day workweek in 1852, the hacienda owners paid their twenty-five peons a cumulative total of 31.8 pesos weekly, or 21 centavos daily to each worker. The workers' earnings were actually much lower because the owners deducted various fees from their wages. The operators of the communal kitchen charged 3.75 pesos per week for the twenty-five workers, while the obligatory weekly church service cost an additional 2.05 pesos. Each worker was thus obligated to pay 23 centavos per week for these services from total weekly earnings of 1.2 pesos. In addition, the hacendado encouraged his twenty-five employees to accept a portion of their salary, 9.70 pesos, in pulque instead of cash. This cost each peon about 39 centavos. Workers who refused to accept the pulque—an intoxicating beverage derived from the maguey plant—suffered the deduction from their wages nonetheless.

The hacendado also charged 3.8 pesos, or about 15 centavos per worker per week, for their only source of corn, the maize allotment. The prorated deductions from employee pay made by the manager of the *tienda de raya* totaled 6.8 pesos, or about 27 centavos per worker. The hacendado made certain of the peons' patronage at the store by issuing 10 pesos of their wages in tokens, almost one-third of the payroll total, redeemable only at his *tienda*. After totaling all the wages and expenditures, a typical worker at San José Buenavista in the early 1850s saw less than 4 centavos per week as liquid cash available for discretionary use. During 1852 the weekly net income of the workers was usually negative, reaching as low as −3.62 pesos, or about −14.5 centavos per employee. In spite of these constraints, the employees and their families somehow found other sources of funds. During two weeks in May, twenty-eight peons earned 10.9 pesos not accounted for by the hacienda bookkeeper through normal worker income and expenditures on the estate. Outside sources of income included the supplementary sale of corn and beans, moonlighting, and the theft of pulque.[35]

Wage figures tell us a great deal more about the material quality of life when they are placed in the context of prevailing prices. Let us enter the *tienda de raya* at San José Buenavista on payday with the peons' base weekly salary of 1.2 pesos. It cost 1.63 pesos to repair a damaged sombrero. A liter of fish was priced at 3.5 pesos. A single fish weighing 4.5 pounds cost 84 centavos. A quarter-liter of shrimp was priced at 63 centavos. A slab of cheese weighing 17.25 pounds was valued at 3.45 pesos. One bottle of Jerez wine was 63 centavos. The workers paid 1 peso for a *media* (measure) of potatoes and 4 pesos for a "*molinda* [bar] of chocolate (small)." A bottle of vinegar cost 22 centavos. A pound of cured sugar was priced at 1.88 pesos. Beans, the staple of the laborers' diet, cost 4.75 pesos per barrel. A *media* of garbanzo beans was 3 pesos. Two barrels of rice cost 3.75 pesos, and two pounds of salt were 3.2 pesos.[36]

Faced with such prices and a lack of convenient alternatives, the estate workers adopted the strategy of group purchases, but this action did not solve their plight. Given culinary preferences and the maize allotment, the peons endured a diet that was not adequately nutritious. Any variation from the basics of beans, corn, and salt carried a prohibitive expense. Eating meat was uncommon. The great volume of *tienda de raya* sales consisted of beans, chiles, and rice, plus very small quantities of fish and shrimp.

At the end of the nineteenth century the agricultural estates were still principally Mexican, but Americans and Spaniards held important properties in those parts of the country that became centers of future political unrest. The Spaniards established an impressive hold over the burgeoning sugar plantation region of Morelos, south of Mexico City. The development of a modern agricultural complex in the state of Morelos, the country's most prosperous and industrialized rural area, created job opportunities, labor mobility, higher wages, and a more complex social structure. The sugar industry led the way. In 1872 the mechanized sugar hacienda of Acamilpa paid its *mozos*, or laborers, which included skilled workers such as stonemasons and mechanics, an average of 44 centavos daily, more than twice the wage received by the workers at the nearby San José Buenavista hacienda. Even the *segunda*, or unskilled workers, earned 39 centavos per day. The administrator was paid 2 pesos for the same period.

When the Americans arrived in the Mexican countryside, they adopted the local labor practices. The economic differences between American and other foreign supervisors and technicians on one side and Mexican workers on the other, found at Rascon, Batopilas, Querétaro, and more than a thousand other places in Mexico before the great revolution of 1910, created separate and antagonistic cultural, economic, and social groups, dividing the Mexican and American populations that were otherwise living side by side. They reduced the merging of peoples and cultures that might have been expected and contributed to the creation of an industrial working class that historian Rodney Anderson has called "outcasts in their own land."[37]

MEXICAN LABOR ON AMERICAN PLANTATIONS

The greatest tension between American entrepreneurs and Mexicans of all social classes was created by the labor practices associated with plantation agriculture. In the late 1890s John R. Markley and Isaiah Benton Miller, both of Chicago, organized the firm of Markley and Miller to develop the resources found in a considerable area of the southeastern coast of the Gulf of Mexico. Markley was a prominent businessman and Miller his right-hand man. They located in the state of Campeche, on the western part of the Yucatán Peninsula, which separates the Caribbean from the Gulf.

As they developed their holdings, other American interests entered the area. By 1910 their neighbors owned a block of land extending from the Gulf of Mexico to the Guatemalan border. Those estates included the 400,000-acre San José de Aguada Seca of Phoebe Hearst, the 300,000-acre International Lumber and Development Company of Victor Du Pont Jr., the 604,000 acres of the Laguna Company of Williamsport, Pennsylvania, controlled by the chief of Marathon Oil, the 625,000 acres held by the Pennsylvania-Campeche Land and Lumber Company, the 75,000 acres owned by the Campeche Land and Fruit Company, the 1,610,000 acres held by the Mexican Exploitation Company, the 1,020,000 acres held by the Frederick Probst Company of New York, and the 760,000 acres owned by the Mexican Gulf Land and Lumber Company of Williamsport.[38]

President Díaz had granted Phoebe Hearst a personal exemption from the constitutional prohibition against foreigners owning land near the border, and he later extended the same courtesy to other American buyers.[39] The large American companies in Campeche owned well over half the land surface of the state. The companies exported chicle and hardwoods, especially cedar and mahogany, and converted some of the cleared lands to fruit orchards, farming, and henequen production. Their rapid gains in the area resulted from the initial consolidation of interests created by Díaz when he issued a surveying grant to Manuel S. Vila in 1886. That concession resulted in 1,630,000 acres passing from Vila through real estate sales firms to the Laguna Corporation, the Pennsylvania-Campeche Land and Lumber Company, and the Mexican Gulf Land and Lumber Company. At that point financial strength, transportation and storage capacity, and market demand in the United States propelled the companies toward profitability.

Markley and Miller replicated the successes of their neighbors, but their story is notable because the abuses that they imposed on their Mexican laborers are extensively documented. They began their operations modestly enough in 1899, when they purchased several fruit ranches and adjacent lands in Campeche. One was a 2,567-acre estate called Los Naranjos, which they acquired from the New Jersey Guarantee and Trust Company for the sum of $7,650. They then acquired neighboring lands, which also might have derived from the Vila tracts, purchasing them for similar prices in Mexico City and elsewhere. By 1904 Markley and Miller had consolidated a production complex of 20,000 acres and were preparing to expand.

Markley made the purchases, and Miller served as a witness to the contracts and then took over direct supervision of the land development program. The men were enjoying success despite the expenses incurred in clearing and planting, which discouraged so many American plantation development efforts in southern Mexico at that time. They raised henequen and other crops and cultivated rubber trees. In 1904, they expanded their operation by signing a contract with the International Lumber and Development Company of Philadelphia to manage the clearing and planting of 300,000 acres of land near their own. The International Company agreed to pay them $250 per acre for the first 20,000 acres they cleared. The directors of the International Company, including Du Pont, continued to market chicle, henequen, and rubber, keeping the proceeds while paying Markley and Miller through the sale of the hardwoods that they cut while clearing the land. The partners gained productive land without a cash expense.[40]

In 1904, by their own admission, they began the practice of employing debt peons. The partners justified the tactic by pointing out that it was legal under the provisions of Porfirian agrarian law and was customary, but they misunderstood the prevailing practices. Although Mexican employers did use their workers' indebtedness to hold on to them, debt peonage varied greatly between regions. In the mining areas of Chihuahua and other, wealthier, regions of the north, indebtedness was an individual contract between employers and the highly mobile workers they wanted to recruit. In the mining camps, the arrangement functioned more as contract labor. In the henequen plantation areas of Yucatán, it constituted forced labor, but the victims were Yaquis transported there from Sonora as prisoners of war. The plantation owners used forced labor more often, as on the Rascon estate, but the entrapment of mestizo Mexican citizens, rather than Huastecos, Mayas, and Yaquis, was a different matter.

Miller managed the enterprises in Campeche while Markley ran the distribution network for their products in the United States and obtained financing. They placed the headquarters for their operations at San Pablo, a camp on the estate of that name, and constructed a series of stone buildings including a civic structure, warehouses, a company store, machine and artisan shops, and houses for the managerial personnel. They also developed their own fleet for shipping lumber and henequen and bringing in supplies. Their largest ship, the *Vueltabago,* was a virtual seagoing barge. It measured 204 feet and drew only 8 feet of water. With those contours it could enter relatively undeveloped ports and carry enormous quantities of lumber across the Gulf. The *Vueltabago* cost $102,000. Their second vessel, the *Virginia,* had a 40-ton capacity. The partners also owned and operated three smaller ships, and they constructed a modern sawmill in Mobile to process mahogany and Spanish cedar. Markley found it imperative to work at least part of the time in Philadelphia, where many of the plantation owners were located, whereas Miller found it necessary to maintain his contacts in Mexico City, where he found new buyers from the United States.

At that point they hired E. Kirby-Smith, namesake of the last Confederate commander in Texas, to take over as the general manager of their operations in Campeche. Kirby-Smith, an American, was an infamous plantation developer who had managed plantations in the states of Tabasco and Veracruz.[41] When Kirby-Smith assumed management in 1905, he inherited the excitement of a dynamic and rapidly expanding plantation business that was clearing the jungle and reaping big profits. He used the debt peon labor system. Indeed, he already had 160 forced laborers of his own whom he sold to Markley and Miller for 23,663 pesos, complementing the 500 to 600 debt peons already working the land. Markley, Miller, and Kirby-Smith retained at least seventeen private policemen to enforce the company's prohibition against workers leaving the property before their obligations had been properly paid off. In defending their methods of labor control, the threesome did not claim that the workers were satisfied with their lot. They viewed the control of the workers as a problem, and they were correct. In 1905 the peons of the nearby Hacienda San Pedro, owned by the Repetto family of Campeche, rebelled, complaining of the "repression and bad treatment inflicted on hacienda workers."[42]

The strategies of Markley and Miller corresponded to those carried out by the other American timber and chicle plantation owners in the area. These firms engaged thousands of peons in the clearing of the tropical forestlands. By 1911 the representatives of the half-dozen American companies that dominated landholding in the southern two-thirds of Campeche claimed that they had "cleared the jungle," as though it was a notable achievement, from the Bay of Carmen on the southern coast of the Gulf of Mexico all the way to the Guatemalan border. They depended on the same profit-making strategies that their mining and timber counterparts used in northern Mexico, applying capital, incorporating technology, maintaining economies of scale, and exploiting the labor force.[43]

COOPERATION IN CAMPECHE

The carefully documented stories of the Laguna Corporation and the Mexican Gulf Land and Lumber Company reveal the competitive yet cooperative and closely linked nature of American private interests in prerevolutionary Mexico. Both companies originated with the purchase of land from Vila, who, like so many of the Mexicans who received presidential land concessions, lacked the resources to fulfill his obligations. He sold his grant in 1886, the same year that he received it, to the partnership of Luis García Teruel and Salvador Malo. After several deals García Teruel, a merchant-banker from the port of Veracruz with large land holdings in Chihuahua, Durango, and Puebla, controlled 604,000 acres in Campeche. Malo had about 580,000 acres. Malo then sold his share to the brokerage house of Sommer, Herrmann and Company, and Mavers, or gave them agency to sell it for him. In 1903 the directors of Mexican Gulf bought the 580,000 acres from the Sommer group.[44]

The Laguna Corporation waited almost two decades for its leaders to mobilize the capital that created the giant that their company became. The process began in 1903 when A. L. and James E. Moore incorporated in Maine and formed what they initially called the Laguna Company. They immediately bought 604,000 acres from García Teruel in Campeche that included 381,000 acres of land from the Vila grant. In 1909 the Moores sold their holdings to Vermont financier Charles H. Thompson, a director of the Colonial Trust Company of Philadelphia and a marketer of Central American hardwoods in the United States. Thompson, a noted advocate of minimum wages and social reforms in the United States, identified the resources in the Vila grant as "virgin forests containing cedar, mahogany and other hardwoods in larger quantities and of better grade than most of the other lands in Mexico and Central America." He paid the Moores $1,000,000 for the land, reincorporated in Maine as the Laguna Corporation, and took out a mortgage for $500,000 on the land with the German Trust Company of Davenport, Iowa.[45]

The directors of Laguna and Mexican Gulf had important similarities and differences. Both groups marketed chicle and hardwoods. The leaders of Mexican Gulf not only mortgaged their assets with the German Trust; they even lived in Davenport. The Laguna directors lived in Pennsylvania, however, and the two firms concentrated their sales in different markets. Mexican Gulf sold most of its chicle to the firm of William Wrigley Jr. and Company of Chicago, while Laguna marketed its chicle to the Sen Sen Company and other firms on the East Coast. Several other American interests in Campeche, including International Lumber and Miller and Markley, were also headquartered in eastern Pennsylvania.

Between 1909 and 1912 the leadership of the Laguna Corporation widened its financial base to include prominent figures from the Philadelphia and New York banking communities. Laguna's new directors included the president of the firm, Charles B. Fritz. Fritz was a son of Bessemer steel pioneer and Bethlehem Steel Company chief engineer John Fritz, director of the Colonial Trust Company of Philadelphia, and the head of the Fritz and LaRue import firm in New York. James Lichtenberger served as Laguna's chief counsel, as a director of Colonial Trust, and as a member of the advisory committee of the Pennsylvania Company for Banking and Trusts. John Gribbel, another director and a board member of the Girard National Bank of Philadelphia, tied Laguna to New York as a member of the boards of the Importers and Traders National Bank and the Leather Manufacturers National Bank of New York. Another director, investment banker A. B. Leach of New York, provided direct ties with the energy industry as a director of the Union Gas and Electric Company of New York. The leadership of the Laguna Corporation provided financial strength from Philadelphia and New York that was capable of developing the industrial complex needed for the sale of remote resources in the United States.

Despite being separate entities, the interests of the Laguna Corporation, the Mexican Gulf Land and Lumber Company, and the Pennsylvania-Campeche Land and Lumber Company overlapped financially in Mexico as well as the United States. In Mexico they frequently cooperated in their dealings with the Mexican government, and they sometimes shared port and shipping facilities as well as migratory labor. The strength of having two directors from the important Colonial Trust of Philadelphia, with another director serving with the Girard National Bank and two major New York banks, enhanced Laguna's ability to expand and take over the operations of Mexican Gulf Land and Lumber.[46]

Laguna and Mexican Gulf, like Markley and Miller, each achieved vertical integration through the development of separate railroad and port facilities in Campeche, their own shipping companies, and lumber mills located on the Gulf Coast. Yet they remained connected. The Mexican Gulf directors established a mill in Mississippi, while Laguna operated one at Mobile, and one of the Laguna directors served on the board of the Mississippi firm that handled some of the transportation for the Mexican Gulf Company. Despite competing for markets, the Laguna and Gulf leaders developed a strategy of cooperation. They filed joint resolutions with the Mexican government and joint representations with the American embassy.[47]

The expanding American interests in Campeche found equivalents in other parts of Mexico, and sometimes the same parties were involved in acquisitions of extensive tracts. Frequently the large American buyers obtained their land in sales from survey companies or from those who purchased tracts from the Mexican government. Apart from performing surveys, most of the sellers appear to have been mere land speculators operating on a grand scale.

On 28 July 1903 García Teruel sold 520,000 acres of timber in Chihuahua to the Pine King Land and Lumber Company. That land, like the property in Campeche, had been obtained through a survey contract accompanied by a presidential concession. In 1889 Díaz issued land titles for the property, known as Pino Gordo, to Ignacion Sandoval, who was identified as the "grantee." Sandoval wasted little time in signing it over to William P. Morrison, who conveyed the title to García Teruel, who in turn transferred it to James McShane, one of the leading lumbermen in the midwestern United States and the president of Pine King. García Teruel had closed land transactions of enormous magnitude in Chihuahua and Campeche, the extreme ends of Mexico, and within a few years important American capitalists emerged as the owners.

In the Pine King case, the John Deere Company of Moline and the Kemper Insurance Company of Kansas City surfaced as the major players ten years later. The separate negotiations of McShane and Moore with García Teruel for land in Chihuahua and Campeche overlapped. The Americans leading in the creation of vast American landholdings in Mexico dealt with relatively few people, particularly García Teruel, Matías Romero, Romero Rubio, and Valenzuela.[48] By 1909, on the eve of the Mexican Revolution, a conglomeration of powerful Americans was in place that would refine itself during the hardships of revolutionary turmoil and emerge in 1919 as a virtual monopoly in Campeche, but with other, far-reaching interests.

Although many among the American financial elite desired the annexation of northern and central Mexico, political leaders in the United States repeatedly cautioned against this desire because the people to be assimilated as Americans would be ill-bred, indolent, and incapable of self-government. The capitalists and political leaders agreed on a strategy of developing Mexico's infrastructure while taking a wait-and-see approach to the "Mexican Question" of territorial acquisition. Both groups anticipated hegemony.

Americans purchased enormous tracts of land from Mexicans whom the rural citizenry often viewed as usurpers, and in doing so they became part of the intense struggle between the elites and the disenfranchised. The Americans sometimes bought lands directly from survey companies that specialized in sales to Americans. The sellers had no incentive to warn buyers about property disputes and litigation, but courtroom arguments did not fend off the newcomers. Americans even bought lands in Sonora and the northern Sierra of Chihuahua that were being violently contested by

Yaquis. American developers did little or nothing to alleviate the situation. They frequently saw themselves as empire builders, and they viewed the Mexican working classes as inferiors—dangerous and stupid. While they frequently claimed to pay their workers more than their Mexican counter-parts, they usually did not.[49] By 1910, in the eyes of the Mexican national-ists, the American landowners had joined Mexican and Spanish hacendados and sugar plantation operators as objects of scorn.

8   Boomers, Sooners, and Settlers

We've come to work, we mean to stay.
We'll raise thy standard, win the day.
                From the official song and yell
        of the Juárez Academy, Chihuahua

During the late nineteenth century and the first decade of the twentieth century American immigrants entered Mexico as colonists and settlers in increasing numbers. Many of those who chose to live in the northern part of
the nation believed that those provinces would soon become a part of the
United States despite the fact that their economic and political leaders no
longer regarded the acquisition of Mexican territory as a desirable undertaking. American financial elites, facing the demographic strength and the
growing resistance of what they regarded as an inferior people, saw commercial empire as not only more desirable than the incorporation of territory, but inevitable.

As the American leadership turned toward economic control of Mexico
rather than annexation, an initial wave of Americans numbering in the thousands was settling in the sparsely populated but fertile valleys of Sonora,
Chihuahua, and Tamaulipas. In contrast to the politicians and financiers,
many of them viewed the thin Mexican population of the far north as too
weak to maintain control. They went to Mexico to fulfill personal ambitions
and dreams, but they were mindful of creating an American way of life. Calling themselves "boomers," they expected the U.S. government to protect
them, and they awaited the acquisition of these territories for an enlarged
American union. They would be sorely disappointed.

AN INFLUX OF IMMIGRANTS

American immigrants, beckoned by economic opportunity, followed the railroads that had opened the way into Mexico, repeating the pattern of exploration, investment, and migration that had typified development on the
American frontier. Just as the railroads and the telegraph and highly

profitable extractive industries provided opportunity for the richest Americans, cheap land and higher-status jobs provided opportunity for those who were less affluent. The railroads brought virtually every desirable region of the north within fifty miles of modern communications and transportation, while land development companies, many of them owned by the directors of the railroads, bought large tracts for timber, mineral, agricultural, and real estate development. Other entrepreneurs and the settlers' own leadership established colonization companies. Between 1900 and 1910 about 3,000 American immigrants entered Mexico each year, swelling their numbers to almost 40,000.

The increasing number of immigrants encouraged American businessmen to offer their services. By 1902 they had opened 1,112 companies and small businesses in Mexico, apart from mines, farms, and ranches, and had invested $511,465,166. By 1910 the numbers were considerably larger. A small group of about 160 American individuals or companies held over 90,000,000 acres, or 18 percent of Mexico's area, and some 20,000 smaller farmers held tracts making up another 40,000,000 acres. They capitalized agriculture and ranching, expanded the economy, and offered employment to Mexican workers.

The Americans also stepped into the middle of the deepening dispute over the ownership of land, frequently employing Mexicans to work on land that the local folk regarded as their own. Growing portions of the Mexican rural working and middle classes, which constituted almost 80 percent of the population, and a significant number of the elite provincial landowners were positioning themselves against a majority of the large landholders, government officials, and their ever less enthusiastic allies in the middle and working classes. The Americans became engaged in the controversy by purchasing former pueblo lands that had been denounced and outbidding Mexican private interests for desirable assets, including land, mines, and other businesses. This process had provoked deep stress in much of the nation between 1856 and the early 1880s and had led to economic polarization, disenfranchisement, geographic dislocation, and violence. It had not led to the creation of the larger, more stable middle class that the Liberals had envisioned.

In the United States land promoters announced their offerings in newspaper and magazine advertisements and in mass mailings. Many of the ads carried wild exaggerations as to the quality of the soil, the nature of the crops produced, and the climate. Slick salesmen, or "sharpers," on the border near Mercedes, Texas, made their pitch to prospective buyers in the spring and fall to avoid showing them land that was dry all summer, when the region suffered from oppressive heat. Their employers, including state judge Victor L. Brooks, Houston mayor Richard Brooks, and other Texas Company officers, also offered millions of acres for sale on the Mexican side of the river. The literature that attracted their clients referred to "giant ebony trees" in an area of Tamaulipas that was actually covered with mesquite and sagebrush. The land on the Mexican side, however, was cheaper than that in the United States, and it attracted Americans interested in small farms and the development of rural communities. In cities such as Colorado Springs salesmen sold land, sight unseen, in Sonora and Chihuahua.[1]

Kent E. Peery, president of the Williams Real Estate Investment Company of Ponca City, Oklahoma, described the situation in positive terms to Díaz.

> If we could locate a desirable body of agricultural land, preferably in the central or northern part of Mexico, and get the proposition financed by Mexican or United States capital, we are in a position to settle the property with energetic Americans.[2]

The American immigrants were searching for independence or a better standard of living. Mexico offered them cheap land and employment opportunities in the burgeoning railroad, petroleum, and mining industries. Some settled in the cities or bought private tracts of land, but the great majority came to reside in enclaves that were designed to accommodate their insecurities regarding an alien culture, language, and rule of law. Of the more than 25,000 Americans who went to Mexico as farmers, between 9,000 and 12,000 of them joined these communities, usually sponsored by colonization and land development companies. Development companies dominated the colonization effort in Tamaulipas, San Luis Potosí, Oaxaca, and Chiapas, but American colonists also occupied properties in Baja California, Chihuahua, Coahuila, Durango, Jalisco, Sinaloa, Sonora, and Veracruz. Most of these Americans possessed limited financial resources. The promoters and the Mexican government called the settlements "colonies." The American newcomers called themselves "sooners" and "colonists" as well as "boomers." While most of those who settled in the north expected to be annexed by the United States, those who established towns in Chiapas, Oaxaca, San Luis Potosí, and Veracruz hoped that protection would be provided by "their" government.

The colony method of settlement made sense for many of the American small farmers. Surrounded by an alien language, culture, and customs, the majority of them were intent on retaining their language, values, and mores. In eastern San Luis Potosí, several hundred American colonists and a few

American estate owners claimed most of the land covering three districts and inhabited by over 100,000 Mexicans of mestizo, Otomí, Nahuatl, and Huasteco descent. In Tamaulipas several American estate owners and two dozen oil companies joined between 2,000 and 3,000 American immigrants on the land. The same pattern of colonization and private ownership also took hold in northwestern Chihuahua, northeastern Sonora, Sinaloa, and the Isthmus of Tehuantepec.

In the less habitable areas, colonization played a minimal role. In Durango vast American holdings took shape in the timber zones and in the desert regions, where aridity required large properties for economic success. In Veracruz individual owners developed small but expensive coffee farms. In Coahuila the newcomers purchased large estates. The Seminole, Kickapoo, and Pottawatomie colonists in Coahuila held large expanses only because Juárez had given them the land as inducement to settle the area and deter Comanche incursions. Under Díaz, these peasants of U.S. parentage suffered the same displacements as their Mexican counterparts.

The San Dieguito colony, situated just south of the Rascon hacienda in San Luis Potosí, typified the strategy of the American settlers who purchased lots in groups from the land development companies.

> Each member of the so-called colony owned in severalty the land purchased by him, the term "Colony" being merely a designation to indicate a community or settlement composed entirely of citizens of the United States, engaged in farming, stock-raising, fruit-growing, gardening and other agricultural pursuits.[3]

The colony concentrated Americans in specific areas and minimized the assimilation of Mexican culture by giving the community a partially closed and culturally isolated character. The great majority, if not all, of the residents at San Dieguito raised sugarcane as their principal cash crop, processed it at the Rascon plantation sugar mills, and transported it via the Mexican Central Railroad. They supplemented that crop with products from vegetable gardens and citrus orchards, which also provided food for the colonists. Almost all of the colonists employed local Mexicans and used sharecropper contracts in lieu of cash. It is not clear if the small-scale American ranchers and farmers in this area used debt peonage as a labor strategy, but the practice was so pervasive that it could have existed.[4]

MORMON COLONIES

Given the importance of religion and idealism to Americans at the time, it is not surprising that various sects either established or attempted to undertake the development of colonies. Members of the Church of Jesus Christ of Latter-Day Saints began their effort to establish communities in Mexico in 1885. By 1910 they had developed nine prosperous settlements. Seven were in northwestern Chihuahua. Díaz and Dublan were located on the rich lands along the Casas Grandes River, and the three mountain colonies of García, Juárez, and Pacheco were situated on the equally rich lands along the Piedras Verdes River. Cave Valley and Chuichupa enjoyed the benefits of running water from streams. The two other settlements, Morelos and Oaxaca, were in northeastern Sonora on the Río Bavispe. The Mormon colonists came from all over the western United States, but principally from Utah, Idaho, and Colorado. Over four thousand farmers inhabited their settlements. Devoutness, a sense of mission, and American patriotism led nearly all of the Mormon immigrants to cluster together.

The Mormons entered Mexico for reasons related to, and yet distinct from, those of the secular colonists. Although like other immigrants they sought a better life, they left the United States in the midst of controversy. In the aftermath of the Civil War, the American government had established its authority and rule of law in the areas occupied by the Mormons, and during the 1880s the Church of Latter-Day Saints began to send its members to Mexico to escape prosecution for polygamy. Another, almost equally compelling, reason motivated Mormon emigration. They were impressed with the achievements of the pre-Columbian Mayan and Aztec civilizations. The indigenous peoples of North America, in the Mormons' view, were descendants of the Lamanites, a tribe of Hebrews who had migrated to America in about 600 B.C. and abandoned their beliefs. The Latter-Day Saints combined their search for refuge with a deep belief in a missionary obligation to convert the Native Americans. They believed that all of "Israel's descendants" would need to be "gathered"—converted and baptized—"before Christ's second coming." Mexico's indigenous population had attracted Mormon missionary efforts for several decades before they established colonies.[5]

From the outset the Latter-Day Saints met with a mixed reception from their Mexican hosts. In 1884 the church leaders sent a delegation to Sonora to investigate resettlement outside the reach of the U.S. government. Benjamin Francis Johnston, a member of the group and later a sugar magnate in Sinaloa, reported that the "normally suspicious and resistant Yaqui received them with open arms." Some citizenry and local officials in northern Chihuahua and Sonora expressed open hostility. Yet they were well received by the governors, the president, and members of his cabinet, who were anxious to attract "hard working" American immigrants. They could see the efficacious effect of European immigration on the society and economy of the United States. The Mormons were also pleased to find their beliefs attractive to some Tarahumara "Lamanites" and mestizos in western Chihuahua.[6]

In 1885 the initial group of Mormon settlers purchased a tract of land just west of Casas Grandes, Chihuahua. Several years earlier they had been warned by Governor Antonio Ochoa of Chihuahua "to beware of fraudulent land titles and worthless land." A title dispute soon forced them to give up their new property. After living in tents and shacks and enduring the hardships of hard freezes, insufficient clothing, food shortages, smallpox, and diphtheria, the Mormon settlers established a series of colonies. The immigrants were successful in this endeavor because, like their entrepreneurial counterparts, they turned the matter over to specialists. They spurned opportunities to buy three large tracts of land in northwestern Chihuahua that included the vast Corralitos hacienda for an asking price of $800,000 because they knew the neighboring villages of Janos and Casas Grandes had challenged the titles. The Latter-Day Saints thus avoided contributing to the antagonism that was growing prevalent among the local officials and Mexican population.[7]

The Mormons made their capital at Colonia Juárez, located in the hills a few miles west of Casas Grandes. They adopted an introverted lifestyle, keeping to themselves "culturally and politically" despite trading with the Mexicans and proselytizing them. They wanted to maintain their "American" way of life, and they paid homage to the flag on Independence Day. The Mexican elites, led by Díaz and General Carlos Pacheco, openly supported them, arranging land concessions and tax exemptions. Pacheco approved several land grants on the Americans' behalf. At the same time the distrust of local Mexican authorities began to percolate upward toward the level of statewide authority. Border guards detained wagon trains and marshals refused to carry out their law enforcement duties in support of the colonists. The governor of Chihuahua unsuccessfully ordered their deportation, and a standoff between national and state officials resulted. Pacheco intervened against the expulsion order, enabling the Mormons to remain. President Díaz apologized for the governor and urged them "to stay and help develop the resources of the country."[8]

In 1887 the Mormons established the Mexican Colonization and Agricultural Company as a Mexican company in order to purchase land from private Mexican sellers and the government with less difficulty. They planned to subdivide it and sell the tracts to individual Mormon buyers. Among their many acquisitions were 50,000 acres at Piedras Verdes, Chihuahua, 60,000 acres at Colonia Díaz, north of the Corralitos hacienda, and 60,000 acres at nearby Corrales. During the remainder of the nineteenth century the Mormons gradually improved their material conditions and increased their numbers. When the church gave up polygamy in 1893, the influx of settlers slowed, but the majority of those already in Mexico chose to stay, some because they refused to accept monogamy. Their numbers increased thereafter largely as a result of large families and material prosperity.

At Colonia Dublan, which was adjacent to Nuevo Casas Grandes, the Mormons developed a civic center that included a school and an iron foundry, while farther west at Colonia Juárez they constructed a furniture factory, a gristmill, a school, a cannery for their orchard and vegetable harvests, and other factories. The colonists achieved a high degree of self-sufficiency. By the end of the century, they were showing their agricultural and industrial products at trade fairs in Mexico City. Despite the growing size and prosperity of Colonia Dublan, they retained Colonia Juárez as their capital, perhaps because of its position in the hills to the west, which reinforced the settlement's autonomy.[9] Charles W. Kindrich, a State Department official, described Colonia Juárez in 1899. To reach the settlement one had to

> cross the foothills of the Sierra Madre Mountains. The road winds through passes and defiles until the colony, nestling like a green garden in the wilderness, comes suddenly into view. . . . The gardens are fragrant with flowers, and the blossoms of the peach, apricot, and plum trees glow in the pure air. Clear water from the *acequia* along the hillside flows down the gutter of each cross street. Neat brick residences are nestled amid grapevines and pear trees. . . . The capital colony is a beautiful village comparable to any in New England.[10]

The spacious, open front yards guarded by white picket fences and the two-story wooden structures with brick chimneys stood in stark contrast to the neighboring Mexican town of adobe houses, which presented only their adobe walls to the street, hiding the patios within.

The Mormon colonies flourished. Even the smaller settlements of Morelos and Oaxaca did well. By 1910, when the revolution began, the Mormon colonies were more prosperous than ever. Five hundred Americans lived at Colonia Díaz. The communities donated clothing, household furniture, kitchen utensils, livestock, and "sometimes even land on which to build a first home" to newlyweds, enabling them to begin their life in Mexico with some financial security. As Thomas Cottam Romney put it, "we had about all we could wish for." Eliza Tracy Allred reported, "For the first time in my married life we had on hand our year's supply of bread and fruit."

The Mormon settlers achieved a complex coexistence with their Mexican neighbors. The Americans were good customers, reliable, and relatively rich—perhaps too rich. They had earned the respect of some Mexicans, including Felipe Chávez, the highest ranking government official at Colonia Juárez. Local Mexicans held mixed opinions. Some thought the Americans were arrogant. Many believed the Mormons lived on usurped land and prospered by exploiting them.[11]

Ernest V. Romney arrived in Colonia Díaz in 1890, and for the next two decades he worked hard and became prosperous. His neighbors Milton Lowry Gruwell and Peter K. Lemmon Jr. also did well. By 1910 Lemmon held a large interest in the mercantile store and served as one of its managers. He owned a two-story, eleven-room brick house with three porches, a bathroom, and lightning rods. It was "well finished throughout" and had a value of $5,000. His barn measured 60 by 120 feet and sported a corrugated iron roof. He also had a one-buggy garage, a granary, a chicken coop, a hog pen, and a six-foot-high corral that measured 100 by 150 feet. The Lemmons employed Mexicans, but they expected the workers to leave at the end of each day. Romney, Gruwell, and Lemmon regularly paid their taxes to the authorities. They had befriended some of the officials, but others remained reserved and a few were confrontational.

In 1890, at the age of thirty, J. W. Palmer left Provo, Utah, and settled at Colonia Pacheco. Palmer established a farm, ranch, orchard, and store. He fenced the properties and raised wheat, horses, cattle, and hogs. By 1910 he owned two houses of five rooms each, one made of adobe and the other of logs. His residences, occupied by his many wives and children, were completely furnished and complemented by outhouses. Palmer built a barn and a silo and a garage for his carriage. His farming assets included poultry, several carts, and blacksmith and carpenter tools. His crops grew on 129 acres of land. The orchard had 170 fruit trees, of which all but 20 were mature and bearing. His assets totaled more than $15,000. His marital practices compounded the grievances of the neighboring Mexicans, who were Catholic.

Palmer and Romney were more prosperous than most of the Mormon colonists. The two men lived in the head settlement and exercised community leadership. Lemmon typified the Mormon middle class. The living comforts of his families did not trail those of Palmer and Romney by much, but he lacked the financial capacity for luxuries and travel.

In 1876, the year Díaz became president, Hyrum Turley was born in Beaver, Utah. As a young man he helped establish the Colonia Chuichupa, which was located in a valley in western Chihuahua thirty-five miles south of the other Mormon colonies. The settlement enjoyed access to the headwaters of the Río Bavispe, which flowed into Sonora. Like many of his compatriots, Turley had only one spouse living with him in the colony. They constructed a modest house made of dried adobe bricks. The house was valued at only $200, but Turley owned a sizeable plot of land on which he farmed and raised livestock. He dedicated some forty-four acres to farming and a larger plot to the support of his cattle. He "completely furnished" the house and built a "lumber barn, granary, and other outbuildings." He stocked the establishment with the "necessary farming equipment, wagons, harness, livestock, and poultry." His most valuable assets were his crops and his cattle. Turley and his family lived a hard but rewarding frontier life. By 1910 their belongings had an assessed value of $3,537.50. They had no excess cash, but they could satisfy their basic needs. Most of the people in Chuichupa were in a comparable economic condition—they were poor but respectable.[12]

The American religious settlers were good trading partners for the Mexicans, prompt redeemers of debt, and steady taxpayers. Despite these attributes, their closed cultural attitudes and sinful practices, including polygamy, alienated many of their Mexican neighbors. By 1910 their Mexican friends were warning them of that resentment and telling them that there was a plan afoot to seize their properties and evict them from the country.[13]

In addition to the Latter-Day Saints, the Knights of Columbus prospered in Mexico. The organization was created in New Haven in 1882 by Father Michael McGivney as a mutual aid society for Catholic men. In 1905 John Frisbie Jr., the son of Díaz's noted railroad adviser, founded the first chapter in Mexico City. The more important early meetings were attended by the national leaders of the American organization. Edward Hearn, the supreme knight, appeared at the inaugural gathering and Patrick McGivney, the chaplain, followed up, conferring rank on the leaders of the chapter. The American chapter of the Knights of Columbus in Mexico City claimed thirty-five "saxon catholics" and seven affluent Mexicans who spoke English. The leaders identified their membership by ethnicity and degree of Americanization. "Their only concession to local custom came when they called it the 'Guadalupe' chapter."[14] By 1911 the Mexican membership had grown and outnumbered the "anglo saxons," but Mexican critics complained vaguely that the "Caballeros" continued to operate under statutes "adapted to the nature and needs of American Catholics."[15]

COLONIES IN URBAN SETTINGS

The most affluent Americans in the cities joined their less wealthy brethren of the countryside in attempting the colony method of settlement. The presence of English-speaking neighbors reassured them, and their numbers provided the basis for an active social life. The largest settlement developed in Mexico City. Smaller ones developed in Guadalajara, Monterrey, Tampico, and Chihuahua.

American venture capitalists and land developers were also interested in urban colonies. They focused on Mexico City, developing the Paseo de la Reforma, Colonia Roma, the Calzada de Chapultepec, and Chapultepec Heights. In 1883 a consortium of New York businessmen headed by architect Stephen D. Hatch, financier Andrew Mills, civil engineer Samuel Keefer, attorney William Henry Butterworth, securities and real estate broker Thomas B. Lewis, and, probably, George Baker, chairman of the First National Bank, organized the Mexico Land and Building Company. The company acquired, surveyed, and prepared lots for construction along the Paseo de la Reforma, including a luxury hotel.

The directors maintained their headquarters on the fifth floor of Number 2, Wall Street, a New York City building that housed both the First National Bank and the Bank of the Republic. The directors of the Mexico Land and Building Company provided an integrated leadership that was as sophisticated in terms of the interplay of functions as the leadership of the railroads. All of the principals were connected with members of the New York banking elite, including Stillman and Morgan. From the 1880s until 1935, when the Mexican government completed the buyout of the Americans' remaining 50 percent interest in the nation's railways, the directors of First National took a leading role in the management of Mexican transportation and communications.

Hatch was an investment banker and one of the world's leading architects. He had designed the Corning, Norwell, and Roosevelt buildings and the Murray Hill Hotel in Manhattan. He took over the task of designing buildings for the Paseo de la Reforma, including an elite hotel with an estimated construction cost of 500,000 pesos. Mills came from a New York banking and railroading family that represented "old money." He served as a director of the Manhattan Life Insurance Company, the Broadway Bank, and the Stuyvesant Insurance Company and as president of the Dry Dock Savings Bank, and he mixed socially as a member of the Union League Club.[16]

Keefer, the owner of the Keefer Hotel in Manhattan, was a high-ranking civil engineer with the Morgan-backed Northern Pacific Railroad when he joined Mexican Land and Building. He had supervised the construction of the suspension bridge over Niagara Falls in 1869 and, later, the site of the Sault Sainte Marie Canals. The combined talents of Hatch and Keefer gave the firm leadership experience in architecture, engineering, finance, and management. Butterworth, a New York attorney, lent expertise in securities and international law. He served as a trustee as well as an incorporator of the firm. Lewis served as a securities broker and as the general manager of operations in Mexico City, where he took up residence. The combined talents of the firm helped make the extension of the Paseo de la Reforma and the residential zone west of Mexico City one of the most desirable areas in the capital region.[17]

In 1903 the Compañía de Terrenos de la Calzada de Chapultepec of Lewis Lamm, E. W. Orrin, and E. N. Brown undertook the development of properties west of the historic Chapultepec Castle and adjacent to the company's holdings. That year they entered into an agreement with the Díaz government to provide "paving of the streets and installing sewer system, sidewalks, etc. in 'Colonia Roma.'" Lamm then bought haciendas in the state of Puebla, one hundred miles southeast of Mexico City, and developed a major oil field there. His Chapultepec Land Company, an American firm that controlled Compañía de Terrenos, carried out urban modernization projects for the Mexican government. Nelson Rhoades of Cleveland served as manager of operations in Mexico and as general manager of its subsidiary, the Chapultepec Heights Development Company. In that capacity he oversaw the construction of the most distinguished housing subdivision in the nation.[18]

Rhoades served as a member of one of the most prestigious law firms in the United States, James R. Garfield and Nelson Rhoades of Cleveland. The firm enjoyed close ties with members of the government in Washington, D.C., the Standard Oil Company, and the New York financial establishment. That background placed him in a strong position with Díaz, who awarded him survey contracts accessing valuable tracts of property across Mexico. He used those arrangements to become president of the Oso and Navito Sugar Companies while still managing urban development projects. By 1913 the government owed the Compañía de Terrenos 917,994 pesos in unpaid bills.

The success of the company's urban development efforts in the capital brought ever more Americans to the scene. By 1910 some 12,000 Americans had registered as residents of Mexico City, but only the richest among them could afford Chapultepec Heights, later known as the Lomas de Chapultepec. John B. MacManus figured prominently in the Chapultepec social scene. He was a member of the steel manufacturing family of Camden and Philadelphia that had been associated with Rosecrans and Scott in the ill-fated Texas and Pacific and Tuxpan railroad projects.[19]

Guadalajara, the nation's second largest city, attracted Americans because of its relatively cheap real estate and pleasant Mediterranean climate. They congregated in "Colonia Seattle," the counterpart of Chapultepec Heights. Some of the residents were Mexican, as were some residents of Chapultepec Heights. The number of Americans in the Seattle Colony is unknown. Most were financially well-off, some even powerful. For example, Charles and Adelaide Dolley lived there until revolutionary conditions forced them out in 1914. Using Guadalajara as their headquarters, the Dolleys operated a network of Mexican enterprises that included a mine in Sinaloa and plantations in Guerrero and Chiapas. Many Americans concentrated in Monterrey, where George Brackenridge held real estate interests. Brackenridge lost interest in those ventures in light of his considerable successes in San Antonio, and he sold his holdings to American, British, and Mexican investors. Tampico Alto, on the high ground above colonial Tampico, attracted a wide assortment of American oilmen and suppliers.

PROMOTING THE LAND FOR COLONIZATION

Private entrepreneurs attempted to establish American settlers across the length and breadth of Mexico. George Blaylock, a real estate developer from Oklahoma and Houston, developed one of the most notable concentrations of American colonists. In 1903 he was the probable head of a consortium that bought the 174,000-acre Chamal hacienda in the southwestern corner of Tamaulipas. His position as the principal buyer is uncertain—more-powerful capitalists in New York, Chicago, and Los Angeles often emerge as the heads of such syndicates when in-depth company records become available or when a sudden death requires a full revelation of ownership of an American firm in Mexico before it can be reorganized.

The Chamal hacienda straddled the municipal districts of Antiguo Morelos and Ocampo, just west of the town of Mante (present-day Ciudad Mante). The Chamal hacienda was a rundown cattle estate with a variety of terrains: mountains, forests, chaparral, grazing lands. The Boquillas River made the low land potentially suitable for fruit orchards and farming if sufficient sums of capital could be committed to irrigation. The burgeoning port of Tampico in the new Mexican oil fields was 120 miles to the west, and its inhabitants were capable of consuming whatever produce the hacienda could provide.

By 1907 Blaylock and his associates had obtained a clear title for the land and clearance to subdivide the estate and sell it to American colonists. They developed a plat for the hacienda that divided the property into farms, ranches, orchards, and a town site. By 1910 Blaylock had sold five hundred farm, ranch, and orchard plots in 160-acre tracts to buyers in Oklahoma and Texas. The majority of the buyers came from Oklahoma, while Houston and San Antonio provided most of the others. Some of the land brought $1.00 per acre, about six times what Blaylock and his partners paid for it. Yet it was a bargain price for his buyers because comparable land in Oklahoma and Texas was selling for $1.50 an acre and more.

Many of the buyers came as families to settle and develop small farms and ranches. They bought guns and barbed wire along with their land titles. The settlers formed an association that purchased an additional 57,000 acres to augment their ranching capacity. Some of their Mexican neighbors resented them. The nearby *municipios* of Antiguo Morelos and Ocampo had been part of land disputes a mere twenty-five years earlier. Much of the violence carried out against the Americans in the area during the revolution of 1910 was committed by their former workers.

Seymour Taylor, one of the more successful settlers in the Blaylock Colony, came to make a better life for himself. He bought several of the 160-acre plots, employed a Mexican workforce, built a home, a silo, a barn, and other buildings, and fenced in his land. He planted one of his parcels with 1,500 orange trees. By 1911 that portion of his land alone grossed 18,000 pesos yearly. Taylor achieved success through wise land selection and investment. He bought land on the edge of the mountains and then diverted water from the mountains to water his crops. His orchard was the best in the colony because "the water being piped from the mountain brings his trees to bearing quicker and keeps them in better condition." His inventive strategy, however, contributed to the later demise of his estate at the hands of the revolutionaries. Mountains traditionally offered the rural populace of Mexico firewood, building materials, and water, which was divided between local estates and settlements—in this case the pueblos of La Roncha and Chamal Viejo. Taylor monopolized the water, firewood, and building materials. He either knew nothing of these arrangements or rejected them.[20]

In 1903 seventeen-year-old Flora Ellen Medlin, a native of Barton County, Missouri, came to the Blaylock Colony from Lampasas County, Texas, with her husband. Expending a considerable amount of cash for 2,000 acres of land, they built a "nice, well furnished home" of pine. They complemented the house with an American-style flower garden. Their property also included twenty-four "tenant houses." The Medlins developed a profitable combination of farming and ranching at Chamal. They owned barns, silos, and modern planting and harvesting equipment, which probably impressed the tenant farmers, who had not seen such expensive technologies applied to the land by its previous owners. Flora's husband, L. A.

Medlin, performed the function of a "dealer in livestock." The couple's principal crop was corn, supplemented by sugar cane and bananas. By 1911 they had 250 acres of cultivated croplands, and they had fenced the ranch, which enabled them to raise and sell cattle and horses. To cut their labor costs, the Medlins offered some of the workers sharecropping contracts. These workers planted beans "and some other stuff as well as corn."

Americans of adequate wealth applied technologies to the land that their Mexican predecessors had not, usually because markets were too remote and the cost of transportation too high. The construction of the Mexican Central Railroad from Tampico to San Luis Potosí and the Monterrey and Gulf Railroad totally altered the profitability of such enterprises. The pattern of American success with livestock and agricultural products at the Blaylock Colony paralleled that of the mining industry. Although the successes of American farmers and ranchers were less spectacular than those of American miners, the elements of success were the same: cheap transportation to previously inaccessible markets and sufficient capitalization to provide the latest technologies.[21]

South of the Blaylock Colony other American immigrants established four settlements along the railroads that terminated at Tampico. The colonists that settled in the southwestern extreme of Tamaulipas formed the communities of Atascador and Guerrero, while their neighbors to the west in the state of San Luis Potosí established Micos and San Dieguito. The affluent colony of Altamira, largely populated by oil company employees, was located north of Tampico. There were several other American colonies in both states of comparable size and similar circumstances, but San Dieguito was exceptional because of the closeness of the settlers and their appreciation for the beauty of the place.

Early in 1903 a group of American investors bought the Hacienda de Micos, located in the heart of the Sierra Madre foothills. They divided the property, more than 50,000 acres, into tracts for farming and ranching. It was a particularly beautiful region of the Huasteca Potosína, named after the indigenous people and the state in which it was located. Technically there were separate colonies at Micos and San Dieguito—the original legal name of the latter was "Elk City, Oklahoma, Mexico Colony"—but the entire area soon came to be known affectionately as San Dieguito. A prospectus described it with reasonable accuracy as "a beautiful mixture of prairie, timber, hill, and valley." The flat valley floor comprised some 22,000 acres. One hundred and sixty Americans settled the area. They raised livestock and poultry and cultivated oranges, hay, wheat, corn, and sugar. The Río del Naranjo, filled with game fish and wildlife, bordered the San Dieguito farmlands on the northeast for twenty-five miles. The town of San Dieguito claimed at least one medical doctor.

San Dieguito lay in the heart of a prosperous zone of American enterprise. To the north, the American-owned San Luis Land and Cattle Company had constructed a sugar mill with an 800-ton daily capacity. To the west, the enormous American-owned Rascon hacienda had over 1,200 acres of sugar cane and a processing mill capable of handling 1,000 tons. Twelve miles to the southwest, alongside the Mexican Central Railroad, the American-owned Tamasopo Sugar Company plantation had "over five hundred acres of cane and one of the finest up-to-date refineries in the republic." A plethora of smaller American sugar producers, farmers, and ranchers surrounded the settlers at San Dieguito.[22]

G. E. and Augusta Fuller bought nine numbered lots totaling some 500 acres of rich, level bottomland located between the town of San Dieguito and the railroad station at Micos. They raised horses and cattle, but their primary emphasis was sugar cane. They bought carts and wagons for hauling cane, plows, machinery, and tools and erected fences, barns, and a sugar mill. The mill featured a boiler, an engine, tanks, and evaporators in an adjacent building. The industrial facilities were worth some $6,000. The Fullers built a large home, a store, and a warehouse near the railroad tracks. They soon found that the sugarcane business was more profitable than retailing and converted the store and the warehouse into sugar storage facilities for themselves and their neighbors. Three large houses, valued at $1,000, were constructed near the mill for their American employees. Nearby they constructed a dozen *chozas* for their Mexican workers. By the start of the second decade of the twentieth century, the Fullers had 170 acres of growing cane and another 80 acres ready for planting. The yearly crop brought a $9,000 net profit.[23]

Many of the San Dieguito promoters established residency there. One was O. D. Jones. He retained a mixed farming and ranching establishment with seventy-five horses. The estate produced at least ten tons of crude sugar, known as *piloncillo*, each year. The income generated by its sales made sugar the most important crop in the region. Within a few years the settlers at San Dieguito and their neighbors were economically prosperous, and that attracted greater numbers of colonists to the scene. Jones, the president of the Tampico Real Estate Company, also held land in the American colony of Doña Cecilia, a suburb of Tampico. The realty, headed by Jones, W. A. Bowie, and Ed Williams, owned twenty-four acres, and Jones held an additional thirty acres of prime suburban land in Tampico. The three men specialized in the sale of homes that attracted American petroleum company employees.[24]

A number of individual settlers took up residence among the concentration of colonists along the border between San Luis Potosí and Tamaulipas. In 1908 Jasper Exendine, his spouse, a daughter, and two sons, all members of the Wichita Delaware Nation of Oklahoma, took up residence near Valles. They bought 2,500 acres of land known as "El Ojo de Agua" from Rinaldo del Campo, a banker and realtor in Valles, where they registered their property titles and paid property taxes. When Exendine decided to live "apart from the tribe to which he had formerly belonged," he became a citizen of the United States. The irony of becoming a citizen by leaving the United States underlines the nature of American immigration to Mexico during the Díaz regime. The newcomers came in search of opportunity, but very few gave up their U.S. citizenship. People who experienced "marginalization" in the United States became "Americans" in Mexico. The Exendines correctly regarded their citizenship as an important asset in Porfirian Mexico. They, and most of the other Americans in the eastern San Luis Potosí–Tamaulipas area, registered with the U.S. consulate at Tampico just in case they had trouble.[25]

The burgeoning oil industry and the rich potential for farming and ranching brought a larger number of American immigrants to Tamaulipas than to any other Mexican state. For the most part the immigrants came from Texas and the midwestern United States. The La Palma colony had an even larger concentration of Americans than did the colonies along the Tamaulipas–San Luis Potosí border. La Palma took root about thirty-five miles northwest of Tampico. In the first decade of the twentieth century an American development company purchased the Hacienda La Palma and "certain lands, adjacent thereto." Known to the residents of the area as the "Columbus Lands," they sold quickly because of their proximity to the port and oil refineries. American purchasers of modest means acquired lots and built homes. The La Palma settlers initially numbered about 300, but by 1913 some 600 American farmers lived there. Many of them developed truck farms to serve Tampico and the oil fields. Michael Bowes owned 40 acres, and Rueben Cox bought 20 acres. Jacob Gergen and George Graff, among the largest landholders, held 320 and 410 acres, respectively. Some of the oil company employees bought homes at La Palma for their families while they worked and lived most of the time in the oil fields.[26]

Several hundred American colonists made their way to Oaxaca and Chiapas in the far south. In Oaxaca, Frederick Stark Pearson, the magnate who owned the Mexican Northwestern Railroad in Chihuahua and various electric companies in central Mexico and South America, attempted a colonization project of his own. In 1904 Pearson and his associates bought the

58,000-acre Agua Fría tract in the jungle near the projected line of the Mexican Southern Railroad, which would run across the Isthmus of Tehuantepec from Veracruz to Salina Cruz. They had visited the site in 1903 and understood the challenge that awaited them. The tract was ideally located because crops could be exported to either coast of the United States. Pearson's group formed the Mexican Agricultural Land Company of Oklahoma and divided up the property that was adjacent to the railroad into town sites. They created a town, composed of American-style houses with streets named after heroes of the American Revolution, out of an older Mexican site named Medina. They changed its name to Loma Bonita.

Using the funds derived from land sales to colonists, they surveyed, "cleared" the jungle, and divided the property into three lots. In Lots 1 and 2 they created parcels of about 640 acres and then subdivided them. Their sales of properties from Lots 1 and 2 totaled some 18,000 acres. The purchasers included stockholders in the company, but in the great majority they were "persons of ordinary means, principally citizens of the United States, who were interested in small farms in a tropical and fertile section." Three hundred and thirty of the buyers were Americans. A few were Mexicans, who purchased 200 acres. The Mexican Agricultural Land Company kept the rest of the property for the production of tropical fruit, especially bananas, for export. In 1908 Pearson and associates sold Lot 3, consisting of 20,000 acres, to a group of farmers from Council Grove, Kansas.

Among the rush of new colonists were Henry Martin Pierce, Mary P. Pierce, and their seven children, who arrived at Loma Bonita in 1909. Pierce and his family had lived in Oklahoma. They purchased fifty-eight acres of land from the Mexican Agricultural Land Company at $10 an acre. During 1909 and 1910 the Pierces employed four or five men for six to seven months each year, clearing the place and planting banana, orange, and other fruit trees. The Pierces built a home, dug a freshwater well, and eliminated fifteen acres of underbrush. They planted a lawn in front of the house and fenced the twenty-five-acre area with barbed wire, placing the posts ten feet apart. The Pierces and their neighbors created a replica of the American dream in Oaxaca with their houses, yards, and small farms and plantations. Henry joined the American Colony and Fruit Growers' Association, which the planters had established in order to represent their interests before local, state, and federal authorities. The association also bargained with private interests over such matters as contract labor, freight rates, and shipping prices. The Americans were charmed by Oaxaca. They marveled at the colorful garb of the indigenous people, the bright flora, and the beautiful landscapes. Local male "Indians" stepped to the side, bowed, and doffed their hats to American passersby.[27]

Joanna Bogy, who settled in Durango as a colonist and established a small ranch, represents a level of wealth and educational background that stands in contrast to that of Cora Townsend, who took over the Rascon hacienda. Bogy was an intrepid woman whose story offers special insights regarding the diverse nature of the immigrant population. She is also another example of those Americans who found that they could transcend marginality by immigrating. In Mexico, Bogy was not "just a woman," she was an American woman.

Bogy gave birth to her oldest child at DeKalb, Texas, in 1887 and later moved to Sapulpa, Oklahoma, with two daughters. Her spouse had sold Sonoran real estate out of an office in Colorado Springs at the turn of the century, but his fate is unknown. In 1908 Bogy bought a 1,280-acre subdivided tract on the beautiful Santa Isabel Ranch in Durango from the American-owned Creek Durango Land Company of Oklahoma. Bogy paid $10 per acre for the land, a mixture of irrigated farmland, pasture, and high ground with timber. Her cost was at least ten times the per-acre sum expended by the operators of Creek Durango when they purchased the Santa Isabel from its Mexican owners only three years earlier. Bogy understood, however, that its beautiful locale, rich topsoil, pine timber, and running water made the purchase a bargain in comparison to prevailing land prices in the United States. Some of the property was titled to her two daughters, Annie and Lillie. Each held one 160-acre plot, probably purchased in their names by Bogy.

In February of 1909 Joanna took her daughters to Durango and established residence on the ranch. A few Americans joined her as neighboring rancho owners. Her daughter Annie was twenty-two years old, and Lillie was in her late teens. The region of Oklahoma where the Bogys had lived offered the family few opportunities for a comfortable lifestyle. The amount of cash that Joanna invested in the endeavor might have facilitated a small country store, at best. The family left the familiar behind when they entered Durango. The area was associated by many Texans and Oklahomans with banditry and danger, and the cultural and social expectations in rural Mexico were different from those of the midwestern United States and presented many unknown variables. Joanna was probably fulfilling plans she made with her deceased husband.

Beyond these considerations we have few facts regarding Bogy's background. She could read and write and had the know-how to negotiate with land agents, Mexican authorities, and Mexican workers. Bogy's purchase of land in her daughters' names suggests that she was setting an example for them as a woman who knew how to manage her affairs. She had the courage, determination, and ingenuity to leave her home, take her daughters with her, and successfully run the ranch.

Bogy's business strategy speaks for itself. In addition to buying the land, she purchased five mules, twenty head of cattle, and eight horses from Creek Durango. Her total investment was $15,000. The women operated the ranch as a single unit and marketed the corn, wheat, and cattle in the city of Durango, some forty miles distant. After establishing the rancho as a working enterprise, Bogy aggressively opposed the Mexican campesinos who, in accordance with local practice, harvested *lena,* or firewood, on her forestland. In the United States this was trespassing. In Mexico it could be a crime, but the practice was common and was provided for in written sharecropping contracts and land leases. Bogy put up fences in a vain attempt to prevent the campesinos from gathering the wood they depended on for heating and cooking. The conflict between Bogy and her neighbors was economic as well as cultural.

Despite their modest circumstances, the American women could afford to hire Mexican cowboys and farm workers by subletting plots of land to them for sharecropping. In that way they obtained inexpensive labor for the difficult farm and ranch tasks while escaping the much more expensive costs of farm machinery, which were a major obstacle to small farming in the United States. Given the Bogys' lack of capital, the enterprise they established would not have been feasible in the United States, where ranch labor was much more expensive. In Mexico not only was their operation economically rational, but it placed them above the hard work and perhaps limited independence experienced by rural middle-class women in Texas or Oklahoma in the early twentieth century. The Bogys enjoyed a lifestyle that included socializing with the elite among the farmers, ranchers, and businessmen who formed the American "colony" in Durango City.

Some of the Americans who entered Mexico at the turn of the century and established small farms and ranches were bold, as Joanna Bogy certainly was, but many Americans clustered in enclaves to protect or insulate themselves from their mysterious, "dirty," and sometimes hostile working-class neighbors. Typically, American colonists and small landholders did not understand Mexican culture, and few could speak the language. The Americans viewed the peasants' practice of gathering firewood on the estates where they worked as theft. The frequent holidays associated with Mexican Catholicism annoyed them and reinforced their stereotype of the Mexicans as "slothful and lazy." The drunken sprees of the poor frightened and repelled them.

Sometimes American "colonies" were quasi-private real estate acquisitions in which American entrepreneurs took advantage of Mexican colonization laws to obtain government support, but the "colonists" were largely Mexican sharecroppers. In 1909 John T. Cave of Alhambra and his partner R. L. Summerlin of Port Hueneme, California, purchased the 78,000-acre Hacienda del Río in the territory of Tepic, bordering the state of Sinaloa. The site was one hundred miles south of Mazatlán by sea or rail and blessed with the waters of the Acaponeta River. The large size of the river allowed for extensive irrigation projects on the hacienda, which featured some 69,000 acres of level land on which fruit and timber grew. The river was navigable for most of the year.

Cave and Summerlin incorporated their investment as the Quimichis Colony. The advantages of incorporation included a government concession for irrigation rights and tax exemptions that were linked to the promotion of immigration and land development by foreign settlers. However, the owners did not recruit colonists like the Bogys; instead, they populated the estate with Mexican sharecroppers. The arrangement, while not fulfilling the provisions of the colonization laws, seems to have satisfied the region's federal authorities. Cash payments frequently encouraged official approval in such situations. By 1911 the sharecroppers recruited by Cave and Summerlin had successfully enlarged the cultivated area of the estate from 4,000 to 12,000 acres, which they planted in corn, beans, cotton, and tobacco. Irrigation made the cultivation of corn for the Mexican marketplace a paying proposition, since the land irrigated with water from the Acaponeta River yielded 3,600 pounds of corn per acre. The timberlands included marketable cedar and pine. By 1912, when revolutionaries invaded the estate, it was realizing healthy profits.[28]

The entrepreneurial vision of Cave and Summerlin combined with the hard work of the Mexican sharecroppers to turn a desolate land into a profitable enterprise. The notion of colonization promulgated by the Americans to gain the government concession was also the source of their undoing. The Mexican workers living in pueblos around the estate, if not those employed on it, resented the wealth and power of the Americans. In 1912 self-proclaimed "Zapatista" revolutionaries from the neighboring settlements entered the property, drove away the sharecroppers, and divided up the land for their own use.[29]

PROFITABLE VICE AND WHOLESOME OCCUPATIONS

In contrast to the settlers who sought to develop agriculture and create colonies consistent with family life, an assortment of American businessmen chose to open bars, casinos, dance halls, and whorehouses rather than enter agricultural, industrial, or ranching endeavors. In doing so they gave the most important population centers in the border area a frivolous and even vicious stamp.

By 1901 an elite group comprising Carl Withington, Baron Long, and James Coffroth had emerged from among these Americans. Withington owned the Tivoli bar and casino, a "sporting house" in Tijuana. He paid the local authorities some $60,000 each month for "gambling rights." Known as the "Czars of the Bars," the three owned nightclubs, gambling establishments, and brothels along the border from the Pacific Ocean to Matamoros on the Gulf of Mexico. They also opened the plush Casino de la Selva in Cuernavaca, a resort and watering place for the Mexican elite some fifty miles south of Mexico City, and the swanky Foreign Club in the national capital. Withington, with Marvin Allen and Frank Beyer, also owned the notorious Tecolote Bar in Mexicali, where they paid the local authorities some $30,000 each month for operating rights.

The cost of prostitutes represented a fraction of the expenses that clubs incurred in the United States, and the promoters faced fewer restrictions for floor shows. The American bar, casino, and brothel operators in the border cities reinforced consumer preferences by dividing their prostitutes into two groups: those who entertained African Americans and Mexicans, and those who did not. The American entrepreneurs and managers in the vice clubs on the border assumed the same superior attitude toward the Mexican and American women who worked for them in the brothels as their industrial counterparts assumed toward their laborers. Their moral justifications for their undertakings, however, were quite opposite. Men such as William Dodge and John McCaughan supported Christian universities and missionary work. They equated their business enterprises with a moral mission that uplifted the Mexicans by introducing the capitalist work ethic and the virtues of individualistic Protestantism. In contrast, Withington and his cohort believed that the women they employed were degenerate. Why not, then, take advantage of what they would do regardless of circumstance?

Tijuana began to attract a cross-section of southern Californians that included Hollywood stars such as Charlie Chaplin, who frequented the track and sumptuous clubs, as well as sailors from San Diego, who patronized the less salubrious climes. Mexico's resort industry began to flourish when Rosarito Beach and the booming tropical resort of Acapulco claimed Errol Flynn, Betty Grable, Clark Gable, and Jean Paul Getty as visitors.[30]

The American organizers of sporting events such as baseball and American football openly expressed their desire to convert Mexicans from bullfighting and cockfighting to more "wholesome" American pastimes, changing their interests and behavior. Baseball and American football entered Mexico late in the nineteenth century. In 1877 American sailors disembarked at the port of Guaymas in Sonora and played a baseball game witnessed by the local citizenry. That same year the construction workers for the Mexican National Construction Company played a game at Nuevo Laredo. Presumably the American railroad workers and sailors continued to play at construction camps and port cities whenever the opportunity presented itself. Meanwhile a Mexican team at Guaymas challenged Hermosillo, and two years later a league emerged involving the townspeople of Guaymas, Hermosillo, Nogales, Cananea, and La Colorada.[31]

During the early 1880s teams made up of American railroad workers began to play in the capital, where there was already a sizeable American colony. The American editors of the *Two Republics* newspaper in Mexico City urged the residents of the colony to give their support to a league of teams made up of Mexican Central employees to ensure the successful introduction of "the American national game." The editors saw the introduction of baseball as part of their "leadership role" in bringing the Mexicans to "healthful and recreative outdoor pastimes not yet known." They believed that the wholesomeness of baseball, in contrast with the butchery of bullfights and cockfights and the gambling associated with these contests, would teach Mexicans patience, attention to detail, individual initiative, and constancy.[32]

In 1887 "large crowds"—"1,000 spectators" in one case—attended baseball games between American railroad workers in Chihuahua and Mexico City. At that point some relatively skilled Mexican players formed the "Mexico" team in Mexico City. They played two American teams and opponents from Chihuahua and El Paso in Sunday afternoon games. In 1888 the Mexican railroad workers formed their own team in emulation of the Americans. In 1889 Bernard Frisbie, another son of Díaz's American railroad adviser, captained a team of American railroad workers from Mexico City called the "Washingtons." They met another American team in a series facilitated by the secretary of the U.S. legation.

By the end of the century the sport had caught on, growing from sandlot teams to municipal leagues. In 1904 two leagues began play, one composed of amateurs, the other of semiprofessionals. In 1907 Charlie Comiskey brought his defending "World Champion" Chicago White Sox to Mexico City for a week during spring training. Ramon Corral, the vice president of Mexico, attended one of the games. A Mexican team, "El Record" of Mexico City, played the White Sox on 12 March and lost 12 to 2 because of poor fielding. The revolution of 1910 subsumed sports reporting for a full decade, but the games continued.

American football was not far behind. In 1895 George Hill from Austin, Texas, an investor in Mexican railroads and land, organized a tour by two college teams. The varsity football teams from the Universities of Texas and Missouri barnstormed the country, playing three games at Mexico City, Guadalajara, and Monterrey. Missouri won the first two encounters, and the third, played while the players suffered from "hangovers," was a scoreless tie. Small but enthusiastic crowds viewed the games.[33]

Other American sportsmen joined those associated with baseball, seeking to become part of Mexican culture. In 1894 Robert C. Pate, a Saint Louis horseman, built a racetrack at Indianilla, outside Mexico City. He introduced pari-mutuel betting and arranged for seventy-five horses, largely from Texas and Kentucky, to race against twenty-five Mexican steeds. The races, held in the fall, lasted two months, and opening day drew 4,000 patrons, including notable contingents of Americans and Englishmen. The metropolitan elite identified with the sport and its rituals. Horseracing prospered and in 1910 the Jockey Club, created by the Mexico City elite, opened its elegant Hipodromo. In 1883 Howard Conkling, a grandson of a former U.S. minister to Mexico and a relative of Edgar Conkling, made a well-publicized climb up Popocatepetl, the volcano that dominates the Mexico City landscape to the southeast. Americans took part in the introduction of boxing, bicycle riding, and even a yacht race at Veracruz. In 1891 a group led by Edward C. Butler of New York created the Lakeside Sailing Club in Mexico City. They staged regattas on Lakes Xochimilco and Chalco. In 1894 Butler became the first secretary of the U.S. legation.[34]

American intellectuals, artists, and political dissidents found Mexican culture to be an irresistibly romantic brew. They were attracted to the endless vistas of mountains and the clear air, the grand Arab-Spanish cupolas and patios, the distinctly indigenous element of the populace, the idealism expressed in art and song, and the direct contact with the past. At first they came to Mexico by the hundreds to study, photograph, draw and write, marry, live, and die. Later they came by the thousands. With them a new and richer cultural relationship came into being.

THE TRANSFORMATION OF MEXICO

Beginning in the late 1870s the Porfirian regime, empowered by foreign capital and the ideology of free enterprise, created a virtually free flow of trade.

In Mexico's metropolitan and provincial cities free trade meant larger enterprises and the considerable replacement of artisan industry with factory production. In the nation's byways it meant the growth of currency exchange and a reduced level of barter. The railroad began to dominate transportation, replacing the *diligencia,* burros, and horses. The telegraph increased the volume of communications, both commercial and personal, hundreds of times over. Liberal laws encouraging free trade and the development of infrastructure encouraged foreign capitalists to expand. By the late 1880s the influx of foreign capital and technology enabled the enlargement of factories and geometric increases in worker productivity. The growth of trade and the expansion of railroad, port, and telegraph services multiplied the value of mineral and timber properties, while complex and expensive technology transformed the extraction, milling, cutting, and transportation of ore and trees. These changes meant different things to peasants, workers, artisans, the *pequeña burguesía,* local elites, and the upper classes.

The transformation of the textile industry, which was the nation's largest manufacturing sector apart from mining, weakened the artisans, who were a fundamental part of local polity and culture until the 1880s. Factory owners needing part-time workers made the best of the difficult labor situation. They commonly established their facilities near autonomous pueblos and on or near roads that afforded them access to urban markets. This strategy gave the industrialists ready market opportunities and access to relatively inexpensive and scarce rural labor, although the workers came and left in accordance with pueblo and family needs rather than those of their employers. The workforce in the textile factories increased from a few thousand in 1876 to 32,000 by 1910, while the number of tailors decreased in number from over 41,000 to only 8,000. The new technology replaced artisan crafts with machine operator tasks and resulted in an alienated form of production that included remote points of consumption and the replacement of local leadership with absentee ownership, external controls, and a more regimented workplace.

Industrial and agricultural workers found more employment and, before 1906, sometimes gained higher wages, but they faced longer workdays despite higher productivity. For a quarter-century large and small mercantile and service businesses in the countryside gained from greater per capita consumption and a growing population. Only near the end of the century, when growing competition created the need for more reliable and sophisticated workers, did the ever stronger capitalists begin to establish their plants in the cities, creating an urban industrial working class. That development began after the Mexican elites achieved two major changes in their society. First, they removed the campesino pueblos from the control of land resources, and second, they attracted a massive infusion of foreign capital, largely French, which helped to transform the textile industry from artisan to factory production. Many of the dispossessed peasantry took up residence on private agricultural estates or at least worked on them, while the remainder migrated to the growing factory towns.

During this period the federal government subsidized municipalities, and state governments replaced the *alcabalas,* or local tariffs. The *alcabalas* were abolished because they had provided revenues to local governments and protected local producers from outside competition, which retarded commercial exchange. As localities became more dependent on federal revenues, a change in the balance of power at the local level took place. The artisans, the most literate and articulate members of the industrial working class, began to lose ground to the business, landholding, and governmental elites in defining local priorities. They lost their strength in community governments and their ability to control prices. As the national and state governments grew stronger, local elites lost their economic and political autonomy but temporarily gained greater prosperity through an integrated and more rapid exchange of goods. Free trade gave wider market access to capitalists from outside the municipalities, the merchants and industrialists of Mexico City, foreign businessmen, and the elites in a handful of provincial centers. The economy of Mexico had become more closely linked to the outside world.

The ideological changes compared, in their impact on traditional culture, with the religious, economic, and political transformation of the sixteenth century. In the rural sector, where over 80 percent of the people lived, traditional loyalties to the community on the part of some peasants, artisans, and local elites turned toward a concern for personal interests and income. Politically, the national elites asserted their desire to control events in far-removed places, while the more affluent among the rural *pequeña burguesía* increasingly asserted their desire to participate in national and state affairs. Local elites increasingly exercised the power of free speech as their business activities and mental horizons grew, while skilled workers and the surviving artisans emerged as the spokesmen for the new working class. Local elites became accustomed to the exercise of personal authority in the conduct of business and, despite their social conservatism, expected to enjoy civil liberties including candidacies for office at the national level. Political activism on behalf of liberalism, trade unions, and more extreme ideologies, including anarchosyndicalism, were articulated along with the pre-Porfirian social projects of elite political clubs and the anarchist, mutualist, and co-operative societies of the working class. Even Church-sponsored political groups reappeared at the local level before 1892 despite their political defeats in the 1860s.

Popular expectations grew after the first two decades of successful Porfirian programs. The experience of shifting from an artisan-based rural society toward a capitalist society in a more urban context caused Mexicans to believe they were capable of changing the destiny of the nation through concerted political action. The instrument for change was the federal government. The elites expected the government to perform ever more tasks in infrastructure and economic development, although they did not wish to pay the taxes needed for such improvements. Mexican peasants and artisans, although facing doom, were tenacious and inventive adversaries for the Liberals. They were fully aware of the legal and extralegal avenues of redress for their grievances. When their demands were crushed, any hope for participatory democracy was ended, at least in the short term.

PRELUDE TO REVOLUTION

By 1910 thirty-five years of economic experimentation was drawing to a close. Clearly, Díaz had succeeded in his quest to increase productivity in Mexico's mining, timber, petroleum, agricultural, and livestock industries, but there were fatal flaws in his strategy.

Foreigners held some 35 percent of Mexico's surface area by 1910. Americans owned the largest share—15,000 American owners controlled 130,000,000 acres, or almost 27 percent of the nation's land. Foreigners held over 60 percent of the nation's coastlines and border areas, and Americans held nearly all this area, just under 60 percent. Some 20,000 Americans owned ranchos. Some 160 American individuals and companies owned estates of 100,000 acres or more, totaling over 90,000,000 acres of agriculture, livestock, mining, and timberlands. This vast amount of land was in addition to the cross-country rights-of-way and the warehousing and other terminal facilities owned by the American railroads and their compatriots in Mexico's cities and ports. These figures are conservative. They do not include the over 18,000,000 acres held by the Lower California Development Company, which was almost certainly controlled by Morgan, nor do they include over 5,000,000 acres that I have been unable to account for among the 7,000,000 acres estimated to have been owned by William Randolph Hearst.[35]

The discrepancy in salaries between American supervisors and Mexican laborers reached a ratio of wild disproportion, 20 to 1 in the mines and 30 to 1 on the plantations. In contrast, the ratio between supervisors and laborers in the United States was only about 2.5 to 1. Menial labor performed by Mexican peasants produced raw materials that were exported out of the country. The standard practice was to apply sophisticated technology to raw materials only after they had reached the United States or, in the railroad, communications, oil, and mining industries, to reserve for American workers the jobs involving high technological skills. These procedures closed off opportunities for the development of skilled Mexican labor.

The difficulties encountered in the recruitment of agricultural labor, the labor shortages in commercialized areas of the countryside, and the use of debt peonage by hacienda and plantation owners continued and even grew in some places as a result of peasant cultural, economic, and political resistance and the imbalance of power between them and the landholding oligarchy. The refusal of local workers to participate in commercial agriculture in areas such as the Valle Nacional in Puebla, the Yucatán Peninsula, and La Laguna in Coahuila caused the powerful landowners and their managerial contractors to resort to *enganche* labor—contract labor—in which the workers were prepaid and therefore indebted, and more long-term peonage.

American landowners used forced labor in Campeche, Guerrero, San Luis Potosí, and the Valle Nacional in the southeast. In the Valle Nacional of southeastern Mexico, Americans invested two-thirds of the area's capital on only one-third of the land, yet they adopted the same forced-labor practices used by their Mexican neighbors. An investigator sent by the U.S. State Department described the system as "slavery."[36] The same condition prevailed in parts of Tabasco and Campeche. The Americans' labor strategy further angered opponents of the Díaz regime, who protested the inequities created by the administration's policies.

Mexico's foreign entrepreneurs directed most of their agricultural output toward the world market. Had these products been finished goods produced by highly skilled labor earning ever higher wages, more of their output could have been sold within Mexico. The limited domestic market received only coarse cotton and *piloncillo*, or granular sugar. The failure to develop a domestic market based on a burgeoning middle class doomed the Porfirian idea that commercial agriculture would provide the basis for modernization, as it had in Western Europe and the United States.

The northerners were driven to desperation when the Porfirian government refused to intervene in the economy after blight and drought repeatedly devastated harvests. Nor would it allow the political pluralism needed for a national debate of its refusal. In the south the decline of U.S. and European sugar purchases forced the plantation owners of Morelos to dump more of their product on the domestic market, which yielded lower revenues, while laying off workers. Many blamed the dictatorial regime for the economic failures just as they had credited it for earlier successes.

The capitalization of the countryside did increase production overall. Sugar output expanded fivefold during the first thirty years of the Díaz regime, reaching 2,503,825 tons in 1907. Henequen became a global commodity, and Mexican production, largely centered in Yucatán, increased eleven times between 1876 and 1907, when it reached 128,849 tons. Modern transportation and productive facilities enabled the American growers in Mexico to respond to the demands of the U.S. marketplace, but not to that of Mexicans.

Had Díaz succeeded in creating a larger group of middle-sized farmers among the Mexicans themselves? The answer is a qualified yes—and therein lies a basic reason for the revolution of 1910. Over 90 percent of the municipal common lands, which had constituted some 25 percent of the nation's surface area, had been acquired by local and higher-level Mexican elites through the application of the privatization laws. By the end of the Porfiriato a small group of private landowners, both Mexican and foreign, had increased the amount of property under their control to about 85 percent of the nation's surface area. Mexican hacendados, or larger holders, numbered over 8,000. Other Mexican private interests totalled about 48,000 small farmers and rancheros, or middle holders—a fivefold increase.[37] The Mexican private owners represented no more than 2 percent of the rural population.[38] The Mexican government held another 13 percent of the nation's lands in *terrenos nacionales,* largely in remote regions. Díaz had envisioned a modern economy based on commercial enterprise, but this group of landowners was too small to provide the domestic market necessary for vigorous economic growth. Many rural Mexicans fell into occasional labor, underemployment, and misery.[39]

In contrast, the educated and commercially active sectors of the Mexican populace had developed a much higher level of public interest than had their ancestors. More people were literate and wished to participate in public policy than ever before. The economic stagnation, their political exclusion, and the obviously preferential positions enjoyed by the oligarchy and foreigners combined to create the desire to replace the government with a popular democratic regime. The economic decline and the failure of dialogue caused rural agricultural workers, miners, townspeople, the *pequeña burguesía,* and provincial elites to join in a chorus of increasingly radical dissent. It was during the last five years of this crisis that the influx of Americans to Mexico reached its highest level.

The district of Cuencame, Durango, serves as an example of the unworkable and distorted situation that developed as a result of Díaz's policies. In 1910 fourteen landholders, at least two of them Americans, held 1,185,900 hectares, or over 99 percent of the area. The three municipalities in the district, with a combined population of 6,400, owned 8,200 hectares, or less than 1 percent. The land was arid, with almost no irrigation, and large sections were necessary for ranching success. In addition, the three former pueblos had been stripped of their rights as incorporated entities and declared mere *rancherías,* unincorporated places characterized by small populations that lived in huts. *Rancherías* were subject to the decisions or whims of the landowners. In early 1909 the owner of the Hacienda de Sombreretillos invited the representatives of the settlements to negotiate their differences with him. On 20 January the state police stood at the side of the owner as he greeted the four campesino leaders. The workers were shot to death on the spot. The working class of the area became radical agrarians, rallied to Calixto Contreras, and soon joined the Villista revolution.[40]

The colonists in Durango such as Joanna Bogy and her daughters and resident entrepreneurs such as John McCaughan and his family became enmeshed in a much wider conflict that began among the Mexicans themselves and grew to include the foreigners living in Mexico. Chinese and Spanish residents were at risk, but anti-Americanism became one of the important aspects of the Mexican Revolution. It deeply affected the lives of the tens of thousands of American colonists and citizens living in Mexico.

A few of the elite American businessmen and politicians who worked closely with top officials in the Mexican government to promote American investments, protect American concessions, and develop the nation's infrastructure advocated a form of political pluralism. Many of them and their professional and working-class counterparts, however, practiced residential segregation while enjoying great advantages in earnings compared to their Mexican neighbors. The settlers and colonists, seeing themselves as the "backbone" of American society, the developers of frontiers, and the clearers of jungles, painstakingly built their homes and workplaces in Mexico. They ignored the land disputes between the rural working class and the government officials even though those disputes often involved their land. As they grew comfortable and even prosperous, most chose to remain apart from Mexican society. Often they employed local Mexicans as day laborers to work on lands that the rural revolutionaries claimed had been "usurped." Usually their children married among their "own kind." The Americans who chose this course failed to merge culturally with their Mexican neighbors. Those who lived among the Mexicans as individuals, merging culturally and sometimes intermarrying, fared far better when the rural Mexicans became revolutionary.

President Lerdo had warned his fellow Mexicans of the dangers of foreign economic control. Obviously the Americans had achieved that control, but was it dangerous? Threats to American businesses or investments in Mexico directly inconvenienced and angered the leaders of Amalgamated, ASARCO, AT&T, International Harvester, Phelps Dodge, Southern Pacific, Santa Fe, Standard Oil, Texaco, and IMM. For this reason most of the American economic leadership found President Díaz acceptable—and they expressed extreme displeasure with Mexican political reform movements. The manifest power of the Americans alarmed the nationalists, who saw their country being engulfed. Even Díaz sought relief by giving Englishmen, Canadians, French, and Germans concessions for mining, oil, lighting and power, and colonization.

Abundant evidence indicates that the Mexican economy was distorted, driven neither by internal consumption nor by the production of essential goods for export unobtainable elsewhere. Government expenditures in support of largely foreign-owned transportation and communications infrastructure drove up the debt, while a flood of imported manufactured goods undercut the value of the peso. Protesters claimed that the Díaz administration's purchase of half of the nation's railroad shares had been made at an inflated price, and they faulted the president for accepting the continued control of the New York directors. In 1905 Díaz decreased the value of the peso from one dollar to fifty cents, putting Mexican businessmen at a severe disadvantage with Americans in the competition for the purchase of new properties.

Other problems soon appeared. Conditions in Mexico and the American financial panic of 1907 and 1908 combined to dry up the availability of new capital. New construction slowed to a crawl and left thousands of railroad track layers, bridge builders, and tunnel excavators unemployed. The economic crisis in the United States provoked declines in Mexico's key export industries of mining, sugar, and timber. Between 1909 and 1910 the rate of American consumption of Mexican products dropped by 1 percent, and prices contracted. The setback rippled through the Mexican economy. In the harvest of 1909 and 1910, the reduced value of sugar produced in Morelos brought about a 7 percent decline in production. The plantation and mill owners reacted by laying off thousands of workers in the state, provoking widespread unrest.

Corn harvest failures in Durango, Chihuahua, and Coahuila in 1908 and 1909 caused domestic shortages because commercial growers shipped much of the surviving crop to the American market. The Mexican government imported low-quality corn that was produced as cattle feed to nourish a starving populace. Riots occurred in several northern cities. The International Railroad of Mexico, now owned by the Southern Pacific, carried 18 percent less freight than it had in previous years, reflecting reduced output and unemployment in timber and mining in the states of Coahuila, Durango, and Chihuahua. Between 1895 and 1910 agricultural wages declined 17 percent, while industrial real wages dropped from 1.92 pesos daily in 1897 to 1 peso in 1907.[41]

No reliable data are available, but the period from 1908 through 1910 was even more dire. Meanwhile, global increases in the cost of food and cotton had a drastic impact on Mexican buyers. Between 1900 and 1910 chile and bean prices increased 193 percent and 64 percent, respectively. Between 1907 and 1910 corn prices shot up 38 percent and wheat 20 percent. In sum, many of the products exported from Mexico dropped in value while the costs of imports and necessities shot up. The weakness of the domestic market against stronger global prices led to the exportation of high-quality products and their substitution with inferior goods. Corn was one such product.

Díaz's policies had produced an unstable economy that benefited relatively few. It had failed to sustain the economic expansion that characterized its first twenty-two years and had shifted the burden of that failure to the working class and the less affluent through the devaluation of the peso, government-endorsed reductions in salary, and longer working hours. The peasantry had been unprepared for the commercialization of commodities and the dislocations of the Industrial Revolution, and they now suffered indescribable misery. Miners and artisans had been denied political expression, and the local and provincial elites lacked political representation. The combination of economic hardship and frustration combined to create a form of political dissension. The dissension was sustained by a widely based popular desire for fuller public participation in decision making and social benefits. It also stemmed from resentment toward Americans and other foreigners, a resentment that had been exacerbated by inside dealings between the highest officials in the Díaz regime and American capitalists.

The Díaz regime had merged the economic leadership of foreign capitalists with the mandates of Mexico's traditional oligarchy and the political leadership in Mexico City. Many Mexicans resented the power and wealth that Americans often manifested to excess. The tension between the Mexican public and the foreigners added a deepening nationalistic dimension to the struggle for political power in Mexico.

Early in the twentieth century critics of the Díaz regime began to point at inefficiencies, and then corruption, and the government and the economic elites proved unequal to the task of assuaging the growing discontent. The Porfirian experiment with free trade and foreign investment ultimately led to disaster for the nation, as a brokenhearted José Ives Limantour later admitted when he said, "We created a social nightmare."[42]

When an economy prospers, the difficulties of modernization can be overcome despite human tragedies, as evidenced in the United States and western Europe, where increasing numbers of people prospered. In contrast, the economic well-being of the Mexican masses, and the local and provincial elites as well, began to erode in the late 1890s. By 1910 a stark contradiction existed between the expectations that had been created by Díaz's policies and the reality of life.

In Mexico growth depended on a process of dependent development—the importation of foreign capital. The failings of the Díaz regime did not become critical until the effects of foreign capital had passed through two of three phases. In the first phase, new investments led to the development of transportation and communications in the form of enlarged and improved ports, streets, and highways, the telegraph, and the railroads. The capital was also used to purchase mines and large tracts of land. The second phase included the application of new, expensive, and sophisticated technology for the handling of timber and minerals, and the organization of land resources for the production of agricultural goods and livestock. It was in the third phase, that of integrating the domestic market by paying wages adequate for greater consumption, that foreign capital faltered. Political instability arose when the flow of foreign capital became erratic, when it was not directed toward needs dictated by changing economic conditions, or when it contradicted the expectations of the public.

The decline in Mexico was widely repeated throughout the world at the end of the nineteenth and in the early twentieth century. The global breakdown of modernization programs took place because of repatriated profits, the imbalanced distribution of benefits, and governmental fiscal insolvencies rooted in the devaluations of silver-based currencies, higher interest rates, and the uneven flow of foreign capital. The lack of growth in domestically oriented businesses and in goods for local consumers and the failure to pay wages commensurate with the greater value of the output produced by workers undermined the regimes in Iran, China, and Russia as well as Mexico. In each nation local citizens acted out their resentments toward their oligarchies and foreigners, and each underwent dramatic political change. In Mexico the oligarchy experienced revolutionary upheaval while the Spanish sugar plantation owners in Morelos, Chinese merchants in the northwest, and Americans everywhere suffered nationalist violence.

Part III

THE YEARS OF REVOLUTION,
1910–1940

9 Mexico for the Mexicans

In general the lower people are beginning to act upon the principle
that might is right and what is here in the country belongs to them
and that all that remains for them to do is to take it.

> Walter Brodie, chief engineer,
> Batopilas Consolidated Mining Company, 1913

[The] agitation and discussions now going on in . . . Mexico with
reference to the ownership and the operation of properties owned
by citizens of other countries . . . has seriously disturbed the
investing public in the United States.

> Daniel Guggenheim, letter to Porfirio Díaz, 1908

The policies of President Díaz were, ultimately, a terrible failure. The Porfirian program of privatization and foreign investment had enriched the oligarchy, failed to deliver economic betterment for the majority, and denied the latter group political power. By 1910, when the revolution began, American financiers and industrialists had successfully established their dominance in Mexico and were strengthening their interests in other nations. They were gaining greater influence in Panama, the Caribbean, and the rest of Central America compared with their European partners and were participating as junior associates of their British partners in South America, Africa, and Asia. The revolutionary challenge in Mexico began as a call for a more participatory government and agrarian reform, but it quickly deepened into a broad-based cultural, political, and nationalist rejection of the political elites in the nation's capital, the great estate owners, and the foreign capitalists—for the most part, Americans.[1]

AMERICANS CAUGHT IN THE MIDDLE

A nationalistic backlash was under way. The influx of American emigrants, which exceeded 3,000 each year in the early 1900s, alarmed a growing number of Mexicans. The foreigners came as property owners, businessmen, miners, petroleum engineers, railroad workers, farmers, and ranchers. They created the economies of scale that generated wealth in the Mexican mining, oil, timber, farming, and ranching industries, and they provided hope for economic growth and fostered the expectation of a greater good for the many. The growth of the Mexican rail network had made the most remote areas of the country accessible, and the Americans who sought to farm and ranch settled in large numbers in the northern states and along the coasts and, to a lesser degree, on the Isthmus of Tehuantepec and Chiapas.

By 1910 more than 40,000 Americans resided in Mexico. Most colonists chose rural settings, but significant numbers, perhaps 20,000, opted to live in cities and towns. Twelve thousand established themselves in Mexico City. Wherever they went, land values skyrocketed, and it did not matter if the properties were urban or dedicated to agriculture, timber, mining, oil, or ranching. Land prices in the more densely populated valleys of central Mexico were so high that only the wealthier newcomers could buy land there.

Mexican critics noted that the benefits of industrialization were going principally, if not entirely, to the Americans and a handful of rich Mexicans. The opposition saw the small group of Mexicans who made up the nation's economic and political elite as "sellouts"—conspiring opportunists who were opposed to democracy. The emerging revolutionary consciousness believed these problems to be internal in origin but inextricably linked to American interests. A leading political opposition group, the Partido Liberal Mexicano, expressed the feelings of its members in a banner headline on the front page of its newspaper, *Regeneración:* "Mexico for the Mexicans." The democratic expectations of Mexico's citizens had been reinforced by the Americans' practice of suffrage for white men, their rhetoric of democracy, and the search for individual opportunity, material success, and happiness. These American goals enthralled the Mexicans, but the outcomes seemed to point in the opposite direction.

The presence of tens of thousands of Americans in the cities and rural areas of Mexico and their ownership of businesses and properties placed them in the middle of the agrarian and nationalistic upheaval. Between 1910 and 1914, peasant and local elite groups, most of them free of external controls, violently attacked American landholders and their foreign and elite Mexican counterparts. The stories of what happened to them during the revolution are as dramatic as their pioneering efforts during the previous forty-five years.

In 1910 Francisco Madero, an heir to a family empire in the northern state of Coahuila, was nominated as the presidential candidate of the anti-reelectionist party, which opposed Díaz's reelection. Díaz, surprised by Madero's campaign and disturbed by his rhetorical attacks on Díaz's administration, had Madero jailed and rigged the election. After being released on bail, Madero fled to Texas, where he made plans for the overthrow of Díaz. Madero's revolutionary document, the Plan de San Luis Potosí, called for the revolution to begin on 20 November 1910.

The early phase of the uprising seemed mild. American colonists in the cities experienced a preliminary wave of anti-foreign unrest in November 1910 after the lynching of a Mexican national at Rock Springs, Texas. At Guadalajara two nights were particularly dangerous. Since 1900 the American population of the city had doubled from an estimated 275 to 500. The Americans were concentrated in an affluent foreign area known as the Seattle Colony. Following the practice of Americans throughout Mexico, the Americans in Guadalajara had developed real estate, mercantile, and industrial concerns while operating Protestant missions and schools, including one attended by a sizeable number of Mexican girls. As in other places, anti-Americanism surfaced occasionally, usually in conjunction with Independence Day celebrations on 16 September, when crowds mixed shouts of "Long Live Mexico" with anti-foreign epithets, including "Death to the Yankees," and anti-Protestant slogans. The unrest had a cross-class nature. Participants included artisans, students, peasants, and members of the middle class.

On 10 and 11 November 1910 angry citizens formed crowds that marched through Guadalajara, attacking American residents, homes, and businesses. One focus of their attack was the residence and person of Charles Carothers, a member of a land-owning American family in Saltillo. Carothers ran the West End Realty Company, a firm noted for the sale of large tracts of land, much like that of the equally resented John McCaughan in Durango. The rioters stoned "definite targets: wealthy and/or Protestant Americans . . . and damaged sites that visibly symbolized the ostentatious American presence and arrogant dominance, which were the focus of their anger." Similar anti-American rioting took place in Mexico City, Puebla, and other cities. In Guadalajara and Mexico City the government failed to act against the unrest at the onset and may have tried to use the Rock Springs incident to direct public attention away from Mexico's internal crisis. If that was the case, the strategy backfired in the capital, where the crowds quickly turned on President Díaz.[2]

Unrest among the industrial workers and the *pequeña burguesía* in the urban areas quickly spread to the sugar mill and field workers of Morelos, whose parents had lost their village communes in the 1850s and 1860s. They joined the miners and townspeople of the north, demanding the return of their land and resisting a government that had offered no relief to the unemployment and food shortages that stalked them after 1906.

Immediately after 20 November, violence erupted at the Stephens brothers' holdings at Cacalutla and El Potrero, near Acapulco. In the following months and years, the rural populace working in and around the estates raided the properties, cut down the trees, and finally occupied parts of them, planting beans, corn, and other staples. Claiming Zapatista and other allegiances, the peasants confiscated the cattle, destroyed the fences and outbuildings, and carried away the supplies and equipment. As Stephens put it later, "Just before the outbreak of the Mexican revolution, we were a prosperous and progressive company. . . . When the revolution ended we were ruined men."[3]

The military successes of Madero supporters Pascual Orozco and Francisco Villa, who seized Ciudad Juárez in May 1911, triggered small uprisings across Mexico and persuaded Díaz to resign the presidency and agree to free elections. Díaz's resignation was also influenced by the growing strength of the revolutionary forces in the south led by Emiliano Zapata. Zapata was a leading citizen of the pueblo of Anenecuilco in eastern Morelos. The land in this rural area had been increasingly capitalized and privatized from the 1840s through the 1870s, anticipating events that later occurred throughout most of the nation. Highly capitalized sugar haciendas occupied the lands formerly held by the pueblos. The wages that the hacendados paid exceeded those earned by campesinos anywhere else in central Mexico, and this produced a certain degree of stability among the rural citizenry. When a crisis in sales and declining income affected the sugar industry in the years immediately preceding the revolution, the long-smoldering resentments of a minority of the region's pueblo citizenry suddenly erupted. Zapata, a horse trainer and head of the Anenecuilco Defense Council, assumed the responsibility of leadership.

Zapata and his advisors created a legacy of idealistic revolutionary proclamations that explained in absolute terms the plight of the rural people who had been dispossessed. Zapata once complained that the rich in Mexico City took better care of their horses than of the people. His declaration "I would rather die on my feet than live on my knees" is one of the more endearing sentiments attributed to him. His idealism and evident unselfishness attracted an intense following among the campesinos in south-central Mexico and, in the far north, locally based rebel bands in Sinaloa, Tamaulipas, and the province of Tepic. The followers called themselves Zapatistas.

After Díaz agreed to free elections, the rebels pulled back, establishing relative accord across Mexico. Further incursions would have lacked legitimacy, since Madero had made peace and had promised them "justice." The elections in October were a triumph for Madero, and in November he replaced Díaz as the Mexican president. Madero enjoyed the support of the American oil companies as well as an important array of Texas interests in Mexico. Joseph Cullinan of the Texas Company and the Rockefeller brothers of Standard Oil had been frustrated by the denial of concessions during the Porfiriato, and they had welcomed Madero's revolution because, as Cullinan put it, they could conduct their affairs "without the constant nightmare of being sandbagged at every turn of the road."[4] Despite the social conservatism of Madero and most of his closest associates, the men who had rallied to put him in power seemed universally radical to some of the Americans with whom they had contact. The Americans feared that Madero and his supporters planned "to completely Mexicanize the railroads."[5] American ambassador Henry Lane Wilson longed for the restoration of law and order by way of a military takeover.

The indirect concessions of *terrenos baldíos* through Mexican *prestanombres*, or middlemen, to foreigners were a source of great tension between the native landowners and the foreign entrepreneurs. Mexican agrarians and elites in the more intensely affected areas grew resentful as the number of American holdings grew. The Mexicans' attitude toward wealthy foreigners in their country had changed, as noted by the American owner of a silver mine in Zacatecas:

> My Mexican servant failed to appear with my saddled horse ready for the trip, until too late. While scolding him in the office for his delinquency, a head was thrust into the door, and a voice shouted; "Why are you abusing the servant?" Shortly after, a man entered, after opening the door without asking permission, and I was told in harsh emphatic tones, that the revolutionary government would no longer suffer servants being spoken to like slaves. Asking whom I had the honor of addressing, the intruder introduced himself as the "*jefe politico*," the practical governor of Zacatecas City.[6]

Each time the local citizenry challenged the Americans' land titles the foreigners sought to upgrade them. In 1911 the officers of the U.S. and Mexican Realty in Durango became alarmed by the hostility of the citizenry and petitioned President Madero to authenticate their land titles. The following year Madero, seeking good relations with the powerful Americans, obliged. In one case Madero acted on behalf of William H. Dent of the Durango Land Company. Dent needed authentication of his title to the 157,000-acre Hacienda El Salto, which the local citizenry disputed. El Salto held some of the finest timber in northwestern Mexico and had attracted powerful American owners. In 1913 the Bank of California proved that it actually owned Dent's land titles and foreclosed on El Salto for mortgage nonpayment.[7]

One of the greatest concerns of the victorious leadership around Madero, and of the defeated government, was the restoration of order, and Madero's choices in the selection of new state governors revealed that order was his highest priority. Indeed, some of the appointees were men who had not even taken part in supporting the revolutionary movement that deposed Díaz. In addition, Madero retained intact the officer corps and the regular army. His strategy went even further—he disbanded the revolutionary forces. In taking those steps Madero disappointed ambitious young men who had expected high rewards for their service. They believed that he had failed to keep his promises. As a result, many of the revolutionaries who had helped depose Díaz took up arms against Madero, and Mexico entered ten years of civil war.

On 25 November 1911, just nineteen days after Madero took the oath of office, Zapata denounced the president. He and his officers signed the revolutionary Plan de Ayala, in which they promised to take back lands that had been stolen by the foreigners—in this case Spaniards and wealthy Mexicans who claimed European descent and lived in Mexico City—and restore them to their former owners. Zapata supported a system of mixed private and pueblo ownership. He proposed that the campesinos receive one-third of the land and that the landowners who did not oppose the revolution be allowed to keep two-thirds of their holdings. The Plan of Ayala identified the cause of the revolution to be the problems suffered by Mexico's rural populace.

> The immense majority of the Mexican pueblos and citizens are owners of no more than the land they walk on, suffering the horrors of poverty without being able to improve their social condition in any way . . . because lands, timber, and water are monopolized in a few hands.[8]

The Americans were not the objects of Zapata's scorn, for in Morelos the landlords were Mexicans and Spaniards. Indeed, Zapata admired and aspired to the democracy practiced in the United States. Nevertheless, when his fragmented followers, who were located in far-flung regions of Mexico, attacked their landlords, many of them were American.

Much of the revolutionary struggle took place at the almost invisible local level and was carried out by disparate bands of insurgents. The Mexicans expressed their grievances toward the Americans in a number of ways that became characteristic of their interaction during the conflict. Americans were the target of moral outrage and indignation, nationalistic rhetoric and appropriation, and class-based violence in accordance with the political position, social status, and social class of the revolutionaries.[9]

The fighting in 1911 had a direct effect on Americans across the countryside. The states of Mexico, Morelos, and Guerrero teemed with "bands who, for want of a better name are still styled Zapatistas, though it is doubtful if more than a small percentage ever received orders from the notorious rebel of Morelos." The Americans expressed deep alarm and disgust when the Zapatistas "slaughtered" fifty soldiers and civilians that they had captured during a train ambush. To the south, in Chiapas, rebels tore up fifty miles of Pan American Railroad track.[10]

In Durango, Americans fled the approach of revolutionaries. In 1911 Joanna, Annie, and Lillie Bogy abandoned their subdivided properties on the Santa Isabel Ranch, some forty miles northeast of Durango City, when their workers and neighbors warned them that revolutionaries were approaching the area. Fearing for their safety, the three Americans fled to Durango City, where they caught "the last train out." Shortly afterward the revolutionaries captured the capital city, sacked it, and set it on fire. The Bogys never returned. In 1925 Joanna's daughters convinced her to write at least some of the story in her own hand.

> i purchased this Land in the year of 1908 in the Month of August. and i purchased 960 Nine Hundred and Sixty acres of Land of my own and i am also Writing for my two Daughters Annie Bogy and Lillie Bogy. each purchased 160 akers of Land. Which was 1280 Akers of Land With Mine, Joanna Bogy and Annie and Lillie Bogy and my two Daughters property are Separate From Mine i am only Writing for them Because they ask me to attend to this for them and the Greater Part of this Land was in cultivation With the Mexicans Rent Houses on the Land and a part of the Land was pasture for my Stock Horses mules cattl and other Stock: and also other Mexican Families Living in the Pasture Timber part of my Lands Burning charcoal that i would have freighted to Durango City 40 miles away on mules.[11]

John McCaughan left behind his real estate business and elegant home in the capital and his properties in southern, western, and central Durango. The McCaughans returned, but things were never the same. Both the Bogys and the McCaughans lost the futures that they had carefully planned.

Their decision to flee was wise. Durango experienced a high degree of violence for the next seven years. During 1911, revolutionary forces under the command of Calixto Contreras and Domingo and Mariano Arrieta occupied the ranches of Mexicans and Americans alike. They seized the livestock, horses, weapons, and other supplies and shot those who resisted. In 1911 the American stockholders of the Creek Durango Land Company lost much of their cattle and supplies on those parts of the Santa Isabel that they still owned. Warrior Grayson, whose property was located ten miles from the Bogys' lands, did not leave in time to avoid the rebels. Threatened and beaten, he suffered serious injuries before he fled to the United States.[12]

Even in Yucatán, where a lower level of unrest was claimed, unhappy locals invaded Edward H. Thompson's Hacienda Chichén Itzá. The Mexican government later charged Thompson with using "slaves" to mine pre-Columbian relics, some made with jade and gold plate, which he "smuggled from the country." Thompson did use his position as the U.S. consul at Mérida to forward relics through diplomatic pouches to the George Foster Peabody Museum with the admonition that "these treasures should not be entrusted lightly."[13]

The leaders of the Mexican Revolution moved against debt peonage throughout the nation. As a result, the Madero administration headed directly into conflict with some of the largest American agricultural interests in Mexico. As the revolution became more radicalized, the administrations that followed Madero's not only abolished debt peonage but also encouraged unions and endorsed many strikes. Their goal was a free labor system. The government's involvement with labor activists continued after the warfare ended. Until the end of the 1930s the revolutionary governments sought accommodation with factions that favored strong anarchosyndicalist or nationalist agitation. The government's support of unions represented a strategy of controlling a new force in society by taking a position between the most reactionary Mexican and American capitalists and the more radical workers.

NO FREE LABOR

The San Pablo complex in Campeche, operated by John Markley and Isaiah Miller, was an early target of the increasing hostility toward Americans. By 1911, Markley and Miller had expended "over 4 million dollars" in the "development of the ranch at San Pablo." Debt peons had cleared the first 20,000 of the International Lumber and Development Company's 300,000 acres. The partners had achieved a gross revenue of some $5,000,000, plus income from chicle production and the sale of cut hardwood. They managed eleven forced-labor camps on the vast expanse of undeveloped land that remained. The camps featured central buildings made of "mahogany with tile roofs, while hundreds of bamboo houses were built for the laborers." Those camps were already producing henequen and other tropical products. One of the coconut groves that they planted extended for fifteen miles along the coast.[14]

The owners had constructed a complex of buildings in the heart of the plantation that included a $35,000 *casa grande* complete with "servants' quarters" for the foreman, E. Kirby-Smith. The town of San Pablo was a complex of sixty-five "modern stone buildings," with "the bookkeepers, doctors, and heads of various departments" housed at its center. The town, formerly a site characterized by thatched huts, held a civic building, a hospital, machine shops, a tannery, a foundry, a carpentry with molding equipment and a turning lathe, and a smithy. It also included the company's *tienda de raya*, which measured ninety by forty feet. "Bamboo houses for the natives," on the periphery of the complex, provided living quarters for the workers.

Forty miles of telephone lines and an equal amount of railroad trackage connected San Pablo with the outside world at Champotón. The estate's machine shops provided over one hundred specially designed cars for the railroad spur. Markley and Miller bought locomotives from the Baldwin Locomotive Works in Philadelphia. To complement their sixty-ton tree slicer, they constructed a new $60,000 building that was especially designed to dry mahogany and Spanish cedar veneer. The Mexican mayor of the town was an employee of the firm. One wonders if this layout approximated what Scott had in mind when he, MacManus, Kennedy, and Rosecrans had bid to open Mexico to American railroads thirty-five years earlier.[15]

Markley and Miller, obliged to fulfill a contractual agreement with the International Lumber and Development Company, arranged for the purchase and transport of 1,320 debt peons in 1911, including 120 women. They obtained the workers from Pedro Tresgallo, a Spanish *enganchero*, or labor contractor, who delivered them to the Americans in Campeche via a steamer that carried them from the port of Veracruz. They paid Tresgallo 129,600 pesos with a check drawn on the Mexico City Banking Corporation, where they maintained accounts. The also bought several hundred additional peons from other agents, bringing their total outlay to $285,000. These expenses included the cost of transporting the workers to the San Pablo Plantation.

Once the workers were there, Kirby-Smith placed them in the far-flung base camps used in the development of the property. Periodically they could travel to the *tienda de raya*, where they obtained credit for the purchases of basic supplies such as food and clothing. The store's inventory reflected the self-contained nature and the simplicity of plantation life. It included simple garments, hats, caps, boots, shoes, a variety of vegetables and fruits, hardware, tobacco, cigars, cigarettes, alcoholic beverages, and inexpensive jewelry. The value of the entire inventory totaled $30,000. The gross annual sales of the store ran between $250,000 and $300,000.[16]

In the late summer of 1911, shortly after Madero assumed power, Markley and Miller had "more than 2,600 laborers on the ranch," which the partners categorized in two groups, according to cost and quality. Reports of harsh treatment prompted a careful study of their labor practices by the U.S. government:

> This labor was of two classes—first, the better class of men with their families, who were purchased from ranch owners mostly from the States of Tabasco, Chiapas, Campeche, and Vera Cruz. There were about 700 of this class of laborers. Markley and Miller paid to the former employers of such labor the amount of their advances to such laborers, which payments, together with subsequent advances made by Markley and Miller, were as high as $400.00 to $450.00 per man and family. The other class of labor was purchased from regular labor agents in Mexico City and other places. The average purchase price, together with transportation cost and subsequent advances made by Markley and Miller, was not less than $100.00 per man. There were about 1,900 of this class of laborers.[17]

Kirby-Smith explained that debt peonage was essential to the operation of the ranch:

> Conditions in Mexico, and particularly at the ranch, at the time mentioned were such that it was impossible for any plantation owner to hold any labor on the ranch unless that laborer owed him money. It was the rule in Mexico at the time that no man could leave the employ of a ranch owner to enter the employ of another person unless the new employer first paid to the former employer the amount of that laborer's indebtedness. This was the general rule and prevailing custom throughout Mexico at the time and, without it, progress on any ranch would have been impossible, inasmuch as no laborers could have been held.[18]

Kirby-Smith then reiterated claims made by many American employers in cases of worker unrest. He declared that the workers on his estates enjoyed "good food" and that there was no "general complaint" among them, just a few malcontents and outside agitators.[19]

One of the reasons that American entrepreneurs got into so much trouble in Mexico was that they perpetuated local labor practices when the Mexicans expected improvements. Frederick Stark Pearson and the managers of the Mexican Northwestern Railroad of western Chihuahua, faced by raids and sabotage, echoed the claims of Kirby-Smith in an effort to placate critical bondholders and the directors of the Empire Bank of New York, which held its mortgage. A few years later oil baron Edward Doheny, while testifying during Senator Albert Bacon Fall's investigation of American losses in Mexico, stated that only a few malcontents and outsiders were the cause of unrest among the oil workers. He failed to note that he segregated the workplace and living facilities and maintained an uneven wage schedule for

Americans and "natives." In fact, his workers were politically divided. Some were loyal employees, but significant minorities joined the most radical factions of anarchist groups and the Partido Liberal Mexicano.[20]

In the late summer of 1911, the new Maderista governor of Campeche, Manuel Castillo Brito, sent two commissioners to the San Pablo Plantation with orders for Markley and Miller. The governor had led the Maderista revolution around Champotón and was not to be taken lightly. The governor ordered the owners to permit inspection of the company's camps "for the purposes of consulting with the laborers and investigating labor conditions on the ranch." His authority to do so was derived from the Plan Política Social, a document produced earlier that year by a small convention of representatives from the southern states and signed by a delegate from Campeche. The document declared that "foreign companies should employ the same percentage of Mexicans in supervisory positions as they did in lower level labor and that they should receive the same wages as foreign employees in comparable jobs." Markley and Miller claimed that Castillo Brito had another, more subversive, intent.

> Instead of fulfilling such pretended mission, however, these commissioners immediately went around among the laborers in the camp at San Pablo and informed the men that they were commissioners at the order of the Governor of Campeche; that the Governor had discovered that the men were being grossly mistreated and underpaid and informed them they could make far better wages on other ranches, in the army or elsewhere. These commissioners further told the men on behalf of the Governor that they need no longer comply with the contract of employment they made with Markley and Miller; that the governor released them from such contract of employment and advised them to go to Campeche to better their conditions.[21]

Markley, Miller, and Kirby-Smith claimed that they paid wages "as high as any ranch in Mexico," and that the workers had made personal contracts with them. In reality they had adopted local labor practices that were harsher than those found in the northern and central parts of the nation. From their perspective these practices counted among the advantages of "doing business" in Mexico. They made deals with the *engancheros,* as did the other plantation operators in the south, and they paid the illiterate and sometimes conscript labor only what necessity demanded. The workers assumed the obligation for repayment of the total cost, including the transportation expenses claimed by the *engancheros* plus interest to Markley and Miller. Given the illiteracy that prevailed among the workers, their inability to defend themselves in court is understandable.

Markley, Miller, and Kirby-Smith claimed that bribery and corruption motivated the governor and other state officials to move against them. First they charged the governor with making threats against Miller and Kirby-Smith, and then they asserted that two commissioners sent to San Pablo had requested bribes and agitated the workers when they were refused. Markley and Miller reiterated the charges to federal government officers in Mexico City, the U.S. State Department, and Ambassador Wilson. The Maderista government dismissed their claims.

The government commissioners, Luciano Caceres and Gerardo Díaz, did indeed foment trouble between the firm and its workers. One of the foremen, Torcuato Telles, "a Mexican," endeavored "to quiet the men in the camp [at San Pablo] to counteract the effect of the governor's agents." Telles, assisted by other men on the ranch "who could speak the Mexican language," temporarily succeeded in forestalling a mass desertion of the San Pablo facilities. A few days later, two hundred workers at Sahcabchen, one of the camps visited by the commissioners, rose up, looted the place, and marched on the city of Campeche. Miller, Telles, Mayor Manuel Pavon of Champotón, and fifteen company policemen tried to intercept them. When the mayor, who worked for Miller and Markley, confronted the march leaders, they said

> that they had been released from their labor contracts by the Governor;
> that they knew from the agents of the Governor that they could make
> higher wages on other ranches and in the army and were on their way
> to Campeche to meet with the Governor.[22]

Miller attempted to negotiate with Castillo Brito, but he charged the Americans with abuse of the workers. Miller later claimed that he agreed to all of the governor's demands for change, and that his troubles stemmed from the introduction of outside agitators and the fact that he had refused to pay a bribe. On 22 November 1911, in desperation, he wrote to Ambassador Wilson.

> About one month ago the Governor of Campeche sent two inspectors
> to our estate who, misconstruing their mission, agitated our laborers
> to such an extent that on the 16th inst. 200 from one camp rebelled
> shouting: "Viva Madero," abandoned their camp, all armed with
> machetes.
>   These peones are now in the City of Campeche and refuse to return
> to our estate. The Governor of Campeche refuses to use his authority
> to return them. They are being fed at our expense.
>   If the authorities continue in refusing to protect us the rest of our
> labor will also leave us and cause the ruin of our business in which

we have invested several million dollars as our henequen is needing immediate cutting and grinding.

As American citizens we ask your honor to intervene with and have Mexico authorities give us the protection that our interest requires.

The situation is most urgent therefore we make use of the telegraph in appealing to you and hope our petition will receive your prompt attention.[23]

The next day the 200 workers at the Allende camp rose up, but this group was armed. They looted the facilities and marched en masse toward Campeche. Within a few months of the onset of the unrest, some 1,800 workers had left the camps after rioting and looting several of them. According to Markley and Miller, the governor had unjustifiably released these men from valid labor contracts under which the firm had paid 1,100 laborers $100 each and 700 more an average of $250 each. This outlay included their transportation costs from Veracruz and the cost of providing them housing and salary "advances." In other words, the workers were debt peons. Castillo Brito probably knew that some workers had been held by Markley and Miller since 1904 and had been unable to pay off their debts. The governor returned all the marchers and their families to Veracruz on the government transport ship *Minerva*. He rejected the Americans' claims and in return charged them $1,643 for the feeding of what he viewed as ill-treated fellow countrymen before they were shipped back to Veracruz. Miller, Markley, and Ambassador Wilson appealed to Madero, alleging that Castillo Brito had insisted on bribes, but their plea fell on deaf ears. Many American businessmen and colonists had long held the stereotypic view that Mexican officials were "immoral," but in Mexico City no one apparently asked for money. The loss of their workers cost Markley and Miller $286,643. They regarded the Mexican laborers in this instance as private property. They advocated free trade and protested state regulations and taxes, but they did not accept the corollary of free labor. By 1913 Miller felt his life was endangered by the revolutionaries. He fled to the United States after troops loyal to Madero raided the plantation twice and left it in ruins.[24]

In 1913, after the overthrow of Madero, rebels sacked the nearby Sakahal Ranch and took the manager prisoner. After a terrifying experience he reported the incident in detail but mentioned no attempts at bribery, undercutting Markley and Miller's assertions that immoral Mexican officials were the cause of the problems. Financier Frederick E. Pittman of 65 Wall Street owned the Sakahal and would have reported any irregularities to the American authorities. The revolutionaries at Sakahal manifested an inflamed anti-Americanism. They warned the Sakahal manager to leave and robbed

him of "thirty-eight horses and mules, cleaned out the store and main building, causing a loss to Sakahal, in his estimation, of about $30,000 Mexican
Currency. . . . [Then] they burned in front of him an American flag which
they found in the house."[25]

RISE OF THE OROZQUISTAS

In 1912 the discontent of increasing numbers of Mexicans with the Madero
regime became apparent, and the violent attacks of Mexican revolutionaries and bandits on Americans and their properties increased in frequency,
intensity, and extent. The supporters of agrarian reform were disappointed
in the president's inaction, and Zapata continued to lead an armed agrarian
revolution against him in south-central Mexico. Madero's temporizing with
his other enemies caused them to mistake his moderation for weakness. The
Porfirian establishment believed the president to be incapable of maintaining order, and extremists among them plotted his overthrow. There was,
however, another problem.

Madero's decision to exclude most of the young revolutionaries from positions of power in his new regime frustrated nationalist zealots, leftists, and
populists and denied the ambitions of those who had hoped for advancement through participation in the armed struggle. Madero's failure to accommodate politically his own most avid followers led to his undoing. One
of these revolutionaries, Pascual Orozco, began a revolution against Madero
in March 1912. Madero had offended Orozco by offering him the position
as head of the rural police in Chihuahua after he had commanded the main
Maderista army and won the greatest military victory of the revolution at
Ciudad Juárez. That victory contributed to Díaz's decision to resign and to
go into exile.[26] Orozco also believed that Madero had broken the promises
he had made to Mexico's working class and rural laborers.

Although Madero's business experience gave him the status and skills
to lead an army of vaqueros and miners, the circumstances of the conflict
worked against him. The new president came from a family that counted
itself among the Mexican oligarchy, and Orozco came from the *pequeña burguesía* of Chihuahua. Orozco had operated pack trains that delivered goods
throughout much of the rugged Sierra Madre in the westernmost area of
the state, including the mining camps at the bottom of the canyons. A close
relative owned the biggest house in the mining town of Batopilas, where
Orozco's *arrieros*, or mule drivers, made frequent deliveries. Despite his
ownership of dozens of burros, horses, and mules, a number of way stations,
and a comfortable home, Orozco was neither a member of the upper class

from which Madero made his appointments to office nor a formally trained soldier. Madero's exclusion of Orozco was the major reason he rebelled against his former leader.

Orozco had far more concern for the plight of the rural poor than did Díaz or Madero. Orozco's political plan, the Plan de la Empacadora, which he announced simultaneously with his revolt, differed from Madero's by offering a radical agrarian reform that included the confiscation of lands wrongfully taken from the peasantry during the Díaz regime. The promise of land reform, although muted, gained the support of Yaquis in Sonora and small groups in the states of Tabasco and Campeche.[27] Orozco's forces included units from a radical arm of the PLM that operated in western Chihuahua. These leftists had been marginalized by Madero's success.

Orozco's professed allegiance to the common man also attracted Zapata, who believed that Madero had betrayed them both. Zapata acknowledged Orozco as the leader of the revolution against the president. The news of Zapata's action triggered an uprising of peasants and townsfolk at the remote Quimichis hacienda in the Territory of Tepic that demonstrated the diffuse and populist nature of the revolution. On 12 April 1912 shoemaker Alejandro Barron, Alejandro Jimenez, Roman Jaramillo, and José Aguayo led citizens from the town of Acaponeta onto the estate owned by John Cave and R. L. Summerlin. The hacienda workers reported that "[a]pproximately three hundred Zapatistas visited us and took horses, mules, furniture, rifles, pistols, and all the money we had." The Zapatistas also took six prisoners, five of them Americans, who later escaped by floating down a river to the coast. The furious Zapatistas accused the hacienda's Mexican sharecroppers of helping the Americans but left without harming them to join in an assault on the capital city of Tepic.[28]

On 15 April the Zapatistas returned and attempted to enter the big house, where five American supervisors and one Mexican stalled them off before fleeing that night with the rebels in hot pursuit. The Zapatistas stayed at the estate until the end of the month, when the majority left to join a large force attempting to capture the capital. The sharecroppers evacuated the hacienda when the Zapatistas confiscated their property and threatened their lives. When the foreman tried to return in 1913, the Carrancistas, another revolutionary group, arrested him and confiscated his funds.[29]

ATTACKS AGAINST THE ESTATES

In December 1912 the Mexican secretary of war, Fidencio Hernández, acknowledged "that the army is not nearly large enough to give protection to haciendas and small towns." In March and April the Orozquistas gained a strong position in Chihuahua and eastern Durango, enveloping the rail hub and manufacturing center of Torreón. Following the victory of Orozco's forces over the army north of Torreón, the American railroad engineers and conductors in the region began leaving their jobs and fleeing the country. Americans fleeing from Durango and boarding the USS *Buford* and other transport ships at Culiacán and Mazatlán were joined by others from neighboring Sinaloa. Some of these refugees drifted back after Orozco's defeat later in the year.[30]

The Orozquistas inflicted great damage at Hidalgo del Parral, in southern Chihuahua near the Durango border. American ranchers Joseph P. Chamberlain of New York City and brothers Charles N., Ernest P., and Ortus B. Fuller of Los Angeles had created the archetypal commercial estate at Hidalgo del Parral. In 1910 they bought the Berendo and Santo Domingo ranches, comprising 448,280 acres, and incorporated as the Southwestern Land and Cattle Company of Los Angeles, California. They spent considerable time on the property and took pride in their 17,000 head of cattle and 4,600 registered Black Angus. In 1911 they added another 3,200 head of registered cattle. At first the revolution to unseat Díaz swept past their ranch, causing minimal damage. The revolutionaries took some horses and cattle, but they had more important objectives in mind.

In 1912, however, the situation changed dramatically. Orozquistas entered the estate, shouting anti-American epithets, and inflicted heavy damage, seizing livestock, horses, and supplies. In November 1912 and January 1913 the situation worsened. The Americans ceased adding to their breed stock. Not satisfied with confiscations, the Orozquistas smashed equipment, wrecked buildings, tore down fences, and took feed. By early March the damages totaled $49,616 and the survival of the ranch was in question. Its great size, however, made some of the herds too remote for the revolutionaries to locate. Maximo Castillo led five raids on the estate. He and his men expressed amazement at the great size of the herds, which was possible because the Americans had developed water resources and disbursed baled hay.[31]

The 376,360-acre Durango estate of meatpacker George Hormel, the president of the Mexican-American Land and Colonization Company, suffered repeated raids. In February 1911 the managers of the estate fled when they heard that Domingo Arrieta was approaching. Following the first wave of invasions, which continued through March of that year, other armed insurrectionists invaded the property, stripping it of assets. Then, after a few months of quiet, violence swept the area again. During 1912 and 1913 the revolutionary forces of Orozco committed even more thorough depredations in the area. In November 1912 they "completely sacked and burned" the Maguey Ranch of Marion Clyde Dyer. The estate managers, who specialized in cattle raising and breeding, could operate only sporadically for the duration of the revolution.[32]

Farther north, situated in the foothills of the Sierra Madre of Chihuahua and twenty-five miles south of the American timber camp at Madera, was the Dolores Esperanza Mining Company, owned by Ernest L. McLean and E. M. Leavitt of New York City. They also owned the El Rayo Mining Company of Chihuahua and the Creston-Colorado Mining and the La Dura Mill and Mining Companies in Sonora. Each of these companies enjoyed sizeable capitalization, operating their own mills and smelters. McLean and Leavitt were closely tied to the Phelps Dodge Company. Ernest's father, James McLean, served as a director of Phelps Dodge and on the boards of virtually all of its myriad enterprises in Sonora, Chihuahua, Arizona, New Mexico, and Texas. Leavitt was equally well connected in Mexico and the American southwest through his relative Gardiner Howland, one of the investors in the Texas and Great Northern Railroad and the Mexican National Railroad. Leavitt's brother was the director of a silver mine in Guanajuato.

McLean and Leavitt had owned the highly profitable Dolores Esperanza for more than a decade when the Orozquistas invaded their property in July 1912.

> An armed band of men estimated in number from 2,200 to over 3,000 came into the Dolores camp and took forcible [control]. They seized the stores and buildings of the company, and took and looted the stores of all food supplies. . . . They entered the company mill and compelled the employees to stop work and threatened the lives of various employees. . . . After removing all supplies they destroyed the cash register, and scales and destroyed all of the interior fittings. . . . Arson was attempted several times. . . .
>
> Many of the American employees lifes were threatened . . . [and] one was seriously injured by being shot.[33]

Generals Antonio Rojas, Luis Hernández, Jesús José Campos, and Emilio Campa commanded the troops. The revolutionaries looted the mine and continued to raid it, intercepting shipments of bullion, for the rest of the year. In early 1913 similar actions at their other sites forced McLean and Leavitt to close down their operations throughout the state.[34]

To the southeast of the Dolores Esperanza, deep in the Copper Canyon complex, the Batopilas Mining Company also became a rich target for the revolutionaries. Its small private army was no match for the highly motivated rebels. It suffered repeated robberies, and on 12 September 1912 the Orozquistas took merchandise valued at over 13,000 pesos from the company store. The general manager summed up the situation:

> Foreign interests have absolutely no security here and under present conditions it will only be a few weeks before looting bands will be out all over the country. . . . The rabble only care for pillage and many who have higher pretensions are quite ready to capture what they can.[35]

Rebel troops and, later, government forces "raided, robbed, dynamited, pillaged, and burned by fire" the housing, offices, and machinery of Bernard Rowe's Arizona-Parral Mining Company. The company, located near Hidalgo del Parral in Chihuahua, suffered heavy losses. The violence spread across the state. In the far north, in 1911, revolutionaries under the command of Villa occupied Edward Morris's 1,237,960-acre T. O. Riverside Ranch. Like so many of the larger American-owned properties, this one had been obtained from the Jesús Valenzuela Survey Company, which sold the estate to Morris some twenty-two years after acquiring it in 1886 from the Díaz government.

The ranch was strategically located. Its northwestern corner reached to within seventy-five miles of El Paso, and its property line extended some sixty miles along the Rio Grande and seventy miles to the south. It afforded to the military force that controlled it almost unlimited access to the United States, a highly important strategic position for the acquisition and transit of arms after such shipments were embargoed in 1914 by the U.S. government. As a result, Morris experienced repeated invasions by Orozquistas and then Villistas, leading to the destruction of his properties. Edwin Marshall suffered repeated losses of cattle and equipment on the Las Palomas hacienda, which shared the U.S. border for about 200 miles, from El Paso–Juárez to the eastern boundary of Arizona. Rebels associated with the PLM and their successors warned the American employees on his estate to get out.[36]

The fate of the Corralitos hacienda, which was located in northwestern Chihuahua, exemplifies the nature of the attacks on American properties from the inception of the revolution and the nature of American responses. In 1910 rebels burned railroad bridges on the property and its approaches. In December twenty-six rebels entered the estate and recruited several of the cowboys to their ranks. The rebels—anarchist, socialist, and radical members of the PLM—espoused nationalism under the banner of "Mexico for the Mexicans." A daughter of one of the foremen at the Corralitos poignantly described the local American attitude toward the Mexican rebels: "Just think, mother, we are staring at them just as if they were not common people." If the Americans remained unimpressed, the *jefe politico* in Casas Grandes was scared stiff, as George Laird, a Corralitos foreman, contemptuously noted: "He has a couple of hundred troops and he wanted us to find out where the men [rebels] were, so he could send up and catch them. Just about like watching a flea and then sending for help to come and catch it."[37]

The *rurales*, or members of the rural police, failed to act, despite reporting to Díaz that they had restored order, and the rebel units continued their activities with unrestricted freedom. At Janos they disarmed a detachment of *rurales*. Laird took note of the situation. He feared that the workers might "start something" and tried to generate goodwill by hiring a doctor to tend to ill employees, rebuilding the church that was located near the big house, and holding an open meeting to discuss grievances. He also offered the laid-off *peones* part-time work despite the fact that the revolution had rendered shipments impossible. By providing some work he hoped to avoid credit advances at the *tienda de raya*, which he knew the laborers would demand if no work was forthcoming. He also anticipated legal challenges to the estate and moved to "perfect" the titles.[38]

In early 1911 the American managers at the Corralitos evacuated their women and children to El Paso on the train. But they also treated the revolutionary violence as a temporary crisis. The leaders of the Corralitos joined the settlers in the colony at Dublan in a joint effort to build a canal that would irrigate 100,000 acres. The hacienda manager also consulted with the U.S. Department of Agriculture for advice on the development of experimental cotton and tobacco fields. Before the political situation turned against them in early 1911, the Corralitos managers remained in good economic shape. The owners had paid off much of the company debt and had reorganized the remainder in 4 percent rather than 8 percent bonds. Meanwhile, more Corralitos workers left the estate to join the forces of Villa and Orozco.[39]

It was not long before the prosperous times ended. In 1912 former PLM generals José de la Luz Blanco and José Inez Salazar joined Orozco. They commanded strong forces in northwestern Chihuahua and northeastern Sonora that quickly drove away the federal garrisons, leaving the Mexican and American landowners at the mercy of revolutionary anarchists, socialists, agrarians, and nationalists. In the course of the year armed Mexican "squatters" from Casas Grandes and Janos occupied the bottomlands of the Corralitos immediately adjacent to the big house and began to farm. The rebel troops took cattle for sale and sustenance. The prestigious American owners of the Corralitos, including the Shearson, Morgan, Morton, and

Peirce families, were powerless to stop them. The two generals encouraged the violence perpetrated by their 1,700 troops by arguing "that Mexico was for Mexicans, that the Americans must be driven out of the country, and their property divided among Mexicans."[40]

THE FATE OF SETTLERS AND COLONISTS

Even as discouraged Americans began to sell their properties for only a fraction of the original value, American newcomers, filled with energy and optimism, bought them with the notion that the revolution was a temporary condition. In a stock market–like interaction, sellers acted as bears, anticipating disaster, while buyers viewed the situation optimistically and adopted the strategy of bulls, rushing in to buy what they considered giveaways. The Americans conducted hundreds of such transactions during 1912 and 1913. The bears turned out to be right. They fared much better than those who held on to their investments or entered Mexico when they thought the land market had hit bottom.

The experiences of the American settlers in Sonora and Chihuahua were even worse than those of the estate owners. They suffered devastating losses and humiliations. The Mormons lost much of their property when Salazar ordered them to leave the country. He issued the first of these orders on 30 August 1912 to the residents of Colonia Morelos in Sonora. Then his forces entered the settlement on 12 September and looted the houses. The Americans who remained were forced to witness the banditry before they were allowed to flee across the border. In December, having replaced Orozco as the commander of the rebel forces in northwestern Chihuahua, Salazar ordered his men to join local citizens in destroying American properties. The rebels were thorough: "In the absence of tenants, the natives are pulling up the posts from fields and city lots and using them for firewood." In 1915 some of the Latter-Day Saints returned, only to be robbed and chased away again, this time by forces loyal to Villa.[41]

In late July 1912 Salazar ordered the Americans at Colonias Díaz, Dublan, Pacheco, and García, and all other settlements in northwestern Chihuahua, to abandon their homes and leave immediately for the United States. On 26 July Junius Romney at Colonia Pacheco was informed that

> all guarantees, for the safety of life and property of American citizens, were withdrawn, and then by command of said General, large forces of his soldiers proceeded to Colonia Dublan, Colonia Díaz, and other towns where Americans resided, and by acts of violence and atrocities made serious threats, against the families of Americans.[42]

Salazar's troops arrived at Colonia García on 1 August. They enthusiastically complied with their orders to expel the Americans. After giving the Americans "peremptory notice" that all guarantees for their safety and that of their fellow citizens in neighboring towns were withdrawn, the revolutionaries disarmed the Americans and "were exceedingly hostile, cruel, and abusive to them."[43] They "seized, appropriated, or destroyed property owned by Americans, as they saw fit." The revolutionaries left Colonia García "in a completely devastated condition" and proceeded to Colonia Chuichupa, where they killed Benjamin Griffith and generally repeated their earlier performances at Dublan and García. During these actions they expressed the same hostility to the Americans that was manifested by the Mexican "squatters" on the private American estates in the area.[44] Some of the Mexican employees working for the Americans at Colonia García joined in the attacks on their employers and took part in the seizure of the property after they fled.

> Hostile subjects emboldened by the acts of the soldiers and their
> officers also invaded claimant's said lot, tore down his fences . . .
> and continued to keep his premises open for army horses and other
> livestock to pasture, until [everything was] seized and appropriated.[45]

Salazar's troops included the Americans in a generalized attack on the great landed estates. They also killed Mexican landowners and their agents found on the Azcarate and Ojitos estates north of the Corralitos, but at no time did they interfere "with property claimed and in the possession of Mexican subjects who were in sympathy" with the revolution. In contrast, Salazar accosted one American and "commanded him to at once leave the country, under penalty of death, if he did not do so, or if he again returned."

Salazar and de la Luz Blanco were anti-American zealots who represented the most radical revolutionary tendencies in Chihuahua in 1912, and they were, for the moment, popular with the people in the Casas Grandes–Janos region. When the citizens of those communities invaded the Corralitos hacienda and constructed shacks, they did so with the generals' approval.[46] The revolutionaries that the two generals commanded, however, were not the only Mexicans to manifest their anger with the Americans in the region. In early September forces loyal to Governor José Maytorena of Sonora arrested a party of several Americans near Colonia García. After stripping them of all their belongings, the Mexicans ordered them out of the country. The soldiers' "acts of violence and atrocities became more and more frequent," and some civilians joined them in making threats and committing thefts.

The cultural and social gap between the American settlers and the Mexicans was deep and generally unbridgeable. James Whetten of Colonia García believed that the newcomers were blameless for the hostilities. The Mexicans "entertained a race-hatred against Americans, were exceedingly envious of their prosperity, and had an insatiate desire to secure and own their property, without payment therefor." Such perceptions were exacerbated by reports of atrocities, such as the

> massacre of more than 300 law-abiding Chinese subjects, at Torreón in May of the previous year, with a savage ferocity indescribable by a force of revolutionary soldiers, under the command of a Mexican officer, who was subject to the command of General Francisco I. Madero. . . . [They were] incited to commit their brutal and inhumane acts by the speech of a prominent Mexican, Jesus C. Flores, a Maderista leader, delivered just previous to the occurrence.[47]

The attacks by revolutionaries on Americans quickly spread to Coahuila, where the Orozquistas occupied the Piedra Blanca hacienda of John Blocker, William Jennings, and Edna Jeffreys Moore for four days in September 1912. Between 800 and 1,500 troops commanded by Colonel Marcello Caraveo "robbed" the estate of cattle and horses valued at over $50,000. They then defeated the federal garrison at neighboring Muzquiz before overrunning the other estates in the region, including the Treviño-Ord hacienda, La Babia. Blocker, who soon afterward became the U.S. consul at Parral, offered a racial perspective on the fighting to the U.S. State Department, stating that "all of the white men on the San Domingo and Piedras Ranches have sought safety in Texas, and that these properties have been virtually abandoned."[48]

The revolutionaries were active in the states of Guanajuato as well. The Americans in the state capital evacuated at least two trainloads of women from the U.S. colony, who took refuge in Mexico City. At the Cubo mines the four *rurales* who were entrusted with guard duty also fled.

INTERNATIONAL SYNDICATES

During the second decade of the twentieth century, as the Mexicans fought, American financial elites extended the power of their monopolies in Mexico and abroad and gained control of strategic resources not available in their own country. One such resource was rubber. In 1902 Baker had led the consolidation of the U.S. Rubber Company, creating a trust that increasingly dominated domestic rubber production and sales during the next ten years. That year J. P. Morgan brought John D. Rockefeller into U.S. Rubber by selling him 30 percent of the preferred stock while keeping 30 percent for himself. Then, in 1910, Morgan managed a $12,000,000 issue of new stock for

U.S. Rubber, of which David Boyle Blair, the firm of Kidder Peabody, George Baker, and Morgan jointly bought $8,000,000. U.S. Rubber gave Morgan the opportunity to establish vertical and horizontal control over the rubber industry. His $2,000,000 investment in 1910 improved U.S. Rubber's production and distribution facilities in the United States.

Simultaneously, Morgan purchased $600,000 of stock in the Intercontinental Rubber Company of Mexico, with options to buy more. Intercontinental's assets were concentrated at Zacatecas, where it owned some 2,500,000 acres of guayule bushes. The company operated a refinery at Torreón, and it held large concessions in Sumatra and the Belgian Congo. The owners of the company still included Morgan associate H. P. Davison; A. H. Wiggin, the president of Chase Bank; William C. Potter of the Brown Brothers Bank and Tlahualilo Estates of Torreón; Charles H. Sabin, the president of the National Copper Bank and the Colima Lumber Company; Bernard Baruch, a financial adviser to President Wilson; the Rockefeller brothers; and Senator Nelson Aldrich.

Morgan thus gained influence in the production of low-grade latex in Mexico and high-grade latex in the Belgian Congo while developing plantations in Sumatra. In 1910 Morgan Jr. acquired 26,700 shares of the Mexican company. That year the financiers arranged for U.S. Rubber to buy all of Intercontinental's output. As a result, the value of Intercontinental's stock increased by almost 50 percent in twelve months.[49] Intercontinental remained important in the production of strategically important rubber products until after World War II.

The bankers also tried to organize timber production in the mountainous regions of Mexico. In 1912 Morgan, Baker, and the investment firm of White and Weld recruited Sabin and created the International Agricultural Corporation (IAC). They also formed other companies to harvest timber in British Columbia and Central America. The IAC took over Sabin's Colima Lumber Company, giving it the capitalization needed for initial outlays until profits caught up with costs. White and Weld took $9,892,000 and Morgan $2,967,600 in IAC bonds. Baker's First National Bank and Sabin's Chase Bank also bought into the venture. The IAC was also supposed to protect smaller entities during the uncertainty of the Mexican Revolution. Between 1913 and 1919 the consortium easily survived the loss of $50,000, but the prolonged land nationalization program that followed caused them to give up.[50]

The South American Group turned their attention toward Africa in 1910, when they purchased the Liberian national debt. Unpaid bills provoked threats of military invasion by Germany, France, and Great Britain and prompted the American financiers to act. Their plan called for a loan of $1,627,418 and gave them control of a world-class iron ore reserve. They achieved their Liberian objective shortly after consolidating the U.S. Steel Corporation. They paid a bargain price for control of the Liberian government and punctuated it with a detailed prescription for repayment of the loan. The Liberians would pay 5 percent annually by means of a "rubber tax [and] head monies [head taxes on the citizenry] . . . to be collected . . . by officials to be appointed by the United States, or by the United States and certain European nations, as may be decided."[51] Kuhn Loeb and the Liberian government agreed that Dr. Roland P. Falkner of Washington, D.C., would be the special agent of the fledgling nation. Falkner was paid $1,000 by Kuhn Loeb, with that sum added to the monies owed to the South American Group, Liberia's new creditor. Falkner went to Europe to negotiate the payment of the Liberian debt to its old creditors. The South American Group advanced Liberia $1,627,000 to pay off the Europeans.[52]

The New York financiers developed an international matrix in which they coordinated direct financial linkages between Mexico and Britain. Two examples demonstrate just how closely related the syndicates that controlled American and Mexican big business were. In 1910 James S. Mackie, the treasurer of the Baltimore and Ohio Railroad (B&O) and a director of various former Huntington enterprises in Mexico, commissioned Morgan to float a bond issue for the line. Morgan already held stock in the B&O, and his bank easily recruited not only the other members of the Trio but also John Stewart, Henry Clay Frick, John and William Rockefeller, and most of the other leading bankers of New York as investors. Mackie and the B&O had strong ties to British capital through the investments of Cassel, the J. S. Morgan investment house, and Morgan's London partners Burns, Gordon, and Lawrence, who appointed James Sloan Jr. of National City to the B&O board of trustees as their representative.

Morgan assembled a syndicate that indicated the layered complexity and underlying unity of American and British capital at that time. Several of the major investors were already Mackie's associates in American and Mexican ventures, holding important interests in Collis Huntington's International Railroad and the Alamo, Fuente, and Coahuila Coal Companies, all former Huntington enterprises in the states of Coahuila and Durango. The railroad Big Four—E. H. Harriman, William Rockefeller, James Stillman, and George Gould—were also Mackie associates. They had taken over the Mexican International after Huntington's death and carried out a stock issue that attracted the same lineup of inside investors buying shares at discounts.

Stillman and Rockefeller, as members of the Big Four, controlled most of the late Huntington's Mexican holdings, including the Southern Pacific Railroad and the Cananea Consolidated Copper Company. The Southern Pacific's Sur Pacifico, which ran along the Mexican west coast, also attracted capital from John Rockefeller. Stillman and William Rockefeller sat with Mackie as directors of the B&O, but they also controlled the National City Bank and the United States Trust Company. Stillman, Rockefeller, and Stewart, who conceived United States Trust and served as its chairmen, were the major owners of the Monterrey Belt Railroad, which surrounded Mexico's most important industrial city in the north. John S. Kennedy, who had worked with Rosecrans on the original Tuxpan Railroad concession in 1868, and Gustav Schwab, whose father, Charles, had pioneered railroading in Chihuahua, also sat on the board of United States Trust. The underlying unity of the B&O syndicate reached beyond the railroad and the former Huntington companies. Members of the syndicate also held stock in the Mexican National Railroad, where Morgan, Baker, and Schiff joined Rockefeller and Stillman as the most powerful figures.

The B&O syndicate serves as but one example of dozens of Anglo-American financial interests that worked together in Mexico and the United States. Their unity in the creation of the Ferrocarriles Nacionales de México in 1905 was a result of years of cooperative effort in high finance despite their competition in many areas. When World War I began, the American associates of the British capitalists felt like they were at war as well.[53]

The second case was one of goodwill and involved Weetman Pearson (Viscount Cowdray). Although British capital intertwined with American investments in the United States and Mexico, it usually remained passive, leaving the Americans to manage the enterprises. The Mexican Central Railroad, Century Real Estate, and United States Trust all had such an arrangement. In contrast, Pearson's industrial and engineering genius earned him great importance in London, Mexico, and New York. He earned early fame in London by constructing the Blackwall Tunnel under the Thames River. His completion of the dam above Khartoum on the Blue Nile and the enlargement of the Dover harbor on behalf of the admiralty brought him even more recognition. In New York his firm completed four tunnels under the East River for the Pennsylvania Railroad, financed by bonds purchased by the New York financial community and sponsored in part by Morgan. In Mexico, Pearson completed the centuries-old drainage project in the central valley that protected Mexico City from flooding, and then he brought in the enormous oil fields in Veracruz. In 1908 his Dos Bocas well became the "largest oil gush on record." In 1910, already highly regarded in New York, he received the title of viscount in London. In 1914 the strategic importance of Pearson's holdings in Veracruz were an important factor in the American decision to invade Mexico at that point rather than farther north, where the less threatened U.S. oil companies were concentrated.

The Trio continued to expand around the world. They joined ventures headed by their British and French associates, usually dividing equally the 15 percent allocated to them. In 1912 the South American Group, now calling itself the American Group, purchased bonds valued at £712,500 from the government of Francisco Madero. This was the first installment of what was slated to be a sale of bonds worth £1,700,000 in the United States market.

In 1913, during a meeting between Woodrow Wilson and James Stillman, William Rockefeller, and Frank Vanderlip, all directors of the National City Bank, the president agreed that American law had to be changed to allow banks to make direct foreign investments and compete more effectively in the world market. Rockefeller and Vanderlip described

> the possibility of American capital capturing foreign markets. Stillman listened. Wilson listened. [They] waxed eloquent upon the glory of American trade penetrating remote countries. They held that the government, as a patriotic duty, should place no restrictions in the path of pioneering capital.[54]

Wilson was a kindred soul. In 1907 he had said:

> Since . . . the manufacturer insists on having the world as a market, the flag of his nation must *follow* him, and the doors of nations which are closed against him must be battered down. Concessions obtained by financiers must be safeguarded by ministers of state even if the sovereignty of unwilling nations be outraged in the process.[55]

Soon after his meeting with the National City directors, Wilson sponsored the Federal Reserve Act, which allowed banks to make direct foreign investments and facilitated their global intentions. Between 1914 and 1917 the U.S. banking and industrial elite combined their economic power, political connections, and global interests to decisively influence their government's decisions to intervene in Colombia on behalf of the Panama Canal project, to influence the outcome of the Mexican Revolution, and to enter World War I.

Other dynamic individuals gained notoriety around the world as the leaders of enterprises that the Trio, the South American Group, and the IBC helped finance. In Mexico, Frederick Stark Pearson stood out as one of the more public figures. A major stockholder in the Mexican Telegraph Company, the Bostonian controlled the Mexican Northwestern Railroad in Chihuahua, which hauled timber and cattle to the Texas and Pacific yards at El Paso, the Medina Land Development Company in Oaxaca, which contained a colony of American settlers whose contact with the outside world came by way of Morgan ships at Coatzacoalcos, and a variety of other enterprises including the power and light plant situated at Nexcaca, which served Mexico City.

Pearson needed capital to expand his Nexcaca power plant. On 1 August 1910 Schiff and Morgan's British associate Ernest Cassel gave Pearson $400,000 in return for 10,000 shares of Missouri Pacific Railroad stock and additional securities. Then Baker, Cassel, Morgan Jr., and Schiff extended Pearson a $2,721,500 loan, of which Baker tendered 37.5 percent and Morgan 12.5 percent. The other 50 percent was divided by Cassel and Schiff. That is how the bankers took control of important Mexican entities without the knowledge of outsiders. They also gained American railroad stocks owned by Pearson and his previous financial backer Percival Farquhar that were valued at $6,400,000. Farquhar, meanwhile, continued his more global plans, generating the $15,000,000 Argentine Railroad Syndicate, of which the American Group—Morgan, Stillman, Baker, and Schiff—took $1,500,000. Mexico was part of a global nexus.[56]

CARRANZA'S REVOLUTION

In February 1913 matters became even more serious for the Americans in Mexico. Soldiers loyal to General Victoriano Huerta, the commander in chief of the Mexican Army, seized President Madero and Vice President Pino Suárez. A few days later, in an obviously prearranged ambush aided by the guards who were transferring them from one prison to another, Madero and Suárez, the two highest executive officials of the nation, were assassinated. Then, through an equally transparent sequence of cabinet-level appointments and immediate resignations, Huerta became president of Mexico.

Madero's assassination seriously damaged the effort to sell Mexican government bonds. Buyers in the Paris and London markets were wary of Huerta's dictatorship in Mexico, and the syndicate's European partners were unable to sell their share of the issue, which was worth £4,300,000. The American Group divided over strategy. Stillman and Baker considered Huerta a bad risk and sold their Mexican bond "participation" at a discounted rate of 92 percent to Morgan, Guarantee Trust, Ladenburg-Thalmann, M. M. Warburg, and Kuhn Loeb, each of which took a one-fifth interest. The American financial community was divided about Huerta, but enough capitalists in the eastern United States supported him to make the sale a success. Six months later, and three months after Morgan's death, the American banks had sold all but £83,000 of the bond issue.[57]

Madero's murder galvanized Venustiano Carranza, the governor of Coahuila, to immediately issue his Plan de Guadalupe and proclaim a new revolution. He initiated the revolt under the rubric "Constitutionalist" to underline the illegal manner in which Huerta had seized the presidency. In Chihuahua, Villa mobilized his followers, who had disbanded during the Madero administration, in support of Carranza. At that point guerrilla fighting spread across the countryside and again enveloped the Americans. Villa's forces congealed and began their sweep of the state of Chihuahua from south to north. One of Villa's first conquests was the Southwestern Land and Cattle Company's hacienda near Parral. General Joaquin Terrazas informed the ranch management that he was carrying out Villa's personal orders when he seized 248 head of cattle. Soon thereafter other Villistas "robbed the ranch, . . . forcibly ejected the employees, and threatened to execute them by firing squad if they returned. The men responsible for these acts did not identify themselves."[58]

Chaotic fighting spread across the state. The superintendent of the Batopilas Mining Company explained the situation to his board of directors on Wall Street:

> From the best information obtainable, the revolutionists are breaking up into small bands making it almost impossible to travel or freight through the mountains. The freighters say they are afraid of having their mules taken from them on the trail. It is hard to say how far off the end of trouble is in the country. The common people are, however, fast coming to the point where they will be unmanageable for the lack of a general Government. In general the lower people are beginning to act upon the principle that might is right and what is here in the country belongs to them and that all that remains for them to do is to take it.[59]

The Batopilas mine, which had suffered repeated occupations during the Orozco uprising, now lost supplies and equipment in addition to money, food, and arms to the Villista revolutionaries.

In 1913 the Orozquistas in Coahuila began fighting on behalf of President Huerta. That summer they reinvaded the Piedra Blanca hacienda in Coahuila, burning the owners' records and confiscating livestock, then fleeing as Carranza's Constitutionalist forces advanced. The actions of the Orozquistas in Coahuila were the same as those in Chihuahua. They took goods, burned records, and warned the "gringos" to go home, combining the foraging strategies of insurgents, the class interests of peasants, and the biases of nationalists. In northern Chihuahua and other areas of the state they explicitly warned the Americans to "get out" or suffer death.[60]

Edward Morris, the owner of the T. O. Riverside Ranch in northeastern

Chihuahua, had experienced a brief respite from the invasions of his land by armed men after Madero came to power. In 1912 the Orozco uprising against Madero led to several destructive incursions. The interlude between Orozco's defeat by Madero's forces in May and the start of the revolution against the Huerta regime in February 1913 passed quickly. Within a few months of the uprising against Huerta, Villista forces under the command of Captain Antonio Castilla occupied the Riverside Ranch and remained until 1914. In 1915 Carrancista troops replaced them, and so it went. During five years of invasions rival groups consumed and confiscated the livestock and broke the equipment. By the end of the fighting in the early 1920s the T. O. Riverside Ranch had been ruined, suffering a claimed $1,298,417 in damages.[61]

The invasions of rival forces also complicated the life of Manuela Breckenridge de Hibler, the owner of the Hacienda Pablillo at Galeana, Nuevo León. Manuela had been there since 1894, when she and her husband, John Hibler, bought the estate. John Hibler, born in Paris, Kentucky, in 1860, went to Mexico as a child when his family migrated to escape prosecution after his father killed a Union soldier. He married Manuela in 1891, and three years later they purchased the hacienda and settled down. The Hiblers improved their properties by fencing them, building barns, silos, and machinery and tool sheds, and enlarging their residence. Before John died they had developed a successful ranch on which they bred sheep and goats and cultivated grain. Following his death Manuela stayed on, raising their four children in the healthful and affluent atmosphere of the large estate. The business prospered even when the revolutionary fighting first broke out in 1911 because the rebels were engaged in adjacent states.

Hibler's luck ran out in the spring of 1913. Constitutionalists supporting Governor Carranza raided the Hacienda Pablillo, and the Hiblers took refuge in Monterrey. The Carrancistas confiscated livestock, equipment, and other materials, but the value of the property taken was only $2,826. In 1913 the Carrancistas sought only those assets needed to support their troops in the field. That situation changed dramatically during the course of 1914, when Villa challenged Carranza. That year damages and confiscations reached catastrophic proportions, bringing the Hiblers to ruin. In 1915 Villista forces under the command of General Eulalio Gutiérrez occupied the defunct estate and added insult to injury by warning the Americans to leave. Manuela's four children could have been Mexican or American by virtue of their place of birth. The family fled Mexico.

Unjustly called an incompetent and poor general by some historians, Gutiérrez was an able and merciless guerrilla leader. Early in 1914 he seized the state of San Luis Potosí, and in one of his first acts he abolished debt peonage in the state. That action was a damaging blow to the American owners of the Rascon Manufacturing and Development Company, which dominated the eastern part of the state, and to the Guggenheim and Towne interests, which held the same position in the mining industry. All three enterprises lost control over their workers and the debts owed by them. Later that year, when the Villistas and Zapatistas created their administration in Mexico City, Villa chose Gutiérrez to serve as president of Mexico because of his radicalism and ability. When the Villista-Zapatista cause lost the military initiative to Carranza's Constitutionalists in early 1915, Gutiérrez renounced the presidency and fled the capital.

Gutiérrez remained a Villista. Between 23 March and 10 May 1915, and again in June, he occupied the Hacienda Pablillo with forces that varied from 700 to 1,100 men. By June the Constitutionalists had driven Villa's forces from central Mexico, and Gutiérrez joined Villa in blaming the Americans for reequipping and harboring the previously routed Carrancistas at Veracruz. Gutiérrez's orders were "to destroy everything of use to the enemy." He chose to destroy the Hacienda Pablillo but spared the neighboring Mexican-owned estates.[62]

Apart from an invasion in June 1911 by unnamed local revolutionaries, the holdings of the Rascon Manufacturing and Development Company had escaped most of the violence during 1911 and 1912. Huerta's overthrow of Madero and the subsequent challenge by Carranza brought the ruin of the estate, which was owned by George Lee and his brothers-in-law in New Orleans.

> [T]hroughout the states of San Luis Potosí and Tamaulipas and especially the portions of those states wherein the claimant's properties were located, armed revolutionary forces, forming a part of the Constitutionalist forces operated. . . . The activities of these forces reached such proportions that in August 1913 the Federal Government of Mexico conceded control of eastern San Luis Potosí to such forces.[63]

In 1913 Magdaleno Cedillo and his followers occupied the estate on four occasions, seizing the sugarcane and others crops as well as store supplies and equipment. They also invaded the 44,800-acre Hacienda San Rafael de Minas Viejas, which was adjacent to both the Rascon estates and the Atascador Colony. Cedillo issued a warning to San Rafael owner Thomas Harding "to deliver the sum of four thousand (4,000) pesos before the 15th of this month, or the property will be burned." Cedillo exacted the punishment shortly thereafter.[64]

The settlers at Atascador fared no better than Harding did. In 1913 David and Desde Duff lived in the Atascador Colony, cultivating land they bought in 1906. In July they fled to the United States because "for several months . . . the natives had been stealing and destroying [Desde's] property."[65] At that point more than a dozen Americans in different places, including Rascon, Atascador, San Dieguito, Ganahl, Micos, and the neighboring Huasteca region, "suffered greatly from marauding bands of men." At Coco the insurgents raped two American women.[66]

The majority of the several hundred American colonists at the Blaylock Colony in Tamaulipas fled in 1912 when raiders entered their ranchos. Blaylock had subdivided and sold plots of land to some five hundred Houston and Oklahoma purchasers between 1907 and 1910. Those who took up residence there developed orchards and ranchos. They fled when attacks on foreign-owned properties intensified during the Orozco revolt against Madero. Some of the settlers returned after Orozco's defeat, but many chose to sell their properties to neighbors or hire caretakers.[67]

During late 1913 and early 1914 the uprising against Huerta to the south along the coast in Veracruz disrupted the coffee harvest. The northern inland area of the state was cut off by rebels calling themselves Zapatistas, who seized plantations and disrupted the delivery of coffee to Arbuckle Brothers. The prominent importers and merchant bankers of New York who dominated the Veracruz coffee business received only 413,799.69 kilograms. The indebted growers and their lender-merchant associates faced a decline in volume of over 60 percent.[68]

Farther south a manifest nationalism had emerged among grassroots revolutionaries at an early stage of the upheaval. On 24 December 1910 rebels lacking outside direction raided and seized the properties of the Mexican Diversified Land Company at Huimanguillo, Tabasco. After that date the American hacienda owners in the state found no relief, with armed parties occupying their lands until 1922. The U.S. Department of State concluded that the "entire state was at one time or another infested with bands of marauders." The directors of Mexican Diversified went further.

> [S]ince the different revolutionary movements occurring in the State of Tabasco, since that date [December 1910] one and another political bands, revolutionists and Government forces, always occupied that zone; especially the revolutionists who in some occasions came to be established in the government.[69]

In 1925 company president M. E. Hay filed a claim with the U.S. government for the damages suffered by his firm, listing supplies, household goods, etc., taken and destroyed about December 30, 1910, under orders of Colonel Ignacio Gutiérrez; other property taken later by other forces; two boats sold at great loss; further losses through failure of oil prospecting contracts.[70]

He then went on to list the generals and other leaders of the revolutionaries who occupied its properties over a twelve-year span.[71]

In late 1912 the Zapatistas attacked the ranch of John and Ellen Lind at Río Colorado in southeastern Veracruz, just inland from Tabasco. John had purchased the property from the Mexican Diversified Land Company, which was attempting to develop an American colony at nearby Acayucan. A sizeable number of U.S. citizens settled in the town, but Lind preferred the ranch. When the local people in that area rebelled, they invoked the name of Zapata, the legendary leader in the state of Morelos, with whom they had no contact. Ellen Lind reported that "the rebel bands murdered and pillaged and her family was visited and threatened several times by said bands." Since the unraveling Madero administration in Mexico City and the local authorities could offer them no protection, the Linds joined most of the other Americans near Acayucan in flight.

There were two waves of American emigration from southeastern Veracruz. The first came in late 1912 and the first month of 1913. A few Americans in the adjoining colonies in Oaxaca and Veracruz joined the second wave of refugees, who remained until the anti-American attacks of late April 1914 forced them out.[72]

During 1912 the American residents in the adjacent Isthmus of Tehuantepec suffered grave losses, and many fled. In April the citizenry at Juchitán, called "Juchitec Indians" by the Americans, rebelled and occupied the town of Reforma, Oaxaca. They threatened the American settlers and Mexican elites alike. Dozens of Americans fled by way of Salina Cruz, where a U.S. Army transport ship picked them up. Similar events took place at the colony of Loma Bonita. In 1912 the Loma Bonita settlers owned extensive holdings purchased from the Fortuna and Agua Fría tracts by the Mexico Land Securities Company, the Fortuna Company, and the Agricultural Land Company. The three firms had originally controlled a tract of 1,500,000 acres. Beginning in the district of Tuxtepec, immediately west of the state of Tabasco, the lands of the Loma Bonita colony extended from the town of Sanborn in Oaxaca fifty miles southward into northeastern Chiapas and terminated near the archaeological site of Palenque. The promoters had renamed a preexisting settlement "Sanborn" in honor of a fellow participant in the Land Securities Company.

In the midst of the violence of 1912, Lewis J. Haskell, the American consul, warned the 330 settlers at Loma Bonita to evacuate because of hostile revolutionaries. He advised them that conditions were "such that they should leave everything and return to the United States." Some of the 330 packed as many of their belongings as they could carry and fled the country: "[W]e had no protection whatsoever from the Mexican Government and [because of] the menacing attitude of the natives and other frequently forming bands for plunder along our river, we therefore considered our lives unsafe."[73] The colonists had settled in Loma Bonita and its environs expecting to pay for their parcels in installments. When the refugees left, they lost their investments and labor, and the land company investors lost everything they had put into the project. Within a few years the jungle covered the once cleared land.[74]

In 1911, immediately to the north, the forces of Zapata had repeatedly attacked the predominately Spanish-owned sugar haciendas. By 1912 the fighting had spread to the state of Guerrero, where the Zapatistas attacked and occupied the Hacienda Atlixtac, which was owned by General John B. Frisbie, who had served as Díaz's railroad adviser throughout the 1880s. The estate comprised about 20,000 acres of irrigated sugarcane fields. The first incident took place while the men who lived in the nearby pueblo of Puente de Ixtla were away serving in the Zapatista fighting forces. The women of Puente de Ixtla marched onto the hacienda and "burned and destroyed large quantities of sugar cane." The Frisbies claimed $40,000 in lost cane. In 1913 the revolution deepened. The Zapatista forces, temporarily aligned with Orozco, occupied the estate and appropriated livestock and supplies, damaging the Frisbies' ability to continue operations. The invasions and destruction continued at about the same level until 1915, when it became even worse. Frisbie claimed that the rebels had destroyed his property.

> Beginning in the year 1912 and continuously for several years thereafter, armed forces invaded and seized the Hacienda Atlixtac, destroying or appropriating personal property, crops, livestock, machinery and buildings located thereon with a result that by the year 1918, the property was in a ruined and devastated condition.[75]

The Mexican Revolution presented the first major political challenge to American hegemony in Latin America during the modern era. The American economic elites had invested far more capital in Mexico and its strategic resources—copper, rubber, zinc, and oil—than in any other country, and those investments were in danger of being destroyed. The tentative responses of American leaders reflected the widespread magnitude and intensity of the upheaval. Ambivalence and uncertainty prevailed among most of the financiers, industrialists, colonists, and political leaders.

By 1914 a mix of Mexican miners, agrarian workers, and village citizens had attacked virtually all of the larger American estates and most of the smaller ones. The rise of anti-Americanism intensified as the fighting among the Mexicans deepened and broadened. The struggle over land possession inevitably drew the Americans into the conflict, as did their growing wealth, their aloofness, and their unequal treatment of Mexican workers. The tensions between the revolutionaries and their American neighbors resulted from a national crisis in which the oligarchy and the foreigners were seen as an increasing threat to the nation and to local interests.

10 Interventions and Firestorms

We have overt support to the Allies by America's principal bankers, and their commitment via cash to Russia, Great Britain, and France. Their investors are likewise committed.

J. P. Morgan Jr., 18 January 1917

After the invasion of the American forces into Veracruz it was impossible to return to the property without taking great chances.

Edward Dunbar, American plantation owner, 1914

When the American Group purchased the bonds issued by the Mexican government in 1912, they hoped that their participation would help stabilize the nation's economy and renew prosperity in the Mexican oil fields. In July 1913, when James Stillman and George Baker withdrew from the loan, the remaining bondholders expected that the revolutionaries led by Venustiano Carranza would win. The revolution continued, however, and investors were discouraged. Colonies, mines, haciendas, and plantations were abandoned. Occasionally the depredations were accompanied with declarations that the "gringos" had to leave. Between late 1912 and April 1914 American interests in Mexico suffered major losses to the rural revolutionaries, and the government of the United States decided to intervene.

THE INVASION OF VERACRUZ

Carranza was supported by a number of influential Americans. He was well connected with the Texans in the Wilson administration through his earlier partnership in a Saltillo bank with the Frost Brothers Bank of San Antonio. As the prerevolutionary governor of Coahuila, Carranza had approved land grants to leading Texas ranchers in his state. Even more impressive to the Americans, he had restored properties confiscated by his own revolutionary forces in Tamaulipas and defended the nearby 2,000,000-acre Sautema tract, which was controlled by the Texas Company.

President Woodrow Wilson had lost confidence in the Huerta administration. He regarded Huerta as a dictator who had imposed himself on the Mexican people after murdering his democratically elected predecessor and had then refused to hold a "fair and free election." The Mexican president could not maintain order and protect American private and public interests in Mexico, including the production of oil, rubber, and copper, which were strategically important to the United States. Carranza's Constitutionalists were engaging Huerta's forces in the north, and the Zapatistas were attacking them from the south. By the end of 1913, presidential emissaries reported back to Wilson that Huerta could not stop the advancing revolutionaries.[1]

In the fall of 1913 William F. Buckley Sr., a graduate of the University of Texas School of Law and legal counsel for the Texas Company in Mexico, described the situation and demanded intervention in a thirteen-page letter to Colonel Edward Mandel House, who was not only President Wilson's chief adviser but a Texan as well.

> We all believe here that there is but one solution of this difficulty, and that is American intervention. . . . The great majority of the Mexican people at this stage in their development care little for political liberty. . . . We hope that if intervention comes, it will not be by the joint action of the great powers, but by the United States alone.[2]

At that time the Texas Company's only paying fields were at Tampico, and Buckley was trying to protect the company from disaster. The problem was that Lewis Lapham, who had financial ties to J. P. Morgan and Company, had outraged Colonel House and his Texas friends when he and his cohorts had gained control of the Texas Company at an almost riotous stockholders meeting in Houston in 1913. Lapham had gained the proxies of John Gates's widow, giving him a majority of shares. He also had a sharp and aggressive lawyer, Arnold Schlaet, who was a major stockholder. The company's Texan president, Joseph Cullinan, and its Texan secretary, Will Hogg, were thrown out of office, and the headquarters were moved to New York. Both men were House's intimate friends. House, who had ties to the Standard Oil Company through his daughter's marriage, wanted revenge. He supported an American invasion, but not at Tampico—Standard's fields were elsewhere.[3]

Wilson's cabinet included a number of Texans, who all supported a military intervention to protect American interests in Mexico. Wilson's Texans—Thomas Watt Gregory, David Houston, Charles Culberson, Albert Burleson, and Sidney Mezes—joined House and Rio Grande Valley landowner William Jennings Bryan in formulating a plan of action. The nationalistic Carranza was not perfect from the administration's point of view, but he respected private property, he offered a degree of safety for the tens of thousands of Americans living in his country, and the Texans liked him as a person. Despite their urging, Wilson wavered on whether the United States should depose Huerta.

Then, during the winter of 1914, Villistas threatened strategically important oil production at Tampico, which was the center of the Texas Company's operations, and other oil fields on the Gulf Coast. Production was suspended for three months, and Wilson, despite serious reservations, felt that he had to act. In January 1914 the cabinet secretly agreed to prepare the U.S. Armed Forces for an armed invasion of Mexico in order to protect American interests in strategic materials such as oil, rubber, copper, and zinc and, as a corollary, to ensure political stability. Secretary of War Lindley Garrison and Secretary of the Navy Josephus Daniels carried out the arrangements. Since "[i]ntervention had already been agreed upon . . . [it was] only a question of an opportune time and sufficient arrangements."[4] The Americans massed 24,000 troops and stockpiled ample supplies at Texas City on Galveston Bay. Additional supplies were stored at the Philadelphia shipyards and at Newport News, as well as at other points. The administration executed the necessary troop movements.

A minor episode at Tampico that preceded the invasion revealed Admiral Frank Fletcher's readiness for a fight if nothing else. In the April the Mexican army detained some American sailors who were working at a fueling station in Tampico harbor, and Fletcher pressed for an armed intervention under his command. Wilson and House resisted because the Texans wanted the invasion to take place at an even more strategic point, and a few days later Wilson ordered the invasion of Veracruz. An occupation of Veracruz would give the Americans better control of the import and export of Mexican oil—and better control over the outcome of the Mexican revolution—than an occupation of Tampico would.

The pretext for the invasion was provided by the freighter *Ypiranga*, which was destined for Veracruz and was carrying arms and supplies for the Hueristas. The ship was identified by American newspapers as a German vessel. The Wilson administration knew that a consignment of Colt machine guns had left New York on 17 April for Veracruz aboard the *Monterrey*, and earlier the president had authorized the arms shipment aboard the *Ypiranga*, a freighter owned by the Hamburg American Packet Line. The arms were being shipped to President Huerta. Certainly the owners of Hamburg American—J. P. Morgan Jr., Peter Widener, Clement Grissom, and Bernard Baker—had nothing to hide. They had received the presidential clearance for the *Ypiranga* to haul its cargo to Mexico well in advance of departure. It should also be remembered that when U.S. authorities wanted to stop a ship, it was boarded at sea.[5]

On 21 April, instead of stopping the ship, the American fleet struck at Veracruz itself. Wilson's goal was to influence the outcome of the Mexican struggle by controlling military supplies while exposing American servicemen to a minimum of risk. By seizing Veracruz, the most important entrepôt for arms entering Mexico, the United States could direct the flow of arms to the combatants. As a part of that effort American warships began patrolling the coasts weeks in advance of the attack.[6] The Mexican army withdrew, following an agreement made between its commander and the American forces.

The Mexican civilian populace resisted, mounting a stout defense, and the attack on Veracruz turned into a tragedy. The American warships bombarded the city for hours, and their upgraded guns took a terrible toll on the populace. The casualty estimates vary so widely, from the United States's figure of less than 300 to the 10,000 reported by the Cronista de la Ciudad de Veracruz (the official city historian), that neither side can be taken seriously. The bombardment allowed the U.S. Marines to occupy the city.[7] After the troops seized Veracruz, the *Ypiranga* was sent first to New Orleans and then to Puerto Mexico, south of Veracruz, where the ship's cargo of arms was discharged to troops loyal to Huerta. In May, the U.S. Army and General Frederick Funston took charge of the American forces at Veracruz, replacing Fletcher and the U.S. Marines under his command. Funston had led covert operations in the Philippines in 1901 when U.S. troops captured Emiliano Aguinaldo, the leader of the Filipino independence movement. Following President Wilson's orders, Funston established a defensive perimeter around the city but did not engage Huerta's troops, which were just outside the city, or the revolutionary forces.

In the following weeks the American troops seized extensive amounts of arms that the Constitutionalists had cached in several arsenals: the fortress of San Juan de Ulloa, which guarded the harbor on the north; the Baluarte of Veracruz, a two-square-block barracks complex facing the harbor on the south; and the one-square-block Benito Juárez lighthouse and supply depot, which was immediately inland from the piers. A large number of weapons were held in the Vivac storage facility in the Civic Building on the city's main plaza. U.S. forces also seized the *Monterrey*'s cargo, including twenty-five machine guns, and impounded three other ships that were unloading at the docks. They seized arms consignments that were stored in the warehouses adjacent to the wharves and awaiting shipment inland. These arms had reached Mexico on the *Morro Castle* and three other ships owned by the U.S. and Cuba Steamship Company. During the summer of 1914 the Americans worked with Constitutionalist officers to store the arms and to establish a joint administration for the customs house and warehouses.

In midsummer and again in November, the Wilson and Carranza administrations were able to reconcile their differences regarding issues of Mexican sovereignty. Wilson agreed to protect the Mexicans who had worked for the Americans during the intervention at Veracruz. In turn, Carranza agreed not to punish them as traitors and to protect American properties and citizens in Mexico. Funston and the Constitutionalists found a valuable ally in British oil magnate Weetman Pearson, whose relationship with the Americans dated from his projects in New York. In August the head Constitutionalist representative in Veracruz telegraphed Carranza, stating that "Lord Cowdray places at our disposal railroad from Alvarado here. . . . Leaders . . . recognizing plan Guadalupe, also capitalists, manufacturers, bankers, merchants, representatives large foreign enterprises."[8]

The American forces concentrated the captured arms in warehouses adjacent to the wharves. The exact size of these caches is unknown, but General Funston described the arsenal seized at the Vivac as "immense." The biggest operation required thirty-four man-days to move 291 crates of arms, some of them enormous, from the warehouse where they were stored to another warehouse. Six crews using wagons took four hours to complete another transfer. The American forces seized many small-arms cargoes addressed to the Mexican government and placed them in the warehouses as well. The impounded items included new Benz trucks, shortwave radios, machine guns, field and mountain artillery, uniforms, and accessories.

The American forces impounded additional shipments as they arrived. In May 467 *bultos,* or conglomerates of crates holding arms, were taken from the *Kronprinzessin Cecile.* One *bulto* weighed 6,300 kilos. Another shipment included 200,000 rounds of ammunition. In mid November the Americans impounded 354 rolls of barbed wire taken from the *Morro Castle.* Some of the arms were redistributed.

> Venustiano Carranza received the arms in Veracruz via Matamoros. These arms were stockpiled and guarded here. The chief intermediary with the Americans in this trade was General Pablo González. The machine guns were taken to the Baluarte de Santiago for the utmost security.[9]

The arms buildup continued until the American occupation ended seven months later, on 23 November 1914. The Carrancistas were now able to compete with the Villistas, and public pressure and the cost of maintaining the presence of U.S. troops encouraged Wilson to pull out. During the last two weeks the flow of arms increased. On 18 November the stevedores began working around the clock, unloading military equipment from five ships.

John Lind, the presidential emissary in Mexico, met several times in Veracruz with Carranza's son-in-law, General Candido Aguilar, and the Constitutionalist officers who were to take over. Army adjutant general W. W. Wright had told his officers at Veracruz that "[i]n the event of the withdrawal of the United States troops from Veracruz, the arms, munitions, and gun implements . . . will be turned over to the Mexican authorities." Funston was ordered by Garrison to "surrender . . . all physical property excepting money to the designated successor."[10]

On the evening of 23 November the U.S. Army guards briskly placed their rifles at "port arms," did an "about face," and moved away at "double time" from the warehouses and piers stacked with arms. Three of the warehouses measured 57.5 yards front to back and side to side and 21 feet in height. These and the other storage facilities were filled to overflowing with military supplies. At that point the Americans neatly stacked the excess on the piers. American officers deposited the keys to the storage facilities at the offices of the Veracruz Chamber of Commerce. The membership of the organization was undoubtedly representative of the landholders in Veracruz— over 96 percent of the property was owned by foreigners, and a good many of those were absentee landlords. The Constitutionalists who marched out of Veracruz two months later to defeat the Villistas and Zapatistas carried a wide array of arms, including strategically important artillery and field radios for spotters, supplied by the U.S. forces.

The Americans held 2,604,051 pesos in Mexican customs revenues in a New Orleans bank until several years later, until the Constitutionalists offered further guarantees regarding the protection of foreign property and those who had worked with the U.S. forces. The American property at stake included elite-owned great estates dedicated to rubber, ranching, timber production, and tropical and temperate agriculture, silver and copper mines, petroleum fields, storage facilities, and even refineries, as well as infrastructure companies including railroads and telegraph and power companies. American settlers and workers were expected to leave, as President Wilson had ordered.

American forces occupied Veracruz for seven months. Their presence provoked a firestorm of protest and resistance. Riots broke out across the country. Mexican troops provided an escort to Veracruz for American colonists, landowners, and estate administrators who lived close to the Gulf in the Isthmus of Tehuantepec. Hundreds of residents of the American colony in Mexico City, joined by refugees from the mining towns in the surrounding countryside, also fled to Veracruz. In Veracruz angry citizens pelted the Americans with eggs, rocks, and tomatoes. Even the conservative young Catholics of the Asociación Católica de la Juventud Mexicana formed a "Guadalupe Battalion" and sent emissaries in search of support.[11]

Tampico seethed with unrest, and the Americans in the area used the U.S. consulate as a refuge until they could be escorted to ships. In northern Chihuahua and Sonora most of the American settlers and miners who earlier had fled for their lives once again had to escape across the border. On the west coast the USS *Buford* picked up refugees from ports as far south as Salina Cruz and carried them to San Diego. The U.S. government set up camps at El Paso, New Orleans, Texas City, and San Diego for the handling of refugees, some of whom were suffering from tropical diseases and abuse from the revolutionaries. Many had lost virtually everything they owned. The evacuations of 1914 were far more widespread than were those of 1913.

Wilson's strategy in Veracruz emulated the actions taken after the occupation of Bluefields, Nicaragua, in 1909, when American forces made weapons available to the conservative rebels. His orders also paralleled those that he gave four years later, in the summer of 1918, to General William S. Graves, the commander of the 7,500 to 10,000 American soldiers in the expeditionary force at Vladivostok, Russia. Wilson directed Graves

> to assist anti-bolshevik groups but also barred interference in Russia's internal affairs. So while he assigned American troops to guard the Trans-Siberian railway that delivered supplies to anti-Bolsheviks in the interior he refused to join in punitive expeditions against Bolshevik units. . . . American firms delivered 800,000 rifles and other weapons, along with a million uniforms, to the anti-Bolshevik troops, which were commanded by Adm. Aleksandr V. Kolchak. . . . [The Americans'] assignment, besides guarding the Trans-Siberian Railway, was to protect the coal mines at Suchan, about seventy-five miles from Vladivostok. . . . [They] helped . . . to preserve a vital supply pipeline for Kolchak's forces. . . . When the American troops arrived in 1918, Vladivostok already was teeming with . . . [t]ons of unopened supplies, including crated cars and trucks, bales of cotton and machinery, [which] were piled on the docks and nearby hillsides, according to contemporary accounts.[12]

The strategy is today referred to by the Pentagon as EAT—equip and train. Varied versions of EAT were carried out at Bluefields, Nicaragua, in 1909, at Murmansk, Archangel, and Vladivostok during the Russian Revolution, and, most recently, in Bosnia in 1997.

British cooperation at Veracruz anticipated their support of the interventions at Vladivostok, Archangel, Murmansk, and Bosnia. The distance of the Alvarado railroad line from Veracruz duplicated the geographical proximity of the Russian line to Vladivostok, which provided transportation and communications, but also indicated that the penetration of the interior was limited.

FORMING THE ALLIANCE AGAINST GERMANY

Although the revolution in Mexico threatened vital American interests, the German threat to the Anglo-American alliance was even more important and required an even stronger response. The military and financial crisis presented by the onset of World War I revealed the depth of the ties between the United States and Britain, and, to a lesser degree, the United States and France.[13]

America's entanglement in the European war and the British financial crisis that ensued began in August 1914 when J. P. Morgan Jr.—who had taken his father's place in the Trio after Morgan Sr.'s death in 1913—ordered his representatives to help the Bank of England stave off a selling binge of its currency. Morgan, responding on his own initiative to a request from the British government, ordered his agents at Morgan Grenfell and Company of London to buy all sterling currency offered in the London market to halt a catastrophic decline in the value of the pound. Then, while continuing to protect the British currency, Morgan, Stillman, and Baker negotiated the terms of a series of "confidential" loans by the Trio to the Bank of England.

The Bank of England used the funds to stabilize its currency and to finance the purchase of arms and munitions in the United States, which meant the establishment of several accounts. The first series of transactions agreed upon, "confidential loan #1," eventually reached a value of $436,821,137 on 25 April 1917, despite paydowns through the liquidation of domestic and foreign assets over the three years. That initial step presaged other loans, including "confidential loan #2," which at one point totaled $344,000,000. The exact amount owed by the British government to the American bankers at any point in time is somewhat obscure owing to the myriad number of transactions—loans, securities and stocks from companies around the world, treasury bills, and gold shipments—that are recorded. In Paris the situation was at least as difficult. Stillman bought a $10,000,000 set of one-year treasury bonds from the French in late 1914 to tide them over, and Morgan accepted one-half of the burden.[14]

On 18 February 1915 the Bank of England asked the firm of J. P. Morgan and Company, the First National Bank, and the National City Bank to buy sterling bills up to an amount of $10,000,000 to stabilize the currency. The loan was financed at 3.5 percent. H. P. Davison, a Morgan partner in London, met with the chancellor of the exchequer and then informed Morgan that he would "take up quietly all sterling bills offered up to $10,000,000." On 24 February the loan was increased to $25,000,000. The First National Bank and the National City Bank each accepted a one-quarter interest, and Morgan and Company assumed the balance.[15]

As the American bankers increasingly realized the depth of the armed conflict developing in Europe they began to diversify. At the darkest moments for Britain, from August 1914 to early 1917, Morgan demonstrated the tremendous depth of the Trio's commitment.

> On March 4th First National Bank requested us to place $2,250,000 of their interest elsewhere. We gave the Corn Exchange Bank $1,000,000 and retained the other $1,250,000 ourselves, making our interest $13,750,000. . . . March 26th—as advances to this date were nearly $25,000,000, it was decided to increase the loan to $50,000,000, with interest at 4%. On May 1st we reduced the interest again to 3.5%.[16]

Morgan, Stillman, and Baker made their monies available at the prevailing interest rates. The Trio's actions were prompted by loyalty, morality, and personal identity—and an unprecedented opportunity for profit and empire.

On 28 May 1915 the French government, using the banking firm of Rothschild Frères, obtained $30,000,000. The bank offered its shares in the Pennsylvania Railroad and the Chicago, Milwaukee, and Saint Paul Railroad as security, but "the entire loan was privately guaranteed . . . by the French government."[17] The participating American banks greatly widened the range of support for the allies among America's elites. The Trio recruited the Corn Exchange and other New York banks, clients such as John D. Rockefeller, the Stillman-controlled Riggs Bank in Washington, and the Illinois Trust and Savings and First Trust and Savings of Chicago, which offered their financial support.[18]

As summer approached, the British financial crisis grew worse. The Trio sought additional financial supporters, probably not because of cash shortages but because they wished a wider participation on the part of the New York banking community for political reasons. By then Stillman held $10,350,000, Morgan $9,605,769, and Baker $4,000,000 in British credits. "On June 1st we gave participation to a few additional banks as shown below. . . . The maximum amount loaned in the period ending July 26th was $41,555,769."[19]

The British currency was now supported by all the leading American bankers. They included the directors of the Chase Bank ($2,000,000), the National Bank of Commerce, the Guarantee Trust, the Bankers Trust, and the Farmers Loan and Trust ($2,500,000 each), the National Park Bank ($1,000,000), the American Exchange Bank ($800,000), and the Hanover Bank and the Mechanics and Metals National Bank ($500,000 each), and others as well. It was not enough. In the summer of 1915 the Trio "agreed to lend a further $50,000,000 on demand at 3.5 percent, secured by [British-owned] American securities," which included holdings in Latin America. The Trio kept this transaction to themselves because it represented an opportunity to capture British-owned Chilean mining stocks. Baker took $4,000,000, Stillman took one-quarter, and Morgan picked up the balance. The British used much of the $45,170,109 for arms purchases, of which Morgan advanced $29,870,109. Meanwhile, Morgan and Kidder Peabody led a syndicate that put together $7,764,816 for the refinancing of the Winchester Repeating Arms Company and the consolidation of the Remington Arms Company's debt, which allowed the firms to increase their productive capacity. Baker and the Chase National Bank were participants. The Trio loaned money to the British in order to sell them arms produced by companies that they controlled.[20]

The strong antiwar sentiment that prevailed in the United States at the time prevented the Trio from making their actions public. The Trio demonstrated their concern in this regard during the fall of 1915, when they issued a loan to Morgan, Grenfell, and Company of London that was actually intended for the Bank of England. They also kept secret their acquisitions of British and French assets around the world. The British asked

> for $10,000,000 to keep [the] sterling exchange above 4.66. By December 18th we purchased in all . . . $9,369,199. All of the above transactions were carried in an account reading "Special Loan to Morgan Grenfell and Co., A/C Client" with the exception of the Chilean loan, which was handled through an account reading "Bank of England Special Loan Account."[21]

In November 1915 the French government borrowed $15,000,000 from a syndicate of American banks headed by the Trio. The monies went directly to Schneider and Company in New York as an export credit for the purchase of war supplies. Schneider carried through on three more loans for the same amount and purpose during 1916 and in March 1917. A number of French banks helped their government meet the demands for payment. Among them were Stillman's contacts: Rothschild Frères, Credit Lyonnais, the Banque de Paris et des Pays-Bas, Mallet Frères, the Société Générale de Crédit Industrial et Commercial, and the Banque Union Parisienne. All had worked in foreign investment syndicates with the Trio and the South American Group in the decades prior to the loan. Two participants, Mallet Frères and Old Colony Trust of Boston, had worked together on the Mexican Central Railroad.[22]

By 1916 bankers across the United States had joined financial syndicates headed by the Trio in support of Britain and the Allies. On 18 January 1917 Morgan reported that the financial support of the principal American bankers was secured "via cash" to Russia, Great Britain, and France and that "their investors are likewise committed."[23] Morgan then informed Wilson that the private resources of American bankers had been exhausted and that the U.S. government would have to step in. Wilson helped by advancing the British $200,000,000 and giving them $80,794,041 for obsolete ships that the United States did not need.

As Morgan enlisted the support of the U.S. government, the Trio continued their private efforts. Beginning on 5 February 1916, they supported the exchange value of the pound sterling at 4.67.5. On 17 February Morgan sold $22,800,000 in British treasury notes at 110.5 percent of their value to the U.S. Steel Corporation, a company that his father had organized. Morgan demonstrated his intent by stating, "We credited the proceeds of the entire block to the British Government Treasury Account."[24] Eleven of the Northeast's leading banks, including the Guarantee and Bankers Trusts and the Chase and Hanover Banks, bought up another $11,000,000 in bonds. Between February and April they drove their balance with the British government up to $92,321,136. The transactions continued.

> [We] applied $50,000,000 out of $200,000,000 advanced British Treasury by the U.S. Government. By May 5th, further advances by us had increased it again to $85,295,531.46. From this point all further purchases in support of exchange were made with funds transferred from Treasury account [from the remaining $150,000,000]. From March 1st interest was charged at 6%.[25]

Baker and Stillman each accepted $5,000,000 in risk, while the Guarantee Trust and Bankers Trust took $10,000,000 and $6,400,000, respectively. The Astor Trust Company and the Union Trust Company took smaller amounts.[26]

That spring the situation again became acute for the British, although not as severe as it would be a year later. By April 1916 the outstanding balances owed by the British treasury to a narrow group of American supporters totaled $344,000,000. At that point the British "applied" $49,195,049.40 from the "$200,000,00 advance made to the Treasury by the U.S. Government" to pay it down. On 4 May 1916 the Trio "agreed to loan Bank of England,

repayable in gold in transit or to be shipped, up to $50,000,000. . . . [W]e
purchased an aggregate amount of L38,690,000, the cost of which was carried on 'Client No. 1 account.' "[27] The Trio, in this case principally Morgan,
minimized their risk. They did not allow payments to fall too far behind.
During this period the First National Bank and the National City Bank each
advanced $2,000,000 to the British, and J. P. Morgan and Company added
$33,659,935.[28]

During January 1916 the Trio opened negotiations with the British treasury for a new series of loans. This arrangement came to be known as "His
Britannic Majesty's Government Loan (Morgan Grenfell and Co., A/C Client
No. 2 Confidential)."[29] These loans would eventually total $384,000,000 and
draw commitments from banks across the United States. The loans constituted a turning point in the American-British global relationship as the interests of the United States assumed primacy.

> January 1916—(see cables 12392 and 13143). During negotiations
> the British Treasury, through its "London Exchange Committee," for
> the sale of American securities [Western Hemisphere] here to provide
> funds to purchase munitions, we were asked if, when the Treasury
> account did not have sufficient funds, would we be prepared to make
> them a loan. On behalf of ourselves, First National Bank and National
> City Bank, (designated "Trio"), we advised we were prepared to lend
> up to $250,000,000 at 4% per annum, such rate to be subject to change
> if money advanced substantially. We stipulated, however, that when
> the loan reached this amount, we would charge .5% per annum on the
> amounts participated.
>
> June 1st, when due to a change in the money situation here (bank
> loans having heavily increased with reserves steadily diminishing)
> we informed treasury (see cable 19760) that although the loan had
> not reached $100,000,000, we were obliged to participate between
> $15,000,000 and $20,000,000 outside the Trio.
>
> June 10th—With amount loaned over $100,000,000, we notified
> Treasury that, unless sales of securities and importation of gold took
> care of future requirements, we were doubtful of being able to continue
> in the same quiet way as heretofore. Replying thereto, Treasury advised
> us of a credit of $50,000,000 to London banks held in New York banks
> which was available to us at any time. On July 10th, with amount loaned
> $140,000,000, we requested that this credit be paid to us.[30]

During the critical months from January to July 1916, the balance of the
loan reached monumental proportions, with $73,150,000 contributed by
Morgan and $66,850,000 by Stillman and Baker and a consortium of sup-
porting banks that Morgan called the "Group." The Group continually grew.

No sooner was it reconstituted than it became outdated owing to the increasing need for funds.

Meanwhile, through an agreement reached by the Brown Brothers Bank and the French government, the Brown Brothers, Morgan Hartjes (the Morgan branch in Paris), and Morgan, Stillman, and Baker formed the American Foreign Securities Company of New York. This firm then extended the French government a $100,000,000 credit on its $50,000,000 note for the purchase of arms and munitions in the United States. The directors of the Santa Fe Railroad and U.S. Steel bought into this issue.[31]

The importance of the Eastern Front to the British and French war effort, and therefore to the Trio's other investments, prompted them to extend loans to Russia. On 6 June 1916 Stillman concluded a $50,000,000 credit in Paris to the Russian state for arms and munitions purchases guaranteed by that government. Led by Stillman, Baker, and Morgan, the subscribing bankers came from every part of the United States. By December 1917 the bonds had fallen to 49 percent of their face value. Temporarily boosted by the American occupations in Russia during the summer of 1918 they reached 75 percent and then declined again. By December of 1918 they had fallen to 47 percent of their face value.[32]

During 1916 Morgan had sought funds from the trusts that he and his father had helped organize during the previous two decades. By October 1916 the limits of the private American lenders had again been reached, and the British treasury issued three-year and five-year notes to drive the debt down by $116,397,000. The war dragged on, the needs for financing continued to deepen, and the interest charged by the Americans reached 6 percent. By 10 November the Continental and Commercial Bank, the Continental and Commercial Trust and Savings, the First National Bank, the First Trust and Savings Bank, and the Illinois Trust and Savings Bank, all of Chicago, had committed $11,500,000. At the same time the leading banks in Boston, Cincinnati, Cleveland, Detroit, Philadelphia, and Pittsburgh joined International Harvester and U.S. Steel in the commitment of $62,750,000. Later, smaller institutions on the West Coast and in the South also enrolled. The demand for war materials made investment in Remington, Winchester, and other munitions suppliers highly profitable. In October 1916, consistent with that logic, Jacob Schiff purchased $60,000,000 in new bonds issued by the flourishing U.S. Rubber Company, giving it a "First and Preferred Mortgage."[33]

On 23 November 1916 the Exchequer encountered yet another shortfall for twelve critical days, and Morgan personally covered the British treasury's embarrassment and a growing crisis in the U.S. banking community.

Due to the fact that Treasury was short of funds so soon after the last
United Kingdom loan, and its possible effect upon our banks, J. P. Morgan
and Co., agreed that so far as possible it would make these loans alone.
This we did up to December 4th, when we were compelled to participate to others of the group. Advances amounting to $229,000,000 were
made to enable us to make transfers from Treasury a/c to Client No. 1
Account.[34]

A month later the Trio, led by Stillman, whose subscribers already had
investments in Russia, joined a new consortium of bankers, revealing their
deepening concern. This group of bankers in Buffalo, Chicago, Detroit, and
Pittsburgh, plus a wide assortment of New York bankers that included the
houses of Harris Forbes and Lee Higginson and Company, loaned the faltering Russian government $25,000,000 at a discounted rate of almost 10
percent. It was a desperate bid to save a faltering ally, and it deepened the
involvement of America's elite in the Russian predicament. It undoubtedly contributed to the U.S. military interventions at Vladivostok and
Murmansk.[35]

On 16 March 1917 many of the same bankers who had loaned money to
Russia committed their institutions to a $100,000,000 loan to the French
government, buying up the French notes at 99 percent of their value. The
Trio led the loan managers, and many of the largest banks in the United
States took part. The French guaranteed their notes with

certain bonds, stocks and other securities . . . to have a value of at least
$120,000,000. . . . $20,000,000 in value is to consist of securities of
American corporations and municipalities (including securities of the
Canadian Pacific Railway Co.), and . . . of the following governments:
Argentina, Uruguay, Brazil, . . . and the Suez Canal Company.[36]

The deal included the French interest in the DeBeers Consolidated Mines
Ltd. of South Africa, although that amount was "not to exceed $10,000,000."
The American financial elites were replacing the French in strategic con-
cerns around the world.[37]

During this period the British also began selling off assets. In January
1917 they offered their majority stock in the Central Argentine Railway
Limited for $15,000,000 to their once junior partners, the South American
Group. The Americans accepted the bargain, and on 6 February they placed
the money in one of the two British loan accounts maintained by Morgan
for the purchase of arms. One hundred and seventy-five investors rushed
to buy the stock. The brokers, besides Morgan, Stillman, Baker, and Schiff,
included the Chase Bank, the Brown Brothers, bankers in Chicago and else-

where, and Kissel, Kinnicutt, and Company, which was a major player in Chilean copper production.[38]

During 1916 the Trio had purchased some of the British share in the Cerro de Pasco, while Morgan led the way in acquiring control of the Penyon Corporation of Anthony Gibbs and Sons in London and its nitrate deposits near Antofagasta, Chile. The participants included the leading American investors in Mexico and their heirs, the American Group as individuals and their institutions as well, and some newcomers. All were interested in Latin America. Among them were William Randolph Hearst, James Ben Ali Haggin, George T. Bliss, Charles T. Barney, Henry Du Pont, Percy Rockefeller (son of William and son-in-law of Stillman), John D. Ryan, E. R. Stettinius, and H. P. Whitney, who had financially supported Díaz in 1876.

This expanded group of Americans bought up the British interests in the Antofagasta and Bolivian Railroad, Argentine government bonds, and the Braden Copper Company in Chile, in addition to four Cuban railroads and sugar companies. The purchases were made through the Trio's new Foreign Securities Company. Daniel Guggenheim and Eugene Meyer Jr. formed a syndicate to buy up $35,000,000 of the British interest in the Chilean Copper Company. This was a major coup. The development of its field at Chuquicamata between 1913 and 1917 had been impressive, growing from a proven reserve of 95,657,000 to 354,000,000 tons, with a rich ore content that ran between 1.89 and 2.98 percent. The Americans, while supporting Britain's war effort, had achieved dominance in a key area of British power and influence in South America.[39]

On 5 February 1917 yet another British bid for cash support brought U.S. Steel forward to take up $25,000,000. E. H. Gary and Ford Frick, two of its leaders, simultaneously bought into the sale of British interests at Cerro de Pasco. Baker, Schiff, and Stillman also committed more cash to the buyouts, while an even wider array of bankers across the nation joined in the effort to save the British currency and enable that government to purchase arms in the United States. In March the Americans even bought into British holdings in Asia. A broad diversity of Americans invested in the Burma Corporation. Future president Herbert C. Hoover assumed 15 percent of the company, or 140,000 shares, probably to help sell them in the American market. Morgan and a partner later bought 75,000 of Hoover's shares and sold them at a loss on the London market when the war ended.[40]

The Trio's commitment to France, Great Britain, and Russia swept the entire U.S. financial system, including the U.S. Treasury Department, into the fray. The rapid transfer of economic resources from Britain and France to the United States that began in August 1914 changed America's determination to sit out the crisis. The situation jeopardized the entire financial structure of America, and political and economic pressures continued to grow in the first months of 1917. Wilson's decision to declare war in April had been made for him. He could hardly remain neutral when by intervening he could save the bankers and the financial system and increase the power of the United States in international politics.

On 7 August 1917 the balance owed by the British treasury to a narrow group of American supporters stood at $313,000,000. American financial support for Great Britain continued throughout the remainder of the war years. The British had already yielded to American hegemonies in Mexico, Cuba, and Panama, and the war heightened the pace of that process. The French repayments are unknown, but they were guaranteed by assets that included Latin American government bonds. By the end of World War I, Latin America was dominated by a new economic and political giant. In 1918 the Trio purchased, at the request of the U.S. government, an $80,000,000 British debt incurred in early 1917 when the American bankers were financially exhausted and unable to meet the needs of the British government. Morgan appealed to President Wilson for government support. He obliged, and a year later the bankers were able to buy the note.[41]

In 1916, in the vacuum of power created by Great Britain's vulnerability, Frank Vanderlip had announced the creation of the American International Corporation (AICorp), a short-lived attempt to create a global holding company. With Stillman occupied in Paris, he also saw a chance to rise even further as an individual financier. He wanted to assume the chairmanships of the IBC, the National City Company, and the new corporation at the same time. The *Wall Street Journal* characterized the AICorp by comparing it to two powerful organizations that reigned in an earlier era: "[I]n its broad charter and unusually broad scope . . . [it] may be likened to such organizations as the East India Company and the Hudson Bay Trading Company, to which England owes much of her supremacy in world finance."[42] The AICorp integrated the most powerful United States capitalists in a global effort, about which Vanderlip said, "Latin America will be the first field to be cultivated." The board included Morgan, Stillman, Baker, Charles H. Sabin, A. H. Wiggin, Percy Rockefeller of Standard Oil, James J. Hill, the head of the Northern Pacific Railroad, Cyrus McCormick, the head of International Harvester, and meatpacker J. Ogden Armour. AICorp expanded to South America, China, Europe, and Russia. Stillman, who was still the chairman of the board of the National City Company and Bank, felt threatened by Vanderlip's ambition and killed the project by withdrawing National

City's support. The beginning of World War I had focused the interest of the American financial leadership in other directions.[43]

REVOLUTIONARY NATIONALISM

During 1914 local insurrectionists, empowered with nationalistic and revolutionary fervor, sacked Mexican- and American-owned estates, especially in the states of Chihuahua, Jalisco, San Luis Potosí, Zacatecas, and the Isthmus of Tehuantepec and in states along the length of the Pacific and Gulf Coasts, including Campeche, Chiapas, Guerrero, Oaxaca, Sinaloa, Tamaulipas, and Veracruz. They also attacked American-owned estates in Coahuila and Durango. In the course of the year, the revolutionaries attacked the properties of more than a thousand American companies and "pioneers." The rebels shot dozens of American citizens and warned the others to leave.[44]

In April 1914 Edward E. Dunbar and his spouse ended seventeen years of residency at their 150-acre sugar cane and coffee plantation known as the Hacienda Santa Inez, at Cuichapa, Veracruz. The Dunbars had gone to Mexico during the late 1890s from their home at Port Huron, Michigan, in search of opportunity and a higher standard of living. By 1914 they had achieved both objectives. The local tax assessor valued their plantation at 66,900 pesos, and they were well on their way to paying off a mortgage held by the National Bank of Mexico for 18,000 pesos. Their workers were harvesting the new sugar crop, and they owned other properties in addition to the plantation.

The American invasion at Veracruz electrified Mexico and unleashed a public fury against the U.S. citizens residing there. When the American navy attacked the port city on 21 April, all hell broke loose in Cuichapa. Dunbar described "disturbances . . . hazardous to our personal security." Their Mexican neighbors broke into their home and seized their cash, furniture, clothing, and kitchen utensils. "[A]ll moveable property of value, particularly horses, saddles, mules, pack saddles, cows, oxen, carts, etc. [and] my iron safe" were taken. Dunbar stated that "[a]fter the invasion of the American forces into Veracruz it was impossible to return to the property without taking great chances of encountering serious difficulty and possibly loss of life." Leaving their belongings, the Dunbars fled to Veracruz and then to the United States. As the unrest spread across the Isthmus of Tehuantepec most of the Americans fled their homes, leaving fifteen haciendas and plantations abandoned.[45]

In the city of Guanajuato the Americans in the 225-member foreign colony fled in two train cars on the day of the invasion. They had barely begun the perilous journey to Mexico City when a railroad employee warned them that a "mob" was waiting for them at the city of Silao. He advised them to leave the car, which was to be put on a side track and attacked. The Americans moved to the middle of the train and, with the windows shuttered so that they could avoid detection, rode it to the nearby city of Irapuato, where they caught a night train coming from the west. They continued to the national capital, where drivers from the U.S. embassy carried them by automobile from the station to the Hotel Genève. The Americans from Guanajuato then learned that a crowd had rioted the night before, breaking the windows of the U.S. embassy and the American Hotel, and threatened the personal safety of individuals. They were divided over what to do. Eleven elected to join other Americans who were leaving the next day on the train for Veracruz under the safe conduct escort of personnel from the British and German embassies. The train carried the flags of those nations.[46]

Irving Herr, the American chief engineer of the Cubo Mining and Milling Company, blamed outside agitators for the hostile feelings of the Mexicans. Nevertheless, a statement he made ironically revealed the deeper causes of the discontent:

> The peon does not hate foreigners. . . . He is, however, very easily influenced, and one or two labor agitators, or political agitators, can work havoc in a well-ordered community, if allowed free rein. Unfortunately he will believe for a time at least anything he hears. . . . For such a people democratic government is not possible. . . . In the meantime the central government should remain a military one, for . . . there must be order.[47]

The refugees reached Veracruz fifty-two hours later. When they arrived they found a chaotic scene in the harbor, which was filled with not only their compatriots in flight but also "all the boats full of Mexicans who had gone there . . . for safety." These ships included several Ward Line steamers specially commissioned for the evacuations.[48]

Near the port of Tampico, the National Oil Company of New York suffered grave misfortunes at its drilling site on the Pánuco River. Earlier in April the company's exploration teams, after prolonged efforts, had finally struck a major gusher. The well started producing 30,000 barrels of petroleum daily. Shortly after the Veracruz invasion, however, revolutionaries occupied the site and carried away construction supplies and other necessities. By the end of May the troops had "compelled" the company to abandon the place. The result of this "forced abandonment" was a runaway well and "the loss of a large quantity of oil." The lost petroleum was valued at $1,880,050. The well was ruined and overflows extended over the adjacent producing sites of other oil companies.[49]

On 25 April 1914 the wave of anti-American outrage reached the Blaylock Colony in Tamaulipas, the San Dieguito colony in San Luis Potosí, and the Loma Bonita colony in Oaxaca. Mexican troops entered Loma Bonita, which was being developed by the Mexican Agricultural Land Company and the colonists, and placed sixty-three American residents under arrest while hunting for thirty-seven others. After threatening "the men of the colony with death" the troops forced them into railroad boxcars and deported them in the company of a British government representative. The governor of Oaxaca and the district chief of Tuxtepec assumed custody of the Americans' property. Two years later several Americans returned to Loma Bonita over "impassable roads," only to find the place abandoned and overgrown with jungle. The Mexican Agricultural Land Company counted its losses at $101,150, a surprisingly low figure considering that more than sixty-three residents and employees had been at the scene.[50]

General Huerta's federal army was defeated in the summer of 1914, but the revolutionary forces divided, each claiming presidency. In the north, Villista commanders took over and administered Mexican-owned estates. A call went out for Carranza to immediately "approve measures for the redistribution of the land." This issue contributed to the second phase of the revolution. Fighting erupted between those who supported Carranza and those who backed Villa and Zapata. Professionals, provincial elites, and the *pequeña burguesía* formed the leadership of the Carrancistas, while peasants, rural workers, and some professionals led the Villistas and Zapatistas.

In the days following the U.S. intervention at Veracruz, revolutionary turmoil gripped the state. The American plantation owners abandoned their estates and fled to the city. The growing hostility engulfed the Arbuckle Brothers Coffee Company. Arbuckle Brothers had dominated merchandising in Veracruz, but during the 1914–15 harvest revolutionary turmoil deepened to such an extent that deliveries from growers to the company dropped to a mere 178,925 kilograms. By 1915 the civil war between the Zapatistas and Carrancistas had become so intense in the state that most Mexican coffee plantation owners also abandoned their estates. The rebels found the properties attractive because they were highly capitalized and the stores of coffee could be sold on the black market. The growers went broke and defaulted on the mortgages held by Arbuckle Brothers. The Americans, however, were in no position to replace them or exercise property rights. It is possible that Arbuckle Brothers bought coffee from the rebels. By 1916, however, the New York directors, comprising Arbuckle and the Jamison heirs, dissolved their insolvent Mexican company.[51]

By the end of 1914 the sense of immediate fury had died down, only to be replaced in many places with a smoldering resentment. On 13 November a concentration of Carrancista troops in Guanajuato changed their allegiances to Villa and threatened the American mines around Cubo. They robbed the Peregrina Mining Company's headquarters and took the horses. Hostilities continued even after the withdrawal of the invasion force on 23 November. The Villistas controlled Guanajuato, but the towns had no police presence. In one incident soldiers attacked mining company employees near Cubo and killed one person, but the Villista and Carrancista leaders largely left miners free to work in the hope of economic benefits through taxation.[52]

In 1915 some of the leaders and soldiers among the otherwise antagonistic Carrancista and Zapatista revolutionaries in Chiapas agreed that the American ranch owners and settlers at the Mapastepec Colony on the Pan American Railroad should be driven out of the state. Violence and threats had caused many of the American colonists to flee aboard the USS *Buford* in 1912. In 1915 Mexican officers and their men began individually warning and threatening the Americans that had stayed behind to leave, but some hung on tenaciously. It took until 1919 for the expulsion effort to succeed.

In November 1915 Carrancista troops entered the La Blanca plantation outside Mapastepec in Chiapas. La Blanca was the home of Cora and Charles Sturgis and Cora's mother, Sarah Keenright. The Carrancistas alleged that the Mexican laborers on the estate were working under conditions of servility. They ordered all of the "servants" to leave the property and during the next two years repeatedly entered the plantation to seize assets. In 1917 the Carrancista desire to oust the Sturgises came to a head. Captain Julio Castellanos and another captain named García entered the big house with ten soldiers. According to the Sturgis family, the men held them at gunpoint and announced, "We are going to drive all the Americans out of here and divide up your property. This property belongs to Carranza." The apocryphal statement captured the reality of the moment. The Sturgises attempted to leave Chiapas, but the U.S. consuls at Frontera and San Juan informed them that Zapatista troops and brigands made the roads too "dangerous [for] traveling and if we had no more trouble, we had better stay at the plantation." Trapped, the Sturgises stayed on until June 1918, when Zapatista General Rafael Cal y Mayor, leading two hundred soldiers, seized the estate, made them prisoners, and took them in tow. For over six months he subjected them to forced marches, hard labor, sleep deprivation, semi-starvation, and beggary as they made encampments across Chiapas and the Isthmus of Tehuantepec. Cal y Mayor sought no pecuniary gain. He did not ask for ransom. Sarah Keenright died during the ordeal because of the harsh conditions. On 18 February 1919 the Zapatista general released the surviving couple, and they fled Mexico.[53]

At the Rascon hacienda in Tamaulipas, similar conditions prevailed. On 23 April 1914, when the news of the American invasion at Veracruz reached the area, soldiers under the command of Captain Reyes Espinosa ranged across the Rascon properties, which extended some 30 by 60 miles. Magdaleno Cedillo led the men at Rascon. There the revolutionaries found vast stores of sugar, sugar cane, alcohol, corn, dry goods, and industrial supplies. They took over the mill, worked the cane, and sold it. They threatened the American supervisors and those among the more than 10,000 Mexican employees who failed to manifest revolutionary zeal. Other troops and armed men invaded the Atascador Colony to the east and the San Dieguito Colony immediately to the south, terrifying the American colonists. Most of the "demoralized" Americans at Rascon and the nearby colonies fled to the United States, and many of the Mexican workers also fled.[54]

During the rest of 1914 and 1915, the situation remained so chaotic that neither the employees living in "approximately one hundred villages" nor the remaining Americans on the Rascon estate or in nearby colonies felt safe. In late 1914 rival Villistas and Carrancistas began fighting in and around the complex, and the workers joined the revolutionary tumult. They burned one of the big houses at the hacienda annex known as La Mula and leveled it. Villista General Tomás Urbina and the Cedillo brothers were hostile to the Rascon enterprise, and they repeatedly raided it. After Villa's defeats in central Mexico during the spring of 1915 his allies in the area attacked the estate even more violently. In 1917 the Rascon directors finally gave up and abandoned the estate. They lost some $880,679, which had been invested in the mill, the power plant, a railroad, company stores, storage facilities, residences, and unsold crops.[55]

The Cedillo brothers were the Americans' major problem. They not only raided properties but also practiced terror to drive the foreigners out. Linton M. McCrocklin had owned 43,000 acres near Micos since 1903. His Espiritu Santo Plantation included 400 acres in sugar cane, 300 in *para* grass, a large area in bananas and citrus fruits, 60 "houses" for his workers, and a large house for his family. On 15 November 1913 Enrique Salas, a local rebel of unknown affiliation, and 1,000 local armed compatriots demanded cash and supplies. Unable to extract sufficient funds, the rebels placed a rope around McCrocklin's neck and lifted him so that his toes barely touched the ground. They left him in that condition while sacking his home, that of the foreman, and the company store. The employees were not molested. The revolutionaries warned McCrocklin that they would be back in a few days to retrieve a payoff of some 3,000 pesos. McCrocklin, the manager, and the employees fled.[56]

To the west, in Zacatecas, the Intercontinental Rubber Company experienced unending troubles during the revolution. Local unrest, disrupted communications and transportation, and labor shortages caused the company to lose money. The nadir was reached in 1914, when, as a result of the invasion of Veracruz, the company's profits sank to .17 of 1 percent, from 9 percent in 1911. An analyst observed that "a return to normal conditions in Mexico would make a great difference in the affairs of the company."[57] During late April and May 1914 insurgents seized $60,000 in cattle, corn, and wheat, destroyed fences, and carried away tools. Men under the command of General Eulalio Gutiérrez repeatedly entered the company's Cedros hacienda in May and carried away horses, mules, corn, wheat—literally anything they could find. During the following six years raids carried out by other rebels continued to disrupt the transportation of Intercontinental's products. Between 1910 and 1917 the Morgan bank lost $144,095.98 on its Intercontinental Rubber investment.[58]

VIOLENCE NEAR THE BORDER

During the early spring of 1915 a force of 2,000 Mayos and Yaquis under the leadership of Chief Felipe Bachomo, aided by Lorenzo Lieba (also known as Cajeme), constituted the strongest Villista force in the northwest. They carried out raids against the great estates in the area around the Río Fuerte in Sinaloa and the Yaqui River in Sonora. The largest properties assaulted were those of the Richardson Construction Company, owned by John Hays Hammond, Harry Payne Whitney, the Knickerbocker Bank of New York, the United Sugar Company, and the Sinaloa Land and Water Company, as well as some anonymous "Californians." The "12 major attacks" on the Richardson estates on the north side of the Yaqui River caused the company to suspend operations. The owners of the smaller ranchos included an even mix of several dozen Americans and Mexicans. The landowners, who almost all supported Villa's rival Carranza, fled their homes and concentrated in the towns of San Blas, Los Mochis, and Ahome. They decided to defend the United Sugar pumping station, which pulled irrigation water from the Río Fuerte. On 27 April they fought the Villista force there and were quickly routed. In the hours that followed, the angry Villistas rounded up a number of noncombatants and killed D. M. Brown, an American rancher.

The Villista rebels in Sonora, Sinaloa, and the mountains of western Chihuahua included a high percentage of indigenous people. Their opposition to outside intruders in addition to the Constitutionalists led to the ruin of virtually all of the Mexican and American landed estates. Benjamin Johnston, whose ruthlessness had given him control of the Ochoa estates and the properties of the utopian colonists at Topolobampo, was the notable American exception. He survived by surreptitiously supplying the Yaqui rebels with arms despite his role as U.S. consul and the Wilson administration's opposition to the Villistas. His support apparently had its limits, however—when Felipe Bachomo, the Yaqui leader, was captured Johnston quietly abandoned him. The destruction of the other sugar plantations in Sinaloa, and in Morelos, Puebla, Veracruz, and San Luis Potosí, eliminated most of Johnston's domestic competition and provided him with high prices in the Mexican sugar market. Then World War I gave him an equally important opportunity in foreign sales. By the end of the war and the revolution Johnston had become one of Mexico's richest and most powerful men.

In early 1914, immediately to the south of the Mayo and Yaqui attacks, local Carrancistas settled in at the Hacienda de Quimichis, owned by partners John T. Cave and R. L. Summerlin. In effect, the revolutionaries nationalized the estate. The troops raised "corn, beans, beef, cattle, horses, and mules." They stayed until the Villistas drove them out in December. Then the Carrancista garrison at Acaponeta changed sides and became Villistas, and they too settled on the hacienda. Each group demanded "taxes" from the Americans. Some workers at the estate summed up the situation:

> Finally, on 6 November 1915, exactly one year after our field foreman had been killed, our general manager and vice-president, Mr. W. S. Windham, was assassinated inside the big house of the hacienda. The superintendent was obliged to abandon the property and retire to Acaponeta.[59]

The Carrancista officers expropriated all production that exceeded the sharecroppers' entitlements. The Americans did not return to the estate until at least 1919.[60]

The wave of public outrage that followed the invasion at Veracruz reached the northern frontier in one day. On April 24 the rebels were already "loading and seizing all live stock belonging to Americans in vicinity of Musquiz" in Coahuila. During the following week Huerta's forces announced the confiscation of "all stock from American owned ranches," but it was the Carrancistas who in early July occupied the "San Miguel Ranch operated by the American firm of Meier and Rose [and] . . . killed three ranchmen and stole horses and other property." At the same time, Carrancista Colonel Ramón Martínez "claimed to be a tax collector came to the Piedra Blanca Ranch and destroyed all of our record books and papers." Martínez tried to eliminate the documentation of well over $61,000 in confiscations, but the Americans had duplicates.[61]

During late 1914 and early 1915 the Villistas gained control of the border region, but in the spring of 1915 the situation suddenly changed. They suffered a series of serious defeats in central Mexico following the massive infusion of U.S. military aid on behalf of the Carrancistas. As the Villistas lost, they widened their attacks on American interests. In Coahuila they invaded the Piedra Blanca Ranch again and laid it to waste, despite the status of the owner, John Blocker, who was the U.S. consul at Ciudad Porfirio Díaz. Under the command of local leaders José Rojas and Antonio Chávez, they appropriated or destroyed livestock, wagons, and grain, and again "burned books, papers, and records." On 15 May Villista captain Felipe Musquiz and his men threatened to kill 116 select breeding bulls unless a head tax was paid. Blocker informed the Villista that there was no such tax law, at which point Musquiz "touched his rifle and told Mr. Blocker that this was the law." Blocker paid him $580 for the release of the cattle. About 5 June Musquiz took ranch foreman G. C. Delamain prisoner and held him for a $2,000 payoff. Musquiz collected the ransom in a bizarre ritual in which the Americans transported the cash across a bridge past soldiers standing at attention and wearing crossed bandoliers. Musquiz counted the money in front of a reporter from the *San Antonio Express* and then released the hostage.[62]

The situation in northern Coahuila deteriorated so badly in the face of Villista hostility that Blocker and his American personnel, who had returned when Villa offered them protection in late 1914, abandoned the ranch in July 1915 and did not return until 1919. The property destroyed during and after 1915 totaled $271,216 in value. In 1912 the ranch management had described the revolutionaries as "respectful and kind to the ranch employees." In 1915 the revolutionaries threatened them with "death." As Villa's regular army disintegrated, his forces adopted a strategy of guerrilla warfare throughout Chihuahua and parts of Sonora and Coahuila. The Villistas found previously overlooked cattle on the T. O. Riverside, Palomas, and Piedra Blanca haciendas and marketed them in El Paso, Columbus, and Eagle Pass, using the monies for arms and provisions. The Villistas confiscated some 17,000 head of cattle, 3,000 goats, and 1,800 horses from the Piedra Blanca. During the next three years the properties fell into virtual disuse. The remaining livestock was scattered and wild, irrigation systems were hopelessly damaged, and houses, corrals, fences, and barns had been destroyed.[63]

Other American and Mexican landowners fared even worse. Nearby, the revolutionaries killed three heirs of General E. O. C. Ord on the 88,560-acre ranch given to him in 1884 by his son-in-law Geronimo Treviño. Local revolutionaries, men and women with rural working-class backgrounds, stayed on the remote ranch for several years. Some claimed membership in the Kickapoo, Pottawatomie, and Seminole settlements that had been denied land tenure status on the estate by Díaz during the late nineteenth century.[64]

Edwin Marshall at Las Palomas hacienda and the heirs of Edward Morris at the T. O. Riverside Ranch suffered a series of devastating losses. After years of raids and occupations by Orozquistas, Villistas, and, to a lesser degree, Carrancistas, the Americans withdrew their own nationals from the properties and established new administrative operations in Texas. In these cases cowboys joined the rebels and betrayed the location of herds hidden away on the vast expanses. In many cases their Mexican neighbors suffered fates that were even worse. Rebels seized a Chihuahua elite family on their estate that neighbored the Palomas and executed them.

After April 1914 and during 1915 the grassroots Villistas in the Sierra Madre of western Chihuahua and eastern Sonora turned against land and mine owners with increasing fury. The Americans paid a high price. In December 1915 an angry Villa attacked Agua Prieta, a smelter town controlled by Phelps Dodge and located opposite Douglas on the Sonora-Arizona border. Villa and his 3,000 troops were defeated by the Carrancistas, who received American artillery support. After Villa's retreat, he occupied the Dolores Esperanza mines, knowing that they were closely tied to Phelps Dodge. His men robbed the stores and shot several Mexican employees and at least one American before departing.

The Villistas also exacted revenge at the Southwestern Land and Cattle Company ranch near Parral, owned by Edwin Chamberlain and the Fuller brothers. On 1 December 1915, in compliance with Villa's orders, a force of retreating Villistas under the command of General Joaquin Terrazas took the last 248 head of cattle on the estate and refused to give the manager a receipt. After that raid there was not much left to take.

THE PUNITIVE EXPEDITION

In March 1916 an embittered Villa attacked Columbus, New Mexico, a U.S. Army garrison town on the border. The Villistas killed eighteen Americans, but the U.S. Army killed more than a hundred Villistas. Wilson reacted to Villa's attack by launching an invasion of Mexico under the command of General John "Blackjack" Pershing from the area of Columbus and El Paso. Villa hoped to expose Carranza's ties to the Wilson administration and the weakness of Carranza's government by provoking U.S. intervention. Wilson hoped to strengthen his position in ongoing acrimonious negotiations with President Carranza and to eliminate the threat that Villa's forces posed to peace along the border. The military action brought disaster to numerous Americans still living in Mexico.[65]

The U.S. forces, 12,000 strong, brought a full complement of military trucks and even observation aircraft with them. Marching in several columns, they made their way deep into Mexico, meeting serious resistance only a few times. The most notable battle, fought at El Carrizal between an American detachment and the Carrancistas, resulted in a Mexican victory. Pershing's contingency plans included establishing his headquarters at Parral, just north of a line extending from Mazatlán to Tampico. The possibility of a U.S. protectorate deeply concerned the Mexican government. The U.S. representatives negotiating the withdrawal of U.S. forces with the Carranza government in late 1916 sought, as explained by Friedrich Katz, to "Cubanize" Mexico by imposing conditions modeled after those in the Platt Amendment, which gave the United States considerable control in Cuba after American troops withdrew following Spanish-American War. The American negotiators demanded the Mexicans accept a clause that stated:

> The Government of Mexico agrees to afford full and adequate protection to the lives and property of the United States, . . . and this protection shall be adequate to enable such citizens of the United States . . . [to operate the] industries in which they might be interested. The United States reserves the right to re-enter Mexico and to afford such protection by its military forces, in the event of the Mexican government failing to do so.[66]

Some of the men around Carranza added a flirtation with Germany to the nationalism directed against American interests. The dialogue with the Germans, which the Carrancistas never considered more than mere talk, led to the Zimmerman telegram, which promised the return of lost territories if the Mexicans would join the war against the United States. The Wilson administration reacted angrily to Carranza's intrigue and the apparent machinations of the Germans. The telegram was probably the work of British intelligence.

The Mexican public and the Mexican administration became increasingly nationalistic in the face of Pershing's advance. Before the American invasion Villa had lost popularity and could gather only slightly more than 500 combatants. Public outrage fueled the Villistas, and soon they could mass as many as 5,000 men. The animosity intensified between the Villistas and the local U.S. mine operators, some of whom had survived earlier surges of anti-Americanism. In March 1916 Villista troops circled behind the forces under Pershing, returned to the Chihuahua-Sonora border region, and overran mines and haciendas. The American miners abandoned their properties, in some cases with only hours to spare. The Dolores Esperanza, Creston-Colorado, El Rayo, and La Dura mines had been abandoned on orders from the U.S. Department of State. These mines were nominally owned by Ernest McLean and E. M. Leavitt of New York City, but in reality they were probably the property of Phelps Dodge. The Villistas attacked the mines at Batopilas and the Phelps Dodge installations at Nacozari during 1915 and 1916. In 1916 James Douglas and President Wilson's close friend Cleveland Dodge reluctantly closed the Nacozari mines and refinery.

In early 1916 chief engineer Herr visited the mines at Cubo and reported on "worker unrest." Using the metaphors of a mining engineer, he stated that "there was something stirring which showed things were hot under the surface." H. L. Hollis, the overseer for Mexican operations for the Palmer family of Chicago, unfortunately ignored his warnings and hired a group of mining engineers to restore operations at the Cusi mine in Chihuahua. Villistas intercepted their train, forced the Americans to disembark, and killed them all. In 1922 the Palmer estate administrators in Chicago rewarded the hard-driving Hollis for his aggressive approach by making him the general manager of all their interests, which included mines in Mexico and the western United States and at least one elegant hotel in the Windy City.[67]

In May 1916 an anti-American backlash to the Punitive Expedition swept across Chihuahua. During the height of the public fury provoked by the Pershing expedition, some Villistas camped about twenty-five miles from Perry Holly's 20,000-acre Hacienda de Sainapuchic, near San Andres. Holly had bought the estate only three years earlier for what he thought was a bargain price of 20,000 pesos. The Villistas had repeatedly raided the ranch since late 1915, however, and stripped it of resources. Holly did not receive the Wilson administration's warning for Americans to evacuate, probably because the estate was so remote. The Villistas suspected that Holly was a "spy." Their desire for vengeance, his resistance, and their frustration at finding no supplies led the Villistas to kill him by gunshot.[68]

After the Villistas left, the Americans at Dolores, Chihuahua, found that the local people were divided in their attitudes. The Americans employed loyal Mexican caretakers, but the caretakers, in turn, were unable to gain the cooperation of the local authorities. Believing that their "lives and property were being threatened," the owners resorted to private police forces. They placed L. F. Castro in charge of the constabulary, which they armed and trained. The guards were "for the most part loyal, but were insufficient in numbers to cope with the throngs of raiders and thieves." For several years there were "twenty or thirty men stealing high grade ore from the mine, with no effort being made by the municipal authorities to stop this practice." The owners did not reopen the mines at Dolores until the 1920s.[69]

Carranza had hoped that the U.S. Army would eliminate the Villistas, but, as the invasion continued, he found that his government was threatened by a loss of public support for its failure to challenge the Americans. In late 1916 the Mexican leader finally demanded that the U.S. forces end their advance. That demand, the hostile reaction of the Mexican public, a riot against Pershing's men at Parral, and Pershing's failure to track down Villa and his followers resulted in a public relations disaster for the United States. Wilson decided it was time to leave. On 5 February 1917 the American troops crossed the border and reentered the United States. The search for Villa and the invasion of northern Mexico had ended.

In the wake of the Punitive Expedition, the Villistas stepped up their attacks on American holdings in Chihuahua. The raiders returned to the slowly recovering Chamberlain–Fuller brothers' estate and took 350 cattle in May 1917, eighteen months after they had stripped it the first time. Chamberlain and his partners, however, would not go away, and they began restocking the ranch. In December 1918 the Villistas confiscated a herd of 692 steers. They also took 266 tons of feed, 419 hectoliters of maize, 118 cattle that had already been slaughtered in the ranch's rendering plant, and various other livestock, horses, and equipment. The ranch was attacked again by Villistas in June and July 1919, and losses were similar.[70]

The Punitive Expedition provoked extreme danger only in the north-central region, but it had long-term effects. Mexico's constitutional convention met at Querétaro in the winter of 1916, and in February 1917 the delegates adopted a new constitution, known as the Constitution of 1917. Article 27 threatened the gamut of American interests. It asserted Mexican ownership of all subsoil resources including oil and minerals, declared the government's right to nationalize properties for agrarian reform, which placed American landholdings in danger, and prohibited foreign ownership of lands along the borders and coasts. The writers of the constitution had pinpointed the areas of U.S. hegemony.

The Carranza government in Mexico City was gaining strength. As it did, it marginalized the Villistas in the north and Zapatistas in the south.

While the government gradually extended its control, it used the courts and diplomacy to advance its interests over those of the American entrepreneurs. The Tampico Navigation Company experienced both strategies. Tampico Navigation, a subsidiary of the Southern Oil and Transport Corporation of Delaware, occupied a centrally located landfill adjacent to the Pánuco River at Tampico. Southern Oil held some 73 percent of the $996,800 in common stocks that had been issued. Capitalized at $2,000,000, and with offices in New York, Tampico Navigation provided pipelines, piers, dock facilities for refining and storage, and transportation services for the American oil complex, which extended from the Laguna de Tamiahua and Tampico to Galveston Bay and New Orleans.

Since 1912 Mexican revolutionists, beginning with the Orozquistas, had repeatedly attacked the company's properties. In 1913, while bands of rebels stole food, money, and equipment, the Constitutionalists and the company began a prolonged conflict. The company directors felt they were performing a vital service by providing oil transportation and delivering supplies. They had absolutely no sympathy for Mexican revolutionary or nationalist goals. Beginning in 1913 Carranza's son-in-law, General Candido Aguilar, who was operating from his headquarters south of Tuxpan, began to harass the company. Aguilar felt justified in exercising martial powers for the revolutionary cause. He seized property and imposed forced levies. These exactions were never very large—the largest totaled only some $6,000—but they infuriated the company directors. On 3 June 1914 a small Carrancista force, led by local leader Francisco Marriel, burned down the company distillery at Ganahl, causing $200,000 in damages. Daniel Morales, the chief of police, compounded the directors' outrage when he "appropriated furniture, etc. taking merchandize to sell it for his own account and using the earnings of our dairy for his benefit."[71] At that point the directors shut down operations.

They reopened three months later, after General Manuel Peláez restored order to the region, a condition he maintained for about two years with the help of some 6,000 well-armed troops. Peláez was supported by the directors of the Tampico Navigation Company and Edward L. Doheny, the head of the Mexican Petroleum Company. Two shipments authorized by President Wilson, totaling 11,000 rifles and 7,000 cartridges, to the Tampico News Company could well have been intended for Peláez.[72] In 1917, however, the Carranza administration was finally able to assert its authority in Tampico. It immediately came into conflict with Tampico Navigation over the rights to the former marshlands, which the company had developed by dredging the river. The local Carrancista representatives, no doubt influenced by Peláez, had recognized the company's claim to the land. Under Mexican law, however, littoral areas could be claimed by the federal government, and that is what it did. The authorities seized nearly three critical acres in the center of the oil complex. The directors protested, litigated, and eventually appealed to the U.S. government, but had no immediate success. The Constitutionalists felt they were restoring order to the countryside and reasserting Mexican ownership over properties adjacent to the nation's ports that had previously been under American control.[73]

North of Tampico, locally based conflicts prevailed. In August 1917 a band of twenty armed local men raided Ingebricht Ole Brictson's San José de las Rusias hacienda. An army unit of about one hundred troops chased the raiders into the nearby hills, but they returned in January, and this time the soldiers offered the American owner no relief. When the "bandits," as Brictson labeled them, realized that official intervention was not imminent, they returned again and again, carrying out "six or seven raids thereafter." The army failed to react despite the defeat of Villa and marginalization of Peláez. Since Carrancistas controlled the area, it appears that the long-standing resentment of the local authorities toward the Brictsons, which dated back to the 1890s, had surfaced again. This time it involved the attitudes of the army officers. Given the refusal of the authorities to provide protection, Brictson tried to operate the estate in absentia by using Mexican intermediaries, but the property lost money and he fell behind in the payment of rapidly increasing, locally imposed estate taxes.[74]

BLACK GOLD

In Campeche political tensions grew more critical each year as the sides recognized the region's potential for oil. The struggle between American and Mexican interests was often hidden. The likelihood of large oil and gas deposits under the Campeche shoreline brought the powerful American interests that were incorporated as the Laguna Corporation into the fray against Carranza and succeeding Mexican administrations. They struggled quietly for the next twenty-five years. A great deal was at stake and both sides were steadfast. Interestingly, neither side mentioned oil. Neither side wanted to reveal its hand. The Mexican government pretended that its major concern in getting rid of the Laguna Corporation was for the purpose of agrarian reform in a vast, almost uninhabited area. The Mexicans wanted control of the Campeche coastline, but they did not want to aggravate the already tense relationship between the two governments. Campeche held strategic importance as well as the certainty of profits and power for entrepreneurs.

The directors of the Laguna Corporation owned 604,000 acres in Campeche, south of the operations of John Markley and Isaiah Miller. Local elites had led campesinos in a strike against the owners of the Laguna estates in 1911, but for the first three and a half years of the revolution Laguna avoided the working-class uprisings that devastated other estates. Laguna and its neighbor, Mexican Gulf Company, were quick to complain about their losses, but they did not degrade Mexican officials. Laguna's damages did not reach the extremes that were incurred by Markley and Miller—the local Mexicans had identified the worst offenders. The directors attributed the loyalty of their employees to director and social reformer Charles H. Thompson's application of enlightened labor policies, including liberal credit and pay in Mexican currency rather than scrip. They were probably right in the short term, but they had many enemies in Campeche, and after April 1914 they experienced their own worker unrest.

The directors of the Laguna Corporation held a strong position relative to their American neighbors. Charles B. Fritz, James Lichtenberger, and Thompson were closely tied to the leading New York and Philadelphia monied interests. They had acquired prime land for a mere $1,000,000 and had established their facilities in Campeche for less than half that amount. Between March 1911 and March 1914 they shipped more than 3,000,000 feet per year of "cedar, mahogany, and other hardwoods" to the United States. The price for hardwood dropped each year, from $95.38 per one thousand feet in 1912, to $82.40 in 1913 and $73.82 in 1914, but those figures provided a handsome margin of profit. In 1912 Laguna grossed $286,143 on its hardwood stumpage alone. The figure fell to $247,200 in 1913 and $221,460 in 1914. Those totals are impressive when one considers that Laguna planted the cleared areas in henequen, that the income from chicle was not available for the first three years of the revolution, and that chicle income exceeded the hardwood earnings in the years thereafter. Laguna succeeded in keeping its costs down once the products reached the United States because the company operated transportation and storage facilities in New York and Philadelphia and because its directors were well connected in that sector of the American import market.[75]

The rise of violence in the state and the raids by outside revolutionaries and government forces in search of supplies finally forced the directors of Mexican Gulf to abandon the business. In 1914 the directors shut down operations and began negotiations with the Laguna Corporation, their erstwhile competitor, to run their estates under a lease arrangement that took effect in 1919. Despite the revolutionary unrest, the Laguna directors increased their operating capital by recruiting new directors, including Charles R. Miller, the governor of Delaware, and General W. D. Snyman. Enjoying the support of important New York and Philadelphia banks and the Du Ponts, they were better equipped to survive the revolutionary crisis than were Markley and Miller and Mexican Gulf. They knew the property rested on a lake of oil. It is no surprise that they tried to outlast the soldiers who repeatedly entered the property and took livestock, food, and other provisions.[76]

In 1915 and 1916, "by reason of friction between Mexico and the United States, and Mexican labor troubles, and restrictions placed on the movement of labor from one place to another," the American forestry and chicle companies fell into a deep crisis. The companies dominated landholding in Campeche and controlled its economy. The labor unrest and continuing raids by revolutionary forces and government troops created an insupportable situation for the Americans. Even the Laguna Corporation's leaders, with their financial strength and their U.S. marketing network, felt the effects of the crisis. In 1915 and 1916 the Laguna reduced its production of cedar, mahogany, and other hardwoods from 3,000,000 to 800,000 feet and sold it at a mere $76.15 per thousand feet. The conditions of unrest and depressed market prices caused a decline in output of almost 70 percent between 1914 and 1919.

Between 1911 and 1915 the Laguna directors, despite labor unrest, had grossed between $200,000 and $300,000 per year from hardwoods alone (there is no data for chicle production). By 1917 their capitalization, which was larger than that of their neighbors, had enabled them to survive the decline while their neighbors became defunct. In 1917 and 1918, after years of turmoil, the directors correctly announced to the Laguna stockholders that the assessed value of their holdings was holding steady. In 1917 those properties totaled $10,467,076 in capitalization and $265,450 in current assets, and in 1918 the respective figures were $10,464,635 and $207,048.

The following year proved to be a watershed for the Laguna directors. Political setbacks and depressed market prices in the United States sent them reeling. The state government and the Carranza regime encouraged peasants to carry out land invasions by issuing agrarian reform proclamations and other nationalistic edicts. Carranza had already challenged the American elites with a tax on petroleum and reminded them that oil was a subsoil resource ultimately owned by Mexico. He wanted to transform their titles into concessions controlled by the government. The company's hardwood exports grossed only $57,990, with a net profit of $12,515 based on a reduced timber harvest of 757,798 board feet, and the volume of sales reached only 25 percent of the level attained in 1913. The directors of the Campeche-Laguna Corporation, which was controlled by the Laguna Corporation, announced a $6,914,000 loss in "real estate and standing timber" to the agrarians between 1918 and 1919 and $50,000 in "fixed improvements."

In 1919 the Mexican government seized several hundred thousand acres of the American properties in Campeche, underscoring the growing differences between Carranza and the highest figures in American finance and polity. In 1919 the Campeche-Laguna Corporation and the neighboring Mexican Exploitation Company were already divisions of the Laguna Corporation. The Mexican Exploitation Company owned 1,610,000 acres of "timber, chicle, and henequen lands" in Campeche. The companies appear to have never exploited those lands, perhaps holding them as a reserve. At this point the Carranza government, without mentioning oil, announced the dissolution of the Campeche-Laguna Corporation and the cancellation of its land concession. The Americans fought back despite the obviously poor prospects for a successful business in that political climate and the hopeless nature of the chicle market.[77]

Until 1919 the directors of the Laguna Corporation had remained in the background. Now, as their assets declined and the political uncertainty grew, they moved to take absolute, public control of their interests in Campeche. They enlarged the Laguna board to include powerful oil men. In 1919 the reorganized and expanded Laguna leadership featured banker and gas impresario John Gribbel, financiers Charles H. Thompson of Philadelphia and Vermont, A. J. Stevens and M. J. Murphy of New York, and oilman and investment banker Arthur B. Leach of New York and Chicago.

Gribbel became a leading figure in Laguna's new brain trust. He exercised considerable influence in Philadelphia and New York banking circles as a director of the Girard National Bank in Philadelphia and the Leather Manufacturers and Importers and Traders National Banks in New York, as the president of the American Gas Meter Company and the Tampa Gas Company of Florida, and as a director of several other oil and gas companies. Stevens owned the investment house and marketing empire that carried his name, and Murphy was a banker in New York.

Arthur Curtis Leach emerged as a principal owner of Laguna. His financial connections were crucial to future oil and gas development. He was a director of Cities Service Power and Light Company, a high-technology firm that was still on the cutting edge of oil discovery and development at the end of the twentieth century. He was president of the Columbia Gas and Electric Company and a director of the Island Oil and Transportation Corporation, the Massachusetts Oil and Refining Company, the Union Gas and Electric Company, and several other gas, oil, and coal companies. He served as the president of the Investment Bankers Association of the United States and as the head of the Leach Brothers investment bank on Wall Street. His political connections were equally impressive. President Wilson appointed him to the Liberty Bond Committee during World War I.

Leach's associates considered him to be one of the most brilliant and successful businessmen of his era. He had business associations with Henry Doherty of New York and other leaders in the fields of utilities and oil financing. Doherty was a leading American investor in Latin America. Leach and his close friend Victor Du Pont Jr. sought to develop the St. Lawrence River as a source of hydroelectric power. Du Pont served as a director of the International Lumber and Development Company, which was adjacent to Leach's Laguna property. Their association in the St. Lawrence Seaway project underscores their joint ownership of vast landholdings and oil deposits in Campeche. Leach's contemporaries noted his "interest in promoting other ventures in power and oil development requiring large capital investments."[78]

The documents later released by the directors to the U.S. Department of State in pursuit of claims for damages say nothing about oil, yet the presence of oil served as the motive behind the actions of the Campeche and Mexican governments and the Laguna directors. Both governments had known for decades that the Mexican subsoil held rich reserves of oil. The Mexican government had asked J. W. Wiley, who was one of America's most famous geologists and mineral experts, to survey the region. He made this report in 1896:

> After making a thorough study of the petroleum fields and many explorations, I find that there is a larger extension of paying oil springs in the republic of Mexico than in any other part of the world. . . . That some six years past I visited the petroleum fields in the state of Tabasco and in my judgement the two oil currents . . . one down the Pacific coast, and the other down the Atlantic coast, come together below the Isthmus of Tehuantepec and form a subterranean lake, or deposit of oil, with a much larger extension than the oil fields of Pennsylvania; that there are more oil seepages to be found in this section than in any other known part of the world and in my opinion more subterranean deposits than perhaps those in the Caspian Sea in Russia.[79]

British oil interests under Weetman Pearson and, later, Royal Dutch Shell had dominated southern Veracruz, Tabasco, and the Isthmus of Tehuantepec in the early twentieth century. The American oil companies had concentrated their exploration and development along the northern coast of Veracruz and Tamaulipas. The Laguna Corporation's holdings in Campeche broke British domination in the south and placed the Americans in control of Mexico's largest oil deposit.

Continuing reports of oil ooze from the southern end of the Gulf kept Gribbel, Leach, Fritz, Lichtenberger, Thompson, Stevens, and Murphy busily engaged. They knew that if they accepted the mandates of Carranza they would lose great opportunities for wealth and power. The extensive interests of Gribbel and Leach in the gas and oil business and their experience in the Gulf of Mexico through firms such as Cities Service, Island Oil and Transportation, and the Tampa Gas Company gave them the knowledge and experience to maintain their position in Campeche. The directors plunged ahead, giving company president F. B. Lasher all the authority for expansion that he needed. Carranza reacted by seizing poor farmlands in sparsely populated and swampy southern Campeche, but he knew the stakes were high.[80]

The struggle that left ever more Americans in Campeche exhausted and unwilling to continue presented the Laguna directors with new opportunities for expansion. Most of the other operations in the region had to shut down. Some were ruined. Economically strong, the directors of the Laguna Corporation were ready to benefit from the adverse conditions that had eliminated their competitors. In 1919, shortly after reorganizing and bringing Leach and Gribbel into the action, the Laguna Corporation took over the Mexican Gulf Company. The merger was made to look like a lease to address the Carranza government's concerns about monopoly ownership. Why would the Laguna directors acquire 760,000 acres and increase their exposure when the Carranza government was taking steps to curtail their operations? First, they risked very little. Investigation reveals that they paid the owners of Mexican Gulf a percentage of the profits, not a preestablished sum. In de jure terms the relationship was a lease, but in fact Laguna took control of the land at no extra cost and held control for at least twenty-eight years.

Moreover, taking over Mexican Gulf's lands and accounts helped the Laguna directors to diversify and at the same time maintain an economy of scale. The acquisition dramatically increased Laguna's production and sale of chicle. Laguna gained the Wrigley chicle accounts in Chicago and added Mexican Gulf's shipping and processing network, which served the Midwest, to their own list of shippers and buyers. In 1919 the directors grossed $430,024 from the sale of chicle and realized a net profit of $229,450. The Laguna directors needed chicle because they had been losing money on hardwoods. Their profit on hardwoods for the year came to only $125,131. The new emphasis on chicle allowed Laguna to survive the inroads caused by the Carranza government and to maintain its dominant position in the forestlands of Campeche and in the chicle market in the eastern half of the United States.[81]

Despite Carranza's seizure of several hundred thousand acres, the Laguna directors still controlled the Pital estate, which had 604,000 producing acres. The acquisition of Mexican Gulf added more than 700,000 acres to their holdings. The long-range interest of the Laguna Corporation was not chicle production and the few hundreds of thousands of dollars that were available through its trade. The Laguna directors sought to maintain their strategic position until new technology made oil production in the region feasible. As a director of Cities Service, Leach would be one of the first to know when it became possible.

Between 1917 and 1920 the Campeche government continued converting property to Mexican ownership by claiming that estates did not have "clear titles" or that taxes were in arrears. The state officials took those actions despite the fact that many of the owners continued to argue the boundary disputes in court.[82] In contrast to the Laguna directors, most of the American landholders in Campeche were willing to sell what they had previously considered valuable. Some faced so much hostility from the government, workers, unions, and revolutionary state administrations that they abandoned their holdings. Mexican owners also left their properties. Hundreds of thousands of abandoned acres in Campeche were purchased, mostly by private Mexican interests and the Mexican government. Most of the buyers, as well as the sellers, were interested in producing and selling chicle, hardwoods, and henequen. They lacked the experience with gas and oil that Gribbel and Leach possessed.

The newcomers bet that the violence and nationalism would abate. They bought land and leases at bargain-basement prices from exhausted owners, many of whom wanted out for whatever price they could get. Some knowledgeable Mexican elites took advantage of the opportunities. One obtained the title to Miller and Markley's vast San Pablo hacienda, where so much violence and controversy had arisen over forced labor. One of the former owners, Victor Du Pont, must have been very unhappy.

Carranza's confrontation with the Laguna interests in 1920 was one more nail in the coffin of his presidency. His hostility to American banking, petroleum, and property interests, especially along the borders and coastlines, ensured that aid from American interests went to General Alvaro Obregón Salido—a major client of the Chase Bank—when he announced his insurrection in 1920. Seven governors of the American Southwest quickly joined the chorus of support for the prospective Mexican administration.[83] When President Obregón, future president Plutarco Elías Calles, and interim president Adolfo de la Huerta challenged the Carranza government, the Laguna directors were still holding fast.

CLOSE OF AN ERA

Between 1916 and 1920, as the Carranza government attempted to gain control over Mexico's natural resources, it developed an ever stronger position in confronting and gradually bringing under control the organized labor movement. In 1916, in central Mexico and along the Gulf Coast from Veracruz to Tampico, anarchosyndicalist union members had challenged company owners and even the government. While rural workers sought control of the land through agrarian reform, industrial workers bargained for a greater voice in and even control of management the organized labor movement. In 1916 the Carranza administration beat back the challenge of the 150,000-member Casa del Obrero Mundial in Mexico City when the organization tried to force concessions that included worker management, higher wages, and improved labor conditions. The Casa's counterpart in Tampico, supported by the Industrial Workers of the World (IWW), fared only marginally better. In the spring of 1918 the Confederación Regional de Obreros Mexicanos (CROM), a more moderate labor group, gained the support of the Mexican government. As a result, American entrepreneurs obtained a somewhat more predictable labor environment. The American Federation of Labor (AFL) quickly supported the CROM, and American labor leader Samuel Gompers delivered a supportive speech at one of the CROM's first congresses.

Working together, the U.S. and Mexican governments, the AFL, and CROM undermined the influence of the anarchosyndicalists and the IWW. In 1918 Mexican government and union officials supported the creation of the Pan-American Federation of Labor (PAFL). The AFL and CROM used the PAFL to promote trade unionism in opposition to the anarchosyndicalist Confederación General de Trabajadores (General Confederation of Workers) in Mexico and the rest of the Americas. In the state of México, the CROM gained rapid headway, backing a membership drive for workers employed in Mexican and American companies and ensuring contracts that contained sizeable increases in wages. Nationwide, however, the unevenness of the Mexican economy and the wage structure left room for the radicals to maneuver and survive, especially in textiles and the construction trades.[84]

Payments on Mexico's foreign debt remained in arrears and required rescheduling. Devaluations of the peso, the overprinting of monies by competing factions, and disrupted trade between 1910 and 1920 had created insolvency. The economic travail of the Mexican government strained its relationships with American bankers and industrialists. By 1920, as a result of nonpayment for services rendered, the Compañía de Terrenos de la Calzada de Chapultepec and the Chapultepec Land Company of Mexico City, both connected to the First National Bank and to leading New York architects, faced bankruptcy. The Mexican government would not pay bills totaling 917,994 pesos for paving, sewers, drainage, water pipes, and other utilities around the Paseo de la Reforma and in Chapultepec Heights and Colonia Roma.[85]

The banks that held the nation's debt, including J. P. Morgan and Company, National City Bank, the First National Bank, and the Chase Manhattan Bank, insisted on stiff payment schedules that could not be met, while the oil companies and landowners sought reassurances regarding their interests. As a result three American committees, one of bankers, another of oilmen, and a third comprising U.S. government negotiators, began a series of meetings in 1917 with Mexican officials that quickly became deadlocked and remained that way until the overthrow of Carranza. The impasse in gaining guarantees from Carranza cost the Mexican leader much of his support among the leading American interests. Many of them supported the revolution led by General Obregón, who overthrew Carranza in September 1920.

When the political leaders of the United States decided to take control of the Panama Canal project in 1904 and invade Mexico in 1914 and 1916, they had reason to consider the interests of the immensely powerful individuals who had planned an American empire by investing in those areas of the world during the previous half-century. The elites who led the United States into the Third World also created a binding economic relationship with the British and French governments that deeply influenced the decision and timing of America's entry into World War I.

The financial leaders had created syndicates of the nation's wealthiest citizens to bankroll the global development of transoceanic cable and steamship companies and then to support the British in the war. They had established their domination of the railroads, ports, and natural resources in Mexico, and then they moved to Panama and Central America. They had created the IBC, the first American multinational bank, and had enlarged their sphere of operations in Latin America, Asia, and Africa. They had increased their economic and political power globally through the Anglo-American alliance and were employing revolutionary innovations in technology, especially the internal combustion engine and electricity. They had expanded on an unprecedented scale.

11 Crisis in the New Regime

After making a thorough study of the petroleum fields and many
explorations, I find that there is a larger extension of paying oil
springs in the republic of Mexico than in any other part of the
world.

J. W. Wiley, American geologist, 1896

In 1920 a new era in relations between Mexico and the United States began. Following the assassination of Carranzo, de la Huerta led the first Mexican government since 1910 that did not face widespread violence. The new
leaders sought stability and, in some cases, social justice. Francisco Villa struck
a deal with de la Huerta, agreeing to retire from politics and to begin ranching in Durango. The four-year term of de la Huerta's mentor, the formally
elected President Alvaro Obregón Salido, began in September.

As American and Mexican officials sought a working relationship satisfactory to both sides, their respective publics continued to pressure them.
Negotiations continued between the governments and the special committees representing the interests of American bankers, petroleum companies,
and the U.S. government. Mexican workers sought the realization of their
rights as written in the Constitution of 1917 and demanded that foreign companies accept national laws.

AN ERA OF REFORM

Mexico was still a primarily rural society after the revolution. Over 80
percent of its citizens lived outside the cities, and the pastoral economy
provided the basis for work and sustenance. During the 1920s both agrarian and labor reforms surged forward. The leaders of the small towns clamored for redistribution of the land and more effective political representation,
while union members in the cities clamored for higher wages. Some union
members sought *auto gestion*—workers' self-management. The Mexican
landholding elites and the agrarian populations of the villages, pueblos, and
rancherías were determined to recapture their self-defined spheres of

343

influence. The era was one of intense conflict, and the government, the agrarians, and industrial unionists frequently carried out threats of violence.[1]

The advocates of land redistribution at all levels intensified their campaign. In 1920 Obregón issued the Plan de Agua Prieta, which proclaimed the exemption of "small properties" from agrarian seizures. Obregón specified that a small property could not exceed 100,000 acres. In the litigation carried forward by American landholders in the Mexican courts and before the various claims commissions, the Americans, whether large estate owners or smallholding settlers, split up their properties and argued that they were exempt from agrarian confiscations because they were small property holders.

In 1921 the Mexican Congress passed an agrarian reform bill, laying out the procedures and rules for the redistribution of land. Local agrarian juntas, or committees, from hundreds of villages, pueblos, and even smaller unincorporated settlements in the countryside interacted with agrarian politicians in the Mexican Congress and the political bureaucracy. Sometimes local citizenries were stimulated into agrarian actions by political administrators, but more often the impetus came from below. During the early 1920s the most important concentration of agrarians was found in the Comisión Nacional de la Refoma Agraria (National Agrarian Reform Commission). In the early 1920s the Partido Nacional Agrarista (National Agrarian Party), headed by Antonio Díaz Soto y Gama, a senator and former Zapatista, became the most visible manifestation of agrarianism. It is clear, however, that the bulk of agrarian unrest and legal actions derived from local campesino constituencies. Local agrarian juntas often used violence against local elites and large landowners who opposed them. The attacks on small and large property owners often forced the government to preempt further attacks by disbursing land.[2]

In 1918, as a result of the threat to their interests, William F. Buckley Sr., a legal counsel for the Texas Company in Mexico and a land and oil company owner in Tamaulipas, and Edward L. Doheny had already created the National Association for the Protection of American Rights in Mexico. In the years that followed they gained important support from Senator Albert Bacon Fall, who carried on a highly polemical Senate committee investigation of Mexican "outrages." Buckley, evicted from Mexico by Obregón for counterrevolutionary activities in 1923, campaigned against the Mexican government for years. Hundreds of Americans, rich and poor, joined the association, determined to "protect American rights." They included George Carnahan, president of the Intercontinental Rubber Company of Mexico, Walter Douglas of Phelps Dodge, Thomas Lamont, a partner at J. P. Morgan and Company, Chester Swain of Standard Oil, Ingebricht Ole Brictson, the Atascador colonists, and hundreds of small landowners. The leaders of the group often met at the Murray Hill Hotel in Manhattan. They and other Americans lobbied the U.S. Congress and the executive branch but, ultimately, had no observable effect on the resolution of the crisis.[3]

Important private American interests continued to litigate and communicate their concerns to the Mexican leaders. They included Robert Towne and George Foster Peabody of the Metalúrgica Mexicana, the International Harvester Corporation, the John Deere Company, ASARCO, the Hearsts, the Marshalls on behalf of their Las Palomas hacienda, and Bernard Baruch and Nelson Aldrich of the Continental Rubber Company. They enjoyed mixed success. Their compatriots who held small properties were even less successful. The U.S. government, especially the U.S. Department of State, largely ignored them while concentrating its efforts on behalf of the financiers and petroleum companies.

In Sonora the combination of Yaqui attacks and agrarian demands finally pushed the Richardson Construction Company into bankruptcy. The Richardson firm, managed by William Richardson and H. A. Sibbett, was actually owned by Harry Payne Whitney, John Hays Hammond, the Knickerbocker Bank, and "anonymous California interests." Richardson had pioneered irrigation in the Yaqui Valley in the last few years before the revolution. During the 1920s the residents of the communities of Huachimoco, El Huarache, Palo Parado, San José, and Bacum demanded and received portions of the Richardson properties. In 1927 Whitney, Hammond, and their partners sold the property to the government and the corrupt Obregón. The latter divided it into two parts, one for himself and the other for agrarian disbursements.[4]

In 1921 Obregón issued an edict against Cargill Lumber Company, a New Mexico subsidiary of the Cargill grain transportation and trading company. Obregón's declaration supported the tenets of agrarian nationalism.

> It being necessary to proceed to the revision of all the contracts and the concessions made by former governments from the year 1876 which have as a result the monopoly of lands, waters and natural resources of the nation; and the Executive being empowered by virtue of the last paragraph of article 27 of the Constitution to declare null such contracts as effect grave injury to the public interest . . . after studying the case it may proceed to make the declaration of nullity.[5]

The Mexican officials held that foreigners had been required to obtain a presidential authorization to acquire lands in border and coastal states in the 1840s and thereafter. In addition, Díaz's transfer of the Cargill properties in Chihuahua to José Limantour was considered a gift because that land had been exchanged for invalid claims to tracts in Baja California. The government's ruling was clear: "The Department of Agriculture and Development had no power to make a gratuitous gift to the Messrs. Limantour either of the lands located in the districts of Guerrero and Abasolo in the State of Chihuahua, nor of those located at Tehuantepec."[6]

The Special Claims Commission took up the Cargill case in 1923. The commission had been established that year by the United States and Mexican governments to settle disputes arising from damages incurred during the Mexican Revolution between 1910 and 1921. Each government had equal representation on the commission, and each side investigated the claims and then negotiated a settlement. The American representatives realized the gravity of the company's situation. Cargill, one of the nation's most powerful private companies, pointed out that it had been unable to develop the property because of recurring Orozquista and Villista threats to the safety of Americans. The company wanted $1,375,000 in damages. The commission delegates noted the lack of development on the site and notified the Cargill interests that they would be paid $642,000. The authorities in Mexico City, however, balked at that figure. They eventually agreed to pay damages totaling $300,000, a far more generous percentage of the original claim than those obtained by less powerful American claimants.[7]

In 1923, as a result of two years of negotiations between the Mexican government and representatives of American special interests and the government of the United States, the Obregón regime was formally recognized by its American counterpart. De la Huerta was in charge of the negotiations for the Mexican government. The agreement, called the Bucareli Accords, resolved the financial and property disputes between the two countries that had grown out of the revolution of 1910 and the Constitution of 1917. As part of the agreement, a committee of bankers representing the leading firms that had financed Mexican development programs since the 1880s negotiated debt repayment schedules with the Mexican revolutionary government. A counterpart committee made up of representatives of the leading oil companies obtained a satisfactory modification of Article 27 that declared that it could not be applied retroactively and that the rights to subsoil resources that had been purchased before 1917 were not subject to seizures. The Mexicans also agreed to the amount claimed against the government by its foreign creditors, including the purchasers of bonds that had been issued by various opposing regimes during the revolution.[8]

SEIZURES AND FORECLOSURES

The Bucareli Accords had little effect on agrarian seizures. On 21 November 1924 Obregón seized another large tract in Chihuahua by invalidating the contracts issued by Díaz in 1889 to Ignacio Sandoval, which the Mexican land surveyor had sold to the Pine King Land and Lumber Company in 1903, 1909, and 1910. The tract contained 517,000 acres of pine forest. The president cited the failure of the company to colonize and improve the concession. Instead, Pine King had harvested trees. The company entered into prolonged litigation that reached the Mexican Supreme Court, but before the judicial decision was handed down, negotiations with Obregón's successors paid off. In 1930 the minister of agriculture recognized the validity of Pine King's titles, allowing them to sell the property on the open market.

As a part of the accord, company representative Harvey Basham agreed to divide the land suitable for farming into 12,500-acre lots and the timber property into 100,000-acre sections for sale to independent buyers. In that way the Mexican proscription against regional monopolies of land and resources would be accommodated. The sales had to be concluded within three years, and the state retained the mineral rights. Basham dropped his claims before the Special Claims Commission to placate the agriculture secretary despite a warning that a grievance once dropped could not be reinstated. Later, the minister of agriculture and Basham learned that the president had appropriated 300,000 acres of Pine King lands for agrarian reform on 26 October 1929.[9]

To satisfy the demands of the rural citizenry in Chihuahua, the governor, Ignacio Enriquez, seized land either through direct decrees against American and other large landholders or, if taxes were owed on the property, through foreclosures. One of the principal motivating factors behind the governor's actions was his desire to maintain public order in an area where support for the Villistas' agrarian programs had made their Division del Norte the largest force in the Mexican Revolution. National, state, and local governments carried out these seizures across the nation, however, even in those areas where agrarian unrest had been minimal. Expropriations were sometimes made to give rural people relief, but they were always made in pursuit of Mexican control over natural resources.

On 10 November 1922 Governor Enriquez seized 11,000 of 220,000 acres along the border that were owned by Alfred Shapleigh of Saint Louis and his American partners. The governor gave the land, part of the Santisima tract, to the inhabitants of the border pueblo of Vado de Piedra. Shortly thereafter he increased that allotment to over 12,000 acres. On 13 November he granted an additional 9,000 acres from the Shapleigh holdings to the nearby pueblo of San Antonio. In 1924 and 1925 Enriquez and the state government of Chihuahua took further action. The state treasurer taxed the Shapleigh holdings 112,043 pesos on an assessed value of 450,000 pesos, or 25 percent. The valuation of the land was four times greater than previous assessments or those given similar properties in the state. In 1925 a U.S. government investigator assessed the northern 100,000 acres, almost half of the property, at $64,384, or 125,000 pesos, far less than the Mexican estimates. Later, during litigation between the two governments, the Mexican side reduced its valuation to a small fraction of the original. Enriquez then changed his strategy. After refuting the complaints of Shapleigh, his associates, and the U.S. officials, the governor seized the 100,000 northern acres of the Santisima tract that fronted the Rio Grande. By leaving the American partners without access to water, this seizure rendered their remaining land worthless, although it remained taxable. Chihuahua officials justified the seizure of the riverfront by claiming that the American owners "had not subdivided their holdings according to law." During the 1940s the land fell into disuse, and the Mexican authorities foreclosed for the failure to pay taxes.[10]

By the early 1920s the American owners who had abandoned estates that exceeded 1,000,000 acres, such as the T. O. Riverside Ranch and Las Palomas hacienda in Chihuahua, and the Piedra Blanca hacienda in Coahuila and the San José de las Rusias hacienda in Tamaulipas, were now vulnerable to foreclosure under laws passed during those years by the state governments. The laws targeted idle lands, lands for which taxes were unpaid, and lands that were valuable to the agrarian reform movement. These laws stood in addition to those of the federal government's agrarian reform program. Mexicans living near the giant estates claimed properties on the basis of need through their state and national agrarian commissions, and local authorities exerted their taxing powers in cases where absentee owners could not prove that payments had been made. Successive presidents ruled that the original land grants given to the survey companies during the Porfirian era were invalid. Those grants had been the source of most of the larger American-owned estates.

The heirs of Edward Morris claimed losses of over $500,000 in livestock and property damage on the T. O. Riverside Ranch during the revolution, and the combine of the Jennings, Blocker, and Lytle heirs itemized damages to the Piedra Blanca totaling $271,216. But those damages paled before the effects of the government-led attacks on foreign property owners that took place during the 1920s. On 26 June 1924 Obregón announced that the northeastern Chihuahua land grant given to impresario José Valenzuela by Díaz on 15 May 1886 was illegal. This ruling invalidated the private title to over 985,000 acres of the Riverside Ranch, about four-fifths of the estate. On 30 March 1925 the governor of Chihuahua expropriated the property that contained the Riverside Ranch for the state agrarian reform program. The trustees of the Morris estate appealed the governor's decision, asking for the right to sell the Riverside to the national government or Mexican private interests at a "reasonable price." The Chihuahua governor seemed to agree with the proposal and temporarily revoked his decree pending the negotiations.

The two sides debated the issues between 1925 and 1929. In 1927 the governor seized 165,000 of the remaining 250,000 acres for agrarian reform purposes. In desperation the trustees retained civil engineer Bruno Trejo, who appraised the value of the lands on the defunct estate at 2,695,915 pesos, a figure the Americans quickly accepted. In 1929 they submitted the Trejo estimate to the Chihuahua authorities, but the authorities balked at paying such a high price and reasserted the 1924 presidential decree, claiming that most of the property that Morris had purchased was illegally obtained. On 18 January 1929 the secretary general of Chihuahua officially notified the Americans of the nullification of 985,000 acres of the Riverside Ranch. At that point local people overran the estate, occupying buildings and the irrigated areas. The Chihuahua authorities seized a total of 1,150,000 acres of the Riverside estate. The Piedra Blanca hacienda, originally purchased from private parties, was taken over later by the national agrarian commission and given to farm workers in northern Coahuila.[11]

In 1928 the surviving Ord heirs sold the Nacimiento hacienda in Coahuila to Dudley Jackson, a physician in San Antonio, and his partners. The Ords were discouraged by the assassinations of three of their kinsmen and the insecure nature of their land titles. The Ords' property had been taken from the Sanchez Navarro family by Benito Juárez for supporting the French and had been given to the Ord family by Geronimo Treviño. The Ords had little hope of retaining the ranch since the Mexican government was nullifying similar disputed land grants throughout the country. Jackson and his friends bought the remote ranch with the expectation of using it for hunting trips.[12]

In Zacatecas the directors of Intercontinental Rubber faced a seemingly endless fiasco. Revolutionaries had attacked their Cedros and Grunidora haciendas for almost ten years, leaving them devoid of assets. Yet the stakes were big enough, given the growing market for latex products in the United States, for the New Yorkers to continue their efforts. In 1917 their common stock peaked at $35, buoyed by a favorable international market and the promulgation of the new Mexican Constitution, which seemed to promise tranquility. The company still harvested guayule and produced about 10 percent of the world's rubber supply. The Torreón plant processed 1,060,851 pounds yearly. The U.S. Rubber Company, which had an "understanding" with Intercontinental, bought much of its product. In 1918 the price of rubber fell because of reduced demand and the rise of synthetics. The earnings available through dividends fell from a high of $2,268,184 in 1910 to a low of $165,000 in 1918. That year the factory at Torreón milled 1,787,131 pounds of rubber, but the directors could sell only 1,285,000 pounds through fiscal 1919. By 1920 the directors were in trouble. A "very serious crisis developed in the world's crude rubber market" and was compounded by Villista guerrilla activity near Torreón, which disrupted fuel shipments and paralyzed rail traffic.

In the early 1920s the Intercontinental directors still held assets of about $28,000,000, including real estate and factories in Mexico, the American Congo Company, transport ships, and factories. By then many of the company's individual leaders, such as Nelson Aldrich, Bernard Baruch, A. H. Wiggin, and Levi P. Morton, had pulled out, although the company still had major banking support, especially through continuing director Charles H. Sabin, who was now the chairman of the Guarantee Trust Company. At that time the directors transferred 1,100 shares of common stock from the Cedros Hacienda Company, a division of Intercontinental Rubber, to Guarantee Trust as security on a new $2,903,000 line of credit. When the directors filed a claim a short time later with the Mexican Department of State to redeem the $1,378,071 in losses they had suffered from revolutionary incursions, they estimated that Guarantee Trust's share in those setbacks was $222,064. Since they had a total capitalization of only $550,000 in the Cedros, it meant that despite grossly inflated estimates, the damages to the estate were extensive. The Cedros hacienda had lost a minimum of 20 percent of its value as a result of the ten years of fighting and the market decline. This was only the beginning of the directors' troubles.

On 3 April 1924 Obregón seized 925,000 acres, or slightly more than 50 percent, of the Cedros hacienda. The president asserted that the Díaz survey grant was invalid because it established a monopoly. The company replied that it acquired all of its properties by purchase, and that Díaz had approved the "detailed survey."

> Our rights were acquired in good faith and in full accord with the then existing laws of Mexico. We know that we cannot be deprived of any part of these rights in fairness and equity. We hope that no further attempts to do so will be made.[13]

The directors and stockholders were sorely disappointed. While the government and the company litigated the expropriation of the 925,000 acres of survey lands in Mexico's Supreme Court, the Mexican authorities resorted to tax and labor strategies. The company's 1926 report to its stockholders noted that "[o]perating conditions in Mexico have tended to become increasingly difficult with new measures of taxation and officially imposed concessions to labor."[14]

During the mid 1930s the directors rushed to negotiate a "provisional agreement" regarding further agrarian land seizures, to no avail. In 1937 the "dismemberment" continued, with 375,000 acres seized through "agrarian expropriations." The land taken included all of the water sources, leaving the American-held portions dry. In 1939 the Torreón rubber plant closed for six months and then reopened, running only one shift. The levies on the Cedros had continued to increase and now included a 12 percent export tax. Only the military's need for rubber and the cooperative economic relationship between the U.S. and Mexico after the onset of World War II saved the Intercontinental's landholdings from expropriation and its industrial facilities from insolvency.[15]

Otto Brictson and his son Louis faced a similar situation. Ingebricht Ole Brictson, Otto's father, had purchased the San José de las Rusias in the early 1900s. The hacienda occupied a beautiful valley between a coastal range of hills and mountains farther inland. It ran southward from the Soto la Marina River of Tamaulipas and supported 8,000 to 9,000 head of cattle. The San José was "covered with black top soil from seven to ten feet thick, very fertile with plenty of rainfall." In the early 1920s Obregón condemned almost 500,000 acres of the property as the product of an illegal survey concession authorized by Díaz. He ruled, as he had in similar cases, that the grant was illegal because it was located too close to the coastline for foreigners to own. His action reinforced the intent of agrarians who had invaded the property and occupied parts of it from 1918 onward. In the meantime the prominent López family of Soto la Marina continued litigation initiated before 1910, contending that part of the property belonged to them. The governor of Tamaulipas also issued decrees condemning parts of the estate. The Brictsons continued to pay taxes on the property despite rapidly rising assessments and continuous land occupations. During the 1920s and, increasingly, the 1930s, survey teams from the national agrarian commission visited San José in anticipation of future allocations to the Mexican residents.

The difficulties faced in the 1920s by American land and mine owners often led to bargain-basement sales and to the reorganization of holdings. In 1928, when Horace W. Corbin purchased the 125,000-acre Chivela hacienda on the Isthmus of Tehuantepec from Gulf Coast Hardwoods, he paid only $70,000. His action staved off, perhaps, an impending presidential nullification of the land title since the original grant, which was given by Díaz to the Land Securities Company, created a "monopoly" in that it created holdings that dominated the region, similar to the Laguna, Riverside, Palomas, Piedra Blanca, and San José de las Rusias estates. These properties had been claimed by the Porfirian government as *terrenos baldios*.

People actually lived on the tracts, however, either as individuals or as a member of a group residing in hamlets known as *rancherías, cuadrillas,* or *aldeas,* which did not have rights of incorporation—that is, they did not have legal standing. Lacking monetary resources, these people could not litigate and were forced to abide the intruders. During the revolution they invaded the disputed lands. Then in the 1920s local agrarians, representatives of the Comisión Nacional de la Refoma Agraria and student volunteers from the Universidad Nacional Autónoma de México encouraged the Isthmian citizenry to demand land grants. Corbin's status as an individual owner allowed him to escape the attention of the authorities, who were looking for companies against which to apply the nullification and antimonopoly provisions of the laws that Obregón enforced with such vigor. During the 1930s, however, Cárdenas seized much of Corbin's land and returned it to the campesinos. Corbin eventually lost it all.[16]

Sometimes newcomers, even sophisticated ones, fell victim to deceptive sellers attempting to recoup from the loss of their properties. In 1925 W. J. Hotchkiss and C. A. Vance bought the 25,000-acre San José de Costilla hacienda in Nayarit. Their firm was the largest grower of cotton and wheat in California. They paid 95,000 pesos for the property, only to discover that the agrarian commission had seized the most valuable portion, including most of the water, leaving it almost unworkable. Vance arrived on the estate in 1925. Shortly thereafter, to his surprise, agrarian surveyors allocated 4,100 acres to the Mexican residents and nearby pueblo citizenry. Vance persisted, however, building new structures and putting 4,000 acres into production. Unfortunately for Hotchkiss and Vance, during the 1930s a significant number of the local population wanted them to leave, and they petitioned President Lázaro Cárdenas for more land. The president obliged them, leaving the American portion of the property without water.[17]

Disputes involving industrial ownership were as intense as the agrarian fights. Until April 1925 the Jalapa Power and Light Company continued to operate the concession it had purchased from John Frisbie in 1898. During the late 1910s and early 1920s, the company faced growing dissatisfaction with its performance from the public, local and state officials, and organized labor. Protests against high rates led to user boycotts, while officials threatened the company with intervention. Even more dangerous from the owners' perspective, the organized workers were anarchosyndicalists and demanded the right to take over and run the company as the Cooperativa de Luz, Fuerza y Transportes de Jalapa.

Anarchist self-management, mutualist self-help, and cooperative efforts to deliver goods and services without profits had created the cooperative. Now nationalism gave new energy to those beliefs. The union leaders campaigned against American ownership, accusing the Americans of price gouging, discrimination in employment and wages, and poor service. The *sindicato* directors knew they lacked the financial resources to run Jalapa Power, but as a first step they hoped to gain government intervention by emphasizing the twin themes of nationalism and revolution. On 26 March 1925 they went on strike and suspended service. Officials at all levels refused the company relief, and on 4 April 1925 the Veracruz state authorities seized the company. The general manager, William K. Boone, feared for his safety and fled to the United States. The state officials then agreed "to some of the demands of the unions." James Rockwell Sheffield, the American ambassador, informed the Mexican government that he was carefully monitoring the situation and advised the Mexican secretary of foreign relations that the U.S. "reserved . . . all rights with respect to the matter." Aarón Saenz, the secretary, retorted that "the Government of Veracruz was obliged to assume management of [the] enterprise since its Manager had left Mexico in violation of the contract which required . . . a representative there."

The management of Jalapa Power, citing its difficulties with "municipal and federal authorities and the public," offered to sell the entire complex to the state of Veracruz for 2,000,000 pesos. After a year of negotiations, the governor and legislature agreed to purchase the company for 1,800,000 pesos, to be paid off at 100,000 pesos monthly at 6 percent interest. The authorities, however, lacked the monies to meet these conditions without curtailing other expenditures and, recognizing the Americans' despair, held off making payments until 1931. At that point they turned Jalapa Power over to the Cooperativa de Luz and promised to pay the owners between 7,000 and 10,000 pesos monthly. The company officials took their money and sued in the courts, losing decisions during the 1930s at the local, state, and federal levels. The strategy backfired because it confronted the Mexicans as nationalizations reached their zenith.[18]

A RENEWED ATTACK ON LAGUNA

In Campeche the Mexican government undertook an attack on the Laguna Corporation, which was owned by some of the most powerful capitalists in the United States. The Mexican officials relied on the laws that promoted agrarian reform, and outlawed monopolies and the foreign ownership of coastline property, to strip Laguna of millions of acres. The intensity of the confrontation between Laguna and an array of local, state, and federal authorities was elevated by growing labor unrest. The company directors defended themselves against accusations of worker abuse by asserting that they had the most liberal labor policies in Campeche. They argued that their problems derived from regulations that restricted the movement of workers at the company's discretion and limitations placed on the amounts of hardwood and chicle that could be harvested.

The rate of hardwood harvesting slowed appreciably, and hundreds of workers lost their jobs. In 1923 the workers cut 330,037 board feet, only 11 percent of the total shipped ten years earlier. In 1924 the total fell to 267,698 board feet, and in 1925 it was a mere 184,811 board feet. The hardwood cuttings earned $85 per thousand board feet in 1925, an increase of 15 percent over the prices that obtained in the late 1910s and 11 percent more than the prices in 1924, but for the first time Laguna lost money on hardwoods. Production in board feet was a mere 5 percent of that in the company's peak years. In 1926 they stopped cutting timber in Campeche but continued to harvest chicle. In 1920 their chicle sales reached $506,000, with a net profit of $235,00, but during the early 1920s chicle output fell to $217,000, and net profits reached a nadir of $59,000. For the rest of the decade, chicle production earned the Laguna directors an average of only $100,000 per year.

The decision to cease working their timber holdings meant that the company no longer used the sawmills, railway, shops, housing, and warehousing facilities that had been developed for that purpose at great expense. They also had to endure the challenges of officials and workers, the associated legal costs, and the time-consuming efforts required to maintain their rain forest properties. With the loss of their timber trade and the minimal returns they obtained from chicle, they would have been hard put to justify their large investment were it not for the vast field of oil under their property.

When the Laguna directors decided to suspend hardwood cutting, they attributed their decision to the official restrictions, which they said made the conduct of business impossible. The directors later claimed that they still held rich reserves of cedar and mahogany forests, but eyewitnesses claimed that southern Campeche had been stripped of trees as far south as the Guatemalan border. The Mexican authorities used the cessation of timber work as an opportunity to eliminate the powerful American oilmen. Without noting that they had restricted cutting and that the hardwoods were depleted, they condemned the directors' cessation order as arbitrary and demonstrative of a monopolistic power that cut off Mexican laborers and merchants from their livelihoods. The cutting restrictions remained in force until 1940. Agrarian reform officials encouraged organizers to form juntas at settlements on the Laguna properties. The officials and other proponents of agrarian reform spoke largely of chicle and farming. They never mentioned oil or hardwoods. The campesinos probably knew nothing of the hidden agendas of the Laguna directors or the government. They wanted to harvest chicle and farm. The workers at Kilometer 47 and Matamoros duly applied for land allocations for chicle harvesting and farming under the agrarian reform provisions of Article 27 and the agrarian reform law of 6 January 1915, statutes that provided that all legal residents of rural communities were entitled to land.[19]

Immediately to the southeast of the American landholding complex in Campeche, on the border between Chiapas and Guatemala, lay the large Agua Buena hacienda, which had been acquired by Francis Skiddy in the nineteenth century. Skiddy had supported General Díaz during the Revolution of Tuxtepec, and, like General Ord, the Lower Rio Grande Valley ranchers, and the railroad magnates, he had benefited by obtaining a large land grant within a proscribed zone adjacent to a foreign border. Skiddy had a deep interest in Mexico and Central America. He held a partnership with Moses Taylor and William Aspinwall in the Pacific Mail Steamship Company, and he was, with Taylor, one of the principal importers of Cuban sugar to the United States in the nineteenth century. He had developed the Stamford Manufacturing Company, an enterprise that specialized in natural dyewoods and chemical extracts from tropical flora. The workers at the Agua Buena produced chicle and harvested mahogany, cedar, dyewood, and logwood from ancient forests that had never been cut. With his son William Skiddy he built a railroad to his docks on the Hondo River and mills and houses on the estate.

It is not clear if the Agua Buena was still exporting goods when the revolution broke out, but in the early 1920s Obregón nullified the Skiddy grant and nationalized the entire estate. In 1919 the Skiddy heirs lost most of their records in a fire at Stamford and could not prove their ownership until the 1940s. When the Roosevelt administration announced a new round of claims settlements in 1942 the Skiddy heirs searched their records. On 30 November 1943 Lillie Skiddy Parker, Adele Skiddy Carle, and Robert Carle applied for compensation, saying they knew they owned something, but not exactly what. One of the Ord heirs did the same. None of the parties even sensed the dramatic roles that their great-grandfathers had played in 1876, when they helped create a foreign government favorable to U.S. interests.[20]

LOSING EVERYTHING

Among the stories of the American estate owners who lost virtually everything, the case of Rosalie Evans stands out for its pathos and tragedy. Born an American, Evans lost her citizenship by marrying a British subject. In 1917, upon the death of her husband, Evans inherited the Hacienda San Pedro Coxtocan, at Huejotzingo, Puebla. The estate comprised 2,500 acres of rich land, some 90 percent of it irrigated. She successfully raised wheat, corn, beans, and chiles. In 1923 Evans expanded, buying the Hacienda El Xuchil, which contained 3,500 acres of largely timberlands in Veracruz. She had endless problems with the campesinos in the region around San Pedro, who wanted the land for their support. They had appealed to the government for relief shortly after it promulgated the principal agrarian reform law on 6 January 1915.

After the death of her husband, the census takers and surveyors studied her property, and Evans had several armed confrontations with the local campesinos. When agrarian reform officials announced their intention to seize some of her property, Evans appealed to the U.S. ambassador, Henry P. Fletcher. He turned Evans away, claiming she was not a citizen because of her marriage to a foreigner. She never accepted that determination and continued to appeal. The men at the U.S. Department of State who investigated the case seemed quite comfortable with the denial of aid, perhaps because Evans also approached the British representatives for help. On 27 November 1920 the agrarian commission seized 1,500 acres of her land at San Pedro and gave it to the neighboring heads of families who had petitioned for it for many years. At that point Evans met with Obregón, argued her case, and volunteered her negative views of agrarian reform. The president admired her spirit, if not her views, and promised to look into her claims. In 1924 unknown persons killed her by gunshot in an ambush near her Puebla estate. Her appeals seem to have caused a reaction in the agrarian bureaucracy in Mexico City, because the next seizure did not take place at San Pedro until 1929. During the 1930s the agrarian commission seized most of the properties on her Xuchil estate.[21]

American landholders in the coastal hills and mountains surrounding Atoyac de Alvarez, located north of Acapulco, all experienced land invasions. The campesinos began invading the holdings of the Stephens Brothers Company and the Silberberg estate during the revolution. Ed Shearson's 200,000-

acre Guerrero Land and Timber Company was more remote, and the campesinos did not begin their permanent occupation of it until 1927. They entered the land bearing arms, planted crops, harvested a few trees at a time, and intimidated challengers. After the invasion the American owners and their personnel stopped their timber operations.[22]

In Nayarit, John T. Cave and R. L. Summerlin had already experienced the violence practiced by the working-class Mexican agrarians who called themselves "Zapatistas." Neighboring campesinos and villagers, especially those from the town of Milpas Viejas (old farms), had repeatedly entered the Quimichis Colony between 1912 and 1920. The Acaponeta River ran the length of the colony's mostly level 78,000 acres, making it the most desirable property in the region. Between 1913 and 1920 the Zapatistas repeatedly set up *ejidos*, only to be dislodged by the Carrancistas. They then counterattacked, retaking the disputed lands. In 1920 Obregón supporters formed a third faction that continued to struggle with the Zapatistas. In the eyes of the original American settlers, these were three groups of "bandits." They alternately invaded the estate during the 1920s, robbing its occupants of cash and property. The colonists finally created a civil militia and prevented the excesses committed on two neighboring properties during the early 1920s, when revolutionaries cut off one finger of each of two American victims and then killed one.

In 1925 the inhabitants of Milpas Viejas occupied 150 acres of the estate and refused to leave. On 15 May, Cave, Summerlin, and the colonists who had purchased parts of the colony's holdings appealed for relief to the Obregonista governor. They also forwarded their complaint to the U.S. Department of State. To their surprise the governor, who was loyal to Obregón, widened the attack. Instead of evicting the "squatters" from the 150 acres, the governor quickly ordered the "expropriation" of 10,000 addition acres for agrarian reform purposes. This marked the beginning of the end for the Cave-Summerlin enterprise. During the late 1920s and the mid 1930s, the state and national authorities seized additional tracts, especially those fronting the Acaponeta River, until the Americans were forced to abandon it. During those years the properties of the defunct Quimichis Company reverted to their pre-American name, the Hacienda del Río.[23]

In nearby Sinaloa large landowner Benjamin Francis Johnston was still defending the favorable position he had gained during the revolution by clandestinely supporting Felipe Bachomo and the Yaquis who were affiliated with Villa. That step had given him immunity from their attacks. After selling his product at high prices, made possible by the destruction of his competitors, Johnston bought more sugar estates. He obtained similar selling advantages during World War I, when fighting caused disruptions in the foreign markets. By 1920 Johnston had become the most powerful figure in the region. During the 1920s he developed a sales network that reached Asia as well as the United States, and he oversaw the development of the Bajolaqui Dam on the Río Fuerte. That project and the accompanying power plant cost some $120,000,000 and not only gave Johnston an improved position in Sinaloa but also underscored his influence in Mexico City and the United States.[24]

Most of the other American sugar growers in Sinaloa failed. The destruction of the revolution and continuing political uncertainty forced even the directors of the Old Colony Trust Company of Boston to sell their holdings. In 1901 they had invested $750,000 with George R. Douglas to support the development of the San Lorenzo Sugar Company and its estates of La Loma and Tecomante. Between 1924 and 1929 the American presence in Sinaloa receded as the Old Colony Trust sold its holdings to the Haciendas de Redo y Compañía, S.A., a firm headed by Diego Redo, the former governor of the state. The governor had served under Díaz and had a long and friendly relationship with American interests in the state. He had supported Johnston and the Boston bankers in their disputes with the American utopian settlers at Topolobampo. In 1911 Redo fled into European exile, returning in 1923 to buy American properties in Sinaloa at bargain prices. The negotiations between the Redo family interests and Old Colony Trust began immediately. For the Boston bankers, the sales to Redo represented the alternative to the absolute losses experienced by their fellow Bostonians, the Peirce family, and by the Shearsons and Mortons, who owned the Corralitos hacienda in Chihuahua.

In 1921 residents of Janos and Casas Grandes forcibly entered the Corralitos hacienda, located midway between their towns, and occupied the bottomlands immediately in front of the big house on the Corralitos River. They occupied 12,000 acres and proceeded to build shacks and plant crops. E. C. Houghton, the manager of the Corralitos, protested to the local authorities and the governor, Ignacio Enriquez, only to be informed that the citizens held lands that were rightfully theirs and that formal seizures of more properties would be forthcoming. During the occupation, Governor Enriquez raised the taxes on the estate several times over. Disputes erupted between the local authorities and the owners in New York. Among Houghton's bosses were Ed Shearson and Ed Morgan, the capitalists who had bought the Corralitos during the Porfiriato, and Judge E. H. Gary, the president of the U.S. Steel Corporation. In December, after consulting with the owners, Houghton visited high-ranking officials in Mexico City in a bid to settle the affair.

Shearson, the president of the Corralitos Company, monitored the situation closely.

Accompanied by a Mexican lawyer, Houghton began his effort to save the estate by holding separate meetings with the secretary of foreign affairs, A. J. Pani, and the head of the Comisión Nacional de la Refoma Agraria. The latter official offered little reassurance. Given the owners' close ties to the Morgan bank, Houghton hoped that their influence would help with Secretary Pani. Houghton explained that the local authorities had done nothing about the seizure of estate lands and the threats of foreclosure made by local, state, and agrarian reform authorities. He then gave Pani a letter from Judge Gary, which expressed "grave concerns." Pani promised Houghton "an immediate interview with the President." When Pani failed to communicate for three days, Houghton forwarded his card to the secretary as a reminder. "Nothing came of it, as I never heard anything more from the Secretary of Foreign Relations."[25]

At the end of 1921 Houghton tried again. He wired Obregón that he was in Mexico City on urgent business for the Corralitos Company. The president received him briefly the same day and arranged a longer meeting for later. They finally met in early January and discussed the application of agrarian law and the land invasion at Corralitos. Obregón informed the American that he

> was obliged to respect the sovereignty of States and the legal actions
> of all governors and would not . . . go against him unless he found that
> the Governor or the Agrarian Commission of the State had exceeded
> their authority.[26]

Obregón added that he thought the Corralitos matter could be resolved easily, and he wrote a letter to be personally given to Governor Enriquez. He then sent a senator from Chihuahua with Houghton to serve as an intermediary.

Houghton met with Enriquez on "Friday the 13th." The meeting went badly for the American. The governor faced pressure from the Villistas. Sporting their own agrarian reform law, they were competing with the state government for the support of the local citizenry, and Enriquez pacified them with land donations from the Corralitos. He and the head of the state agrarian commission argued that the individuals described by Houghton as squatters were in fact legal occupants of the land under the state agrarian reform law of 23 June 1921. The American charged the "squatters" with stealing timber, firewood, and water that the estate used for irrigation. Water usage had long been an issue between the estate owners and the people of Casas Grandes. Enriquez informed Houghton that the people were within the law.

Furious, Houghton told the governor, the state agrarian reform official, and the senator that

> the government of Mexico had made it impossible for the large land-owners to continue in business; that they had destroyed the Corralitos property as a cattle breeding enterprise; also that they had destroyed the farming scheme of the corporation by allowing squatters to take water from the river.[27]

He added that the company would have difficulty selling the farming sections because of the squatters and that Mennonites from Canada were preparing to buy "the very lands that were occupied by Mexicans." Governor Enriquez replied:

> It is an utter impossibility for the government to remove these people; they have started to make homes and to cultivate the land, and at the end of the period set forth by the Idle Land Law, it will be necessary to apportion and donate lands to them.[28]

Enriquez then issued an order to the squatters to stop pilfering water from the river and promised to buy between 100,000 and 150,000 acres for the agrarian reform effort at the rate of $8.50 per acre for bottomlands and $5 per acre for hillsides. Unfortunately for the American owners, who had capitalized the Corralitos at $313,260 by issuing stocks, Enriquez failed to purchase the lands.[29]

In 1923 the owners of the Corralitos met in New York and voted to abandon the enterprise and to sue Mexico for damages via the Special Claims Commission. That year Villa accepted peace with the Obregón administration, and the political need to pacify the local citizenry abated. The people of Casas Grandes and Janos did receive most of the Corralitos, but Canadian Mennonites fulfilled Houghton's prophecy by purchasing vast tracts of land in the southeastern part of the hacienda and taking up residence. A community of small landholders, specializing in vegetables and cheese, replaced the American capitalists there.

Two Americans on the scene devised a way of gaining parts of the Corralitos properties. On 23 April 1927 Francisco Irigoyen purchased a 62,000-acre tract of the Corralitos located immediately northwest of Casas Grandes and the American community of Colonia Dublan. Irigoyen immediately conveyed control of his purchase to John Steinkampf and Harry Smith. They held an unaffected mortgage until 1937 and 1938, when President Lázaro Cárdenas and the Comisión Nacional de la Refoma Agraria seized 37,000 of those acres in two steps and distributed them to local workers.

Billy Wallace, a foreman at the defunct hacienda, gained ownership of the big house and 35,000 acres around it, including fine soils on both sides of the Corralitos River. In the late 1980s Billy Wallace III, a graduate of New Mexico State University at Las Cruces, still held the core element of the old Corralitos. Sixty years after his father and other New York financiers had lost the property, Jack Wentworth Peirce remarked, "I would like to know how the Wallaces obtained their present title. I bet there is a story behind that one."[30]

LABOR DISPUTES AND THE CRISTERO WAR

Plutarcho Elías Calles became president in 1924. A son of the Sonoran oligarchy, Calles was deeply influenced by Ambassador Dwight Morrow, a partner in the Morgan Bank. Calles believed in state control over the unions and private ownership of the land. He achieved a degree of the former, at least to the extent of suppressing strikes, but agrarian unrest continued to grow. The rural population was deeply divided. Significant groups sought to preserve traditions, including pueblo autonomy and clerical authority, and to exclude all forms of external authority including agrarian surveyors and even school-teachers. A much larger but less publicized group sought the redistribution of land and water resources to the pueblos and working class. They had important allies among the local and state revolutionary elites who sometimes shared the sense of mission of the *agraristas* and sometimes sensed opportunities for personal advancement through the redistribution of rural assets.

Mining had always been one of the most fractious areas of labor relations, but the American mine owners in Guanajuato were not ready for the hard economic and political realities of the 1920s. The organizers of mine workers were less numerous, but they repeated the threats and violence of their agrarian counterparts. At the Cubo mines, Irving Herr, the engineer in charge, found his objectives challenged by radical workers and depleted ores. Workers guilty of infractions could no longer be summarily dismissed, and the CROM, which organized the workforce around Cubo, dominated the government's arbitration board. The CROM's powerful position resulted largely from the fact that the union chief, Luis Morones, served as Mexico's secretary of labor.

In 1922 the Cubo drillers gained concessions when they went on strike over working conditions. In 1924 new legislation established minimum wages and required "just cause" for the firing of employees. Labor organizers in Guanajuato, including "Communists," published a newspaper called *Rebeldia* (Rebellion) in which they charged Herr with abuse. The American protested to the governor, who sent the police chief and the colonel in charge of the state police to smash the presses. But Herr had no influence in Mexico City. The national government merely sent investigators to examine conditions in the mines, and more regulations ensued.[31]

As the authorities increased their surveillance of labor practices, challenging the ability of Herr and other mining engineers to run their facilities with the autonomy they had previously enjoyed, reduced production in the mines forced salary cuts and layoffs. Among other things, the examiners questioned the workers' exposure to cyanide during ore separation. The use of cyanide had provoked the ire of cattlemen in Chihuahua, who found the Díaz administration uninterested when they protested the poisoning of water holes before the revolution. In 1925 an American-owned mine employing 1,400 Mexicans in Guanajuato closed as a result of the "lower grades of ore," "complaints of the authorities and workmen," and the higher labor costs resulting from a new minimum-wage law.[32]

As the revolutionary government sought to extend its authority into the realm of health, education, and welfare services, it came into direct conflict with the Roman Catholic Church, which had traditionally directed those affairs. The Church hierarchy had reacted strongly to provisions in the Constitution of 1917 that called for secular education and prohibited clerical schools. Denouncing the constitution as the work of Satan, many of the Church's leaders promised disobedience. In 1923, in reaction, Calles—then the minister of defense—began deporting priests. After he became president, a series of confrontations between his officials and the clergy ensued. The new executive was not radical, but he was anticlerical. Finally, in 1926, a guerrilla conflict known as the Cristero War erupted. The most fierce and persistent fighting took place in the area centered on the states of Jalisco, Michoacán, Guerrero, Zacatecas, Durango, and Aguascalientes.

The Cristeros were largely campesinos, indigenous people, and lower clergy who supported the Church hierarchy. The members of the grassroots movement resisted the rural public education program and were usually against agrarian reform and other forms of state intrusion into the way of life in rural communities. Some Cristeros in Durango and neighboring states favored agrarian reform, however, and had been denied its benefits. These contradictions underscored the complexity of the movement and of the attitudes of rural Mexicans. The Cristero War was also a source of political instability in Guanajuato, but there the Cristeros limited their objectives to the defense of traditional social practices and attracted support from the Americans. Mining engineers such as Herr were relieved to find that the

Cristeros demanded little. When they entered the properties of the Cubo Mining and Milling Company, they asked for only 200 pesos in the form of a loan and refused a larger amount when it was offered.

President Calles correctly perceived the Cristeros as a threat to public order and state power. Between 1926 and 1929 he set out to crush them. The fighting and reports of violent excesses on the part of the army, both propagandistic and somewhat accurate, caused alarm in the American Catholic community. Church publications in the United States offered wild tales of rapine inflicted upon innocent believers and branded Calles and his officials "Bolsheviks," as did William Buckley. Catholics in the United States protested to their elected representatives, and William Randolph Hearst campaigned against the use of Mexican troops in his newspapers.

The American and Mexican governments wanted peace and stability, but the Mexican leaders could not surrender what they considered state sovereignty to a foreign-controlled church. The new American ambassador, Dwight Morrow, faced the difficult task of cooling matters down. Morrow was welcomed by the Americans in Mexico, who knew that he was a tough bargainer and a partner in J. P. Morgan and Company. In 1929, after the army had reduced the Cristero threat, Morrow succeeded in negotiating a peace settlement. He convinced Calles that improved bilateral relations and internal tranquility presented a better choice for Mexico's future than the continued prosecution of a militarily weak enemy.[33] The hierarchy of the Church returned to its normal religious functions and accepted its removal from social and political affairs. The formal fighting ended, but grassroots violence in the rural populace continued, especially over village autonomy and agrarian and educational issues. So did the mutual antagonism of American Catholics and the Mexican regime.

In 1929 another, more menacing wave of social unrest swept Guanajuato. This movement, led by José Padrón, shifted between banditry and a leftist-nationalist political effort. To protect the Cubo mine against "the rebels," Herr obtained a detachment of federal troops. His spouse, Luella, described events as a "reign of terror in the foreign colony of Guanajuato." Padrón kidnapped Americans on at least two occasions and killed two of them. The governor, Arroyo Che, "didn't much care if the Americans were killed and . . . frankly said so." In a raid of the Tajo mine they sought the "gringo" foreman for execution, but he escaped. Other American engineers fled the state. Herr wondered "whether foreign companies will continue to be allowed to exist in Mexico. At present the political atmosphere is not favorable." The end came for the American mining companies of Guanajuato, however, not only because of revolutionary nationalism but also because of the long-term slide in silver prices, the wage increases and improved working conditions that pushed operating costs higher, and the Great Depression, which increased the downward pressure on silver prices. The mines became financial liabilities. In 1932 Herr and the mine's owners gave up. Management cited the higher cost of labor as the Cubo joined a growing list of American mine closings.[34]

PARACAIDISTAS, DIVES, AND BISTROS

By 1927 the cancellation of land grants had challenged the interests of many American and Mexican property owners in the border region. In Tijuana the government's strategy for the control of frontiers, coastlines, and essential natural resources coincided with local conflicts among the American and Mexican elites. The Tijuana area had been occupied in 1911 by a group of revolutionary anarchists from the PLM. Their leader, Ricardo Flores Magón, had remained in Los Angeles. He was the archrival of Harry Chandler, who opposed the unions and owned large tracts of land in Mexico adjacent to Tijuana (then known as Tía Juana) and Mexicali. The Magonistas had set up a short-lived "Anarchist Republic of Baja California" and abolished large landholdings. That memory and local animosities toward Chandler and his associates were still close to the surface in the 1920s. Social unrest in Tijuana over squalid living conditions and the demeaned lives of many who lived there compounded the situation.

Two powerful groups of American investors, expecting rapid demographic growth in southern California and northern Baja California, sought to dominate the real estate market and business development in the region. The members of the first group represented the "old money" of Los Angeles—the established elite. Among them were the Bandini and Wolfskill families, who owned the 26,000-acre Tía Juana Ranch in the center of what is now metropolitan Tijuana. They claimed that their titles derived from an 1829 land grant, although Mexican officials judged them to come from an 1886 colonization company grant issued to Luis Huller. They were the heirs of the Arguello family, Californios who had intermarried with the elite families of southern California during the one hundred years that had elapsed since the original cession.

The twenty-nine members of the second group were land developers and capitalists whose wealth was more recent. These men included Chandler, Ed Fletcher, George Griffith, H. W. Keller, Epes Randolph, T. A. Riordan, and H. H. Timken. They had created the Compañía del Rancho de San Isidro in 1911 to administer the affairs of their hunting and fishing club, located on a 32,000-acre rancho near the Bandini and Wolfskill property.[35] In 1927 local agrarians overran the Rancho de San Isidro and local, state, and national officials refused to act against them. The agrarians usually acted with unannounced audacity and were difficult to dislodge because any movement against them would generate the negative publicity of an attack by the rich on the needy. The police rarely succeeded in efforts to remove the squatters if they were determined to stay.

Capitalized at $80,000 in 1911, the Rancho San Isidro was one of the most valuable properties on the northern frontier. A bitter dispute followed the land invasion as the American owners appealed to local authorities. Chandler had changed the name of his interest to the Chandis Security Company in 1924, and this allowed him to avoid overt exposure as a litigant. The Americans demanded that the police remove the agrarians, and when that was not done they claimed that higher-ups in the Mexican government had encouraged the squatters to invade the ranch. The agrarians built houses and began farming. The Mexican officials claimed they had no control over the actions taken by the intruders because they were acting in accordance with the laws regarding invalid concessions and vacant lands. The Mexican officials probably had not approved the action in advance. The squatters were often led by political radicals, but in this case neither radical nor governmental leadership was apparent. Later in the twentieth century squatters came to be known as *paracaidistas*.

The San Isidro invasion took place simultaneously with the confiscation of the Tía Juana Ranch. In 1929 Emilio Portes Gil, the president of Mexico from 1928 to 1930, canceled the land grant for the Tía Juana. The president declared the entire Tía Juana tract, which extended the length of the eastern side of the old town, to be national property. Immediately after the nationalization, the president turned over the southeastern part of the ranch, known as Agua Caliente, to Governor Abelardo Rodríguez, a future president of Mexico. The owners of the Tía Juana hired lawyers and protested to the Mexican and American courts and the U.S. State Department, to no avail. The rapidly escalating value of the San Isidro and Tía Juana ranches made them attractive to reformers. In addition, the Mexican leadership clearly wanted national control of an important port of entry into the United States, as it did over all of its frontiers and coastlines. Here in the border region the actions of elites and workers coincided.

The opportunities in Tijuana, as well as in Acapulco, Tampico, Soto la Marina, and other key areas, attracted the interest of Mexican elites who knew how to work the system and could apply their influence. Governor Rodríguez profited from the Tía Juana seizure through an ensuing presidential grant for a racetrack at Agua Caliente. Apart from that, the government officials apparently realized little benefit other than Mexican occupancy of lands previously held by powerful American interests. The new agrarian and elite occupants of the Tía Juana and the San Isidro held on to their gains.[36]

Meanwhile, other issues came to bear in U.S.-Mexico relations on the border. The enactment of anti-drinking laws in the United States culminated in passage of the Volstead Act in 1920, which prohibited the consumption of alcoholic beverages on the American side of the border. The law had a massive effect on cultural and social life in Tijuana and the entire border region. Brothels, bars, casinos, a few swanky hotels, and the racetrack drew throngs of Americans to Tijuana and, on a smaller scale, to towns along the length of the border. American investors dominated these businesses in Tijuana, where the fanciest and largest amusement facilities emerged. Rodríguez and James Wood Coffroth, a San Francisco boxing promoter, created an extensive bar and prostitution operation. Ed Baker handled the liquor imports. Coffroth bought the Agua Caliente Racetrack in 1913 and managed it until 1929. Coffroth and his American associates invested some $285,000, and the track became noted for its elegance and clubhouse facilities despite pervasive rumors that many of the races were fixed. Americans Wirt Bowman and Baron Long, both of southern California, joined Coffroth and Rodríguez as the owners of a string of bars and whorehouses largely in Tijuana and Mexicali, but also including the noted Casino de la Selva in Cuernavaca.

One of the benefits for the Americans of having Rodríguez as a partner in their nefarious enterprises was his utter lack of scruples. His participation ended the need for high payouts to local authorities for "gambling permits." Together the associates developed the Agua Caliente Hotel and Casino, the finest club of its kind in northern Mexico, where West Coast celebrities could relax and enjoy themselves. Wallace Beery, Clara Bow, Jean Harlow, Rita Hayworth, Al Jolson, and many others enjoyed the free-living atmosphere of Agua Caliente. The racetrack prospered beyond the most avaricious dreams of its owners, and it became too tempting for Rodríguez and the federal authorities. In November 1929, a short time before Rodríguez was chosen as the president of Mexico, federal and state authorities seized the track, shutting out the American partners and giving the governor power.

Elsewhere in the city, less sumptuous facilities awaited working-class visitors and the ubiquitous sailors from the San Diego Naval Base and the marines from Camps Pendelton and Matthews. The clubs along Avenida Revolución offered inexpensive entertainment and "girls." By the early

1930s there were at least five hundred prostitutes in Tijuana alone, but the depression discouraged the development of fancier places. During the 1930s Mexican owners trimmed expenses, opened ever cheaper and more primitive establishments, and effectively ended American dominance of the bars and brothels. On the eve of World War II, the Mexicans controlled both extremes of the Tijuana entertainment industry.[37]

Other border points, especially Ciudad Juárez, Nuevo Laredo, and Matamoros, benefited from the dry ordinances in the United States that encouraged young men to seek illicit pleasures on the "other side." The "dives," far less opulent than the bistros that catered to the Hollywood and Los Angeles elites, were owned by an assortment of Americans and Mexicans. They offered women for sex and as dance partners, and alcohol as well, to Texas cowboys and businessmen. All along the two thousand miles of the border, the bar and club owners practiced racial discrimination with their employees and customers. "Girls" with lighter complexions enjoyed preferences, and those who refused customers of color, including Mexicans, Asians, and African Americans, held higher status. Remarkably, the "yanqui" population in southern Texas formed a narrow but persistent definition of Mexican character, one based on the moral climate of Ciudad Juárez, Nuevo Laredo, and Matamoros, without reflecting upon their own role in the creation of such conditions.[38]

ALTERING THE IMAGE OF THE REVOLUTION

During the 1920s a group of American bohemians, intellectuals, and leftists took up residence in Mexico City, and with their art and their writings they began to alter the image of the Mexican Revolution in the United States. By the end of the decade they had challenged the earlier and enduring vision of Mexico—one formulated by Richard Harding Davis, Jack London, and the Hollywood cinema—as a chaotic "half-breed" nation in need of Anglo-Saxon direction. Mexico became a nation of indigenous people and those with mixed blood who had risen up in search of regeneration and justice.

A vibrant artistic community that included muralist Paul O'Higgins, model Tina Modotti and her lover, photographer Edward Weston, writer Katherine Ann Porter, journalists Carleton Beals and Francis Toor, and Ernest Gruening, the editor of the *Nation*, led an American cultural elite that befriended Diego Rivera and his wife, Guadalupe Marín. Together they challenged the elite orthodoxies promulgated by the American embassy and the business community and newspapers in the United States. The American literati and their Mexican companions formed a cultural elite that experimented with photography, art, and literature and portrayed dramatic land-scapes and workers, peasants, Indians, and others in heroic postures. Weston, like the best of contemporary photographers, used sharp imagery and contrasting shadows and light while focusing on his model and lover, the beautiful Modotti. She joined him in dramatizing people in everyday lives. Together they sought to transmit human sensitivity and evoke mood.[39]

A number of academics quietly joined their artistic and literary counterparts. Helen Phipps, a Columbia University history student, lived in Mexico City, researching her doctoral dissertation. In her book Phipps expanded on Díaz Soto y Gama's heroic depiction of Emiliano Zapata and provided depth to the idea of the Mexican Revolution as an agrarian struggle to overcome age-old abuses and to provide justice to the indigenous population and peasantry. Other former Zapatistas also produced histories that replaced versions of the revolution in the south that focused on Zapata as a "Crimson Jester" and his slaughter of innocents. Phipps presented her argument, however, to a society of American historians that was almost entirely male, and she offered her findings during the wave of anticommunist hysteria that characterized the presidencies of William G. Harding and Calvin Coolidge. Historian Howard Cline rendered a critical review of Phipps's work despite the pleas of historian Charles Gibson, who, unfortunately, did not defend her publicly. Emotionally crestfallen, Phipps gave up a promising career as an interpreter of the revolution.

Frank Tannenbaum, a younger colleague of Phipps in the history graduate program at Columbia, finished his doctorate in the mid 1920s. He gained acclaim ten years later by reintroducing the revolution as a struggle for land and bread. Tannenbaum expanded on Phipps's work to include the agrarian reform program of President Cárdenas as the fulfillment of Zapata's just cause. His interpretation of the revolution and its results became the fodder for succeeding generations of American social scientists and tourists.[40] Anita Brenner completed the argument that had been introduced by Phipps and elaborated by Tannenbaum in her classic and widely read book *The Wind that Swept Mexico,* which was published in 1942. It gave the English-speaking world sympathetic photographs of the revolutionaries and their world, although it reinforced stereotypes of revolutionary women. Brenner portrayed mothers with children wrapped in rebozos on their backs, rather than showing the battlefield nurses and armed fighters who took part in the conflict.

During the late 1920s Lesley Byrd Simpson of the University of California at Berkeley also took up residence in Mexico City. An independent leftist, he adopted a more critical view of Mexico than the bohemians did.

In his famed *Many Mexicos,* Simpson bemoaned the nation's historic lack of democracy and political corruption, themes that still characterize the work of historians and social scientists who write about Mexico. His critical viewpoint, however, stemmed from sympathy for the Mexican revolutionary cause and was distinct from that of his contemporary H. H. Dunn, who hated revolutionary chaos and any notion of an uprising of the masses. Dunn wrote *Zapata, The Crimson Jester,* citing Zapatista atrocities and then embellishing them.

American literary and cultural diversity produced at least three Mexicos. J. Frank Dobie examined the deepening integration of the United States and Mexico from a completely different perspective than that of Hollywood or the American intelligentsia in Mexico. Dobie's family owned a rancho in Tamaulipas before and during the revolution. He employed the vivid experiences of his childhood in the writing of novels about the Great Southwest and the border region. Dobie's portrayals of sensitive, wise, colorful, and tough vaqueros and his descriptions of rodeos, romantic ranchos, and harsh landscapes were all rooted in his lifelong rural experience in the border region.[41]

Even when the two peoples seemed to be maintaining their distinct cultures, a merger was under way. The two countries entered the "car culture" era within forty years of each other. The American mass adoption of the Ford Models T and A anticipated the arrival in Mexico of the Volkswagen Beetle a generation later. Another, more subtle, example of cultural merger was found in *raree.* Traditional *raree,* a street theater staged with only greasepaint, simple costumes, spirit, sometimes talent, and no money, continued to attract crowds of Mexican working-class onlookers in cities and small mining camps alike. Mexican mime performers adopted Charlie Chaplin and his characters as some of their most prominent themes.

Immigration from the United States grew during the late nineteenth and early twentieth centuries as an adjunct of westward expansion. The related economic opportunities presented by the development of new properties carried important cultural components. The American settlers were determined to recreate their society in what they usually considered "Indian" Mexico. They reproduced their religions, cuisine, clothing, and pastimes in the new environment and introduced them to the Mexicans. The great social revolution that broke out in 1910 interrupted the Americans' effort to introduce Mexicans to "wholesome" pastimes such as organized sports, but it began again as soon as the violence subsided. The two peoples grew closer together through sports as well as through the performing arts and economic interactions. Despite the overtly nationalistic reaction of the Mexican public to foreign political and economic power in the aftermath of the revolution, pervasive American cultural influences helped ameliorate the political antagonisms that had developed. The seemingly unimportant processes of integrating cuisine, clothing, religion, and pastimes all contributed. The growth of baseball and sports offer a measure of the subterranean, unconscious reconciliation under way in the midst of economic and political disputes.

In 1919 the public regained its interest in baseball as higher-level teams appeared in Mexico City and the revolutionary turbulence subsided. That year an international tournament in the capital involved three teams from Cuba and two from the United States, including one made up of major league "All Stars" and "a black team" called the "American Giants." The sport became entrenched. Ban Johnson, a former president of the American League, attended a game in Mexico City in 1921 and gave a trophy to the winning team. Later he enlarged on this generosity with a two-foot bronze trophy presented to the league playoff winners, and in 1928 he donated a set of uniforms to the champions. The American sportsmen sought to acculturate Mexican workers through entertainment. Historian William Beezley explained that Johnson "wanted to educate Mexicans away from the savage and cruel practice of bullfighting." By 1924 some fifty-six teams played Sunday baseball in Mexico City municipal leagues. In 1925 the Mexican Professional League inaugurated a summer schedule involving clubs from the capital and other major cities in central Mexico.[42]

During the 1920s Mexican leaders mixed realpolitik, opportunism, idealism, and corruption in the struggle to take charge of local and national resources. National and local elites often sought personal political and material advantages during the process of agrarian reform and land seizure. Major American interests lost heavily in the nationalizations, but the universal losers were the small American investors. They lacked the assets that the Mexican government found valuable, such as high technology, capital, and marketing networks in the United States for products that the Mexicans wished to export. But nationalism was growing among the general populace and the elites, and they began pressing for the Mexicanization of all national assets.

12   Nationalization of Land and Industry

The person and property of a citizen are a part of the general
domain of the nation, even when abroad, and there is a distinct
and binding obligation on the part of self-respecting governments
to afford protection to the persons and property of their citizens,
wherever they may be.

Calvin Coolidge, 1927

Foreigners cannot own real estate under any conditions.

Manuel C. Tellez, 1926

The agrarian and labor demands asserted during the revolutionary decade
became increasingly tied to the state and its programs during the 1920s and
1930s. Presidential and gubernatorial land seizures through nullifications of
grants, assertions of eminent domain, agrarian reform, and sheriffs' auctions
of properties for unpaid taxes redistributed over 100,000,000 acres of Mexico's surface to its citizenry and provided a broadly participatory material
basis for the emergence of the one-party state.

Although Plutarco Elías Calles was the Mexican president for only four
years, from 1924 to 1928, he controlled the government until 1935. Subsequent presidents—Emilio Portes Gil, Pascuál Ortiz Rubio, and Abelardo
Rodriguez—were dominated by Calles and continued his policies. In 1935,
at the height of the Great Depression, the reformists and nationalists
among the Mexican leadership seized power from the supporters of Calles.
He had kept a leash on rural and urban working-class unrest, but the new
president, Lázaro Cárdenas, promptly turned the agrarians and labor organizers loose. His campaign for the presidency had benefited from the public's sense that the agrarian, labor, and nationalist goals of the revolution
had not yet been fulfilled. Agrarian unrest and labor agitation grew expo-
nentially during his administration, which meant trouble for American
landowners, investors, companies, and settlers.

SWEEPING OUT THE AMERICANS

Cárdenas was the president of Mexico from 1934 to 1940. During the revolution he had served and adhered to the *agrarista* politics of his mentor,

371

the radical General Lucio Blanco. His rise in rank was so rapid that he was often identified as the "youngest general in the Mexican Army." He was the governor of the state of Michoacán between 1932 and 1934, leading an administration noted for its active pursuit of agrarian reform.

The agrarian seizures carried out during the agrarian reform totaled around 49,000,000 acres, with about 44,000,000 disbursed by Cárdenas. He also seized many millions of acres of American-owned properties located on the coasts and frontiers through presidential decrees. In doing so he invoked the constitutional prohibitions against foreign ownership in those areas and the illegality of large landholdings that created de facto conditions of local monopoly, which restricted Mexicans in their pursuit of economic well-being. The agrarian administrators, local tax collectors, and sundry other authorities singled out the landholdings of foreigners and gave them high priority for seizure. The government also seized land through foreclosures for abandonment and tax arrears, unclear titles, and public utility.

The sweeping land reform affected almost everyone, including the Mexican rural landholding elite. American companies that provided communications, transportation, and high technology—including the railroads, which were still controlled by the directors in New York—and the oil companies came under attack. To the chagrin of the Americans who owned property and companies in Mexico and the U.S. government, the personnel of the Comisión Nacional de la Refoma Agraria and the Mexican Department of Labor cooperated with the restless elements in the agrarian and urban working classes. American owners of small holdings and large estates continued to litigate their claims, arguing that they were exempt from agrarian confiscations. Larger property owners divided up their holdings and cited Article 27, which exempted small properties from agrarian seizures, and Obregón's Plan de Agua Prieta, which defined a small property to be no more than 100,000 acres.

By 1940 a high percentage of Mexican campesinos had received lands through the satisfaction of claims either that they needed land *(dotación)* or that they had been defrauded during the prerevolutionary era and merited restitution. Most of the land taken from large foreign-owned haciendas near the borders and coasts, however, was not specifically acquired for agrarian reform. As a result, estimates of land seizures during the Obregón and Cárdenas eras have been routinely understated. The actual amount of land taken from the American landholders was much greater than the amount taken by Cárdenas for agrarian reform. In cases of lands near seacoasts and borders, the nationalization of land was more important, with seizures for tax arrears, abandonment, and unclear title also playing a major role.

Early friction with local Mexican authorities and then the disruptions of the revolution had set the stage for the land seizures of the 1930s. Between 1906 and 1911 the public registry officials refused to record many of the land titles and bills of sale when the newly arrived Americans presented them. They gave no reason for the refusals, but accepted tax payments. Many of the titles were never entered into the public registry. This fact surprised a number of American settlers when the land disputes intensified during the 1930s. A sizeable number of them, in effect, held de facto but not de jure possession of the land. Their claims to ownership had been further undermined in 1912, when the wave of violence that swept Mexico reached them. Most of the settlers fled, encouraged by President Wilson's warning to do so. That act caused many of them to lose control of their properties. Some stayed away for only a few months; others were away for longer periods. Many never returned. Those who returned within eighteen months repeated the evacuation experience when U.S. troops invaded Veracruz in April 1914 and attacks against Americans spread across the nation.

Agrarian reform edicts often singled out for seizure land on larger estates that enclosed water sources. Those actions rendered the estates operated by Americans dysfunctional, often leading to their abandonment and then reversion to Mexican control. For example, the San José de las Rusias hacienda in Tamaulipas, owned by the heirs of Otto Brictson, became a complete liability when Obregón ruled that Díaz had created a foreign-owned monopoly near the border and coast and nationalized almost 500,000 acres of the 1,200,000-acre estate. Agrarians occupied parts of the San José during the revolution and throughout the 1920s. During the 1920s and 1930s the governor of Tamaulipas issued eight decrees expropriating 70,000 acres of the estate. The Comisión Nacional de la Reforma Agraria and President Calles approved three seizures in the late 1920s and early 1930s. No less than six agrarian expropriations were made against the estate in 1937 and three more seizures occurred in 1938. The confiscations of the late 1930s totaled only 65,000 of almost 700,000 acres, but the lands taken bordered both sides of the river that ran through the estate. The remaining parts of the hacienda became unusable when the agrarians gained control of the river.

The Brictsons found themselves in an impossible situation, one that prevailed in most parts of the country. In 1938 the axe fell on the San José de las Rusias. In the late 1930s President Lázaro Cárdenas signed agrarian decrees creating nine *ejidos*, each comprising 50,000 acres, situated along both sides of the stream that ran north and south across the estate. Four other agrarian grants were also processed. At the same time the authorities were pacifying the complaints of local elites. They authorized 38,536 acres for

Señora Refugio de León, the surviving head of the López family, and the governor condemned 156,137 acres for unpaid taxes that were then auctioned off to individuals capable of purchasing land. Brictson complained to his sister in Mexico City that the hacienda was also being "continuously invaded by Mexican citizens of the State of Tamaulipas and from the State of Texas, who have returned as repatriates."[1] A combination of agrarians, local elites in Soto la Marina, state leaders, and federal officials brought about the end of Brictson's estate. Very few investors would buy a property lacking access to water and facing further expropriations. If they did, the price reflected the risk being taken. In the late 1930s the Brictsons, seeking to save their holdings, appealed to the government "to guarantee that no additional land would be expropriated." Given the high level of nationalism, agrarian unrest, and the social democratic program of the Cárdenas administration, the Mexican officials refused to "bind the government to not exercise the right of eminent domain."[2]

In the early 1940s, beset by the local citizenry and without access to water, Louis Brictson and the other heirs turned to Senator Bob La Follette of their native Wisconsin and the American Mexican Claims Commission set up by the administrations of Franklin D. Roosevelt and Manuel Avila Camacho, who was elected to succeed Cárdenas in 1940. But there was no evidence to indicate that they "made any attempt to use the land after 1937," and that undermined their argument. In 1937 the Brictsons had ceased to pay what they regarded as futile property taxes. After an appropriate interval the local, state, and national authorities foreclosed on the remaining property for nonpayment of real estate taxes. The land involved still exceeded 600,000 acres. The fate of the Brictsons duplicated that of numerous Americans who owned great estates, especially near the coasts and frontiers. National concerns at the presidential level and long-simmering disputes between the American estate owners and their Mexican neighbors over land titles and water rights turned into land invasions, denial of water rights, and foreclosures by local Mexican officials for unpaid taxes and the frequent claim that property titles had not been legally registered since no record existed in local archives.[3] By 1940 three generations of Brictsons had fought for the San José properties in the Mexican courts, and they had lost almost everything. Their only chance lay with the continuing work of the claims commission and the intercessions of Senator La Follette. During the 1940s the attractiveness and wealth of the estate would attract powerful Mexican outsiders and lead to the partial displacement of the agrarians.[4]

Nearby, the survivors of the five hundred Blaylock Colony pioneers in Tamaulipas had a similar experience. They had purchased small tracts of land from George Blaylock's original acquisition, the 173,000-acre Chamal hacienda, "as far back as 1906 and 1907," but largely between 1908 and 1910. The Mexican workers living in settlements around Chamal claimed that they were the "rightful owners" of the property, and they applied to have their titles restored. They considered themselves victims of the Americans, forced to work on land that had been taken from them. The American settlers claimed with pride that prior to the revolution many of them had installed irrigation facilities and improved the land, converting it from neglected open range into "developed" farmland. They had employed the nearby citizens of the pueblos Chamal Viejo and La Roncha as workers to carry out the improvement projects on their "ranchos." Some of the American settlers contrasted their achievements with what they characterized as the "neglect" practiced by the estate's former Mexican owners.

The Mexican agrarian authorities, backed by Cárdenas, replied to the settlers' legal case by asserting that the Blaylocks still owned the 173,000-acre Chamal hacienda. No registered property titles could be found by the authorities. They also pointed out that many of the Americans who claimed these unregistered properties had in fact not lived in the region for many years. The Mexican officials brushed aside their tax receipts because they did not constitute land titles.[5]

For the Mexican national leadership, the area around Acapulco was at least as important as Tamaulipas. Acapulco was the most important port on the Pacific Ocean and the center of the most desirable resort area in the nation. The Mexican leadership's desire to secure absolute control over the area brought it into conflict with the Stephens Brothers Company, the owner of the Cacalutla and El Potrero haciendas.

In the mid 1920s Stephens Brothers committed an error in judgment by filing with the claims commission for compensation from the Mexican government for the damages incurred during the revolution. That step reenforced the strong sense of alienation that the regional authorities felt toward the brothers. When the local agrarians carried out their next land invasion on the Cacalutla, the local and state officials did not try to evict them. The agrarians then used firearms to maintain their hold on the land against the private police employed by Stephens Brothers.

The municipal, judicial, and state officials, led by the "ultra-nationalist" governor of Guerrero, General Adrian Castrejón, denied every request for relief from the American consular officials in Acapulco, who protested the invasions. The U.S. representatives understood things. The Mexicans intended to end the American "monopoly" over the production of oil from *coquito* palms in the Costa Grande—and the authorities did not like the

Stephens brothers. Castrejón made his position and that of the Mexican government clear.

> The governor is a firm believer that foreigners should be deprived of all rights to properties lying within the zone of fifty miles from the seacoast, and during his last visit to the North or *Costa Grande* district of Guerrero, he conceded to certain individuals the right to buy and sell the coquito produced on the American owned ranches, without considering the rights of the owners of the same ranches.[6]

Shortly afterward, in 1927, the government issued an agrarian reform decision granting a large portion of the Cacalutla properties to the citizenry of three pueblos in the municipal district of Atoyac de Alvarez. More was at stake, however, than agrarian reform. Part of the land came directly under the control of General Amadeo Vidales, "who for several years had been terrorizing the coast. The government was of the opinion that peace could be bought in this manner." In the Costa Grande the government sought to fulfill the need for national ownership, buy off local troublemakers like Vidales, and appease the agrarian rebels.[7]

In 1930 the Mexican agrarian commission attempted to finish off the Stephens Brothers Company. It confiscated the remainder of the Cacalutla and all of the El Potrero property and issued titles to twenty-three pueblos around the Cacalutla. Corruption played a role in the appropriation of the El Potrero, which was located in the Costa Chica, immediately south of Acapulco. In 1930 future presidential aspirant General Juan Andreu Almazán, the secretary for communications and public works, took personal control of 1,900 acres of land immediately south of Puerto Marques and began collecting rents from the Mexican inhabitants. The property owners in the area, including the Stephens brothers, claimed that Almazán had usurped the property, but the general claimed to hold the power of attorney for the absentee Turkish owner, Jacobo Harootian, who had lived in Cuba or Santo Domingo since the revolution—no one knew where. As the agrarian commission carried out the partitions of adjacent American properties, those controlled by Almazán—the acreages that were the most populated and the best suited for farming, acreages for which he held no valid title—remained the only tracts unaffected.

It was in this setting that five families moved onto the El Potrero lands south of Puerto Marques in the late 1920s. They constructed crude houses made of wooden stakes and palm leaves and called their settlement La Zanja. In 1935 visitors encouraged by Governor Castrejón joined the original families at La Zanja in a special gathering held for an agrarian census. Officials from the agrarian commission solemnly counted thirty families, the male members of which were "armed with rifles and pistols," and took no notice that only a few days earlier most of these "agrarians" had lived in Acapulco, about nineteen miles from the settlement.

Having mustered the needed number of residents, the residents of La Zanja filed a land claim and awaited the adjudication of their petition. An engineer sent by the Comisión Nacional de la Reforma Agraria noted that the law required that all claims filed by campesinos must be for lands situated within seven kilometers of their places of residence. He decided to abide by that dictate and, in the words of the agrarians and some local officials, ruled in favor of the "gringos." Miguel Bonilla, a friend of Generals Almazán and Castrejón, promptly telegraphed the agrarian reform headquarters in Mexico City and obtained the removal of the engineer. William Stephens described Bonilla as the local "agrarian agitator." The commission then sent a replacement, who duly allotted the lands to the workers. During the next few years, however, the "agrarians" did not work the land they had successfully claimed at El Potrero. Instead, without a public record of who controlled the proceeds, other ranchers "rented" the parcels from an anonymous "owner."

Successive presidential agrarian decrees consolidated Mexican control over 13,000 acres of the El Potrero during the 1930s, and agrarian "squatters" overran another 2,400. In 1938 the government even leased 3,750 acres to "third parties" while Stephens Brothers appealed to the courts and the authorities of two nations.[8]

In spite of all the adversity experienced by the Stephens brothers and thousands of other American landowners, newcomers continued to enter Mexico and buy land at what they considered bargain prices. The disasters experienced by their predecessors represented opportunity to the aggressive newcomers. They joined the earlier arrivals just in time for the forthcoming agrarian disaster. In late 1914 Frank Young bought 3,000 acres fronting the La Boquilla River in Tamaulipas from Claude and Willie Blaylock, the heirs of George Blaylock. His property fronted the river for one-half mile and featured a deep freshwater well at the back of the property. He paid only 580 pesos for the entire tract. Like many of his neighbors he feared remaining in the area during the revolution and did not return until 1920. At that point he discovered that most of the improvements, including the irrigation network, had been destroyed. During the 1920s and 1930s, with the campesinos from the nearby pueblos of Chamal Viejo and La Roncha invading their properties and "stealing fruit," Young and his neighbors were loath to invest in improvements. They did, however, continue to pay taxes on the land, hoping that conditions would change. Instead they grew worse, and in 1938 the agrarian authorities confiscated 1,200 of Young's 3,000 acres, including all of the river frontage and his well. The best orchards on other properties in the area were also confiscated and meted out to the former employees on the "ranchos" and their descendants, who qualified for the land because of their residency in Chamal Viejo and La Roncha.

The experience of Young and his American neighbors, who found their access to water blocked by the land and water allocations, was duplicated countless times throughout Mexico. The government correctly perceived that if the reform was to serve any purpose, then the campesino recipients of land should gain access to water. Moreover, the denial of water to the foreigners encouraged their departure.

Horace Corbin, a New York financier, purchased the 125,000-acre Chivela hacienda at Juchitán, Oaxaca, from the Gulf Hardwoods Company in 1928, paying a bargain-basement price of $70,000. Corbin took a bold move, considering the rising tide of nationalistic and purely agrarian land foreclosures that local campesinos were pressing for at the time. He got a "bargain," and the sellers no doubt felt a mix of chagrin and relief. Perhaps Corbin believed that Dwight Morrow's influence on Mexican strongman Calles meant an end to the federal reform effort, or perhaps he took Calles at his word when the president strongly hinted that agrarian seizures would end. Corbin believed that "the Agrarian laws affecting the foreign owned property in Mexico would be revoked and the property itself would return to the holders of the title in fee simple." Those hopes, whatever their source, were soon dashed. Campesino land seizures without government authorization plagued him and an increasing number of landholders, Mexican and American, across southern Mexico.

In 1932 the government responded to local political pressure by announcing no less than four annexations of Chivela lands. Two more seizures followed in 1933. Corbin responded to the challenge by appealing to local and state judges and police authorities, the national agrarian commission, the U.S. embassy, and the U.S. State Department. In 1933 he decided to follow the strategy used by William Randolph Hearst and many other large estate owners. Corbin created a dummy corporation registered in Mexico. He called the new firm the Compañía Maderas del Golfo, S.A., and sold 100,000 acres of the hacienda for a mere 50,000 pesos. He kept 25,000 acres under his name. Corbin's division of the Chivela placed all of the estate within Obregón's 100,000-acre definition of a "small property," and it was therefore exempt from the agrarian expropriation laws. The Mexican authorities, however, discovered that Corbin held the majority of stock in

Maderas S.A., and by 1937 the agrarian commission had taken 50,000 acres. The effect on the viability of the estate, however, was greater than the amount of land lost. Once again the nationalized properties provided the only access to water and were already developed. The agrarian seizure rendered a crippling blow to Corbin's commercial activities.[9]

The new American buyers continued to grab Mexican haciendas and large properties at the height of the agrarian seizures because they saw "exceptional opportunities" and dismissed the agrarian reform as a temporary aberration. In 1937 Octal Dewitt Jones purchased a large part of the haciendas owned by the Rascon Manufacturing Company in Tamaulipas and San Luis Potosí. The properties had almost sold in 1922 for $1,500,000, but Jones bought them from Cora Monro Lee, the heiress of Cora Townsend, for a mere $40,000. Jones thought he could circumvent the agrarian foreclosures and moved quickly on a preconceived plan to colonize the estate and further develop its resources with a new electrical plant at the El Salto waterfall, a mill, and even a tourist resort. He intended to go over the heads of the agrarian reformers to the president of Mexico.

In February 1938 Jones submitted his plans and blueprints to José Parres, the Mexican secretary of agriculture, and Pablo Fernández, the chief of the Colonization Department. He was racing against time. The Mexican agrarian reform surveyors were already at Rascon when he returned from Mexico City. On 5 May 1938 Jones met with President Cárdenas and explained his projects in the context of developing that region of Mexico. The president encouraged him but made no promises. During the spring and summer of 1938 insurgents supporting regional leader General Saturnino Cedillo demanded donations from the estate owners in and around the Rascon. Jones survived Cedillo's campaign, but after peace was restored Cárdenas visited the area. The president must have thought that Jones had supported Cedillo in the manner that Doheny had supported Manuel Peláez— Doheny had virtually created the general who had defended oil properties against the *agraristas*. While Jones was asking Cárdenas for government guarantees so that he could attract more capital for his projects, Parres ordered a massive land seizure in the region, including 67,000 acres at El Salto. Jones confronted Parres, accused him of deception, and asked him for rectification. He received none.

In July 1939, while Jones raged, civil engineers subdivided the lands and supervised the construction of housing for refugees from the Spanish Civil War. Cárdenas personally invited the refugees to Mexico and watched over the resettlement program. Later the government established a large sugar factory at El Salto that processed the output of the small producers established by the agrarian reform. The determined Jones, however, would not give up. He asked the American Mexican Claims Commission, which had been established to settle disputes between the U.S. and Mexican governments arising from the Cárdenas program, for $365,000 in damages. The Mexicans rejected his claims, and the litigation continued into the 1940s.[10]

In Yucatán, Cárdenas punished what he considered another American wrongdoer, and, once again, local support made his task easier. During and after the revolution campesinos had invaded and started to farm portions of the Hacienda Chichén Itzá, owned by Edward H. Thompson. The American fought with the national agrarian commission for the return of his lands for two decades before his death in 1935. Cárdenas closed off the debate with the agrarian reform officials. Then, in the American Mexican Claims Commission, he not only denied Thompson's claims but also charged him with the "enslavement of Mexican workers" and the "theft of national treasures." Thompson sued in the Mexican courts, where the government attorneys described in detail how Thompson had misused his position as U.S. consul at Mérida to smuggle Maya treasures out of the country to the Peabody Museum of Boston. In 1942 the Mexican Supreme Court ruled in favor of the government and against the Thompson heirs and the museum.[11]

GAINING CONTROL OF COASTS AND BORDERS

The Mexican government's drive to control the nation's coasts and frontiers required the elimination of all the prosperous American estates on the Pacific Coast, not just those of the Stephens Brothers Company. Between 1907 and 1910 Abraham and Robert Silberberg, the heads of the Knickerbocker Wall Paper Company of New York, had purchased 198,000 acres of mixed forest, coffee trees, and fruit orchards at Atoyac, Guerrero. This land, located seventy-five miles north of Acapulco near the Stephens brothers' Hacienda de Cacalutla, was one of the most valued rural areas in the state. The Southern Pacific, headed by its directors E. H. Harriman, Henry Huntington, Charles Peabody, and Frank Vanderlip, had offered the Silberbergs $600,000 for the property shortly after they had purchased it.

The Silberberg holdings survived the incursions by revolutionaries between 1910 and 1920 without fatal effect and somehow eluded the local elite-led and nationalistic land invasions experienced by the Stephens brothers, but they could not escape from the agrarians and their supporters in the national government. In the 1930s they had one of Mexico's finest plantations, with 57,000 acres of coffee trees. Local peasants had claimed much of the Silberberg estate for years. The end became evident when survey parties from the agrarian commission arrived on the estate in the mid 1930s. On 8 November 1939 Cárdenas appropriated 90,000 acres of the Silberg lands on behalf of the heads of families living in the neighboring pueblos. An aging Abraham Silberberg filed a claim for $1,092,162 in lost assets with the American Mexican Claims Commission. The amount awarded him remains unknown, but similar claimants rarely received more than 10 percent of the appraised value of their losses.[12]

Nearby were the extensive tracts of land held by the Guerrero Land and Timber Company. Like the Silberbergs and the Stephens brothers, the owners of the Guerrero Company had not visited their properties since agrarians overran them in 1927. The peasants had used armed force to defend them against interlopers. On 8 November 1939 Cárdenas formalized the de facto situation, nationalizing the company's 200,000 acres and giving them as collective *ejido* lands to the pueblos of Agua Fría, San Andres de la Cruz, and others.[13]

In Sinaloa, in contrast to Guerrero, Cárdenas had to deal with Edwin Marshall's Sinaloa Land and Water Company and Benjamin Francis Johnston's United Sugar Company interests. Johnston had figured out ways to prosper and grow during the diverse conditions of the Porfiriato, the revolution, and the 1920s, and he was still prosperous in the mid 1930s because he had found markets in Asia. A few intensely contested land seizures took place on Johnston's estate, but the property stood intact and functional. In 1937, however, Johnston died in his sleep in Hong Kong, and his legal struggles with Cárdenas ended. On 9 December 1938 the president seized the land that was historically the most controversial: the 216,478 acres around Las Mochis and Topolobampo. Cárdenas reorganized society in the region by creating thirty-two *ejidos* for 4,663 peasant families living in fifty-six settlements. The peasants and the government completed the property's return to Mexican control by organizing the *ejidos* and mills into a sugar refining collective that they called "Emancipación proletaria" (proletarian emancipation).[14]

Edwin Marshall, who owned the Las Palomas hacienda in Chihuahua and plantations in Chiapas, controlled tracts throughout Sinaloa that he had subdivided and sold through the Sinaloa Land and Water Company of Los Angeles. His influence during the 1930s rested on his close relations with the leadership of the Democratic Party, which controlled the presidency and both houses of the U.S. Congress. Cárdenas cited the Sinaloa Land Company as a survey company that had come by its holdings wrongfully when, between 1900 and 1909, President Díaz had given the company one-third of the properties it delineated. Cárdenas claimed that the sites had been falsely identified as "vacant lands." In addition, Cárdenas pointed out that Marshall had gained options on the other two-thirds of the lands that his men surveyed. The American had taken advantage of the opportunity to become the largest landowner in Sinaloa. Cárdenas declared that the resulting monopoly denied the citizenry the right to pursue opportunities in the profession of their choosing and expropriated 256,000 acres of Marshall's holdings throughout the state. He distributed them to the pueblos using the agrarian commission as his vehicle.

In the late 1930s and the 1940s Marshall appealed to the American Mexican Claims Commissions for assistance, but to his surprise the commissioners gave him little help. In 1944 they cited his failure to appeal estimates that had been made earlier on the value of his holdings. They also rejected as "dummy companies" the firms he had established to gain exemptions under the 100,000-acre small property rule. Marshall had also attempted to deceive the government by using the denomination "Limited" and claiming part-British ownership. His real partner, Nelson Rhoades, ran a Cleveland law firm with James R. Garfield, the son of the American president. In 1939 the commissioners offered him recompense of only $32,211.11 for the seized properties, about 2 percent of their actual value.[15]

Through strenuous and sustained efforts the Mexican leaders and local citizenries eliminated virtually all of the American settlers from the coasts, frontiers, Tehuantepec, Chihuahua, and Durango. They seized the assets of larger landowners in a variety of ways, including restricting access to water, tax foreclosures, the illegal monopoly law, local, state, and national agrarian reform, and the prohibitions against the foreign ownership of coastal and frontier lands. In addition, as in the case of Nayarit, they used the amendment to the law of *tierras ociosas*, or unoccupied lands. The lawmakers intended to increase agricultural output by decreasing the amount of idle land. In Nayarit the law stated that "any property not in cultivation by June 15 [of a given year] could be occupied and cultivated by outsiders." Early in 1934 the governor, Francisco Parra, supported an amendment to the law "to make the date May 5."[16]

The implications of the amendment were not comprehended at first by W. J. Hotchkiss and C. A. Vance of San Francisco, owners of the agricultural firm Hotchkiss and Vance, the largest cotton and wheat grower in California, or their tenant farmers in Nayarit. The partners owned the Hacienda de San José de Costilla, which they purchased in 1925, and raised cotton on it each year until 1934. Their problems with local agrarians and the agrarian commission had already resulted in the alienation of 4,140 acres from the 20,000 acres that made up the estate, but that settlement left both sides dissatisfied.

In 1934, as usual, Hotchkiss and Vance timed their spring planting for completion on 15 June, when the rainy season began. Lacking an irrigation system, the company usually began breaking the soil in mid or late May, although some of the tenant farmers began tilling their own plots before 5 May in order to finish in time to join in the preparation of the company's land. On 5 May 1934 the tenant farmers had already begun to work on their own plots when "150 men, each of whom carried a rifle," from the neighboring pueblos occupied all 15,860 acres of the company's and tenant farmers' lands. The agrarians acted when they saw that the outnumbered tenant farmers had begun work, and they easily dislodged them along with the company administrators. In accordance with the newly amended idle land law, which allowed the seizure of idle properties, they immediately went to work tilling the soil for their own use.

Vance and a delegation of the tenant farmers went to the capital at Tepic and protested to the governor, but he rejected them. The losers came away from the meeting fully convinced that the governor, whom the agrarians politically supported, had planned the seizure. They complained to the American embassy and the U.S. State Department of a "land steal" and joined the more than 3,000 other American owners in Mexico who were filing claims with the claims commission. Hotchkiss and Vance underestimated their problem. Usually state orders, which emanated from governors and state agrarian commissions, resulted after consultation with national authorities. The Nayarit idle land law was the vehicle used for seizure, but a mandate from Mexico City likely reinforced it. The nature of the San José de Costilla invasion and the owners' appeals to higher authority in Washington caused the dispute to last well into the 1940s.[17]

CONFRONTATION IN CAMPECHE

The greatest confrontation between Mexican officials and U.S. property interests took place in Campeche, where Cárdenas and the governor combined in a campaign to neutralize the American latifundio complex that dominated the state. Both sides recognized the importance of the area as a site for future oil production. During the revolutionary violence two contending powers had emerged: the increasingly assertive state and national governments, and the consolidation of U.S. interests represented by the Laguna directors. The Campeche government was claiming sections of the hardwood forests and leasing them to small operators. The Laguna directors girded for battle in the courts by creating a Mexican company, the Compañía de los Terrenos de Laguna. The Cárdenas administration called Terrenos de Laguna a front for a "monopoly."

The lineup of American estate owners in Campeche in the mid 1930s remained remarkably intact, although the properties were largely inactive. Some of the smaller firms were insolvent and some of the entities had changed directors. Three of the estates had been consolidated, and one, Miller and Markley's Hacienda San Pablo, had been sold to Mexicans at discounted prices. The Laguna Corporation emerged as the leading American presence. It still held its 604,000 acres and it had taken over effective control of at least two other large interests: the Mexican Gulf Land and Lumber Company of Davenport, Iowa, and the Pennsylvania-Campeche Land and Lumber Company of Williamsport. The owners of other large American interests—the Campeche Timber and Fruit Company, the Campeche Lumber and Development Company, Adolph Vietor's Proskauer Company, and the Hearst Estate, which was still held by William Randolph Hearst—do not appear to have been actively working their holdings, but they continued to hold title to a mass of land extending southward from Champotón to Guatemala.

By 1919 the Laguna Corporation had extended the firm's operations and control of the market, consolidating control over hardwood and chicle production in Campeche, but its net profits were only $125,131 that year. Under the leadership of Charles B. Fritz, John Gribbel, and Arthur B. Leach, the Philadelphia firm had harvested hardwoods until 1926 and then focused on chicle production while hoping for an oil bonanza. During the 1930s the company harvested chicle on 1,840,000 of the more than 2,000,000 acres that it controlled.

The joint interests of the Laguna directors derived from their business relationships in the United States and Mexico. Fritz owed his involvement in Mexico to the deep ties of his father, John Fritz, and those of his associate, Alexander Lyman Holley, to John Edgar Thomson and Thomas Scott, the leaders of the Pennsylvania Railroad. Thomson and Scott had pioneered the introduction of high technology and massive capital infusions into the neighboring republic. Holley had designed and served as the head engineer of the Edgar Thomson Steel Works in Pittsburgh. Scott and Thomson had been the largest consumers of Bessemer Steel products in the United States from the Civil War until the end of the century. Holley and John Fritz were associates of John Griswold, Mexican railroad pioneer and patent holder of the Bessemer process, to which Fritz had dedicated his career and from which he made his fortune. Their efforts contributed the rails and locomotives that traversed Mexico.

The directors' ties to the Americans and Mexicans of the past went even further. In the 1860s John Fritz's associates, Thomson, Scott, Griswold, and Rosecrans, had striven to build the first American railroad system in Mexico. After Griswold changed sides and joined Moses Taylor's New York group, the others eventually merged with the Pennsylvanians and created the Mexican National Railroad. A grandson, Sylvanius Griswold Morley, had worked on the Hacienda Chichén Itzá in Yucatán, not far from Campeche, assisting in the extraction of Maya artifacts for the Peabody Museum. In the 1880s Charles Schwab, father of the Bethlehem Steel Corporation chairman for whom John Fritz worked, had pioneered the development of American railroads and mining in western Chihuahua. He had sought to establish the route between El Paso, Chihuahua, and the Pacific Ocean before realizing that the Chihuahua Sierra Madre and the Yaquis in Sonora were insurmountable problems. Both Schwab and Bethlehem Steel continued to operate mines in Michoacán well into the twentieth century.

The merged interests of Laguna and Mexican Gulf brought even more Mexican relationships into play. Mexican Gulf stockholder Frances Tifft of Massachusetts came from a family whose interest in Mexico dated from the 1860s, when New York investment banker Jonathan Tifft had sold Mexican government bonds for Juárez. The John Deere Company, a major purchaser of Bethlehem Steel products, held 20 percent of the stock of Mexican Gulf and was a major customer of the steel products manufactured by Schwab and Fritz. At the same time, Willard Deere Hosford, a director of John Deere and of the Federal Reserve Bank of Kansas City, owned the Pine King timber tract of 516,000 acres in Chihuahua. Hosford gained control of the largest block of stock in the Pine King Company through the holdings of his spouse, Mary Lee McShane, the heiress of James McShane. By then the John Deere firm was probably the largest single interest in the Mexican Gulf Land and Lumber Company. John Deere joined Thompson, Fritz, and Gribbel as the leading forces in the affairs of the Laguna Company.[18] The reports of possible oil production whetted the desire of these men and women to possess Campeche.

Laguna's survival in the face of Cárdenas's challenge and the company's continued domination of Mexican chicle sales in the United States was no accident. The directors constituted a powerful, well-organized, and experienced leadership that included representatives from the industrial, marketing, and financial centers of the nation. The Laguna directors used board member A. J. Stevens of New York to create a marketing Goliath, while Leach and Gribbel provided durable financing during the revolution and the 1920s. Leach, as president of the American Investment Bankers Association and other sensitive posts, and Gribbel, as a director of the Importers and Traders National Bank and the Leather Manufacturers National Bank, enabled the firm to survive the Great Depression. Gribbel had worked with John Arbuckle, the largest U.S. importer of Mexican coffee, on the board of the Importers and Traders National Bank. Arbuckle knew as much about Mexican investments as any financier in the world.

The Laguna directors had survived where others had failed, but their minimal profits point to the fact that their passion for Campeche was rooted in the promise of oil production. In 1934 they netted only $83,652 from chicle sales. They continued to sell the resin to the Wrigley Chewing Gum Company in Chicago as well as to the Sen Sen Company and other buyers in New York. Smaller American and Mexican companies operated on the fringe of the market. Laguna lost money in 1935, 1936, and 1938, but the directors persisted, as they had during the Mexican Revolution and World War I.

The Laguna directors successfully stalled the threat of Mexican nationalism until 1940. It probably would not have mattered given the determination of the Mexican government to secure its coasts, frontiers, and subsoil wealth, but unfortunately for the Americans the most important leaders of Laguna died in the midst of Cárdenas's effort to gain control of Campeche and its resources. Gribbel died in 1936, and his less powerful son, W. Griffen Gribbel, replaced him on the board. Leach followed Gribbel to the grave in 1939. Fritz passed away in 1944. In the midst of Laguna's greatest crisis, financier Charles W. Bayliss and James B. Lichtenberger, a director of the Colonial Trust Company of Philadelphia, assumed the leadership.

In 1935 Cárdenas launched a campaign to diffuse ownership of the Campeche coastline and infuse it with Mexican producers. The president wanted to eliminate the Laguna Corporation. Between 1935 and 1939 he imposed four agrarian land seizures on Laguna, seizing over 200,000 acres. The small settlements of Kilometer 47 and Matamoros received land grants of Laguna properties totaling 77,000 acres. Cárdenas clearly used agrarian reform as a tactic to dissolve the powerful company. Kilometer 47, which was a *poblado* (an unincorporated rural settlement), received more than 2,000 acres for each of its thirty-one citizens.

The Americans rallied their workers in an effort to block the agrarian measures. Eighty-five signed an appeal to the governor that claimed that "Matamoros and Empalme Escarcega" (Kilometer 47) had agrarian committees only because the secretary of agriculture had sent in outsiders. The appeal pointed out that the Laguna Corporation was a key economic factor in the state, having paid 542,491 pesos in salaries during 1938. It also cited the company hospital, school, and store, where (it claimed) goods were sold at cost as benefits to Campeche.

In the courts the Mexican government argued that Laguna constituted a monopoly because it restrained trade, development, and opportunity for Mexican producers. During 1939 business operations were interrupted for all but three months. It is not clear if the disruption came about as the result of government action or because of the directors' reaction to agrarian reform efforts. But the agrarian reform was only a skirmish. Cárdenas planned to nationalize the American property complex in Campeche before leaving office in 1940.[19]

REFORM IN CHIHUAHUA

In Chihuahua agrarian reform had begun in earnest during the early 1920s. The movement engaged American companies accustomed to wearing out their opponents in the courts through protracted litigation, a strategy that proved disastrous in confrontations with the Mexican government. Agrarian surveyors infuriated John McShane when they studied his properties during the 1920s. In 1929, as president of the Pine King Land and Lumber Company, McShane embarked on a decade-long struggle to undo the expropriation of 300,000 acres that occurred after President Emilio Portes Gil invalidated the concession that Díaz had made to the Valenzuela survey company. McShane's problem was not just that loss, but the minister of agriculture's insistence that the 1929 action required McShane to sell the remaining 216,000 acres of Pine King forests within three years in tracts of 12,500 to 100,000 acres. That action would end Pine King's monopoly as the only major commercial enterprise in the area. McShane learned that Calles, the strongman of the Mexican government, opposed further agrarian reform, so in 1930 he agreed to sell the remaining 216,000 acres and dropped his suit with the claims commission. McShane, thinking the agrarian reform program had ended, did not sell the land.

Three years later, on 29 April 1933, the minister of agriculture noted that no transactions had taken place and annulled McShane's contract. A stunned McShane and his partners appealed to the U.S. Department of State, but the American claims investigators showed no sympathy for the Pine King owners. They noted that McShane had accepted the nullification of the 1880s survey titles when he agreed to drop the Pine King suit in return for the opportunity to sell the 216,000 acres. The U.S. officials agreed with their Mexican counterparts that the presidential cancellation of the land grant to the survey company negated the sale to Pine King and that McShane and his associates had lost their rights to compensation through their maneuvers and stalling.[20]

During the 1920s the rural populace of Chihuahua, many of them former Villistas, continued to demand land reform. Vaqueros, *foresteros* (timbermen), and agrarian laborers, the rural workers of the area, had periodically invaded the great estates in north-central and western Chihuahua since

1910. The Chihuahua government invalidated the titles to almost 80 percent of the T. O. Riverside Ranch properties. It pursued two objectives: to
establish public tranquility through agrarian reform, and to secure Mexican ownership of the borderlands. The state agrarian commission gave much
of the land to campesinos, many of whom were former Villistas who already
occupied parts of the estate. The rest were retained by the state of Chihuahua.
Despite those actions, the heirs of Edward Morris and the Swift packing-
houses continued to pay their taxes in order to maintain their legal standing and not fall victim to further seizures under the idle land laws also passed
during the early 1920s. Between 1925 and 1938 the Morris-Swift heirs paid
$39,901 in taxes. They also employed a tactic common among the more pow-
erful American interests in Mexico. They attempted to avoid offending the
Mexican authorities by not appealing their troubles to the U.S. Department
of State, and in 1929 they advised President Portes Gil that they were not
protesting the previous Mexican seizures. The strategy failed. Between 1929
and 1938 the state seized 138,000 acres and the federal government seized
30,000 of the remaining 300,000 acres still held by the heirs. The Mexican
officials distributed the properties to the farmers and vaqueros who lived
on and near the estate.

In 1938 the Morris-Swift heirs recognized the futility of their position
and turned to the U.S. government for help. They were disappointed again.
The investigation and negotiations with the Mexican government took five
years. During that time World War II began and the Roosevelt administration redoubled its efforts to reconcile with the Mexicans. The American
members of the claims commission ignored the 1910 purchase price of
$525,000 and the improvements, and they noted that the value of the prop-
erty as assessed for taxes in 1930 totaled only 481,000 pesos. Then they
agreed that their mandate only applied to the agrarian reform decrees between 1927 and 1938 and awarded the Morris-Swift heirs $72,263. The
trustees of the estate appealed again, and the struggle continued into the
1950s era of "confidential" information, much of which remains classified.[21]

The combined strategies of the Mexican national and state governments
regarding the seizure of American properties were the result of both ad hoc
reactions to immediate conditions and applied strategy. Governors and local officials tolerated land invasions by the citizenry of neighboring towns
and pueblos. State administrations imposed high property taxes followed
by foreclosures. Agrarian expropriations were made by state and federal
officials throughout the process. The land seizures involved careful planning. At countless sites, including the Blaylock Colony, the San José de las
Rusias hacienda, the T. O. Riverside Ranch, and the Santisima hacienda, the

adjudicators awarded the access to water to the Mexican claimants, leaving the Americans literally high and dry. The agrarian measures and the tax impositions so devastated the Americans psychologically, as well as materially, that many gave up. That happened to the colonists everywhere and to the Shearsons, Mortons, and Peirces at Corralitos, the Shapleighs at Santisima, and the Brictsons at San José de las Rusias.

Elsewhere, the survivors of the Mormon colonies in Chihuahua and Sonora also had a difficult time maintaining their holdings. At Colonia Díaz, Ernest Romney lost everything he had brought to Mexico. The Mormons had originally evacuated the colony on 27 July 1912, following the killings of residents William Adams and J. D. Harvey by rebel soldiers. The shootings took place in full view of the Americans, with Harvey's daughter standing beside her father pleading for his life. The soldiers who committed the atrocities came from northwestern Chihuahua, and their actions underscored the complexity of local Mexican attitudes toward the Americans that still prevailed in the 1930s. They were followers of General Pascual Orozco and his subordinate, radical and former PLM general José Ines Salazar. During the revolution Salazar had expressed his hostility to the Americans on several occasions prior to the killings and had pointedly "withdrawn" his "guarantees for the safety and life." Other forces fighting for Orozco in the area included Yaquis who were opposed to both mestizo and American landholdings in the territories they claimed.

Many of the more persistent American settlers attempted to return to rural Chihuahua in the ensuing decades, but by the 1930s only a fraction remained because the local and state authorities made only sporadic and unenthusiastic efforts to protect them. They had good reason not to. From 1915 to 1923 a combination of Villistas and hostile neighbors empowered by the anti-American killings carried out by the Villistas blocked their return. The enmity was deepened in 1916 when the U.S. Punitive Expedition so incited the populace that Villa's forces in Chihuahua increased from 500 to 10,000 strong that year. During the rest of the 1920s and 1930s neighbors and newcomers, both those who were hostile to the Americans and those who recognized an opportunity to benefit, blocked the colonists' return. The Mormons concentrated their remaining numbers in Dublan, Colonias Juárez and Garcia, and Cuauhtémoc, where they remain to the present.

FURTHER FORECLOSURES

When Mexican authorities waited before offering to protect the settlers it was often because they felt they needed a strong presence of Mexican citizenry among the Americans who lived in the area. The quicker-paced agrarian actions in the region also reflected local extremes. At Colonia Díaz the potency of those who seized the American properties precipitated the formalized proceedings.

> [S]aid properties were taken into the possession of Mexican citizens, most of whom were ex-soldiers of the Mexican Revolution and the Mexican Army, and such squatters have continued to exercise domain and control over said property without the consent of the owners thereof, but with the approbation and approval of the government of Mexico.[22]

The issue of unpaid taxes haunted the Latter-Day Saints. Peter Lemmon, a former resident of Colonia Díaz, appealed to the Mexican government for twenty-five years to no avail. He offered to pay his back property taxes if they would afford him protection, but "in each instance, they refused to receive any money for taxes, or to permit him to take charge of or manage any of his property." Romney was also rebuffed when he attempted to pay property taxes. During the 1920s and 1930s the Mexican government approved a series of land seizures for unpaid taxes and granted the lands to the citizens of nearby communities, establishing *ejidos* on the former American properties.[23]

Observers rightfully remember 1938 as the year of the oil nationalizations, but American landholders also experienced serious challenges from agrarians, local and state officials, and the federal agrarian reform commission. In Durango, Cárdenas nationalized 58,500 out of the 91,000 acres that James and Robert Long had owned since 1907. Some of the Long brothers' land, situated some forty miles from the railroad running from Parral to Durango City, was suitable for grazing, but the estate existed as an investment for the future exploitation of its stand of virgin timber. The national agrarian commission seized the central and accessible portions of the estate, gave them to the hamlet of El Palomo, and left disconnected areas on the fringe of the estate for the Longs. The seizure disjointed the estate's system of roads and separated its milling facilities, setting the stage for abandonment and ensuing tax foreclosures on the remaining parcels. In effect, the Longs lost all 91,000 acres. A well-planned partial seizure meant a de facto taking of all the property. In numerous cases the demoralized owners opted not to pay their land taxes and the local authorities then seized the properties and sold them at auction to regional elites.[24]

In 1934 and 1937 Charles A. Miller lost over 78,000 acres of his remaining 225,000 acres of the old Hacienda San Marcos south of Acapulco. Miller's father had bought the properties in a series of purchases between 1877 and 1910 for a total outlay of only 36,300 pesos. After the revolution the Millers reoccupied their abandoned estate, reorganized its production, and in good years earned over 600,000 pesos. They enclosed the property with a wire fence, installed windmills, built housing for the workers, and constructed the facilities for a dairy farm and fruit orchards. By 1923 the land was valued at eight pesos per acre. The Millers maintained their own constabulary for the protection of their interests, meeting the land invasions carried out by the local peasantry with armed force, and they protested to their government as soon as the Mexican authorities moved to seize some of the grazing lands and orchards.

The Millers believed that the agrarians, encouraged by Cárdenas's program, had rendered their properties useless. They demanded $1,580,082 through the Agrarian Claims division of the American Mexican Claims Commission. The Cárdenas administration objected, pointing out that the Millers had acquired lands despoiled by Díaz from some fourteen indigenous villages, the rightful owners. The Mexicans also showed that Charles Miller Sr. had employed armed horsemen for years and that his son continued to do so to keep the local Mexican citizenry from entering the disputed properties. About the only issue the two governments could agree on in the Miller case was the fact that the Millers had controlled vast properties that extended from the Costa Chica south to the neighboring state of Oaxaca. In 1940 they turned the unresolved and controversial dispute over to the American Mexican Claims Commission, which maintained classified files.[25]

The establishment of political stability in the countryside deeply concerned the government and led some campesinos to exploit that preoccupation to their advantage. In the 1930s Burton Dike was one of the few surviving Americans at the colony of Pijijiapan in Chiapas. In 1911 he had bought the 5,000-acre Hacienda las Tortugas in the name of the Soconusco Land and Colonization Company for a little over $11,000. Over the years he watched most of his American neighbors lose their land because of foreclosures for unpaid taxes and squatters. The majority of the Americans had not been there to defend their property, having evacuated Mexico aboard the USS *Buford* twenty-five years earlier.

During the 1930s Dike and almost all of the scattered Americans that remained in the area lost their property titles. Dike's troubles began in earnest in 1933 when citizens of the nearby *poblado*, named Joaquin Miguel Gutiérrez, invaded his property and appealed to the governor of Chiapas for a land grant. In 1934 the governor duly ordered some 500 acres of Las Tortugas, plus some other properties, to be given to the campesinos. Abelardo Rodríguez, the provisional president of Mexico, approved the governor's action on 9 April. Usually agrarian petitioners faced long delays if they represented an unincorporated rural place. The authorities normally waited for agrarian claims to pass through years of surveys and studies carried out by the agrarian commission before issuing such grants, but when the peasants created political instability by violently seizing land, as they did at Las Tortugas, they moved more quickly. The peasants usually took violent action in highly inflammatory cases involving earlier usurpations of property, American or Spanish ownership, or titleholders who claimed lineage from the colonial nobility.

That same year the citizens of another *poblado*, El Carmen, asked the governor and the federal government for their own grant of land from Las Tortugas. They too were given land in unusual haste, receiving 225 acres the same year. In 1937 the Mexican government gave the *poblado* of Guanajuato 750 acres that it claimed from Dike, citing unpaid taxes. Finally, in September 1940, Cárdenas gave another 500 acres to the *poblado* of Joaquin Miguel Gutiérrez. At that juncture Dike still held some 300 acres but was loath to pay taxes on the property. Like his compatriots in Chihuahua, he demanded protection from land invasions in return for his tax payments. Like those compatriots, he had no bargaining position. His failure to pay taxes made seizure easier for the authorities. By the end of the Cárdenas regime in 1940, the Mexican authorities had succeeded in the elimination of foreign interests from the coastal and frontier regions of Chiapas.[26]

MINERAL LOSSES

During the 1930s the American-owned mining industry in the north suffered the same fate as the landholdings did. The Mexican leadership moved against the largest American interests in an effort to gain control of the nation's mineral resources and productive potential. From the American perspective, deep troubles plagued the industry. At Cubo the combination of depressed silver prices and new government rules regarding job security for the miners discouraged the owners, who resented the "interference" and compared the Mexican government to "Bolsheviks." In 1932 Irving Herr, the chief engineer at Cubo, gave up his thirty-year career in Mexico and returned to the United States.

> I like our home and like living here. But I do not like working in Mexico anymore. There is too much government interference with one's business. I feel as though our Company, instead of being a

business concern, were simply a sort of institution for the purpose of supplying work to a lot of down and out Mexican workmen.[27]

Yet Herr retained an abiding affection for Mexicans and their culture. Before departing he and his spouse took a tour of the capital and southern Mexico and extolled the people of Cuernavaca and Oaxaca, where they stopped. The Cubo joined a growing list of American-owned mines that closed.[28]

By the 1930s steel production had become an important industry in Mexico, with its own complement of domestic capitalists. In that context American companies were welcome only if they remained productive. The Bethlehem Steel Corporation had entered Mexico in 1907, but the company's primary focus was the export of processed ore to the American market. Given the sluggish level of consumption at home during the Great Depression, it was logical for the Bethlehem directors to cut back and even suspend production.

When the Bethlehem directors established their operation in Michoacán, they used a strategy common to American companies in Mexico that wished to downplay their presence. They created a "Mexican" corporation, the Compañía de Minas de Fierro Las Truchas, S.A. The company entered Mexico under the leadership of chairman Charles M. Schwab, whose father had pioneered railroads in Chihuahua during the early 1880s. Las Truchas posed as a Mexican corporation, but Bethlehem actually owned 9,960 shares out of 10,000.

The company's problems began when the directors suspended operations. In 1916 Carranza had issued a mining law that declared, "All concessionaires of mines are obligated to work the same under penalty of forfeiture, if they suspend work for more than two consecutive months, or in any event for more than three months during any one year." Article 27 of the Constitution of 1917 codified the nation's ultimate, inalienable, and retroactive ownership of natural resources. During the revolution Schwab's company had been buying mining concessions for future development. In 1919 Las Truchas bought a valuable tract of iron ore in the state of Michoacán for $325,000. It had been forfeited by its former owners in 1918 for failure to perform. The tract was reinstated to the company, and all seemed well until the 1930s.

In 1936, "for the first time," the federal official in charge of mining in Michoacán cited the 1916 law and informed the company that the government of Mexico was declaring Bethlehem in forfeiture because it had not worked the mines continuously. The authorities noted that Las Truchas was a dummy corporation in violation of the law. Cárdenas had intimate knowledge of the Bethlehem situation and the Las Truchas site because the property was located in his home state, of which he had been governor from 1928 to 1932. The law of 1916 was the principal vehicle used to invalidate most U.S. mining claims in northern Chihuahua and Sonora, but Bethlehem was a major American company. The government granted the directors the right to appeal and to submit documents as a Mexican corporation. All negotiations failed, however, and Bethlehem lost its most important Mexican mines. During the 1940s the company settled for an unknown amount of cash and gave up its operations in Mexico. The Mexican metallurgical industry was fully capable of providing domestic consumers with basic steel products.[29]

For the Mexican authorities, mining was only one area of concern in their drive to regain control of the national economy. In 1935 Cárdenas began a series of moves designed to end foreign domination of Mexico's infrastructure industries. He began with the railroads, carrying through a buyout of the predominantly American stockholders. By the end of the year the national government had taken over the rail network. In 1937 the Mexican Supreme Court took the next step, ruling on the case of the Jalapa Power and Light Company and its railroad versus the state of Veracruz and the Cooperativa de Luz, Fuerza y Transportes de Jalapa. The court held that the state's seizure of the American-owned company in 1925 was lawful. The decision anticipated the nationalization of the petroleum companies in 1938. That year the American owners of the Jalapa Company received yet another setback, this time from the Veracruz legislature. That body declared that the agreement of 1926, wherein the state had agreed to pay 2,000,000 pesos for the property, was too much. It found that the assessed value of the company was really 1,168,616 pesos and that amount, less the payments that had already been made, constituted its entire obligation. The owners of the company appealed to the U.S. Department of State and were referred to the claims commission.

By 1936 American ambassador Josephus Daniels believed that the worst of the trials between the United States and Mexico were past. The recovery of "Good Neighbor" status seemed to be appreciated by both governments. Daniels saw the binational American Mexican Claims Commission as an effective way to settle the ongoing disputes between U.S. property holders and the Mexican government over damages incurred during the revolution and the seizures that were sweeping away the remaining American holdings. The Good Neighbor Policy, adopted at the Pan American Conference in 1933, meant taking a positive view toward the Mexican effort to restore national ownership over the land, and the claims procedure had already compensated hundreds of aggrieved parties.

Former president Calles had given Daniels, the bankers, and the oil company owners repeated reassurances. Through his friend Ambassador Morrow and industry representatives, Calles had repeated the assurances for seven years during the late 1920s and early 1930s. The Americans felt that their property rights were secure despite repeated difficulties with what they regarded to be labor extremists and nationalistic politicians.

Cárdenas, however, had other ideas. In 1936 his government enacted a law that gave it the power to claim properties through eminent domain if it served the national interest and the discretion to postpone compensation for up to ten years. Meanwhile, the government encouraged the various unions in the oil industry to come together as one union. They formed the Sindicato de Trabajadores Petroleros de la República Mexicana, an entity with close government ties. The new union immediately demanded a 65,000,000-peso pay raise per year. The counteroffer made by the companies totaled only 14,000,000 pesos. The Cárdenas administration attempted to arbitrate the dispute, but the union called a strike when negotiations broke down. Mexican officials undertook a study of the industry to determine its financial condition and to undermine the companies' obviously false claims that they could not afford the demanded raises.

That step altered the dispute from one of company versus union into a confrontation between the companies and the government. The Cardenistas quickly decided that the profit status of the companies was such that they could afford to increase employee pay by 26,000,000 pesos annually. In addition, to strengthen the government's hand, they observed that the foreign companies were monopolies that operated in a manner contrary to Mexico's best interests. This laid the companies open to presidential nullification of their grants and to seizure via new eminent domain legislation passed a year earlier. The struggle over the pay raise and the government's authority to arbitrate the dispute went to the courts.

On 1 March 1938 the Mexican Supreme Court ruled in favor of the government. After prolonged and heated negotiations the American oilmen agreed to the 26,000,000-peso raise, but they would not accept the demand for union control of the work sites. The demand for control was not just anarchosyndicalist—the Mexican workers were fed up with segregation and discrimination. The companies' refusal gave the Cárdenas government the justification it needed for seizure. On 18 March 1938 Cárdenas announced his decision to nationalize the American companies in a dramatic speech at Mexico City that galvanized the nation. The date, once referred to as Mexico's "Economic Independence Day," was remembered for decades by the American oil company owners, managers, and employees as a day of "robbery" and "theft." Soon afterward Cárdenas offered to pay back the companies based on the ten-year compensation provision written into the eminent domain law of 1936.

In early 1939, with war in Europe looming, the Mexicans entered into negotiations with some of the most powerful capitalists in the Western world. The Mexican leadership chose the most propitious time possible. In 1940 Sinclair Oil accepted an $8,500,000 buyout, to be paid in part with petroleum. American oilman William Rhodes Davis helped break an embargo of Mexican petroleum by the big companies, a strategy that was working until he intervened. Davis owned fifty wells and oil technology in Texas and Louisiana and held a part interest at Pozo Rica in Mexico. He knew the head of the consolidated Mexican labor movement, Vicente Lombardo Toledano. Through that association and his connections with the Mexican government and with oilmen in Europe, Davis was able to reach some sections of the European market. From 1939 to mid 1941 Davis sent tankers filled with Mexican oil to Germany and Scandinavia, putting pressure on the Americans to settle their dispute with Cárdenas over the nationalization of their assets.

The U.S. government and Federal Bureau of Investigation treated Davis as a security risk, while British Security Coordination "may have acted to quicken Davis's journey into the next life." He died in late 1941 under "mysterious circumstances." Despite the important sales to Germany and Scandinavia, domestic consumption claimed most Mexican oil during the war. The American oil companies and the Mexican government negotiated until 1941, when the Americans and the administration of Avila Camacho agreed upon a settlement of almost $24,000,000 for the nationalized properties and a schedule for payment. The United States lifted the boycott in 1942, and the Mexican government made the payments punctually. In 1949 it paid off the debt in full.[30]

During 1939 the Cárdenas administration backed off its support of labor unrest and the formation of unions. The number of strikes adjudicated by the government dropped to zero at one point. In the most notable case the administration, in the face of declining copper, lead, and zinc exports, pressured the union workers to reach an agreement with ASARCO, ending a bitter strike. ASARCO was the largest mining operation in Mexico.[31] Labor unrest threatened economic development by scaring off venture capitalists, and an accommodation with the Americans made sense to the Mexican leadership as long as they controlled the bulk of their national economy. In contrast to Díaz's efforts to bring capital into Mexico a half-century earlier, during World War II the nation's business and political leadership developed a joint venture system in which they played a central role. Indeed, in 1945 they wrote the practice into law, providing that 51 percent of all enterprises deemed "critical" by the government would be owned by Mexicans. The Mexican elites adopted a pragmatic nationalism that allowed foreign participation in any walk of life as long as they saw the endeavor as beneficial to the "national interest."

For the American elites, using their influence in the highest circles of Mexican polity was not enough during the Cárdenas regime. But if their services were essential—like the mineral exports of Phelps Dodge, Anaconda, and ASARCO, the flow of new technology from General Electric and General Motors, and capital services from National City Bank—the Americans survived until working relationships with Mexican elites or the government could be arranged.[32]

GROWING CLOSER

Despite the rivalries between American property interests and Mexican nationalists during the 1930s, the American and Mexican people and their cultures continued to grow closer together. They did so through such unspectacular everyday activities as going to the cinema. In 1931 urban Mexicans enjoyed American cinema in sometimes palatial theaters in Mexico City, while rural workers, such as the miners of Cubo, also watched the films. In 1931 the Cubo workers wanted to see and enjoyed "some really good movies." They objected when local incompetence interfered with the screenings.

> Mexicans substitute, off stage, in talking for the American actors. It was awful. . . . it became unsynchronized and the girls mouths were moving and no sounds coming out. Then the scene changed and two men drew guns on each other on the screen and the girls went on talking—amid howls and hissing and stampings on the part of the Mexican audience.[33]

Beginning in the 1930s Hollywood found Mexico and its revolution fertile areas for fantasy. In its first major production treating the revolution, *Viva Villa*, the American cinema joined Dunn in the bashing of rebels. In the film, which was produced by Metro-Goldwyn-Mayer, the filmmakers reinvented the notion of a "half-breed" Mexico out of control. Ignoring the fact that Francisco Villa was a teetotaler, Wallace Beery portrayed him as a stereotypic "Pancho," a vile, drunken rapist. That image of Villa, reinforced by American and Mexican politicians, novelists, and filmmakers, withstood contradiction for decades until Freidrich Katz of the University of Chicago published his monumental *Life and Times of Pancho Villa*. Katz argued that Villa's plan for a decentralized Mexico and a broad base of land ownership in which the oligarchy was destroyed would have resulted in a more democratic nation.

In Mexico City the American intellectuals grew in number, and the bo-
hemian aura of their community shifted to one better characterized as predominately socialist. Bertram Wolfe, Elyer Simpson, Waldo Frank, and Frank
Tannenbaum debated the meaning of the revolution and the future of Mexican society. Tannenbaum, a close friend of Frank and President Cárdenas,
wanted industrialization to proceed but in a gradualist manner that would
allow the indigenous population to adapt to the changes in their lives. Wolfe
and Simpson agreed with them, but Wolfe, an intense admirer and authorized biographer of muralist Diego Rivera, emphasized an idealized view of
indigenous life. Simpson, a sociologist at Princeton, foresaw rural transformation through the onset of the industrial age and also supported the *ejido*
as the basis of a gradual transformation of rural life.[34]

During the 1930s an array of Americans escaped to Mexico, seeking relief from the pessimism of the Great Depression and the pressure of life in
the United States. This group of intellectual expatriates was larger and more
diverse than the group that arrived in the 1920s, but it was almost as romantic. Intellectuals, most of them on the political left, found hope in the
idealistic propaganda of their predecessors and the government, and they
embraced the beautiful scenery, the slower pace of life, and the lower cost
of living. The new residents spread out from the capital, where the intelligentsia of the 1920s had concentrated. The American population in Mexico's urban areas continued to grow steadily, remnants of the rural colonies
stayed on as individual citizens, and art and retirement colonies took shape
at San Miguel de Allende, Lake Chapala, Guadalajara, and Cuernavaca.

In the 1930s James Michener resided at Lake Chapala, where he became fast
friends with D. H. Lawrence and a small group of largely American writers
then living by the lake. Lawrence was working on his famous novel *The
Plumed Serpent*. The fledgling Michener attempted his own essay at the time,
which he called "Mexico," but deemed it his worst writing effort and shelved
it. Fifty years later I argued with him that the artist should not be the critic
and that he should publish it for posterity. Unfortunately, his negative view
of the manuscript proved correct.[35]

During the late 1930s, while Mexicans and Americans fought over the
control of strategic resources inside Mexico, the countries became more en-
twined. U.S. government officials, concerned with the rising threat of Germany and Japan, sought every means at their disposal to maintain friendly
relations with their southern neighbor. The final nationalization of the railroads in 1936 and the oil industry in 1938 led to hard bargaining. The Mex-

icans had the advantage because the approach of World War II gave the Americans adequate incentive to resolve both conflicts. The Roosevelt administration negotiated payments for the oil nationalization but was unwilling to jeopardize American alliances on the eve of World War II by refusing to support a boycott on behalf of the oil companies or private landholders, especially mere small property owners. The Mexicans had perfectly timed their confrontation with the giant to their north.

By the onset of the war the great concentration of American wealth in the railroad, petroleum, mining, and electrical power industries and the telephone and telegraph services that had dominated Mexico at the start of the revolution had been displaced by Mexican ownership or control. Agrarian reform and foreclosures had returned most of the American ranching and agricultural holdings to the Mexicans. American companies had been nationalized or bought out. Tens of thousands of Americans still lived in Mexico, although the value of their properties had declined from a probable $1.5 billion in 1910 to a mere $300,000,000 in 1940. Now the two countries would merge even more intimately than before, and the inequalities of wealth and power, despite the changes wrought by the revolution, would once again come into play and shape the future.

Part IV

THE REENCOUNTER, 1940–2000

13　Cooperation and Accommodation

We have 50 percent of the world's wealth but only 6.3 percent of
its population. . . . Our real task in the coming period is to devise a
pattern of relationships that will allow us to maintain this position
of disparity.

> George F. Kennan, director of policy planning
> for the U.S. Department of State, 1948

Mexico remained independent of direct U.S. economic and political control during World War II and its aftermath, despite the American move toward global hegemony that gained momentum after December 1941. After
the war the United States assumed the role of leading the Western nations
in economic recovery and anticommunist political reorganization. Americans, Japanese, and Western Europeans developed a market economy that
underscored a global network of military alliances against the Soviet Union,
and the partners recognized the hegemony of the United States over Latin
America and Mexico.

During the 1940s the role of Americans in Mexico moved from the lost
ownership of productive properties to an overwhelming domination of bilateral trade and high technology. American residents increasingly accepted
living as individuals in towns and cities in lieu of rural and urban colonies.
The Americans also adapted to greater control of their private enterprises
by the Mexican government. The nationalism of the Cárdenas era had
demonstrated that the Mexicans wanted control of their resources, and the
U.S. elites preferred cooperation to confrontation.

LAST DAYS FOR LAGUNA

The climactic moment for the agrarian reform program occurred in the last
few months of the Cárdenas administration, when the president began his
attack on the Laguna Corporation, the last great American landholding in
Campeche, and the most powerful consortium of private American capital
left in Mexico. Laguna still dominated the state and its valuable oil lands.
The company had come to control virtually all of the Vila tract in 1919
through lease arrangements with the Mexican Gulf Land and Lumber Com-

pany and then with the Pennsylvania-Campeche Land and Lumber Company. From the late 1930s through 1943, Laguna extracted chicle from trees covering 1,773,437 acres.

On 2 January 1940 President Cárdenas nullified the titles to land in Campeche that were given by President Díaz to Manuel Vila in 1886. He declared that Laguna's leases were not leases at all, but a disguised single ownership. The arrangements that Laguna had made with Mexican Gulf and Pennsylvania-Campeche were, in Cárdenas's eyes, mergers. When the Laguna and Mexican Gulf Companies protested, the Mexican Supreme Court consolidated their cases and considered them as one. The companies complained that the government wanted the hardwoods and chicle industries for itself or special interests. They did not mention oil. To increase the compensation they might receive the Laguna directors asserted inaccurately that "practically the entire area is covered with virgin forest of mahogany, cedar, *zapote* [chicle] and other hardwoods." In reality, they no longer cut hardwoods—their principal commodity was chicle. The companies had decimated the hardwood forests between the Gulf and the Guatemalan border as early as the mid 1920s. An observer at the time noted that the companies had created a "desert" in the jungle.

The nullification of the 1,630,000-acre Vila grant did not just threaten the U.S. ownership of those lands, which produced hardwoods, chicle, and henequen. It removed the basis for property rights for the entire American-owned complex in Campeche. Among the interests that had originally benefited from the Vila grant and now lost out to nationalization were the Colonial Bank and Trust of Philadelphia, the Leather Manufacturers and Importers and Exporters National Banks in New York City, the John Deere Company, financier Victor Du Pont, and newspaper publisher William Randolph Hearst, who had inherited the holdings of his mother, Phoebe.[1] The nullification escalated the confrontation between the American consortium and the Mexican government. Cárdenas also canceled the follow-up grant originally given by Díaz in 1891 for the Compañía de Colonización y Deslinde de Terrenos Baldios. The action further undermined Laguna's claims to legitimacy. Citing Article 27, Cárdenas concluded that the American companies were "rendering grave injury to the public interest" and declared that Laguna had violated the Mexican constitution.[2]

The Mexican secretary of agriculture, represented by general agent José Falcón Dominguez, took steps to support Cárdenas's decree and to drive the Americans out. *Todo*, a magazine published in Mexico City, reported that the government's program of property seizures had given it "hundreds of thousands of hectares of cultivable lands, which have remained unoccupied or idle to this day; and that the government desires to take advantage of the lands under cultivation by the said companies." The agricultural secretary systematically "reduced the permits for the gathering of chicle from the lands of each of the companies aforesaid in proportion to the areas affected by said decree. The Laguna directors sensed that disaster was forthcoming from the Mexican Supreme Court.

> Our lawyers, who incidentally are friends of the Judges and are known to review their cases in private, have suddenly become panicky over the ultimate decision on the stay of action before the Supreme Court. For some unknown reason they expect an adverse decision.[3]

Inside connections were essential to success in the agrarian disputes of the time, but the Americans found that theirs were not good enough. In 1940 the Mexican Supreme Court found for the government, and Laguna began a series of appeals to the American Mexican Claims Commission.

Cárdenas's term ended in July 1940. The Laguna owners may have welcomed the end of his administration, but they fared no better with his successor, Manuel Avila Camacho. Avila Camacho's representatives reiterated Cárdenas's position before the American Mexican Claims Commission in Washington. The Mexicans claimed that Laguna restrained commerce, trade, and opportunity for Mexicans as a result of

> the monopoly of extensive tracts of land and the natural wealth therein existing because by virtue of said contract 659,600.1059 hectares of surveyed and located lands were deeded to Manuel S. Vila and the Compañía de Colonización y Deslinde and this constitutes a true monopoly by only one person or corporation.[4]

The Mexican government carried the argument further, maintaining that the nullification did not require compensation for the companies because the Laguna monopoly had violated the constitutional right of the Mexicans of that region to earn their living from the nation's natural resources. The government also echoed Cárdenas's objection to Laguna's merger with Mexican Gulf and lease arrangements with Pennsylvania-Campeche and Campeche Timber. Whatever the de jure status of the leases was, the arrangements reinforced Laguna's control of timber and real estate in Campeche. The extreme concentration of power in the hands of the Laguna directors even violated the objectives of Díaz, who ostensibly issued the grants to achieve diverse and productive ownership of Mexico's resources. It made no difference to the Mexicans that the land had been bought by the companies from parties other than Vila in the first decade of the twentieth century, almost twenty years after the original concessions had been granted.

The Laguna directors did their share to alienate the Mexican government. The owners had vigorously fought Cárdenas and his allies in the state government of Campeche, in the courts of law, with public opinion in Mexico, and with appeals to the ambassador and the U.S. Department of State after the government gave them leases to continue limited chicle and hardwood harvests. During the war years they continued to fight for greater rights and ultimately the restoration of their concessions. They opposed not only agrarian reform and the cancellation of the Vila concession but also the reforms in labor law that had improved the conditions of Mexican workers to a considerable degree during the previous ten years.

> Labor in the industry has had a most thorough overhauling during the last ten years and particularly within the last five years—so much so that the pendulum has swung so far back in favor of labor that every advantage is in his favor.[5]

The Laguna representatives noted that wages had increased for the chicle harvesters from 18 pesos per one hundred pounds of chicle in 1934 to 65 pesos in 1940, and that "the current Mexican labor law relieves the chiclero [chicle gatherer] of all indebtedness if he has not discharged his debt at the end of a twelve-month period."

The Laguna Corporation's salary scale during the 1930s and 1940s did not confirm the government's fears that the company maintained an imbalance of rewards between a handful of supervisory personnel and the rank-and-file employees. In 1946 the ratio between the highest-paid and lowest-paid employees at Laguna was considerably lower than it had been in earlier decades at either the Rascon Manufacturing Company in San Luis Potosí–Tamaulipas or the Batopilas Mining Company in Chihuahua. Cecil L. H. Branson, the general manager and the only foreigner on the estate, earned $970 monthly, and Maria Reyes, the only female employee and the lowest-paid office clerk, earned $100. The accountant at Laguna received $508, the general agent $495, the chicle inspectors $304, the paymaster $302, the pharmacist $275, the warehouseman $250, the storekeeper at Carmen $225, the watchman $180, and the schoolteacher $179 monthly. The average monthly earnings of the *chicleros* are not known because they were paid $22 for each *quintal* (a chicle unit of 100 pounds) they produced. The 485 *chicleros* delivered chicle valued at $292,289 during the 1941–42 harvest. The value of the chicle harvest varied wildly, from $137,911 to $495,738 between 1940 and 1946.

The Laguna directors argued that, unlike the American oil companies, they had on their own initiative forged ahead of everyone in providing their workers with decent pay, working conditions, and benefits.

> Our central camp . . . has been equipped with public services that are not even enjoyed by many of the lesser towns in the state of Campeche. For instance, the company drilled a well to supply potable water, said installation costing $37,418 U.S. This water was piped into the houses of the employees and was to take the place of the water customarily used in all small towns . . . the "cenote." An electric light plant was also installed and a small refrigerator supplying ice. The company has on its payroll two doctors . . . with a fully equipped hospital and free medicine for the employees, the entire cost of which is borne by the company. The houses and buildings provided for the employees are of a type far superior to that usually found, even in the towns.[6]

The American entrepreneurs argued further that they provided their workers with accident and disability insurance through a company headquartered in Mexico City, "an adequate school house," and games and amusements. Photographs of the headquarters area reveal that thatched huts and one-room shacks typical of rural Campeche served as housing for the workers.

The company was politically overmatched in its confrontation with the Mexican and Campeche governments. Cárdenas's timing had been perfect. In 1940 Laguna's battle became merely a secondary concern as the U.S. Department of State dealt with the war in Europe and the crisis with Japan, not with the protection of oil, chicle, and lumber companies in Mexico. Negotiators from the U.S. Department of State and their counterparts from the Relaciones Exteriores (the Mexican Department of State) had already agreed upon $200,000,000 as the total sum to be dedicated to the payment of damages caused to American property as a result of the agrarian reform program. The U.S. Congress appropriated the monies and paid the claimants. The amounts of the settlements were then applied to the Mexican national debt. The negotiation of the disputes themselves was left to the American Mexican Claims Commission. The Laguna directors found themselves surprisingly isolated. In November 1942 Avila Camacho's secretary of agriculture, Marte Gómez, forbade Laguna to produce more than 550,000 pounds of chicle annually despite an appeal by the directors to allow them to ship 1,100,000 pounds.

The Second District Court of Mexico agreed to hear a special pleading by the Laguna owners on 16 April 1942, but first it required that they submit their "original titles and deeds." When the companies complied with the request the judge turned the documents over to the Mexican Department of Agriculture. The court then decided it could not proceed until the documents were returned. Secretary Gómez refused to release them. Seven postponements ensued. Finally, in 1944, the secretary decreased the amount of acreage from which Laguna could harvest chicle by one-third, from 1,773,437 acres to 1,185,000 acres. At the same time he offered the Laguna directors 125,000 acres in unconditional ownership if they would sell 750,000 acres of their land within two years.

The owners responded that 125,000 acres were insufficient for their timber operations. In addition, they faced losing fifty-eight kilometers of railroad including bridges, plus eighty-four buildings, two mills, a machine shop, an electrical power plant, a water plant, and other facilities. The Laguna directors protested that they had already lost heavily from previous agrarian reform land grants. During 1945 and 1946 the Americans struggled to survive, leasing 75,000 acres of chicle-producing trees owned by the Campeche Timber and Fruit Company in an effort to satisfy customer demand. But Gómez again thwarted their efforts and dealt the company a final blow, reducing their producing area by another two-thirds, to 375,000 acres. This was the aggregate amount that Laguna, Gulf, and Pennsylvania-Campeche were entitled to when calculated at 125,000 acres per company, the formula originally ordered by the government in 1944 and then offered during litigation.

The decline of chicle exports from the company's original 604,000 acres testifies to the extent of the damages inflicted on Laguna between 1937 and 1946. Output ranged from a high of 455,242 pounds in 1937 to a low of 85,813 in 1939, when the Laguna directors cut production because they had been forewarned that their operations might be attacked by the government. In 1940 exports from the tract recovered to 348,515 pounds. In 1941 the total dropped to 267,354 pounds, but it reached 333,696 pounds in 1942. The government denied Laguna the right to expand operations in late 1942. During the following year the corporation succeeded in exporting some 419,622 pounds. After the secretary of agriculture made his acreage proposal, production dropped off to 263,409 pounds in 1944, 219,409 pounds in 1945, and 190,295 pounds in 1946. Given that Laguna's directors had asked to export 1,100,000 pounds and that the chicle producing areas adjacent to Laguna's were comparably rich, normal output would have been at least triple the amount actually shipped.[7]

Laguna's confrontation with the Mexican government had outlived all but two of the directors who had emerged after the company's reorganization in 1919, and they were no longer active in management. Considering the enormous resources of the owners, the minimal economic returns of the company seem hardly worth the trouble until one remembers that the unspoken issue was the lake of petroleum under the state and its coastline, which continually oozed to the surface of Laguna's lands. The directors spent more than their total earnings defending lands that had been largely depleted of hardwoods by 1926 and that had only limited potential to produce profit from the sale of chicle. On the other side, the Mexican government had seized "hundreds of thousands" of acres without putting them into any kind of production.

The Laguna directors held on to the hope for favorable settlements until 1945. The claims commission considered their petitions until 1947. In 1942 a claims commissioner informed Charles Fritz that only $3,000,000 was immediately available for compensation out of an eventual $40,000,000 to be applied at the slow pace of $2,500,000 per year. The Laguna directors pointed out that in 1945 their hardwoods sold for only $6 to $15 per thousand feet and that it took an entire hectare to produce that amount. They had begun cutting the trees again, but the value of the lumber had declined $65 per thousand feet since 1919. Meanwhile, their chicle sales, after subtracting enormous carriage and processing expenses, had netted only $25,000 to $52,000 per year since 1934, with an average of $31,000 during the 1930s and $17,000 during the 1940s. Those gains, which were never divided among the major stockholders of the Laguna Corporation, were simply too small to warrant the time and consideration that were expended. The presence of oil changed the stakes.

The American Mexican Claims Commission had advised the companies affiliated with Laguna that it would be wise to plead their cases separately. As a result, the shareholders of Mexican Gulf sued the Mexican government and presented their case for $798,345 to the commission. The largest shareholders in Gulf included Rowe and Company, the John Deere Company, and the French Investment Company, a group of bankers from Davenport, Iowa. Lewis Eliphalet Tifft also held stock in Mexican Gulf. In the late 1860s one of his ancestors had pioneered the modern American presence in Mexico by brokering the sale of bonds during the Liberal government's struggle against the French.[8]

The directors of Mexican Gulf had acquired 660,000 acres in Campeche for $288,377 in 1903. In the ensuing forty years, the firm had paid a total of between $160,000 and $200,000 in local, state, and national taxes. The directors failed in their attempt to defend the company in the Mexican appeals courts during 1940 and 1942. They then turned to the American Mexican Claims Commission, pleading that they owned the lands in Campeche and that Laguna had only controlled them through a long-term lease. They submitted evidence of the continuing value of their properties by demonstrating that between 1941 and 1943 they had realized a yearly average net profit of $4,746 despite being virtually closed down. During the previous twenty years, the average annual profit had been a barely more respectable $19,397. When one considers the purchase price, tax payments, and improvements, they had gained a pitifully low return for a large capital outlay.

On 5 January 1944 the directors of Mexican Gulf tentatively allocated the $133,057 in compensation offered by the American Mexican Claims Commission to their stockholders, but the Mexican government held off final authorization for the payment because the Mexican Gulf directors continued to press for further compensation in the Mexican courts. As a result the payment was delayed pending the outcome of the suit. In 1946 the case finally reached the Mexican Supreme Court, which ruled that Mexican Gulf had no basis for the argument that it had been victimized by retroactive laws in violation of the Constitution of 1917. The company's holdings were reduced to 82,000 acres of disconnected and isolated tracts. The directors asserted that the remaining properties were worthless and again appealed to the American Mexican Claims Commission for redress. In January 1947 the commission, headed by Edgar E. Witt, awarded the Mexican Gulf shareholders a total of $190,710. The commissioners also denied Mexican Gulf its request for interest on the $133,057 that they had failed to distribute in 1944.

In 1947 the American Mexican Claims Commission moved toward closure of the confrontation between American and Mexican interests in the southern Gulf of Mexico. The claims negotiators reached a settlement, but their action was not intended to satisfy the wealthy and powerful American losers. The settlement placated the Mexican government and defused the situation. The Mexican government had forced some of the most powerful citizens of the United States to subdivide their vast properties into tracts and sell them, or lose them, during the 1920s and 1930s. During the early and mid 1940s the American capitalists in Campeche were largely replaced by the Mexican government and, to a much lesser degree, its citizens. The Laguna directors grudgingly accepted $224,597 as compensation for the loss of 604,000 acres and the railroad. Laguna's directors, like their counterparts at Mexican Gulf, then applied for an additional $700,000, pointing out that their position was supported not only by tax assessments of 1,000,000 pesos but also an estimated value of 1,385,008 pesos for the railroad and other capital improvements and a yearly income that sometimes approached $500,000. The appeal passed from the commission to the next era of negotiations, of which the documents are still classified by the U.S. government and protected from the historian's eye.

In 1947 the surviving Laguna directors finally accepted defeat and took a cash settlement, as had the directors of the oil companies located on the Veracruz and Tamaulipas coastlines. James Lichtenberger, one of the firm's legal counsels and a director of the Colonial Trust Company of Philadelphia, and Harvey A. Basham, another legal counsel who was from Charlottesville, Virginia, constituted Laguna's active leadership. The two men lacked experience in the oil business and their financial resources were too limited to successfully direct a petroleum development operation. More important, the political situation in Mexico had become impossible for Laguna or any foreign oil company. During World War II the Colonial Trust leaders, like the powerful public authorities, had no time for Campeche.[9]

STRATEGIC ACAPULCO

The multifaceted confrontation of Mexican and American interests reached high levels of tension whenever the properties carried monetary or strategic value. In many cases multiple forces were at work. Geopolitical interests, the avarice of members of the military and local politicos, and the ambitions of peasants all clashed with American interests.

The coastline south of Acapulco was both strategic and rich in resources. The struggle to control it was generated by the Mexican government's desire to recapture control of its shorelines and frontiers from foreign powers, the greed of army officers and public officials, the juggernaut of agrarian reform, and the involvement of new American interests. On 8 October 1941 William Stephens of Harlingen, Texas, protested to his lawyer, L. W. Larsen of El Paso, that a portion of the land from his 8,800-acre El Potrero hacienda had been seized by the government and sold to wealthy American oilman Jean Paul Getty and the "wealthy Mexican construction engineer Laribera" of the Presidente Hotel interests.

> We own land on the island of El Potrero, located about six or seven miles South of Acapulco. This land extends from the Port of Marques to the River Papagallo, most of which has been taken away from us by the Mexican Government.
> The Mexican Government has sold a strip of this land five-eighths of a mile wide along the coast to a company, known as Presidente de la compañia Mexicano de Golf de Laribera Getty.[10]

The growth of Acapulco from a small seaside town to a burgeoning city brought a wide range of interests into the competition for seashore ownership. With its natural harbor and scenic beauty, Acapulco had already become a favorite vacation spot for Hollywood celebrities, including Betty

Grable, Clark Gable, and Erroll Flynn. Anticipating the value that resort and airport properties would have, both the Getty-Presidente interests and the government sought to control the zone immediately south of the city. The need for land to develop an airport reinforced the authorities' desire to recapture the coasts and borders from American control. That objective could be obtained while still making money.

In 1941 the Avila Camacho administration suddenly abandoned the government's position that El Potrero was needed for agrarian reform. The authorities seized the estate and sold the northern portion of the property to Getty. The Getty-Presidente interests, represented by Laribera, paid the government four pesos per square meter for the 900 acres needed for an elite country club and hotel. Constructed in 1956, it was dubbed the Puerto Marques Hotel and Golf Club. Getty's biographer explained that the oilman used Laribera to find "a way around a law forbidding foreigners to own land on the coast." The government made its decision after Getty consulted with his longtime close friend Miguel Alemán, the Mexican secretary of government and the most powerful Mexican politician in that part of Mexico. Having Alemán's support helped Getty's cause and probably accounts for the southern one-third of the estate becoming the airport.

According to Getty, he and Alemán, two of the world's richest men, became friends in 1940, "when he was a minister in Mexican President Manuel Camacho's government." In 1941 Alemán visited Los Angeles, and he and Getty "spent much time together." Dave Hecht, one of Getty's chief lawyers in New York, flew to Acapulco to finalize the deal with the Mexican government. The government retained control over the remainder of the property from which the Acapulco International Airport and Acapulco Princess Hotel and Golf Club were created in the 1950s. Getty and Alemán remained "good friends" for the remainder of their lives.[11]

Located in the hills immediately inland and along the coast south of El Potrero was the Hacienda San Marcos, owned by Charles and Laura Miller. The government had given 78,000 acres of their holdings to the heads of families in the nearby pueblos in the 1930s. During the 1940s the Millers changed to a more conciliatory strategy to defend their remaining interests against further agrarian seizures. They believed that the removal of the water and other important sections of their hacienda had rendered it useless. Hence they encouraged the citizens of the rural settlements of Lo de Soto and El Quiza to occupy 7,500 acres of the estate while they appealed to the American Mexican Claims Commission for compensation at the rate of $75 per hectare (2.47 acres). The Mexican government reported to the commissioners that the Millers "have been endeavoring to have the alleged taking of their property formalized according to the agrarian laws but that their efforts to date have been unavailing." In 1944, facing the denial of their larger claim, the Millers denied the charge that they had given up the 7,500 acres without request and asserted that they had been trying to address the demands of local agrarians. The Millers' ploy was only partially successful. On 24 March 1945 Witt, the chairman of the commission, signed a voucher giving the Millers $184,742 plus interest for 68,000 of the 78,000 acres taken from the Hacienda San Marcos.[12]

Later that year the Miller heirs filed claims for new losses totaling $1,580,082. With "voluminous" documentation, they described losing an enterprise with some 3,000 head of cattle, more than 200 horses, and several thousand lemon, coconut, cherry, guava, and banana trees, in addition to sugar cane, salt, and other products. They documented that the hacienda had produced corn, chiles, cotton, beans, and tobacco crops worth some 1,500,000 pesos annually. In a detailed brief the Mexican representatives rejected Witt's case in support of the Millers in strongly worded terms. The Mexicans pointed to the outrages committed by the Millers, including usurpations of village land holdings and the use of armed men to suppress dissidents. Charles Miller Jr., who carried the litigation forward, had served as a U.S. consul in the area, but even the U.S. government's interest in his case, which was no doubt generated by his ties to the U.S. State Department, could not save him. The amount received by the Miller heirs is unclear, but it was a fraction of what they claimed.[13]

North of Acapulco, at Cacalutla, President Cárdenas had foreclosed on 27,000 acres of the holdings of the Stephens Brothers Company. That action, taken in 1939 to eliminate American hegemony around Acapulco, was the last in a series of challenges that went back to the agrarian invasions of 1910. As a result, the 50,000-acre Hacienda Cacalutla no longer dominated the Costa Grande near Atoyac de Alvarez. Although officially the government carried out the seizure largely on behalf of peasants, the facts reveal that various officials had other goals in mind and that agrarian reform was a mere pretext in the thinly populated region. Indeed, the struggle between the Stephens brothers and the local and state elites paralleled the experience of Brictson in Tamaulipas. Once again a small number of peasants figured in a dispute of a large and economically important piece of land. By the early 1940s only 7,500 acres of denuded land remained nominally under the control of the Stephens Brothers Company, but they were choice seaside lands immediately south of Puerto Marques.

Throughout the process the Stephens brothers continued to protest to Josephus Daniels, the American ambassador, Cordell Hull, the secretary of state, and the Mexican officials at the municipal, state, and national levels. The Stephens' contemptuous attitude toward the Mexicans, whom they had labeled "insolent," had undermined their cause. The American consular officials in Acapulco maintained their protests, pointing out the collaboration of the Mexican authorities, especially that of Generals Adrian Castrejón and Encarnación Vega Gil, the commander of the Acapulco military garrison, with the land invaders and those who illegally seized *coquito.* But the higher figures at the U.S. State Department took no interest in the situation and referred the Stephens brothers to the American Mexican Claims Commission.[14]

During the 1940s William Stephens did gain the attention of at least one U.S. senator, but no action was taken on the partners' behalf. Finally, after the "four-million-dollar Puerto Marques Hotel" opened at Revolcadero Beach, the Mexican government paid the Stephens brothers a pathetic sum, based on the original purchase price and the low Porfirian tax appraisals on the El Potrero lands.[15]

A WORKING RELATIONSHIP WITH AMERICAN INDUSTRY

The overwhelming needs for strategic materials created by World War II deepened the ties between Mexico and the United States. American entrepreneurs who competed with Mexican interests suffered, but those who developed working relationships prospered. In 1942 a delegation of oil and construction executives that included John McCone of Bechtel, who was later head of the CIA, surveyed Mexico's petroleum reserves at the invitation of the Mexican authorities. The United States then paid Bechtel $20,800,000 to build a refinery and pipeline in Mexico. That year ARMCO International Company joined a Mexican consortium in the construction of an integrated steel mill at Monclova, Coahuila, and Anderson Clayton and Reynolds Metals completed negotiations for vegetable oil and foil paper manufacturing plants. Anderson Clayton built plants at Monterrey and Empalme. Reynolds built its plant near Mexico City. The tax concessions made to encourage these projects are not known. In 1943 Presidents Roosevelt and Avila Camacho created the Mexican-American Commission for Economic Cooperation to increase the production of strategic materials for the U.S. war effort and to stabilize the Mexican economy. By the end of Avila Camacho's presidential term in 1946 some 350 new foreign companies had set up operations in Mexico. Most of them were American.[16]

The war stimulated new profitability for the mining companies. Most of the independent miners and smaller mining companies that proliferated in Mexico between the 1880s and 1910 had withdrawn, but the larger firms, such as American Metals, ASARCO, and Phelps Dodge, continued to function. They had survived the period from 1910 to 1940 largely as a result of their integrated operations, but also because the Mexicans still needed American capitalization, patents, and access to foreign markets.

As the production of copper, lead, silver, zinc, and other minerals grew more important during World War II, the Mexican government moved to give itself more power against the American behemoths. This time, rather than nationalization, the Mexicans tried accommodation. On 29 June 1944 the foreign secretary, Ezequiel Padilla, promulgated a measure giving him the power to arbitrarily require any company in which foreign capital was involved to have a Mexican ownership of 51 percent. Despite American protests and pressure, the measure opened a long-range process in which the government increasingly demanded the presence of Mexican interests in American firms that were seeking licenses to operate in Mexico. Roosevelt aided the Mexicans by refusing to pressure them on the companies' behalf, and the Mexican leadership exploited his critical opinion of the often heavy-handed behavior of the American capitalists.

Avila Camacho bought 32,500 of the 40,000 shares outstanding in the Pan American Trust Company of New York in 1944. This move gave the Mexican government control of an American institution tied to the New York financial community, which could serve as a vehicle for investments and the conduct of intimate banking services associated with government operations. Meanwhile, the Chase Bank, the National City Bank, and J. P. Morgan and Company continued to interact with the Mexican government in its modernization program, while the Import-Export Bank helped finance the expansion of Mextelco, a subsidiary of the International Telephone and Telegraph Company.[17]

Mexico still needed capital, high technology, and economies of scale to modernize its economy, which enabled American bankers, industrialists, and construction company directors to position themselves as essential participants in Mexico's drive to build factories, highways, dams, bridges, and port facilities. In the postwar years American high technology firms demanded and sometimes received control of the new installations that they constructed in Mexico. Mexican interests also made headway. In 1946 Reynolds Metals built a plant at Tlalnepantla, north of Mexico City, and retained 51 percent of the ownership. Notably, Mexico's largest private bank, the Banco Nacional, assumed a 49 percent minority ownership in the aluminum plant. The strategy provided the Mexicans with knowledge of what went on inside the company and the aluminum industry at large. The Mexicans' lack of capital, expertise, and patents, however, meant they could not always demand a 51 percent ownership in the new endeavors. Companies such as Kraft Paper, Maytag, Bendix, Studebaker, and Cities Service entered sectors of the marketplace where the authorities were less intrusive.[18] In 1947 Sears opened a major retail store in Mexico City.

Successful new American businesses sprang up alongside older, beleaguered ones. Among the firms that began operations in Mexico were the industrial engineering firms Arthur D. Little and Ebasco Services, the Armour Research Foundation, and modern accounting firms, including Arthur Andersen, Peat, Marwick, Mitchell and Company, and Price, Waterhouse. American builders accepted contracts for the modernization of the port at Veracruz, although established enterprises in the state continued to suffer. The exhausted owners of the Jalapa Railroad and Power Company continued to demand compensation for their losses. In 1944 the U.S. representatives on the Mexican American Claims Commission accepted a compromise that surrendered control of the company to the Mexican government in return for the 2,080,000-peso settlement that had been rejected during the 1930s.[19] During the 1940s the leaders of educational institutions developed closer ties. The California Institute of Technology established links with the Tecnológico of Monterrey.

As the American role in high technology grew, the Mexican leadership continued to push for national control of basic infrastructure. In 1948 Miguel Alemán, who had been elected to the presidency two years earlier, announced the government's buyout of the Mexican Telegraph Company on terms favorable to the foreign stockholders. Mexican Telegraph, a Western Union subsidiary, had been expanding its lines and service area in the postwar years. The parent company continued to sell equipment to the new Mexican firm. When the development of the country's basic infrastructure required more expertise than the Mexicans could provide, Alemán employed Americans. He also retained American companies to assist in the building of dams on the Yaqui River in Sonora and the Rio Grande between Tamaulipas and Texas.[20]

The Mexican officials wished for American participation in the economy at a cooperative rather than a hegemonic level and in areas of enterprise that were characterized by high technology and large-scale capitalization or that offered access to American markets. They wanted help in areas in which the Mexicans could not perform the tasks at hand. The leading industrialists in the United States adjusted to the new working relationship. In 1952 the leaders of Du Pont, Ford, Monsanto, Anaconda, B. F. Goodrich, Sears, Nation's Business, Chemical Bank, and others met with President Alemán to arrange the enlargement of their operations or their initial entry into the Mexican economy. Alemán, following the practice of American municipalities, enticed them with tax breaks. For example, he gave the National City Bank an exemption on the earnings on its deposits with the Banco de México, the nation's federal reserve institution.

NEW RESILIENCE FOR AMERICAN INTERESTS

Intercontinental Rubber in Zacatecas and Torreón was another of the companies that benefited from the war effort. The strategic interests of the United States led to a Mexican retreat from agrarian reform where Intercontinental was concerned, and the demand for rubber provided an unexpected return to profitability. America's involvement in the war enabled the crippled operations of Continental Rubber to continue for another fifteen years. Important capitalists still headed the firm, including William Potter, the chairman of the executive committee of the Guarantee Trust Bank, John Morron, a director of the First National Bank of New York, Walter Drury, a director of ASARCO, and Herbert Vreeland, the chairman of the Royal Typewriter Company. Intercontinental also enjoyed the benefit of an important Mexican director in Alfonso P. Villa, who served as a contact with Mexican officials.

During 1940, as the American war machine geared up, continuous work shifts produced 8,325,200 pounds of guayule rubber at the Intercontinental factories at Torreón and Catorce, an increase of more than 40 percent over the 5,764,400 pounds of output recorded in 1939. In 1941 the Mexican operation expanded another 20 percent to 10,121,200 pounds, and the company reported eased pressure for agrarian reform measures: "Progress is being made toward settlement of the litigation over the Cedros hacienda." During 1942 workmen expanded the capacity of the plant at Torreón, resulting in 12,663,800 pounds of rubber the following year, which brought handsome profits. The seizure of Sumatra by the armed forces of the Japanese empire in 1942 emphasized the importance of Mexican production. Intercontinental sold all of its rubber to the Rubber Reserve Company for the war effort, as per an agreement between the governments of Roosevelt and Avila Camacho. As a result, the U.S. Treasury Department informed the Intercontinental stockholders that their dividends were nontaxable. In 1943 and 1944 rubber production in Mexico averaged 14,000,000 pounds per year. The company had nearly doubled its 1940 output, and it had reached the limits of its Mexican factories and workers. In 1943 the Mexican government benefited as well, collecting $959,674 in taxes from Intercontinental. A mutually beneficial arrangement had emerged.[21]

The U.S. Department of Agriculture sent agronomists to Mexico to perform experimental work on the soil and plants of the Intercontinental haciendas with the goal of increasing yields. At the same time the directors applauded a Mexican government ruling that allowed the company "to proceed with reasonable safety as regards land tenure and government protection." On 12 August 1944 they announced that the "Cedros law suit has been definitely settled . . . and a contract has been executed with the Mexican Department of Agriculture for the wild shrub on the hacienda during the next fifty years." During 1945 and 1946 the company planted 6,500 acres of newly bred guayule plants in an effort to maintain postwar prosperity. It was not to be. Unfortunately for the directors, drought devastated their Zacatecas harvest in the summer of 1945, and the market value of guayule diminished sharply during the rest of the decade.

By 1948 only the Cedros factory operated, and that was on a limited scale. Production was less than a thousand tons. Having survived the revolutionary agrarians and the government's attempted nationalization, Intercontinental struggled to stay afloat. Higher-grade rubbers and the rapidly advancing production of synthetics had substantially weakened the market for guayule. In 1948 the president of the company, A. W. Edelen Jr., concluded that "this type of rubber may no longer be considered as a commercially sound enterprise." On 20 August 1949, when it moved to "smaller and lower cost space," the company had already sold many of its holdings. It died quietly in the 1950s.[22]

The Mexican government used the crisis of the war to expand sugar exports. Mexican producers supplied their neighbors with 25,000 tons yearly, despite the fact that demand from Mexico's domestic market exceeded national production. The United States suffered from a yearly shortfall of 1,900,000 tons of sugar during the war. Mexico's strategy helped its balance of payments, reestablished Mexican sugar in the U.S. market, and created goodwill between the political and business leadership of the two nations. Indeed, through agencies and firms such as the InterAmerican Development Commission, the Import-Export Bank, and the World Bank, U.S. officials and international bankers authorized and helped finance companies to build mills, dams, and irrigation systems in nationalized agricultural centers such as La Laguna in Coahuila and in sugar producing zones such as El Azúcar in Veracruz and the former United Sugar complex in Sinaloa. At the former American colony at Xicotencatl in Tamaulipas, Americans helped develop 36,000 acres of irrigated *ejido* sugar lands. Other industries also profited from the American war effort. ASARCO, through its subsidiary, the Compañía Carbonifera de Sabinas, gained U.S. funding to increase the production of guano in Baja California as a fertilizer for sugarcane. Celanese Mexicana received $2,750,000 for the production of artificial fibers, and in 1943 the Watson-Flagg Engineering Company of New York provided hydroelectric equipment through its Mexico City office for the construction of three power plants.[23]

The cooperative economic ties developed by the Mexican and U.S. governments during the war years in rubber, oil, and mineral production facilitated the settlements that were reached in the disputes over agrarian reform and land nationalization. On 25 October 1943, after years of litigation, the Morris and Swift heirs to the massive T. O. Riverside Ranch in Chihuahua benefited from the cooperative spirit and won an indemnity of $466,150. It was a major increase from the paltry $72,000 that had been awarded in the atmosphere of confrontation during the 1930s. The payment authorized in 1943 probably represents the ultimate settlement of the T. O. Riverside case, although some of the more powerful American interests such as Cargill and Laguna continued in secret arbitration well into the 1960s.[24]

During the 1940s and 1950s the Mexican and American peoples, despite economic and political rivalries and linguistic and cultural differences, developed ever closer relationships. President Alemán and his successor, Adolfo Ruiz Cortines, recruited commitments from the chief executives of major American chemical companies, including Monsanto, and mining firms, such as Anaconda (the modern name for Amalgamated Copper), and they secured financial backing from the Bank of America, National City Bank, the Chemical Bank, and J. P. Morgan and Company. The transmittal of American technology reached every corner of Mexican society. During the 1940s Morrison, Knudsen, and Company, the contractor for the Hoover and the Grand Coulee Dams, undertook the construction of the Sanalona Dam in Sonora. In 1946 entrepreneur Ed Hugetz introduced the ballpoint pen to Mexican consumers. In 1949 Gillette opened a factory near Mexico City capable of producing 50,000,000 razor blades per year.[25]

During the 1950s an array of strong American companies, including Westinghouse, Goodyear, and Reynolds, opened factories in Tlalnepantla, an industrial suburb immediately north of Mexico City. They operated amid a much larger number of less capitalized Mexican-owned plants. The Americans remained powerful in investments and high-technology industries and gained new strength in construction, film, and trade. By the 1980s the Americans were 49 percent interest holders in the few surviving older enterprises such as Cargill. Companies that had entered Mexico after World War II, such as Sears, Roebuck and Company, the Coca-Cola Company, and the Ralston Purina Company, and a host of new ventures accepted the arrangement.

Among the earlier mining firms, ASARCO, Gold Fields, Phelps Dodge, and National Lead joined Anaconda in compromises with Mexican nationalism and survived. In the countryside, American high-technology manufacturers continued to lead the way. The directors of International Harvester and John Deere offered expensive tractors to those Mexican farmers wealthy enough to buy them.[26]

The role of American interests in transportation is indicative of the transformation that had taken place throughout the Mexican economy. A decade after the 1935 buyout of the American railroad owners, the American capitalists had moved into airlines, leaving the operation of the trains and buses to the Mexicans. Pan American and Braniff Airlines were early providers of air travel in Mexico. The airlines received their capitalization through many of the same investment banks and industrial lenders that had financed railroad construction. Meanwhile, Chrysler, Ford, General Motors, Hudson, Mack, Packard, and Studebaker began to compete for sales in a country with only 238,000 cars. Beginning in the late 1940s, however, the Volkswagen Beetle was produced in Mexico under the franchise of Miguel Alemán. It met U.S. competition more than halfway and dominated the highways.

CONTINUING AGRARIAN CHALLENGES

Despite cooperation between the federal government of Mexico and the industrial leaders of the United States, many state and local governments continued to challenge American interests through agrarian reform actions. By the 1940s the bastions of American power in Campeche, Tamaulipas–San Luis Potosí, the Isthmus of Tehuantepec, Sinaloa, Sonora, Chihuahua, and Durango and along the Guatemalan border had been reduced to mere remnants. Most of the former settlers in Chiapas, Oaxaca, and Tamaulipas had fled, although many Latter-Day Saints in Chihuahua and Sonora stayed on, as had some of the colonists at Blaylock and San Dieguito. Local politicians did not always share the wider concerns of the national authorities, and they continued to respond to public pressure, demanding the removal of virtually all economically important Americans from the rural areas.

Most newcomers now settled in the cities. In some cases, however, nostalgic and opportunity-seeking Americans returned to sites that their parents had left. In 1907 George West acquired a tract of the Chamal hacienda from George Blaylock and settled in the colony named after its promoter. In 1951 his descendants George West, George Allen, Charles and Harriet Allen Talbot, Harvey Houck, and Tom Hale returned and bought 70,000 acres of the Chamal for $1,500 by paying back taxes. At first, annual property taxes were a mere $200. The new owners built a gray and white wooden frame house and set about harvesting mahogany and other hardwoods. To their amazement, Semour Taylor, one of the original colonists, still lived nearby. During the 1960s the taxes imposed by local authorities shot upward, and in 1971 the West heirs made a last payment, a one-year assessment of $10,000, and then gave up. Harriet Talbot seems to have been the driving force in staying on that long. By then the residents in the area were all Mexicans.[27]

In Tamaulipas, at the San José de las Rusias hacienda, the Brictson heirs and their neighboring agrarian rivals had made their choices. During the 1940s the local citizenry continued to occupy sites on the estate that had been left to the Americans by the Comisión Nacional de la Refoma Agraria. By 1942 the "agrarians were overrunning the property," grazing cattle on its vast expanses without waiting for official authorization. In the early 1940s a new group of contenders emerged in the competition to control and occupy the beautiful and rich hacienda. A recently formed colony of retired veterans headed by General Alfredo Jaimes in Soto la Marina applied to Governor Magdaleno Aguilar for the right to colonize the estate. Jaimes and Aguilar were descended from a long line of Tamaulipas elites who had historic relations with the King and Kenedy families of the Lower Rio Grande Valley and the Frost Brothers, bankers in San Antonio. Jaimes enjoyed good standing with the Cárdenas faction, which continued to run the Department of Agriculture and the National Agrarian Reform Commission. The colonists found that the land granted to them earlier by the government was of inferior quality. Hence, they "took advantage of the very rich lands on the cattle ranch known as San José de las Rusias." At that point, in 1942, Governor Aguilar offered the colonists 60,000 acres that the state had seized from the hacienda two years earlier.

In 1946 the political pendulum swung to the right. Alemán took the presidency in Mexico City, and Aguilar's handpicked successor, Hugo Pedro González, became the governor of Tamaulipas. Larger sharks arrived at the San José. Governor González, an ally of Alemán, informed General Jaimes that "it would be convenient for him to look for land elsewhere" because his rancho was situated on a 183,000-acre parcel "purchased" from the state by General Juan Almazán and his partner, Plutarcho Elías Jr., son of former president Calles. Jaimes was given an alternate tract for his colonists, probably on the hacienda. Elías Jr. and Almazán, a defeated right-wing presidential candidate who had worked with Alemán in the Stephens debacle at Acapulco, were heirs to the political factions Cárdenas had displaced when he established control over the government in the 1930s. The "immensely wealthy" and amoral Almazán and Elías Jr. far exceeded General Jaimes in power and influence. The agrarian reform at the San José hacienda produced a mix of *ejido* farmers in some areas and the "new rich" in others. Both groups took advantage of the U.S. government's decision to cooperate with the Mexican leadership in the spirit of the Good Neighbor Policy and bilateral cooperation in the war effort.[28]

Officials at the U.S. Department of State, concerned about maintaining good relations with their neighbor, did little on the Brictsons' behalf. The family had protested earlier seizures to the American Mexican Claims Commission, along with hundreds of other Americans who had suffered losses. Those protests did little good. Even moderately large companies found their complaints shunted aside by the claims bureaucracy. The U.S. commissioners found little merit in the Brictsons' plea for full compensation, saying that it did not appear that there was "sufficient evidence to justify the conclusion that the entire property has been expropriated, nor that the severance damage to that portion not taken is proven." The rejections of American claims were classified as "confidential," and U.S. officials, who did not want to inflame public opinion, did not report them to the media. The interests of the American losers in Mexico were sacrificed on behalf of larger political considerations.[29]

In early 1940 the Mexicans and Americans continued to haggle over the status of New York financier Horace Corbin's Hacienda Chivela in Oaxaca. By the 1940s the Mexican negotiators had accepted liability for 16,000 of the 32,500 acres confiscated during the 1930s, but they and their American counterparts agreed that the first 16,500 acres pertained to another concern, the Gulf Hardwoods Company. Corbin had created Gulf Hardwoods in an effort to reduce his individual titles to less than 100,000 acres each and therefore avoid expropriations under the monopoly and agrarian reform laws. Ironically, that subterfuge cost him dearly because now he could not collect damages on one-half of his losses. Corbin's disappointments did not end there. The two governments agreed to award him only $15,686 of the $171,557 claimed. The U.S. officials in charge of claims performed professionally, but they showed no sympathy for either the citizens who had been caught up in the revolution and agrarian reform or their survival stratagems. On occasion the officials were outraged by the practices of forced labor and shady land deals that the hearings uncovered. Corbin continued to protest that he had been wrongfully deprived of compensation for his losses.[30]

At that point the situation worsened. On 13 November 1940 President Cárdenas approved the confiscation of 3,750 acres of land from the Chivela hacienda, which the governor of Oaxaca ordered given to the *poblado* of

Mena. Corbin, residing in Shelburne, Vermont, did not find out about the confiscation until 17 June 1941, when the American embassy at Mexico City reported it. Corbin lacked the ability to fight back in person, and he filed a new complaint, this one with the recently formed American Mexican Claims Commission (Extended Claims). The new agency was created to settle unresolved disputes, but it faced a new wave of seizures involving agrarians and local political officials.

Corbin's problems ran deeper than just another expropriation. Invading peasants from the *poblados* of Mena, Almoloya, and four other settlements immediately occupied another 22,250 acres of the estate. At first Corbin complained to the commission, but when he understood the extremity of the situation, he went directly to the U.S. secretary of state. The largest American interests—the banks, oil companies, and railroads—had all been using the highest officials in the State Department as their intermediaries with the Mexican authorities. Corbin had that level of influence. In 1945 the acting secretary of state, James F. Byrnes, reported to the commission on Corbin's behalf that his losses were total and illegal. The "expropriations . . . consisted of invasions of the property by groups of agrarians for the purpose of exploiting the timber resources and that resolutions or decrees of expropriations do not exist." The occupations had left the Chivela dysfunctional.

Even with high-level intervention on his behalf, Corbin found he still had to go through the commission if he wanted compensation. Like Edward Shearson and the Peirce and Morton heirs, he would have little satisfaction. The commissioners denied his request for $200,000. They reported that he had not provided them with the exact date that the peasants of Mena had taken possession of the 3,750 acres and that the ownership of the 100,000 acres titled to the Gulf Hardwoods Company and Maderas del Golfo, S. A., was still "unclear": "There is no allotment from the Mexican company . . . or any explanation of its absence, as required by Section 3(b) of the 1942 Act." That reference hinted that Corbin had created Maderas del Golfo to meet Mexico's 100,000-acre limit for small properties. The commissioners stated that if Corbin controlled that company, then he would have to apply in its name as well. If, in turn, the Mexican government learned of an intent to deceive it, then all claims would be disallowed. To his dismay Corbin also learned that although the Mexicans had seized all 25,000 acres that he still held under his own name, a previous award given by the American Mexican Claims Commission in the late 1930s had covered 16,000 acres of that total, leaving him a mere 9,000 acres that were eligible for compensation.

Sometimes American property owners succeeded in subdividing and keeping some of their holdings. On other occasions the maneuver left them to explain the contradictions as best they could when they tried to establish ownership. If they proved ownership of the companies they created, such as Gulf Hardwoods, they were revealing their efforts to defraud the Mexican government. In either case it meant near-total defeat.[31]

The case brought by W. J. Hotchkiss and C. A. Vance of San Francisco received cautious consideration from the American negotiators. The firm's use of sharecroppers seemed to grate on the ethical values of the U.S. government officials. Hotchkiss and Vance lost the 20,000-acre Hacienda de San José de Costilla in Nayarit in two stages during the 1930s. First, an agrarian foreclosure took 4,140 acres. The partners received some compensation for that loss. Then, in 1934, campesinos living near the hacienda had taken 15,860 acres by force. On 1 November 1943 Hotchkiss and Vance sought $79,300 in consideration for this forced occupation. The campesinos took the property in accordance with the law of *tierras ociosas,* not the agrarian reform program. As a result, the loss did not fall under the jurisdiction of the claims commissions of the 1930s. The State Department referred the case to the Extended Claims Commission. The name "extended claims" given to that litigation was appropriate—the outcome remains classified.[32]

THE CUBAN CRISIS

The struggle between the Mexicans and Americans for national sovereignty and control of economic assets that had been unleashed by the Mexican Revolution was apparent in disagreements over policy toward Cuba and inter-American affairs. Following the success of the Cuban Revolution in 1958, the Mexican political leadership offered support to the Castro regime. In contrast, Cuban nationalists garnered boycotts, embargoes, and nonrecognition from the United States, in a repeat of Mexico's experience with the U.S. government earlier in the twentieth century. The Mexicans opposed the hostile maneuvers of the United States toward Cuba in the Organization of American States (OAS). Mexico's opposition began in 1959 and continued for more than three decades. U.S. officials, obsessed with their power and the risk-free political opportunity presented by opposing a "communist dictator," were encouraged in their policy of confrontation by the lingering animosity toward Fidel Castro on the part of the American sugar, tobacco, banking, hotel, power and light, and transportation interests that had suffered when Castro nationalized these industries. Many of those corporations, such as the National City Bank and J. P. Morgan and Co., entered Cuba during the U.S. occupation of the island after the Spanish-American War. Other companies, such as General Electric and Spreckles Sugar, came later and extended the American presence before Castro brought them down. American companies demanded that they be reimbursed in accordance with their estimates of damages before the U.S. government offered any political accommodation. This stance was reinforced by the less significant, but still important, political activities of exiled Cubans and Cuban-Americans.[33]

The Cuban missile crisis, the war in Vietnam, and the persistent efforts of U.S. officials to isolate Cubans from international bodies and trade during the 1960s gave Cuban revolutionaries ample opportunity to convince a large part of the Mexican public that the political stance of the United States was essentially imperialistic. Since the 1940s the Mexican government's public attitude of independence—to "stand up to the Americans"—had been demonstrated more through its support of Cuba than in any other way. A barter arrangement provided Cuba with Mexican oil from the 1960s through the 1980s. Meanwhile, the Mexican authorities, defending their sovereignty as well as Cuba's, stood fast for three decades against American efforts to isolate the island nation through the OAS and various hemispheric forums.[34]

THE INTEGRATION OF POPULAR CULTURE

American sports continued to be an important vehicle for the assimilation of American culture by the Mexican public. In 1945 the Mexican Pacific Coast League began play, offering off-season training to American baseball players. The Mexican League, which had its headquarters in Mexico City, also came into its own during this period. The league attracted a few American players, and it served as a refuge for some. Willie Wells, the three-time U.S. Negro League batting champion, explained why he loved playing in Veracruz, with its strong Afro-Mexican and Caribbean influence:

> Not only do I get more money playing here, but I live like a king. . . .
> I am not faced with the racial problem. I didn't quit Newark and join
> some other team in the United States, I quit and left the country. . . .
> I've found freedom and democracy here, something I never found in
> the United States. . . . Here, in Mexico, I am a man.[35]

In 1997 Wells finally entered the Baseball Hall of Fame in Cooperstown, New York, but during his lifetime white Americans showed little interest in his achievements.

In the late 1940s Jorge Pascual, the nationalistic president of the Mexican League, decided to compete directly with the major leagues in the United States. In order to do so he offered large signing bonuses to well-known American ballplayers, including Max Lanier, pitcher Sal Maglie of the Giants, and Mickey Owen of the Dodgers. The Major League club owners immediately blackballed the players to stop the hemorrhage of talent. Pascual's effort soon failed for financial reasons. The American players cost a great deal, and the Mexican public could not offer enough buying power at the ticket windows despite strong interest in the games. By the end of the 1940s the Mexicans were playing a game originated and dominated by Americans and large crowds were turning out to watch.[36]

American football gained an ever widening acceptance, if in a less notable manner, along with other elements of American culture including the Coca-Cola, Pepsi-Cola, hot dogs, and hamburgers served alongside tortas and Mexican drinks at the ball games. Universities in Mexico City, Guadalajara, and Monterrey began fielding American football teams that played before small audiences but still earned press coverage. At the same time smaller communities and sports clubs took up basketball in addition to football. This less visible participation reflected the deepening integration of American culture.

During the 1960s American professional football began to make headway with Mexican consumers. Tex Schram, the marketing wizard of the Dallas Cowboys of the National Football League, began his successful presentation of the "Vaqueros" to the public in Mexico City. Schram appealed to a sense of manhood, virility, and bravery—the "machismo" of his Mexican male audience. By the 1970s the Cowboys had become "Mexico's team," with television coverage throughout central Mexico and an audience that was larger than that of any soccer team.

The J. Walter Thompson advertising firm entered Mexico at the end of World War II. By 1994 it handled $108 billion in annual billings. Its rival, McCann-Erickson, was even larger, billing $153 billion. Leo Burnett and Panamericana Ogilvy & Mather followed closely at $98 and $92 billion per year. Several other large American advertising firms joined them in a costly media campaign that included television (65 percent), radio (11 percent), and newspapers (10 percent).[37]

During World War II and the postwar years the Rockefeller Foundation provided important cultural and scientific advancements through the introduction of modern nutrition and public health programs. The nutrition program offers an example of how the two nations developed mutual respect through cooperation. In 1942, with foundation support, William D. Robinson carried out dietary research that detailed extensive malnutrition, especially in the Mexican countryside. The undertaking paralleled similar research and results in rural areas of the southern United States. Then Richmond K. Anderson conducted a second research project. Among their joint findings was a new respect for the Mexican rural diet. They concluded that rural Mexicans, unlike their poor American counterparts, did not suffer from pellagra despite the deficiencies in niacin normally found in narrowly maize diets. They traced the reason to the fact that the Mexicans soaked their corn in mineral lime, which freed up the niacin for digestion.

Impressed, Robinson offered the famous conclusion that the Mexican diet "of tortillas, beans, and chiles may be much more satisfactory than has hitherto been believed." Anderson and Robinson presented the first comprehensive reports on Mexican nutrition and demonstrated the need for improvements in the diets of nursing and pregnant women and their children. The Rockefeller Foundation then provided training and materials for the Mexican Instituto Nacional de Nutrición, an agency charged with improving the dietary intake of the public, and endowed the training of nutritionists, including José Calvo de la Torre. In 1951 Calvo became director of the institute. As a result, a matrix of nutrition and health maintenance programs emerged between the United States and Mexico. Health care programs have proliferated since the 1960s. In the 1980s and 1990s the epidemiology division of the University of Texas Health Center at Houston worked in Guadalajara in an effort to control intestinal diseases. Cooperation in the fields of health care and nutrition continued through the 1990s, providing outstanding examples of successful bilateral relations between the citizens of the two countries.[38]

American academics have not always been as forthright with their Mexican counterparts as the University of Texas epidemiologists were. In 1960 Frank Tannenbaum proposed an elite seminar to C. M. Brinckerhoff, president of the Anaconda Corporation. The company would finance the undertaking in order to alter the thinking of the leading Latin American intellectuals, who would undertake one-year residencies at Columbia. This deeper agenda was overlooked in the proposals of intellectual discourse made to Latin Americans. Tannenbaum, who had helped Anaconda settle labor unrest in Latin America several times over the years, including one strike in Mexico, explained in a "Private and Confidential" message to Brinckerhoff the purpose of a "Columbia Social Science Research Council."

> Our problems in Latin America are many, but the one we have been least able to find a handle to is the critical and somewhat hostile attitude of the intellectuals toward the United States in general and toward American business in particular.
>   This is a matter of concern . . . especially to American business in Latin America because the intellectuals have great influence upon public opinion. . . . Fortunately, the really important intellectual figures who have a continental influence and whose writings reach the youth

everywhere are not numerous. . . . Within ten years we would have had, for a year's residence each, forty of the most distinguished intellectuals in Latin America. . . . It would also . . . provide a continuing opportunity for personal contacts with people our businessmen almost never get to know . . . and quite unconsciously they would make their readers and followers partake of the better and deeper insight they would have of the United States.[39]

Brinckerhoff, whose corporate holdings at Cananea were under duress, appreciated the subtlety of the message and its importance. A year later Tannenbaum assumed the title "Director of University Seminars," hosting intellectuals from Mexico and other Latin American countries for yearlong stays.

Advertising, foundation-based health and agricultural programs, and sports and cuisine all helped to "Americanize" Mexico, but more subtle forces were also at work. During the 1930s and 1940s, Rotary International and Lions Clubs spread across the nation. In the postwar era, American consular officials such as Vice Consul Victor Niemeyer of Monterrey spread the gospel of hard work and civic involvement to the businessmen of small towns and cities in the Bajio and across the north. The Mexican small businessmen who joined the Lions Club and Rotary found the emphasis on participation in local political affairs and civic betterment gratifying. It gave them a role in the formidable one-party state created by those who seized political control of the nation in the aftermath of the revolution.[40]

Contemporary Mexican and American libraries reflected the pervasive cultural interactions that were under way. The holdings of the Universidad Iberoamericana and Colegio de México, both in Mexico City, reveal the deep interest of Mexican academic leaders in the production of American culture. The Americans also amassed large collections of Mexicana in libraries in the United States, such as the Bancroft Library in Berkeley and the Benson Collection in Austin. Nettie Lee Benson of Sinton, Texas, began a Mexican odyssey in the late 1920s when she boarded a train bound for Monterrey via Laredo. The trains running from Corpus Christi through Sinton toward Mexico had captured her imagination and that of her sisters during childhood. She took a teaching position in a private school in Monterrey and held it until the early 1930s before returning to Texas, where she enrolled at the university in Austin. After gaining her doctorate in Latin American history, she embarked on a career training Mexican historians and amassing the largest collection of Mexicana literature in the world. During her frequent visits to the Mexican capital and other cities, she purchased private archival materials and forwarded them to the University of Texas. Benson gathered the materials for more than three decades until she had developed the most important aggregation of Mexican archival resources outside Mexico and long-standing friendships with leading Mexican historians, including the distinguished Josefina Vázquez of the Colegio de México.[41]

During the 1950s the scene at Mexico City College, located on the highway between Mexico City and Toluca, reflected the cultural syncretization under way between the two peoples. Paul Vincent Murray served as president of the school from 1940 to 1961, as it became the center of American cultural life in Mexico for a generation. In 1956 Professor Lyle Brown, a devout member of the thirty-five-member Baptist church in Mixcoac, offered political science courses to an array of young American citizens interested in learning about Mexico firsthand. His salary of $240 a month barely supported a rudimentary existence. In 1958 Richard Greenleaf arrived as a new instructor as Brown was leaving to fill a post at Baylor University.

Mexico City College produced some of the leading Mexican historians of the next generation. Instructors Greenleaf and Frank Savage offered Mexican history courses to later professors and authors Tim Harding, Colin Maclachlan, Michael Meyer, William Sherman, and James Wilkie. The students traveled about the country before returning to the United States, where they completed doctorates and trained dozens of university professors in Mexican history. Their memories of youthful romance and adventure captured the attraction that Mexico still held for young American intellectuals.

Religious devotion characterized the culture of many Americans who came to Mexico in the nineteenth century and again after World War II. In 1959 the Mixcoac Baptist congregation continued to grow and attract American members, but most of the seventy parishioners were "poor" Mexicans. The more prosperous Presbyterians grew even more rapidly and were the largest Protestant denomination in the capital, but many of the most prominent American Protestants melted into the expanding Mexican professional classes. Minister Robert Bidwell married the daughter of the Mexican leader of the American Bible Society in the capital.[42] In the post–World War II era, charismatic Christians made great headway among Mexico's ever growing poor population. Exact data are lacking, but in 2000 the number of evangelical Protestants exceeded 10 percent of the population.

While politicians and businessmen fought over policies, opportunities, and natural resources and compromised and accommodated one another during the 1930s, 1940s, and 1950s, other, more subtle processes continued to interweave the two cultures. The film industry exemplified the altered relationship. After a relatively slow start, Hollywood films entered Mexico on a large scale during the 1930s. They glamorized American values and lifestyles for the Mexican public. Then, during World War II, the Hollywood moguls turned out war propaganda films that the Mexican public received with more skepticism. Whistles, the Mexican form of public rejection, filled the theaters during the showing of the more racist potboilers. Walt Disney cartoons provided the saving grace. Mexican adult audiences and children loved Mickey Mouse, Donald Duck, and friends. In the late 1940s, after the demise of their property ownership in Mexico, the Americans gained more acceptance than ever through film presentations that focused on glamorous actors and actresses, an uncritical emphasis on American affluence, and the appearance of leading Mexican stars such as Dolores del Río and María Felix alongside Betty Grable and Jane Russell. In more recent decades, romantic films like *Love Story* and films stressing unmitigated violence found profitable acceptance.[43]

A new image of Mexico's rural revolution began in the 1960s when the American and Mexican viewing publics saw Marlon Brando star in *Viva Zapata*. Brando portrayed a heroic figure leading an equally proud people in search of justice, but, as Hollywood would have it, complex matters ultimately overwhelmed Zapata. During the same decade Hollywood filled out its cinematic caricature of Mexico with *The Magnificent Seven*, in which hopelessly weak Mexican villagers gain protection from evil, degenerate mongrel bandits in their own country through the intervention of American gunslingers who annihilate the "bad guys." This production presented the phenomenon of armed U.S. intervention as an act that provided hope and resolved Mexican chaos. The Seven even employed the Pentagon's strategy of EAT.

As multinational businesses with U.S. leadership developed, corporate culture became an ever more important element in the growth of American influence in Mexico. During the 1970s Jesús Luis Zuñiga of San Antonio, Texas, worked his way up in the staff of the Japanese-owned Sony Corporation until he became president of Sony de México. During the 1980s and 1990s, Zuñiga was the linchpin of a three-way cultural interaction between the directors of the firm in Japan, the American distributors, financiers, and supervisors, and the Mexican workforce. He "taught American corporate culture" to the Mexicans while mediating the cultural differences that arose when the more closed and tacit concerns of the Japanese met the more literal directness of the Americans. Zuñiga successfully convinced the Mexican workers that they stood to benefit personally and materially from efficiency, the ability to deliver products as quickly as possible, and day-to-day reliability.[44] Charles Robinson of Total Systems Development Inc., a management and training firm, explained.

> Such training courses are important to the transformation of the ma-
> quiladoras into self-contained production centers. . . . The reason you
> don't graduate from high school in Mexico may not be that you aren't
> smart enough or didn't want to. . . . Here you get a line worker with
> the same analytical skill as an engineer in the U.S. The reason he isn't
> an engineer? He didn't have the opportunity.[45]

Zuñiga took quality control to higher levels and reduced manufacturing defects to an absolute minimum. These objectives required a career-long series of seminars for the workers.

During the middle and late decades of the twentieth century, the Americans amplified their introduction of Protestantism and sports with cuisine, music, films, and consumer goods, which the Mexicans adroitly adopted, converting them to their own use. Then, to the Americans' surprise and ambivalence, the Mexicans exported their own art, dining, sports, and musical choices to the United States.

Fortunately for the Mexicans, the war needs of the United States in the 1940s dictated that they overlook the hard feelings that came from the struggle to control fields, mines, and ports during the previous two decades. Despite the previous and ongoing conflicts with American interests, the Mexican government used the crisis of World War II to reestablish American business operations in the country and at the same time expand exports to the north.

The technological revolution that followed the war offered new opportunities in Mexico for American investors seeking to introduce high technology and use local labor. The issues shifted from resource ownership and exploitation to industrial labor productivity. The two cultures, which had been largely exclusive, began to merge. The relationships of Americans and Mexicans continued to evolve in the 1980s and anticipated those of the "new world order" of the 1990s.

14 Return of the American Financiers

Informal control requires congenial collaborating elites.
Alan Knight, 1996

Economic stagnation continued to concern Mexico during the 1980s and 1990s. The disparity of per capita income between Americans and Mexicans increased at a rate comparable to that between the industrialized West and the underdeveloped world in general. The Mexican leadership, noting the rapid economic growth of Asia's "Four Tigers"—Hong Kong, Singapore, South Korea, and Taiwan—adopted the strategy of selling private industries and encouraging free trade with the United States. The privatization of most of Mexico's state-owned enterprises and the ratification of the North American Free Trade Agreement brought the largest U.S. firms back to the Mexican marketplace. American investors "dominated the rush" into Mexican stocks, and those of other Latin American countries as well.[1] The financial relationship between Mexico and the United States continued to deepen and broaden. By the late 1980s drug trafficking had largely replaced the illicit activities of gambling and prostitution that had drawn Americans to centers of sin along the border earlier in the century.

AMERICAN CAPITAL AND MEXICAN DEBT

Despite the losses suffered during the revolution, agrarian reform, and the nationalizations, the American financiers had never fully broken their ties with Mexico. The banks that had led U.S. financial activities in Mexico during the Porfiriato, particularly National City Bank and J. P. Morgan and Company, joined by Chase Manhattan, once again assumed leadership. In the decade following the Cold War they came to dominate foreign economic presence in Mexico.

The full reentry of American finance capital into the Mexican economy came about both as part of a broader-based, global movement and as a response to events particular to Mexico. In general, U.S. capital flowed into the underdeveloped world during the 1980s and 1990s in response to opportunities that resulted from trade liberalization, privatization, less regulation of stock markets, and tighter international controls over the monetary policies of Third World nations. In Mexico these general conditions all prevailed, but in the extreme. Mexico led the world in capital inflow and the leading investors were Americans. J. P. Morgan and Company was one of the first to see new opportunities in Mexico. In 1980 the firm opened an office in Mexico City and joined the long-present Citibank in serving wealthy Mexican patrons. Since that time the bank leaders have been "advising Mexico on its financing strategy."[2]

Part of the connection between the two neighbors was rooted in the historic financial dependence of Mexico on the United States. When Mexicans sought investment capital, the leading American capitalists lent money in return for business advantages. In 1964 Mexico owed only $2.3 billion in external debts to public, private, and government lenders. The government began to borrow more heavily for infrastructure development later in the decade, and by 1972 the debt stood at $7 billion, with the government owing 70 percent and the private sector 30 percent. The temporary oil embargo decreed by the Organization of Petroleum Exporting Countries (OPEC) in 1973 increased exports of Mexican oil to the United States. Money poured in, and the Mexican government and Mexican capitalists gambled on a quick expansion of petroleum production and industrial capacity.

By the end of 1974 the debt had reached $14 billion, and by 1977 it totaled $29 billion. In 1982 Mexican foreign indebtedness reached $87 billion, with the ratio of government and private obligations holding at 70 and 30 percent, respectively. At that point interest rates on Mexico's debt exceeded 20 percent. That year the oil market collapsed, leaving the Mexican government insolvent. The International Monetary Fund (IMF) extended an emergency loan of $4.5 billion for interest payments, and other international banks contributed more than $2.85 billion. Citibank faced the possibility of losing $12 billion in defaulted loans to Mexican interests, which would have exceeded its total capitalization by $1 billion. The loans literally saved the bank.

In 1982 José López Portillo, Mexico's president from 1976 to 1982, nationalized the nation's banks in an effort to keep private capital in the country. He also suspended payments on the foreign debt. These events, combined with further devaluations and the flight of additional capital, compounded the crisis. In 1989, in response to a panic among investors, President Ronald Reagan announced the Brady Plan. Countries that were deep in arrears could restructure their commercial bank debt by issuing Brady bonds, which would be guaranteed by the U.S. Treasury Department. The first Brady bonds were issued by the Mexican government in 1990.

The return of American capital began in earnest in 1982 with the collapse of oil prices. The administration of President Miguel de la Madrid was caught in the vise of reduced revenues and astronomical interest rates, which exceeded 20 percent for much of its external debt. The Mexican government renegotiated the terms of payment to its American creditors and, citing a national economic disaster, began to sell state assets as a part of the bargain. De la Madrid privatized over 900 of Mexico's 1,600 *paraestatales*, or state-owned enterprises, during his six-year term. His decision brought American capital into the economy on a scale not seen since the Porfiriato. His successor, Carlos Salinas de Gortari, sold 300 of the remaining firms, including many of the larger ones. Among them was the telephone system. Ernesto Zedillo Ponce de León, whose six-year term began in 1994, privatized the railway system.

In 1982 the Morgan bank, the Chase Manhattan Bank, and Citibank— the result of a merger between the National City Bank and the First National Bank in 1955—each bought a 10 percent share in the Grupo ALFA of Monterrey in return for the retirement of ALFA's outstanding debt. The arrangement was a good investment for both sides. ALFA, a privately held conglomerate, had long led the way in Mexican metallurgy and high-tech industries. In the 1980s, it was the largest consortium of private capital in Latin America. Bernardo Garza Sada, one of Mexico's most powerful businessmen and the head of the oligarchic Garza Sada family, led ALFA and held wealth estimated at $1.2 billion.

Each bank gained one representative on the ten-member board of directors and a voice in Mexico's most forward-looking metals, fiber, and petrochemical company. Between 1988 and 1994 ALFA enjoyed national and international influence through its association with President Salinas and the big three of American banking. Government approval of its projects was ensured, and it gained enormous cash reserves from its American banks while escaping the burden of high-interest debt. ALFA became highly profitable. It expanded into every sector of the Mexican economy imaginable. At the end of the century it was Latin America's leading producer of metals, minerals, construction materials, and beer.

Much of ALFA's diverse activity continues to be hidden from public view. For example, two of Mexico's leading fiber manufacturers, Nylon de México and Fibras Quimicas, are subsidiaries of ALPEK, a petrochemical division of ALFA. The ALFA conglomerate earns some 40 percent of its income in the foreign sector, most of it in the United States. The arrangement with the American banks probably assisted ALFA in its efforts to market products in the United States and may even have helped gain high-level support for NAFTA among New York bankers.

The largest fifty of the former *paraestatales* privatized by the Mexican authorities in the 1980s and early 1990s utilized the American Depository Receipt (ADR) as one of the mechanisms by which they marketed their stocks in the United States. Brokers from Citigroup, Morgan, Chase, Chemical Bank, Bankers Trust, U.S. Trust, Lazard Frères, Lehmann Brothers, Goldman Sachs, Salomon Brothers, Smith Barney, Kemper Financial in Chicago, and a host of other American financial institutions sold ADRs to their clients. Some of the surnames of the leaders of these firms stand out because of their forebears' investments in Mexico—for example, Ames, Buckley, Higgins, Kennedy, Potter, Salomon, and Sanford—but the large majority were new, reflecting the vitality of American capitalism.[3] In 2000 these firms were still selling ADRs to their clients.

Goldman Sachs and Company, where Robert E. Rubin was co-chairman before his appointment as U.S. secretary of the treasury, has a history in Mexico that dates back to the government bond issues in the 1860s. During the early 1990s, while Rubin served in the cabinet, the investment house placed $5.17 billion in Mexican bonds. Salomon Brothers, whose founder helped finance the petroleum undertakings of Edward Doheny in Veracruz and Tamaulipas in the late nineteenth century, brokered some $15 billion in U.S. investments in the Mexican privatization program between the late 1980s and 1999.

The role of Citibank reflected the larger picture of American influence in Mexico during the 1980s and 1990s. The institution's effect on Mexican society had been alternately constructive and destructive since the 1860s, when the leaders of the National City Bank supported the Liberals in their struggle against the French invaders. Taylor then supported the overthrow of Sebastian Lerdo de Tejada. Between World War II and the mid 1990s the National City Bank, now known as Citibank, was the most important American financial institution in Mexico. Indeed, it is no surprise that Citibank, as the only U.S. bank offering full services in Mexico during the 1980s and early 1990s, became the strongest and its investments the safest in the country. In 1995, aside from its overwhelming advantage in assets and facilities, Citibank's past-due loans as measured against all loans were a mere 0.8 percent, while the average for all Mexican banks was 9.5 percent. John Reed, Citibank's chairman, and H. Richard Handley, the vice president in charge of Latin American operations, loomed large in the contemporary relationship between the two countries from the early 1980s through 1997. They negotiated with Mexican presidents, guided private and institutional investments, and participated in myriad businesses. The institution assumed a leading role in the corporate campaign to gain congressional approval of NAFTA.[4]

Although Citibank was the only bank to operate openly in the decades after the revolution, J. P. Morgan and Company developed accounts with about one hundred major Mexican corporations. In late 1994, benefiting from the new tolerance of American financiers underscored by NAFTA, Morgan led an array of over seventy American and other foreign banking houses, sixteen brokerage houses, and twelve insurance companies. These firms set up operations throughout Mexico.

The American insurance companies that entered Mexico in the 1990s, such as the Equitable and New York Life, were old-timers. Their participation in the Mexican economy originally began in the nineteenth century, when they were among the most powerful economic interests in the United States. Their original interest was institutional and individual. Through their directors they connected with the most important new businesses in the land—the railroads and mining and communications companies—and introduced new forms of economic security to wealthy Mexicans. The same strategies are employed in the modern era. In addition to the traditional companies, new combinations will play major roles in the Mexican future.

All of the American banks that were involved in Mexico before the revolution and were still in existence returned to Mexico after a hiatus of over half a century. By 1995 some twenty-eight American banks, led by Citibank, Chemical Bank, Bankers Trust, Bank of America, Continental Illinois Bank, American Express, Bank of Boston, Chase Manhattan Bank, First National Bank of Chicago, Republic National Bank of New York, J. P. Morgan and Company, Pittsburgh National Bank, Wells Fargo Bank, and Texas Commerce Bank (acquired by Chase Manhattan in 1998), had established operations in Mexico. The National Commission on Foreign Investment regulated the entry of these interests and the special investments they sought. In the year 2000 all restrictions on the percentage of Mexican financial capital that these institutions could control were removed, allowing the banks to move into the acquisition of natural resources on a scale reminiscent of the Porfiriato.

The government's decision to sell its assets in 1982 attracted the highest level of American portfolio investment in the world, and the second highest total of individual investments in companies, the latter totaling over $16 billion in 1994 alone. As a result of the privatization of much of Mexico's

Dead bodies on Mexico City street following Huerta's insurrection, February 1913. (Foto Ramos/Library, Getty Research Institute, Los Angeles. Acc. no. 99.R.9)

Demonstration by the U.S. flotilla, April 1914. (Library, Getty Research Institute, Los Angeles. Acc. no. 98.R.5)

American troops disembarking at Veracruz, April 1914. (Photo courtesy Tom Hale)

Mexican federal troops fighting in Veracruz, April 1914. (Photo: L&L Photo/Library, Getty Research Institute, Los Angeles. Acc. no. 89.R.46–13)

Mexican women and children begging food from U.S. sailors, April 1914.
(Library, Getty Research Institute, Los Angeles. Acc. no. 89.R.46–38)

Venustiano Carranza's troops in Matamoros, fall 1915. (Library, Getty Research
Institute, Los Angeles., Acc. no. 89.R.46–40)

Emilio Zapata entering Cuernavaca, 1915. (Library, Getty Research Institute, Los Angeles. Acc. no. 98.R.5)

A Zapatista soldier, no date. (Library, Getty Research Institute, Los Angeles. Acc. no. 89.R.46–23)

American refugees at El Paso camp, 1913–14. (Photo courtesy Otis A. Aultman Collection, El Paso Public Library)

Salido Alvaro Obregón, Pancho Villa, and John Pershing, 1914. (Library, Getty Research Institute, Los Angeles. Acc. no. 89.R.46–29)

American cavalry in Chihuahua during the Punitive Expedition, 1916.
The group is led by General John J. Pershing. (Harry Ransom Humanities
Research Center, University of Texas, Austin)

J. P. Morgan Jr., president of J. S. Morgan and Company, New York,
no date. Morgan, Baker, and Stillman were known as the Trio.
(© Oscar White/Corbis)

George Fisher Baker,
president of the
First National Bank,
New York, no date.
(Culver Pictures)

James Stillman,
president of the National
City Bank, New York,
no date. (Culver Pictures)

J. P. Morgan with French bankers, no date. (© Bettmann/Corbis)

Chief Justice WilliamTaft, President-Elect Plutarco Elías Calles, and President Calvin Coolidge, c. 1923. (© Bettmann/Corbis)

President Emilio Portes Gil and Plutarco Elías Calles at a regional banquet, c. 1928–30. (Library of Congress. LC-USZ62–89457)

Ambassador Josephus Daniels and President Lazaro Cárdenas at a reception in 1936. (Library of Congress. LC-USZ62–75088)

An American-built dam in Sonora, 1940s. (U.S.-Mexican Claims Commission, National Archives and Records Administration /NARA).

Striking Ford employees, no date. (© Bettmann/Corbis)

PRI banners with the likenesses of Luis Colosio, Carlos Salinas, and Ernesto Zedillo Ponce de León, 1988. (© Sergio Dorantes/Corbis)

President Carlos Salinas de Gotari, President George H. Bush, and Prime Minister Brian Mulroney at the signing of the North American Free Trade Agreement, 1992. Chief trade representatives Jaime Serra Puche of Mexico (left), Carla Hills of the United States (center), and Michael Wilson of Canada (right) are seated signing. (© Bettmann/Corbis)

A *maquiladora* near Tijuana, no date. (© Annie Griffiths Belt/Corbis)

A Mexican woman washes clothes in a polluted stream near the U.S.-Mexico border, no date. (© Annie Griffiths Belt/Corbis)

A Zapatista banner in Mexico City, no date. (© Sergio Dorantes/Corbis)

A street vendor in Mexico City sells Subcomandante Marcos dolls, no date. (© Danny Lehman/Corbis)

social security system, the American companies are now managing pension funds. It seems probable that they will do as well as they have in Chile, where U.S. firms controlled some 70 percent of the nation's retirement funds in the 1990s. Nationalistic resistance to the new American presence in Mexico revolves around the issue of whether foreigners will be allowed to export Mexican capital. For the nationalists, the results of this debate promise to be a catch-22 unless they steer a middle course. If they win outright, the U.S. retirement fund managers will be required to invest in Mexico and there will be even more foreign control of the economy than otherwise. If they move their capital out, Mexico will lose investment resources.[5]

Estimates made by the Mexican government in 1995 for the sale of state-owned enterprises revealed the nation's growing dependence on new capital. Electrical production would attract $6 billion, satellite communications $1.5 billion, petrochemical refining $1.3 billion, long-distance telephone $1.25 billion, toll highways $1.25 billion, the government stake in the second largest bank $750,000,000, natural gas pipelines $100,000,000, and the railroads over $1 billion, with undetermined revenues from the sale of airport and port facilities.[6] The recruitment of foreign capital on such a large scale promised a revolution in the financial, material, and political life of modern Mexico.

During the early 1990s over 24,000 multinational corporations based in the United States, Western Europe, and Japan invested in the underdeveloped world. One percent of these enterprises owned fifty percent of the foreign-owned assets in those countries. The leading bankers in the U.S. participated directly through their institutions and in collaboration with one another through the International Finance Corporation (IFC). The IFC functions exactly like the IBC of prerevolutionary Mexico. It is the investment banking division of the World Bank, and it brings together the world's leading capitalists in investment syndicates for entrepreneurial projects throughout the Third World. The IFC's advantage over the IBC is that it is tied not only to private capital but also to the most powerful governments, and it automatically brings their influence to bear when there are problems with recalcitrant regimes, such as the administration of López Portillo.

FREE TRADE

During the early 1990s the American economic and political leadership reached a final accord on NAFTA—the North American Free Trade Agreement—with what Alan Knight calls the "congenial and collaborating elites" of Mexico.[7] NAFTA was at the cutting edge of free-trade arrangements in the Americas at the end of the twentieth century. It reflected changes in the trade relationship between the United States and Mexico that had already taken place. The American propagation of NAFTA derived from long-standing business and geopolitical needs. The treaty satisfied a sense of urgency on the part of the American elite to stabilize a large and potentially chaotic neighbor caught in a state of rapid population growth and economic stagnation.

The leaders of the United States, Mexico, and Canada created NAFTA as the legal framework for a restructuring of their economies. The pact was signed on 17 December 1992 by American president George Bush, Mexican president Carlos Salinas de Gortari, and Canadian prime minister Brian Mulroney. Its ratification in 1993 marked the opening phase of what President Bush called the "new world order," an era of worldwide free trade in which local "democracies" were willing to accept American economic leadership. The governments agreed that the United States would handle the high end of electronic, industrial, and farming technology and that Mexico would provide labor for a range of jobs, from menial to highly skilled.

NAFTA's creators publicly argued that the agreement would encourage U.S. workers to fill jobs with higher productivity while Mexicans performed the tasks requiring less skill and consumed more American goods because of increased employment. This rise in employment was supposed to produce enough demand to create tens if not hundreds of thousands of jobs in the United States, while the transfer of employment engendered prosperity in the Mexican north. Indeed, in the late 1990s the border states of Nuevo León and Baja California Norte were already Mexico's most prosperous zones, and Chihuahua, Coahuila, and Tamaulipas were also better off than most of the nation. Trade with the United States, however, was not a product of the 1990s. The far north had long enjoyed a material advantage over the rest of the country. By the end of the decade, the promised rewards of NAFTA had been minimal in the economy of central and southern Mexico. In the United States NAFTA largely produced higher profits, warehouse retail outlets, and malls.[8]

As a result of American job transfers in the garment industry and the threat to Mexican small businesses represented by warehouse retailing, NAFTA became the focus of continuing criticism in both the United States and Mexico. The more important problems of the agreement, problems that were unsolved at the end of the twentieth century, were less obvious. One of the dangers was that U.S. business executives would develop relations with local strongmen, which could contribute to the entrenchment of the political fraud, use of force, and exploitative labor conditions that many of them used. It has happened in Central America, and it is logical to expect it in parts of Mexico. A second danger, already manifest in Chihuahua, Guerrero, and Chiapas, was the ecological devastation wrought by high-tech, clear-cutting timber companies such as Boise Cascade, International Paper, and Georgia Pacific.

NAFTA's advantages would have pleased J. P. Morgan. It offered U.S. financial elites a historic opportunity for a systematic restructuring of capital, labor, and resources in Mexico that can be compared to the introduction of railroads and industry in the nineteenth century. American bankers reentered the Mexican market and, after the year 2000, they could do so with few limitations. NAFTA provided the Mexican elites several benefits as well. The most significant were the opportunity for partnerships with powerful U.S. financial interests, market opportunities that were more profitable than those in Mexico, and the creation of jobs in a nation where population growth had previously outstripped economic expansion and job growth.

The appearance of the new industrial work force, of Mexican junior partners participating with Americans, and the emergence of a handful of extremely wealthy individuals among the strategically placed repeated the early Porfirian pattern. The boom that began in the 1880s with a surge of employment centered on 50,000 workers used in the construction of the railroads. In the present era, over 1,000,000 workers in American-controlled businesses, many of which have Mexican minority ownership, provided the same impetus. The merging of national entrepreneurs of the past and present with American capitalization and marketing opportunities enabled a few of them to advance to world-class wealth while exercising ever greater power in Mexico.

The ratification of NAFTA provided the sense of permanence needed to attract the very large, as distinguished from medium-sized, investors that could provide economies of scale and high technology. By 1999 Mexico's privatization program had transformed about 80 percent of the 1,600 *paraestatales* that dominated the economy in the early 1980s. Some of the newly privatized companies depended on the American market for the consumption of their products as well as the sale of their stocks. The Internacional de Cerámica, the Grupo Industrial Minera México, the Transportación Maritima Mexicana, the Sociedad de Fomento Industrial, which specializes in auto parts, and ALFA all earned high percentages of their income from the American market.

The open economic arrangement provided by privatization and NAFTA aided the American capitalists who wanted to use Mexican labor for products shipped directly and tax-free into the United States. The border region offered the transfer of goods with minimal lost time and transportation costs. President Zedillo and his advisers sought foreign capital for *maquiladoras* to overcome low levels of domestic savings. Zedillo and his predecessors de la Madrid and Salinas made Mexico

> the darling of the [World Bank's] economists (and its major share-holder, the U.S.). The bank does not need to force Mexico to do anything; the two sides agree on almost everything. . . . World Bank economists and Mexican officials often spend weekends together brainstorming on policy issues.[9]

As a result of NAFTA, Americans had the inside position in the race to privatize Mexico's industries. Concerns with long-standing connections in Mexico, such as AT&T, Chase Manhattan, Citibank, and J. P. Morgan, continued to have unique opportunities. As a result of American penetration of the Mexican marketplace, American residents in Mexico gained more ready access to the many U.S. products they sought. Relative newcomers such as the American Oil Company, the Bechtel Group, El Paso Natural Gas Transmission Company, the General Electric Company, and the Kimberly-Clark Corporation joined the older firms like Cargill, Ralston Purina, and Anderson Clayton that quietly continued to conduct business in Mexico. Cargill was still litigating its differences with the Mexican government over land seizures in Chihuahua as recently as the late 1950s, but both sides seemed oblivious to the past as they looked for markets and good investments.[10] NAFTA also increased American access to Mexico's natural resources. American agricultural companies exported cattle and produce from ranches and farms in Sonora, Chihuahua, Coahuila, and Tamaulipas, shipping it to the major metropolitan areas of the southwestern United States. American firms carried out petroleum exploration and development ventures with Petróleos Mexicanos (Pemex), Mexico's national petroleum company.

American financial interests began to acquire Mexican properties by establishing real estate investment trusts (REIT). In early April 1995 the Mexus Real Estate Investment Trust of San Diego, the first REIT in Mexico, obtained approval for the purchase of properties in three regions: around Mexico City, just inside the border, and along the Pacific Coast. The former locale could increase urban housing choices, but the latter two will ultimately bring controversy. The REIT directors used the services of Alejandro Beuchot, the executive vice president of the Mexican Investment Board, as an intermediary with the finance ministry. In early 1995 Zedillo made Guillermo Ortiz Martínez, his finance minister, responsible for REIT concessions, a connection that recalls the relationship between Matías Romero and the banking elites of the eastern United States. Ortiz, as "a government economist favored by New York investors," tied the present to the past.[11]

Like their American predecessors, the Mexus directors gained a concession that modified the constitutional prohibitions on "foreign"—meaning American—ownership along Mexico's coasts and frontiers. Michael Dunigan, a southern California real estate developer, Malin Burnham, the chairman of the board of the First National Bank of San Diego and president of Burnham Pacific Properties, and George Codling, a land developer, headed Mexus. Like the American land developers of the prerevolutionary era, they took advantage of depressed property values. Their connections with American businessmen seeking properties along the border and their intimate relations with government officials promised to make their venture a success. Dunigan articulated the classic motivation of American investment in Mexico when he stated that "whatever risk is involved will be offset by much higher yields."[12]

The economic relationship between the two countries will continue to deepen with or without NAFTA as businesspeople make choices regarding costs and sales opportunities and seek to create larger markets. There are, however, some serious pitfalls. NAFTA itself could fail through a possible, though not likely, political reaction in the United States to job losses. In Mexico the massive influx of American goods contributed to the devaluation of the peso and the economic panic that swept the country in 1994 and 1995. By May 1996 real wages for the Mexican public had fallen 35 percent below precrisis levels. At that point they stood at less than 50 percent of wages in 1982. Estimates of immediate job losses in the United States in 1995 through 1996 as a result of devaluation ran between 10,000 and 45,000 jobs, although NAFTA-driven employment growth in the transportation and warehousing industries of U.S. border cities and Houston more than offset the losses at manufacturing centers like Flint and Saginaw.[13]

NAFTA is much more likely to have disastrous results in Mexico than in the United States because of the country's volatile economy, the open corruption in the privatizations, and a violated sense of nationalism. If American entrepreneurs make the mistake of aggressively seeking concessions in Mexican natural resources, the nationalists will unite with the political left in a powerful combination. The Mexicans have already proved that they can work politically and economically with such leadership. They operated nationalized industries for long periods during the twentieth century despite boycotts and political pressure from the United States.

COLLAPSE AND BAILOUT

Mexico's debt continued to grow. In the 1990s the situation reached depths matched only by the economic crisis that had prevailed in Mexico between 1865 and the mid 1880s. The larger Mexican companies depended on American financing for expansion and modernization because they were extremely vulnerable to recurring national economic crises and because the adaptation of foreign business practices promised increased efficiency. In December 1990 Southwestern Bell and other American interests purchased a large part of Telmex. Telmex lost over 15 percent of its value (as measured by the ADRs sold on the New York Stock Exchange) when AT&T announced that it would compete with the Mexican company for long-distance business rather than joining it in a consortium, graphically illustrating the dependence of the new private Mexican enterprises on American capital. This should not have surprised anyone, since AT&T had long demonstrated its competitiveness toward the "baby bells." The investment bankers of New York have historically performed badly in Mexico, a condition that has stemmed largely from wishful thinking instead of recognizing Mexico's deep cultural, economic, and political nationalism and its weak markets.

The stock market plunged shortly after President Zedillo took office on 1 December 1994. Telmex stock fell an additional 10 percent. On 14 December Zedillo devalued the peso, and Telmex's stock lost $862,000,000 in foreign exchange value. Other leading concerns demonstrated the same weakness. The Grupo Mexicano de Desarrollo, a mammoth construction company, lost 19.39 percent of its value, the diversified banking company Grupo Financiero Serfin fell 18.39 percent, and the PepsiCo bottler Grupo Embotelador de México dropped 16.78 percent. Empresa La Moderna, one of the leading tobacco companies, lost 14.47 percent of its value, and the Consorcio Grupo Dina SA de CV, the engine manufacturing monopoly formerly run by the government, fell 13.89 percent. Grupo Televisa, the television conglomerate, dropped over 10 percent. They were but a few of the larger Mexican companies that depended on American ADRs and other forms of investment. Some of them, such as Telmex and Dina, were still heavily bureaucratized and notoriously inefficient at the end of the decade. In December 1994 and January 1995 the Mexican stock exchange lost 43 percent of its dollar value.[14]

Frightened by the stock market's rapid descent, capitalists began dumping their currency. During the NAFTA debate, to create a sense of stability, the Mexican government had quietly bought up pesos that were being dumped in Mexico and the United States and publicly maintained that the

Mexican economy was healthy. In the course of 1994 it used up 90 percent of its approximately $25 billion in reserves. Then, with the ratification of NAFTA, the built-up consumer demand in Mexico for American products created a much larger trade deficit. The resulting imbalance dangerously undermined the already weak peso. Treasury Secretary Rubin and his aides were aware of the trouble, but they did not wish to upset the NAFTA debate.[15]

The economic collapse at the end of 1994 was blamed on short-term factors—a new administration and the rise of the Zapatistas in Chiapas—but the problem was systemic. The Mexican public, living adjacent to the consumer society of the United States, sought at least a semblance of that lifestyle. They produced far less value than they imported, and, as a result, large trade deficits developed with Japan, China, and Western Europe, as well as the United States. To deny the public these imports would have created political dissatisfaction. By the end of 1994 the peso's value had fallen by more than 40 percent. Mexican debtors could not pay their bills because their currency lost value at the same time that interest rates became prohibitive. In addition, the Mexican economy could not import American goods at the levels needed to justify the goals set by NAFTA supporters. Analysts at the Federal Reserve Bank at Dallas estimated that the peso devaluation and resulting decline in U.S. exports to Mexico resulted in the loss of 20,000 to 30,000 American jobs in 1995.[16]

The devaluation of the peso reduced the cost for Americans investing in Mexico by a third. Zedillo's strategy constituted a reversion to the program of recruiting foreign capital followed between 1876 and 1910 and removed the need for foreign bankers to "discipline" the Mexican government with the threat of capital flight. The World Bank noted that disinvestment can "accentuate a country's vulnerabilities through large external imbalances." By threatening to withdraw their support, American bankers could fight a Mexican government that was following policies that they deemed "capricious and irresponsible."[17]

American exposure was so great that the collapse of the peso meant trouble for middle America as well as the financial elite. In 1995 President Bill Clinton and Treasury Secretary Rubin arranged yet another bailout. The U.S. Congress backed away from supporting the Mexican loan because of public opposition, so Clinton used his executive powers to do it. The president acted after Rubin explained that a default by Mexico on its external debt could "touch off a panic in large emerging markets around the world." Rubin, as the former co-chairman of Goldman Sachs, a firm with long-standing ties in the Mexican economy and large investments in Mexican stocks and bonds, understood that stabilizing the peso and rescuing the Mexican government were necessary to save American interests. He recognized that the Mexican financial markets held a significant share of America's more speculative investment capital and that these investments had been made by a cross-section of elite American financial interests that included leading bankers, Wall Street investors, import-export companies, mutual funds, 401(k) plans, and major American companies with plants and markets in Mexico. They stood to be hurt badly by a Mexican default.[18] Clinton stated, "It isn't a bailout for Wall Street. First of all, helping the economy stay strong down there is more important than anything else for our working people and our businesses on Main Street that are doing such business in Mexico."[19]

The U.S. loan of $12.5 billion was supplemented by $10 billion from the Bank for International Settlements in Basel. An even greater amount came from the IMF. In early 1995 the IMF advanced Mexico $10 billion and made another $8.5 billion available as needed. The IMF then sent a team of experts to help in the privatization of the larger *paraestatales*, arranging their sale to foreign investors.[20] As a result, Mexico received a $47 billion line of credit. Clinton's refunding of the debt stabilized Mexico's markets and, contrary to his disclaimers, protected American bankers and an array of foreign investors.

Citibank had invested some $42 billion between the beginning of 1992 and the end of 1994. The Mexican government's obligations to foreign creditors in the form of *tesbonos* (short-term government bonds guaranteed by the U.S. Treasury) totaled $29 billion. Over $22 billion in obligations to foreigners came due during 1995. The international investors, led by the Americans, had put $10.6 billion in the bonds issued for Telmex alone. The Mexican payout to American creditors began immediately after the Americans turned over the first installment of funds.

> Of the $17.1 billion the Mexicans had borrowed as of March 31, they had spent $14.7 billion: $6 billion to redeem the . . . *tesbonos,* $3 billion to redeem other public debt . . . , $4 billion to pay off dollar deposits withdrawn from the Mexican banking system and $1.7 billion to enable Mexican companies . . . to redeem their foreign debts. . . . [M]ost of the bailout money extended to Mexico has stayed in New York and Boston to relieve pressure on wealthy Mexicans, U.S. mutual funds and other institutional investors.[21]

In reality, Clinton had identified two priorities. The first was institutional investors; the second was mutual funds. The bailout restored investor confidence, and the foreign capital that had fled Mexico quickly returned.[22]

The efforts of American financiers to stabilize the peso were similar to the strategy that the Trio, led by J. P. Morgan Jr., followed to help the British during World War I. The crisis also underscored Mexico's importance to the international banking community. Its associate institution, the Bank for International Settlements, is directed by the heads of the thirty-two central banks that hold 84 percent of its stock and are "able to shift billions of dollars and alter the course of economies at the stroke of a pen." It holds ten closed-door meetings per year. Unknown individuals own 16 percent of the institution. Its $10 billion loan came at a critical juncture.[23]

For Americans the new opportunities in Mexico transcended the concerns of finance, insurance, infrastructure, petroleum, real estate, and labor. The ramifications of American expansion reached into every aspect of Mexican life. American residents needed temporary lodgings and restaurants. McDonald's, Kentucky Fried Chicken, and other fast-food chains entered Mexico, seeking the patronage of middle-class Mexicans as well as the more than 1,000,000 American residents and visitors who were present in the country at any given moment. In 1998 fifty-two McDonald's hamburger outlets graced Mexico City alone, appealing to the 20 percent of the population that could afford such extravagance. Most Mexicans thought of Fanta as a national drink. Few realized that it was produced by a division of the Coca-Cola Company. Levi's jeans were ubiquitous. Holiday Inn worked hard for decades to establish a thriving presence in most of the Mexican resorts and large cities. Indeed, temporary housing for American travelers, both vacationers and businesspeople, attracted increasing interest. In 1994 Gary L. Mead, the chief executive of the La Quinta hotel chain, which is headquartered in San Antonio, noted the dearth of comfortable facilities in many cities: "We expect our competitors to be there. . . . We are going after our fair share of the market." In 1998 the politically powerful Meditrust, led by chairman Abraham Gosman and former New York governor Hugh L. Carey, took over La Quinta. Meditrust's influential political position is due to long-term American-Mexican connections: for example, the influential law firm of Nutter, McClennan, and Fish provides its legal services.[24]

Wal-Mart, headed by S. Robson Walton, has been in Mexico since 1991 and has taken control of Cifra, the large Mexican retailer. Jerónimo Arango, the owner of Cifra, had an estate valued at $1 billion, only a fraction of the Walton family's $19 billion in financial and retailing power. Arango could not help but benefit as the junior partner with the American retailing giant. In 1996 Wal-Mart had 431 stores and restaurants distributed across the country. The Wal-Mart directors anticipated the devaluations of the Mexican currency in 1994. They provided for 70 percent of the goods they marketed in Mexico to be produced within the country. In February 1995 they stopped construction on twenty-four stores and reduced shipments from the company's U.S. warehouses. Those maneuvers were good enough to withstand the shocks to business evoked by an automatic devaluation system in the mid 1990s, before the economy stabilized in late 1999.

Not all American retailers proved as adept at adapting to the uncertain Mexican economy. The actions taken by the Wal-Mart directors were a response to the continued recession in the retail market that caused the leaders of Sears, Roebuck and Company to sell most of their Mexican assets to the Grupo Carso. Sears, its Mexican operations headed by Warren E. Flick, had been successful as the largest retailer in Mexico since the 1940s, weathering the ups and downs of the economy in fairly good shape. The directors of Kmart gave up altogether, selling their share of a joint venture to the Controladora Comercial Mexicana. Kmart, which specializes in inexpensive products, failed because the directors tied themselves to an incompatible concern, the El Puerto de Liverpool, a department store chain with an upper-end clientele. During the late 1990s newcomers J. C. Penney, Dillards, and Saks Fifth Avenue also moved cautiously into what was becoming a highly competitive and uncertain Mexican retailing sector.[25]

Some aspects involved in the establishment of new businesses in Mexico had changed very little since the late nineteenth century, as the advice of Jeffrey Peters, the chief executive of the U.S. Mexican Development Corporation, revealed: "Start at the top, close at the top. Mexicans are much more hierarchical than Americans so don't 'spin your wheels with underlings.' "[26] In 1994, following the practice described by Peters, Laurance E. Hirsch, the head of the Centex Corporation, America's largest low-cost home builder, considered the establishment of manufacturing plants in Mexico: "We were waiting to see the results of the election before we did anything. . . . An election that didn't elect the PRI would have led one to wonder about consequences."[27] The company spun off its home construction unit in 1994 and, after several years of poor profits in its U.S. operations, canceled its plans for expansion in Mexico.

AMERICAN *MAQUILADORAS*

The Great Depression ended the predominant role of American club and casino owners and the services for the affluent in the border towns of northern Mexico, but World War II brought a surge of new customers. Marines and sailors from Camp Pendelton, Camp Matthews, and the San Diego Naval Base flooded Avenida Revolución in Tijuana with avid, if not rich, clients.

Soldiers from Fort Huachaca in Arizona went to Nogales, and GIs from Fort Bliss visited Ciudad Juárez. The numerous military bases further east along the Rio Grande each had a Mexican town for an outlet.

The border towns matured in the years following the war, and the rowdier nightclubs were no longer in plain view in the 1990s, having been set aside in *zonas de tolerancia*. Yet some of the old remained in spite of the new. At Miguel Alemán, near Roma, Texas, hundreds or more Americans crossed the border each weekend to watch and wager on cockfights, which were illegal in Texas. The *zonas* found in the larger cities, such as Boys Town in Nuevo Laredo, attracted hundreds of sexually focused American men each Friday and Saturday night. But it was the vast, largely American-owned and American-operated industrial complexes, the *maquiladoras*, that changed the border into a far more complicated urban environment.

The complexes began in 1965 with the inauguration of the Mexican government's Border Industrialization Program. Under the auspices of the program, Mexican authorities offered American businessmen cheap labor and tariff relief and advertised their lower transportation costs to businessmen in the United States. The first focus of the program was the clothing and electronics industries. *Maquiladoras* emerged in Tijuana, Ciudad Juárez, Nuevo Laredo, and Matamoros. They were assembly plants—intermediate facilities in which Mexican workers put together imported American parts and immediately exported them to the United States. The plants usually did not manufacture basic components or ship out finished products. As a result, some 83 percent of the jobs were low level, and only 10 percent were technical. Even fewer, 6.5 percent, were administrative. During the 1980s a new, more sophisticated, form of *maquiladora* emerged. These high-end factories produced computers and automotive parts and displaced skilled as well as unskilled American workers. The ratification of NAFTA exacerbated the tensions between management and labor. The loss of jobs enraged some American workers, who blamed the situation on the trade agreement and the politicians who had supported it.

From 1994 through 1997, fueled by the reduced cost of exports to the United States that was brought about by NAFTA, the number of American-dominated *maquiladoras* in Mexico grew rapidly. From January 1994 to January 1997 the plants in the state of Chihuahua increased by 161. Americans created 147 new plants in Coahuila, 66 in Nuevo León, and 143 in Tamaulipas between 1995 and 1997. In July 1997 Tijuana hosted over 700 of these factories. The *maquiladoras* specialized in apparel, electronics components, automobile parts, and construction materials such as nails. Between 1984 and 1994 the new *maquiladoras* spread beyond the border regions to the rest of Mexico, increasing in those areas from 4 to 238. The states of Baja California Sur, Jalisco, Puebla, San Luis Potosí, Mexico, and Yucatán led the way, but by the end of the decade all of the state governments were promoting the factories and other forms of foreign investment.[28]

The dimensions of the manufacturing complexes along the border were striking to the eye. The rise of these largely American-owned assembly plants created a vast new Mexican industrial working class. In 1996 women accounted for over 60 percent of the 800,000 million workers then employed in 3,233 *maquiladoras*. The program gave women at least some choice in occupation and created numerous households in which women were the breadwinners, an unusual situation in Mexico. By mid 1997 the advantages of lower taxes and wages had stimulated *maquila* growth to a total of 3,508 plants, most of them along the border. These industries employed about 900,000 workers, or some 24 percent of the Mexican manufacturing labor force. At the end of the year GM, Ford, and United Technologies installed new plants in diverse parts of the country, including the states of León and Tamaulipas. In 2000 Tijuana had over 1,000 plants, most of them American owned, with almost 150,000 workers. Job and plant estimates for other cities are less precise, but Ciudad Acuna claimed that 95 percent of its workers were *maquiladora* employees. The factories at Matamoros manufactured garments, electronics, and auto parts. Some processed seafood, which meant they could take advantage of the NAFTA-based exception to the U.S. ban on the distribution of tuna caught in nets without dolphin protection devices.

The number of jobs in the *maquiladoras* at Juárez increased by 77,000 in the two-year period 1995–1996 and reached a total of 218,000 jobs in 350 factories in 1998. These 350 tax-free *maquiladoras* paid women assembly line workers $3 per day. Such low wages, earned in a setting devoid of social welfare services, forced some of these women to work as prostitutes on the weekends in order to feed their children. Border-hopping American executives who resided in El Paso crossed the Rio Grande daily to supervise the Mexicans working in cheap modular facilities built on lands leased from the Juárez and Chihuahua elites. The growth of the *maquila* industry continued into the new century. In 2000 the number of workers in the *maquiladoras* far exceeded 1,000,000, and 65 percent were women.

American workers complained that their Mexican counterparts earned only one-tenth of their salaries in the United States while performing the same tasks for the same employer. Experts have agreed that the wage differentials between Mexican workers and their American counterparts inspired the motives of American entrepreneurs who built factories in Mexico. Indeed, the earning differentials between American and Mexican workers in electricity-related industries were enormous. According to one estimate, Mexican electronics workers earned $1.54 per hour in 1996 with very few, if any, fringe benefits, while their American equivalents earned $13.95 per hour plus health care, retirement, and disability support supplied by their employers. The contrast between the benefits received by Mexican workers and those of American workers was stark. Another observer pointed to a somewhat narrower 7.2 to 1 ratio between the earnings of American and Mexican electronics workers. The two sets of estimates, however, are essentially in agreement if the data that produced the second ratio did not include fringe benefits, which in the United States are typically valued at 15 percent of earnings.

In the automotive industry the differences were even greater. In 1996 workers in Mexican automobile parts factories earned $2.75 per hour, a high wage for Mexican laborers, whereas the average American automobile parts worker made $21.93 per hour plus substantial fringe benefits that were not offered to the Mexicans. Alexander Trotman, the chief executive of Ford, made 20,000 times the salary of these workers. Mexican employees manufacturing doors for Sears, Roebuck in Nogales were paid 55 cents per hour in 1997, about 5 percent of the earnings of their American counterparts.[29]

Two examples demonstrate the comparable strategies of American garment manufacturers with factories in Mexico. In 1994 apparel workers earning $10 per hour plus benefits at Magnetek Inc. in Huntington, Indiana, noted that workers performing the same tasks at the company's new plant in Matamoros earned $1 per hour. The owners of Cone Mills of North Carolina, the largest textile exporters in the United States and a leading producer of denim fabric for Levi Strauss of San Francisco, formed a partnership with CIPSA, one of Mexico's leading fabric producers. In 1998 their installation in northern Mexico employed 3,500 workers. Those employees earned about 70 cents per hour, or $38 for a forty-eight-hour week. Their American counterparts, on average, received $10 to $15 per hour, or $400 to $600 for a forty-hour week. In 1998 Levi Strauss announced plant closings in the United States.

Some 1,000 skilled American seamstresses lost their jobs each month during 1994, while in the same year about 100,000 Mexican apparel workers were employed in the American-owned plants on the southern side of the border. Between 1985 and 1993 *maquiladora* garment exports to the United States increased 381 percent, growing from $1,075,000 in sales to $282,000,000. The clothing produced at the Mexican plants ranged from the lowest in quality to the highest. In contrast, most of the apparel factories that remained in the United States were located in small cities and towns in the Midwest. They primarily produced ready-made clothing directed to the middle and lower end of the market. One observer of the American garment industry noted that during 1994 "[m]ore than a dozen apparel plants now shut each month, and the number grows."[30]

The Mexican leaders followed the same approach in electronics that worked so well in the apparel industry. During the 1970s they introduced tax incentives for the establishment of electronics factories on the border. Once again low wages, tariff exemptions, and reduced transportation costs stimulated growth. From the 1970s until the 1990s, however, the American computer producers hesitated at Mexican demands for joint ventures and the requirement that the factories use locally produced parts. During the early 1990s, in the face of Asian gains in electronics exports to the United States and American resistance to their demands, the Mexicans capitulated. They allowed full foreign ownership and reduced local content requirements to 30 percent and less. The directors of International Business Machines were operating in Mexico on a limited basis during the earlier period, but following the concessions they expanded production.[31]

By 1998 the promise that more American jobs would be created through increasing imports of American goods to Mexico had been realized. U.S. exports increased from $50,843,500,000 in 1994 to $79,010,100,000 in 1998.[32] Although job opportunities for Mexican workers increased in the industrial sector, the real value of the minimum wage dropped by more than 50 percent between 1980 and 1989, and real wages for all workers decreased an estimated 35 percent following the devaluation of 1995. This was the result of one of the goals of the Mexican leaders. They supported devaluation in part because it would reduce the real cost of labor. Mexican labor had to compete with the even lower wages earned by Asian, African, Haitian, and Central American workers. The real advantages for American companies in Mexico were lower transportation costs and, perhaps, lower tariffs.[33]

In the mid 1990s some of the most powerful unions in the United States, including the United Auto Workers, the International Ladies Garment Workers Union, the International Brotherhood of Electrical Workers, the Machinists, and the International Brotherhood of Teamsters, began helping their independent Mexican counterparts along the border. In 1993 the Teamsters filed a complaint under the regulatory provisions of NAFTA on behalf of a group of workers who had challenged the Honeywell Corporation in Chihuahua. The company had fired about twenty workers for attempting to organize an independent union. The NAFTA arbiters and the secretaries

of labor in the United States and Mexico refused to act on the workers' behalf. American and NAFTA officials argued that the dispute came under the
jurisdiction of the Mexican government. That entity determined that because the workers had accepted severance checks they were rightfully terminated. The Teamsters, however, saw the question differently, positing that
the acceptance of the checks resulted from a misunderstanding on the part
of the workers. The union continued to organize but gained no relief. A
Teamsters official declared, "We view our relationship with workers in Mexico as one of supporting independent and democratic unions and putting
pressure on the U.S. multinationals."[34] In the opening years of the new millennium the Teamsters and Electrical Workers redoubled their efforts, but
without measurable success.

Labor problems also cropped up at Zaragoza, a GE plant outside Ciudad
Juárez that specialized in the making of industrial motors. On 24 August
1994 the workers voted 914 to 159 against the United Electrical Union (UE)
and averted a threatened strike. The union charged that management had
told the workers that it was willing to meet all of their demands, but that it
would close the plant if the union won the election. The Mexican authorities dismissed the complaints of workers who supported UE, and the U.S.
Department of Labor and NAFTA arbiters rejected the appeals of the union
organizers.

The negative rulings coincided with the coordinated search for lower labor costs on the part of the capitalists and both governments. When the costs
of employee benefits are included, American factory workers in the electronics industry earned an average of $16 per hour in 1994, while their Mex-
ican counterparts made less than that per day. In rural Chihuahua during
the early 1990s, prior to the enactment of NAFTA, the Farm Labor Organizing Committee, prominent among agricultural workers in the American
Southwest, developed ties with a counterpart union in Mexico. Their first organizing efforts were directed at the tomato and cucumber pickers working
for Vlasic Products. That concern, a wholly owned subsidiary of Campbell
Soup Company, strongly resisted organizing efforts. After the NAFTA treaty
was signed, the American union appealed to the U.S. government, which rejected its claims that the workers' rights under NAFTA were being violated.[35]

RETURN OF THE ZAPATISTAS

Between 1910 and the 1980s over one-half of Mexico's surface, some
259,350,000 acres out of 485,000,000, including about half of the arable land,
was redistributed to cooperatives and small holders through agrarian reform

and other repossession efforts. The American landholding, mineral, and timber interests, so strong in the first decade of the century, yielded to Mexican ownership, although a few large mining interests such as Phelps Dodge, Anaconda, and American Metals still held shares of their former enterprises and therefore partial ownership of the lands around them.

In the 1980s the administration of de la Madrid changed tack, and in 1993 the government's privatization effort led to the revision of Article 27 of the Mexican Constitution and the creation of individually owned plots in 87.5 percent of the 28,000 cooperatives and *ejidos* across the country. This controversial action opened the interior of Mexico to American land ownership once again. Luis Tellez Kuenzler, a Ph.D. in economics from the Massachusetts Institute of Technology, led the planning of this effort. Fear of privatization among the rural working class and the indigenous population contributed mightily to the rise of the Ejército Zapatista de la Liberación Nacional (EZLN, the Zapatista Army for National Liberation), a predominantly Native American movement active in Chiapas. The Zapatista rebels resisted the privatization program, expressing fear of foreign domination and calling for the restoration of the previous version of Article 27.[36]

On 1 January 1994 the Zapatistas launched the "Twelve Days' War" by seizing a number of small towns. The Zapatistas, who demanded the return of indigenous rights, had already built up a considerable base of support among the Tzeltals and Tzotzils in the center and south of the state. The rebel leaders viewed neoliberalism and privatization as a threat to the life and values of rural Mexicans, and they called for the government to negotiate their grievances, provide more social services, and abandon privatization. President Zedillo and his supporters were loath to make concessions of power and wealth to what they viewed as left-wing and illegal insurrectionists. On 2 January UH-1H military helicopters, or "Hueys," strafed Ocosingo and other pro-Zapatista towns. Then airborne troops parachuted into action against the poorly armed Indians.

The market disaster of early 1994 followed on the heels of the Zapatista uprising. The rebellion, which undoubtedly deeply damaged Mexico's capital recruitment effort, provoked a strong reaction from the leadership of the Chase Manhattan Bank, which included men, such as Richard Aspinwall, with surnames from the Mexican past. An adviser for Chase announced in a report not intended for public disclosure that financial tranquility required the elimination of the Zapatistas. Riordan Roett authored this "Political Update" under the firm's auspices:

> While Chiapas, in our opinion, does not pose a fundamental threat
> to Mexican political stability, it is perceived to be so by many in the

investment community. The government will need to eliminate the Zapatistas to demonstrate their effective control of the national territory and of security policy.[37]

This thinly veiled threat of violence was consistent with the quiet involvement of the U.S. government in offering military support to maintain political stability. The American presence in Chiapas went beyond that of the big companies such as the International Paper Corporation. Americans also directly equipped and trained the military personnel deployed against the Zapatistas.

The U.S. government, American arms manufacturers, and the U.S. Army had been central to the modernization of the Mexican military since 1989. An important step in the militarization of Mexico was taken in 1990 when the Drug Control Planning Center of the United States, with the approval of the Mexican government, increased surveillance of that nation's airspace, seaports, highways, railroads, and ports of entry, as part of a "hemispheric network." The Mexican army was already beginning to reequip, and between 1990 and 1992 the government purchased $400,000,000 in U.S. arms and began to buy helicopters on an impressive scale. Between 1989 and 1994 the Mexican military deployed forty-eight American-made helicopters, ostensibly for the War on Drugs. In 1995 they added 608 "laser designators," 208 "night vision devices," 1 Hercules C-130 transport, and 6 Sikorsky, 20 Bell, and 22 McDonnell helicopters.[38]

The Zapatistas found important support in the United States from liberals, Native Americans, and a wide array of humanitarian and activist organizations that were concerned that American military aid intended for the War on Drugs had been misused by the Mexican army to suppress the rebels. Milo Yellowhair, vice president of the Oglala Lakota, represented 455 Native American groups in a pro-Zapatista lobbying effort with the U.S. government. The Pastors for Peace acted on those sentiments and carried supplies to the needy in Chiapas, while the Conference of American Bishops expressed support for their counterparts in Mexico who were sympathetic to Zapatista demands. In March 1997 these groups joined Yellowhair in meetings with Clinton administration officials at the White House.[39]

DRUGS, THUGS, AND LAW ENFORCEMENT

The United States is the world's largest marketplace for drugs, as it is for most products. Smaller-scale American drug importers obtain their goods at border towns and transport them to the interior. Denver serves as a principal distribution center for the upper Midwest, handling goods brought across the Rio Grande from a variety of points extending from Matamoros to Ciudad Juárez. On 17 April 1999 the *Houston Chronicle* editorialized that "[d]rug lords are bribing federal agents for information, paying them to wave smugglers through checkpoints, even hiring them to smuggle drugs." The *Chronicle* pointed out that only twenty-eight agents had been "prosecuted for corruption." It wondered how many "are suspected of being in bed with the drug lords, but not yet prosecuted" and asked, "What about those corrupted but not yet suspected?"

American participation in the drug trade dates from much earlier than the late 1990s, and participation goes beyond the level of functionaries and involves the elites. The most powerful drug dealers operate throughout Mexico, but they concentrate their activities in the border region next to their market. Zones of hegemony allow regular contacts and easy transportation. The Tijuana cartel, run by the Arellano Félix brothers, the Gulf Cartel, headquartered in Matamoros and headed by Juan García Abrego until his arrest in 1996, and the Chihuahua cartel, led by the successors to Amado Carillo Fuentes in Juárez, interact with American and Mexican associates at all levels.

Before the FBI began to press him, García Abrego frequently met with associates in Brownsville. He even helped finance the construction of a country club at Harlingen, Texas. García Abrego's American drug collaborators regularly visited his ranch near Matamoros, where the Mexicans stored about 33,000 pounds of marijuana brought each season from southern Mexico. They moved it across the Rio Grande to sites near Brownsville in vehicles and inner tubes. They also shipped cocaine into Texas from their positions across the border.

The *New York Times* estimated the street value of the cocaine and marijuana passing along the corridor between Matamoros and Houston in 1996 at $10 to $20 billion per year. Traffic between Tijuana and Los Angeles was estimated to be three to four times greater. García Abrego and his partners, American and Mexican, who, beyond Raúl Salinas, have not been identified, used banks in Texas, Mexico, Switzerland, Grand Cayman, and elsewhere to process cocaine and marijuana profits. The decision of Tony Canales, the former U.S. attorney for the Gulf Coast, to represent García Abrego in his Houston trial shocked this observer and further clouded the situation.

American gangsters sometimes provide professional assassins for killings committed in the border towns and pilots for transporting the goods. In one case, Ramón Arellano Félix of the Tijuana cartel recruited assassins from street gangs in San Diego. In another, American gunrunners in El Paso crossed the border to supply drug runners with over "1,000 firearms, including hundreds of AK-47 rifles." An older drug smuggling operation on the border involved retired American pilots living in Sonora. The pilots flew private planes to remote landing strips in the Sierra Madre Occidental of Chihuahua, including the mesas above Batopilas and near Boborigame, picked up bundles of marijuana and cocaine, and then delivered the drugs across the border to a private airport in southern New Mexico. One of the pilots informed me that following his deliveries in New Mexico he reported to his boss, a hotel and casino operator in Las Vegas, for payment.

The connections between American financial institutions and the drug cartels remain obscure. Court proceedings in the United States only rarely focus on bankers and their connections with the Mexican cartels. During the 1980s, American banks laundered $110 billion in drug monies yearly. During the early 1980s, Manufacturers Hanover Trust and the Chemical Bank (both since merged with the Chase Manhattan Bank), Chase, the Bank of America, the First Boston Corporation, Crocker National Bank, and the Irving Trust all paid "civil penalties, some in the millions of dollars, because of money laundering." In 1986 the Bank of America paid fines totaling $4,750,000 for failing to report 17,000 large cash transactions. The money-laundering practices continued through the 1990s. Citibank moved $300,000,000 through the M.A. Bank Ltd. of Grand Cayman over a two-year period in the late 1990s "despite indications that the money had come from drug dealers in Mexico." Correspondent accounts are found in as many as 2,000 tiny banks "scattered around the world." These banks interact with the large financial institutions in New York.[40]

The Central Intelligence Agency (CIA) has been active in gathering drug-related evidence in Mexico since the 1950s. In 1951 it reported that "some of the unscrupulous chiefs" of the Mexican Federal Security Bureau were smuggling narcotics instead of interdicting the flow. American drug agents continue to work in the most active areas inside Mexico. The most sophisticated operation is the Information Analysis Center (IAC), a clearinghouse for intelligence gathered by all U.S. operatives in Mexico. The IAC operates out of the U.S. embassy in Mexico City and provides information that enables Mexican authorities to interdict drug shipments. The IAC also helped in the pursuit of drug kingpin Carillo Fuentes, who died 4 July 1997 after a "fatal reaction" while undergoing plastic surgery. Unknown assassins killed all three of the doctors involved in the operation, and authorities have identified two of the bodies. The cartel continues to operate at full efficiency under the direction of his former associates.

American presidents Reagan, Bush, and Clinton, concerned primarily about protecting trade ties and NAFTA, repeatedly gave Mexican drug enforcement officials high grades in the War on Drugs for what in reality is a miserable performance. In fact, Mexican military and police authorities fought highly visible and fatal gun battles in recent decades, one side protecting drug shipments while the other attempted interdiction.

President Salinas chose Enrique Alvarez del Castillo, the former governor of Jalisco, as his attorney general in charge of the War on Drugs. Alvarez reportedly had ties with the Guadalajara drug cartel members who ordered the death of DEA agent Enrique Camarena.[41] In February 1985 drug traffickers, probably associated with cartel leader Ramiro Mireles Félix in Guadalajara, kidnapped, tortured, and killed Camarena, who was working in that city. Testimony in a Los Angeles court hearing regarding the Camarena case named the former Mexican secretary of defense, Juan Arevalo Gardoqui, as a coconspirator. Eighteen months after Camarena's death, the Jalisco state police kidnapped and tortured Victor Cortéz, another American agent.

U.S. authorities requested that their thirty-nine drug agents be allowed to carry firearms in Mexico for personal protection and that they be given diplomatic immunity. Mexican officials publicly refused these requests on the grounds that it would compromise Mexican sovereignty but tacitly allowed the practice. The U.S. drug agents working in Mexico City, Guadalajara, Monterrey, Hermosillo, and two unidentified cities carry weapons and technically violate Mexican law. Mexican concerns for national sovereignty were misdirected. The Mexican officials claimed concern about DEA agents carrying arms, yet in 2000 the IAC gathered information on whatever topic it wished, nationwide, with impunity.[42]

At least a few American border authorities have worked with the syndicates for personal gain. The more sophisticated drug runners present them with deposits to numbered accounts in offshore banks. Detection through normal surveillance procedures is almost impossible. The activities of the CIA in Mexico cannot be assessed because of the secrecy that surrounds them. There are, however, strong indications that rogue members of the agency have worked with Colombian drug syndicates. The leading Mexican drug lords were working with the same Colombians during the 1980s, at the same time that CIA members were abetting drug imports to the United States to finance the Nicaraguan contras' war against the government. Hence, while agents of the DEA faced death in situations like that at Guadalajara, and FBI investigators tracked the drug traffickers in the United States and Mexico, members of the CIA, guided by their own priorities, worked with the criminals. Prior to the revelations regarding the CIA-contra drug smuggling scheme, the secrecy of the CIA caused Mexican media commentators to imagine the worst. Their suspicions were provoked by the assassination of Manuel Buendia, Mexico's leading investigative reporter, in the early 1980s. Buendia, who was gunned down in traffic while stopped at a red light, was in the midst of publishing the names and personal data of CIA personnel in Mexico. Although he was also working on stories that exposed the drug cartels, many media reports identified the CIA as the leading suspect in the murder.[43]

The CIA claims authority over activities far removed from the needs of American national security in Mexico, and it probably continues to obtain intelligence regarding drug traffic. In the early 1980s, for example, a CIA taskforce of approximately ten agents entered Monterrey to investigate a small labor and urban land occupation movement that used Maoist rhetoric while negotiating with the government. Their objective was to penetrate the labor movement in Monterrey and determine the extent of radical politics in the working class.

U.S. military intelligence operates independently of the CIA in Mexico. In a secret U.S. Army operation during the 1960s and 1970s, attachés at the American embassy in Mexico City taught courses to Mexican officers at the Estado Mayor, the "Mexican Pentagon," in counterinsurgency and political ideology. This classified American government activity was occurring during the suppression of guerrilla insurgencies in Oaxaca, Guerrero, Michoacán, and Chihuahua in the 1970s. The campaign in Chihuahua even involved the delivery of American armor and other weapons, although, according to them, the officers involved did not participate directly with the Mexican troops in the field. In the late 1990s at least one U.S. officer from the School for the Americas was teaching counterinsurgency to Mexican officers under the auspices of the American embassy.

In 1997 the leaders of the American and Mexican governments bypassed the less reliable CIA by assigning the FBI the responsibility of screening all applicants to Mexico's new antidrug agency. Created that year, after its predecessor had been disbanded and its chief arrested, the new agency confronted serious political challenges. Jeffrey Davidow, the U.S. assistant secretary of state for inter-American affairs, inadvertently pointed to the problem by explaining that the restructuring of Mexico's drug enforcement agency had led the bilateral agenda of the two nations. Mexican critics charged that U.S. officials were "dictating" the nation's drug policy. Attorney General Jorge Madrazo, in the face of nationalist concerns, cautiously described the relationship: "We have requested the advice of some people of the FBI who specialize in polygraph tests . . . to look at the way we conduct the tests and make suggestions." He disingenuously added that other countries were taking part. The role of the FBI in selecting the Mexican drug agents and training them remains secret.[44]

Goods moving in the opposite direction were also important. The smuggling of electronic goods such as VCRs, television sets, and computers from the United States into Mexico went on for decades prior to NAFTA, which has undercut the need for these clandestine operations. During that time Miller International Airport in McAllen, Texas, served as the major point of departure for electronics smugglers in the Lower Rio Grande Valley.[45]

Mexico had become a minor consideration for the leadership of the United States during the Cold War and the war in Vietnam. That situation changed beginning in the 1980s, when neoliberal economics and the War on Drugs propelled Mexico to the forefront of American attention once again. During the 1980s and early 1990s, capital flowed into the countries of the Third World from the industrialized nations. Chile, Argentina, Korea, and Indonesia were primary recipients of American capital, but the largest amount of American money reached Mexico, just as it had in the nineteenth century. The opportunities presented to any impoverished economy when it ties into the largest market in the world are almost limitless. Mexico's leaders were well aware of the possibilities—and the dangers.

15   Mexico in the New World Order

Drug lords are bribing federal agents for information, paying
them to wave smugglers through checkpoints, even hiring them
to smuggle drugs.

Editorial, Houston Chronicle, 17 April 1999

As the end of the millennium approached, the political leadership of Mexico continued to pursue foreign investments, privatization, and free trade despite a lack of evidence that the program was actually benefiting the majority of its citizens. Members of the Mexican elite profited enormously in the new partnership arrangements, as had their Porfirian predecessors, but farmers, laborers and the middle class faced increasing hardship brought on by stagnant wages, rising inflation, and skyrocketing interest rates.

President Ernesto Zedillo Ponce de León, whose term began in 1994, believed that the only solution for Mexico's economic woes was privatization combined with the recruitment of foreign capital. He continued the policies of his predecessors, Miguel de la Madrid and Carlos Salinas de Gortari, by inviting American bankers and entrepreneurs to actively participate in the Mexican economy. These three leaders sought more capital for privatization, which could provide employment for a rapidly growing population. They believed that the private sector would be more efficient than public services and that partnerships with Americans would ensure access to the U.S. market.

BENEFITS OF A DEBACLE

The last four years of the twentieth century offered American enterprises their greatest opportunities in Mexico since 1910. The market collapse and devaluation in 1994 and the bailout financed by the United States and the IMF deepened the American-Mexican relationship once again. The devaluation of the peso directly benefited wealthy investors, whether American or Mexican. Private Mexican debtors owed between $12 billion and $15 billion

459

that would be redeemed in pesos to mainly American creditors, allowing the Mexicans to save about $3 billion, given the exchange rate of December 1994. At the same time the devaluation offered American investors who were willing to plunge ahead offered inexpensive opportunities for the purchase of Mexican properties, stocks, and natural resources. The U.S. government bailout benefited elite interests. The Mexican regime was confident of several more years of solvency and the American creditors and elite Mexican debtors had their crisis resolved. The American investments in capital goods intended for the production of exports were essentially inflation-proof. The cost for the setback in the mid 1990s was borne by Mexican workers and American taxpayers. Relative to other burdens it was a small cost for Americans, but the economic penalty Mexican workers paid was severe.[1]

President Zedillo worked hard to reestablish his credibility with the American bankers. He guaranteed the loans by giving the United States the right to draw on Mexican earnings from oil exports. For precedents in the United States one would have to return to the exposure of the American railroad financiers who were advancing toward the border in 1876 and the loans to the Allies before the U.S. entry into World War I. In Mexico the attachment of oil earnings compared to the situation in the nineteenth century, when European creditors collected from the customs earnings at Veracruz and the Americans took the revenues from the border entrepôts of Nuevo Laredo and Matamoros as recompense them for the completion of the railroads.

By March 1995 Zedillo was able to repay $1.7 billion. In Mexico, however, a sense of public outrage developed because the president cut social programs to make the payment. "To pay for the bailout, Mexico cut the standard of living for most people by 20 percent." The political leaders associated with the Partido de la Revolución Democrática (PRD), most of the intelligentsia, and much of the press felt that Zedillo had surrendered an important part of national sovereignty—the ability to determine the extent of domestic social spending—when he allowed the IMF and the United States to dictate terms.[2]

In 1996 the Mexican government funded the payback of almost three-quarters of its obligation to the U.S. government by selling five-year notes to Americans through investment banks while the U.S. Treasury Department allowed the transfer of the petroleum earning guarantees to the private bondholders. J. P. Morgan and Company facilitated the purchase of the major part of the bonds by private interests. That year the Mexicans also made a $1.5 billion early payment to the International Monetary Fund (IMF) while continuing to owe that institution an additional $10 billion.[3] By August 1996 the Mexican leadership had paid back $9 billion of the $12.5 billion loaned them by the Clinton administration in 1995 plus $1.29 billion in interest. The well-publicized availability of financial support for Mexico reassured the investment community and enabled the Mexicans to escape bankruptcy in the face of demands from their bondholders. By October 1996, however, the erosion of peso reserves once again threatened the confidence of foreign investors and sent tremors through the Mexican stock market.[4] At the end of 1996 the Mexican foreign debt reached $157 billion, with public obligations standing at $98.2 and short-term accounts totaling $70 billion. In mid 1997 the Mexican government secured new loans of $3.5 billion for use in repaying $6 billion in five-year notes.

Just as Duncan, Sherman and Company, J. P. Morgan and Company, Corlies, and the National City Bank did in the nineteenth century, Citibank bought Mexican bonds at discounted rates. The recession made it difficult for Mexican entrepreneurs to pay their debts. In 1995, because of the devaluation of 1994, some $14 billion in bad loans—an 87 percent increase over 1993—weighed down Mexico's banks. The government's debt stood at $180 billion, burdening the currency, undermining infrastructure development, and providing the likelihood of another currency devaluation and economic contraction. Citibank officials hoped that hedge funds, which would provide some insurance for American investors, would help offset the difficulty of removing their capital during Mexico's recurrent crises.[5] The IMF and the Morgan bank helped the Mexican government in the same manner utilized under Juárez and Díaz. The IMF gained a guarantee of $50 billion in revenues from Pemex as security, and J. P. Morgan and Company floated the Mexican bond issue in the New York financial community.[6]

Citibank benefited from Mexico's financial crisis in two ways: as a beneficiary of the bailout, and as a sponsor of future government and private infrastructure projects. It was already active in government undertakings, especially in electric power, before the crisis began. Citibank became involved in a wide range of ventures including financing the latest modernization of the Gran Canal del Desague and a possible future disaster at the Laguna Verde nuclear power plant. Like Weetman Pearson and the foreign financiers who sponsored the repeated enlargements on the Desague during the late nineteenth century, the Americans will provide the bulk of the capital needed for the completion of the project. In the present era, however, Mexico has the engineering skills to carry out the engineering and construction projects on its own. The Dirección General de Construcción y Operación Hidraulica del DDF will oversee the project. The drainage system will protect the new suburbs from floods during the torrential downpours that take place during the rainy season.[7]

By the end of the 1990s the New York banking establishment had a new face. In 1998 Citicorp, a company incorporated to hold the stock of Citibank and its subsidiaries, reorganized with the Travelers Group as Citigroup. J. P. Morgan and Company merged with the Chase Manhattan Bank. The Chemical Bank had already united with the former Hanover and Manufacturers Banks. The new threesome—Citigroup, J. P. Morgan Chase, and Chemical—wielded tremendous power in Mexico. Their ties with high finance, politics, and industrial ownership connected them to the highest levels of Mexican business and government. In particular, Citigroup was one of the largest and most influential forces in the United States and Mexico, just as Citibank had been since the late nineteenth century. It is only natural that the leaders of this powerful company have placed themselves in the position to provide massive infusions of capital for new technology and infrastructure development.

The Travelers Group, which included Morgan Stanley, was not the only American insurer in Mexico. In 1996 the TCW Group of Los Angeles and Greenwich Street Capital partners bought 13.3 percent of Seguros Commercial America, headquartered in Mexico City, for $153,000,000. The new firm controlled 32.6 percent of the Mexican insurance market. It interlocked with other consortiums. Seguros Commercial became part of Pulsar Internacional, a Mexican conglomerate that ironically included tobacco among its products. The Dallas firm of Hicks, Muse, Tate, and Furst Inc. also sought a share of the Mexican insurance market, a further reflection of the regional diversity of the American firms in that industry.

The self-interested search for power and profits on the part of American financiers could go wrong, as evidenced by the underhanded dealings that have been connected to some of the most prestigious U.S. financial institutions in Mexico. Since Citibank had been in Mexico for the longest period of time, intimately serving the highest figures in the economy and polity, it was logical for Raúl Salinas de Gortari, the president's brother, to attempt to use the firm to launder illicitly obtained funds. Salinas, long rumored to be involved with fraudulent real estate transactions and to have connections with Mexico's narcotics industry, was arrested in February 1995 for masterminding the murder of the secretary general of the Partido Revolucionario Institucional (PRI), who was also believed to be involved with Mexico's drug trade. U.S. law enforcement agencies found that Salinas had transferred over $114,000,000 out of Mexico through Amy Groves Elliott of the private banking department at Citibank in New York. At Citibank the money was "disguised" by mixing it in "concentration accounts"—that is, mixing it with other cash. Elliott then "sent the funds to an account in the Citibank Private Bank in Switzerland," and they were then forwarded to Trocca Ltd., a shell corporation controlled by Salinas in the Cayman Islands. Elliott created "a labyrinth of accounts for Salinas between the United States and Europe that allowed him to move millions of dollars out of Mexico quietly."[8]

The private banking branch of Citibank moved the cash to Swiss banks from 1988 through 1994, the six years that Carlos Salinas de Gortari served as the Mexican president. Raúl Salinas's declared income of $200,000 per year was inconsistent with the amount of funds transmitted. The *New York Times* explained that the bank

> has a long and cozy relationship with the Salinas family and the Mexican elite in general. For years, Citibank was the only United States bank with a branch in Mexico. Citibank's top officials customarily stop by the President's office when they visit Mexico.[9]

Citibank officials in Mexico and New York handled some of Salinas's funds through a Swiss affiliate with the interesting name of Confidas. Salinas also used the private banking department of Citibank to transfer other monies to the Union Bank of Switzerland and the Banque Pictet. Mexican authorities have found that Salinas sent some $84,000,000 to Swiss banks by this means. The *New York Times* reported on the front page that

> [t]he instructions from Citibank's New York headquarters to clerks at the bank's Mexico City office were clear: Ask no questions.
>
> Every few weeks throughout 1993, a mysterious courier made his way to the 16th floor of Citibank's glass-walled headquarters in Mexico City, carrying a cashier's check in pesos with a value of $3 million to $5 million. The clerks accepted the checks, which were made out to a Citibank subsidiary, and converted the proceeds to dollars. Then the money was wired to Citibank in New York, which sent it to accounts in Switzerland. No questions asked.[10]

Reed, Handley, and lesser Citibank executives refused to discuss the case, including their relationships with the Salinas family, with the press or to surrender documents to the U.S. government. Authorities in the U.S. Department of Justice obtained a federal grand jury order in New York giving them the power to force Citibank to relinquish control of documents relating to the Salinas case, but only limited public disclosure had been made by the end of the decade. In that instance the federal regulators reported that "Citibank, while violating only one aspect of its then policies, facilitated a money-managing system that disguised the origin, destination and beneficial owner of the funds involved."[11] Given Citicorp's deep interests in Mexico, the closed nature of polity and high finance in that country, and the historically secret relations between the political leadership and the largest American bankers, it is no wonder that the directors were intent on keeping as much hidden as possible. Salinas was convicted in 1999.

In a similar case Antonio Giraldi, a former private banker at Citibank and American Express International, was found by a federal jury in Texas to be guilty in the early 1990s of laundering millions of dollars for Ricardo Aguirre Villagomez, an associate of Matamoros drug syndicate leader Juan García Abrego. American Express, led by chairman Harvey Golub and notable directors that have included Henry A. Kissinger, has had a continuous relationship with Mexico that dates back to Ed Shearson's ownership in the enormous properties held by the Corralitos Company of Chihuahua and the Guerrero Iron and Timber Company during the Porfiriato.

Equally troublesome was Citibank's purchase of Banca Confia, a Mexican financial institution with 250 branches throughout the country, but with a high concentration in the drug-ridden border area. The bank's president, Jorge Lankenau Rocha, led his institution into countless bad loans and eventual bankruptcy while committing frauds totaling $170,000,000 that led to twelve criminal charges and imprisonment. In August 1997, two days after Lankenau's clients first accused him of fraud, Citibank announced plans to buy Confia. When Lankenau fled prosecution the police found a secret door in his residence leading to an underground escape tunnel. Instead of halting the acquisition, Citibank officials, led by Julio de Quesada, the chief of operations in Mexico, launched a publicity campaign putting the purchase in a positive light. On 12 May 1998 Citibank completed the purchase of Confia for $195,000,000, and the Mexican government assumed 75 percent of its $4 billion in non-performing loans. The authorities placed Citibank in charge of collecting the bad debts in Mexico. Six days later a federal grand jury in Los Angeles charged Confia, Grupo Financiero Bancomer, and Banca Serfin, three of Mexico's largest banks, and twenty-six Mexican bankers "with laundering millions of dollars in drug profits."

> Three Mexican banks—Bancomer, Banca Serfin and Banca Confia—were indicted as institutions. United States Justice Department officials said they felt that the pattern of money-laundering through these banks was so systemic that it would not be enough to indict individual employees. U.S. authorities seized $122 million deposited in U.S. banks but found no evidence of wrong doing by the Americans.[12]

The American authorities failed to indict high-ranking U.S. bankers in the case. In fact, they worked with officials of the Bank of America to trap the

Mexican culprits. Citibank then launched an advertising campaign to improve Confia's image. In both the Salinas and the Giraldi–García Abrego cases, far more money was transferred out of the country than has been uncovered.

The involvement of American banking institutions in the Mexican drug trade undoubtedly goes beyond these cases. U.S. prosecutors have charged that drug cartel operatives "used Citibank accounts to launder huge proceeds." Money laundering takes many forms, but the most frequent practice involves wire transfers. In a simple and direct method American bankers create subsidiaries in foreign countries. Those affiliates are exempt from "the tight regulations that govern other cash transactions," presumably because the money involved has not left the firm. The bank officials then send the funds via "internal bank wire transfers" to those affiliates, which in turn place the money in accounts with fictitious names. In addition, affiliates in Mexico can legally issue cashier's checks without checking identifications. That facilitates the movement of drug-generated funds in and out of the accounts.[13]

To their credit, the executives of the Chase Bank, headed by Thomas G. Labrecque, refused to accept Raúl Salinas as a client when he approached them, but they also become involved in the Mexican drug trade as a result of the prevailing practices of money processing between Mexican and American banks. In multistep transfers, Mexicans move millions of dollars through the Clearing House Interbank Payments System of the U.S. Federal Reserve. Chase belongs to that system. In one case in which the laundering of drug money was detected, Serfin transferred $15,000,000 to the Banco Union, which then wired the funds to an account at Chase. The Chase officials dutifully forwarded the money to Mercury Bank and Trust Ltd., the Grand Cayman subsidiary of Grupo Financiero Bancomer.[14] By not examining individual accounts closely American bankers stand to profit enormously through the great amounts of cash being handled and can usually claim innocence in those rare cases where the authorities uncover the transactions.

In 1995 and 1996 the political leaders of Mexico and the United States meshed the two economies and essentially re-created the dependence on American private capital on one side and the promise of grand profits on the other that characterized the economic relationship of the two countries during the regimes of Juárez and Díaz. The directors of the large financial institutions that reentered Mexico after a long hiatus exhibited no understanding of the events that generated the revolution, and they reinstated practices that had succeeded in the past. A sizeable number of investment bankers joined Chase, Morgan, and First Boston in offering Mexican elites letters of credit and the ability to make discreet foreign investments. Citibank traded in Mexican corporate loans, sold the bonds to its clients, and offered all forms of insurance and monetary services. By early 1996 foreign investors had committed $33 billion to Mexican stocks and bonds. Between 1995 and 1997 they doubled their share of Mexican banking assets from 7 to 15 percent of the system's total. At the same time Mexican banks were burdened with $14 billion in overdue loans. In contrast, American banks owed $134,000,000, less than 2 percent of the Mexican total. The continued weakness of Mexican banks and the greater resources and better global business contacts of the U.S. financial institutions were testimony to growing American domination.[15]

THE NEO-PORFIRIAN ECONOMY

The short-term economic picture for Mexico brightened in the late 1990s. Economic growth resumed during the second quarter of 1996 and continued through 2000. Protected by the loans from the IMF and the United States, Mexican stocks and bonds dramatically increased in value during the same period. American investment advisers, in their euphoria, seemingly ignored the fact that the peso, which in the early twentieth century was equal in value to the dollar, had degenerated in repeated crises during the past ten decades to the point that in 2000 its value was one eight-thousandth of its worth in 1900. Private American buyers and portfolio investors continued to pump money into the Mexican stock market in the late 1990s, buying Telmex and other high-technology issues. In 1997 and 1998 the government sold $1 billion in ten-year bonds at reduced rates over its previous issues and saved money by paying off the more expensive earlier bonds.[16]

As Mexico's economy gained strength, contemporary American and Mexican elites moved to railroad acquisitions, as had their ancestors. American banking and railroad interests began re-creating their nineteenth-century hegemonic relationship with Mexico, moving from financial control, to market penetration via NAFTA, to the direct ownership of infrastructure and control over the movement of goods. They combined Mexican lines with their more highly capitalized American counterparts. The railroads provided the transportation needed to ship American products to the Mexican interior and large amounts of Mexican raw materials to America. American agribusiness benefited from modern trucking, which facilitated the transport of crops from northern Mexico, an area with sizeable expanses of fertile soil and low land and labor costs. American businessmen shipped produce from Sonora into Arizona and southern California, and from Chihuahua and Tamaulipas into Texas. NAFTA and the trend toward more open trade will continue to facilitate that process.

In 1996 the Union Pacific and the Southern Pacific Railroads merged—a unification blocked by the U.S. Supreme Court in 1913 when George Baker, J. P. Morgan, William Rockefeller, and James Stillman attempted it—and the new company planned to handle 75 percent of the freight traffic borne by rail between the United States and Mexico, while the merged Burlington Northern and Santa Fe lines would carry 13 percent. Their expectation was reasonable. The new company ties in with Mexico at every major border city, and Union Pacific now controls two-thirds of the shipments of chemical, plastics, and other industrial goods through Texas and Louisiana to the rest of the United States. With their wide access to the Mexican border these firms seemed capable of achieving Morgan's dream of a centrally controlled rail system covering all of North America.[17]

The merger of Kansas City Southern Industries (KCSI) and Transportación Maritima Mexicana (TMM) altered that possibility. Arthur Stilwell, the founder of KCSI in 1887, established the firm's original ties to Mexico when he created the Kansas City, Mexico, and Orient Railroad over a hundred years ago. That line, which ran from Kansas City through the Copper Canyon to Topolobampo, was never finished. KCSI and TMM created a transportation network capable of moving Mexican raw materials quickly into the U.S. market.

Late in 1995, as Zedillo privatized the 16,000-mile Ferrocarriles Nacionales network, Paul H. Henson, the chairman of KCSI, and company president Landon H. Rowland merged their operations in northern Mexico with those of Luis Gutiérrez, the president of TMM, Mexico's largest oceanic transportation company. At first Zedillo considered leasing the national system for fifty years, but Mexican railroad "experts" decided that a breakup of the network into five divisions would provide better service than a unified line.

On 5 December 1996 the Zedillo administration sold a fifty-year concession for 80 percent of the Northeast Railroad to the partnership of KCSI and Transportación Ferroviaría Mexicana (TFM), a division of TMM, for $1.4 billion. TFM took a 51 percent share of the 80 percent of the enterprise sold, and KCSI obtained 49 percent. The Burlington Northern, Union Pacific, and Norfolk Southern Railroads submitted unsuccessful bids. The government sold the remaining 20 percent of the stock on the open market over the next two years while the partners cut the workforce by more than one-half, to 4,100 employees. American financial analysts for Bear Stearns estimated that the lower labor costs would lead to a profit margin of 45 percent for the new firm, in contrast to the 20 percent margins that prevailed in the United States at that time. In 1999 TFM enjoyed a profitable operating revenue of $450,000,000.[18]

Gutiérrez explained the purpose of the merger: "We believe this strategic alliance between two strong North American transportation companies will be an effective vehicle for investment and development of a surface transportation business, both cross-border and within Mexico." The rail network connected Chicago, Kansas City, Houston, Corpus Christi, and Laredo, plus other cites throughout the southern United States, with Monterrey, Saltillo, Mexico City, and the Mexican ports of Lázaro Cárdenas on the Pacific and Tuxpan and Madero, near Tampico, on the Gulf Coast. TMM also purchased concessions to operate the ports of Mazatlán and Tuxpan and a fuel terminal on the Gulf Coast.

The KCSI-TMM combination virtually monopolized sea and rail transportation in eastern Mexico north of Veracruz. The firms had direct access to the Pacific and operated warehousing facilities throughout the center and north of the country. They also purchased a 49 percent share in the Texas-Mexican Railway, which connects Laredo, the "gateway to Mexico," with Corpus Christi, the nearest American port. The Americans originally created the "Tex-Mex" in the nineteenth century as a division of the Mexican National Construction Company. The line ran across the King Ranch. In some respects KCSI-TMM is a Porfirian-style merger of a stronger American enterprise with a weaker Mexican partner, but in this case both sides benefited. The Americans gained a concession in Mexico, and the Mexicans got a stronger economic base and access to global markets. The volume of trade grows. During 1996 the once small towns of Nuevo Laredo and Laredo profited from over 1,000,000 truck crossings.[19]

The leaders of KCSI-TMM achieved the nation-girding transportation network envisioned by Rosecrans and his associates in the 1860s. The network connects the center of Mexico to both coasts and ties into the American trunk roads at Laredo. The American owners are free to merge their operations with others in the United States, much as Pacific Enterprises, the owners of the Southern California–Northern Baja energy grid, already have done. The financial support behind KCSI-TMM follows historic patterns. The companies enjoy close financial ties to J. P. Morgan Chase and Merrill Lynch. Those financial institutions provide operating funds and may have been involved in the acquisition. The biggest financial problems for KCSI and TMM in 2000 were low Standard and Poors bond ratings of BBB+ and BB, respectively.[20]

On 7 March 1997, FERROMEX, a consortium comprising Union Pacific and two Mexican firms, bought the North Pacific line, which connects Mexico City with Guadalajara, Mazatlán, Nogales, and Mexicali, for $524,000,000. The acquisition included 405 locomotives and 12,591 cars. The buyers planned to eliminate the majority of 13,000 jobs. Other lines that were sold were the Southeast Railroad from Mexico City to Mérida, the Valley of Mexico line, which provides urban services, and the Chihuahua Pacifico, running from Ojinaga to Chihuahua across the Sierra Madre to Los Mochis. By 2000 almost the entire Mexican railroad system had been privatized with major infusions of American capital.[21]

The weakness of Mexican companies often prompted their owners to sell out to American and other foreign companies that were seeking new markets. The Mexican owners of La Moderna, the cigarette manufacturer, gave up control to British investors in 1997 for $1.5 billion, and Philip Morris bought 50 percent of La Tabacalera, La Moderna's competitor, for $400,000,000. John Reed, a member of the Philip Morris board of directors, was at that time the co-chairman of Citicorp, giving the merged tobacco company tremendous financial resources. Meanwhile Procter and Gamble bought out its Mexican counterpart Loreto y Peña Pobre for a paltry $170,000,000. Eduardo Cepeda, the chairman of J. P. Morgan of Mexico, reported that Grupo Modelo, one of Mexico's strongest beverage companies, sold a 50.2 percent interest to Anheuser-Busch because "[i]t is one thing to sell beer in many markets, but it is another thing to compete with the likes of an efficient Anheuser-Busch plant in a free-trade environment." The Morgan bank advised Anheuser-Busch on the transaction.[22]

The mining sector also entered a neo-Porfirian synthesis of elite Mexicans and more-powerful Americans. In the mid 1990s Jorge Larrea purchased the Cananea copper mines once owned by William Greene, Amalgamated Copper, Anaconda, and the Mexican government. Larrea paid $500,000,000 for the complex through Medisma, Mexico's largest copper producer. Medisma, which is partly owned by ASARCO, produces 98 percent of Mexico's copper.[23]

PEMEX AND NATIONAL OWNERSHIP

In 1995, as part of its effort to privatize Mexican industry, the Zedillo administration made plans to sell off Pemex, the government petroleum monopoly. The leading American financiers and their counterparts in the oil industry expected that the Mexican petroleum business would be one of their most profitable endeavors. Pemex averaged a gross income of $21 billion yearly in the mid 1990s, much of it in domestic retail sales. In the late 1990s it was the fourth largest petroleum company in the world. The nationalization of oil resources in 1938 still stands as a proud moment in the eyes of the public, however, and in September 1996 the rank and file of PRI resolved to oppose its privatization.

In 1996 Santiago Levy, an economist trained at Boston University and the president of the Federal Competition Commission, established by Salinas, ruled that Pemex had to sell its products to competitive retail stations. The ruling opened the door for Amoco/Femsa, an American-Mexican combination dominated by the U.S. partner, to challenge Pemex in the Mexican retail gasoline market. The decision to break the retail monopoly of Pemex threatened one of the psychological pillars of national pride. That year the American Petroleum Institute, which represents the collective interests of the two companies in research and government and public relations, joined with the U.S. Department of State in calling for the development of deepwater fields in the Gulf of Mexico, some within Mexican waters, which extend 200 nautical miles from the Mexican coastline. The Agujero de Doña, as the oil field is known in Mexico, contains an estimated 12.5 billion barrels of oil and natural gas. Officials from the U.S. Department of the Interior met with representatives of the American Petroleum Institute and the Shell Oil Company regarding the potential of the field and possible jurisdictional conflicts with the Mexican government. The Department of the Interior officials then notified the U.S. Department of State that clarification of the boundaries with Mexican authorities should be a priority.[24]

President Zedillo and Energy Secretary Jesús Reyes Heroles grudgingly yielded temporarily to popular opposition to the privatization of Pemex. Oil workers and businessmen who traded with Pemex favored the continuation of national ownership of oil resources and production of ethane and butane. Zedillo and Reyes Heroles, however, took the next best step from their point of view by reducing the extent of Pemex's control over the preparation of "dozens of other petrochemicals, including polyethylene used for plastic bags, styrene used in tires, and ammonia used in fertilizers." Between 1995 and 1997 the president and the energy secretary had arranged the sale of the sixty-one plants for secondary petrochemicals to Exxon, Chevron, and Shell, among others. In 1996 the government issued stock valued at 49 percent of the plants' worth to private interests, retaining the other 51 percent.[25]

Reyes Heroles justified the action by claiming that he and the president were "expanding oil production," but this rationale is not supported by all the facts. Pemex is highly profitable and fully capable of expansion into the area of "secondary petrochemicals" without the intervention of foreign capital. Under the 51–49 percent proviso, extra economic and political influences will shift control from the periodically bankrupt Mexican government to multinational corporations. The actions taken by Zedillo and Reyes Heroles suggest their purpose was to integrate the Mexican economy more fully with that of the United States and to placate the Americans who wish to restore their ownership of Mexican energy production, which was lost in 1938.

The Mexican public viewed Pemex as the strongest element of the economy and as a symbol of national sovereignty. In 1995, when Chevron, Exxon, Phillips, Union Carbide, and other foreign firms competed for the purchase of the large refinery at Coatzacoalcos on the southern Gulf Coast, oil workers resorted to street demonstrations protesting the sale as unpatriotic. They won widespread public support. The effort to place Pemex in foreign hands provoked a nationalistic backlash against the entire privatization program and contributed to a sweeping victory for the left-of-center PRD in the 1997 Mexico City mayoral elections.[26]

The relationships between many of the specialized American oil firms and Mexican producers date back to the revolutionary and postrevolutionary eras. Koch Industries, based in Corpus Christi and Wichita, operated the Ganahl oil field outside Tampico in the 1910s, and Cities Service, which remains one of Pemex's principal American drilling subcontractors in the Bay of Campeche, was also active in the region in the early years of the century. Higher levels of capitalization and technology and a wider merchandising network will be the key elements in the relationship between American and Mexican oil interests for the foreseeable future. American oil exploration and field development companies have worked with Pemex for decades. These firms have exercised considerable control in the Mexican petroleum industry over the application of high technology, a function that the Mexicans need badly. The American companies were powerful in the world market and in U.S. politics. Pemex continues to operate a refinery on the Houston Ship Channel jointly with Shell Oil to facilitate the marketing of Mexican oil products in the United States. Many of the oil companies that sell specialized technological services to Pemex continue to maintain privileged access to the U.S. government. Valero Energy of San Antonio became involved in the 1997 White House fund-raising scandal when Stan McLelland, its executive vice president, enjoyed four visits with President Bill Clinton. The company had earlier lobbied Congress on behalf of NAFTA.

Other firms have had even better connections to the political inside. For many years Dresser Industries and the Zapata Corporation of Houston enjoyed the leadership of future president George W. Bush. Even more powerful firms such as Halliburton of Dallas and its subsidiary Brown and Root Marine of Houston carry out the brunt of the work in developing the new fields assigned to them by the Mexican government. Halliburton is especially well connected in Mexico City and Washington. Thomas H. Cruikshank, of a notable family in Mexican railroad history, headed Halliburton in the early 1990s. Dick Cheney, vice president in George W. Bush's administration, succeeded him for several years in the late 1990s. Other companies supply power and light to large cities. Houston's NorAm Energy will provide service to Chihuahua, and the AES Corporation of Arlington, Virginia, will sell their product to Mérida.[27]

In 1997 Mexican officials authorized American companies and investors to participate in four major oil production projects. The development of the Cantarell offshore field near Campeche received $4 billion from the Mexican government for 120 "development wells" and 24 gas injection wells to tap the heavy crude. The development expenditures were evenly divided over four years, with $1.02 billion spent in 1997. The Cantarell field is crucial to Mexico's economy. It has provided 35 percent of the nation's oil production over the past fifteen years. The government earmarked $485,000,000 for a light crude processing center to serve the nine oil and gas fields off the shoreline of Tabasco, while the Burgos Basin Gas Field in the northeast received $150,000,000 for exploration and development. The modernization of the gas processing center and refinery for the Burgos Field at Cadereyta Jiménez near Monterrey cost the Mexican government $403,000,000.[28]

The participation of U.S. oil and gas exploration companies has been long standing in projects such as these. American firms have rented rigs, technical equipment, and employees to Pemex for many years. That relationship prompted the Mexican company to place its international headquarters, with its some 350 engineers, in Houston rather than Mexico. CitiService and Brown and Root are two of the largest sources of expertise available to Pemex. The American companies offer support for Pemex's exploration efforts and furnish technical assistance, providing work crews, platforms, housing, and drilling packages including jackets and valves for the ongoing offshore work in the Bays of Campeche and Carmen. Unfortunately, Mexico already has 3,000 idle wells and a record of massive overspending in oil production projects. At the beginning of the twenty-first century, proven oil reserves total 48.8 billion barrels but the possibility of inefficient extraction threatens the success of these projects and their profitability.

The supporters of privatization in the Mexican government continued to work for the sale of refineries to American and other foreign interests despite nationalistic reaction. Ten new Pemex affiliates will spin off from their parent company, each tied to one of ten Pemex complexes. Private funds raised through sales in the Mexican stock market made them possible. The first two energy "distribution zones" will be focused on the northern state capitals of Chihuahua and Hermosillo. After these ventures have success-fully incorporated foreign capital, probably American, eight more will be formed: Northwestern, including Tijuana and Mexicali; La Laguna, centered on Torreón; Tampico; the Bajio; a zone including Querétaro on the north, Cuernavaca on the south, and Toluca midway between the two; and greater Mexico City, which comprises three entities. American companies built ma-jor fuel pipelines to power plants at Rosarito near Tijuana, Samalayuca in the Bajio, Guaymas on the Sea of Cortez, and Mérida in Yucatán. In 1997 the Midcon Corporation of the United States undertook a problematic ef-fort to construct a fuel transmission line from Monterrey to the U.S. bor-der at Ciudad Alemán. A similar project under the direction of the Bechtel Corporation failed in the late 1970s when the administrations of Jimmy Carter and Luis Echeverria failed to agree on the price of Mexican gas.[29]

The delivery of energy from oil and gas is a key element in the devel-oping relationship between the Americans and the Mexicans. Pemex offers natural gas services to southern and central Mexico, but the border region is far removed from the wells of the Gulf Coast, and Presidents Salinas and Zedillo recognized the financial opportunity presented by the desire of American natural gas companies to gain new assets and markets. In 1995 the Mexican leadership estimated $5 billion in new capital could be garnered by opening up the north to American bidding.[30] The natural gas providers in the United States, some with solid connections in Mexico, competed for contracts to provide monopoly services throughout the border region. For example, Mexicali, a city of 750,000 in the Imperial Valley, is a major prize. A large producer of steel, glass, and paper, the city depends on propane and fuel oil provided largely through deliveries by train and truck.

In August 1996 the Mexican authorities awarded a thirty-year monop-oly contract to provide natural gas to Mexicali to three companies, the Enova International Corporation of San Diego, Pacific Enterprises of Los Angeles, the parent company of the Southern California Gas and Southern Counties Gas Companies, which together serve the second largest urban area in the United States, and Proxima, a Mexican firm. Originally the companies sub-mitted competing bids, but the American concerns were so powerful and in-timate that it is likely that Zedillo's administrators decided to combine their interests rather than alienate one of them. Two months later the leaders of Enova and Pacific merged their companies, creating the largest utility in the United States, with a market value of $5.2 billion, and the greatest number of consumers in the nation. Richard D. Farman, the president of Pacific, be-came the chairman, and Stephen L. Baum, the head of Enova, became the vice chair and president. Farman and Baum sought to dominate the delivery of energy from Los Angeles to Ensenada and inland to Mexicali. With the capacity to deliver both natural gas and electricity, the new company enjoyed an enviable position in competition with the Southern California Edison Company. Farman and Baum's search for market growth and control brought them to Ensenada and Mexicali, which are the southernmost and easternmost points of the Southern California–Northern Baja population mass.

The Enova-Pacific combination joined with El Paso Natural Gas for the Mexicali market, a logical extension to their control over energy deliveries to the 1,500,000 inhabitants of Tijuana. Before the merger with Pacific, the Enova leaders bought electricity from Mexican plants in Baja. Then El Paso Natural, a transmission company, built a line extending from Yuma to Mexicali, Tecate, and Tijuana. The consolidation and interconnected nature of the energy industry along the international boundary led to an American-dominated energy grid encompassing the most rapidly growing region in Mexico.

The directors of El Paso Natural and Tenneco constructed a 600-megawatt power plant at Rosarito, just south of Tijuana, which will serve the affluent American and Mexican suburbs extending south toward Ensenada. The resulting energy grid blends markets in the United States and Mexico with sources in those two nations and Canada.[31] The new energy company has wide ties with other energy-related firms in the Southwest, and together they constitute a virtual conglomerate. In addition to its long-standing relationship with El Paso Natural, Pacific also has old ties to Chase, which expanded dramatically across the region during 1998. El Paso Natural, in turn, shares a partnership with General Electric (GE), Bechtel, and Empresas, Mexico's largest construction company, in the construction and long-term development of the $700,000,000, natural gas–driven electric power plant at Samalayuca, south of Ciudad Juárez. Fluor Daniel built the pipelines to and from that installation. GE, led by financier Gary C. Wendt, contributed $150,000,000 to the Samalayuca project, which gained public praise from Zedillo.[32]

Further east the integrated energy delivery system extends far beyond the border to Monterrey, the bailiwick of the ALFA heavy industry complex. Tenneco is well positioned there as a result of its long-standing relationship as a provider of technology and skills to Pemex. The Tenneco directors made an initial investment of over $40,000,000 in energy-related projects around Monterrey and planned new plants and pipelines for the next decade. Across the Gulf, at Mérida, Kenneth Lay, the chief executive of Enron and a close friend of President George W. Bush and his father joined the Tenneco directors in the construction of pipelines and a natural gas power plant to serve the capital of Yucatán.

PROFITS FROM LABOR AND LAND

The most important aspect of operating expenses is the cost of wages, and NAFTA afforded American entrepreneurs access to inexpensive labor. Mexico has an enormous number of underemployed workers. In January 1997, 43 percent of the Mexican working population earned less than $2 per day. In 1997 the minimum wage varied between $2.86 and $3.36 per day, and it only averaged $3 in mid 1998. American employers can pay far more than these amounts and still save 90 percent on labor costs.[33]

The fall of real wages and the rise of the *maquiladora* complexes led to greater assertiveness on the part of Mexican union leaders. In 1991 the Co-ordinación de Trabajadores Mexicanos (Coordination of Mexican Workers) lost 100 of its organizers to dismissals when they first attempted to bring together the workers at PepsiCo Inc.'s Sabritas snack food division in Mexico City. In January 1996 the workers rejected the company's offer of a 10 percent raise. At that point the organization included some forty affiliated unions outside of the Confederación de Trabajadores de México (CTM), the government-controlled union. During the four-day walkout the workers in neighboring plants offered the strikers refreshments and toilet facilities. The company, which enjoyed healthy profits, finally granted its employees a 26.5 percent pay raise. Nationally, wage increases averaged 19 percent during 1996, while the inflation rate reached 27 to 30 percent. Economic travail and the complacency of the CTM have led to the rise of independent unions and, in the border region, to affiliates of American unions.[34]

Wage disputes between Mexican unions and American employers that ended in strikes usually meant calamity for the workers. One of the earliest strikes against an American company took place at the Cuautitlán Ford plant near Mexico City in July 1987. The workers gained nothing from their action. On 8 January 1990 the company's representatives broke up an anticipated strike at the plant by hiring armed thugs, who killed one worker and injured others. Ford dismissed 3,200 workers and ended their strike effort. Ford's response was symbolic of the "new world order." The Mexican government, estranged from the unions that were militant, was already emphasizing an economic restructuring based on low wages, nonunion *maquiladoras,* and international financial investment. The use of specially trained thugs by Mexican and foreign companies to break up strikes became a common practice during the 1990s.

Another disaster occurred in 1997 at the Itapsa plant of Echlin Incorporated, a subsidiary of the Dana Corporation of Toledo. The chairman of the company, Southwood J. Morcott, and its president, J. Magliochetti, had acquired some thirty foreign production firms since 1990, a good number of them in Mexico. The Dana Corporation, named after New York financier Charles Dana, has remained on the cutting edge of economic relations between the United States and Mexico since the 1860s, when Dana's grandfather was one of the first to buy Liberal bonds. Utilizing cheap Mexican labor, the company produces a wide range of accessories for automobiles and trucks but specializes in driveshafts and transmissions. When the Mexican workers at Itapsa attempted to organize a legitimate union in place of the "white union," the company-controlled union that had been imposed by the Mexican government, the Dana Corporation management "allowed scores of thugs" from the white union to attack the law-abiding workers. In August 1998 the U.S. Labor Department finally objected to this violation of the NAFTA accords while continuing to ignore more subtle infractions elsewhere.[35]

Wage differentials between American and Mexican workers explain the moves that were made by the auto industry executives in the late 1990s. General Motors (GM), Ford, and, more recently, Chrysler greatly expanded their production facilities in Mexico. Beginning in 1978 the directors of GM placed almost all of fifty new components plants across the northern third of Mexico while ordering the construction of only eleven in the United States. Chrysler's directors projected that the company would invest $1.5 billion in production facilities for pick up trucks and new models between 1998 and 2003. Output at the plant at Ramos Arizpe increased from 140,000 yearly in 1998 to 180,000 in 2000.

In 1998 GM employed 72,000 workers in Mexico in its Delphi Automotive Services plants. The Mexicans employed by Delphi earn $1 to $2 hourly while finishing instrument panels and steering wheels, whereas at Flint and Saginaw their displaced American counterparts had earned close to $22 an hour. GM ships front-end assemblies from Hermosillo to Arizona, and GMC trucks manufactured in León are marketed in both countries. The León plant replaced one in Mexico City that GM officials closed to escape labor strife and higher wages. The salaries at León in 1988 represented a two-thirds reduction from those paid to the workers in Mexico City because of devaluation and because the union was under the control of CTM. The leaders of CTM belonged to the PRI, and before Mexico adopted a system of primary elections, the head of the organization helped select PRI's presidential candidate. In 2000 independent unions were still being kept out of the Mexican plants.

Ford began producing parts in Mexico during the early 1980s and then turned to the manufacture of larger assemblies for export. By 1996 over 150,000 Ford Escorts and Mercury Tracers emerged yearly from Hermosillo and entered the United States at Nogales. By the end of the century the company operated eleven parts factories in Mexico. It also produced the Ford Contour and the Mercury Mystique at Cuautitlán. Chrysler produces cars in Mexico, but primarily for purchase there.

The vicissitudes of the Mexican domestic market constantly threatened the American auto producers. During the first five months of 1994 Ford sold 31,578 vehicles in Mexico. In the same period in 1995 Ford sales reached only 10,999 units. During the rest of the year matters improved very little, and Ford ended up with a mere 25,000 sales of cars and trucks to cash-starved Mexican consumers. Chrysler has assembled and sold cars in Mexico for decades, and at one point in the late 1960s it was the largest industrial concern in the country. The company's directors, until the Daimler-Benz takeover in 1998, limited their reliance on Mexican consumers by shipping components to Mexico for assembly only as needed. The directors of the automotive big two and other U.S. manufacturers will continue to take advantage of the lower labor costs caused by the weakness of the peso and minimize their dependence on the Mexican market by exporting their products.

The executives of the Goodyear Tire Company installation at Tultitlán near Mexico City adapted quickly to the devaluation of the peso. Instead of mourning the loss of 20 percent of their domestic sales because Mexican customers were unable to pay for higher-quality goods, the Goodyear managers began exporting to the United States. With Mexican workers earning only $3 per hour and their American counterparts some $17 per hour, their effort quickly paid off. In 1995 the Mexican plant sold some 50 percent more tires than before the devaluation. Goodyear's strategy portends the future. The losers were the Mexican retailers who could not sell the tires, the Mexican consumers who could not afford them, and the American tire factory workers who lost jobs.[36]

NAFTA has had some effect on wage negotiations in the United States. In 1997 the United Auto Workers union attempted to organize ITT, an auto parts manufacturer in northern Michigan. They gained wide support, but as the

> election was drawing near . . . the company brought in workers from Mexico . . . to film U.S. workers as they went about their jobs. An assembly line was shut down, the equipment shrink-wrapped and stacked onto flatbed trailers marked: "Mexico Transfer Job."[37]

The ITT workers changed their minds and voted down the union.

As NAFTA matures, Mexico will contribute not only an ever larger low-wage labor force but also, compared to Asia, lower transportation costs. This encourages higher profits and a low rate of inflation in the United States. The skills of the relatively well trained Mexican workers range from completing simple assemblies to the operation of robotics and the manufacture of pharmaceuticals. American capitalists regard further labor cost reductions as critical to the success of their enterprises despite the fact that in the late 1990s the United States had one of the highest ratios of labor productivity to cost worldwide. American workers received less for the value that they produced than workers did in all but three other industrialized nations. One survey ranked the U.S. economy first in this category during this time span. In 1998 the number of *maquiladora* jobs totaled 1,052,000. The process of labor substitution will continue to grow if left to the economic self-interest of American and Mexican business and banking elites.

In contrast to the situation with Asia and the rest of Latin America, the transfer of goods between the United States and Mexico is direct, rapid, and inexpensive because of the border shared by the two countries. The NAFTA highway extending from Guadalajara and Mexico City will connect Monterrey with the port of Houston, the largest bulk shipping center in the world, the oil refineries around it, and Chicago. Initial construction began in 2000 and will continue for a decade. Branch highways will tie into other American cities, including Corpus Christi, the still-important terminus of the Texas-Mexico Railroad, formerly the property of the Mexican National and belonging now to Kansas City Southern Industries.

The American role in agriculture is now more indirect than in the past. Americans no longer have large-scale ownership of Mexican land, but, with the help of NAFTA, they have achieved domination over Mexican agricultural exports and imports. American agricultural companies exported cattle and produce from ranches and farms in Sonora, Chihuahua, Coahuila, and Tamaulipas to the major metropolitan areas of the southwestern United States. In 1996 imports of basic staples to Mexico from the United States were triple those prior to the implementation of NAFTA. In that year U.S. produce accounted for almost 50 percent of Mexico's consumption. The influx included 6,000,000 tons of corn, 2,500,000 tons of soybeans, 2,500,000 tons of sorghum, and 2,000,000 tons of wheat. These imports cost Mexico $3 billion. Imports of beans, celery, and rice each reached approximately 250,000 tons. The Commodity Credit Corporation financed almost $500,000,000 of the agricultural purchases made by Mexico from the United States. The small, undercapitalized farms that are typical in Mexico are unable to compete with the economies of scale that prevail in U.S. farming. As a result,

12,500,000 acres of Mexican farmland had fallen idle in 1996 because of depressed prices and the lack of government support.[38]

During the 1990s the United States expanded its global agricultural exports from $40 billion to $60 billion per year. Among the largest American players in Mexican agriculture today, as in the past, are Dow, Du Pont, Monsanto, Cargill, and Anderson Clayton. Their principal competition in the sale of higher-yield seeds come from European firms such as Ciba-Geigy, Hoechst, and Zeneca. The Mexicans are now so dependent on the essential patented seed products of the multinationals and their imports that famine would result without them.[39]

The timber industry presents a far more ominous threat to the indigenous population than any undertaking in recent memory. During the 175 years since national independence the indigenous people of Mexico have suffered many defeats at the hands of liberal and conservative government administrations who have steadily reduced their capacity for home rule and self-sufficiency. The Cardenista years, between 1934 and 1940, stand out as the time in which they made the greatest material gains, but they paid the price in the form of increased cultural and political interference from the central government. In the late 1990s Mexican timberlands still had considerable cedar and pine reserves, but the timber industry was threatening the remaining resources, which extended from Chihuahua to Guerrero, Oaxaca, and Chiapas.

Remarkably, considering the resistance to outsiders long maintained by the local peasantry, the Boise Cascade Corporation chose the mountainous area inland from the old Stephens hacienda of Cacalutla in the Costa Grande of Guerrero for exploitation. This land, made up of timber *ejidos,* is near the former properties of the Guerrero Iron and Timber Company. During the 1910 revolution Zapatista revolutionaries attempted to secure control over the entire region on behalf of the peasantry. This time, however, in a contract signed by the governor, Rubén Figueroa Alcocer, and Costa Grande Forest Products, a division of Boise Cascade, the company gained the right to harvest trees for five years. The *ejidatarios* retain nominal ownership of the land and obtain temporary employment at $4.74 per day, which is about 5 percent of the daily earnings of their American counterparts. The massacre of seventeen campesinos who were protesting logging operations by a Mexican company at nearby Aguas Blancas points to the destabilizing effect that NAFTA has had in the region. The long-term problem with the arrangement with Boise Cascade is that in many areas of Mexico the forest does not grow back. The barren mountains west of Durango and the depleted shoreline of Campeche, both rich in forests a hundred years ago, render mute testimony to the ecological losses that occurred during in the early twentieth century. Boise Cascade expanded its operations to Oaxaca, Malaysia, Chile, and Siberia in the late 1990s.[40]

In 1996 the International Paper Company, headed by John A. Georges and John T. Dillon, began logging operations in the *ejido* of San Alonso in the Baja Tarahumara of Chihuahua. This exercise was a test run for exploitation. The mountainous forestlands are occupied by 56,000 Rarámuri, a people who survived the Spanish Conquest, colonialism, and the upheavals of the past 175 years. A huge extent of this land, 186,000 acres, was threatened by government privatization plans that granted 25 percent of the timber to a local firm, Proveedora Industrial de Chihuahua, and the other 75 percent to International Paper, which had become the largest business operating in the state. The companies claimed that the projected increase in output, from 11,000 to 30,000 tons per year, will have no negative effect on the Mexican market because the entire cutting is destined for export. San Alonso had at that time 275 *ejidal* families and was surrounded by crops and grazing land. The majority of citizens in San Alonso opposed the increased cutting because the incredible pace and the removal of green trees threaten the ecosystem of the region. The tree cutting will benefit those 5 percent, largely mestizos, who will cut the trees and drive the trucks for as long as the trees last. Clear-cutting will leave lifeless ground because the thin soil and arid climate prevent regrowth. As in the mountains west of Durango, a barren habitat awaits those who come after the machines have finished their work. In 2000 the cutting was greatly slowed by litigation in the Mexican courts.[41]

The leaders of International Paper also entered into an agreement with two Mexican firms for the planting of 730,000 acres of eucalyptus trees on *ejido* properties in Chiapas. The area includes pueblo lands where some of the citizenry actively support the Zapatista revolutionaries. The project, supported by a World Bank loan for the development of forestry, includes the Indians as minority stockholders. The problem is that eucalyptus allows virtually nothing to survive under it. During the late 1990s the government of President Zedillo consistently rejected a call from the Zapatistas for the recognition of the Indians' autonomous rights to their *ejidal* lands. That recognition would have given them added authority over operations like those of International Paper. In December 2000 the new president, Vicente Fox, accepted the San Andres Pact, which had been signed years earlier by the Mexican government and the Zapatistas. The agreement—which included, among other provisions, assurances of land, political authority, and protection against exploitation by petroleum and logging companies—was suspended during ongoing disputes. The new president offered the villagers of Chiapas limited autonomy, a concession that was removed from the congressional bill that was forwarded to Fox in early 2001. The Zapatistas rejected the congressional version and in the summer of 2001 the confrontation continued.[42]

RESOURCES ON THE ENDANGERED LIST

Ecological problems plagued NAFTA and the deepening American involvement in Mexico at the beginning of the twenty-first century. The Laguna Verde nuclear power plant, which uses GE technology, is some 1,000 miles directly downwind from Houston. During the summer the prevailing winds push northward across the Ohio Valley, the Middle Atlantic states, Pennsylvania, New York, and New England. The plant began operations in 1991. Since that time its directors have maintained a low standard of safety, and GE has assumed no responsibility for maintenance, resulting in repeated emergencies. The former head of the federal Departmento de Protección Radiológica reports that there have been "failures because of obsolete equipment, technical improvising, the use of counterfeit replacement parts, and errors and negligence on the part of security personnel." More specifically, "the oven originally destined to burn the collective waste has no filters, nor a pressurized containment system for particles, nor beds of activated carbon in order to absorb the toxic gases expelled during the incineration of radioactive waste." When that waste reaches nearby beaches employees are sent out to burn the contaminated areas with gasoline. The last independent safety and maintenance review was ordered in 1989 by the governor of Veracruz. In 1992 the successful gubernatorial candidate, Patricio Chirinos, promised petitioners that he would look into the situation. As of 1996 the inquiry had not been carried out. The combined negligence of the American firm and Mexican authorities and the corrupt practice of counterfeiting parts endangers large parts of North America.[43]

A wide range of ecological problems plague the border areas. In 1992 the General Accounting Office of the U.S. Congress found that all of the American plants operating on the border violated Mexican environmental laws. Put bluntly, there is no enforcement. As political scientist Stephen Mumme reported in 1995, "Clearly there is much to be done. Current projects and activities fall well short of meeting the infrastructure needs of the border community." The New River, which flows through Mexicali and into the Imperial Valley of California, has been rightfully labeled "the most polluted waterway on earth." At present only 10 percent of Mexico's annual output of 7,000,000 tons of hazardous waste receives adequate treatment. In 1988 only 1 percent of the *maquiladora* operators reported to the EPA that they were sending their hazardous waste back to the United States for treatment, despite the La Paz agreement between the United States and Mexico, which requires the return of all waste to the country of origin. The waste is "poured into clandestine waste dumps and municipal sewers." Americans contribute waste to Mexico as well. Mexicali is inundated each afternoon by smog flowing from the densely populated and automobile-dependent Los Angeles–San Diego area.[44]

The Border Environment Cooperation Commission meets in closed, often unannounced sessions at Ciudad Juárez. It has jurisdiction over 100 kilometers extending along the border in both directions from Juárez–El Paso. No public participation is allowed during its deliberations. Meanwhile the engorged population of Nuevo Laredo and its *maquiladora* complex pump 24,000,000 gallons of untreated sewage into the Rio Grande. The GM plants in Matamoros and Ciudad Juárez and the United States Ink factory at Tijuana have been identified by critics as major polluters that engage in dumping practices prohibited in their homeland.

In the early 1990s pollution victims in Brownsville sued GM and three other firms that enjoy major savings in labor costs by operating in Matamoros. GM operates three factories at Matamoros. Until the suits and the resulting bad publicity forced its hand, the company expelled solvent-laden sewage from its plants by way of open ditches. Donald Williams, a GM plant manager, admitted the problem. The company higher-ups, however, denied responsibility for a surge in the birth of deformed and brainless babies in the area in the late 1980s and early 1990s, blaming a "lack of proper nutrition by their mothers." The other three defendants in the litigation were Magnetek, headed by Andrew Galef, which is a leading electrical components manufacturer; Trico, headed by R. L. Wolf, which is the leading U.S. windshield wiper manufacturer; and Kemet, headed by David McGuire, which is a supplier for Southwestern Bell. Mark Feldstein, a reporter for the Cable News Network, accused Kemet of dumping methylene chloride at intensities "20 to 30 times greater" than what is allowed in the United States. The suit was settled for $17,000,000. American companies still routinely dump dioxin-laden waste in the Matamoros garbage dump. After testing a sample of water from a tap in a Brownsville building, a chemist declared, "No one could live very long drinking that water."[45]

Texas authorities claimed that polluting practices at Brownsville had been "cleaned up," but late in 1994 none of the official positions responsible for the enforcement of NAFTA environmental regulations had even been filled. In 2000, despite many reports of pollution violations by official committees set up by NAFTA, no apparent action had been taken by the authorities to clean up the air or the water. The Environmental Protection Agency has an active role in helping arrange NAFTA environmental oversight procedures, but little or nothing has been accomplished in the major pollution problems that have developed along the New River and the Rio Grande and at the Big Bend National Park, where contaminated air from Mexican coal-fired power plants leaves the countryside shrouded in smog more than half the year. Reduced governmental vigilance is a major cost saver for American and Mexican businessmen, and Mexican authorities hide behind the canard of "national sovereignty" when reacting to the pleas and complaints of American environmentalists. NAFTA negotiator Mickey Kantor inadvertently explained why U.S. regulators have not acted when he described government and business as "two heads connected at the hips."[46]

The Mexican fishing industry exports on a large scale, and Mexican authorities routinely rebuff complaints and charges rendered by American environmentalists. During the mid and late 1990s Mexican negotiators demanded the right to export tuna caught by Mexican fishermen with purse seine nets, which also ensnare dolphins. American negotiator Kantor and Vice President Albert Gore informed President Zedillo that President Clinton "didn't want embarrassing demonstrations of how U.S. laws could be overturned by GATT" and that they would seek a legislative fix in Congress. In 1996 Congress passed the "dolphin death bill," as it was called by its critics, which allowed the use of nets with a finer mesh than that of older nets. The older nets allowed dolphins to escape, but tuna were lost as well. Surprisingly, Greenpeace joined a number of less militant Green organizations in endorsing a "compromise" that permitted "the unlimited sale" of dolphin-lethal tuna in the United States.[47]

Galaxy Latin America and Sky Entertainment, the dominant international communications, news, and entertainment companies in Mexico, cannot be expected to offer the Mexican public a great deal of information about the dumping of pollutants by *maquiladoras* and GM into the river systems and groundwaters of the Mexican north. Galaxy Latin America has a powerful GM presence on its board, and Rupert Murdoch is a director of Sky Entertainment. Nor can we can anticipate dissemination of these concerns from Fox, CBS, NBC, or ABC.[48]

POWERFUL FOREIGNERS AND DOMESTIC ELITES

The privatization of *paraestatales* provided the Americans and Mexicans in ALFA with new opportunities while shedding light on the results of the intimate ties that exist between American high finance and leading Mexican political figures. The Mexicans at the top profited greatly with the influx of American capital, just as they had in the era preceding the revolution.

Until 1995 Telmex, the national telephone company and the second largest enterprise in Mexico, was the only provider of long-distance service in Mexico. That year Salinas opened up the long-distance market to competitors. According to John N. Palmer, the chief executive of Mobile Telecommunications Technologies Corporation, the new consortiums would "encourage the penetration of modern communications services to Mexican business and residential customers." Companies from the United States and Canada would "play the key role in bringing those services southward." By 2000 Telmex had spent $10 billion on modernization and still retained over 70 percent of the market.[49]

In 1995 the directors of Grupo ALFA joined their counterparts at AT&T and Grupo Financiero Bancomer, the second largest bank in Mexico, to form Alestra, the first consortium approved by Salinas. AT&T controls 49 percent of the enterprise, with ALFA holding 25.6 percent and Bancomer 25.4 percent. American participation is actually greater than AT&T's 49 percent, however, because of the 30 percent participation that Citibank and J. P. Morgan Chase have in ALFA. Alestra committed $1 billion to the development of its network. By the late 1990s it had already spent over $450,000,000 and projected even greater expenditures. AT&T's gains in the long-distance business have been realized much more slowly than the company directors expected. Innovations carried out by Carlos Slim Heliu, such as a credit card phone system, have enabled Telmex to retain a predominant position.

President Salinas, a member of the board of directors of Dow Jones, held interests in both sides of the struggle between Telmex and the Alestra partners. The politically powerful Salinas had obtained a private interest in ALFA in the early 1980s. Telmex was purchased by a consortium led by Slim, who was a close Salinas ally, France Telecom, and SBC Communications of Texas (SBC is the parent company of Southwestern Bell). In December 1990 Slim and his partners bought control of Telmex for $1.7 billion. Shortly after the sale the assets of the firm were estimated at $12 billion. Telmex then joined a technology exchange with France Telecom, SBC, Pacific Telesis, and Ameritech. Each of these companies provided Telmex with the necessities of advanced technology and a 10 percent capital infusion. SBC controlled phone service in Texas, California, and Illinois. Its chairman, Edward E. Whitacre Jr., "wanted to rule the telecommunications world." During the 1990s Telmex obtained a 49 percent share in the cable division of Televisa, Mexico's largest media company. Since then, however, Emilio Azcarraga Jean has assumed control of all Televisa operations. The details of these arrangements are not known, and the ties between Telmex—particularly Salinas, Slim, and Southwestern Bell—and its "competition"—Alestra, the Spanish company Telephonica Internacional de España, and GTE—are not fully understood. Related events suggest an underside to Mexican privatization and the reentry of American capital into Mexican communications and transportation services.[50]

Seven other companies joined the contest to provide long-distance service in Mexico. The larger enterprises had American capital to buttress the resources of their Mexican associates. The first consortium to obtain government permission to compete with Telmex was Avantel. Avantel—a combination of Grupo Financiero Banamex–Accival (known as Banacci), a Mexican holding company, and MCI—started with the greatest capitalization of all the new companies. MCI provided 45 percent of the 1.8 billion in capital being invested. MCI and Banamex combined spent $900,000,000 to link thirty-three cities in Mexico. The fiber-optic connection between Mexico City and Monterrey opened on 12 August 1996 with a call from President Zedillo to Benjamin Clariod, the governor of the state of Nuevo León. In 1998 Worldcom, a British concern, took over MCI. In 2001 Citigroup acquired Grupo Financiero Banamex–Accival for $12.5 billion. That action gave Citigroup chairman Sanford Weill and vice chairman Robert Rubin control of the nation's second largest bank and a partnership with MCI in the Mexican long-distance telephone business. It also diversified Citigroup's operations in Mexico and rendered useless the efforts of the U.S. Justice Department to regulate the flow of monies from Mexico to offshore accounts.

Protel, another entry into the communications fray, brought together Mexican investors, who hold 51 percent of the firm, with three American firms—Nextel Communications, LCC International Incorporated, and the Carlyle Group—who together hold the other 49 percent.[51] Another consortium was formed by GTE, which held 49 percent, Bancomer, with 26.5 percent, and Telefonica, with 24.5 percent. Yet another consortium, Arcatel, projected expenditures of $500,000,000. This firm combined the capital of Gustavo de la Garza, the owner of Radio Beep in Mexico City, who holds a 51 percent interest, with that of IXC Communications and Westel of the United States, and Teleglobe of Canada, which own a combined 49 percent of the firm.

In 1997 the directors of Bell Atlantic entered the fray by investing $1 billion in Iusacell of Mexico City. Iusacell offers wireless local telephone service in an industry characterized by an insufficient number of hookups to meet demand. The Bell Atlantic leaders increased their firm's ownership in

Iusacell from 23 to 42 percent, which gave them full control of the company. Their commitment is one of the largest investments by an American firm in Mexico since the advent of NAFTA. The vice chairman of Bell Atlantic, Lawrence T. Babbio Jr., serves in that capacity with the Mexican firm, and a majority of the Grupo Iusacell directors also come from the American firm.

Carlos Peralta Quintero, the head of the Peralta family of Mexico City, was forced to step down as the head of Iusacell because of the scandal that arose from his donation of $50,000,000 to Raúl Salinas while the latter's brother still served as president. Peralta moved $10,000,000 of Salinas's money through the Bankers Trust Corporation of New York "to a Zurich account in the name of Mr. Salinas's wife," $4,700,000 to Bears Stearns, and $15,000,000 "to a small bank in Brussels." Peralta continues to serve on the Iusacell board, but his ties to Raúl made it necessary to place the Americans in direct control of the firm in order to gain approval for the merger from nervous American investors and Mexican officials who had grown "cold" to the deal. The Bell Atlantic directors and Peralta made a marriage of convenience. Bell Atlantic needed Iusacell to obtain market access, and Peralta needed his powerful new allies during government investigations of his multitudinous transactions in Switzerland and Grand Cayman and an offshore money center on the Isle of Man. The list of Iusacell subscribers grew rapidly, reaching 379,000 in 1997. The Atlantic Bell directors, perhaps taking advantage of Peralta's embarrassment, obtained Iusacell on the cheap. They invested $150,000,000 to expand its long-distance and wireless services.[52]

The fleshing out of a successful capitalistic endeavor goes beyond infrastructure development. A successful venture provides individual and privileged opportunity coupled with technological and material advancement in every conceivable area of activity. The interconnectedness demonstrated by Mexican political leaders and the leaders of Citibank, J. P. Morgan Chase, ALFA, and AT&T supports that formula. In 1997 and 1998 Citibank official William R. Rhodes "led the negotiating team for hundreds of foreign creditor banks in their talks with Mexico over the country's tens of billions of dollars in bank debt." Rhodes headed the negotiations with Mexico on behalf of the Banker's Steering Committee, which represented 530 international banks concerned directly or indirectly with Mexico's debt. They successfully renegotiated the obligations, but their conditions required the Mexican government to restrict social spending. That provision and the devaluation of the peso led to enormous hardships for the poor and the collapse of the Mexican middle class. In 1999 the Mexican government acknowledged that 40 percent of its people lived in "extreme poverty," and in

October of that year the World Health Organization reported that 60 percent of the Mexican population suffered from malnutrition. The man in charge of negotiating with the American bankers, Angel Gurría Treviño, was made secretary of foreign relations by President Zedillo. The association recalls that of Matías Romero and Benito Juárez in the 1860s and Adolfo de la Huerta and Alvaro Obregón Salido in the 1920s.[53]

During the late 1990s the Anheuser-Busch Company of Saint Louis increased its already important stake in Mexico's largest brewery, the Grupo Modelo. With a $477,000,000 stake making up 17.7 percent of Modelo, Anheuser-Busch netted a modest $12,000,000 in annual profits from the relationship in the mid 1990s. The Mexican firm, with eight breweries, is the twelfth largest beer producer in the world and markets the popular Corona brand in the United States. It sells Modelo products in over 100 countries. Mexico attracted Anheuser-Busch because it is the seventh largest market in the world for the beverage and demand has increased at a rapid 8 percent annually for the past several years. Anheuser-Busch's investment offered its happy Mexican partner, Pablo Aramburuzabala Ocaranza, greater capitalization and therefore increased advertising and production capacity. In 1999 Aramburuzabala was worth over $1 billion. His seat on the board of Anheuser-Busch allowed him to function as a mediator with the state, affording him the same influence enjoyed by the Mexicans who served on American boards during the Porfiriato.[54]

The relationships between the elite and the powerful in Mexico can be compared to similar configurations in the American business world. In Mexico and other less diverse polities and economies, however, when one party or regime entwines with oligarchic economic elites and multinational companies, the entrenched interests can sometimes become criminal in nature. The insider relationship between Citibank and President Salinas and his brother Raúl led directly to a scandal that shook global confidence in Mexico's political system. The virtual takeover of the Mexican transportation and communications infrastructure by a handful of domestic elites and much more powerful American consortiums reveals the advantages that insiders have had.

MANEUVERS IN CHIAPAS

The U.S. Department of State claims that its military assistance to Mexico has been legal because the United States "provides material assistance to the Government of Mexico, not to individual units, while training is provided to individual members of the Mexican military, who are later assigned to units." In 1996 the Mexican government bought and installed four telecommunications transmitters in Chiapas and acquired seventy-three Hueys from the U.S. government. Fifty-three of the Hueys were reconditioned at San Antonio. This equipment supplemented the helicopters, laser designators, night vision devices, and Hercules transports that the Mexican government had purchased from the United States during the early 1990s, items valued at $400,000,000. The helicopters ostensibly were intended for deployment in Sinaloa, Sonora, and Baja California, where they would be used in the interdiction of drug traffic. The arrangement freed up the movement to Chiapas of other helicopters already in Mexico, some with fresh paint and markings.

The Mexican armed forces deployed the Hueys during 1997 at newly constructed bases in and around Chiapas. At the same time the government began construction of a naval base capable of docking supply and warships on the Pacific Coast between Arriaga and Tapachula. The claim that the military equipment was intended solely for the War on Drugs rang hollow. Although the General Accounting Office reported the "misuse" of the helicopters against the rebels in 1997, the U.S. Department of Defense continued to help equip the Mexican army. In 1997 the United States "transferred four C-26 transport aircraft to Mexico." In 1999 dozens of the Hueys were found "unfit for service" and were reportedly returned by the Mexican armed forces to the United States.

In contrast to the official American presence in Chiapas, humanitarians, who operated at the discomfort of the authorities in both governments, offered aid to the needy. In April 1998 the Pastors for Peace delivered thirteen tons of medicine, clothing, and food that had been contributed by a variety of American groups to the impoverished Mayan Indians. The U.S. authorities provided nothing.

The American military assumed a critical role in Chiapas through aerial photography and the equipping and training of troops. The latter two activities were disingenuously justified by U.S. officials as part of the War on Drugs because the rules imposed by the U.S. government for military aid projects required the equipment and training to be employed in the northern part of Mexico. In fact it is a simple matter to transfer war materiel from the north to Chiapas and to replace it with the American exports. Many of the commanding officers in Chiapas studied at the U.S. Army's School of the Americas (SOA) in Georgia. Between 1996 and 1998 the American military trained 3,200 Mexican soldiers at a cost of $41,100,000 at seventeen bases in the United States, creating the Grupos Aeromoviles de Fuerzas Especiales (GAFE), or Airborne Special Forces. During the same period the U.S. Department of State financed the training of 603 Mexican troops under a program called IMET. The U.S. government also gave the Mexican military $3,000,000 in special assistance for the War on Drugs. Again, State Department officials announced that this effort was part of the War on Drugs and had nothing to do with the suppression of the pathetically armed Zapatistas.

Mexican military leaders, however, expressly viewed the purpose of GAFE, the military aid, and the other training programs in a broader context, one that included counterinsurgency. In 1998 the Clinton administration, in the face of pointed criticism, insisted on the explanation that the program applied only to drugs despite the fact that the 7th Special Forces Group at the John F. Kennedy School of Special Warfare at Fort Bragg, North Carolina, was in charge of the training. This unit advised indigenous troops in Bolivia, Colombia, Ecuador, Laos, Peru, South Vietnam, and Thailand during uprisings between the 1960s and 1980s. In Central America it prepared the counterinsurgency forces of El Salvador and Honduras during the mid 1980s.[55]

The graduates of the SOA and GAFE have committed atrocities in strife-ridden Chiapas, Oaxaca, and Guerrero, and in Jalisco. Three of the officers originally placed in charge of operations in Chiapas after the rebellion began have been cited by Amnesty International for human rights violations. All three—Generals Gaston Menchaca Arias, Juan López Ortiz, and Manuel García Ruiz—attended the SOA. Following the Zapatista uprising, Menchaca Arias served as the head of the military district that includes San Cristobal de las Casas. López Ortiz, who took part in the fight against the "Army of the Poor" in Guerrero during the 1970s, ordered his men to treat the Zapatistas as "criminals." Mexicans remember his Guerrero campaign because of the large number of citizens who "disappeared." In 1994 his troops massacred peasants at Ocosingo, Chiapas. Soldiers under García Ruiz occupied Zapatista strong points and were used against rebels in Oaxaca, where numerous civilians also "disappeared."

In 1998 the distinguished Mexican magazine *Proceso* identified four SOA graduates, Colonel Augusto Moises García Ochoa, Lieutenant Colonel René Herrera Huizar, General Luis Montiel López, and General Fernando Perez Casanova, as under investigation for suspected participation in the drug trade. These suspects were using equipment sent by the United States allegedly to interdict the drug trade.[56]

General José Rueben Rivas Peña, who completed instruction at the SOA in 1980, served as the field commander of the Mexican army in Chiapas in 1994. His intelligence officers already knew a great deal about the civil unrest and prepared a comprehensive plan of counterinsurgency. Article "r" announced some of his intentions: "To secretly organize civilian groups, among them small ranch owners and individuals characterized by a high sense of patriotism, who, under our command, will assist our operations."[57] This step led to the empowerment of local right-wing extremists, including paramilitary groups. Other graduates of the SOA holding key positions in Chiapas included Colonel Julian Guerrero Barrios, who studied commando operations, and Colonel German Antonio Bautista, whose troops entered Tzotzil communities in Chiapas shortly before the elections of 6 July 1997 and threatened the inhabitants. Other important SOA graduates involved with Chiapas include General Carlos Demetrio Gaytan Ochoa, the commander of the "Gaytan" task force at Monte Libano, and General Enrique Alonso Garrido of the 83rd Infantry at Rancho Nuevo, where Native American inhabitants were threatened.

In July 1997 General Mario Renan Castillo Fernández, who received instruction in the GAFE program at Fort Bragg, served as the commander of the 7th military region in Chiapas and masterminded the counterinsurgency effort against the Zapatistas. In July he participated as an "honorary witness" in the agreement reached by the governor of Chiapas with the paramilitary terrorist group Paz y Justicia, in which the gunmen were given over $450,000 for "agricultural and infrastructure development." In December 1997 Paz y Justicia members, using military arms, slaughtered forty-five unarmed Tzotzil supporters of the Zapatistas at the pueblo of Acteal as they fled the church where they had been praying. Police and military personnel manned barricades in the vicinity of the atrocity and periodically fired their weapons into the air. The killing continued for five hours. Most of those killed were women and children. The American-trained GAFE manned barricades at Majomut only 2,413 meters, or five minutes by truck, from the slaughter. They did not intervene. Less than two days after the killings they moved closer to Acteal and restricted the movement of civilians. The lines of command for the police security forces and GAFE are distinct, but in the Acteal case it became clear that they were coordinated when GAFE moved in to close off communications and transportation. The exact time of their arrival and their positions at the time of the killings is unclear. Less than two weeks later the Mexican special forces began periodic sweeps through Acteal and neighboring communities in a search of Zapatista arms. In reality, this was an effort to demoralize the Zapatista sympathizers and encourage government supporters. Drive-by shootings were a virtually daily occurrence at Acteal in May 2000. The gunmen usually fired over the heads of the pedestrians and above homes—but not always.

The Mexican army was well prepared for the paramilitary aspect of the struggle in Chiapas. In addition to the 3,200 GAFE troops prepared in 1996 and 1997 and the 500 men who attended the SOA between 1953 and 1992, American military officers attached to the American embassy have long offered counterinsurgency courses to their counterparts at the Estado Mayor in Mexico City. Despite official denials, the existence of this program during the 1960s and 1970s is certain. The curriculum, originally established to counter the "Soviet threat," includes training in the use of marginal indigenous groups against their neighbors. That strategy, which surfaced in the slaughter at Acteal and continued there into 2000, is standard fare in modern counterinsurgency operations. In 1997 the director of the FBI complicated the scene in southern Mexico by ill-advisedly sending two agents to Oaxaca to teach security police how to identify and eliminate subversives.[58]

Another, more threatening, armed guerrilla group, the Ejército Popular Revolucionario (EPR, the Popular Revolutionary Army) surfaced in Guerrero in 1996. The EPR vowed "fierce opposition to Mexican government policies favoring free-market economics and closer ties to the U.S." In 1996 the guerrillas even threatened to attack the resort of Cancún, popular with American tourists, and swore "to halt the continuing sale of our land to Yanqui investors."[59] In the first week of December the Mexican army occupied and searched for EPR members at Pijijiapan in Chiapas and Loma Bonita in Oaxaca, once predominately American communities that had been invaded by their Mexican neighbors in 1914, forcing the American colonists to evacuate. The army leaders believed that Loma Bonita was a center of support for the EPR insurrection. In June 1998 the Mexican army employed its high technology against the EPR in the otherwise impossibly rugged mountains of Guerrero. They inflicted a terrible defeat on the small EPR by ambushing a detachment, killing eleven, wounding five, and arresting twenty-one.[60]

Favorable outcomes for the peasantry in political disputes are increasingly rare, but, sometimes, when Mexican indigenous people stand fast in defense of group interests they earn more than the cultural rewards of community pride and identity. On Friday 10 January 1997 President Zedillo awarded 32,000 Yaquis in Sonora control over 1,140,000 acres of land in the Yaqui River Valley and surrounding territories. This land was invaded by Spanish *conquistadores* and then colonized by provincial elites. They were followed by hundreds of Americans, including the owners of the Wheeler Land Company and the Richardson Construction Company, and, finally, President Obregón, who retained a considerable portion for himself when the Americans sold their holdings to the government. The land has now returned to indigenous control. President Zedillo issued the residents a land grant and promised to provide treated drinking water and a gift of forty pesos per resident annually, presumably for seeds.[61]

CULTURE AND RELIGION

At the beginning of the twenty-first century, well over 500,000 Americans were officially registered residents of Mexico. Most are retirees and immigrants to urban areas. Border residents and the employees of American companies make up the remainder. Following the practice initiated by those who moved to Mexico during the Porfiriato, the Americans often concentrate in identifiable colonies in the cities and countryside.

Americans are not as discernible in the cities as they were in the earlier era, but they provide a cultural and physical presence in Mexico's multicultural landscape. Over 350,000 of them live in Mexico City alone, and Tijuana and Guadalajara each claim in excess of 50,000. The border cities of Ciudad Juárez and Matamoros have 21,461 and 12,000, respectively, while picturesque Mérida in the Yucatán Peninsula claims 4,500. Those using tourist cards, which grant six-month stays and can be replaced simply by leaving the country and reentering, double the total of American residents in Mexico to over 1,000,000. In addition, in 1996 and 1997 an average of over 20,000,000 American tourists visited Mexico.[62]

Many people are partly American by family lineage but Mexican in citizenship. Some of them, especially those in cities like Hermosillo, Monterrey, Torreón, Chihuahua, Cuauhtémoc, and Nuevo Casas Grandes, are descendants of the first great wave of American immigrants to Mexico during the 1890s and 1900s. Mixed marriages have resulted in countless children with citizenship in both Mexico and the United States. American retirees choose Mexico for the low cost of living and often scenic surroundings. Centers such as Ajijic at Lake Chapala, a mere half-hour from Guadalajara, are populated by fairly large groups of retired Americans, many of them former members of the armed services. Other retirees have concentrated in Alamos, Sonora, San Miguel de Allende, and Oaxaca, where colonial architecture and traditional lifestyles are venerated from within the confines of modern comforts.

By the late 1990s the media were highly developed in Mexico and had deep connections with American multinational companies. Grupo Televisa, a television and radio conglomerate of 200 stations in Mexico and the southern United States, was also the largest seller of Spanish-language magazines in the world. Bankers in New York, Florida, Texas, Arizona, California, and London and a wide array of television broadcasters and investment bankers joined this important complex. Televisa partnered with Sky Entertainment Services of Los Angeles to broadcast via satellite to remote areas of Mexico. In 2000 naturalized American Rupert Murdoch owned 30 percent of Sky. Murdoch, owner of the Los Angeles Dodgers baseball team, planned to televise his games to as much of the world as possible, and broadcasting in Mexico was the first step. Tele-Communications Inc., the largest cable operator in the United States, and Oranizacoes Globo of Brazil were the other participants. Guillermo Canedo White, the chief financial officer of Televisa, regarded the Sky venture as his firm's "most important project" because of the potential of reaching the entire Mexican and Latin American middle class on a hemisphere-wide communications grid within the next twenty years. Patricio Milmo (Mullins) would be proud to know that Emilio Azcarraga Milmo helped create Televisa.[63]

Galaxy Latin America, headquartered in Miami, is the alternative to Sky Entertainment and Televisa. José Antonio Ríos, the president of Galaxy, was also creating a satellite-based television network that would embrace Mexico and the rest of Latin America. In 1996 the U.S. and Mexican governments contracted with Galaxy and Sky for these two companies to beam entertainment, news, and advertising into Mexico. They also planned to send Spanish programming to American markets along the border and in Florida, where large numbers of Mexican Americans and Cuban Americans and immigrants reside. The directors of the General Motors Corporation in Detroit control Galaxy through their Hughes Electronics division, which holds a majority of the stock. Their minority partners are MVS Multivision, a Mexican pay-television company, Grupo Cisneros, which runs a cable television network in Venezuela, and Televisão Abril, a Brazilian communications conglomerate. The partners made an initial outlay of $800,000,000 to ensure the project's success. The participation of cooperative Latin American elites benefits these ventures, as the *New York Times* reported in 1996:

> Although the countries in the region share similar cultures and common languages, they have different legal and economic systems. Any company hoping to tap the entire market must balance control from corporate headquarters with the flexibility needed by local partners to handle the different laws, tax structures, and currencies in Latin America's mosaic of nations.[64]

The new American presence in Mexico had a broader cultural and geopolitical context, as Ríos noted: "Latin Americans will have a common telecommunications bond; there will be a common point of reference for all of Latin America."[65]

The American-owned television networks also entered Mexican broadcasting. Westinghouse subsidiary CBS and General Electric's broadcasting division NBC, along with cable networkers such as Time Warner unit CNN and Univision of Miami, gave Mexican viewers and U.S. citizens living in Mexico an American corporate outlook on the news and provided popular programming. In the late 1990s the directors of NBC sought an even broader opening into the Mexican television market first, and then into all of Latin America. The greater American presence includes an English-language news channel. The staff of Telenoticias, a division of CBS headquartered in Miami, underscores the new interconnectedness of American and Mexican communications companies. It employs newscasters from eight countries, and Cuban-born Ricardo Brown serves as the company's news director.[66]

The growth of hemispheric broadcasting through the vehicle of American-owned satellites and cable networks stood in stark contrast to the multinational efforts of the late 1970s and early 1980s to create a media system controlled by Third World governments through UNESCO. Headed by the director general of UNESCO, Amadaou Mahtar M'Bow of Senegal, the UN agency attempted to counterbalance what its leadership saw as a monopoly on the flow of information to the underdeveloped world and the denigration of cultures. President Ronald Reagan saw the UNESCO effort as "anti-Western" and appointed Jean Gerard to confront M'Bow as the American representative to the agency. Girard informed the UNESCO leader of the American withdrawal from the agency on 31 December 1984. The British resignation followed. The U.S. action alone cost UNESCO 25 percent of its revenues. Economically disabled, the media project foundered. M'Bow left office in 1987 and UNESCO abandoned its effort to create a Third World communications alternative. That history has left Sky and Galaxy, largely American-controlled private entities, without an effective challenge in Mexican and Latin American television. The role of the wealthy Azcarraga interests in the multinational conglomerate parallels the Porfirian-era relationships of García Teruel with the Laguna, John Deere, and Cargill corporations.[67]

In recent decades television exposure has contributed to a dramatic growth of public interest in American sports. A broad base of public participation and even municipal basketball leagues sprang up across the nation. The games between teams from the communities of General Zua Zua, headed by Miguel González, and Cienega de las Flores in Nuevo León are spirited and intense. During the 1990s the schoolchildren of the Tarahumara pueblo of Quirare in the Sierra Madre of Chihuahua waited patiently for more than a year before their makeshift and worn-out basketball backboard and hoop could be replaced. At the same time, in the barranca below them in the Copper Canyon complex, the people of Batopilas gathered in the evening on the narrow street that surrounds the plaza with its single light and watched the youth play basketball on a court that takes up most of the area.

Reflecting the growing interest in spectator sports, numerous baseball players from United States teams, especially the Los Angeles Dodgers and San Diego Padres, have played in Mexico. American scouts and training personnel also work there. Baseball is probably the second national sport, trailing only soccer in popularity. In 1996 the Padres played a well-attended three-game series against the New York Metropolitans in Monterrey, amid speculation that the American Major League would expand to Mexico City in the near future.

During the 1990s the Dallas Cowboys played exhibition games in Mexico with various opponents. In the mid 1990s they played an exhibition game with the Houston Oilers at the 105,000-seat Estadio Azteca in Mexico City before a sellout crowd. The Cowboy's general manager, Tex Schram, demonstrated that media exposure was the key to success. The American advertising industry needed no such instruction, promoting the images that its leaders deemed necessary to sell products in Mexico.

American motion pictures are not only seen in Mexico; they are produced there as well. John Wayne used the Chupadero site outside the city of Durango for many of his westerns, and, as a result, many American viewers equated the "Wild West" with the landscapes of the state of Durango. Wayne, a popular figure in Durango, built a hacienda-type home in a draw overlooking the valley that runs northeasterly from the state capital. Another site near the state capital was used for the filming of *Fat Man and Little Boy,* a film about the making of the atomic bomb starring Paul Newman. Farther north, Rupert Murdoch, the owner of the Fox Studios, installed a studio at Rosarito Beach. The first film he made there was *Titanic.* Americans made up the overwhelming majority of technical personnel employed during its filming, despite the large Mexican film industry. A large tank filled with chlorine-treated water was used to make the movie. The discharges of effluent ruined the neighboring fishing village at Popotla Beach. After *Titanic* was released Steven Spielberg and the producers of the James Bond films released *Fox Baja.*[68]

All of the major Hollywood film companies enjoyed distribution in Mexico by the end of the decade. American films played in all of the larger theaters of Mexico City and could often be found in small towns. The Mexican public generally received Hollywood films well, but occasionally they complained about the gratuitous violence that pervaded American cinema. During the 1980s the outcry against the "glorification" of death squads in *Cobra,* a film starring Sylvester Stallone, provoked a public reaction at a time when the use of police and government violence swept Mexico's neighbors in Central America. Many of the Mexican populace who were interested in politics believed that the violence in Nicaragua, Honduras, El Salvador, and Guatemala was supported by the U.S. government. Boycotts against *Cobra* ensued, and the cinema owners of Guadalajara agreed that it should not be shown in that city during its first run.

NAFTA gave more prominence to the increasing presence of American corporate culture in Mexico. Companies offered weekly seminars to their employees on the importance of punctuality, sobriety, thrift, and hard work to achieve personal and material advancement. In reality, the development of American corporate culture was gradual, not sudden. Advertising, foundation-based health and agricultural programs, and the introduction of sports, cuisine, and cultural indoctrination all helped to "Americanize" Mexico.

The growth and promotion of Protestant individualist values have been a corollary aspect of American expansion throughout the history of the United States. Baptist, Episcopalian, Methodist, Latter-Day Saints, Pentecostal, and Presbyterian missionaries entered Mexico to uplift the people and rescue them from "Romanism." In recent years the number of American Christian sects in Mexico has multiplied to over 300, with the northern border area playing host to at least 250 separate Protestant groups and missionaries from the United States.

The Mormons had considerable success, and they endured in Chihuahua, Sonora, and Mexico City despite the expulsions and violence they suffered during the revolution. In 1978 the church's leaders opened a temple in Mexico City, where other denominations also prosper. At the end of 1994 the Latter-Day Saints announced the establishment of a stake there. In 1998 a polygamous sect of Mormons concentrated at Cuauhtémoc enjoyed considerable local influence. A prosperous group that includes merchants and farmers, its members have held city offices. The authorities quietly overlook their marital practices, which are in violation of the law. There are some 2,700,000 Mormons in Latin America, with the largest number of them located in Mexico. The appeal of Mormonism, like that of the charismatic sects, centers on Mexican family values coupled with American individualism. That combination enables new urban workers and commercialized former peasants to maintain family ties while distancing themselves from practices such as fiestas, masses, and ancestor memorials that consume individual savings and distribute them throughout the local community.[69]

Well before NAFTA codified the process, the American-Mexican commercial relationship had deepened to the point of establishing a new culture in Mexico. From Coca-Cola and Pepsi-Cola to Marlboro Cigarettes, prepackaged chickens from Ralston Purina, Chryslers, Fords, baseball, movies, American football, Tejano music star Emilio Navaira, and artist Barry Wolfryd, U.S. products and the visions that sell them have permeated Mexican society. In 1996 Navaira undertook what he called the "NAFTA tour" of Mexico. He signed albums for sale at Wal-Marts in Monterrey and Mexico City.[70] Wolfryd moved to Mexico City from Los Angeles in the 1970s, developing an art form known as New Jersey–Aztec. He acquired a taste for things Mexican while growing up in East Los Angeles. His work reflects the cultural miscegenation that he saw.

> You might see Lil' Lulu with an Aztec chief roasting marshmallows and hotdogs over the flames of an animal. It's a purgatory scene and the definition of a universe that's just developing; it's also an attempt to explain that universe. I'm taking some elements 400 years old and others 20 years old and expressing their coming together.[71]

Wolfryd presents a more serious side when he portrays the "disenfranchisement, abuse and exploitation of street children." He mirrors the concerns expressed by some people in the First World when they witness the economic hardships endured by the poor in underdeveloped countries. Those concerns are addressed through the intervention of UNICEF and UNESCO.

The geographic proximity of the United States and Mexico and the growing complex of relationships between the countries have led to the inevitable mixing of the cultures. The blending process was especially evident in the Mexican north and American Southwest. Author Carlos Fuentes and historian W. Dirk Raat call this syncretic area "MexAmerica." Today, it extends for hundreds of miles north and south of the border. The cuisines, music, housewares, architecture, pastimes, languages, and decor of the neighboring peoples have mixed into a delightful new culture. While American interests of a baser sort shaped the evolution of casinos, red light districts, beach resorts, and *maquiladoras* just across the border, south and north of MexAmerica the process of immigration and the blending of cultures continued unabated throughout the 1990s.

The whole American people have a part in the new world order in which the U.S.-Mexico relationship holds special significance. In the nineteenth century the frontiersmen and soldiery fought the wars in Texas and Mexico, the bankers financed Mexican modernization and supported dictatorship, the industrialists brought transportation and communications technology, and the miners, technicians, ranchers, and farmers went there to work and settle down. Many took advantage of ethnic discrimination and all of them enjoyed a stronger currency. In the modern era the Americans control the making and marketing of most products available in Wal-Mart, Price Club, and similar American-owned stores in urban Mexico. Consumers who wish to can completely immerse themselves in U.S. culture by acquiring goods ranging from headboards, mattresses, and bed sheets to use at night, to alarm clocks, appliances, foods, clothing, and automobiles for use during their waking hours. At the end of the century, the advertising of American products, the promises of prosperity, and the call for Mexicans to abandon nationalism and embrace NAFTA represented a

> rhetoric of power [that] all too easily produces an illusion of benevolence when deployed in an imperial setting. Yet it is a rhetoric whose most damning characteristic is that it has been used before . . . with deafening repetitive frequency in the modern period, by the British, the French, the Belgians, the Japanese, the Russians, and now the Americans.[72]

Mexico's ideology of free trade in the late 1990s was based on faith rather than empirical evidence. The need of the American financial elite to advance its position became, once again, a powerful force in the financial decisions of Mexican leaders. Doubts about how free trade served the interests of the underdeveloped agricultural sector of the Mexican economy and small retailers were not allowed to soften the discussion.

Despite short-term economic setbacks in Mexico between 1980 and 1999 and repeated failures in the Third World, free trade might work in Mexico, as any fair-minded critic would admit. Some questions, however, remain. Will the Mexican masses benefit if American capital is attracted only by low wages? Will the owners of new infrastructure improve services if the Mexican consumers cannot pay the higher costs? Will the uneven economic relationship allow Mexicans to act independently of American political and economic power? And, finally, can Mexican culture survive in recognizable form given the onslaught, not just of material products from the United States, but also of higher levels of American television, advertising, and corporate culture?

Conclusion
Imperial America

In the United States political power flows from economic power,
not the other way around.

                    Tom Wicker, *Nation*, 17 June 1996

The American presence in Mexico constitutes a continuing story in which
thousands of new faces appear every day in the midst of profound conti-
nuities. By 2000 the descendants of immigrants from the United States lived
in virtually every town in Mexico, and every city had a visible American
presence. American anthropologists and archaeologists scoured the most remote regions, American sociologists examined urban complexities, and
American historians searched the archives. Many other Americans, retirees
and those seeking escape, went to Mexico with high expectations. Some have
stayed, and others have left in disappointment.

By 2000 the Mexican presence in the United States had also grown to
impressive proportions. The maize of long-marginalized Native Americans
had become the basic staple in omnipresent Mexican restaurants. Mexican
art and architecture could be found in Montana and New York, and Mexican music could be heard everywhere. The southwestern states became bilin-
gual. Mexican workers were a major force in Chicago. Oaxacans raised mush-
rooms on truck farms in eastern Pennsylvania and marketed them in New
York City. Universities offered de facto Ph.D. programs in Mexican history,
albeit under the rubric of Latin American history. In Mexico, Mexican political leaders prospered with degrees from Harvard, Yale, and Nebraska,
while academic leaders used American doctoral degrees as passports to higher
status. The poorest of Mexican workers, encountered in Michoacán or even
Chiapas, might tell an American acquaintance that he had lived in Chicago,
Houston, or Los Angeles. American consumer goods were essential elements
of the marketplace, and Wal-Mart and Taco Bell were well established.

Millions of Mexicans lived in the United States, including 500,000 in Ma-
hattanlán, the Mexican barrio in New York, and close to a million Americans lived in Mexico. Millions more visited every year. Tens of thousands

intermarried, as did their offspring, despite the fact that millions of people still had only symbolic or stereotypic visions of the others' beliefs and motives. By 2000 the cultures and economies of Mexicans and Americans interacted in myriad ways. Mexicans and Americans had become integrated to an extent that American leaders could not have foreseen 135 years before.

During the 1990s wildly unequal economic growth and benefits in Mexico exacerbated poverty and led to social banditry, such as the kidnapping of rich individuals and the insurrectionary conditions represented by the Zapatistas and ERP. Meanwhile, social displacement caused by the privatization of land and economic hardship led not only to crime and social unrest but also to the flow of poor and poorly educated migrants, who entered the United States without legal sanction.

The privatization of agricultural lands in 1992 unleashed considerable amounts of capital for investment, offering that sector of the Mexican economy a running start. Unfortunately, the admission of American grain to the Mexican marketplace that was allowed under the provisions of NAFTA and the removal of government price supports for Mexican grain produced uneven competition. Because products from family-sized Mexican farms are labor-intensive and therefore more costly, these farmers could not compete with American agricultural corporations that, through economies of scale, could offer lower-priced products. This economically driven form of enclosure will mean ruin over the next few decades for most of the over 10,000,000 Mexican rancheros and farm families who earn their livelihood on tiny plots of land in *ejidos* and collective farms. Between 1995 and 2000 over 600,000 of them left the land, many of them abandoning the homesteads of revered ancestors. Their hardships have contributed to the flow of unskilled and poorly paid labor to Mexico's cities, border zones, and the southwestern United States. The United States Immigration and Naturalization Service reports that some 2,700,000 illegal Mexican immigrants resided in the United States by 1996. They were joined by 89,000 legal Mexican immigrants in 1995, 163,500 in 1996, and 146,000 in 1997. Since 1988 an average of 150,000 undocumented Mexican immigrants have entered the United States each year. The migrating poor will continue to depress working-class wages in the border area.[1]

Mexico was the first formally legitimated nation that the United States encountered as it began to disseminate its values, doctrines, and practices in less economically and technologically advanced nations. A small group of merchants and financiers, led by Moses Taylor, the New York bondholders of the Mexican debt, and then J. P. Morgan, James Stillman, and George Baker, pioneered American expansion into Mexico and the Third World.

They planned for an American empire by laying undersea cables, building and consolidating shipping lines and railroads, and controlling the debts of weaker nations. In Mexico they started by financing government debts and then took over infrastructure, industry, and real estate development. In the rest of the Third World they became junior partners with the British, joining syndicates in South America, Africa, and Asia.

In Mexico the financiers were quickly followed by the infrastructure men. The most powerful were Rosecrans, Palmer, Scott, Harriman, and Huntington. Then came the large and small investors in industry, agriculture, and ranching, including the Dodges, the Guggenheims, the Hearsts, and the Du Ponts. They were followed by the settlers. In the late nineteenth and early twentieth centuries, in the wake of their Mexican experience, they financed and engineered railroads in Peru and established telephone and telegraph companies in South America, plantations in Central America, and mining operations in Africa. Today, we find American oilmen in Indonesia, American ranchers in South America, American timber companies throughout Latin America, and American mining interests in Liberia and Ghana.

The influence of American money, technology, and ideas has been a mixed blessing for the Mexicans. Often, vested American economic interests influenced U.S. policymakers at the expense of democratic ideals, as evident in their opposition to Sebastián Lerdo de Tejada, their support of Porfirio Díaz, and their help in the overthrow of Francisco Madero and the unseating of Venustiano Carranza. Despite this, American values have sometimes influenced the Mexicans in valuable ways throughout the 135 years between the end of the American Civil War and the end of the twentieth century, reinforcing the Mexican thirst for democratic government. The American dream has become a symbol of progress for many among the elites in the Third World. All too often, however, the ideals of the Americans are contradicted in practice by their support for monarchies in the Middle East or military dictatorships and civilian oligarchical regimes in Latin America. On the positive side, American health research programs, along with their Western European and United Nations counterparts, have contributed to the development of immunization programs and cures for tropical diseases such as malaria.

The important role of special economic interests in shaping the policies of the United States toward Mexico is an integral part of the "strategic interests" consistently invoked by officials of the U.S. Department of State. Appointees of the department often displayed utter disregard toward the middle-class or less influential American citizens with interests in Mexico when they were in trouble and approached the embassy for some kind of relief or consideration. Although larger interests also experienced considerable official indifference, especially on the eve of the two world wars, those at the highest financial and industrial levels clearly had the advantage of influence, and they often were able to gain representation and compensation as a result. U.S. government support for the murderous regime of General Augusto Pinochet in Chile during the 1970s represents the opportunistic and amoral strategies adopted by these public employees in cases where major American economic interests, such as the copper companies, and relatively minor political interests are at stake.

The American experience in Mexico offers a partial answer to the question of why the United States has so frequently supported oppressive tyrants with material aid, even while criticizing other governments for doing the same. Overriding material concerns, specifically the desire to extract wealth without opposition despite moral pronouncements, prompted financiers, railroad men, and ranchers to support military strongman Díaz against democratically elected Lerdo. Subsequently they backed Victoriano Huerta. Wilson supported Huerta with arms for over six months, hoping that the Mexican dictator could restore order, because he respected American property interests. Next the American financial elite briefly supported Francisco Villa but then shifted to Carranza as the lesser of two evils. Finally they lent their support to Alvaro Obregón Salido and Plutarcho Elías Calles. In every case the powerful Americans in the private sector had a far-reaching influence on official U.S. policy. During the 1990s those sectors of the American business community seeking relief from the demands of American labor supported President Bill Clinton and Treasury Secretary Robert E. Rubin in the approval of NAFTA. Meanwhile, they rushed to help Presidents Carlos Salinas de Gortari and Ernesto Zedillo Ponce de León in their privatization efforts.

The American elites' continuing interest in access to strategic resources in other parts of the world is an integral part of U.S. policymaking. The interests of elite American property holders and investors has been the most important factor in relations between the United States and other nations throughout the Western Hemisphere, outweighing objections to dictatorships in the countries in question even in the cases represented by "Papa Doc" Duvalier, the Somoza patriarchs, and the Argentine, Brazilian, Chilean, Uruguayan, and Central American generals of the 1970s and 1980s. Although the CIA-supported overthrow of the democratic government of Guatemala in 1954, the boycott of Nicaraguan products in 1980, and the ensuing support for the Contras were explained by the U.S. government in purely political terms, it is clear that a perceived nationalistic danger to the elaborate structure of American land ownership and trade hegemony in Central America was the deeper concern. Cooperative collaborating elites gained power as a result of U.S. intervention.

In Africa, American support for the deployment of Belgian troops in Zaire by the North Atlantic Treaty Organization during the early 1960s provides another example of a misleading political emphasis given to strategies rooted in the effort to control strategic resources. Zaire contained one of the world's largest copper producing complexes, and American support for the creation of a client state run by a right-wing dictator instead of his nationalistic and left-wing counterpart ensured continued Western ownership of the copper mines. The violent, CIA-supported overthrow of the Sukarno government in oil-rich Indonesia underscores the mix of political and economic considerations behind American activism in the creation of client regimes. American corporate leaders and liberal and conservative U.S. administrations have worked with these antidemocratic regimes, including Nigeria in the mid 1990s, because they supported private enterprise and free trade, which were controlled by American elites.

Middle-class Americans were also a strong cultural force in Mexico, and they remain so today. During the twentieth century their actions and attitudes reinforced the Mexicans' need to participate more fully in public affairs. Today American immigrants—retirees, spouses, scholars, students, and workers—continue to bring the American dream to Mexico. Their complexity of interests and activities sometimes creates an impression of fractionalization. Yet if we remember that most applied themselves to an occupation in order to survive, then we will understand why the main thrust of day-to-day middle-class American activity in Mexico has been in the workplace and in home life. This vision of individualism, competition, efficiency, religious practice, free markets, social mobility, and democracy was and continues to be passed to Mexico's people with an intensity possible only between neighbors. As Americans have immigrated to Mexico on a massive scale, Hollywood movies, television shows, fast-food joints, baseball, blues, disco, jazz, and folk and rap music have permeated Mexican culture.

The American dream represents a unique mix in which Western ideas about progress and individualism combine with a preoccupation with individual perfectibility and a belief that consumerism represents the ultimate path to human happiness. These American values and ideals transcend even the attraction of electoral democracy and political liberty. At its deepest level the American dream teaches that individuals are perfectible when emphasis is placed on education, personal and public hygiene, and physical fitness. The search for individual happiness has an even more common course. It is achieved through the materialism that developed alongside the growth of American businesses, first in Mexico during the late nineteenth century and now in the rest of the Third World. Happiness through consumerism is achieved by competition, efficiency, and productivity. In daily life the people of Mexico and the Third World learn these lessons via advertising, television programs, and Hollywood movies that promise fulfillment through the acquisition of elegant clothing and sporty cars.

The new individualism has replaced the community and family economic and cultural commitments once found in the traditional villages of the countryside. A major cultural component of the change has been the rise of Protestantism. The American Protestant sects that grew in Mexico during the nineteenth century are now flourishing in Brazil and Guatemala and spreading to the rest of Latin America. It relieves individuals of the responsibility to donate their savings to community welfare through fiesta rituals, and it offers them the right to communicate directly with God, removing the village priests from their mediating role between the deity and the people.[2]

America is an imperial force in Mexico because U.S. government authorities and privileged American citizens assert their power there in search of advantages. Beyond their personal resources, they use the World Bank, the International Monetary Fund, and multinational banks and corporations as instruments of that power. With their demands for reducing investment in social programs that would benefit Mexico's citizens and awarding budget priorities to debt payments for foreign creditors, the leaders of these institutions emphasize the goal of development. This ideology distinguishes them from middle-class Americans who hold more democratic beliefs. The elites who participate in these institutions are distinct from their counterparts during the age of European colonialism, when the rich and powerful sought the direct exploitation of openly enslaved peoples.

The attempts to link the economies and peoples of Mexico and the United States have always been problematic and sometimes disastrous, but they have also been mutually beneficial. The benefits, however, are lopsided, since the continuing relationship indicates roles for Mexican labor in American industrialism and American capital in the Mexican marketplace. Probable benefits include an increased per capita output for Mexico, which could potentially relieve the Mexican government of its onerous national debt by creating a larger economic base and providing a substantial marketplace for both Americans and Mexicans.

The challenge of and problem with NAFTA, however, lie in the idea of economic growth induced and effectively controlled by capitalists from outside Mexico rather than from within. Under the coordinated plan of trade and investments represented by ADRs and NAFTA, the Mexican leaders are attempting to bypass the gradual, centuries-long, internalized process of commercial and then industrial growth that acculturated the peoples of Western Europe, the United States, and Japan. Mexican prosperity, like that of the Four Tigers of Asia, depends upon outside investments and buyers and oscillates accordingly. In Mexico's case the outsiders are Americans. Unlike the Four Tigers, Mexico is a geographically large and socially diverse nation. It has the world's thirteenth largest economy and a population of approximately 100,000,000, half of whom live in what the government admits is extreme poverty. The rural population—30 percent of Mexico's citizens—lacks educational opportunities and will not be able to participate in an economic expansion in either the short or the mid term, except as menial laborers.

NAFTA can bring Mexico more prosperity if it avoids the pitfalls that trapped the Díaz program, which was driven by foreign capital and government expenditures. That crisis, which began in the last years of the nineteenth century, left the Mexican state with fewer monies for social programs in the face of increased expectations and need while the public faced overwhelming foreign control of the nation's industrial productivity, natural resources, and lands. The decline in contemporary Mexico in the real value of minimum wages, increasing numbers of people living in poverty, and the lack of sanitary, health, education, and other social services was serious by the end of the 1990s. These conditions contributed to the defeat of the PRI and victory of presidential candidate Vicente Fox.

In the modern era the activities of the two governments have grown more important, but they are still exceeded in significance by the almost invisible deeds of individual citizens. Those acts come in a variety of forms—corporate partnerships and mergers, work and family relationships, the consumption of goods, reading and viewing material, population growth, immigration, and modes of production—that cumulatively define culture, constitute the economy, and create self-images and political beliefs.

When evaluating contemporary behavior we do not have the advantages of the historical archive, but it is clear that American motives and expectations at the end of the twentieth century were different from what they had been in the past. The political leaders of the United States no longer entertained ambitions for territorial expansion, nor did they believe that the Mexicans would fade away as they had assumed in the nineteenth century. They did pursue policies rooted in the belief that trade and the free movement of American capital to Mexico and the Third World offer the United States ac-

cess to hardworking cheap labor and an enormous supply of natural resources, a combination that can result in wealth beyond the dreams of the
newspaper editors so long ago.

That belief is challenged by the concern of union leaders for the fate of
the once well-paid American industrial worker. How will Americans benefit
as American capital leaves the United States, with investors seeking greater
profits through lower labor costs? Their products will flow back into the
United States tax-free. If the Mexicans choose to fill their *canastas,* or bas-
kets, with American goods, then at least the lower-wage earners in Mexico
will join with the consumers of the small middle class and help fund American jobs. The Clinton administration and Secretary Rubin laid plans for a
new free-trade and capital investment zone that would extend from Mexico across the Western Hemisphere. The successful implementation of
NAFTA in Mexico is an important step toward this new phase of American
expansion. The real question for Mexico and the rest of the underdeveloped
world is whether the neoliberal model of development can provide a better
way of life for the majority.

The relationship that evolved between the United States and Mexico beginning at the end of the American Civil War anticipated the issues of glob-
alism that emerged during the 1990s. That experience provides a vital global
lesson for understanding the potential for the positive and negative in the
relationships between expansive great powers and their less powerful neighbors in the human community, and it offers important insights regarding
the role of the Americans in the new world order. Led by a small group of
merchants and financiers and aided by political leaders, American industrialists, agriculturalists, and ranchers played a central role in the transformation of Mexican society from the 1870s to 1910.

The international banks and corporations that entered Mexico before
1910 adapted to the preexisting contours of wealth and authority that they
encountered. They generated a great amount of money but left it concentrated largely among themselves and a handful of congenial, cooperative
Mexican elites. The great majority of Mexicans actually lost ground, given
their cultural values, through the loss of their municipal autonomy, independent means of production, and self-sufficiency. On the eve of the great
revolution they had also lost buying power, and many faced famine.

In today's world the international banks and corporations have concentrated their power in global organizations that are collecting enormous revenues in the form of interest payments from Mexico and other Third World

nations. The economies of the underdeveloped nations strain under the pressure to maintain just the interest payments on their debt, and these extreme burdens limit their ability to provide social services and humane living conditions for vast numbers of the world's people. Yet even as the global division of wealth and the economic disparity between Mexico and the United States remain extreme, the introduction of American elite and popular culture—religion, literature, scholarship, food, political values, manners of dress, and arts and entertainment—has brought an even greater diversity to Mexico, and a corresponding Mexican influence continues to flourish in the United States.

Although the postindustrial West, led by the United States, controls vast amounts of capital and levels of technology unimagined in Mexico, it has failed to benefit Mexico in the sense of making it a better place to live. Environmental destruction and drug trafficking are but two symptoms of the problem. Mexico, like its many even less fortunate Third World counterparts, has been left stagnant and falling ever further behind despite overall economic growth, the profits of a few, and the oft-repeated insistence that it is a "developing nation."

Mexicans should face the fact that Americans have decisively affected the history of their country from the early nineteenth century to the present. The proximity of the United States has created often unrealistic hopes for a generalized prosperity for the masses in an underdeveloped and undercapitalized country that is dominated by an economic and political oligarchy. The people of Mexico, and the Third World as well, must recognize the interconnectedness of their country's elites with their globalized American partners. Only a high degree of public awareness and political mobilization in support of wider social benefits can bring about the improvements so desperately needed by the great majority.

Endpiece

The Americans are still a part of Mexico.

> Farewell, farewell! but this I tell
> To thee, thou Wedding-Guest!
> He prayeth well, who loveth well
> Both man and bird and beast.
> He prayeth best, who loveth best
> all things both great and small;
> For the dear God who loveth us,
> He made and loveth all.

Coleridge, *The Rime of the Ancient Mariner*

Excuse me. I meant: recommend to the ambassador that he study the situation calmly and offer our government his disinterested opinion, influenced only by his natural concern for the interests of American citizens in Mexico. Let him explain that a favorable climate for investment must be maintained, and that with these riots . . .
Okay, okay.

Carlos Fuentes, *The Death of Artemio Cruz*

Appendix 1   Partial List of American Landholdings and Ownership in Mexico, 100,000 Acres and More, 1910–1913

The following list does not include properties in which ownership or the nationality of ownership is in doubt. It specifically excludes most American railroad holdings, of which the rights-of-way alone totaled 8,200,000 acres. Also excluded are the purchases made from 1874 to 1883 by railroad entrepreneurs Colis Huntington, Thomas Wentworth Peirce, and George Crocker, who bought 140,000 acres of the Encinas and Alamos haciendas in Coahuila. They continued buying estates of indeterminate size until Peirce's death in 1883. The 1883 and 1884 purchases made by Jean B. La Coste of San Antonio of 1,575,000 acres of estates of the disenfranchised Sanchez Navarro family in Coahuila and of 180,000 acres extending forty miles along the Mexican side of the Rio Grande above Del Río are also excluded because the exact boundaries of those purchases cannot be confirmed in the Saltillo archives. The few railroad properties included are identified specifically in the sources. Petroleum properties are cited only when the tracts are individually noted as being under the control of the American oil companies. This list therefore excludes most of an estimated 8,000,000 acres held in lease or outright ownership, including the majority of 4,000,000 acres that Texas Company officers estimated to be held by their firm.

Daniel Cosio Villegas, a noted Mexican historian who as a young man worked for several years in the archives of the Banco de México (Mexico's federal reserve bank), informs us that William Randolph Hearst owned 7,000,000 acres in Mexico. The properties that devolved to Hearst upon the death of his mother, Phoebe, are restricted in this list to those specifically identified in the documents. Those estates included the Aguada Seca in Campeche and the Babicora in Chihuahua. Hearst's 70,000 acres in oil lands in Chihuahua just south of Ojinaga and his properties in the states of Guerrero and Tabasco are not listed because the former tract was far removed from his other holdings and totaled less than 100,000 acres in size, and the dimensions of the latter tracts have not been determined. A number of properties owned by Americans in 1902, as cited by J. Fred Rippy in *The United States and Mexico,* are omitted from this list because they could not be confirmed to comprise over 100,000 intact acres between 1910 and 1914 or to be in the possession of U.S. citizens.

Finally, this list does not include the enormous properties, which totaled some 18,000,000 acres, of the Baja California Land Company, a firm that was supposedly British. Available evidence indicates that while a majority of the stock in that company was held by British citizens, J. P. Morgan of the Morgan Bank of New York had put together the investor syndicate through his trading house of Drexel Morgan in Philadelphia and London. Morgan exercised managerial control of the company through Edgar T. Welles, the son of Gideon Welles, who was secretary of the navy during the Civil War and a business associate and friend of J. P.'s father, Junius Morgan, and Anthony Drexel. After the Baja Company closed, Edgar served for many years as a director of the Wabash Railroad, Morgan's railway holding company for the upper midwestern United States.

Properties	Source[a]	State	Size in Acres	Owners
The Agricultural and Colonization Co. of Tabasco and Chiapas tract	12	Chiapas and Tabasco	316,000	The Agricultural Colonization Co. of Tabasco and Chiapas, and American colonists
Agua Blanca	1	Quintana Roo	660,000	William W. Skiddy
Agua Prieta	12	Sonora	162,000	Various
Alamos Altos Ranch and La Asencion	1	Chihuahua	171,000	Lewis E. Booker, Alfred Isaac Boyd
American International Fuel and Petroleum	1	Tamaulipas and Veracruz	185,000	H. M. McIntosh (Chicago)
Atotonilco	7, 8	Durango	120,000	Raymond Bell
Babicora Ranch	1	Chihuahua	1,192,000	William R. and Phoebe Hearst
La Barra San Marcos	12	Tabasco	330,000	Arthur C. ?
Batopilas mines	17	Chihuahua	122,500	Alexander Shepard Jr., George Quintard, and George Pullman
Blaylock Colony	1	Tamaulipas	230,000	George Blaylock and American colonists
California-Mexican Co. tracts	1, 12	Baja California Norte	1,949,702	California-Mexican Co.
El Camalote, Mesa de los Venados, La Siberia, Rincon Grande and annexes	1	Guerrero	198,000	Abraham and Robert Silberberg
Campeche, Esperanza, Laguna, and Tuxpena	1	Campeche	1,610,000	Mexican Exploitation Co.
La Canada	1	Sonora	300,000	Thomas Negri

Properties (continued)	Source[a]	State	Size in Acres	Owners
Cananea Cattle Co. and Cananea Consolidated Copper Co. tracts	22	Sonora	2,560,000	William C. Greene et al.
Cargill Lumber Co.	5	Chihuahua	542,000	William Wallace Cargill and George T. Gould et al.
Chacamax Plantation	1	Chiapas	116,000	Chacamax Development Co.
El Chamal	5	Tamaulipas	133,000	George Reeder
American Chicle Development Co.	22	Yucatán and Quintana Roo	3,000,000	Horatio, John, and Thomas Adams, James C. Parish, and Henry Rowley
Chicle, Resin, and Hardwood Concession	1	Yucatán and Quintana Roo	3,601,000	C. C. Mengel Co.
Chico Zapote	1	Tabasco	117,182	Mexican Diversified Land Co.
Circle Bar Ranch	1	Baja California	1,000,000	R. H. Benton and Norte Circle Bar Cattle Co.
Colorado River Land Co.	12, 20	Baja California Norte	860,655	Harrison Gray Otis and Harry Chandler et al.
Compañía de Terrenos El Nuevo Mundo	1	Sonora	293,632	Samuel Epler, William B. Raymond, and Carl F. Schader
Compañía de Terrenos y Ganados La Sanoita	12	Sonora	1,500,000	J. M. Chittins and A. J. Vick (San Antonio)
Compañía de Terrenos y Minas tract	12	Tamaulipas	104,000	Compañía de Terrenos y Minas
Compañía Deslindadora de Tamaulipas	21	Tamaulipas	123,000	Joseph A. Robertson
Compañía Terrenos de Sonora (Altar)	12	Sonora	618,000	Compañía Terrenos de Sonora Inc.

Property		State	Owner
Compañía Terrenos de Sonora (Hermosillo)	12	Sonora	Compañía Terrenos de Sonora Inc.
Conway Ranch	12	Sonora	Elena P. Conway
Corralitos	1	Chihuahua	Edward Shearson, Edwin D. Morgan, Thomas W. Peirce, and George Bliss
Los Coyotes Ranch	7, 8	Durango	Edward Hartmam
Culiacan Land Co.	1	Sinaloa	C. F. Van de Water
Del Río tract	1	Sonora	Guillermo Andrade heirs
Diversos Baldios	12	Baja California	Delbert J. Hoff
Durango Estates	1, 7, 8	Durango	Marion Clyde Dyer and Durango Estates Co.
El Cebollin y Anexos	1	Chihuahua	Louisiana Mexican Timber and Investment Co., Lamar Otis, J. R. Newton, and H. B., D. R., and C. E. Watson
El Chamal	1	Tamaulipas	George Blaylock and American colonists
El Ebano Ranch and annexes	19	San Luis Potosí and Veracruz	The Mexican Petroleum Co., Edward L. Doheny et al.
El Ojo	8	Durango	Otto Funk
Colonia Díaz	1	Chihuahua	Andrew Peterson and American colonists
Esperanza	1	Chiapas	Esperanza Timber Co.
San Tiburicio	12	Zacatecas	Espiritu Santo Agricultural Co.
Finca Pital and annexes	5, 13	Campeche	A. J. Stevens, Hugh A. Johnston, Charles H. Thompson et al., Laguna Corporation

Note: the numeric values shown in the image (148,000; 108,000; 890,000; 100,000; 130,000; 300,000; 1,480,939; 256,000; 180,000; 116,000; 450,000; 195,000; 100,000; 167,000; 282,250; 604,000) correspond to an acreage/area column between the reference-number column and the state column.

Properties (continued)	Source[a]	State	Size in Acres	Owners
Fomento Blocks 1 and 2, San Juan Jaltepec, and Terreno Fortuno	1	Veracruz and Oaxaca	500,000	Mexico Land Securities Co. (Kansas City) and George Straight
Frederick Probst and Co. tract	1	Campeche	1,020,000	Adolph Vietor
Grand Union Mining	1	Sonora	192,000	Rudolph Erve
Greene's Cananea Copper Co. tract	22	Sonora	380,000	Thomas Fortune Ryan, William Rockefeller, and James Stillman et al.
Guerrero Iron and Timber Co.	1	Guerrero	990,950	Edward Shearson, Severo Mallett Prevost, Charles Schwab, and Charles H. Foote
Carrera Brothers tract	1	Guerrero	200,000	Guerrero Land and Timber Co.
Hacienda de Acatita	7, 8	Durango	225,000	I. A. Porter
Haciendas Cerro Prieto, el Aguila, Los Arenales and annexes	5, 7, 8	Durango	542,001	Edward Hartman, Compañia Maderera de la Sierra de Durango (New York)
Haciendas de Chapacao, Tulillo, Pitahaya, Cerro Viejo, La Merced, and others	19	Tamaulipas and Veracruz	950,000	Mexican Petroleum Co. Ltd., Edward Doheny et al. (Doheny claimed to own 1,400,000 acres)
Hacienda Chivela	1	Oaxaca	125,000	Gulf Hardwoods Co.
Hacienda de Corrales and annexes	1	Chihuahua	362,000	International Land and Livestock Co., H. E. Bullock, James D. Sheahan, Palmer Montgomery, and Morgan F. Edwards
Hacienda El Corte	12	Oaxaca	171,000	F. Henry and Sons
Hacienda Grunidora	12, 22	Zacatecas	680,000	Nelson Aldrich, Bernard Baruch, Alexander J. Hemphill, Daniel Guggenheim et al., Intercontinental Rubber

Hacienda				
Hacienda de Huitrón	7, 8	Durango	300,000	I. A. Porter
Hacienda del Cañon de Santa María	7, 8	Durango	150,000	Marion Clyde Dyer
Hacienda El Maguey and annexes	7, 8	Durango	250,500	Marion Clyde Dyer
Hacienda El Salto and annexes	7, 8	Durango	157,000	Leonard Heid, William H. Dent, and Louise Willard
Hacienda de Janos	1	Chihuahua	105,000	E. K. Warren and Son
Hacienda Jicayan de Tovar	5	Guerrero	274,000	Henry A. Meyer, Patrick Beirne, and A. E. Pleak et al.
Hacienda La Bayona y Nieblas and annexes	5, 13	Province of Tepic	650,300	Land Finance Co., William Lemke, and Senator William Langer et al.
Hacienda La Montana	7, 8	Durango	285,000	J. S. McCaughan
Hacienda La Quemada	7, 8	Durango	171,000	Mr. Kraft
Hacienda de Los Angeles	7, 8, 12	Durango	105,000	W. Elton Brock and Forest R. Lowry
Hacienda San Ignacio	7, 8, 12	Durango	109,000	Mexican Highlands Co.
Hacienda San Xavier Otinapa	1, 7, 8, 12	Durango	185,000	Fred L. Morris, J. D. Bowersock, Patrick Ducey, and Walter Bishop
Hacienda Pelayo y Cadena	1, 7, 8, 12, 13	Durango	467,525	I. A. Porter, William Harold Albritten, Charles S. McCaughan, and Alexander Sessions
Hacienda Pericos	1	Sinaloa	200,000	Guillermo and Pablo Retes
Hacienda Río del Parral	1	Chihuahua	318,611	Torreon Construction Co. and I. A. Porter
Hacienda San Diego	1, 7, 8, 12	Durango	218,000	Durango Land Co.
Hacienda San Geronimo and annexes	7, 8	Durango	410,000	Angela Flores de Flores
Haciendas San Juan and El Chamal	1	Tamaulipas	189,000	Harold H. Reeder

Properties (continued)	Source[a]	State	Size in Acres	Owners
Hacienda San Juan de Cedros	1, 12, 22	Zacatecas	1,867,520	Nelson Aldrich, Bernard Bautista Baruch, Alexander J. Hemphill, Daniel Guggenheim, Intercontinental Rubber Co.
Hacienda San Luis and annexes	1	Chihuahua	174,000	J. Paul Ginther
Hacienda San Marcos	1, 12, 13	Guerrero	480,000	Charles Miller and Guerrero Trading Co.
Hacienda San Pablo	1, 12	Campeche	445,000	George S. Baily, G. W. Edmunds, United Security Life Insurance and Trust, International Lumber and Development Co., Victor Du Pont Jr.
Hacienda Santa Ynez	1	Veracruz	148,750	Edward C. Denbar
Haciendas Surumuati and Santa Ana	1	Michoacán	465,100	Charles and Dolores Markassuza
Haciendas El Tintero, Santa Clara and annexes, Carmen de Namiquipa, and Santa Ana de Torreon	1, 13	Chihuahua	1,250,000	George C. Douglas, George J. Douglas, and David E. Douglas (heirs of Henry Muller)
Hacienda Union en Cuale	13, 15	Jalisco	100,000	Alfred W. Geist and Mexican Tropical Fruit Co.
Hearst properties in Tehuantepec	5, 14	Veracruz	351,804	William Randolph and Phoebe Hearst
Hearst properties in Tehuantepec	5	Oaxaca	389,120	William R. and Phoebe Hearst
Hearst properties	14	Sonora	200,000	William R. and Phoebe Hearst
International Lumber and Development Co.	5	Campeche	300,000	Victor Du Pont Jr., Judge John B. Barnes, and W. H. Armstrong et al.

Property		State	Area	Owner
Isla del Carmen	12	Baja California Norte	540,000	Pacific Salt Co.
Jantha Plantation	13	Oaxaca	270,500	American colonists
Kansas Sinaloa Investment Co.	23	Sinaloa	468,000	A. Foster Higgins and Solon Humphries
La Fortuna Plantation	5	Oaxaca	153,340	Hugh Rogers and Benjamin Stonum et al., Fortuna Development Co.
La Santísima	5, 13	Chihuahua	225,000	Thomas Smith Lytle, James L. Davis, and Charles Davis
La Montana	7, 8, 12	Durango	340,000	Edward Rotan
La Zacatosa and El Juncal	3	Coahuila	174,864	T. F. Ragsdale
Land and Mining Co. tract	21	Tamaulipas	105,000	Cía de Terrenos y Minas
La Rosita	3, 8	Coahuila	139,387	John Long
Las Bagues	7, 8	Durango	173,000	Marion Clyde Dyer
Las Encinas	12	Nuevo León	144,000	George Reeder
Las Lomas	12	Nayarit	221,000	William D. Fisk
Las Palomas	8	Chihuahua	2,500,000	Edwin J. Marshall
Lewis Booker Timberlands	5, 13	Chihuahua	165,000	Lewis E. Booker
Look properties (four ranches)	5	Chihuahua	238,000	George Look
Los Otates Ranch	5	Sonora	140,000	Sonora Land and Timber Co.
Lote de Banderas	7, 8	Durango	376,205	Mexican American Land and Colonization
Edward Hartman Timberlands and Rubber	1, 8	Chiapas	204,360	Edward Hartman
McClellon properties	5	Coahuila	240,000	McClellon interests

Properties (continued)	Source[a]	Size in Acres	State	Owners
Mexcalapa Timber tract	5	136,000	Chiapas	Texas-Mexico Development Co., Otto Koehler and Otto Wahrmund
Mexican-American Land and Colonization Co.	5	376,360	Coahuila and Durango	Charles P. Reeves and George Hormel
Martinez del Río tract	5, 9	300,000	Chihuahua	Unidentified "American syndicate"
Mexicali town site	1	100,000	Baja California Norte	Guillermo Andrade heirs, Hiram W. Blaisdell, and William Hefferman
Mexican Candelaria Co.	7, 8, 13	161,000	Durango	Daniel Burns et al. (San Francisco)
San Rafael and annexes	1	760,000	Campeche	Nathaniel French (Davenport, Iowa), John Markley (Chicago), and Edgar H. Ryan et al., Mexican Gulf Land and Lumber Co.
Mexican Pacific Coal and Iron Mining and Land Co.	13	250,000	Guerrero	The Mexican Pacific Co., syndicates of Morgan, National City Bank, First National Bank, and Ladenburg-Thalmann
Mexican Pine Lands Co.	5	400,000	Chihuahua	A. J. McQuatters
Mexican Northwestern Railway Co.	10	2,700,000	Chihuahua	Frederick S. Pearson and American, Canadian, and British capitalists, First Mortgage Empire Bank
Mexico Lands Co.	13	1,500,000	Tamaulipas	Charles E. Moore
Moctezuma Copper Co.	13	302,000	Sonora	Cleveland Dodge, James Douglas, and A. H. Danforth of Phelps Dodge Corp.
Motzorongo Plantation and Hacienda Josefinas	5	365,000	Veracruz	Motzorongo Co., Herbert A. Parkin, James O. Rice, and Joseph A. Robertson

Nacimiento and annexes	5	Coahuila	302,000	A. E. and J. W. Noble
Ojitos Ranch	5	Chihuahua	107,606	Edward and Charles K. Warren
Parral y Durango Railroad tract	7, 8	Durango	185,500	American Smelting and Refining Co.
Pennsylvania-campeche tract	1	Campeche	625,000	Pennsylvania-Campeche Land and Lumber Co., and Laguna Corporation
Piedra Blanca	13	Coahuila	1,250,000	John Blocker, William Jennings, and Alva Heywood syndicate
Pijijiapan Estates	5	Chiapas	130,000	Pijijiapan colonists and Pan-American Railway
Pine King Timber tract	5, 8	Chihuahua and Durango	524,000	John A. McShane et al.
Pino Gordo Timber tract	7, 8	Durango	416,000	Patrick Ducey and Thomas Willard
Pinos Altos	7, 8	Durango	120,000	Edward Hartman
Puxmetacan	1	Oaxaca and Veracruz	130,000	John C. McConnell
Querendaro	5	Michoacán	247,500	Charles Haghembeck
Rancho La Arizona	5	Sonora	100,000	William Barnett
Rancho Ensenada	1	Baja California Norte	1,100,000	María Amparo Ruiz de Burton
Rancho San Jorge and Tamaulipas	13	San Luis Potosí	256,000	Richard Meade
Ranchos Laguna Colorado, Olote, Jaral, Soldado, Mimbres San Francisco, Santa Barbara, Cienega de Ibarra, Aguinaldo	7	Durango	501,080	A. H. Featherston (Henrietta, Texas) and A. E. Baird (Nashville)

Properties (continued)	Source[a]	State	Size in Acres	Owners
Rascon	24	San Luis Potosí and Tamaulipas	1,400,000	George Lee (Galveston)
Richardson Yaqui River Valley tract	1, 2, 25	Sonora	750,000	Anonymous "California interests" of Yaqui Valley Land and Water Co., William Richardson, John Hays Hammond, and Harry Payne Whitney
Rincon Grande, El Canalito, and San Esteven	1	Guerrero	150,000	Charles Newman and Abraham and Robert Silverberg
Río Bravo Tract	12	Tamaulipas	988,440	Río Bravo Agriculture Co.
Río Bravo Land and Cattle tract	1, 5	Chihuahua	120,893	Río Bravo Land and Cattle Co.
Río Cajones	20	Coahuila	126,000	Río Cajones Co. (Cisco, Texas)
Rodrigo Ranch	1, 5	Coahuila	163,320	F. M. Rose et al.
Las Rusias	18	Coahuila	161,000	Nelson and Weller and Co.
Salinas de Tehuantepec	13	Oaxaca	128,000	Charles, Frederick, and Rafael Parraga, Parraga and Co.
San Antonio, Santisima Vado de El Comedor	15	Chihuahua	222,000	Alfred L. Shapleigh, Thomas Rankin Jr., John Piedra, J. O'Fallon, and Charles Davis et al.
San Estevan Ranch and Timber tract	7, 8	Durango	290,000	United States Land and Lumber Co., John P. Eiken
San Javier and annexes	7, 8	Durango	100,000	Marion Clyde Dyer
San José de Aguada Seca	1, 14	Campeche	389,120	William R. and Phoebe Hearst
San José de las Rusias	4, 15	Tamaulipas	1,200,000	Otto Brictson

San Juan de Michis	7, 8	Durango	180,000	J. S., A. E., and F. L. McCaughan, J. Lanham, and Joseph Higginbothan
San Pedro	5	Chihuahua	206,000	A. B. Urmsten
San Pedro and annexes	5	Chihuahua	346,643	Greene Cananea Copper Co., James Stillman, William Rockefeller, William Rogers
San Pedro Martyr	5	Baja California Norte	288,000	Sam A. and Frank T. Thing
San Rafael de la Noria	1, 12	Sonora	110,000	Lewis Henry Lapham, Merritt M. Shearman, and F. H. Rockwell
San Tiburcio	12	Zacatecas	812,750	Espiritu Santo Agricultural Co.
Santa Isabel Ranch	7, 8	Durango		Warrior W. Grayson and Creek Durango Co.
Santa Ana de la Florida	1	Nuevo León and Tamaulipas	148,500	International Land and Investment Co.
Santo Domingo Ranch	1	Chihuahua	480,000	O. B. Fuller, A. W. Tenant, and Southwestern Land and Cattle Co.
Sautema tract	12	Tamaulipas	550,000	Compañía de Terrenos y Minas, La Sautema, and The Mexico Co.
Sinaloa Land Co. tract	1, 20	Sinaloa	1,607,000	Edwin Marshall and Nelson Rhoades Jr.
Sociedad Irrigacion land tract	1, 13	Baja California Norte	100,000	Sociedad de Irrigacion S.A.
Sonoita Valley Land tract	1, 13	Sonora	232,000	Sonoita Valley Land Co.
Sonora Land Co. tract	1, 13	Sonora	524,400	Sonora Land Co. Inc.
Sonora Land Co. of Hermosillo	1, 13	Sonora	150,000	Sonora Land Co. of Hermosillo

Properties (continued)	Source[a]	State	Size in Acres	Owners
Sonora Land and Cattle Co. tract	1, 13	Sonora	1,525,000	Sonora Land and Cattle Co.
Tamaulipas Land and Cattle Co. tract	1, 13	Tamaulipas	130,000	Tamaulipas Land and Cattle Co.
T. O. Riverside Ranch	1	Chihuahua	1,250,000	Edward Morris
Turkey Track Cattle Ranch	6, 12	Sonora	148,000	Turkey Track Cattle Co.
United Sugar Co. tract	13	Sinaloa	264,000	Benjamin F. Johnston and Charles Hudson et al.
Unnamed, adjacent to San Juan Nepomuceno	6	Chihuahua	485,000	George M. Holmes
Unnamed	1	Jalisco	125,000	Francis Lake
Unnamed, adjacent to Corrales, Babicora, and Chuichupa	6	Chihuahua	497,000	Smith, Davis, and Hartman
Unnamed, adjacent to San Estevan	16	Durango	165,000	Buckeye, Arthur, and Reid of New York
Various tracts	12	Baja California	235,000	Heirs of John MacManus
Victoria Land and Cattle Co.	5	Chihuahua	199,000	James Ben Ali Haggin
Wheeler Land Co.	11, 13	Sonora	1,610,000	George F. Wheeler, Stanton Hyer, George S. Bisbee, Louis Gates, James McClelland, Walter Douglas, and Phelps Dodge
Yaqui Valley Land and Water Co.	13	Sonora	750,000	John Hays Hammond et al.

[a]*Sources*

1. Records of the Special Claims Commission, Washington National Records Center, College Park, Maryland

2. Special Collections, The University of Arizona, Phoenix

3. Nettie Lee Benson Latin American Collection, University of Texas, Austin

4. Brictson Family Papers, Madison, Wisconsin

5. Entry 185, Special Claims Commission, Washington National Records Center, College Park, Maryland

6. Archivo Historico del Registro Publico de la Propiedad, Estado de Chihuahua, Chihuahua

7. Archivo Historico del Registro Publico de la Propiedad y el Comercio, Estado de Durango, Durango

8. Decimal file 312, records group 59, Diplomatic Branch, National Archives and Records Administration, Washington, D.C.

9. David Walker, Department of History, Michigan State University, East Lansing

10. *Engineering and Mining Journal,* 2 October 1909

11. Albert Bacon Fall Collection, Huntington Library, San Marino, California

12. Frank Tannenbaum Papers, Butler Library, Rare Book and Manuscript Library, Columbia University, New York

13. Entry 125, General Claims Commission, Washington National Records Center, College Park, Maryland

14. Gray Brechin, "Imperial San Francisco," unpublished manuscript, Berkeley, California

15. Entry 107, Underwood, General Claims Commission, Washington National Records Center, College Park, Maryland

16. *El Paso Herald*

17. Batopilas Mining Company Papers, Hart Collection, Houston

18 . Nicolau d'Olwer et al., *El Porfiriato, la vida economica,* in *Historia Moderna de México,* ed. Daniel Cosio Villegas (Mexico: Editorial Hermes, 1965), 1108.

19. Edward Doheny, *Mexican Petroleum,* 49

20. Colección Porfirio Díaz, Universidad Iberoamericana, Mexico City

21. Registro Publico, Ciudad Victoria, Tamaulipas

22. Marvin Scudder Collection, The Thomas J. Watson Library of Business and Economics, Columbia University, New York

23. Topolobampo Papers, Mandeville Collection, University of California, San Diego

24. Townsend-Stanton Family Papers, Howard-Tilton Memorial Library, Tulane University, Tulane

25. *Who's Who in California, 1928–1929*

Appendix 2   Partial List of American
Properties of More Than
100,000 Acres or of Special
Significance, Derived via
Government Portions of
Land Surveys or from the
Land Survey Companies,
1876–1910

Purchaser or Name of Estate	Source[a]	Seller	State or Territory	Size in Acres
Agua Blanca, Francis Skiddy	2	Mexican government	Quintana Roo	660,000
Andrade, Guillermo	1, 2	Luis García Teruel	Sonora	150,000
Andrade, Guillermo	1, 2	Mexican government	Sonora	100,000
Babicora Ranch, William R. Hearst	2	Jesús Valenzuela	Chihuahua	1,192,000
Cargill Co.	2	Mexican government via Limantour Grant	Chihuahua	537,000
Hacienda Chamal, Blaylock Colony	2	Mexican government	Tamaulipas	230,000
Circle Bar Ranch	2	Mexican Land and Colonization Co.	Baja California Norte	1,000,000
Compañía de Terrenos, El Nuevo Mundo	2	J. B. Jecker and Co. via Martínez del Río	Sonora	293,632
Compañía de Terrenos de Sonora, Simeon Tucker	1	General Francisco Olivares	Sonora	4,200,000
Corralitos	2	Jesús Valenzuela	Chihuahua	860,795
Patrick Ducey	4	Joaquin Casasus	Durango	81,627
Patrick Ducey	2	Joaquin Casasus	Durango	416,000
Patrick Ducey	2	Mexican government	Durango	117,000
Durango Land Co.	4	Francisco Armendariz Durango and Rafael García Martínez	Durango	219,000
L. C. Dyer	2	Mexican government	Durango	250,000
Guerrero Iron and Timber Co.	2	not named	Guerrero	723,500
Hacienda El Toruno	2	Compañía de Terrenos, El Toruno	Sinaloa	24,752

Purchaser or Name of Estate (continued)	Source[a]	Seller	State or Territory	Size
Edward Hartman	4	Luis Vazquez	Durango	81,627
Edward Hartman	4	Jesús Valenzuela	Durango	69,000
Edward Hartman	4	Joaquin Casasus	Durango	414,000
Durango Land Co.	2	Joaquin Casasus	Durango	212,000
Fred Morris, San Javier Otinapa hacienda	3, 4	Joaquin Casasus	Durango	185,000
Intercontinental Rubber, Cedros hacienda	2	Mexican government (unconfirmed)	Zacatecas	1,867,520
Intercontinental Rubber, Grunidora hacienda	2	Mexican government (unconfirmed)	Zacatecas	680,000
International Co. of Mexico, Edgar T. Welles, J. P. Morgan et al.	2	Luis Huller (a naturalized American)	Baja California	18,000,000
International Lumber and Development Co.	2, 3	Luis García Teruel	Campeche	288,000
Laguna Corp.	2, 3	Manuel Vila via Luis García Teruel	Campeche	604,000
Peter MacArthur	4	Cía. Mexicana Deslindadora de Terrenos	Durango	30,000
Peter MacArthur	4	Cía. Mexicana Terrenos Baldios	Durango	75,000
Col. C. C. Mengel	2	Reyes concession and Mexican government	Quintana Roo	966,000
Col. C. C. Mengel	2	Faustino Martínez via Banco de Londres y México	Quintana Roo	1,735,000

Name		Source	State	Acres
Mexican Diversified Land Co.	2	Rafael Dorantes	Tabasco	117,000
Mexican Exploitation Co., Campeche, Esperanza, Laguna, and Tuxpena tracts	1	Manuel Vila via Luis García Teruel	Campeche	1,610,000
Mexican Gulf Land and Lumber Co.	2	Manuel Vila via Luis García Teruel	Campeche	581,000
Charles S. Moore	2	Mexican government	Sonora	48,500
Las Palomas, Edwin Marshall	2, 3	Luis Huller	Chihuahua	2,500,000
Thomas MacManus and Co.	1	Luis García Teruel	Chihuahua	375,000
Daniel J. Murphy, Hacienda Dolores	4	Francisco Valenzuela	Durango	378,000
Daniel J. Murphy	4	Mexican government	Durango	85,000
Daniel J. Murphy	4	Mexican government	Durango	501,080
Pijijiapan Colony	2	Compañía Mexicana de Terrenos y Colonización	Chiapas	
Pine King Co.	2	Ignacio Sandoval	Chihuahua	516,000
Pino Gordo Timber Co.	2	Mexican government	Durango	118,000
Richardson Construction Co.	2, 5	Charles Conant and Sonora and Sinaloa Irrigation Company	Sonora	329,075
Richardson Construction Co.	5	Luis García Teruel via Mexican Land and Colonization Co.	Sonora	86,959
Richardson Construction Co.	5	Max Muller et al.	Sonora	123,500
Richardson Construction Co.	5	Mexican government	Sonora	37,324
Davis Richardson	5	Mexican government	Sonora	44,035
T. O. Riverside Ranch, Edward Morris	2	José Valenzuela	Chihuahua	1,250,000

Purchaser or Name of Estate (continued)	Source[a]	Seller	State or Territory	Size
Sinaloa Land and Water Co., Edwin Marshall	2, 3	Sinaloa Land Company and Luis Martínez de Castro	Sinaloa	1,300,000
Sinaloa Land Co., Francis T. Wheeler	3	Manuel Teniche	Sinaloa	1,610,000
Sinaloa Land Co., Francis T. Wheeler	2	Manuel Teniche	Sinaloa	256,000
Union en Cuale, Alfred W. Geist	2	Mexican government	Jalisco	100,000
Adolph Vietor and Frederick Probst and Co.	2	Manuel Vila via Luis García Teruel	Campeche	1,020,000
William Wallace Varn et al.	4	Pablo Valenzuela	Durango	106,000
Edward and Charles Warren	2	Ignacio Gomez del Campo (controlled by Luis Huller), via Beresford	Chihuahua	107,606
Wheeler Land Company	2	Manuel Teniche as Sonora Land Co.	Sonora	1,316,000

[a]Sources

1. Colección Porfirio Díaz, Universidad Iberoamericana, Mexico City
2. Records of the American Mexican Claims Commission, Washington National Records Center, College Park, Maryland
3. Deferred Miscellaneous Claims, AKA Extended Claims, Washington National Records Center, College Park, Maryland
4. Archivo Historico del Registro Publico de la Propiedad y el Comercio, Estado de Durango, Durango
5. Richardson Construction Company Papers, Manuscripts Room, University of Arizona Library, Tucson

Appendix 3   American Banking Syndicates Formed to Render Financial Support to Britain and Her Allies during World War I, September 1914–April 1917

DATE	February 1915–25 April 1917
LOAN RECIPIENT	Bank of England
AMOUNT OF LOAN	$436,821,137
ACCOUNT	"Client #1" Demand Loans One and Two (Confidential) (To Support Sterling Exchange)
SYNDICATE MANAGERS	J. P. Morgan and Co. National City Bank, and First National Bank (known as "the Trio")
SYNDICATE PARTICIPANTS	J. P. Morgan and Co.; National City Bank; First National Bank; National Bank of Commerce; Guarantee Trust Co.; Bankers Trust Co.; Chase National Bank; National Park Bank; Bank of Manhattan Co.; Corn Exchange Bank; American Exchange National Bank; Hanover National Bank; Mechanics and Metals National Bank; Liberty National Bank; Title Guarantee and Trust Co.; Chemical National Bank; Union Trust Co. of New Jersey; and Astor Trust Co.; negotiations for Loan One initiated in September 1914
DATE	28 May 1915
LOAN RECIPIENT	Rothschild Frères
AMOUNT OF LOAN	$44,436,395, in 5 percent notes guaranteed by the

531

French government and secured by bonds of the
Pennsylvania Railroad and Chicago, Milwaukee, and
St. Paul Railroad

SYNDICATE MANAGER
J. P. Morgan and Co.

SYNDICATE PARTICIPANTS
Kuhn Loeb; J. P. Morgan and Co.; First National
Bank; National City Co.; Chase National Bank;
Chase National Bank a/c Clients; Mechanics and
Metals National Bank; National Bank of Com-
merce; Farmers Loan and Trust; Hanover Bank;
National Park Bank; Illinois Trust and Savings
(Chicago); First Trust and Savings (Chicago);
Riggs National Bank (Washington, D.C.)

DATE
November 1915

LOAN RECIPIENT
French Commercial Export Credit

AMOUNT OF LOAN
$15,000,000, secured by French treasury notes

SYNDICATE MANAGER
National City Bank

SYNDICATE PARTICIPANTS
National City Bank; Bankers Trust; Irving National
Bank; American Exchange National Bank; Chase
National Bank; Farmers Loan and Trust Co.;
Guarantee Trust Co.; Hanover National Bank;
Mechanics and Metals National Bank; J. P. Morgan
and Co.; Central Trust Co.; First National Bank of
Boston; National Park Bank; Old Colony Trust of
Boston; U.S. Mortgage and Trust; Liberty National
Bank; Broadway Trust; National Shawmut Bank
(Boston); Metropolitan Trust Co.; Astor Trust;
National Bank of Commerce of Toledo; Union Trust
and Deposit Co. of Ithaca; and thirteen French banks
including Mallet Frères of Paris

DATE
January 1916–April 1917

LOAN RECIPIENT
His Britannic Majesty's Government

AMOUNT OF LOAN
$344,000,000

ACCOUNT   Loan (Morgan Grenfeld & Co. a/c "Client #2")
(Confidential)

SYNDICATE   J. P. Morgan and Co., National City Bank, and
MANAGERS   First National Bank

SYNDICATE   J. P. Morgan and Co.; National City Bank; First
PARTICIPANTS   National Bank; American Exchange National Bank;
American Telephone and Telegraph; Bank of Man-
hattan; Bank of New York; Bankers Trust Co.; Brown
Brothers and Co.; Central Trust Co.; Chase National
Bank; Chatham and Phoenix National Bank; Colum-
bia Trust Co.; Corn Exchange Bank; Drexel and Co.;
Chemical National Bank; Empire Trust Co.; Farmers
Loan and Trust Co.; Fifth Avenue Bank; Guarantee
Trust Co.; Hanover National Bank; International
Harvester Co.; Irving National Bank; Liberty
National Bank; Mechanics and Metals National
Bank; National Bank of Commerce; National Park
Bank; George W. Perkins; Title Guarantee and Trust
Co.; New York Trust Co.; United States Steel Corpo-
ration; Union Trust Co.; United States Trust Co.;
Citizens Savings and Trust Co. (Cleveland); Conti-
nental and Commercial National Bank (Chicago);
Continental and Commercial Trust and Savings
(Chicago); Corn Exchange National Bank (Chicago);
First National Bank (Boston); First National Bank
(Chicago); First National Bank (Cincinnati); First
National Bank (Cleveland); First and Old Detroit
National Bank; First Trust and Savings Bank
(Chicago); Illinois Trust and Savings Bank (Chicago);
Mellon National Bank (Pittsburgh); Merchants
Loan and Trust Co. (Chicago); National Shawmut
Bank (Boston); Northern Trust Co. (Chicago); Old
Colony Trust Co. (Boston); Peoples National Bank
(Pittsburgh); Saint Louis National Bank; and Union
Trust Co. (Pittsburgh)

DATE   March 1916

LOAN RECIPIENT   French Commercial Export Credit

AMOUNT OF LOAN $15,000,000, secured by French treasury notes

SYNDICATE
MANAGER
National City Bank

SYNDICATE
PARTICIPANTS
National City Bank; Bankers Trust; Irving National Bank; American Exchange National Bank; Chase National Bank; Farmers Loan and Trust Co.; Guarantee Trust Co.; Hanover National Bank; Mechanics and Metals National Bank; J. P. Morgan and Co.; Central Trust Co.; First National Bank of Boston; National Park Bank; Old Colony Trust of Boston; U.S. Mortgage and Trust; Liberty National Bank; Broadway Trust; National Shawmut Bank (Boston); Metropolitan Trust Co.; Astor Trust; National Bank of Commerce (Toledo); Union Trust and Deposit Co. (Utica); and thirteen French banks; including Mallet Frères of Paris

DATE 6 June 1916

LOAN RECIPIENT Russian Government Credit of 1916

AMOUNT OF LOAN $47,600,000

SYNDICATE
MANAGER
National City Bank

SYNDICATE
PARTICIPANTS
J. P. Morgan and Co.; National City Bank; Guarantee Trust Co.; Lee Higginson and Co.; Claude Ashbrook and Co. (Cincinnati); Astor Trust Co.; Bankers Trust Co.; E. T. Bedford (NYC); Commercial Trust Co.; Fidelity Trust Co. (Philadelphia); First National Bank (Utica); First National Bank of Cuba (NY); Girard Trust (Philadelphia); Frazier and Co. (Philadelphia); Irvine National Bank; Mary Goldsborough (Cambridge, Md.); Liberty National Bank (NY); National Bank of Commerce; National City Bank (Troy); William E. Paine (NY); Philadelphia Trust Co.; J. S. Rippel and Co. (Newark); Sun Life Assurance Co. (Montreal); with other subscribers in St. Paul, Charlotte, Jersey City, Chicago, and San Francisco

DATE 8 June 1916

LOAN RECIPIENT Purchase of Argentine 5s of 1909

AMOUNT OF LOAN $10,000,000, in Paris for resale in this market

SYNDICATE J. P. Morgan and Co.
MANAGER

SYNDICATE J. P. Morgan and Co.; First National Bank Guarantee
PARTICIPANTS Trust Co.; Harris Forbes and Co.; National City Co.;
via Bernhard, Scholle and Co., Paris agents

DATE 21 June 1916 and 6 July 1916

LOAN RECIPIENT Conversion of Sterling Debt of Governments of
Manitoba, Saskatchewan, and Winnipeg at London

AMOUNT OF LOAN $8,000,000

SYNDICATE J. P. Morgan and Co.
MANAGER

SYNDICATE J. P. Morgan and Co.; Harris Forbes; First National
PARTICIPANTS Bank; National City Bank; and Brown Brothers and Co.

DATE July 1916

LOAN RECIPIENT American Foreign Securities

AMOUNT OF LOAN $100,000,000; three-year 5% notes

ACCOUNT French Commercial Agency

SYNDICATE J. P. Morgan and Co.
MANAGER

SYNDICATE Morgan Hartges & Co., $1/6$; Brown Brothers, $1/3$; First
PARTICIPANTS National Bank, $1/6$; J. P. Morgan, $1/3$; sold $5,000,000
to United States Steel, Santa Fe, and Brown Brothers;
National City Bank, slightly less than $1/6$ [sic]

DATE September 1916

LOAN RECIPIENT French Commercial Export Credit

AMOUNT OF LOAN $15,000,000, secured by French treasury notes

SYNDICATE National City Bank
MANAGER

SYNDICATE PARTICIPANTS — National City Bank; Bankers Trust; Irving National Bank; American Exchange National Bank; Chase National Bank; Farmers Loan and Trust Co.; Guarantee Trust Co.; Hanover National Bank; Mechanics and Metals National Bank; J. P. Morgan and Co.; Central Trust Co.; First National Bank of Boston; National Park Bank; Old Colony Trust of Boston; U.S. Mortgage and Trust; Liberty National Bank; Broadway Trust; National Shawmut Bank of Boston; Metropolitan Trust Co.; Astor Trust; National Bank of Commerce of Toledo; Union Trust and Deposit Co. of Utica; and thirteen French banks including Mallet Frères of Paris (this syndicate and contract duplicate those of November 1915 above)

DATE — October 1916

LOAN RECIPIENT — French Industrial Credit

AMOUNT OF LOAN — 50,000,000, secured by $50,000,000 in French treasury bonds

SYNDICATE MANAGERS — Guarantee Trust Co. and Bankers Trust Co.

SYNDICATE PARTICIPANTS — Guarantee Trust Co.; Bankers Trust Co.; J. P. Morgan and Co.; and numerous other financial institutions

DATE — 1 November 1916

LOAN RECIPIENT — United Kingdom of Great Britain and Ireland

AMOUNT OF LOAN — 272,095,000, in three- and five-year 5.5 percent secured notes

SYNDICATE MANAGER — J. P. Morgan and Co.

SYNDICATE PARTICIPANTS — J. P. Morgan and Co.; First National Bank; National City Co.; Brown Brothers; Harris Forbes and Co.; Wm. A. Read and Co.; J. & W. Seligman and Co.; Kidder Peabody and Co.; Lee Higginson and Co.; Lazard Frères; Kissel, Kinnicutt and Co.; Guarantee Trust Co.; Central Trust of Illinois; White, Weld and

Co.; Bankers Trust; Farmers Loan and Trust; Central
Trust Co. of Illinois; Union Trust Co. of Pittsburgh;
Continental and Commercial Trust and Savings
Bank (Chicago); Marine National Bank (Buffalo);
First and Old Detroit National Bank (Detroit)

DATE	December 1916
LOAN RECIPIENT	Imperial Russian Government Bonds
AMOUNT OF LOAN	$25,000,000, at 5.5 percent, due 1 December 1921
SYNDICATE MANAGER	National City Bank
SYNDICATE PARTICIPANTS	J. P. Morgan and Co.; National City Co.; Guarantee Trust Co.; Lee Higginson and Co.; and Harris Forbes and Co.

DATE	15 December 1916
LOAN RECIPIENT	Argentine Government
AMOUNT OF LOAN	$16,800,000, six-month notes taken up to enable the Argentines to pay $15,000,000 due British holders of Argentine bonds
SYNDICATE MANAGER	National City Bank
SYNDICATE PARTICIPANTS	J. P. Morgan and Co.; National City Bank; and Guarantee Trust Co.

DATE	18 January 1917
LOAN RECIPIENT	United Kingdom of Great Britain and Ireland
AMOUNT OF LOAN	Total $250,000,000: $100,000,000 for one year, and $150,000,000 for two years at 5.5 percent
SYNDICATE MANAGERS	J. P. Morgan and Co., National City Bank, and First National Bank
SYNDICATE PARTICIPANTS	J. P. Morgan and Co.; First National Bank; National City Co.; Harris Forbes and Co.; Brown Brothers and Co.; Wm. A. Read and Co.; J. & W. Seligman and Co.; Kidder Peabody; Lee Higginson and Co.;

Lazard Frères; Kissel, Kinnicutt and Co.; White, Weld and Co.; Guarantee Trust Co.; Bankers Trust Co.; Farmers Loan and Trust; Central Trust Co. of Illinois (Chicago); Union Trust Co. (Pittsburgh); Continental and Commercial Trust and Savings Bank (Chicago); Marine National Bank (Buffalo); First and Old Detroit National Bank

DATE	March 1917
LOAN RECIPIENT	French Commercial Export Credit
AMOUNT OF LOAN	$15,000,000, secured by French treasury notes
SYNDICATE MANAGER	National City Bank
SYNDICATE PARTICIPANTS	National City Bank; Bankers Trust; Irving National Bank; American Exchange National Bank; Chase National Bank; Farmers Loan and Trust Co.; Guarantee Trust; Hanover National Bank; Mechanics and Metals National Bank; J. P. Morgan and Co.; Central Trust Co.; First National Bank of Boston; National Park Bank; Old Colony Trust of Boston; U.S. Mortgage and Trust; Liberty National Bank; Broadway Trust; National Shawmut Bank of Boston; Metropolitan Trust Co.; Astor Trust; National Bank of Commerce of Toledo; Union Trust and Deposit Co. of Utica; and thirteen French banks, including Mallet Frères of Paris (this syndicate and contract duplicate those of November 1915 and September 1916 above)
DATE	16 March 1917
LOAN RECIPIENT	Government of the French Republic
AMOUNT OF LOAN	$100,000,000, two-year 5.5 percent secured loan convertible notes
SYNDICATE MANAGERS	J. P. Morgan and Co., National City Bank, and First National Bank
SYNDICATE PARTICIPANTS	J. P. Morgan and Co.; First National Bank; National City Co.; Harris Forbes and Co.; Kidder Peabody;

J. & W. Seligman; Lee Higginson; Wm. A. Read and
Co.; W. P. Boatright; Lazard Frères; Kissel, Kinnicutt
and Co.; White, Weld and Co.; Spencer Trask; Chase
Bank; National Bank of Commerce; Guarantee
Trust; Bankers Trust; Central Trust Co.; Farmers
Loan and Trust; Union Trust Co.; Equitable Trust;
Union Bank (Pittsburgh); Mellon Bank (Pittsburgh);
First National Bank (Cleveland)

Notes on Archival Sources

This book is based on a multiplicity of archives in the United States and Mexico. Important papers of many of the large American corporations and those of Americans of considerable standing, as well as of small property holders active in Mexico during the nineteenth and twentieth centuries, are available in the Archives of the United States because they submitted crucial data from their records as part of the Bucareli Accords in 1923. That agreement established a procedure for the satisfaction of claims against personal and property damages incurred during the Mexican Revolution. These documents are buttressed by similar submissions made by Americans in Mexico after the agrarian reform agreements of 1938, under which the Mexicans agreed to pay out $200,000,000 in bonds underwritten by the U.S. Treasury to satisfy claims made as a result of property confiscations.

University library archives in the United States, such as Columbia University's, which guards the Marvin Scudder Collection and the papers of Frank Tannenbaum, James Stillman, and Edgar Turlington, contain the papers of many important American entrepreneurs. The Madison Building of the Library of Congress holds the papers of many key Americans with political and business interests in Mexico, including Edward Lee Plumb. The manuscripts room of the UCLA Graduate Research Library contains the William Stark Rosecrans Papers, which, combined with those of Plumb, explain how and why the Americans moved into Mexico so avidly. Local and personal collections pertinent to the study of the Americans in Mexico, such as the Rascon Hacienda archive and the Brictson, Hearst, Towne, and Huntington Papers, are found throughout the American Union.

In Mexico the records of concessions given out by that government are found in the Archivo General de la Nación, the Porfirio Díaz and Manuel González Papers at the Universidad Iberoamericana, the Archivo Historico de la Secretaria de Relaciones Exteriores, the Matías Romero Papers in the Banco de México, and in the Condumex Archive, all in Mexico City. The central and state archives of the Secretaria of Reforma Agraria and the Tribunal Superior del Distrito y Territorios Federales, both found in Mexico City; the notarial archives of Coahuila, Nuevo León, Durango, and Tamaulipas; and municipal archives provide a wide range of cross-checks for an otherwise blurred picture of the ever changing makeup of property ownership and ongoing litigation.

The research problems are immense. The United States government, its officials, and American businesses, entrepreneurs, and persons who went to live in Mexico have lost or kept secret many of the facts regarding their experiences there. The papers of Wilson and Roosevelt administration officials in private collections, the National Archives, and the Library of Congress have been carefully culled to remove damaging or embarrassing material. The highly sensitive Claims Commission materials for the period since 1947 are still classified and not available to the National Archives. The materials pertinent to Americans in the Comisión de Reclamaciones Extranjeras (Mexican Foreign Claims Commission) are still classified at the Secretaria de Relaciones Exteriores archive in Mexico City.

Fortunately, the archive of the military government of Veracruz (records group 141) and related papers in the National Archives were too complex for the censors to control before they were released to the U.S. National Archives. The censors cleaned up the bulk of the correspondence relative to the vast array of weaponry left behind for the Constitutionalists at Veracruz, but they missed letters attached to transmittal slips and the warehouse inventories, which must have looked like ancient Greek to them. They left behind sufficient evidence to reveal the significance of the Veracruz intervention in 1914. The complexity of these documents was also a tangle for this researcher, however, who spent six months over a period of five years sorting them out. Fortunately the voluminous materials treating the Mexican Revolution found in the U.S. National Archives are well ordered and relatively accessible.

The most useful U.S. records for the study of American property interests are those of the United States and Mexican Claims Commissions (records group 76), housed in the Washington National Records Center, College Park, Maryland, and the Department of State documents on Mexico, series 312 and 412 (records group 59), at the Archives of the United States in Washington, D.C. These documents record much of what went on before and during the revolution, and onward to the post–World War II era. The themes treated include concessions of land and national resources by the Mexican government to American entrepreneurs, border conflicts, countless anti-American acts carried out by revolutionary groups, and the nationalizations and agrarian reform actions of the Mexican government during the 1920s, 1930s, and early 1940s. Those events complicated the American experience in Mexico.

The 312 and 412 decimal files are the most important records of the U.S. State Department that treat the United States and Mexico because, while they contain diplomatic materials as do the other files, their assigned purpose is to provide detailed reports on American individuals and on American business and property interests in Mexico. They include inventories of American assets in various consular districts, accounts of local disturbances when they affected Americans, evacuations, and political intelligence. Unlike the better-known, but less useful, 812 files, the 312 and 412 files are not available on film. They also have three ranges—A, B, and C—at the archives. Ranges B and C are superior to A range, contain more declassified materials, and are placed behind the A boxes in the stacks. When requesting them, the scholar should go to the boxes and specifically point them out to the archivists.

The records of the American-Mexican claims commissions, like the 312 and 412 files, have been almost entirely overlooked by scholars studying American-Mexican relations. Sometimes they have even been misrepresented by historians who have called them mere "insurance adjusters' estimates" or "exaggerated claims" by American "opportunists" seeking compensation with unjustified claims. These assertions are completely without basis and do the profession a disservice. The document collections with which this author worked, including those of the Special Claims Commission, which treated the period from 1910 to 1920, and the Agrarian Claims Commission and American Mexican Claims Commissions of the 1930s and 1940s, respectively, contain well over 1,000 cubic feet of materials. These documents detail the histories of the Americans in Mexico and include short biographies and autobiographical sketches, titles of property ownership, sworn and notarized eyewitness narratives, proof of the claimant's citizenship, and on-site reports by investigating teams from both governments. The document group titled "Extended Claims" contained some twenty boxes with even more detailed previously classified information.

Historians have misread the importance of these collections for two principal reasons. One reason was that in the 1930s Frank Tannenbaum and Edgar Turlington were both working on behalf of President Franklin Roosevelt's Good Neighbor Policy when they published their important books on Mexico. As Turlington's papers reveal, he was concerned that the American public would react negatively to the settlements and create uncertainty between the Americans and the Mexicans on the eve of World War II. The commissions offered little compensation to the great majority of less wealthy and powerful American litigants and to individuals who tended to have less complete records to support their claims than did their corporate counterparts.

Turlington worked with the claims commissions and then as a representative of some of the claimants. Tannenbaum served as a labor consultant for the American Metals Corporation of New York for more than two decades as a labor consultant in Mexico and Chile. He helped the company develop strategies for the control of Mexican labor unions and unrest. Both Tannenbaum and Turlington were anxious to protect the interests of American corporations, such as American Metals, that made private arrangements with the Mexican government. Turlington, like Tannenbaum, appreciated the gravity of the political tension that existed between the two countries as World War II began. Too much public outcry against the nationalizations and the small settlements being forced on over 3,000 American claimants could have strained relations on the eve of World War II.

Beyond their larger political concerns, Tannenbaum and Turlington had great sympathy for the agrarian reform efforts of Mexican president Lázaro Cárdenas. As a result they both understated the size of American interests, the numbers of American colonists affected by the agrarian reform, and the violence that had been directed toward them by the Mexicans during the revolution. The strategy of smoothing over the rough spots between the Americans and the Mexicans has deeply affected the thinking of historians. Another reason for the lack of attention given the claims commission archives has been the wounded pride of a few historians. Two prominent contemporary scholars, relying on Tannenbaum, have denounced the claims commission documents without ever reading them.

Records group 141 in the Washington National Records Center is invaluable for understanding the military government of Veracruz. Censored long ago, the index for the mass of documents offers no hint of the enormous military buildup and political intrigue that went on in Veracruz between April and November 1914. The innocuous-appearing invoices of the warehousemen that describe damaged shipments were left untouched, however. For example, a warehouseman would typically report that he had dropped a crate of rifles, damaging a few or even crushing a crate. In the course of his report he would include the identifying marks of the merchandise. By finding these markings in the warehouse inventories, I could, with the aid of the prominent Mexican arms historian James B. Hughes, identify shippers and confirm the size and nature of the consignment. Hughes could also determine the contents of some special shipments by their markings and weight. We were able to match large batches of arms and ammunition with the damage reports and transferral notes made in the warehouses. The markings and reports provided the basis for locating these items among the tens of thousands of shipping crates in the harbor. The Mexican Intervention and Villa's Revolution collections in the National Archives complement records group 141 by detailing the intense concern of U.S. Army intelligence officers in the populist Villista and Zapatista movements.

The Barker Texas History Library in Austin, Texas, is invaluable for data on the Brownsville merchants during the Tuxtepec Revolution, the growth of the oil industry, the economic and political backgrounds of entrepreneurs who ventured into Mexico, and politicians who exercised national influence during the Wilson administration. The Mexican holdings in the rare books and manuscripts room of the adjacent Benson Latin American History Library in Austin contains important information regarding American colonists and investors in Mexico from the late nineteenth century through the 1920s. This data is found in the Northwestern Railroad Records and in the Sherman Kile, Graham Ker, William F. Buckley, Robert S. Towne, and Lazaro de la Garza Papers. Kile was a U.S. military intelligence officer in Fort Sam Houston, near San Antonio, Texas, and the manager of a Mexican land development company. His papers provide a unique combination of perspectives on American business and military concerns. Towne's papers are excellent for insights regarding capitalization, daily business, and the crisis that developed in the mining industry once the revolution began.

In Houston, the Metropolitan Research Center holds the valuable John Henry Kirby and Joseph Cullinan Papers. These documents, and the papers of James Autry and W. B. Sharp at the Woodson Research Room at Rice University, provide the history of the Texas Oil Company as it entered Mexico, the intricacies of the oil business, and the roles of the Texans and New York financiers involved in American undertakings in Mexico. These men had long-standing business ties with James Stillman and were also longtime allies of Colonel House. They supported the Wilson presidential campaign and the American administration's policies during the Mexican Revolution.

In the Rio Grande Valley the James L. Allhands Papers, found in the John E. Conner Museum, Texas A&M University at Kingsville, Texas, proved invaluable in reconstructing the manner in which U.S. enterprises connected with New York capital and expanded across Texas and into Mexico. Allhands recorded interviews in the Lower Rio Grande Valley and along the border with railroad directors, land developers, and settlers in shorthand. They are stored in two boxes. The Rio Grande Valley Historical Collection at Pan American University, Edinburg, Texas, provided links between the land development companies along the border and Texas and northern financial interests.

The Bancroft Library at the University of California, Berkeley, contains a microfilmed set of the Collis F. Huntington Papers, the Hearst Family Collection, the papers of Placido Vega, and the interviews of Mexican industrial and political leaders conducted by Hubert Howe Bancroft. The Huntington, Hearst, and Vega Papers provide insight into American entrepreneurs and the Mexicans who invited them into their country. The first two collections complement the Rosecrans and Plumb materials. The Bancroft interviews carry that understanding further by drawing out the progressive mentality of the men who wished to see themselves and Mexico prosper. The Vega Papers provide an American West Coast version of the bond-selling efforts depicted in the materials left behind by Matías Romero and others that track events on the East Coast during the Revolution of Tuxtepec. The Huntington Library, San Marino, California, holds the Albert Bacon Fall Papers, within which the Franklin Lane Papers are an unusually rich source of information regarding American economic interests in Mexico, especially Sonora. The Tulane University Library, New Orleans, Louisiana, houses the Stanton-Townsend Family Papers, which include the rich files of the Rascon sugar hacienda at San Luis Potosí.

The Houghton Library at Harvard University and the Butler Library of Columbia University contain the papers of Charles and James Stillman, which, combined with the sources available in the Rio Grande Valley and Barker collections, demonstrate the Stillmans' deep commitment and manner of operation as investors in Texas and Mexico. The papers also demonstrate the role of the National City Bank as a source of finance capital for land development and railroad construction in Texas and Mexico. The Butler Library also holds the W. R. Grace Papers, which complement the Grace files in the Claims Commission Records at College Park. The Sterling Library Rare Books and Manuscripts collection at Yale University holds the papers of Colonel Edward Mandel House and John Lind. Although the House Papers reveal almost nothing of his economic life, they do have the letter by William F. Buckley, as the legal counsel in Mexico of the hated Texas Oil Company, that urges U.S. intervention in Veracruz. There is also an array of important correspondence, including letters from cousin Henry House, that allows the researcher to piece together at least some of House's non-public life. The Lind Papers are useful in their depiction of his hostility toward Villa and sympathy for Carranza.

Abbreviations

Many references to archives and holdings are abbreviated in the notes, using the following list. The bibliography contains a list of pertinent holdings for each of the archives.

AGN Archivo General de la Nación, Mexico City

AGNL Archivo General del Estado, Monterrey, Nuevo León

AHSRA Archivo Historico, Seis de Enero de 1915, de la Secretaria de la Reforma Agraria, Mexico City

AJTS Archivo Judicial del Tribunal Superior de Justícia del Distrito y Territorios Federales, Mexico City

AMCC Records of the American Mexican Claims Commission, Washington National Records Center, College Park, Maryland

ARGLI American Rio Grande Land and Irrigation Company Papers, Rio Grande Valley Historical Collection, Pan American University, Edinburg, Texas

ARPD Archivo Historico de la Propiedad y el Comercio, Registro Publico, Durango

BL Butler Library, Rare Book and Manuscript Library, Columbia University, New York

BLAC Nettie Lee Benson Latin American Collection, University of Texas, Austin

BTHC Barker Texas History Collection, University of Texas, Austin

CLP-NYHS   Charles F. de Loosey Papers, New York Historical
              Society, New York

CPD   Colección Porfirio Díaz, Universidad Iberoamericana,
              Mexico City

ELPP-LC   Edward Lee Plumb Papers, Library of Congress, Wash-
              ington, D.C.

FJHP–NYHS   Francis Jay Herron Papers, New York Historical Society,
              New York

HC   Hart Collection, Houston

HL   Houghton Library, Rare Books and Manuscripts Room,
              Harvard University, Cambridge

HMRC   Houston Metropolitan Research Center, Houston

HPC   Hayes Collection, Rutherford B. Hayes Presidential
              Center, Spiegel Grove, Ohio

HTML   Howard-Tilton Memorial Library, Tulane University,
              New Orleans

JECM   John E. Connor Museum, Texas A&M University,
              Kingsville, Texas

JPCM   Junta Protectora de las Clases Menesterosas, Archivo
              General de la Nación, Mexico City

MBR   Memorias del General Bernardo Reyes, Monterrey

MGV   Records of the Military Government of Veracruz,
              College Park, Maryland

ML   The Morgan Bank Syndicate Books, Morgan Library,
              New York

MR-BM   Archivo Historico de Matías Romero, Banco de México,
              Mexico City

NARA   National Archives and Records Administration, Wash-
              ington, D.C.

RGVHC   Rio Grande Valley Historical Collection, Pan-American
              University, Edinburg, Texas

RPD   Registro de la Propiedad, Registro Publico, Durango

SCC   Records of the Special Claims Commission, Washington
              National Records Center, College Park, Maryland

SC-TWL   Marvin Scudder Collection, The Thomas J. Watson
              Library of Business and Economics, Columbia University,
              New York

TOPO   Topolobampo Papers, Mandeville Collection, University
              of California, San Diego

WNRC   Washington National Records Center, College Park, Maryland
WRC   Woodson Research Center, Rice University, Houston
WSRP   William Starke Rosecrans Papers, Special Collections, University of California, Los Angeles

Notes

INTRODUCTION. IMPERIAL AMBITION

1. William Appleman Williams, *The Tragedy of American Diplomacy* (New York: Dell, 1962), 1–13.

CHAPTER 1. ARMS AND CAPITAL

1. John Austin Stevens, *The Valley of the Rio Grande, Its Topography and Resources* (New York: William C. Bryant, 1864), 21, 32.

2. *Correspondencia de la Delegación Mexicana en Washington durante la Intervención Extrangera 1860–1868. Colección de documentos para formar la historia de la Intervención.* (Mexico City: Imprenta del Gobierno, 1870), vol. 5 (Matías Romero), no. 425, p. 606.

3. For John S. Kennedy see Saul Engelbourg and Leonard Bushkoff, *The Man Who Found the Money: John Stewart Kennedy and the Financing of the Western Railroads* (East Lansing: Michigan State University Press, 1996). Kennedy entered the Mexican railroading with Taylor, via the lines in Texas; see 16–17. *New York Times,* 20 May and 5 June 1868.

4. William Dodge Jr., New York, to Matías Romero, New York, n.d.; see *Correspondencia de la Delegación Mexicana,* vol. 4, no. 413, p. 589. Information on arms can be found throughout six volumes of this work; see, for example, in vol. 2, no. 36, p. 588; annex no. 8, p. 674; and no. 395, pp. 678–679. In vol. 3 see no. 11, pp. 83–34; no. 29, p. 135; no. 289, p. 396; and no. 204, pp. 300–302.

5. For more on Romero's support, see Henry Clews, *Twenty-Eight Years in Wall Street* (New York: Irving, 1888), 45–57.

6. *Correspondencia de la Legación Mexicana en los Estados Unidos de America sobre los contratos celebrados por Don Juan Bustamante, 1862–1863* (Mexico City: Imprenta del Gobierno, 1869), 5, 12.

7. *Correspondencia de la Legación Mexicana con el Ministerio de Relaciones Exteriores de la Republica de Julio a Diciembre de 1867,* in *Correspondencia de la Legación Mexicana en Washington,* vol. 10, p. 241. For Tifft's role and the contract with the firm of John W. Corlies, see Henry R. Tifft, New York, 22 December 1887, to Matías Romero, Washington, D.C., vol. 3, document 35563, four pages, Archivo Historico de Matías Romero, Banco de México, Mexico City (hereafter cited as MR-BM); and Herman Sturm, *The Republic of Mexico and Its American Creditors. The Unfulfilled obligations of the Mexican Republic to citizens of the United States, from whom it obtained material aid, on credit— the nature and extent of that aid* (Indianapolis: Douglas and Conner, 1869), 18–94. The Woodhouse Bonds are discussed by several authors; see Edgar Turlington, *Mexico and Her Foreign Creditors* (New York: Columbia University Press, 1930), 162–164.

8. For the delivery of arms to Díaz, see Sturm, New York, to Romero, Washington, 6 August 1867, in *Correspondencia de la Legación Mexicana en Washington,* vol. 10, p. 241.

9. Numerous applications are found in the papers of Matías Romero, MR-BM.

10. Entry 47, box 18, case 822, Boundary and Claims Commission, U.S.-Mexican Claims Commission of 1868, Opinions and Decisions, 1870–1876, records group 76, Washington National Records Center, College Park, Maryland (hereafter cited as WNRC) and Hart Collection, Houston (hereafter cited as HC).

11. Ibid.

12. Jasper Ridley, *Maximilian and Juárez* (New York: Ticknor and Fields, 1992), 226.

13. General P. H. Sheridan, *Personal Memoirs,* 2 vols. (New York: Webster and Company, 1888), 2: 224–226.

14. Ridley, *Maximilian and Juárez,* 237–238.

15. David Smith forwarded supplies valued at $113,678. George Ramsay held bonds valued at $212,090 in return for "torpedo boats," and James T. Ames and the Massachusetts Arms Company claimed $160,800 in obligations, an increase of $46,000 over an earlier claim. Other arms suppliers and the value of their Mexican bondholdings included J. J. Wright Jr., $61,600; C. W. Mitchell, $197,166; A. C. Campbell, $208,000; the Philadelphia Arms Company, $120,000; plus the $131,622 of the American Arms Co. *Correspondencia de la Legación Mexicana en Washington,* vol. 4, no. 413, p. 589; vol. 4, no. 81, p. 161; vol. 5, no. 411, pp. 584–586; and vol. 10, pp. 90–577. Henry du Pont is discussed in Sturm, *Republic of Mexico,* 59.

16. Entry 47, box 2, docket 73, Boundary and Claims Commission, U.S.-Mexican Claims Commission of 1868, Opinions and Decisions, 1870–1876, records group 76, WNRC and HC.

17. For Herman Funke see *New York Times,* 16 September 1890 and 9 February 1884. Funke's complaints and references to associates in the Mexican enterprise are found in Sturm, *Republic of Mexico,* ii–iii.

18. *Correspondencia de la Delegación Mexicana,* vol. 5 (Matías Romero), no. 425, p. 606.

19. For the Liberal La Reforma program, see Richard Sinkin, *The Mexican Reform, 1855–1876: A Study in Liberal Nation-Building* (Austin: University of Texas Press, 1979).

20. Court affidavit, comun de Santa Maria Ozumbilla contra los vecinos de San Pedro Atrompan sobre tierras, Ramo Pueblos, Archivo Judicial del Tribunal Superior de Justícia del Distrito y Territorios Federales, Mexico City (hereafter cited as AJTS).

21. Ibid. For several thousand examples of colonial-era court litigation in which rural localities submitted their cases to the state for arbitration and won total or partial victories, see the Ramo de Tierras, Archivo General de la Nación. Perhaps one thousand similar cases from the nineteenth century are available to the researcher in the AJTS.

22. The Junta Protectora archive consists of local complaints that reflect the divisions that existed in the countryside and the policies of the political faction in control of the government at Mexico City. For examples of unrest in the region of Chalco, see Ixtapalapa, vol. 3, claim 19, pp. 184–203; San Pedro Actopan, vol. 2, claim 19, pp. 174–182; San Pedro Xalostoc, vol. 2, claim 21, pp. 260–270; Santiago Tianguistengo, vol. 3, claim 2, pp. 10–17; Coatepec, Chalco, vol. 3, claim 27, pp. 397–405; and pueblo documents from the *municipio* of Chalco throughout the Junta Protectora de las Clases Menesterosas (hereafter cited as JPCM).

23. La Junta Auxiliar Municipal, Cocotitlán, to Faustino Chimalpopoca, Mexico, 1866, vol. 4, claim 5, pp. 27–28, JPCM.

24. Faustino Chimalpopoca, Mexico, to La Junta Auxiliar Municipal, Cocotitlán, May 15, 1866, vol. 4, claim 5, page 33, JPCM. This strategy is made clear by the program of the Junta Protectora and underscored by the regime's alternative rural development program detailed in the Archivo Historico de la Secretaria de Transportes y Comunicaciones, which contains surveys of rural resources and economic potential, analyses of local population skills and feasibility studies for telegraph, road, and railroad services, and recommendations for government reform in order to achieve more efficiency.

25. See San Bartolo Tepetitlan and San Francisco Sayula, Ramo Pueblos, AJTS.

26. E. Basse and Robert H. Hord, *To the Public: A Brief Description of the Title to the Lands upon which the City of Brownsville is Situated* (Brownsville: n.p., n.d.), 5; in the Barker Texas History Collection, University of Texas, Austin, Texas (hereafter cited as BTHC).

27. For an extended discussion of Stillman, Kenedy, and King and the history of the Texans and Mexicans in the Lower Rio Grande Valley in the nineteenth century, see John Mason Hart, *Revolutionary Mexico: The Coming and Process of the Mexican Revolution* (Berkeley: University of California Press, 1987), 105–128. For Samuel Belden and Simon and Jacob Mussima, the other owners of Brownsville, see Simon and Jacob Mussima, Brownsville, to General Francis Jay Herron, n.p., 20 January 1864, box 1, Francis Jay Herron Papers, New York Historical Society, New York (hereafter cited as FJHP-NYHS).

28. See the "Ratificacion de una compra-venta del Sr. Bruno Lozano a favor de José Morell[.] el vendedor recibe una letra de $27,700 contra la casa de los

Sres. Stillman y Compañía de Brownsville," letter 131, 26 August 1852, pp. 235–236, Notario Bartolome Garcia, Ramo de Notarias, Archivo General del Estado, Monterrey, Nuevo León (hereafter cited as AGNL).

29. See Hart, *Revolutionary Mexico,* 105–128. Also Reynolds, Vallecillo, to Charles Stillman, Brownsville, 5 June 1852, box 3; Villareal, China, to Charles Stillman, Brownsville, 25 December 1852, box 3; and Morell, Monterrey, to Charles Stillman, Brownsville, 8 February 1962 and 9 June 1862, box 3, Letters, Letterbooks, Accounts, Bills, and Other Business Papers of Charles and James Stillman, 1850–1879, Houghton Library, Rare Books and Manuscripts Room, Harvard University, Cambridge (hereafter cited as HL). See also Flores, Vallecillo, to Charles Stillman, Corpus Christi, 29 July 1853, box 2, Butler Library, Rare Book and Manuscript Library, Columbia University, New York (hereafter cited as BL). See also Estadistico de diversos romos [sic] administrativos, Vallecillo, 23 July 1878, box 4, page 10, 1877–1881, AGNL.

30. Hart, *Revolutionary Mexico,* 105–128.

31. Ibid. For Brackenridge reporting as a "Secret Service" agent to Union forces on the movement of cotton across the border, see Brackenridge, Memorandum, 1 May 1864, box 1, folder "May 1864," FJHP-NYHS.

32. Hart, *Revolutionary Mexico,* 105–128. For Civil War cotton receipts, see Charles Stillman, Bills of Lading, clients 1859–1861; 1860 Account Book; 1861 Receipt of Francisco R. Rendon; 1863 Account Book; Morell, Monterrey, to Charles Stillman, Brownsville, 8 and 16 February 1862; and 1865 Diary, James Stillman, Diaries and Personal Account Books, 1860–1918, HL. The story of the Civil War cotton trade is told in L. E. Graff, "The Economic History of the Rio Grande Valley 1820–1875," Ph.D. diss., Harvard University, 1942, 496–607; Tom Lea, *The King Ranch* (Boston: Little Brown, 1957), 1:179–214; William Broyles Jr., "The Last Empire," *Texas Monthly* (October 1980), 238; and John Kennedy Winkler, *The First Billion: The Stillmans and the National City Bank* (New York: Vanguard Press, 1934), 25–31.

The Liverpool and Manchester figures are found in Charles Stillman, 1863 Account Book; and James Stillman, Diaries and Personal Account Books, 1860–1918, HL. For Matamoros transactions including those involving T. W. House, see Charles Stillman, 1860 Account Book, 1 July, 8 July, and 30 July 1860, in James Stillman, Diaries and Personal Account Books, 1860–1918, HL. See also Frederick Huth, Liverpool, to House, Houston, 1 February 1865; Huth, Liverpool, to Droge, Oetling and Company, Matamoros, 14 February 1865; Huth, Liverpool, to House, Houston, 22 March 1865; and Huth, Liverpool, to House, Houston, 12 August 1865, T. W. House Papers, vol. 2, BTHC.

33. For the charge that Stillman was a "traitor," see Simon and Jacob Mussima, Brownsville, to Herron, 20 January 1864, FJHP-NYHS.

34. Stillman discusses his bonds in James Stillman, New York, to Romero, Mexico City, 1 April 1887, document 34841, MR-BM. For Carbajal and the Republic of the Sierra Madre, see Hart, *Revolutionary Mexico,* 111. For Lewis Wallace and Carbajal, the latter's background, and details on the maze of intrigue

and conflicting interests involved in the sale of bogus and undercapitalized Mexican bonds, see Sturm, *Republic of Mexico,* 1–33; and James Morton Callahan, *American Foreign Policy in Mexican Relations* (New York: The MacMillan Company, 1932), 305–309.

35. Entry 47, box 10, case 440, Boundary and Claims Commission, U.S.-Mexican Claims Commission of 1868, Opinions and Decisions, 1870–1876, WNRC and HC.

36. *New York Times,* 20 May 1868 and 30 July 1868. The firm went through myriad name changes; it was also known by two other names: the International Company of Mexico and the International Company of Lower California.

37. Entry 47, box 18, case 891, Boundary and Claims Commission, U.S.-Mexican Claims Commission of 1868, Opinions and Decisions, 1870–1876, WNRC and HC.

38. Ibid.

39. Entry 47, box 8, dockets 149, 347, 535, 539, 713, 850, and 966, Boundary and Claims Commission, U.S.-Mexican Claims Commission of 1868, Opinions and Decisions, 1870–1876, WNRC and HC.

40. Entry 47, box 18; dockets 48, 49, 855, 856, and 857, Boundary and Claims Commission, U.S.-Mexican Claims Commission of 1868, Opinions and Decisions, 1870–1876, WNRC and HC.

41. For the Tehuantepec Canal Concession to the London bondholders of 1851 and 1864, see H. Guedella, London, to William Starke Rosecrans, 5 August 1870, folder 8, box 18, William Starke Rosecrans Papers, Special Collections, University of California at Los Angeles (hereafter cited as WSRP).

42. *New York Times,* 27 August 1868. For the complaints see book 2, entry 47, dockets 69, 190, 340, 439, 555, 782, 783, 784, 961, 967, Boundary and Claims Commission, U.S.-Mexican Claims Commission 1868, Opinions and Decisions, 1870–1876, records group 76, WNRC and HC. See also MR-BM and the indexes with brief descriptions of the contents in Guadalupe Monroy, ed., *Archivo historico de Matías Romero: Catalogo descriptivo, correspondencia recibida, 1837–1884,* 2 vols. (Mexico City: Banco de México, 1965 and 1970).

43. *New York Times,* 20 May 1868.

44. *New York Times,* 20 May, 5 June, and 13 July 1868. *Correspondencia de la Legación Mexicana en Washington,* vol. 10, pp. 288–291 and 302–303. For the sale of monitors, see pp. 309, 353, 360–363, 400–409, and 415.

45. For representative descriptions of the lobbying efforts, see C. Brink, n.p., to Rosecrans, Mexico City, 7 May 1869, folder 59, box 14; John McManus, Reading, Pa., to Rosecrans, New York, 14 January 1870, folder 18, box 16; Colonel Sylvester Mowry, n.p., to Rosecrans, New York, 17 February 1870, folder 77, box 16; and Salmon Portland Chase, Washington, D.C., to Rosecrans, New York, 22 February 1870, folder 87, box 16, WSRP.

46. *New York Times,* 5 June 1868.

47. *New York Times,* 13 July 1868.

48. William Hunter, Acting Secretary of State, "Appointment and Commis-

sion as Envoy Extraordinary and Minister Plenipotentiary of the United States to the Republic of Mexico," Washington, D.C., to Rosecrans, 31 July 1868, folder 10, box 12, WSRP.

49. For Edward Lee Plumb's efforts to advance the interests of the Pacific Mail Steamship Company, obtain Baja California, and gain other concessions for the United States in return for the payment of the accrued unpaid interest of the Mexican government's foreign debt, see Plumb, New York, to Senator Charles Sumner, n.p., 3 January 1866, items 8818–8822; Plumb, Mexico City, to N. P. Banks, Chairman of the Committee on Foreign Affairs, The House of Representatives, Washington, D.C., 3 January 1866, items 8823–8829; Plumb, Mexico City, to Banks, Washington, D.C., 9 May 1866, item 8841; Plumb, Mexico City, to William Pitt Fissenden, Washington, D.C., 20 July 1866, item 8865; Plumb, Memorandum, Mexico City, 9 June 1866, items 8845–8848; and Plumb, Mexico City, to J. Edgar Thomson, Philadelphia, 9 December 1867, item 8992, vol. 7, Edward Lee Plumb Papers, Library of Congress, Washington, D.C. (hereafter cited as ELPP-LC).

50. For the acquisition of Baja California by the United States, see Joseph H. Dulles, Philadelphia, to Rosecrans, New York, 28 October 1868, folder 94, box 12, WSRP.

51. For examples of Rosecrans's organizing efforts, see Edgar Conkling, Cincinnati, Ohio, to Rosecrans, New York, 6 August 1868, folder 17, box 12; 25 September 1868, folder 65, box 12; and 24 October 1868, folder 84, box 12; David S. Hoffman, San Francisco, to Rosecrans, New York, 21 August 1868, folder 28, box 12; Dulles, Philadelphia, to Rosecrans, New York, 28 October 1868, folder 94, box 12; Sturm, Newport, to Rosecrans, New York, 28 August 1868, folder 34, box 12; Thomas Stewart Sedgwick, Washington, D.C., to Rosecrans, New York, 30 August 1868, folder 36A, box 12; Major General Schuyler Hamilton, Newport, to Rosecrans, New York, 15 September 1868, folder 53, box 12; and Francis Darr, Cincinnati, to Rosecrans, New York, 17 December 1868, folder 132, box 12; Robert Symon, New York, to Rosecrans, Mexico City, 12 August 1869, folder 20, box 15; John Jacob Astor, New York, to Rosecrans, New York, 7 February 1870, folder 13, box 16; and Royal Phelps, New York, to Rosecrans, New York, 28 February 1870, folder 99, box 16, WSRP.

52. For the establishment of an American-controlled National Bank of Mexico with sweeping powers, see folder 4, box 59, WSRP.

53. Romero, Mexico City, to Rosecrans, New York, 5 October 1869, folder 68, box 15; and Antonio D. Richards, Mexico City, to Rosecrans, Mexico City, 29 December 1869, folder 159, box 15, WSRP.

54. William Mackintosh, New York, to Rosecrans, Mexico City, 12 August 1869, folder 18, box 15; Mackintosh, New York, to Rosecrans, Mexico City, 12 August 1869, folder 57, box 15; and Symon, New York, to Rosecrans, Mexico City, 12 August 1869, folder 20, box 15, WSRP.

55. Stewart Auld, Pachuca, to Rosecrans, Mexico City, 13 March 1869, folder 8, box 89; and William A. Winder, Los Angeles, to Rosecrans, n.p., n.d., folder 8, box 89, WSRP.

56. For Sebastián Lerdo de Tejada's opposition to Rosecrans and Romero, see Carlos Merighi, New York, to Rosecrans, Mexico City, 8 May 1869, folder 56, box 14, WSRP. For Brink see folder 7, box 12; Brink, New York, to Rosecrans, Mexico City, 7 May 1869, folder 54, box 14; and Romero, New York, to Rosecrans, Mexico City, 16 June 1869, box 14, WSRP.

57. For Lerdo's repudiation of the Mexican national debt incurred by Maximilian, see "The Mexican Debts," *New York Times,* 19 May 1867. American disgust with Lerdo's debt repudiation is best expressed by Funke, New York, to Sturm, n.d., quoted in Sturm, *Republic of Mexico,* ii–iii.

58. For Plumb's efforts to obtain Baja California and other concessions for the United States and private interests in return for the payment of the Mexican government's staggering foreign debt and Lerdo's strategy to delay the acquisition, see Plumb, New York, to Senator Charles Sumner, n.p., 3 January 1866, items 8812–8822; Plumb, Mexico City, to Banks, Washington, D.C., 3 January 1866, items 8823–8829; Plumb, Mexico City, to Banks, Washington, D.C., 9 May 1866, item 8841; and Plumb, Mexico City, to William Pitt Fissenden, Washington, D.C., 20 July 1866, item 8865, vol. 7, ELPP-LC. For the transfer of European-owned Mexican debts to the United States, see Plumb, Mexico City, 9 June 1866, items 8845–8848, vol. 7, ELPP-LC.

59. For the quote describing Lerdo, see Merighi, New York, to Rosecrans, Mexico City, 8 May 1869, folder 56, box 14, WSRP.

60. Francis Darr, New York, to Rosecrans, Mexico City, 19 February 1869, folder 18, box 14, and 17 April 1869, folder 42, box 14; A. Willard, Guaymas, to Rosecrans, Mexico City, n.d., folder 39, box 14; Conkling, Cincinnati, to Rosecrans, New York, 6 August 1868, folder 17, box 12; 25 September 1868, folder 65, box 12; and 24 October 1868, folder 84, box 12; and Darr, Cincinnati, to Rosecrans, New York, 17 December 1868, folder 132, box 12, WSRP.

61. Ibid.

62. For the acquisition of Baja California by the United States, see Joseph H. Dulles, Philadelphia, to Rosecrans, New York, 28 October 1868, folder 94, box 12, WSRP.

63. John McManus, Reading, to Rosecrans, Mexico City, 4 March 1869, folder 24, box 14; McManus, Reading, to Rosecrans, 4 August 1871, folder 2, box 15; William Jefferson Galewood, to Rosecrans, San Diego, 9 August 1869, folder 13, box 15; Sedgwick, n.p., to Ephraim W. Morse, Cincinnati, 4 July 1869, folder 13, box 15; Morse, Cincinnati, to Rosecrans, San Diego, 9 August 1869, folder 15, box 15; and Romero, Mexico City, to Rosecrans, Mexico City, 27 August 1869, folder 37, box 15, WSRP.

64. For the International Banking Corporation, see vol. 1, 1902, of *La Tierra de México;* the newspaper is archived at Hermeroteca Nacional de México, Mexico City. For the Hegemons see the *Directory of Directors of New York, 1910* (New York: Audit Company of New York, 1910), 268, 279, 310, 446, 492, and 732; or see any year between 1899 and 1910.

65. For the Mexican bondsmen, see "Bondsmen for the Railroad," 10 December 1870, folder 15, box 90, WSRP. The British concern of Barron and Gibbs

also opposed the Americans. For the racist reference regarding President Juárez, see John A. Gadsden, Mexico City, to Rosecrans, New York, 27 August 1869, folder 29, box 15, WSRP. For Romero see Romero, Mexico City, to Rosecrans, New York, 27 September 1869, folder 59, box 15; Romero, Mexico City, to Rosecrans, New York, 5 October 1869, folder 68, box 15; Romero, Mexico City, to Rosecrans, New York, 1 November 1869, folder 100, box 15; and Antonio Richards, Mexico City, to Rosecrans, New York, 31 August 1869, folder 41, box 15, WSRP. The Mexicans and their investments (in pesos) in the project included Matías Romero, 25,000; Solorzano e Hijo, 48,000; Vicente de Pontones 40,000; Juan de Dios Pradel, 40,000; José Acevedo, 30,000; Primitivo Serrano, 10,000; Manuel de la Hoz, 5,000; and Manuel M. Fuentes, 2,000.

66. *New York Times*, 15 March 1868. For the quote see Astor, New York, to Rosecrans, New York, 7 February 1870, folder 57, box 16, WSRP. For an insightful discussion of the power struggle between the state elites and Juárez government, see Barbara Corbett, "The Political Economy of the Alcabala: Taxation and Dependency in Mexico's Restored Republic, 1867–72," unpublished ms., Princeton University, 1987, 40. See also Astor, New York, to Rosecrans, New York, 13 January 1870, folder 13; Astor, New York, to Rosecrans, New York, 17 March 1870, folder 138; Joseph Brennan, Veracruz, to Rosecrans, New York, 1 January 1870, folder 1; Romero, Mexico City, to Rosecrans, New York, 24 January 1870, folder 30; McManus, Philadelphia, to Rosecrans, New York, 16 February 1870, folder 76; Royal Phelps, New York, to Rosecrans, New York, 28 February 1870, folder 99; Romero, Mexico City, to Rosecrans, New York, 9 January 1870, folder 11; Romero, Mexico City, to Rosecrans, New York, 24 January 1870, folder 30; Blas Balcarcel, Mexico City, to Rosecrans, New York, 26 January 1870, folder 33; and Colonel Sylvester Mowry, New York, to Rosecrans, Washington, D.C., 12 February 1870, folder 64, all in box 16, WSRP.

67. William Henry Seward, Auburn, New York, to Rosecrans, New York, 28 June 1870, folder 138, box 17; Thomas A. Scott, Philadelphia, to Rosecrans, New York, 24 March 1870, folder 156, box 17; George Peabody Este, Washington, D.C., to Rosecrans, 7 May 1870, folder 77, box 17; McManus, Reading, to Rosecrans, New York, 14 January 1870, folder 18, box 16; McManus, Reading, to Rosecrans, New York, 20 January 1870, folder 24, box 16; and McManus, Reading, to Rosecrans, New York, 21 January 1870, folder 26, box 16, WSRP.

68. Astor, New York, to Rosecrans, New York, 7 February 1870, folder 57, box 16, WSRP.

69. "International Railroad Project between Mexico and the United States," *New York Journal of Commerce*, 1 January 1872, box 16, WSRP.

70. Caleb Cushing, Washington, D.C., to Rosecrans, New York, 4 March 1870, folder 105; James Abram Garfield, Washington, D.C., to Rosecrans, New York, 17 March 1870, folder 140; Rutherford Birchard Hayes, Columbus, Ohio, to Rosecrans, New York, 21 March 1870, folder 147; and John Thompson Hoffman, Albany, New York, to Rosecrans, New York, 24 March 1870, folder 155, all in box 16, WSRP.

71. Elisha Dyer, Providence, to Rosecrans, New York, 19 February 1870, folder

84; Salmon Portland Chase, Washington, D.C., to Rosecrans, New York, 22 February 1870, folder 27; and Matthew Hale Carpenter, Washington, D.C., to Rosecrans, New York, 24 February 1870, folder 91, all in box 16, WSRP.

72. Horace Austin, Saint Paul, to Rosecrans, New York, 2 April 1870, folder 3, box 17, WSRP.

73. Nahun Capen, Boston, to Rosecrans, New York, 5 August 1870, folder 7, box 18, WSRP.

74. Symon, n.p., to Rosecrans, New York, 27 February 1870, folder 141; James William Simonton, to Rosecrans, n.p., n.d., folder 137; Richards, Mexico City, to Rosecrans, n.p., n.d., folder 136; and Romero, Mexico City, to Rosecrans, n.p., 23 December 1870, folder 126, all in box 18, WSRP.

75. Benito Juárez, Mexico City, to Rosecrans, New York, 21 January 1870, folder 41, box 16, WSRP.

76. For the sale and purchase of the San Antonio Lizardo Concession, see Richards, Mexico City, to Rosecrans, 27 January 1871, folder 43, box 19, WSRP. See also Balcarcel, Mexico City, to Rosecrans, 18 January 1871, folder 29, box 19, WSRP. For the original American involvement in the Tehuantepec Railroad project, see Maximilian's grant to the San Antonio Lizardo Company, Concession of Charles B. Stuart, Edward M. Serrel, and C. F. de Loosey, of the Mexican Imperial Railway, 17 March 1866, vol. 22, p. 21, Charles F. de Loosey Papers, New York Historical Society, New York (hereafter cited as CLP-NYHS).

77. For the American missionary effort, see Melinda Rankin, *Twenty Years among the Mexicans* (Cincinnati: Chase and Hall, 1875); and Deborah J. Baldwin, *Protestants and the Mexican Revolution: Missionaries, Ministers, and Social Change* (Urbana: University of Illinois Press, 1990). For specifics on Hickey see Milo and John Kearney, "A Historical Sketch of the Baptist Church in Brownsville and Matamoros," in *Studies in Brownsville and Matamoros History,* ed. Milo Kearney, Anthony Knopp, and Antonio Zavaleta (Brownsville: University of Texas at Brownsville, 1995), 270; and Ramon Eduardo Ruiz, *On the Rim of Mexico: Encounters of the Rich and Poor* (Boulder: Westview, 1998), 124.

78. Court affidavit, ciudadanos de San Salvador Tisayuca, 1866, Ramo Pueblos, AJTS.

79. Clews, *Twenty-Eight Years,* 369.

CHAPTER 2. RIVAL CONCESSIONAIRES

1. Benjamin Franklin Grafton, n.p., to Rosecrans, Washington, D.C., 4 August 1870, folder 5, box 18; Grafton, n.p., to Rosecrans, Washington, D.C., 25 August 1870, folder 18, box 18; H. Guedalla, London, to Rosecrans, 5 August 1870, folder 8, box 18; Richards, Mexico City, to Rosecrans, 24 November 1870, folder 88, box 18; "Decree of 10 December 1870," folders 3 and 4, box 90, WSRP. Article 7 reads "4000 hectares de terrenos baldios por cada kilometro de ferrocarril y telegrafo que se ponga en explotación."

2. Mark Saad Saka, "Peasant Nationalism and Social Unrest in the Mexican

Huasteca, 1848–1884," Ph.D. diss., University of Houston, 1995. For the Tehuantepec Canal Concession to the London bondholders of 1851 and 1864, see H. Guedella, London, to William Starke Rosecrans, 5 August 1870, folder 8, box 18, WSRP.

3. For the participation of Hyde, representing the Equitable Insurance Company, and James, representing Phelps Dodge, see D. Temple, New York, to Rosecrans, 13 March 1871, folder 121, box 19, WSRP. For excellent discussions of events in Sonora see Miguel Tinker Salas, *In the Shadow of Eagles: Sonora and the Transformation of the Border during the Porfiriato* (Berkeley: University of California Press, 1997); Ramon Eduardo Ruiz, *The People of Sonora and the Yankee Capitalists* (Tucson: University of Arizona Press, 1988); and Evelyn Hu-Dehart, *Yaqui Resistance and Survival: The Struggle for Land and Autonomy, 1821–1910* (Madison: University of Wisconsin Press, 1984).

4. Carlos Butterfield, *United States and Mexico Mail Steamship Line and Statistics of Mexico* (New York: J. A. Hasbrouck, 1859).

5. *Project of the International Railroad Submitted to the Congress of Mexico 1872, Documentos Relativos a La Compañía del Ferrocarril Internacional de Texas* (Mexico City: Imprenta de I. Cumplido, 1872), 71, in box 91; and "Comite Ejecutivo de las dos compañías unidas," folder 71, box 91, WSRP.

6. Henry G. Stebbins, New York, to Rosecrans, 4 April 1871, folder 9; Moses Taylor, New York, to Rosecrans, 5 April 1871, folder 12; and Rosecrans, to Balcarcel, Mexico City, 2 May 1871, folder 49, all in box 20, WSRP. Plumb, Mexico City, to Sanford Barnes, New York, 23 December 1871, items 9208–9210; and 26 December 1871, item 9216, vol. 8, ELPP-LC. See also McManus, n.p., to Rosecrans, n.p., n.d., folder 56, box 19, WSRP.

7. *Project of the International Railroad*, box 91; and "Comite Ejecutivo de las dos compañías unidas," folder 71, box 91, WSRP.

8. The membership of the executive committee also included experienced railroad financiers David Parish Barhydt, Thomas W. Pearsall, and Paul N. Spofford. For the executive committee of the International Railroad of Texas, see the 1872 memorandum, item 9851, vol. 11, ELPP-LC; and folders 67 and 69, box 91, WSRP. For Kennedy as interim president of the International Railroad of Texas, see Kennedy, New York, to Plumb, Mexico City, 5 August 1872, items 9499–9503, vol. 9, ELPP-LC. The Mexican government's reaction is found in Plumb, Mexico City, to Barhydt, New York, 21 February 1873, item 9981; and Plumb, Mexico City, to Barhydt, n.p., 23 April 1873, item 10087, vol. 11, ELPP-LC.

9. Item 9813, vol. 10, ELPP-LC.

10. For the railroad syndicate see Barhydt, New York, to Ignacio Mariscal, Washington, D.C., 10 February 1873, items 9924–9925, vol. 11, ELPP-LC; and the *Project of the International Railroad*, 3–4, 12, and 29, box 91, WSRP.

11. For the meetings held in an attempt to reconcile the Texas and Pacific Company's leaders with the New Yorkers, see Plumb, n.p., to Pearsall, New York, 13 September 1873, items 10201–10213, vol. 12, ELPP-LC. The participants at the negotiations to consolidate the lines are found in Barnes, New York, to Plumb,

Mexico City, 27 September 1872, items 9606–9609, vol. 10, ELPP-LC. Further efforts to "harmonize" and end the dissension among American financiers are described in Barhydt, New York, to Percy R. Pyne, New York, 10 June 1872, items 9452–9456, vol. 9, ELPP-LC. See also folders 65, 66, 67, 69, and 71, box 91, WSRP. For references to the Pennsylvania Railroad's Scott and Thomson, see Plumb, Mexico City, to Barhydt, New York, 9 January 1872, item 9230, and 17 January 1872, item 9235, vol. 8, ELPP-LC. For Plumb's attempt to block the Tuxpan concession, see S. M. Felton, n.p., to Barnes, New York, 14 November 1872, item 9749, vol. 10, ELPP-LC; and Rosecrans, San Francisco, to unnamed, n.p., 1 May 1873, folder 30, box 90, WSRP.

12. *Project of the International Railroad,* box 91, WSRP. Also Plumb, Mexico City, to Barnes, New York, 23 December 1871, items 9208–9210; and 26 December 1871, item 9216, vol. 8, ELPP-LC. For King, Brackenridge, and the border see Hart, *Revolutionary Mexico,* 105–128. The career highlights of individual financiers and their business relationships are found in the obituaries of the *New York Times* and the biographies of central figures.

13. The Stillmans maintained their $200,000 stock interest in Brackenridge's San Antonio National Bank from the 1870s until his death in the twentieth century. For interest payments see Brackenridge, San Antonio, to James Stillman, New York, 1 December 1876, box 11, Diaries and Personal Account Books, 1860–1918, HL. Regarding the payment of $12,000 as a 6 percent dividend, see James Stillman, New York, to Brackenridge, San Antonio, 15 December 1890, Letterbook, 15 March 1890–11 February 1891, box 4; and James Stillman, New York, to Brackenridge, San Antonio, 4 January 1907, box 6, BL. The extensive cooperation between James Stillman and Brackenridge is further documented in the Swenson XIT Ranch transaction with Lord Balfour, 20 January 1908, box 3, BL.

14. For the railroad concessionaires see *Documentos relativos a la compañía del Ferrocarril Internacional de Texas* (Mexico City: Imprenta de I. Cumplido, 1872), 1–43, in box 91, WSRP.

15. Rosecrans renewed the Tuxpan concession. See Plumb, Mexico City, to Barnes, New York, 29 May 1872, items 9395–9397; and Plumb, Mexico City, to Barhydt, New York, September 1872, items 9585–9586, vol. 9, ELPP-LC. Union Contract Company, Philadelphia, to Rosecrans, n.p., n.d., folder 11; "North American Railroad Proposal," 11 December 1871, folder 6; Scott, et al., Philadelphia, to Juárez, Mexico City, April 1872, folder 9; and "Estimate of Crop Shipments: Cuernavaca Valley and Vicinity to Mexico via Mule, 1872," folder 16; all in box 90, WSRP. See also Mariscal, *El Monitor Republicano,* [27 November] 1872, book 2, box 91, WSRP.

16. Mariscal, *El Monitor Republicano.*

17. For Vice President Lerdo's opposition to the Union Contract Company proposal, see Plumb, Mexico City, to Barhydt, New York, 30 August 1872, item 9565, vol. 9, ELPP-LC. *El Federalista,* 6 December 1872, book 2, box 91, WSRP. For the substitution of cash subventions for land grants, see folder 30, box 91, WSRP. For Plumb's attempt to block the Tuxpan concession, see S. M. Felton,

n.p., to Barnes, New York, 14 November 1872, item 9749, vol. 10, ELPP-LC; and Rosecrans, San Francisco, to unnamed, n.p., 1 May 1873, folder 30, box 90, WSRP.

18. See Rosecrans's resignation, 1 May 1873, folder 30, box 90, WSRP; see also Rosecrans, to the editor, *Diario Oficial*, 28 November 1872, book 2, box 91; and Rosecrans, n.p., to the editor, *Diario Oficial*, Mexico City, 26 April 1873, folder 29, box 90, WSRP.

19. For the network of interests in the Lower Rio Grande Valley and their interactions with New York finance capital, see Hart, *Revolutionary Mexico*, 105–128; and L. E. Graf, "The Economic History of the Rio Grande Valley 1820–1875," Ph.D. diss., Harvard University, 1942. For Texan attitudes toward Mexico, see *The San Antonio Express*, 7 March 1876; and "Our Relations with Mexico," *The San Antonio Herald*, 13 January 1876. For Mexican-American relations and conflicts in southern Texas see David Montejano, *Anglos and Mexicans in the Making of Texas, 1836–1986* (Austin: University of Texas Press, 1987); and Arnaldo de Leon, *They Called Them Greasers: Anglo Attitudes toward Mexicans in Texas, 1821–1900* (Austin: University of Texas Press, 1983).

20. Testamentaria de Gral. Gabriel Duran, 1838, Ramo Haciendas A (haciendas are usually located by the first letters of their name), AJTS.

21. For an excellent discussion of Chalco, see John Tutino, "Agrarian Social Change and Peasant Rebellion in Nineteenth-Century Mexico: The Case of Chalco," in *Riot, Rebellion, and Revolution: Rural Social Conflict in Mexico*, ed. Friedrich Katz (Princeton University Press, 1988), 95–140; and John M. Hart, "Agrarian Precursors of the Mexican Revolution: The Development of an Ideology," *The Americas* 29 (1972): 131–150.

22. Hacienda de Buena Vista, Ramo Haciendas A (misfiled because the owner's name Araoz, began with the letter A), AJTS.

23. Ibid.

24. Ibid.

25. For an expanded discussion of the development of banditry, nighttime flier posting, and other forms of peasant resistance in Morelos, see Paul Brian Hart, "Peasants into Workers: The Social Transformation of Morelos, 1865–1910," Ph.D. diss., University of California, San Diego, 1997.

26. Hacienda de Acamilpa, Ramo Haciendas A, AJTS.

27. For Lerdo's cancellations of the American railroad and other concessions, see J. Fred Rippy, *The United States and Mexico* (New York: F. S. Crofts and Company, 1931), 296. For a useful treatment of the Revolution of Tuxtepec, see Laurens Ballard Perry, *Juárez and Díaz: Machine Politics in Mexico* (DeKalb: Northern Illinois University Press, 1978).

28. *Corpus Christi Gazette*, 5 March 1876.

29. Hart, *Revolutionary Mexico*, 122–128.

30. *Chronicle of Finance and Business*, 6 February, 27 March, 13 June, and 22 August 1875.

31. Plumb, n.p., to Secretary of State, Hamilton Fish, Washington, D.C., n.d., item 10363, vol. 12, ELPP-LC.

32. Francisco Z. Mena, San Rafael, California, to Rosecrans, San Francisco, 17 January 1876, folder 31, box 31, WSRP.

33. Mena, n.p., to Rosecrans, San Francisco, 24 January 1876, folder 33, box 31, WSRP.

34. Juan Fermin Huarte, Colima, to Rosecrans, San Francisco, 13 February 1876, folder 35, box 31, WSRP. Emphasis on "we" in the second sentence is mine.

35. *Corpus Christi Gazette,* 5 March 1876.

36. *San Antonio Daily Herald,* 21 February 1876. For Buckley see Tehuantepec Inter-Oceanic Railroad Company Folder, Marvin Scudder Collection, The Thomas J. Watson Library of Business and Economics, Columbia University, New York (hereafter cited as SC-TWL). Information on the others in attendance is available in the *New York Times* obituaries or in biographical directories.

37. John Salmon Ford, "Memoirs," vol. 7, box 7, pp. 1237–1238, BTHC.

38. For the contribution to Díaz by the "New York Bondholders Committee," see Alberto Castillo, Havana, Cuba, to Juan Bustamante, Mier, Mexico, 15 July 1877, document 000921, Colección Porfirio Díaz, Universidad Iberoamericana, Mexico City (hereafter CPD). Castillo was the courier. For cash contributions see Sabas Cavazos, Brownsville, to Díaz, Mexico City, 30 August 1877, document 001000; Díaz, Mexico City, to Cavazos, Brownsville, May 1877, document 001403; and General Placido Vega, Brownsville, to Díaz, Mexico City, 26 April 1877, documents 000877–000879, CPD.

For Díaz's order to Cortina to turn over the command of his forces to General Geronimo Treviño, see Cuartel General, Guadalajara, to Juan N. Cortina, n.p., 31 January 1877, documents 000867 and 000918; Cuartel General, Guadalajara, to General Servando Canales, n.p., 31 January 1877, document 000867; and Cortina, Military Prison, Mexico City, to Díaz, Mexico City, 26 December 1885, document 11580, CPD. For Cortina's resistance to earlier Díaz-led uprisings, see manuscript 15575, MR-BM.

39. "Expecting a Revolution in Mexico Instigated by Díaz," *Galveston Weekly News,* 26 February 1876 and 20 March 1876. For Díaz in Bagdad see Porfirio Díaz, Bagdad, bundle 1, 1876, passim, CPD. For Mexican correspondence detailing the supply and shipments of arms, see Alexander K. Coney, New York, to Porfirio Díaz, Mexico City, 30 July 1877, documents 000825 and 000826; and the Wexel and De Grees Company, New York, to Díaz, Mexico City, 31 July 1877, documents 000823 and 000824, CPD.

40. Tom Lea, *The King Ranch,* 2 vols. (Boston: Little, Brown, 1957), 1:292; Broyles, "The Last Empire," 161. See also James B. Wells Papers, box 2H 207; and Ford "Memoirs," vol. 7, box 7, p. 1238, BTHC. For Brownsville merchant and Stillman confidant José San Roman as an intermediary between General González and the Americans, see Laura M. de González, n.p., to San Roman, 19 February 1876; and Charles A. Whitney and Company, "Agents Shipping on the Morgan Line," New Orleans, to San Roman, Brownsville, February 1876, box 2G 102, letters 1875–1876, San Roman Papers, BTHC. For arms shipments see the Armendaiz Receipt, March 1876, Samuel Baker and Company, Liverpool, to Armendaiz, Brownsville, and various inventory documents listing arms

in box 2G 102, letters 1875–1876, San Roman Papers, BTHC. For a detailed discussion of the network of south Texas interests directly involved or connected with intervention in the Revolution of Tuxtepec, see Hart, *Revolutionary Mexico*, 105–128.

41. For an expanded discussion of Díaz's guerrilla war strategy and the recruitment of provincial elites and military officers with their troops, see Perry, *Juárez and Díaz*, 215–284. For Lerdo's economic collapse see Hart, *Revolutionary Mexico*, 105–128.

42. Quoted in Turlington, *Mexico and Her Foreign Creditors*, 182.

43. See the commentary on Mexico and the rejection of the annexationist argument in the *New York Times*, 15 July 1885; and "Land Speculators' Interest in Fostering Revolutions and War with U.S.," *New York Times*, 15 August 1886.

CHAPTER 3. UBIQUITOUS FINANCIERS

1. Hamilton Fish, Washington, D.C., to John W. Foster, Mexico City, 12 February 1877, no. 370, vol. 19, *Mexican Instructions (1848–1898)*, Department of State, Bureau of Indexes and Archives; cited by Rippy, *United States and Mexico*, 297–298.

2. House Ex. Doc. No. 13, 45 Cong., 1 Sess. (Ser. 1773), pp. 14–15; cited by Rippy, *United States and Mexico*, 299.

3. For an extended discussion see Hart, *Revolutionary Mexico*, 124–125. For Díaz's grant to Treviño and the latter's contribution to Ord, see claim 328 (especially Lucy Ord Mason, Reno, to Secretary of State, Washington, D.C., 24 July 1939), Approved Agrarian Claims, 1936–1947, American Mexican Claims Commission (hereafter AMCC), record group 76, WNRC and HC.

4. Rippy, *United States and Mexico*, 294–295. For Ord's near court martial and reprimand, see Vega, Brownsville, to Díaz, Mexico City, 20 May 1877, documents 000877–000879, CPD.

5. Cortina, Atzcapotzalco, 27 October 1890, to Díaz, Mexico City, bundle 15, box 24, document 11968, CPD.

6. French financiers dominated Mexican domestic banking, controlling the Banco Nacional de México, the Banco Central Mexicano, and the Bank of Londres y México. They held 47.5 percent of bank capitalization, or a total of 130.6 million pesos out of the 286 million pesos invested in the industry. See José Luis Cecena, *México en la orbita imperial: Las empresas transnacionales* (Mexico City: El Caballito, 1979), 57.

7. Albert W. Atwood, "John Pierpont Morgan," in *Dictionary of American Biography*, 11 vols., ed. Allen Johnson et al. (New York: Scribner, 1958), 182.

8. For an example of the intensive financial ties between Morgan and Drexel, see "The Southern Improvement Company," syndicate book 2, p. 290, The Morgan Bank Syndicate Books, Morgan Library, New York (hereafter cited as ML); and Vincent P. Carosso, *The Morgans, Private International Bankers, 1854–1913* (Cambridge: Harvard University Press, 1987). Morgan's other connections in Great Britain included Brown Shipley, C. J. Hambro, and Knowles and Foster.

9. "International Company of Mexico," syndicate book 1, pp. 228, 261, and 272, ML.

10. Ibid.

11. Ibid., 261 and 272.

12. Carosso, *The Morgans,* 413 and 420.

13. Ibid., 420.

14. Ibid.

15. Ibid., 524–525.

16. "International Mercantile Marine," syndicate book 4, pp. 111–112; and "Consolidation," syndicate book 3, p. 6, ML.

17. Among the many studies of Morgan, see Ron Chernow, *The House of Morgan: An American Banking Dynasty and the Rise of Modern Finance* (New York: Atlantic Monthly Press, 1990); Ron Chernow, *The Death of the Banker* (New York: Vintage, 1997); Lewis Corey, *The House of Morgan* (New York: Grosset and Dunlap, 1930); Andrew Sinclair, *Corsair, The Life of J. Pierpont Morgan* (New York: Little, Brown, 1981); George Wheeler, *Pierpont Morgan and Friends* (Englewood Cliffs, 1973); Edwin P. Hoyt Jr., *The House of Morgan* (New York: Dodd, Mead & Co., 1966); Stanley Jackson, *J. P. Morgan* (New York: Stein and Day, 1983); and John Douglas Forbes, *J. P. Morgan Jr.* (Charlottesville: University of Virginia Press, 1981).

18. For more on Stillman's career see Winkler, *The First Billion;* and Hart, *Revolutionary Mexico.*

19. "Mexican Government External Loan 4% of 1910," syndicate book 6, pp. 55–56, ML. See also Carosso, *The Morgans,* 414–420. For the Panic of 1907 see "Loans on the Stock Exchange at the Time of the Panic," syndicate book 5, pp. 4–5, ML.

20. "Mexican Government External Loan 4% of 1910," syndicate book 6, pp. 55–56, ML; and Carosso, *The Morgans,* 584–586.

21. For the Paseo de la Reforma project, see "Mexico Land and Building Company—Paseo de la Reforma hasta la entrada del Castillo de Chapultepec . . . ," document 2710, bundle 1, 1885, CPD. For the articles of incorporation, see "Mexico Land and Building Company," County Clerk's Office, Division of Old Records, New York.

22. Morgan allowed Schiff to participate only when the latter's clients were needed to fill out syndicates. This happened more frequently during the first decade of the twentieth century.

23. "Chinese Development Company," syndicate book 3, pp. 18–20; "Pacific Development Company," syndicate book 9, pp. 215–216; "Burma Corporation Syndicate," syndicate book 9, pp. 69–70; "New York Orient Mines Company," syndicate book 10, p. 15; and "Oriental Development Company," syndicate book 10, p. 121, ML.

24. The Mexican railroads and their American holding companies were refunded several times by the Trio. For examples see "Mexican Central Refunding Syndicate, an issue of $35,000,000 at 5%," syndicate book 4, p. 156; and "National Railways of Mexico, June 1909, $24,000,000, Prior Lien 4½%

Bonds," syndicate book 4, pp. 151–152, ML. Citibank represented its clients on the Mexican Railroad's New York board, but Stillman refused to invest personally in the National Lines after the late 1880s because of their indebtedness, which totaled $25,000 per mile. Stillman made the highly intelligent choices of the Monterrey and Gulf, Monterrey Belt Railroad, and the National only via the merger of his Matamoros-Monterrey rights and his Santa Fe and Southern Pacific holdings. See Stillman, New York, to Balfour, London, 9 January 1891, box 4, p. 387, BL. For the directors see the voting trust agreements 1879–1900, Mexican National Railway Company Collection, New York Public Library. See also Cyrus H. McCormick, Chicago, to Stillman, New York, 6 January 1898, box 2; Stillman, New York, to Sterling, New York, 2 January 1890, box 3; and Frank Vanderlip, Seattle, to Stillman, Paris, 6 April 1911, box 3, Frank Vanderlip Papers, BL.

25. Winkler, *The First Billion*, 201–203 (emphasis mine).

26. Ibid., 48.

27. James Stillman, New York, to A. Balfour, London, 30 December 1890, Letterbook 1886 to August 1891, p. 366; Stillman, New York, to Balfour, London, 9 January 1891, Letterbook 1886 to August 1891, p. 387; and Stillman, New York, to Balfour, London, 16 February 1891, Letterbook 11 February 1891 to 31 August 1891, pp. 13–14, all in box 4, James Stillman Papers, BL. For a list of holdings see the Balfour Letterbook, 14 February 1893 to 8 February 1894, box 5, BL. For other transactions see Stillman, New York, to John Sterling, New York, 20 January 1908, box 2; Baring Brothers, London, to Stillman, New York, 17 May 1912, box 2; Stillman, New York, to Balfour, London, 14 December 1906, box 6; Balfour, London, to Stillman, New York, 4 December 1908, box 3; and Frank Vanderlip, New York, to Prince A. Poniatowski, New York, 8 December 1910, box 3, James Stillman Papers, ML.

28. Stillman, New York, to Gaspard Farrer, London, 13 September 1909, p. 926, box 6, Stillman Papers, BL. See also Stillman, New York, to Baron Von Andre, Paris, 10 September 1909; Stillman, New York, to Prince Poniatowski, Paris, 10 September 1909; Stillman, New York, to Count de Montsaulnin, Paris, 10 September 1909; and Stillman, New York, to Princess Poniatowski, 13 September 1909, pp. 919–925, all in box 6, James Stillman Papers, BL.

29. Biographical information on Stillman's British associates is available in many encyclopedias.

30. For ownership of the *Ypiranga* see "Steamship Lines Combination, Hamburg American Packet Company," syndicate book 3, pp. 1–2, ML. Morgan noted "best avoid publicity" when he acquired the Hamburg American line. For the *Titanic* see "International Mercantile Marine," syndicate book 4, pp. 1–2, and "Consolidation," syndicate book 3, p. 6, ML.

31. "International Mercantile Marine," syndicate book 3, pp. 3–6; and "Steamship Lines Combination, Hamburg American Packet Company," syndicate book 3, pp. 1–2, ML.

32. "Cerro de Pasco Corporation," syndicate book 3, pp. 59–60, syndicate book 8, pp. 101–102, and syndicate book 9, pp. 185–186; "Penyon Syndicate," syndi-

cate book 9, pp. 95–96; "Chile Copper Company" (Chuqicamata), syndicate book 9, pp. 21–22; "Anaconda," syndicate book 10, p. 150; "Braden," syndicate book 9, pp. 121–122; "Guggenheim-Braden," syndicate book 5, pp. 99–100; "Chile Nitrate," syndicate book 10, p. 29; "Peruvian Mining Properties," syndicate book 3, pp. 59–60; "Andes Copper Mining Company," syndicate book 10, p. 216; "Kennecott Copper," syndicate book 9, pp. 133–134, and syndicate book 10, p. 155, ML. See also "Prospectus: Central and South American Telegraph Company," syndicate book 1, p. 1; "Brazil Railroad Advance," syndicate book 5; "Brazil Railway Loan," syndicate book 7, pp. 5–6; "Republic of Chile External Loan," syndicate book 9, pp. 167–168; "Argentine Railroad Syndicate," syndicate book 8, p. 89; "Purchase of Argentine 5s of 1909 in Paris," syndicate book 9, pp. 23–24; "Transandean Construction Company," syndicate book 3, pp. 21–22; and "Chilean Transandean Railroad," syndicate book 3, p. 22, ML.

33. "Cerro de Pasco," syndicate book 3, pp. 59–60, ML. The other participants were Darius Ogden Mills, 11 percent, and H. McK. Twombley of U.S. Steel, 22 percent.

34. The list included British citizen John Jacob Astor, Belmont for the London Rothschilds, Isaac Guggenheim, and Cornelius Vanderbilt, all of the National Park Bank, $1.8 million. See "Panama Canal," syndicate book 3, pp. 221–222, ML.

35. The other banks and their shares were Morgan Hartjes of Paris, $5 million, Seligman Frères & Cie., $2 million, Lazard Frères & Cie., $2 million, and two French-controlled banks, $6 million; see "Panama Canal," syndicate book 3, pp. 221–222, ML.

36. "Harvesting Companies Consolidation," syndicate book 3, pp. 93–96, ML.

37. The initial board of directors included some of the most powerful and wealthy Americans: Jules Bache, of the Empire Trust Bank, which held the mortgages of the Mexican Northwestern Railroad, George Crocker of Southern Pacific, Marcellus Hartley Dodge of Remington Arms, Haley Fiske of Metropolitan Life, Henry Clay Frick of U.S. Steel, Isaac Guggenheim of ASARCO, Edwin Gould of AT&T, Harriman of Southern Pacific, the Mexican International, and the National City Bank, Marcellus Hartley of Remington Arms, John R. Hegemon of the Mexican Telegraph Company, Henry E. Huntington of Southern Pacific, James Hazen Hyde of the Equitable, John James McCook of the Equitable and Wells Fargo, William H. McIntyre of the Western National Bank (Morgan controlled) and Aransas Pass and San Antonio Railroad (controlled by the Big Four: Stillman, Rockefeller, Gould, and Harriman), Henry Clay Pierce of the Mexican Central, Henry Rogers of Standard Oil and the Cananea Copper mines, William Salomon of the Mexican Petroleum Company, and Alfred G. Vanderbilt of the Mexican National Railroad. For an announcement of its arrival in Mexico City, see *La Tierra de México*, September 1902, Hermeroteca Nacional.

38. For an excellent study of the American frontier experience, see Richard Slotkin, *Regeneration through Violence: The Mythology of the American Frontier, 1600–1860* (Middletown: Wesleyan University Press, 1973).

39. For the Gould hacienda see Benton White, *The Forgotten Cattle King* (College Station: Texas A&M University Press, 1986), 70.

40. For the corporate ties of IBC directors, see the *Directory of Directors in the City of New York* for 1898, 1899, 1900, 1901, 1902, 1908, 1910, etc. The Marvin Scudder Collection, Columbia University, contains an extensive file on the Continental and Intercontinental Rubber Companies.

41. *La Tierra de México,* September 1902. For other sources of financial aid for Doheny, see Jonathan C. Brown, *Oil and Revolution in Mexico* (Berkeley: University of California Press, 1993), 43. For a more biographical treatment of Doheny, see Dan La Botz, *Edward L. Doheny: Petroleum, Power, and Politics in the United States and Mexico* (New York: Praeger, 1991).

42. Andrew D. Barlow, House Doc. No. 305, 57 Congress, 2 Session (Serial 4520), p. 436; as cited by Rippy, *United States and Mexico,* 315–316.

43. See the *Directory of Directors of New York,* any year, for the directors and their interests.

44. William Schell Jr., "Integral Outsiders, Mexico City's American Colony (1876–1911): Society and Political Economy in Porfirian Mexico," Ph.D. diss., University of North Carolina, 1992, 305–314.

45. Ibid., 314–316.

46. For the steel, copper, rubber, and shipping trusts, see "U.S. Steel Common Stock," syndicate book 5, pp. 153–154; "U.S. Steel," syndicate book 5, pp. 1–2; "Amalgamated Copper," syndicate book 6, p. 153; "U.S. Rubber," syndicate book 3, pp. 65–66; "Consolidation," syndicate book 3, p. 6; and "International Mercantile Marine," syndicate book 3, pp. 111–112, ML.

CHAPTER 4. BUILDING THE RAILROADS

1. Edward Lee Plumb, Mexico City, to Pearsall, New York, n.d., item 10204, ELPP-LC.

2. Ibid.

3. Ibid.

4. George F. Henderson informed Rosecrans that Díaz had issued Cesar Cousin, a Pennsylvania Railroad supporter, the "Oceanic Concession" connecting Mexico City with Veracruz and the Pacific Ocean; see Henderson, Mexico City, to Rosecrans, San Rafael, 7 April 1877, folder 10, box 32, WSRP.

5. Henderson, Mexico City, to Rosecrans, San Rafael, 21 April 1877, folder 10, box 32, WSRP. For the contracts between the Mexican government and the Philadelphia-centered consortiums, see Huarte, Colima, to Rosecrans, San Francisco, 16 July 1877, folder 58, box 32, WSRP.

6. For the contracts see folders 1–8, box 92; folders 3 and 4, box 90; and books 1 and 2, box 91, WSRP.

7. See the contract in box 91, WSRP.

8. David N. Pletcher, "Mexico Opens the Door to American Capital, 1877–1880," *The Americas,* 16 (1959): 1–14; and Karl M. Schmitt, *Mexico and the United States 1821–1973: Conflict and Coexistence* (New York: John Wiley and Sons, 1974), 90–97.

9. See the "Concessions, Amendments, Transfers, Contracts" and "By laws"

with the American and Mexican participants in folder 67 and vol. 1, box 41; and books 1–4, box 91, WSRP. For additional information on the participants, see items 8898 and 9016, vol. 7; items 9178–9181, vol. 8; item 9539, vol. 9; item 10265, vol. 12; and elsewhere throughout the collection, ELPP-LC.

10. For the quote see Rutherford Birchard Hayes, *The Diary of a President, 1875–1881. Being the Diary Continuously Kept by Rutherford B. Hayes from His Nomination, through the Disputed Election of 1876 and to the End of His Presidency,* ed. T. Harry Williams (New York: David McKay Co., 1964), 104–105. For an excellent discussion of the Díaz-Hayes confrontation that views Evarts and Hayes as unified, see Rippy, *United States and Mexico,* 298–310. For the extensive economic involvement of Hayes and his advisers in Mexican agriculture, mining, and railroads, see William King Rogers Papers, box 3; Stanley Matthews Papers, box 2; and Pamphlets, all in Hayes Collection, Rutherford B. Hayes Presidential Center, Spiegel Grove, Ohio (hereafter cited as HPC).

11. Rogers, Washington, D.C., to Hayes, Washington, D.C., 8 April 1880, Correspondence, William King Rogers Papers, box 2, HPC.

12. Hayes, Columbus, to Rosecrans, New York, 21 March 1870, Rutherford B. Hayes Outgoing Correspondence; Matías Romero, New York, to Rogers, Washington, D.C., 22 March 1881, Correspondence, box 2; John C. Brown, Marshall, Texas, to Rogers, Washington, D.C., 5, 8, and 28 January 1881, Correspondence, box 2; and several letters in box 3, William King Rogers Papers, HPC. Also "Report of the Special Committee, the Cincinnati Land and Mining Association of Sonora," Pamphlets, HPC; and the property descriptions in the John C. Fremont Papers, HPC. Investors in the "Mexican American Railroad" included President Hayes, President-Elect James Garfield, General Fremont, President Díaz, and Romero; see Brown, n.p., to Rogers, n.p., 5 January 1881, William King Rogers Papers, HPC. See also General William G. Le Duc, *Report of a Trip of Observation over the proposed line of the American and Mexican Pacific Railway through the states of Sinaloa and Sonora, Mexico, in the months of May and June, A.D. 1883* (Washington: Gibson Brothers, 1883), Pamphlets, HPC.

13. For the San Antonio and Border Railroad Company, see the incorporation papers, July–December 1881, box 3, William King Rogers Papers, HPC; and folder 18, box 14, WSRP. Frémont acquired one-half of Cincinnati Land's Sonora tract in 1881.

14. Clews, *Twenty-eight Years,* 369.

15. Ibid., 430.

16. "The Boston Blind Pool of 1880–81," folder 53, box 4, Topolobampo Papers, Mandeville Collection, University of California, San Diego (hereafter cited as TOPO). The other syndicate members were bankers Henry Hastings, Thomas Gargan, A. E. Buck, and Walter C. Gibson.

17. Folders 1 and 8, box 1; and the memorandum October 1900, box 4, TOPO.

18. J. H. Rice, New York, to Díaz, Mexico City, 2 September 1895, folder 13, box 1, TOPO. The additional directors included several more bankers as well as political individuals. They included Benjamin R. Carman of the Santa Fe Railroad, William S. Crosby, Drake De Kay, Theodore Dodge, and Prince.

19. B. R. Carman, New London, to A. K. Owen, n.p., 29 November 1881, folder 2, box 1; Rice, New York, to Díaz, Mexico City, 2 September 1895, folder 2, box 1; and Memorandum, October 1900, box 4, TOPO. Also Thomas B. Lewis, Boston, to Rosecrans, San Rafael, 4 February 1881, folder 67, box 41, WSRP. For Higgins see folder 16, box 1, TOPO.

20. Report of Capt. R. I. Leary, USS *Iroquois*, Guaymas, to the Hon. W. C. Whitney, Secretary of the Navy, Washington, D.C., 13 December 1887, folder 30, box 3, TOPO.

21. J. H. Rice, New York, to Díaz, Mexico City, 2 September 1895, folder 13, box 1, TOPO.

22. James Campbell, n.p., to Walter C. Gibson, New York, 29 June 1885, folder 6, box 1; A. Butterfield, Topolobampo, to Rice, New York, 1 September 1895, folder 14, box 1; and A. J. Streeter, n.p., to Owen, n.p., n.d., folder 14, box 1, TOPO.

23. A. M. Gibson, Berlin, to Owen, n.p., 9 May 1896, folder 15, box 1, TOPO.

24. A. F. Higgins, n.p., to James P. Ramey, New York, n.d., folder 29, box 2; E. S. Herrera, Mexico City, to Rice, New York, n.d., folder 12, box 1; and list of assets and memorandum of land subsidy, folder 50, box 4, TOPO.

25. Rice, New York, to Díaz, Mexico City, 2 September 1895, folder 15; Gibson, London, to Owen, New York, 27 April 1896, folder 15; Gibson, London, to Owen, New York, 24 April 1896, folder 15; and Owen, New York, to Díaz, Mexico City, 22 April 1896, folder 15, all in box 1, TOPO.

26. Owen, New York, to Díaz, Mexico City, n.d., folder 1, box 1; and A. M. Gibson, Berlin, to Owen, New York, 22 April 1896, folder 15, box 1, TOPO. For the Pacific Colonization Company, see Assets of the Pacific Colonization Co., folder 50, box 4, TOPO.

27. Terrell, to Owen, New York, 31 May 1899, folder 19, box 2; Creel, to Owen, Chihuahua, 10 March 1900, folder 20, box 2; and Owen, to Creel, Chihuahua, 5 March 1900, folder 20, box 2, and folder 50, box 4, TOPO.

28. The company was known as the Texas Fuel Company until 1902, when it became the Texas Company.

29. Contract Stilwell-Owen, 21 April 1900, folder 35, box 3; W. A. Rule, New York, to Whom it May Concern (Owen), n.p., 15 March 1900, folder 20, box 2; Stilwell, Kansas City, to Owen, Chihuahua, 12 March 1900, box 2, TOPO. Also David N. Pletcher, *Rails, Mines and Progress: Seven American Promoters in Mexico, 1867–1911* (Ithaca: Cornell University Press, 1958), 266–268 and 270–271.

30. Pletcher, *Rails, Mines and Progress,* 270–271.

31. Stilwell, Mexico City, to Díaz, Mexico City, 28 May 1907, bundle 32, box 16, CPD.

32. Assets and Memorandum, folder 50, box 4, TOPO.

33. For Manuel González see Donald M. Coerver, *The Porfirian Interregnum: The Presidency of Manuel González of Mexico, 1880–1884* (Fort Worth: Texas Christian University Press, 1979).

34. For Díaz's acceptance of the Carbajal bonds, see the *Commercial and Financial Chronicle,* 23 October 1878. For the approval of the Interoceanic Railroad concession, see 6 June 1878.

35. *Lone Star*, 3 May 1884

36. The concessionaires included Harriman, Jay Gould, Sage, Morgan, John D. and William Rockefeller, Meyer and Daniel Guggenheim, Grenville M. Dodge, Huntington, Rosecrans, Abbott, Coolidge, Symon, Scott, and Henry Clay Pierce.

37. For an excellent discussion see Saka, "Peasant Nationalism and Social Unrest."

38. John H. McNeely Papers, box 17, Archives, Library of the University of Texas, El Paso.

39. "Texas and Pacific Syndicate," syndicate book 1, p. 169; and "Denver and Rio Grande Railroad Company," syndicate book 2, pp. 71–72, 244, and 260, ML.

40. "Mexican Central Refunding Syndicate," syndicate book 4, p. 156, ML.

41. Hart, *Revolutionary Mexico*, 135.

42. "Prospectus: Central and South American Telegraph Company of New York" (1881), syndicate book 1, p. 1; "The Mackay Companies Stock," syndicate book 3, pp. 237–238, ML. See also "The Mexican National Railway and Leased Lines," box 2; and "Note on Central & South American Telegraph Co. and Mexican Telegraph Company," James Stillman Papers, BL and HC.

43. "Atcheson, Topeka and Santa Fe Railroad Company," syndicate book 3, p. 36; and "Atcheson, Topeka and Santa Fe Convertible Bonds," syndicate book 4, pp. 23–24, ML.

44. "Southern Pacific Stock Syndicate," syndicate book 7, p. 135; and "Mexican Central Refunding Syndicate," syndicate book 4, p. 156, ML.

45. "Mexican Central Refunding Syndicate" (consolidating the "Mexican Pacific, Tampico Harbor, Mexican Central, and National Railways of Mexico"), syndicate book 4, p. 156, ML.

46. Hart, *Revolutionary Mexico*, 133.

47. Ibid., 141. A description of railroad management is found in the Lazaro de la Garza Papers, Nettie Lee Benson Latin American Collection, University of Texas, Austin (hereafter cited as BLAC).

CHAPTER 5. SILVER, COPPER, GOLD, AND OIL

1. Marvin D. Bernstein, *The Mexican Mining Industry, 1850–1950* (Albany: State University of New York, 1964), 23; see also "Our Relations with Mexico," *The San Antonio Herald*, 13 January 1876. For the quote see *The San Antonio Express*, 7 March 1876.

2. For Batopilas see Special Claims Commission (hereafter SCC), agency 55, entry 184, records group 76, WNRC and HC. For ownership and capitalization see Batopilas Letterbooks, vol. 1, HC. The directors and some of their notable directorate memberships were Nicholas F. Palmer of Chicago, the Quintard Iron Works; A. W. Zimmerman, Wells Fargo; Shepherd; Edgar Jorgensen, the Indestructible Fiber Company; Morgan O'Brien, Metropolitan Life Insurance Company; Henry E. Howland, Lawyers Title Insurance and Trust Company of New York; Samuel Elliott, Issaquah Coal Company; George Rowland, The Realty Trust of Atlanta; Louis Scott, the New York Cement Stone Company; and Dud-

ley Evans, Mercantile Trust of New York, Knickerbocker Trust, and the president of Wells Fargo.

3. For the shipments to the Park National Bank, see Walter Brodie, Batopilas, to the Batopilas Mining Company, New York, 23 May 1911, Batopilas Letterbook (unnumbered), p. 329, HC.

4. For the construction of Shepherd's Castle, see Lisa June Hart, "Shepherd's Castle: Documentation of a Gothic Revival House in a Mexican Silver Mining Town," M.A. thesis, University of Texas, Austin, 1988. For the artisans, craftsmen, and influences on design, see esp. 50–67.

5. Ibid. For the hospital see 46; see also Grant Shepherd, *Magnate de plata (Batopilas)* (Chihuahua: Centro Librero La Prensa, 1994), 61. The English version of this work is Grant Shepherd, *The Silver Magnate: Fifty Years in a Mexican Silver Mine* (New York: E. P. Dutton & Co., 1938).

6. Batopilas Letterbook (unnumbered), p. 306, HC. For salaries and extensive documentation of the sugar operations at Rascon, see the Minor Family Papers, Howard-Tilton Memorial Library, Tulane University, Tulane (hereafter HTML).

7. For context and overview see Bernstein, *Mexican Mining.* For Palmer and the Cubo, see Robert Woodmansee Herr, "¿Quien Vive?": An American Family in the Mexican Revolution (Wilmington: Scholarly Resources, forthcoming), chap. 12, p. 7.

8. For more on living conditions in the mining towns, see Batopilas, agency 55, docket 2490; and box 8, Approved Agrarian Claims, Extended (Declassified), AMCC, records group 76, WNRC and HC. Also the Batopilas Letterbooks, HC; and Rios Bustamante, "As Guilty as Hell!: Mexican Copper Miners and Community in Arizona, 1920–1950," in *Border Crossings: Mexican and Mexican American Workers,* ed. John Mason Hart (Wilmington: Scholarly Resources, 1998).

9. Batopilas Letterbook (unnumbered), p. 338, HC; Bernstein, *Mexican Mining,* 23; and Hart, *Revolutionary Mexico,* 43.

10. Bernstein, *Mexican Mining,* 19.

11. Ibid., 21.

12. Towne Papers, BLAC; and the files pertaining to Towne and the Metalurgica Mexicana in the records of the various U.S.-Mexican claims commissions, records group 76, WNRC.

13. For the investors see "List of Common Stockholders," Compañía Metalúrgica Mexicana, 22 March 1892; and "Purchases of Stock, 1895–1907," Towne Papers, BLAC.

14. Harvey O'Conner, *The Guggenheims: The Making of an American Dynasty* (New York: Arno Press, 1976), 95, 100, 104, 108, 110, 118–124, 163, 169, and 496. See also Bernstein, *Mexican Mining,* 50; and Thomas F. O'Brien, *The Revolutionary Mission: American Enterprise in Latin America, 1900–1945* (Cambridge: Cambridge University Press, 1996), 253–256.

15. Bernstein, *Mexican Mining,* 56.

16. Ibid., 54–55.

17. Moctezuma Copper Company, claim 48, entry 125, AMCC, records group 76, WNRC and HC.

18. Bernstein, *Mexican Mining,* 59–60; Moctezuma Copper Company, Department of State decimal file 312.115, National Archives and Records Administration, Washington, D.C. (hereafter cited as NARA).

19. Hart, *Revolutionary Mexico,* 142; Mario Cerutti and Juan Ignacio Barragan, *Juan F. Brittingham y la industria en México, 1859–1940* (Monterrey: Urbis Internacional, 1993); and *El Paso Herald,* 2 January 1905.

20. Bernstein, *Mexican Mining,* 45.

21. For Palmer and the Cubo, see Herr, "¿Quien Vive?," chap. 2, p. 17.

22. Ibid., chap. 2, p. 18, and chap. 6, pp. 29–30.

23. Ibid., chap. 12, p. 7. For context and overview see Bernstein, *Mexican Mining.* The gap between the American and their Mexican workers was so universal that historian Rodney Anderson called the Mexican industrial working class of this era "outcasts in their own land." See Rodney D. Anderson, *Outcasts in Their Own Land: Mexican Industrial Workers, 1906–1911* (DeKalb: University of Northern Illinois Press, 1976).

24. See Greene's report, Arispe Sonora, 29 May 1868?, folder 33, box 91, WSRP.

25. "Report of the President," 11 October 1905, Greene Cananea Copper Company, SC-TWL. The Southern Pacific directors with Cananea were William D. Cornish, Henry Huntington, and Epes Randolph. The Wells Fargo directors who joined the Cananea board were Cornish, Huntington, W. T. Van Brunt, and W. V. S. Thorne.

26. Green Consolidated Gold Company File, SC-TWL.

27. O'Connor, *The Guggenheims,* 281.

28. Harold van B. Cleveland and Thomas F. Huertas, *Citibank, 1812–1970* (Cambridge: Harvard University Press, 1985), 38–43.

29. *Anaconda Copper Company: State of Earnings and Dividends Paid* (pamphlet), Anaconda Copper Company File, SC-TWL. "Braden Copper Mines Company," syndicate book 9, pp. 121–122, ML.

30. "Amalgamated Copper," syndicate book 6, p. 153; and "Mexican Refunding Syndicate," syndicate book 4, p. 156, ML.

31. "Amalgamated Copper," syndicate book 6, p. 153, ML.

32. Hart, *Revolutionary Mexico,* 142.

33. Ibid., 143.

34. Ibid., 144.

35. Pan American Petroleum & Transport Company, *Mexican Petroleum* (New York: Pan American Petroleum & Transport Company, 1922), 17.

36. Ibid., 49 and 52.

37. Ibid., 20.

38. Ibid., 56.

39. Ibid., 74 and 80.

40. Brown, *Oil and Revolution,* 43; Pan American Petroleum & Transport Company, *Mexican Petroleum,* 35 and 52. For the quote see La Botz, *Edward L. Doheny,* 2.

41. Brown, *Oil and Revolution,* 55, 59, 63, and 67.

42. Agency 1643, box 39, Approved Agrarian Claims (Declassified), AMCC, records group 76, WNRC and HC.

43. Ibid. John O. King, *Joseph Stephen Cullinan: A Study of Leadership in the Texas Petroleum Industry, 1897–1937* (Nashville: Vanderbilt University Press, 1970), 115–118; and Hart, interview with John O. King, 3 September 1993, Houston.

44. Walter B. Sharp, San Antonio, to the Texas Company Directors, Houston, 21 September 1901, box 1, Walter B. Sharp Papers, Woodson Research Center, Rice University (hereafter cited as WRC).

45. Sharp, Report to the Texas Company Directors, Houston, box 13, file 579a, James B. Autry Papers, WRC.

46. Hart, *Revolutionary Mexico,* 148–152.

47. Ibid., 147–157.

48. Ibid., 148–152.

49. Brown, *Oil and Revolution,* 68. For an excellent discussion of northern Veracruz during this era, see Glenn Kuecker, "A Desert in a Tropical Wilderness: The Porfirian Project in Northwestern Veracruz," Ph.D. diss., New Brunswick: Rutgers University, 1998.

50. Mario Treviño Villareal, *San Carlos de Vallecillo, real de minas, 1766–1821* (Monterrey: Archivo General del Estado de Nuevo León, 1987), 68–102.

51. Miguel Nieto, Secretario del Estado, Monterrey, 10 February 1826, box 1, AGNL.

52. Correspondencia de Alcaldes Primeros, Real de San Carlos de Vallecillo, box 1; Estadistica de varios ramos Administrativos, 1854, box 2; Colección de Cuadros para la Estadistica, Cuadro Estadistica de Vallecillo, 1854 y 1856, box 2, folder 6; and Estadistica de habitantes and Estadistico de diversos romos [*sic*] administrativos, Vallecillo, box 4, page 10, 1877–1881, AGNL.

53. Estadistica de habitantes and Estadistico de diversos romos [*sic*] administrativos, Vallecillo, box 4, page 10, 1877–1881, AGNL. For wages in 1881 see Estadistico de diversos romos [*sic*] administrativos, Vallecillo, 1881, box 4, page 11, 1881, AGNL. For the school enrollment see Estadistico de diversos romos [*sic*] administrativos, Vallecillo, Bienes Particulares, 1882, box 5, AGNL.

54. For Stillman's income at Vallecillo, see Colonel J. R. Reynolds, Vallecillo, to Charles Stillman, Brownsville, 5 June 1852, box 3; and José Maria G. Villareal, China, Mexico, to Charles Stillman, Brownsville, 25 December 1852, box 3; and Jose Morell, Monterrey, to Charles Stillman, Brownsville, 8 February and 9 June 1862, box 3, all in Letters, Letterbooks, Accounts, Bills, and Other Business Papers of Charles and James Stillman, 1850–1879, Rare Books and Manuscripts Room, HL. Also Patricio Flores, Vallecillo (Mina de Jesús), to Charles Stillman, Brownsville, box 1; and N. Jarvis to Charles Stillman, Corpus Christi, Texas, 29 July 1853, box 2, BL. Later ownership by James Stillman of the Vallecillo mines

is found in Estadistico de diversos romos [sic] administrativos, Vallecillo, 23 July 1878, box 4, page 10, 1877–1881, AGNL.

CHAPTER 6. ABSENTEE LANDLORDS

1. For the rebellions see Hart, *Revolutionary Mexico,* 21–51; and Leticia Reina, *Las rebeliones campesinas en México (1819–1906)* (Mexico City: Siglo XXI, 1980), 291–321.

2. Santa Cruz Baltierrilla, vol. 5, pages 237–241, JPCM. San Andres Apaseo el Alto, Ramo Pueblos, and Santa Maria Mazatla, AJTS.

3. File 82168c, folder 10, Hearst Family Papers, Bancroft Library, University of California at Berkeley.

4. Ibid.

5. Agencies 618 and 1887, SCC, records group 76, WNRC. For the growth of foreign economic interests, see also Bernardo Sepulveda Amor, Olga Pellicer de Brody, and Lorenzo Meyer, *Las empresas transnacionales en México* (Mexico City: El Colegio de México, 1974); and Sepulveda and Antonio Chumacero, *La inversion extranjera en México* (Mexico City: Fondo de Cultura Economica, 1973), 57–58.

6. Letter 3a, page 203, vol. 1; letter 1711, page 240, vol. 2; letter 4565, page 44, vol. 26; letter 1213, page 100, vol. 9; and letter 3188, pages 241–244, vol. 18, Registro de la Propiedad, Durango (hereafter cited as RPD).

7. José Ignacio Gallegos (Cronista de la Ciudad de Durango), *Compendio de historia de Durango, 1563–1910* (n.p.: Biblioteca de la Camara de Durango, n.d.), 465; and letter 1583, page 90, vol. 2, RPD.

8. Cargill Lumber Company, file 1154, agency 94, SCC, records group 76, WNRC and HC.

9. Ibid.

10. Ibid.; and Cargill Lumber Company, file 1154, box 25, AMCC, records group 76, WNRC and HC.

11. Ibid. For an excellent study of the political background and cultural and religious tension at Tomochic, see Paul Vanderwood, *The Power of God against the Guns of Government: Religious Upheaval in Mexico at the Turn of the Nineteenth Century* (Stanford: Stanford University Press, 1998).

12. Wayne G. Broehl Jr., *Cargill: Trading the World's Grain* (Hanover, N.H.: The University Press of New England, 1998), 161; and White, *The Forgotten Cattle King,* 73, 76, and 95.

13. Report of Ed Morgan, Corralitos Hacienda Papers, BLAC and HC.

14. Nellie Spilsbury Hatch, *Colonia Juárez: An Intimate Account of a Mormon Village* (Salt Lake City: Deseret Book Company, 1954), 14.

15. Hart, interview with Lois Archer, Pacific Palisades, 8 January 1984; and Palomas Land and Cattle Company, agency 6153 (especially the Marsh affidavit), SCC, records group 76, WNRC and HC.

16. Ibid.

17. Ibid.; and Rhoades to Díaz, 1 June 1908, bundle 33, box 18, CPD.

18. For Hearst and Haggin see the indexes to the records of the United States and Mexico Claims Commissions, records group 76, WNRC. These include Haggin's properties in Chihuahua and his Jalapa Power and Light Company, the Tevis–Wells Fargo investment in the Batopilas mines, and Hearst's holdings at San Pablo in Campeche, Babicora in Chihuahua, and El Oro in Durango. For an excellent analysis see Joan Didion, "California," *New York Review of Books* (New York), 21 October 1993. For Anaconda and Amalgamated see Isaac F. Marcosson, *Anaconda* (New York: Dodd, Mead & Company, 1957).

19. See the exhibit describing the Hearst properties, Deming Regional Museum, Deming, New Mexico.

20. Agency 1582, boxes 37 and 38, AMCC, records group 76, WNRC and HC.

21. Alfred Shapleigh et al., dockets 1915 and 3084, entry 107, AMCC, records group 76, WNRC and HC.

22. Ojas 8 and 335–340, Indice, Apendice, Notary Rafael Flores, 1913; Ramo Notarias, Archivo General del Estado de Coahuila, Saltillo.

23. For excellent studies regarding the Yucatán henequen trade, see Alan Wells, *Yucatán's Gilded Age: Haciendas, Henequen, and International Harvester, 1860–1915* (Albuquerque: University of New Mexico Press, 1985); and Gilbert Joseph and Alan Wells et al., *Yucatán y la International Harvester* (Mérida: Maldonado, 1986).

24. Bernard Baruch, *My Own Story* (New York: Henry Holt and Co., 1957), 208–214.

25. Intercontinental Rubber Folder, SC-TWL; and Intercontinental Rubber, agency 5820, entry 125, Special Claims Collection, records group 76, WNRC and HC. See also Marco Antonio Velazquez et al., "Guayule; reecunetro en el desierto," La realización de la Conferencia Internacional sobre Guayule (n.p.: Gobierno del Estado de Coahuila, n.d.), 27–70.

26. Hart, *Revolutionary Mexico,* 97–103.

27. Arbuckle Brothers, agency 937, entry 184, SCC, records group 76, WNRC and HC.

28. Ibid.

29. Ibid. For the Batopilas connection see agency 53, entry 184, SCC, records group 76, WNRC and HC. For details regarding the Monterrey Belt Railroad and the Monterrey Railroad and Terminal Company, see Cresencio Pacheco, Archivo de Notarias, AGNL, especially letter 222 of 1899. The American banks active in Monterrey included American Surety, the American Trust Company, and the Traders National Bank, all of New York.

30. Agencies 53 and 76, entry 184, SCC, records group 76, WNRC and HC.

31. Agency 937, entry 184, SCC, records group 76, WNRC and HC.

32. Sergio Reyes Retana et al., *Historia del azucar en México* (Mexico City: Fondo de Cultura Economica, 1988), 1: 101–103; and H. C. Prinsen Geerligs, *The World's Cane Sugar Industry, Past and Present* (Manchester: Norman Rodger, 1912), 164.

33. Carosso, *The Morgans,* 535–536; Cleveland and Huertas, *Citibank,* 52;

and *Financial Chronicle*, no. 2253, 29 August 1908, and no. 1302, 14 November 1908.

34. Geerligs, *World's Cane Sugar*, 164.

35. The details are found in United Sugar Company, claim 185, docket 137, boxes 65–69, Approved Agrarian Claims, AMCC, records group 76, WNRC. See especially the Mexican pleadings. For Albert Owen and the consortium of Boston, Chicago, and New York capitalists who wrested control of Topolobampo from utopian settlers, see the Topolobampo Collection. See especially the Pacific Colonization Company, folder 1, box 1; and the Memorandum, folder 50, box 4, TOPO.

36. Ibid.; and Sinaloa Land and Water Company, claim 305, docket 258, AMCC, records group 76, WNRC and HC.

37. United Sugar Company, claim 185, docket 137, AMCC, records group 76, WNRC. See also Reyes, *Historia del azucar*, 105–106.

38. Stephens Brothers, Acapulco, to unidentified U.S. senator, n.p., docket 23, AMCC; and agency 2265, box 79, entry 125, SCC, records group 76; WNRC and HC.

39. Ibid.

40. Parraga Brothers, agency 2330, boxes 85 and 86, entry 125, SCC, records group 76, WNRC and HC.

41. Horace W. Corbin, docket 189, box 15, AMCC, records group 76, WNRC and HC. For early sales promotions of properties in the Isthmus of Tehuantepec, see the Romero Papers; and the Mexican Agricultural Land Company (which promoted the American colony at Loma Bonita, Oaxaca), agency 136, entry 125, SCC, records group 76, WNRC and HC.

42. Agencies 135, 136, and 2452, entry 125, SCC, records group 76, WNRC.

43. Castilloa Rubber Plantation Company, agency 153, entry 125, SCC, records group 76, WNRC and HC.

44. Mexican Rubber Culture Company, agency 1435, entry 125, SCC, records group 76, WNRC and HC.

45. Guerrero Iron and Timber Company, claim 321, docket 221, AMCC, records group 76, WNRC.

46. Alfred Geist, agency 2278, box 83, entry 125, SCC, records group 76; also Geist, agency 2278, docket 592, box 188, AMCC, records group 76, WNRC and HC.

47. Letters 486 and 487, page 68, vol. 4; letter 5010, page 95, vol. 29; letter 2492, page 115, vol. 15; letter 2666, page 290, vol. 15; and letter 2667, page 292, vol. 15, RPD. The Ramo Terrenos Nacionales of the Secretariat of Agrarian Reform is notable for its incomplete data. For the Corralitos see claim 2, Composiciones; Babicora is found in claim 8, Composiciones; and the Palomas in claim 108, Diversos. For the lack of registered complaints regarding land seizures, see Robert H. Holden, *Mexico and the Survey of Public Lands: The Management of Modernization, 1876–1911* (DeKalb: Northern Illinois Press, 1994).

48. Jantha and 623 individuals, agency 1359, entry 125, SCC, records group 76, WNRC and HC.

49. Schell, "Integral Outsiders," 367–369.

50. Ibid.; and document 018590, bundle 35, box 38, CPD.

CHAPTER 7. RESIDENT AMERICAN ELITE

1. John Sheppard McCaughan, *Personal Recollections* (n.p., n.d.), 121, HC.

2. Ibid., 92–93.

3. John S[heppard]. McCaughan, agency 2526, entry 125, SCC, records group 76, WNRC and HC.

4. Ibid.

5. Letters 3181 and 3182, pages 229–233, vol. 16; letter 2811, page 158, vol. 16; letter 3184, 1907, page 235, vol. 18; letter 3190, page 249, vol. 18; and letter 3647, page 148, vol. 21, Archivo Historico del Registro Publico de la Propiedad y el Comercio, Durango (hereafter cited as ARPD).

6. Letter 4589, 1912, page 69, vol. 26, ARPD.

7. McCaughan, *Personal Recollections* (n.p., n.d.), 132–133.

8. Letter 4615, page 105, vol. 26; letter 1583, page 90, vol. 11; letter 1583, page 90, vol. 11, ARPD; and Hart, interview with Manuel Avelar, Durango, 25 July 1992.

9. William Vernon Backus, agency 6519, SCC, entry 125, records group 76, WNRC.

10. Felix E. Godoy Dardano, "Transferencia de nuevas tecnologias: La electrificación del alumbrado en las principales ciudades de México (1880–1910)," *Siglo XIX* 5, no. 15 (1996): 50.

11. For the divorce settlement see Notaría José Saninana, letters 486 and 487, page 68, vol. 4, 1898; and letter 7, pages 14–15, ARPD. For Chamberlain see agency 6063, entry 125, SCC, records group 76, WNRC.

12. Notaría José Sarinana, letter 34, page 34, 1898, ARPD.

13. Louis E. Booker, agency 943, entry 125, SCC, records group 76, WNRC and HC.

14. Ingebricht Ole Brictson Biography, Brictson Family Papers, home of Marion Rauschenberger, Madison, Wisconsin (hereafter cited as BFP); and Matías Guerra, n.p., to Porfirio Díaz, Mexico City, 6 February 1908, document 1695, bundle 33, box 5, CPD.

15. Ibid.

16. Ingebricht Ole Brictson Biography, BFP; and Matías Guerra, n.p., to Porfirio Díaz, Mexico City, 6 February 1908, document 1695, bundle 33, box 5, CPD.

17. Archibald Hart, n.d. (Victoria, Texas?), to John H. Joice, n.d., Stoughton, Wisconsin, BFP.

18. Agency 1737, entry 125, SCC, records group 76, WNRC.

19. Agency 946, entry 189, SCC, records group 76, WNRC.

20. Ibid.

21. Helen Swift Morris Neilson et al., agrarian claim 240, box 16, AMCC, records group 76, WNRC and HC; and the Las Palomas Inventory, box 3703, Department of State decimal file 312, records group 59, NARA and HC.

22. Notary Jesús Cincunequi, 1884, cited in *Los archivos regionales y el trabajo en equipo* (Durango: Universidad Juárez del Estado de Durango, 1989), 3; Ladislao Gomez Palacio, vol. 1, 1892, pages 31–35, letter 15, RPD; and Pastor Rouaiz, *Geografia del Estado de Durango* (Tacubaya: Taller Grafica de la Secretaria de Agricultura y Fomento, 1929), 169. The legal dispute is found in "Statement of the Candelaria Gold and Silver Mining Company, April 1901," p. 56, Manuscripts and Rare Books Room, New York Public Library; see especially "Birmingham vs Burns," p. 3.

23. Folder 2, box 1, Townsend-Stanton Family Papers, HTML.

24. Folder 6, box 1, Townsend-Stanton Family Papers, HTML.

25. "Mexico MSS," boxes 7, 8, and 9, Townsend-Stanton Family Papers, HTML.

26. Folder 16, box 1, Townsend-Stanton Family Papers, HTML.

27. Ibid.

28. The quote is found in folder 16, box 1; see also folder 2, box 2, Townsend-Stanton Family Papers, HTML.

29. Ibid.

30. Ibid.

31. Folder 3, box 2, Townsend-Stanton Family Papers, HTML.

32. Folders 1, 2, and 3, box 2, Townsend-Stanton Family Papers, HTML.

33. Hacienda San Antonio Acolman, Ramo Haciendas SA, AJTS.

34. Ibid.

35. Hacienda San José Buenavista, Ramo Haciendas SB, AJTS.

36. Cumulative data are available in the AJTS and are scattered in other public and private archives.

37. For the classic study of Mexican labor during this era, see Anderson, *Outcasts in Their Own Land.*

38. Mexican Gulf Land and Lumber Company, docket 18, AMCC, records group 76, WNRC and HC.

39. For the Phoebe Hearst exemption, see Hearst, Washington, D.C., to Romero, Washington, D.C., 15 February 1895, document 44851, MR-BM.

40. Isabelle Miller et al., agency 1396, entry 125, AMCC, records group 76, WNRC and HC.

41. Ibid.

42. Ibid. For a brief description of the uprising on the Hacienda de San Pedro, see *Diccionario historico y biografico de la revolución mexicana* (Mexico City: Instituto Nacional de Estudios Historicos de la Revolución Mexicana, 1990), 1: 220.

43. Isabelle Miller et al., agency 1396, entry 125, AMCC, records group 76, WNRC and HC.

44. Laguna Corporation, docket 31, AMCC, records group 76, WNRC and HC.

45. Ibid.

46. Laguna Corporation, dockets 18 and 31, AMCC, records group 76, WNRC and HC.

47. Ibid.

48. Laguna Corporation, docket 109, box 44, AMCC, records group 76, WNRC and HC.

49. For an excellent analysis of the origins and depth of settler attitudes in the American West, see Slotkin, *Regeneration through Violence;* see also Reginald Horsman, *Race and Manifest Destiny: The Origins of American Racial Anglo-Saxonism* (Cambridge: Harvard University Press, 1981).

CHAPTER 8. BOOMERS, SOONERS, AND SETTLERS

1. For examples of the land promotions, see "An Open Letter to American Farmers and other discriminating Land Buyers," Mexico American Land Co., Kansas City, n.d., bundle 40, box 14, document 734, CPD. Also the Rio Grande Land and Irrigation Company Papers, Shary Collection, Rio Grande Valley Historical Collection, University of Texas Pan-American, Edinburg, Texas. The Sonoran land promotions in Colorado Springs are found in Annie Stevens, Lillie Mitchell et al., agency 2132, SCC, records group 76, WNRC and HC.

2. Kent Peery, Ponca City, to Díaz, Mexico City, bundle 32, box 6, 1907, CPD.

3. Frederick Nuffer (San Dieguito Colony), agency 141, docket 14, entry 189, SCC, records group 76, WNRC.

4. Ibid.

5. F. LaMond Tullis, *Mormons in Mexico: The Dynamics of Faith and Culture* (Ogden: Utah State University Press, 1987), 4.

6. Ibid., 53.

7. Hatch, *Colonia Juárez,* 14.

8. Tullis, *Mormons in Mexico,* 57 and 60; and Hatch, *Colonia Juárez,* 7–14.

9. Hatch, *Colonia Juárez,* 57–59.

10. Ibid., 59.

11. Ibid., 92 and 94.

12. Hyrum Turley, agency 5998, entry 125, SCC, records group 76, WNRC and HC.

13. J. W. Palmer, agency 5947, entry 125, SCC; and Peter K. Lemmon Jr., agency 111; and Milton Lowry Gruwell, docket 114, AMCC, records group 76, WNRC and HC.

14. Randall S. Hanson, "A Day of Ideals: Catholic Social Action in the Age of the Mexican Revolution, 1867–1929," Ph.D. diss., Indiana University, 1994, 141–147.

15. Palomar y Vizcarra to Padre David Ramirez, March 9, 1924, Palomar y Vizcarra Archive, cited in Hanson, "A Day of Ideals," 147.

16. Document 2710, 1885, CPD. For the capitalists see *Who Was Who in America.*

17. See *Who Was Who* and *New York Times* obituaries.

18. Lewis Lamm, E. N. Brown, and E. W. Orrin, agency 6021, entry 125, SCC, records group 76, WNRC and HC.

19. Lewis Lamm, E. N. Brown, and E. W. Orrin, agency 6021, entry 125; and C. and A. Dolley, agency 2175, SCC, records group 76, WNRC and HC. Also

document 2710, year 1885, CPD. Also see the Rosecrans Papers and "Nelson Rhoades" in the index to the Approved Agrarian Claims, AMCC, records group 76, WNRC.

20. Claims 4, 112, 174, 176, 177, 278, and 299, box 10; claims 155, 174, 254, 255, 266, and 278, box 15; and Memoranda, claims 12, 101, 118, 120, and 121 (consolidated as one claim), AMCC, records group 76, WNRC.

21. Flora Ella Medlin, agency 5279, entry 125, SCC, records group 76, WNRC.

22. G. E. Fuller, agency 2190, entry 125, SCC, records group 76, WNRC.

23. Ibid.; and Hiram Blagg, agency 2124, SCC, records group 76, WNRC.

24. Blagg, agency 2124; and O. D. Jones, agency 6054, SCC, records group 76, WNRC.

25. Jasper Exendine, agency 677, SCC, records group 76, WNRC.

26. Michael Bowes, Mrs. R. P. Cox, Jacob Gergen, and George W. Graff, agency 6173, SCC, records group 76, WNRC. Also Department of State decimal file 312.451/37, box 3812, records group 59, NARA.

27. Henry Martin Pierce, agency 111, entry 125, SCC, records group 76, WNRC. See also claims listed under agency numbers 34, 47, 76, 81, 115, 118, 135, 140, 150, 172, 1992, 2135, 4546, and 4547.

28. John T. Cave and R. L. Summerlin, agencies 53 and 53a, entry 189, SCC, records group 76, WNRC and HC.

29. Ibid.

30. Ruiz, *On the Rim of Mexico*, 45–56.

31. William H. Beezley, *Judas at the Jockey Club and Other Episodes of Porfirian Mexico* (Lincoln: University of Nebraska Press, 1987), 22.

32. Ibid., 19–20.

33. Ibid., 19–22.

34. Ibid., 26–66.

35. Alberto Robles Gil (Secretario de Fomento), *Memoria de fomento, 1911–1912* (Mexico City: Imprenta del Gobierno, 1912), 408. The Madero administration found 22,731,678 hectares of *terrenos nacionales* for potential use in its agrarian reform effort. For a useful study of the continuing industrialization effort, see Stephen H. Haber, *Industry and Underdevelopment: The Industrialization of Mexico, 1890–1940* (Stanford: Stanford University Press, 1989).

36. For the quote see the investigator's report, Edward Herbert Thompson, agency 254, docket 14.7, box 24, Approved Agrarian Claims, AMCC, records group 76, WNRC and HC. For examples of the critique, see John Kenneth Turner, *Barbarous Mexico* (Austin: University of Texas Press, 1969). For additional information see agency 2343, entry 125, SCC, records group 76, WNRC and HC.

37. James Wilkie, *The Mexican Revolution: Federal Expenditure and Social Change since 1910* (Berkeley: University of California Press, 1967).

38. Hart, *Revolutionary Mexico*, 161. The original analysis of the failure to create a landholding middle class was offered in Wilkie, *The Mexican Revolution*. See especially Moisés González Navarro, *El Porfiriato: La vida social,*

vol. 4 of *Historia moderna de México,* ed. Daniel Cosio Villegas (Mexico City: Editorial Hermes, 1957), 210, for land ownership data.

39. Wilkie, *The Mexican Revolution.*

40. Rouaix, *Geografía de Durango,* 155–156; Arnulfo Ochoa Reyes, *Historia del Estado de Durango* (Durango: Editorial Patria, 1934), 312; and David Walker, " 'Una Gran Familia': The Social Topography of Cuencame, Durango, Mexico, 1890–1930," unpublished manuscript.

41. Hart, *Revolutionary Mexico,* 163–164.

42. Letter, no name, n.p., n.d., to Edith O'Shaughnessy, New York, Edith and Nelson O'Shaughnessy Papers, box 4, 1910–1915, Rare Books and Manuscripts Room, New York Public Library.

CHAPTER 9. MEXICO FOR THE MEXICANS

1. For the Spaniards, who were also singled out but far less dominant, see the records of the Secretaria de la Reforma in the new Archivo Agrario in Mexico City and the regional centers of the Secretaria throughout Mexico.

2. For a discussion of the Guadalajara incident and a differing interpretation, see Avital H. Bloch and Servando Ortoll, " '¡Viva Mexico! ¡Mueran los yanquis!': The Guadalajara Riots of 1910," in *Riots in the Cities, Popular Politics and the Urban Poor in Latin America, 1765–1910,* ed. Silvia M. Arrom and Servando Ortoll (Wilmington: Scholarly Resources, 1996), 195–223.

3. Stephens Brothers, Acapulco, to unidentified U.S. senator, n.p., 9 March 1935, docket 23, AMCC, record group 76, WNRC and HC.

4. For Cullinan, Texaco, the Rockefellers, and Standard Oil, see Hart, *Revolutionary Mexico,* 147–149 and 281–299. For the quote see Joseph Cullinan, Houston, to Arnold Schlact, New York, 11 March 1913, file 619, box 16, James Autry Papers, Woodson Research Center, Rice University, Houston (hereafter cited as WRC).

5. *El Paso Herald,* 14 August 1912.

6. Illegible, agency 2343, entry 125, SCC, record group 76, WNRC and HC.

7. Letter 4565, page 44, vol. 26; letter 4614, page 105, vol. 26; letter 4614, page 105, vol. 27; and letter 4707, page 37, vol. 27, ARPD.

8. For the Plan de Ayala, see John Womack Jr., *Zapata and the Mexican Revolution* (Vintage: New York, 1968), 400–404.

9. For examples of the attacks on American properties in 1912, see agency numbers 289, 331, 436, 1315, 1316, 1318, 1341, 1343, 1396, 1399, 1524, 1553, 1568, 1700, 1737, 1740, 1921, 2343, 2346, 2381, 2450, 2452, 2606, 4486, 5817, and 5820, SCC, record group 76, WNRC and HC; and the Department of State decimal files, series 312.11 collection, NARA. For Markley and Miller see Isabelle Miller, agency 1396, docket 2693, entry 125, AMCC, record group 76, WNRC and HC.

10. *El Paso Herald,* 9 May, 14 August, and 12 October 1912.

11. Annie Stevens, Lillie Mitchell et al., agency 2132, entry 125, SCC, record

group 76, WNRC. See also Creek Durango Land Company, letter 3647, page 148, vol. 21, ARPD.

12. Agencies 1315, 2132, 2134, and 2704, entry 125, Approved Agrarian Claims, AMCC, record group 76, WNRC and HC.

13. Edward Herbert Thompson, agency 254, docket 147, box 24, Approved Agrarian Claims, AMCC, record group 76, WNRC and HC.

14. Isabelle Miller et al., agency 1396, docket 2693, entry 125, AMCC, record group 76, WNRC and HC.

15. Ibid.

16. Ibid.

17. Ibid.

18. Report of Commissioner Underwood, agency 2693, entry 107, AMCC, record group 76, WNRC and HC.

19. E. Kirby-Smith, agency 1396, docket 2693, entry 125, AMCC, WNRC and HC; see also International Lumber & Development Company and Tropical Products Company, dockets 1 and 2315, AMCC, WNRC and HC.

20. For attacks on the Northwestern Railroad, see boxes 10 and 11, John Mc-Neeley Papers, Special Collections, University of Texas at El Paso Library. The opposed views of Doheny's behavior are found in La Botz, *Edward L. Doheny;* and Brown, *Oil and Revolution.* The anarchist presence at Tampico is represented in their newspapers *Fuerza y cerebro* (Tampico, 1917–1918) and *Hermanos rojos* (Villa Cecilia, 1918). See also Syndicate of Workers of the Mexican Gulf Oil Company, Tampico, to management, Tampico, 8 September 1924, agency 1436, AMCC, WNRC and HC.

21. Isaiah Miller and John Markley, Ciudad del Carmen, to Henry Lane Wilson, Mexico City, 22 November 1911, agency 1396, docket 2693, entry 125, AMCC, records group 76, WNRC and HC.

22. Ibid.

23. Ibid.

24. Ibid.

25. American Manufacturing Company, "Sakahal Ranch," agency 1752, entry 125, SCC, record group 76, WNRC and HC.

26. Michael C. Meyer, *Mexican Rebel: Pascual Orozco and the Mexican Revolution, 1910–1915* (Lincoln: University of Nebraska Press, 1967), 48–93.

27. Ibid., 67–93.

28. John T. Cave, agencies 53 and 2052, entry 189, 1935–1938 awards, claims of 1924–1938, SCC, record group 76, WNRC and HC.

29. Batopilas Mining Company, agencies 53 and 53a, entry 189, 1935–1938 awards, claims of 1924–1938, SCC, record group 76, WNRC and HC.

30. Herr, "¿Quien Vive?," chap. 4, pp. 10–12. For the quote see Marion Clyde Dyer, agency 1922, entry 125, AMCC, record group 76, WNRC and HC.

31. The Southwestern Land and Cattle Company, agency 2381, entry 125, 1935–1938 awards, claims of 1924–1938, SCC, record group 76, WNRC and HC.

32. Marion Clyde Dyer, agency 1922, entry 125, AMCC, record group 76,

WNRC and HC. Also Department of State decimal files 312.11/1001a, NARA and HC. Also "Americans Still Flee from Sin," *El Paso Herald,* 9 May 1912; and *El Paso Herald,* 22 November and 10 December 1912.

33. Ernest L. McLean and E. M. Leavitt, agency 954, entry 184, 1935–1938 awards, claims of 1924–1938, SCC, record group 76, WNRC and HC.

34. Ibid.

35. Batopilas Mining, agency 53, entry 184, 1935–1938 awards, claims of 1924–1938, SCC, record group 76, WNRC and HC.

36. Neilson, agency 240; and Palomas Land and Cattle, agency 6153, entry 125, AMCC, record group 76, WNRC and HC.

37. George A. Laird, San Pedro Chihuahua, 28 December 1910, to Ed Morgan, New York, Corralitos Collection, BLAC and HC.

38. Report of Ed Morgan, New York, to the Corralitos Directors, New York, 8 November 1911; and Reports of Houghton, Corralitos, to the Directors, New York, 28, 30, and 31 December 1910, Corralitos Hacienda Papers, BLAC and HC.

39. Ibid.

40. For the quote see James E. Whetten, agency 334, entry 125, SCC, record group 76, WNRC and HC. Identical and highly specific reports are also found in Abel Hardy, agency 289; Eddie L. Cluff, agency 331; and Parley Fenn, agency 5811, entry 125, SCC, record group 76, WNRC and HC.

41. Parley Fenn, agency 5811, entry 125, SCC, record group 76, WNRC and HC. Also *El Paso Herald,* 10 December 1912.

42. Hardy, agency 289, entry 125, SCC, record group 76, WNRC and HC.

43. For the quotes see Whetten, agency 334, entry 125, SCC, record group 76, WNRC and HC. For examples of a large body of supportive testimony, see Hardy, agency 289; and Cluff, agency 331, entry 125, SCC, record group 76, WNRC and HC. Also Peter K. Lemmon Jr., docket 11; and Estate of Milton Lowry Gruwell, docket 114, entry 125, AMCC, record group 76, WNRC and HC.

44. Ibid.

45. Hardy, agency 289, entry 125, SCC, record group 76, WNRC and HC.

46. Ibid.

47. The quote is from Whetten, agency 334, entry 125, SCC, record group 76, WNRC and HC.

48. See Department of State dispatch number 812.00/5128 in William Henry Jennings, John Rufus Blocker, and Edna Jeffreys Moore, agency 1737, entry 125, SCC, record group 76, WNRC and HC.

49. "U.S. Rubber Syndicate," syndicate book 3, pp. 65–66; "U.S. Rubber Collateral Funding," syndicate book 5, pp. 37–38 and 85–86; "Intercontinental Rubber Company Stock," syndicate book 5, p. 201; and "Penyon Corporation Series B Receipts held by Intercontinental Rubber Company," syndicate book 9, pp. 95–96, ML.

50. "International Agricultural Corporation," syndicate book 7, p. 47; and syndicate book 10, p. 102, ML.

51. "Liberia," syndicate book 6, p. 142, ML.

52. Ibid.

53. "The Baltimore and Ohio Railroad Company," syndicate book 2, p. 46; and "The Baltimore and Ohio Railroad Company," syndicate book 6, p. 20, ML.

54. For Vanderlip's description of his meeting with Stillman, Rockefeller, and Wilson, see Winkler, *The First Billion,* 210.

55. Hart, *Revolutionary Mexico,* 276 (emphasis mine).

56. "Pearson-Farquhar Syndicate," syndicate book 6, p. 58; and "Argentine Railroad Syndicate," syndicate book 7, p. 89, ML.

57. "Mexican Government Ten-Year 6% Bonds," syndicate book 7, pp. 155–156, ML; and Carosso, *The Morgans,* 589.

58. Southwestern Land and Cattle Company, agency 2381, entry 125, SCC, record group 76, WNRC and HC.

59. Batopilas Mining Company, agency 53, entry 184, SCC, record group 76, WNRC and HC.

60. Jennings, Blocker, and Moore, agency 1737, entry 125, SCC, record group 76, WNRC and HC.

61. Helen Swift Morris Neilson et al., agency 240, entry 125, AMCC, record group 76, WNRC and HC.

62. Manuela Hibler, agency 105, entry 125, SCC, record group 76, WNRC and HC.

63. Dr. George Townsend Lee, agency 1524, entry 125, SCC, record group 76, WNRC and HC.

64. Ibid. Also Consul William Bonny, San Luis Potosí, 1913, annex to agency 4, entry 125, SCC, record group 76, WNRC and HC.

65. Desde Duff, agency 2618, entry 125, SCC, record group 76, WNRC and HC.

66. Ibid.

67. Estate of J. F. Briscoe, J. C. Edwards, P. E. Crabtree, F. P. Gorham, A. C. Kinnard, C. B. Pettas, and F. M. B. McElroy, claims 112, 114, 174, 176, 177, 278, and 299, boxes 10 and 15, AMCC, record group 76, WNRC and HC.

68. Margaret A. and Martha A. Jamison, agency 937, entry 184, SCC, record group 76, WNRC and HC.

69. Mexican Diversified Land Company, agency 1703, entry 125, SCC, record group 76, WNRC and HC.

70. Report of Mexican Diversified Land Company, agency 1703, special docket 292, general docket 3116, SCC, record group 76, WNRC and HC.

71. Mexican Diversified Land Company, agency 1703, entry 125, SCC, record group 76, WNRC and HC.

72. John C. Lind, agency 1343, SCC, record group 76, WNRC and HC. Also Department of State decimal files, series 412.11 h64/2, NARA and HC.

73. Mexican Agricultural Land Company, agency 136, entry 125, SCC, record group 76, WNRC and HC.

74. Ibid. For the return of the jungle, see Myrtle Isabel Logan, agency 135, entry 125, SCC, record group 76, WNRC and HC.

75. L. P., and Juana C. Frisbie, agency 4486, entry 125, SCC, record group 76, WNRC and HC.

CHAPTER 10. INTERVENTIONS AND FIRESTORMS

1. Excellent analyses of the Wilson-Huerta confrontation are found in Friedrich Katz, *The Secret War in Mexico: Europe, the United States and the Mexican Revolution* (Chicago: University of Chicago Press, 1981), 156–203; Kenneth Grieb, *The United States and Huerta* (Lincoln: University of Nebraska Press, 1969); and Peter N. V. Henderson, "Woodrow Wilson, Victoriano Huerta, and the Recognition Issue in Mexico," *The Americas* 41 (1984): 151–176.

2. William F. Buckley, Tampico, to Edward Mandell House, Washington, D.C., 3 November 1913, folder 664, box 20, Edward Mandel House Papers, Sterling Library, Yale University, New Haven.

3. Ibid.

4. Thomas P. Littlepage, Washington, D.C., to A M. Trueb, New York, 9 January 1914, Northwestern Railroad Collection, BLAC.

5. The preparations for the Veracruz intervention included a large buildup of military supplies and personnel. See the *Texas City Monthly* , March 1914. Ownership of the *Ypiranga* is established in "Steamship Lines Combination, Hamburg American Packet Company" syndicate book 3, pp. 1–2, ML. Morgan's desire to "avoid publicity" regarding the acquisition of the Hamburg American Line was realized for 84 years.

6. Hart, *Revolutionary Mexico,* 290–292.

7. Hanson, "A Day of Ideals," 167.

8. Hart, *Revolutionary Mexico,* 296.

9. Hart, interview with Professor Antonio Salazar Paz, city historian and director of the Museo de la Ciudad, Veracruz, 28 July 1983.

10. Hart, *Revolutionary Mexico,* 298.

11. Hanson, "A Day of Ideals," 167.

12. William J. Eaton, "Forgotten War: Yanks in Russia," *Los Angeles Times,* 10 March 1987.

13. The origins of the American entry into World War I have been examined many times, but the financial ties between the United States and Great Britain, and to a lesser degree France, left President Wilson with the choice of declaring war or accepting the collapse of the U.S. monetary system.

14. "Bank of England Demand Loans, 1915," aka "Special Loan to Morgan Grenfell & Co.," ($436,821,136.51), syndicate book 9, pp. 185–186 and 203–206; "American Foreign Securities Company," syndicate book 8, pp. 207–208; "Loan to Rothschild Frères," syndicate book 8, pp. 127–128; "Winchester Repeating Arms Company Notes," syndicate book 8, pp. 167–168; "Central Argentine Railway Ltd.," syndicate book 9, pp. 1–2; "Imperial Russian Government," syndicate book 9, pp. 7–8; "Imperial Russian Government Credit of 1916," syndicate book 9, pp. 27–28; "$300,000,000 United Kingdom of Great Britain and Ireland Secured Notes," syndicate book 9, pp. 5–6; "Government of the French Repub-

lic," syndicate book 9, pp. 45–46; and "French Commercial Export Credit, 1915," syndicate book 9, pp. 59–60, ML.

15. "Bank of England Demand Loans," syndicate book 9, pp. 203–204, ML.

16. Ibid.

17. "Loan to Rothschild Frères," syndicate book 8, pp. 127–128, ML.

18. "Bank of England Demand Loans," syndicate book 9, pp. 203–204, ML.

19. Ibid.

20. Ibid.; and "Winchester Repeating Arms Company Notes," syndicate book 8, pp. 167–168, ML. The other banks were Liberty ($300,000), Chemical ($250,000), and Title Guarantee ($250,000).

21. "Bank of England Demand Loans," syndicate book 9, pp. 203–204, ML.

22. "French Commercial Export Credit," syndicate book 9, pp. 59–60, ML.

23. "Bank of England Demand Loans," syndicate book 9, pp. 31–32, ML. See also "Russian Government Credit of 1916," syndicate book 9, pp. 27–28, ML.

24. For the quote, see "US Steel Corporation First Mortgage," syndicate book 8, pp. 193–194, ML.

25. "Bank of England Demand Loans," syndicate book 9, pp. 203–204, ML.

26. Ibid.

27. Ibid.

28. Ibid.

29. Ibid., 205–206.

30. Ibid.

31. "American Foreign Securities Company," syndicate book 8, pp. 207–208; and "French Industrial Credit of 1916," syndicate book 9, pp. 61–62, ML.

32. "$50,000,000 Russian Government Credit of 1916," syndicate book 9, pp. 27–28, ML.

33. "United States Rubber, First and Preferred Mortgage," syndicate book 9, pp. 13–14; and "Winchester Repeating Arms Company Notes," syndicate book 8, pp. 167–168, ML.

34. "Bank of England Demand Loans," syndicate book, 9, pp. 205–206, ML.

35. "Imperial Russian Government $5^1/_2$% External Loan," syndicate book 9, pp. 7–8, ML.

36. "Government of the French Republic Two Year $5^1/_2$% Secured Loan Convertible Notes," syndicate book 9, pp. 45–46, ML.

37. "United Kingdom and Ireland, Convertible Notes" ($250,000,000), syndicate book 9, pp. 31–32; and "Government of the French Republic Two Year $5^1/_2$% Secured Loan Convertible Notes," syndicate book 9, pp. 45–46, ML.

38. "Central Argentine Railway, Ltd, $15,000,000 Bond Note Convertible to Stock," syndicate book 9, pp. 1–2, ML.

39. "Cerro de Pasco Copper Corporation, 10 Year 6% Convertible Bonds," syndicate book 8, pp. 101 and 205; "Chile Copper Company Series A Convertible 6% Bonds Syndicate," syndicate book 9, pp. 21–22; "Purchase of Argentine 5s of 1909 in Paris June 8, 1916 on Behalf of Group," syndicate book 9, pp. 23–24; "$250,000,000 United Kingdom and Ireland, Convertible Notes," syndicate book

9, pp. 31–34; "Central Argentine Railway, Ltd., Bond Note Convertible to Stock, syndicate book 9, pp. 1–2; and "Penyon Syndicate," syndicate book 9, pp. 95–96, ML.

40. "U.S. Steel Corporation First Mortgage 5% Bonds," syndicate book 8; and "Burma Corporation Syndicate," syndicate book 9, pp. 69–70, ML.

41. "Bank of England Demand Loans," syndicate book 9, pp. 203–206, ML.

42. *Wall Street Journal,* January 1916, as cited in Cleveland and Huertas, *Citibank,* 94.

43. Frank Vanderlip Papers, part A: incoming correspondence, BL. Also Cleveland and Huertas, *Citibank,* 94.

44. For the clash between Villa and Carranza, see Adolfo Gilly, *La revolución interrumpida* (Mexico City: Ediciones El Caballito, 1971), 106–109; and Katz, *Secret War,* 260–262. For samples of the innumerable attacks and land seizures against American farmers and hacienda and mine owners by rebel groups outside the control of the revolutionary elites, see docket 78, and agency numbers 88, 89, 90, 135, 136, 170, 226, 236, 296, 435, 437, 438, 520, 1344, 1391, 1396, 1428, 1524, 1568, 1572, 1701, 1721, 1726, 1733, 1737, 1740, 1751, 1752, 1804, 1913, 1914, 1920, 1921, 1922, 2336, 2346, 2350, 2381, 2605–2608, 2618, 2691, 2692, 4493, 4978, 5104, 5820, and 5830, entry 125, SCC, records group 76, WNRC. See also the Department of State decimal files, 312 series, NARA; the Townsend-Stanton Family Papers, HTML; the John Henry Kirby Papers, Houston Metropolitan Research Center, Houston; the Corralitos Hacienda Papers, BLAC; the Batopilas Letterbooks, HC; and the Northwestern Railroad Collection, BLAC.

45. List of plantations on the Isthmus of Tehuantepec, 350.1, entry 152, AMCC, records group 76, WNRC and HC.

46. Herr, "¿Quien Vive?," chap. 6, pp. 21–25.

47. Ibid., chap. 6, pp. 29–30.

48. Ibid., chap. 6, p. 31.

49. National Oil Company, agency 2607, entry 125, SCC, records group 76, WNRC and HC.

50. Logan, agency 135, and Mexican Agricultural Land Company, agency 136, entry 125, SCC, records group 76, WNRC and HC. Also agencies 15, 18, 91, 140, and 394, entry 189, SCC, records group 76, WNRC and HC.

51. Jamisons, agency 937, entry 184, SCC, records group 76, WNRC and HC.

52. Herr, "¿Quien Vive?," chap. 7, pp. 8–10.

53. Cora Lee Sturgis, agency 52, entry 184, SCC, records group 76, WNRC and HC.

54. Lee, agency 1524, entry 125, SCC, records group 76, WNRC.

55. Ibid.

56. Minerva A. R. McCrocklin, agency 1804, dockets 2121 and 2897, SCC, records group 76, WNRC.

57. Unknown, New York, to Louis Batzelle, New York, 10 February 1916, Intercontinental Rubber Company Papers, SC-TWL.

58. "Intercontinental Rubber Company Stock," syndicate book 5, p. 201, ML;

Intercontinental Rubber Company Papers, SC-TWL; and Intercontinental Rubber, agency 5820, entry 125, SCC, records group 76, WNRC and HC.

59. Batopilas, agency 53, entry 189, AMCC, records group 76, WNRC and HC.

60. Ibid.

61. Jennings, Blocker, and Moore, agency 1737, entry 125, SCC, records group 76, WNRC and HC; and Department of State decimal file 812.00/509, NARA.

62. Jennings, Blocker, and Moore, agency 1737, entry 125, SCC, records group 76, WNRC.

63. Blocker Testimony, agency 1737, entry 125, SCC, records group 76, WNRC; and Department of State decimal file 812.00/509, NARA.

64. Lucy Ord Mason, claim 328, Approved Agrarian Claims, Extended (Declassified), AMCC, records group 76, WNRC and HC.

65. The best analysis for Villa's behavior is found in Katz, *Secret War*, 305–314.

66. Friedrich Katz, *The Life and Times of Pancho Villa* (Stanford: Stanford University Press, 1998), 578–579

67. For Sinaloa, see United Sugar Company, claim 185, docket 137, boxes 65–69; and Sinaloa Land and Water, claim 305, docket 258, AMCC, group 76, WNRC and HC. For Chihuahua see Batopilas, agency 53, entry 189, AMCC, records group 76, WNRC and HC; and Batopilas Letterbooks, HC. See also Reyes, *Historia del azucar*, 110; and Herr, "¿Quien Vive?," chap. 8, pp. 3–9 and chap. 10, pp. 2–3.

68. Perry Holly, agency 149, docket 5, entry 189, 1935, Awarded Claims 1924–1938; and Dolores Esperanza Mines, agency 954, entry 189, SCC, records group 76, WNRC and HC.

69. McLean and Leavitt, agency 954, entry 125, SCC, records group 76, WNRC and HC.

70. Southwestern Land and Cattle Company, agency 2381, entry 125, SCC, records group 76, WNRC and HC.

71. Tampico Navigation Company, agency 1495, entry 125, SCC, records group 76, WNRC and HC.

72. See the applications for embargo exemptions for the Tampico News Company, items 2405 and 2508, 4 June and 23 June 1913, and item 3592, 21 September 1914, roll 167, microfilm publication M973, Purport Lists for the Department of State Decimal File, 1910–1914, 812.10–812.345/17, NARA. For Doheny, see La Botz, *Edward L. Doheny*, 59–65. For the shipments, see Department of State Purport Lists for the Decimal File, 1915, records group 59.

73. Tampico Navigation Company, agency 1495, entry 125, SCC, records group 76, WNRC and HC.

74. Otto Brictson, docket 2441, entry 107, SCC, records group 76, WNRC and HC; and Tom Hale Papers (unsorted), Houston.

75. Laguna Company, agency 1391, entry 125, SCC, records group 76, WNRC and HC. Also docket 31, box 14, Approved Agrarian Claims, Extended (Declassified), AMCC, records group 76, WNRC and HC.

76. Ibid.

77. Ibid.

78. *New York Times,* 15 January 1939.

79. *Journal of Commerce,* vol. 6, no. 4.

80. *New York Times,* 15 January 1939; and Laguna Corporation, docket 31, Approved New Agrarian Claims, AMCC, records group 76, WNRC and HC.

81. Laguna Corporation (balance statements), docket 31, Approved New Agrarian Claims, AMCC, records group 76, WNRC and HC.

82. American Shareholders of the Mexican Gulf Land and Lumber Company, docket 18; and Laguna Corporation, docket 31, Approved New Agrarian Claims, AMCC, records group 76, WNRC and HC.

83. For Obregón's $1.8 million debt to W. R. Grace, see W. R. Grace and Company, case 306, docket 136, box 30, AMCC, records group 76, WNRC and HC. For the support of the U.S. southwestern governors for Obregón, see James A. Clark, with Weldon Hart, *The Tactful Texan: A Biography of Governor William Hobby* (New York: Random House, 1958).

84. Norman Caulfield, "Mexican Labor and the State in the Twentieth Century: Conflict and Accommodation," Ph.D. diss., University of Houston, 1990, 19–23.

85. Lamb, Brown, and Orrin, agency 6021, entry 125, SCC, records group 76, WNRC and HC.

CHAPTER 11. CRISIS IN THE NEW REGIME

1. The Archivo Agrario, Secretaria de la Reforma Agrario (formerly the Archivo Seis de Enero de 1915) contains tens of thousands of bundled documents that display the interaction of local militants who wanted "too much" versus the bureaucracy, and local conservatives who wished to maintain the status quo versus the same administrators. For the history of labor during this period, see Jacinto Huitron, *Origenes e historia del movimiento obrero en México* (Mexico City: Editores Mexicanos Unidos, 1975); Barry Carr, *El movimiento obrero y la politica en México, 1910–1929* (Mexico City: SepSetentas, 1976); John Hart, *Anarchism and the Mexican Working Class, 1860–1931* (Austin: University of Texas Press, 1978); Alfonso López Aparicio, *El movimiento obrero en México* (Mexico City: Editorial Jus, 1958); Luis Araiza, *Historia del movimiento obrero mexicana,* 5 vols. (Mexico City: n.p., 1964–1966); and Juan Felipe Leal, *Agupaciones y burocracias sindicales en México, 1906–1938* (Mexico City: Terra Nova, 1995).

2. Senator Antonio Díaz Soto y Gama, the head of the Mexican Agrarian Party during the early 1920s, headed the propagandists who eulogized the campesinos and rewrote agrarian history. Díaz Soto y Gama culminated his work with the path-breaking *La revolución agraria del sur y Emiliano Zapata su caudillo* (Mexico City: private printing, 1961), which was critical in redefining Zapatismo from terrorism and brigandage to a noble cause. For the social content of the 1920s labor and agrarian movements, see Rosendo Rojas Coria, *Tratado de cooperativismo* (Mexico City: Fondo de Cultura Economica, 1952).

3. For the National Association for the Protection of American Rights in Mexico, see the William F. Buckley Sr. Papers, BLAC; and LaBotz, *Edward L. Doheny,* 78.

4. Richardson Construction Company, docket 44, claim 72, Approved Agrarian Claims (Declassified), AMCC, records group 76, WNRC; and Richardson Construction Company, folder 1, Manuscripts Collection, University of Arizona Library, Tucson. See also Department of State decimal file 812.5200, NARA.

5. Cargill Lumber Company, agency 1154A, AMCC, records group 76, WNRC and HC.

6. Ibid.

7. Pine King, docket 109, Approved Agrarian Claims, Extended (Declassified), AMCC, records group 76, WNRC and HC; and Broehl, *Cargill,* 219.

8. For a broader context see Peter Smith, *Talons of the Eagle: Dynamics of U.S.–Latin American Relations* (New York: Oxford University Press, 1996). The postrevolutionary era is covered by several important works. See the classic by Robert Freeman Smith, *The United States and Revolutionary Nationalism in Mexico, 1916–1932* (Chicago: University of Chicago Press, 1972). Other significant contributions are Lorenzo Meyer and Josefina Zoraida Vázquez, *México frente a Estados Unidos: Un ensayo historico, 1776–1980* (Mexico City: El Colegio de México, 1982); Sepulveda Amor, Pellicer de Brody, and Meyer, *Las empresas transnacionales en México;* Schmitt, *Mexico and the United States;* Brown, *Oil and Revolution;* W. Dirk Raat, *Ambivalent Vistas: Mexico and the United States* (Athens: University of Georgia Press, 1992); Cecena, *México en el orbita imperial;* and Hall, *Oil, Banks and Politics.*

9. Pine King, docket 109, Approved Agrarian Claims, Extended (Declassified), AMCC, records group 76, WNRC and HC.

10. Alfred Shapleigh, docket 1915, claim 3084, entry 107, Approved Agrarian Claims (Declassified), AMCC, records group 76, WNRC and HC.

11. Pashal Brown, agency 2451, entry 125, SCC; Helen Swift Morris Neilson et al., claim 240, Approved Agrarian Claims (Declassified), AMCC; and Helen Swift Morris, Approved Agrarian Claims, Extended (Declassified), AMCC, records group 76, WNRC and HC. For the Piedra Blanca, see the Blocker affidavit in William Henry Jennings, John Rufus Blocker, and Edna Jeffreys Moore, agency 1737, entry 125, SCC, records group 76, WNRC.

12. Lucy Ord Mason, claim 328, Approved Agrarian Claims, Extended (Declassified), AMCC, records group 76, WNRC and HC.

13. Intercontinental Rubber Company, Report to Stockholders, 1926, p. 22, SC-TWL.

14. Ibid.

15. Ibid.; and Intercontinental Rubber Company, agency 5820, entry 125, SCC, records group 76, WNRC and HC; and Reports to Stockholders, 20 March 1936, 15 March 1937, 16 March 1938, 27 March 1939, and 16 August 1940, SC-TWL.

16. Horace W. Corbin, docket 189, Approved Agrarian Claims, Extended (Declassified), AMCC, records group 76, WNRC and HC.

17. J. M. Hotchkiss, docket 257, claim 31, Approved Agrarian Claims, Extended (Declassified), AMCC, records group 76, WNRC and HC.

18. Jalapa Power and Light Company, docket 42, Deferred Miscellaneous Claims Approved after 1935 (Declassified), AMCC, records group 76, WNRC and HC.

19. Laguna, docket 31, Approved Agrarian Claims, Extended (Declassified), AMCC, records group 76, WNRC and HC.

20. Cove Investment and Improvement Company, docket 94, Approved Agrarian Claims, Extended (Declassified), AMCC, records group 76, WNRC and HC.

21. Estate of Rosalie Evans, docket 98, claim 153, Approved Agrarian Claims, Extended (Declassified), AMCC, records group 76, WNRC and HC.

22. Guerrero Land and Timber, claim 1471, Approved Agrarian Claims, Extended (Declassified), AMCC, records group 76, WNRC and HC.

23. John T. Cave, agencies 53 and 2052, entry 189, Awarded Claims, 1924–1938, SCC, records group 76, WNRC and HC.

24. Reyes, *Historia del azucar,* 110–111.

25. Houghton, El Paso, to Shearson, New York, 16 January 1922, Corralitos Papers, BLAC and HC. Also Ed Shearson et al., the Corralitos Company, agency 1156, dockets 1220, 1953, 3343, and 3344, boxes 27 and 28; Ed Shearson et al., the Ramos Company, agency 4381, box 168, Approved Agrarian Claims, Extended (Declassified), AMCC, records group 76, WNRC and HC.

26. Ed Shearson et al., the Ramos Company, agency 4381, box 168, Approved Agrarian Claims, Extended (Declassified), AMCC, records group 76, WNRC and HC.

27. Ibid.

28. Houghton, El Paso, to Shearson, New York, 16 January 1922, Corralitos Hacienda Papers, BLAC and HC.

29. Houghton, El Paso, to Shearson, New York, 16 January 1922, Corralitos Papers, BLAC and HC. Also Ed Shearson et al., the Corralitos Company, agency 1156, dockets 1220, 1953, 3343, and 3344, boxes 27 and 28; and Ed Shearson et al., the Ramos Company, agency 4381, box 168, Approved Agrarian Claims, Extended (Declassified), AMCC, records group 76, WNRC and HC.

30. John Steinkampf and Harry Smith, docket 235, box 16, Approved Agrarian Claims, Extended (Declassified), AMCC, records group 76, WNRC and HC. Also Jack Wentworth Peirce, Topsfield, to Hart, Houston, 9 April 1984, HC.

31. Herr, "¿Quien Vive?," chap. 15, pp. 5–7.

32. Ibid., chap. 15, p. 6.

33. For the Cristeros see Jean Meyer, *La Cristiada,* 3 vols. (Mexico City: Siglo XXI, 1973); and David Bailey, *Viva Cristo Rey! The Cristero Rebellion and the Church-State Conflict in Mexico* (Austin: University of Texas Press, 1974).

34. Herr, "¿Quien Vive?," chap. 19, p. 9, and chap. 20, pp. 3–11.

35. Suzie Lucero de Regnier, docket 87; and H. W. Keller, document 125, 1944, Approved Agrarian Claims, Extended (Declassified), AMCC, records group 76, WNRC and HC.

36. H. W. Keller, document 125, 1944, Approved Agrarian Claims, Extended (Declassified), AMCC, records group 76, WNRC and HC.

37. Ibid.; and Ruiz, *On the Rim of Mexico*, 42–60. For Coffroth and the Agua Caliente Racetrack, see R. L. Dinley et al., docket 138, decision 129, Deferred Miscellaneous Claims Approved after 1935 (Declassified), AMCC, records group 76, WNRC.

38. For a searching discussion of border conditions and practices, see Ruiz, *On the Rim of Mexico.*

39. For a brilliant discussion of the American artistic and literary community in Mexico during the twentieth century, see John A. Britton, *Revolution and Ideology: Images of the Mexican Revolution in the United States* (Lexington: University of Kentucky Press, 1995).

40. Hart, interview with Charles Gibson, 29 December 1978, Dallas; and Elizabeth Smith, "Against the Grain: Nettie Lee Benson and Higher Education," unpublished ms., University of Houston, 1995.

41. Britton, in *Revolution and Ideology*, discusses these scholars at length. Dobie's experience is best recorded in his books and in the files of the U.S.-Mexican Claims Commission, records group 76, WNRC.

42. Beezley, *Judas at the Jockey Club*, 23–25.

CHAPTER 12. NATIONALIZATION OF LAND AND INDUSTRY

1. Brictson, docket 55, Approved New Agrarian Claims, 1939–1947 (Declassified); and docket 205, claim 228, Approved Agrarian Claims, Extended (Declassified), AMCC, records group 76, WNRC and HC.

2. Brictson, claim 228, docket 205, Approved Agrarian Claims, Extended (Declassified), AMCC, records group 76, WNRC and HC.

3. Ibid.

4. Brictson, docket 55, Approved New Agrarian Claims, 1939–1947 (Declassified), AMCC, records group 76, WNRC and HC.

5. For an excellent beginning on the Blaylock Colony, see Viola Young, docket 101, Approved Agrarian Claims, Extended (Declassified), AMCC, records group 76, WNRC and HC.

6. For the quote see Stephens, docket 23 (Cacalutla), Approved New Agrarian Claims, 1939–1947 (Declassified), AMCC, records group 76, WNRC and HC.

7. Brictson, docket 55; and Stephens, docket 23, Approved New Agrarian Claims, 1939–1947 (Declassified), AMCC, records group 76, WNRC and HC.

8. William Henry and Hugh Stephens (El Potrero), agrarian docket 160 and docket 57, Approved Agrarian Claims, Extended (Declassified), AMCC, records group 76, WNRC and HC.

9. Young, docket 101; and Horace W. Corbin, agrarian docket 189 and docket 71, Approved Agrarian Claims, Extended (Declassified), AMCC, records group 76, WNRC. For the Hearst estate see dockets 28 and 29, Approved Agrarian Claims, Extended (Declassified), AMCC, records group 76, WNRC.

10. Octal Dewitt Jones, docket 206, claim 290, Approved Agrarian Claims, Extended (Declassified), AMCC, records group 76, WNRC.

11. Thompson, docket 147, claim 254, Approved Agrarian Claims, Extended (Declassified), AMCC, records group 76, WNRC.

12. Abraham Silberberg, docket 82, Approved New Agrarian Claims, 1939–1947 (Declassified), AMCC, records group 76, WNRC and HC.

13. Guerrero Land and Timber Company, claim 1471, Approved Agrarian Claims (Declassified); and Guerrero Land and Timber, claim 1471, Approved Agrarian Claims, Extended (Declassified), AMCC, records group 76, WNRC and HC.

14. United Sugar, docket 137, claim 185, Approved Agrarian Claims (Declassified), AMCC, records group 76, WNRC; and Reyes, *Historia del azucar*, 110–111.

15. Sinaloa Land and Water, docket 90, Approved Agrarian Claims (Declassified); and Sinaloa Land and Water, Approved Agrarian Claims, Extended (Declassified), AMCC, records group 76, WNRC and HC. For Palomas see Palomas Cattle Company, agency 6153, Approved Agrarian Claims (Declassified), AMCC, records group 76, WNRC and HC.

16. C. A. Vance, agencies 6290–6292, Approved Agrarian Claims, Extended (Declassified), AMCC, records group 76, WNRC and HC. See also Land Finance Company, agency 231, docket 46, agrarian docket 175, Approved Cattle Claims, 1933–1947, AMCC, records group 76, WNRC and HC.

17. Vance, agency 6291, docket 3464; and Hotchkiss, claim 31, docket 257, Approved Agrarian Claims, Extended (Declassified), AMCC, records group 76, WNRC and HC.

18. Laguna Corporation, docket 109, box 44, Approved Agrarian Claims, Extended (Declassified), AMCC, records group 76, WNRC and HC.

19. Laguna, claim 154; and docket 31, Approved Agrarian Claims, Extended (Declassified), AMCC, records group 76, WNRC and HC.

20. Pine King Land and Lumber Company, docket 109, Approved Agrarian Claims, Extended (Declassified), AMCC, records group 76, WNRC and HC.

21. Neilson, claim 240, Approved Agrarian Claims, Extended (Declassified), AMCC, records group 76, WNRC and HC.

22. Gruwell, Docket 114, Approved Agrarian Claims, Extended (Declassified), AMCC, records group 76, WNRC and HC.

23. Lemmon Jr., Docket 111, Approved Agrarian Claims, Extended (Declassified), AMCC, records group 76, WNRC and HC.

24. Report of James B. Barker, AMCC Investigator, p. 23, AMCC Decisions, Approved Agrarian Claims, Extended (Declassified), AMCC, group 76, WNRC and HC.

25. Carlos Miller, Claim 105; and docket 60, Approved Agrarian Claims, Extended (Declassified), AMCC, records group 76, WNRC and HC.

26. Burton Dike, Claim 350, Approved New Agrarian Claims, 1939–1947 (Declassified), AMCC, records group 76, WNRC and HC.

27. Herr, "¿Quien Vive?," chap. 20, p. 11.

28. Ibid., chap. 19, p. 9, and chap. 20, pp. 3–11.

29. Bethlehem Steel Corporation, docket 66, Deferred Miscellaneous Claims Approved after 1935 (Declassified), AMCC, records group 76, WNRC and HC.

30. Meyer and Vázquez, *México frente a Estados Unidos*, 167–172; and Stephen R. Niblo, *War, Diplomacy, and Development: The United States and Mexico, 1938–1954* (Wilmington: Scholarly Resources, 1995), 54 and 71–74; the quotes are from p. 74.

31. Niblo, *War, Diplomacy, and Development*, 49.

32. Claims 12, 101, 112, 114, 118, 120, 121, 155, 174, 176, 177, 254, 255, 278, 279, and 299, Approved Agrarian Claims, Extended (Declassified), AMCC, records group 76, WNRC and HC.

33. Herr, "¿Quien Vive?," chap. 20, p. 6.

34. See Britton, *Revolution and Ideology*.

35. Hart, interview with James Michener, July 1985, Austin, Texas.

CHAPTER 13. COOPERATION AND ACCOMMODATION

1. The others were George Bailey, G. W. Edmunds, Charles Fritz, John Gribbel, Hugh Johnston, Arthur B. Leach, John Markley, Frederick Probst, Edgar H. Ryan, A. J. Stevens, and Adolph Vietor.

2. Laguna Corporation, docket 31, Approved New Agrarian Claims, 1939–1947 (Declassified), AMCC, records group 76, WNRC and HC.

3. Ibid.

4. Mexican Gulf Land and Lumber, docket 18, Approved Agrarian Claims (Declassified) and Approved New Agrarian Claims, 1939–1947 (Declassified), AMCC, records group 76, WNRC and HC.

5. Laguna Corporation, docket 31, Approved New Agrarian Claims, 1939–1947 (Declassified), AMCC, records group 76, WNRC and HC.

6. Ibid.

7. Ibid.

8. Mexican Gulf Land and Lumber, docket 18, Approved Agrarian Claims (Declassified) and Approved New Agrarian Claims, 1939–1947 (Declassified), AMCC, records group 76, WNRC and HC.

9. Laguna Corporation, docket 31, Approved New Agrarian Claims, 1939–1947 (Declassified), AMCC, records group 76, WNRC and HC.

10. Docket 23, Approved New Agrarian Claims, 1939–1947 (Declassified), AMCC, records group 76, WNRC and HC; and Russell Miller, *House of Getty* (London: Michael Joseph, 1985), 148.

11. Charles and Laura Miller, docket 105, Approved Agrarian Claims (Declassified) and Approved New Agrarian Claims, 1939–1947 (Declassified), AMCC, records group 76, WNRC and HC; J. Paul Getty, *As I See It* (Englewood Cliffs: Prentice-Hall, 1976), 148 and 158; and Miller, *House of Getty*, 148.

12. Charles and Laura Miller, docket 105, Approved Agrarian Claims (Declassified) and Approved New Agrarian Claims, 1939–1947 (Declassified), AMCC, records group 76, WNRC and HC.

13. Charles Miller Jr., claim 105, box 15, Approved New Agrarian Claims, 1939–1947 (Declassified), AMCC, records group 76, WNRC and HC.

14. Stephens, docket 160, Approved Agrarian Claims (Declassified) and Approved New Agrarian Claims, 1939–1947 (Declassified); and docket 57, Approved Agrarian Claims, Extended (Declassified), AMCC, records group 76, WNRC and HC. Also Stephens, n.p., to Secretary of State, Washington, D.C., 11 August 1930, in Department of State decimal file 312.1156, M57, NARA.

15. Miller, *House of Getty*, 214.

16. Stephen R. Niblo, *War, Diplomacy, and Development: The United States and Mexico, 1938–1954* (Wilmington: Scholarly Resources, 1995), 110–111 and 228.

17. Sanford Mosk, *Industrial Revolution in Mexico* (Berkeley: University of California Press, 1954), 85–93; and Niblo, *War, Diplomacy, and Development*, 202, 214, and 274. For strategic metals see an excellent discussion in chapter five of Maria Emilia Paz, *Strategy, Security, and Spies: Mexico and the U.S. as Allies in World War II* (University Park: Pennsylvania State University Press, 1997). See also Carmela Elvira Santoro, "United States and Mexican Relations during World War II," Ph.D. diss., Syracuse University, 1967.

18. Mosk, *Industrial Revolution*, 185–187.

19. Jalapa Power and Light, docket 42, Deferred Miscellaneous Claims Approved after 1935 (Declassified), AMCC, records group 76, WNRC and HC.

20. Niblo, *War, Diplomacy, and Development*, 184–185, 191, and 239.

21. Reports to the Stockholders, 8 April 1941; 8 April 1942; 6 April 1943; 6 August 1943; and 12 August 1944, SC-TWL and HC.

22. Reports to the Stockholders, 6 August 1943; 12 August 1944; 13 August 1946; 3 September 1948; and 12 August 1949, SC-TWL and HC; and Velazquez et al., "Guayule," 55–66.

23. Niblo, *War, Diplomacy, and Development*, 44, 94, 114, and 176–177.

24. Neilson, claim 240, box 12, Approved Agrarian Claims, Extended (Declassified), AMCC, records group 76, WNRC and HC.

25. Niblo, *War, Diplomacy, and Development*, 213.

26. Ibid., 184–185, 213, and 229; and Hart, interview with Ed Hugetz, Houston, 16 April 1988.

27. Hart, interview with Harvey Houck and Tom Hale, 10 March 1998, River Oaks Country Club, Houston.

28. Andres Lona Almaraz, "Gobernantes Impuestos, Gobernantes Arbitrarios," in Brictson, docket 55, Approved New Agrarian Claims, 1939–1947 (Declassified), AMCC, records group 76, WNRC and HC.

29. Brictson, docket 205, Approved Agrarian Claims (Declassified) and Approved New Agrarian Claims, 1939–1947 (Declassified), AMCC, WNRC and HC.

30. Corbin, docket 189, Approved Agrarian Claims (Declassified) and Approved New Agrarian Claims, 1939–1947 (Declassified), AMCC, WNRC and HC.

31. Corbin, docket 71, Approved Agrarian Claims (Declassified) and Approved New Agrarian Claims, 1939–1947 (Declassified), AMCC, WNRC and HC.

32. Vance, agency 6291, Approved Agrarian Claims (Declassified) and Approved New Agrarian Claims, 1939–1947 (Declassified), AMCC, WNRC and HC.

33. Editorials in the *New York Times,* 1995–1996.

34. For oil deliveries and the best discussion of the Mexican, Cuban, and American triangle, see Arthur K. Smith Jr., *Mexico and the Cuban Revolution: Foreign Policy-Making in Mexico under President Adolfo López Mateos (1958–1964)* (Ithaca: Cornell University Press, 1970).

35. Quoted in Rob Ruck, *The Tropic of Baseball: Baseball in the Dominican Republic* (London: Meckler, 1990), 35.

36. Peter C. Bjarkman, *Baseball with a Latin Beat* (Jefferson, N.C.: McFarland and Co., 1994), 23 and 238.

37. Anthony DePalma, "Mexican Attitudes Shift in Flood of U.S. Goods," *New York Times,* 22 November 1994.

38. Jeffrey Pilcher, "The Rockefeller Foundation and Mexico's National Cuisine," research report from the Rockefeller Foundation, 1996.

39. Frank Tannenbaum, New York, to C. M. Brinckerhoff, New York, 1960, folder Anaconda, box 23, Frank Tannenbaum Papers, Rare Books and Manuscripts Room, BL.

40. Hart, conversations with Victor Niemeyer, Austin, 1985–1996.

41. Hart, conversations with Nettie Lee Benson, Austin, 1978–1988.

42. Hart, interview with Lyle Brown, Morelia, 9 December 1997.

43. Julia Tunon Pablos, "Mujeres de luz y sombra en el cine mexicano: La construcción masculina de una imagen (1939–1952)," Doctoral thesis, Universidad Nacional Autónoma de México, 1992, 79; and Niblo, *War, Diplomacy, and Development,* 203.

44. Hart, interview with Jesús Luis Zuñiga, Guadalajara, 13 December 1997.

45. Joel Millman, "High Tech Jobs Transfer to Mexico with Surprising Speed," *Wall Street Journal,* 9 April 1998.

CHAPTER 14. RETURN OF THE AMERICAN FINANCIERS

1. Doug Henwood, "The Free Flow of Money," *NACLA Reports,* January–February 1996; and "UN Conference on Trade and Development, Programme on Transnational Corporations," in *World Investment Report 1993* (New York: United Nations, 1993), as cited by Henwood.

2. Peter Truell, "Big Investor Relations Task: Selling Mexico to Wall St.," *New York Times,* 15 March 1995.

3. Remarks by Miguel de la Madrid, Colegio de la Frontera Norte, 29 April 1995. Also Anthony DePalma, "Casualty of the Peso: Investor Confidence," *New York Times,* 27 December 1994; David E. Sanger, "Accord's Dark Side," *New York Times,* 4 January 1995; and Susan Diesenouse, "Financial Advisors to the Rich Set a Conservative Course for '95," *New York Times,* 31 December 1994.

4. Anthony DePalma, "Mexico's Banks: A Weak Link in the Rescue Plan," *New York Times,* 9 February 1995; Ken Silverstein and Alexander Cockburn, "Who Broke Mexico?: The Killers and the Killing," the *Nation,* 6 March 1996.

5. Anthony DePalma, "Mexico Tries to Restrict Some Foreign Investments," *New York Times,* 5 April 1996; and Anthony DePalma, "Hicks, Muse and Travelers in Mexico Deal," *New York Times,* 9 August 1996.

6. Anthony DePalma, "Mexico's Garage Sale," *New York Times,* 2 June 1995; Henwood, "The Free Flow of Money"; and Doug Henwood, "Investing Abroad," *New York Times,* 28 August 1995.

7. Alan Knight, public presentation, Texas Christian University, Fort Worth, 1996.

8. Wayne A. Cornelius, "Designing Social Policy for Mexico's Liberalized Economy: From Social Services and Infrastructure to Job Creation," in *The Challenge of Institutional Reform in Mexico,* ed. Riordan Roett (Boulder: Lynne Rienner, 1995), 143.

9. *World Bank Development Report* (Washington, D.C.: World Bank, 1997); see also *Partnerships for Global Ecosystem Management: Science, Economics, and Law,* Proceedings of the Fifth International Conference on Environmentally Sustainable Development, October 1997 (Washington, D.C.: World Bank, 1999); and Silverstein and Cockburn, "Who Broke Mexico?"

10. For Cargill see docket 94, Approved New Agrarian Claims, 1939–1947 (Declassified), AMCC, records group 76, WNRC and HC.

11. Anthony DePalma, "Mexico's Leader, Breaking Silence, Outlines a Rescue," *New York Times,* 30 December 1994.

12. Anthony DePalma, "An American REIT Will Invest in Mexico," *New York Times,* 7 April 1995.

13. For Chrysler see "Chrysler to Invest 1.5 Billion in Mexico," *The News,* 3 July 1998. For General Motors see Sam Dillon, "A Twenty-Year G.M. Parts Migration to Mexico," *New York Times,* 25 June 1998. See also *New York Times,* 25 August 1994.

14. Anthony DePalma, "Mexican Telephone Shares Drop Sharply," *New York Times,* 11 November 1994; and Anthony DePalma, "Casualty of the Peso: Investor Confidence," *New York Times,* 27 December 1994; and Kenneth N. Gilpin, "Investors Weigh a Market's Safety," *New York Times,* 23 December 1994.

15. Silverstein and Cockburn, "Who Broke Mexico?"; and Lawrence Chimerine, "Mexico Bailout Needed U.S. Strings Attached," *New York Times,* 1 September 1995.

16. Anthony DePalma, "Some Mexican Bonds Go Unsold," *New York Times,* 25 January 1995; Anthony DePalma, "The White House Moves to Increase U.S. Aid for Mexico," *New York Times,* 12 January 1995; Paul Lewis, "Bailout Plan for Mexico Wins Praise," *New York Times,* 29 December 1994; Paul Lewis, "Peso Bounces Back, and Mexican Stocks Are Sent Soaring," *New York Times,* 1 February 1995; Alan R. Myerson, "Peso's Plunge May Cost Thousands of U.S. Jobs," *New York Times,* 30 January 1995; Thomas L. Friedman, "The Coffin's Free," *New York Times,* 13 December 1995; and Thomas L. Friedman, "Parent of Mexico's Banamex Improves Operating Results Despite Loan Woes," *Wall Street Journal,* 26 January 1996. See also *The News,* 20 June 1997.

17. *World Bank Development Report;* and Silverstein and Lockburn, "Who Broke Mexico?"

18. David E. Sanger, "Clinton Offers $20 Billion to Mexico for Peso Rescue; Action Sidesteps Congress," *New York Times,* 1 February 1995; David E. Sanger, "An Old Wall Street Pro's Voice in the Campaign," *New York Times,* 22 September 1996; and Patrick J. Lyons, "Mexico's Ripple Effects: Subtle Risks for Americans," *New York Times,* 1 February 1995.

19. For a brilliant and comprehensive examination of the debt problem, see Carlos Marichal, *A Century of Debt Crises in Latin America* (Princeton: Princeton University Press, 1989). For the specifics regarding Mexico, see Carlos Marichal, "The Vicious Cycles of Mexican Debt," *NACLA Reports,* November–December 1997, 25–31; Alicia Salgado, "Suma 157 mil 548 mdd la deuda externa total," *El Financiero,* 14 May 1997; and Todd S. Purdum, "Clinton Pushes Hard on Plan for Mexican Aid," *New York Times,* 31 January 1995.

20. Jeff Gerth and Elaine Sciolino, "I.M.F. Head: He Speaks, and Money Talks," *New York Times,* 2 April 1996 and 30 January 1995; and Anthony DePalma, "Mexico to Get 2nd Half of Its I.M.F. Aid Package," 1 July 1995, *New York Times.*

21. Walker F. Todd, "Dollar Drain," *The Nation,* 10 July 1995.

22. Peter Passell, "A Mexican Payoff," 12 October 1995, *New York Times;* and Anthony DePalma, "After the Fall: Two Faces of Mexico's Economy," 16 July 1995, *New York Times.*

23. Keith Bradsher, "Obscure Global Bank Moves into the Glare," 1 September 1995, *New York Times.*

24. "Trust to Buy Hotel Chain for $2 Billion," 5 January 1998, *New York Times.*

25. James Bennet, "Mexican Shock for U.S. Concerns," *New York Times,* 23 December 1994; Francis Flaherty, "Foraging for Stocks with Life in Mexico," *New York Times,* 24 December 1994; Gary Gereffi and Lynn Hempel, "Latin America in the Global Economy," *NACLA Reports,* January–February 1996; and "Wal-Mart Shows Strong Sales and Plans Expansion Abroad," *New York Times,* 9 October 1996; Bloomberg Business Wire, 13 April 1997 and 11 July 1999.

26. *New York Times,* 21 July 1993.

27. Alan R. Myerson, "Strategies on Mexico Cast Aside," *New York Times,* 14 February 1995; Robyn Meredith, "The Brave New World of General Motors," *New York Times,* 26 October 1997; Sara Anderson and John Cavanaugh, "Nafta's Unhappy Anniversary," *New York Times,* 7 February 1995; Julia Preston, "Mexican Peso Fall Leads to Auto-Sales Standstill," *New York Times,* 10 August 1995; Bennet, "Mexican Shock for U.S. Concerns"; and DePalma, "After the Fall." Also, *Chiapas95,* report 33, 30 March 1997.

28. Alan R. Myerson, "Out of a Crisis, an Opportunity," *New York Times,* 26 September 1995; Alan R. Myerson, "Borderline Working Class," *New York Times,* 8 May 1997; Millman, "High Tech Jobs"; Anthony DePalma, "Economics Lesson in a Border Town: Why That Asian TV Has a 'Made in Mexico' Label," *New York Times,* 23 May 1996; and Ruiz, *On the Rim of Mexico,* 76–81.

29. Ruiz, *On the Rim of Mexico*, 76–81; and DePalma, "Economics Lesson in a Border Town."

30. Bertrand Frank, "Apparel Workers Lose in World Trade Pact," *New York Times*, 24 November 1994.

31. Gereffi and Hempel, "Latin America in the Global Economy."

32. *Statistical Abstract of the United States* (Washington, D.C.: U.S. Census Bureau, 1999), 807.

33. Hector Figueroa, "In the Name of Fashion: Exploitation in the Garment Industry," *NACLA Reports*, January–February 1996; Gereffi and Hempel, "Latin America in the Global Economy"; and Anderson and Cavanagh, "Nafta's Unhappy Anniversary."

34. Alan R. Myerson, "Big Labor's Strategic Raid in Mexico," *New York Times*, 12 September 1994.

35. "NAFTA'S Opposition," the *Nation*, 14 June 1993; *Wall Street Journal*, 4 April 1996; Alan R. Myerson, "Reich Supports Mex on Union Organizing," 13 October 1994, *New York Times*; and Myerson, "Big Labor's Strategic Raid."

36. Merilee S. Grindle, "Reforming Land Tenure in Mexico: Peasants, the Market, and the State," in *The Challenge of Institutional Reform in Mexico*, ed. Riordan Roett (Boulder: Lynne Rienner, 1995), 39–56.

37. Cited in Silverstein and Cockburn, "Who Broke Mexico?"

38. For the data see *Proceso*, 3 May 1998. See also Stefan John Wray, "The Drug War and Information Warfare in Mexico," Master's thesis, University of Texas, Austin, 1997, 70, 73, 87–88, 90–95, 106, 114, 121, 123, and 133; *La Jornada*, 17 April 1998; and Barbara Larkin, Assistant Secretary, Legislative Affairs, Department of State, Washington, D.C., to Senator Patrick Leahy, Washington, D.C., in *Chiapas95*, 3 March 1998.

39. *La Jornada*, 19 March 1997.

40. "Border Corruption," *Houston Chronicle*, 17 April 1999. For money laundering and drugs, see "Sam Marcy on Drug Lords and Bankers," *Chiapas95*, 14 December 1998; *New York Times*, 22 January 1986; Sam Dillon, "Mexican Traffickers Recruiting Killers in the U.S.," *New York Times*, 4 December 1997; Sam Dillon, "Mexico Detains U.S. Brothers, Linking Them to Gunrunning," *New York Times*, 14 January 1998; Sam Dillon, "With Drugs and Gangs Rife, Mexican Governor Resigns," *New York Times*, 13 May 1998; and Andrew Reding, "Narco-Politics in Mexico," the *Nation*, 10 July 1995. For Citibank and money laundering in the 1990s, see Tim Golden, "The Citibank Connection: Real Money, Shadow Banks," *New York Times*, 27 February 2001.

41. Tim Golden, "To Help Keep Mexico Stable, U.S. Soft-Pedaled Drug War," *New York Times*, July 1995; Ruiz, *On the Rim of Mexico*, 169–193; and Martin Edwin Anderson, "Civil-Military Relations and Internal Security in Mexico: The Undone Reform," in *The Challenge of Institutional Reform in Mexico*, ed. Riordan Roett (Boulder: Lynne Rienner, 1995), 163.

42. "U.S. Intelligence Center Played Key Role in Mexico Drug Busts," *Associated Press*, 14 November 1997; and Sam Dillon, "U.S. Drug Agents Want Mexico to Ease 'Rules of the Game,'" *New York Times*, 16 March 1997.

43. For the CIA in Mexico, see Manuel Buendia, *La CIA en México* (Mexico City: Ediciones Oceano, 1983).

44. Andres Oppenheimer and Christopher Marquis, "FBI Helping Mexico Screen Agents," *Miami Herald*, 7 May 1997. For a report on present activities, see Darrin Wood, "Campus Mexico," *Chiapas95*, 20 March 1998.

45. Deborah Tedford, "Cousin Tells Jurors of Murders Ordered by a Reputed Drug Lord," *Houston Chronicle*, 4 October 1996; and Ruiz, *On the Rim of Mexico*, 169–193.

CHAPTER 15. MEXICO IN THE NEW WORLD ORDER

1. Louis Uchutelle, "U.S. Losses in Mexico Assessed," *New York Times*, 26 December 1994.

2. Anthony DePalma, "U.S. Aid Plan Is Hardly a Cure All," *New York Times*, 23 February 1995; Anthony DePalma, "Dollar Duress," *New York Times*, 22 February 1995; Bradsher, "Obscure Global Bank"; and Thomas L. Friedman, "The Critics Were Wrong," *New York Times*, 25 September 1996.

3. Reuters, 16 January 1997.

4. David E. Sanger, "Mexico Says It Will Repay $7 Billion to the U.S.," *New York Times*, 26 July 1996; and David E. Sanger, "G.A.O. Study Cites Benefit of Mexican Bailout," *New York Times*, 24 February 1996.

5. Bloomberg Business Wire, 8 January 1997.

6. *New York Times*, 19 June 1996.

7. "Entubamiento del Gran Canal," *La Jornada*, 27 October 1994; and *New York Times*, 25 August 1994.

8. Julia Preston, "Mexican Fights Swiss for Honor and Millions," *New York Times*, 30 December 1997; and Julia Preston, "Swiss to Seize Salinas Funds, Tying Money to Drug Trade," *New York Times*, 4 April 1997; and Tim Golden, "U.S. Report Says Salinas's Banker Ignored Safeguards," *New York Times*, 4 December 1998.

9. Anthony DePalma with Peter Truell, "A Mexican Mover and Shaker and How His Millions Moved," *New York Times*, 5 June 1996.

10. Ibid.

11. Peter Truell, "Citibank's Records Examined as Part of Mexican Inquiry," *New York Times*, 30 March 1996.

12. Julia Preston, "Mexicans Belittle Drug-Money Sting," *New York Times*, 20 May 1998.

13. Peter Truell, "In Case Tied to Mexico, a Citibank Witness Is Called a Liar," *New York Times*, 4 December 1996; Julia Preston, "For Citibank, a Problem Plum," *New York Times*, 21 November 1997; Preston, "Mexicans Belittle Drug-Money Sting"; Don Van Natta Jr., "U.S. Indicts Twenty-six Mexican Bankers in Laundering of Drug Funds," *New York Times*, 19 May 1998; and Jonathan Friedland, "Citibank Buys Confia of Mexico," *The Wall Street Journal*, 12 May 1998.

14. Craig Torres and Laurie Hays, "Alleged Launderer Moved Millions Despite Scrutiny by U.S., Mexico," *The Wall Street Journal*, 1 April 1997.

15. Interpress Third World News Agency, 26 April 1997.

16. "Mexico Plans One Billion Dollar Bond Sale," *The News,* 4 January 1997.

17. *New York Times,* 28 June 1996.

18. "Kansas City Southern in Deal with Mexican Rail Operator," *New York Times,* 6 September 1995; "The Right Track," *Barron's,* 30 March 1998; and Reuters Security News, 6 February 1997. For TFM revenues see Luther S. Miller, "Mexico's Hot: Come On Down," *Railway Age* 6, no. 4 (1999), at www.railwayage .com/jun99/inside.html.

19. Reuters Security News, 6 February 1997.

20. DePalma, "Mexico's Garage Sale"; Julia Preston, "Mexico Says It Plans More Privatizations," *New York Times,* 7 December 1996; Joel Millman, "Mexico's TMM Plans to Buy Shipper, But Spending Binge Rattles Investors," *Wall Street Journal,* January 1997; and Bloomberg Business Wire, 6 December 1996.

21. Debra Beachy, "Mexico Selling Rail Line," *Houston Chronicle,* 10 August 1996.

22. Craig Torres, "Sudden Targets: Foreigners Snap Up Mexican Companies; Impact Is Enormous," *The Wall Street Journal,* 30 September 1997. For Reed see Timothy L. O'Brien, "Prince of the Citi," *New York Times,* 7 May 1998.

23. "The Americas," *Forbes,* 17 July 1995.

24. *Chiapas95,* report 16, 30 March 1997.

25. Sam Dillon, "Mexico Drops Its Effort to Sell Some Oil Plants," *New York Times,* 14 October 1996.

26. Sam Dillon, "Mexico's Lifeblood on the Auction Block," *New York Times,* 4 November 1995.

27. "White House Klatsches: Who Went, What They Got," *Counterpunch,* 1–15 March 1997; and Toni Mack with José Aguayo, "The Education of Jesús Reyes," *Forbes,* 24 March 1997.

28. *The News,* 4 January 1997.

29. Sanger, "Mexico Says It Will Repay $7 Billion"; Anthony DePalma, "New Ethics in Mexico," *New York Times,* 10 September 1994; Anthony DePalma, "Mexican Banking's New Scorecard," *New York Times,* 19 December 1994; Louis Uchitelle, "Pemex's Barrier to Its Grand Plans," *New York Times,* 4 March 1993; and *The News,* 4 January 1997.

30. For the total of *maquila* jobs in 1998, see *La Jornada,* 29 December 1998, as cited in *Frontera-Border Archives,* 22 January 1999. "Mexico Seeks Funds for Gas Industry," *New York Times,* 24 April 1995. For U.S. exports see *Statistical Abstract of the United States* (Washington, D.C.: U.S. Census Bureau, 1999), 807.

31. Julia Preston, "New Era of Phone Competition in Mexico," *New York Times,* 13 August 1996; Sam Dillon, "Foreign Business to Put $6.3 Billion in Mexico," *New York Times,* 5 December 1996; and Agis Salpukas, "Two Utilities in California Merge to Fight Competition," *New York Times,* 15 October 1996.

32. Hillary Durgin, "U.S. Natural Gas Firms Eye Mexico," *Houston Chronicle,* 30 May 1995; Preston, "New Era of Phone Competition"; and Alan R. Myerson, "U.S. Companies Competing to Be First in Gas to Mexico," *New York Times,* 7 December 1995.

33. Reuters, as cited in *Chiapas95*, 19 January 1997.

34. Myerson, "Out of a Crisis"; Myerson, "Borderline Working Class"; and James G. Samstad and Ruth Berins Collier, "Mexican Labor and Structural Reform," in *The Challenge of Institutional Reform in Mexico*, ed. Riordan Roett (Boulder: Lynne Rienner, 1995). See also "En tres anos las maquiladoras surtiran el mercado nacional," *La Jornada*, 12 May 1997; and Millman, "High Tech Jobs."

35. For the Dana Corporation's abuse of Mexican workers, see Sam Dillon, "Abuses Reported in Mexico at American-Owned Plant," *New York Times*, 5 August 1998; and Samstad and Collier, "Mexican Labor and Structural Reform," 16 and 25.

36. Myerson, "Out of a Crisis"; Myerson, "Borderline Working Class"; and Samstad and Collier, "Mexican Labor and Structural Reform," 15.

37. *Business Week* (International Edition), 7 July 1977.

38. *Chiapas95*, 30 December 1996.

39. Ibid. For a discussion of the companies, see Youssef M. Ibrahim, "Genetic Soybeans Alarm Europe," *New York Times*, 7 November 1996.

40. John Ross, "Treasure of the Costa Grande," *Sierra*, July–August 1996; and John Ross, "Boise in Guerrero," *Sierra*, November–December 1996.

41. "La riqueza de la Tarahumara, a una trasnacional," *La Jornada*, 9 December 1996; and "Ejido Tarahumara," *La Jornada*, 10 December 1996.

42. *La Jornada*, 15 February 1997 and 1 March 1997.

43. Ricardo Ravelo, "Laguna Verde es un gran negocio para algunos y no les importa el peligro; puede haber una catástrofe," *Proceso*, 21 July 1996.

44. Anderson and Cavanagh, "Nafta's Unhappy Anniversary"; Sara Anderson, John Cavanagh, and David Ranney, "NAFTA: Trinational Fiasco," the *Nation*, 15–22 July 1996; Stephen P. Mumme, "The North American Commission for Environmental Cooperation and the United States–Mexico Border Region: The Case of Air and Water," in *Transboundary Resources Report* (Albuquerque: International Transboundary Resources Center, 1995); "New Directions in United States–Mexican Transboundary Environmental Management: A Critique of Current Proposals," reprint from the *Natural Resources Journal*, n.d.; and Ruiz, *On the Rim of Mexico*, 222–233.

45. Mark Feldstein, "Death on the Border," *Impact*, Cable News Network, 18 May 1997.

46. *New York Times*, 16 October 1994; and Ruiz, *On the Rim of Mexico*, 222–233.

47. Alexander Cockburn, "Al Gore, Green Groups and Narco-Traffickers," the *Nation*, 12 August 1996.

48. For the agreement between the U.S. and Mexican governments regarding the establishment of a virtual monopoly on transnational broadcasting, see Anthony DePalma, "U.S. and Mexico Reach Accord over Satellite TV Transmission," *New York Times*, 9 November 1996.

49. Preston, "New Era of Phone Competition"; Anthony DePalma, "MCI Wins Mexican Long-Distance License," *New York Times*, 7 September 1995; Anthony DePalma, "Avantel of Mexico Entering Long Distance," *New York*

Times, 12 August 1996; Edmund L. Andrews, "Minister of Objection Nettles Washington," *New York Times,* 21 May 1997; and "Telecom Firms Call on Mexico," *North County Blade Citizen,* 24 September 1995. See also *New York Times,* 21 July 1993.

50. "Two More Ventures for Mexico Long Distance," *New York Times,* 7 December 1995.

51. Julia Preston, "A Telecom Revolución in Mexico," *New York Times,* 14 November 1996. For the acquisition of Banamex-Accival, see Riva D. Atlas and Tim Weiner, "Citigroup to Buy Mexican Bank in a Deal Valued at $12.5 Billion," *New York Times,* 18 May 2001.

52. Ibid. See also Julia Preston, "Scandal Spurs Bell Atlantic Shift in Mexico," *New York Times,* 27 November 1996; Preston, "Mexican Fights Swiss for Honor and Millions"; Kerry A. Dolan, Stephen S. Johnson, and Joel Millman, "The Billionaires; The Americas," *Forbes,* 17 July 1995; and Craig Torres, "Bell Atlantic Bucks Mexico's Gatekeepers," *Wall Street Journal,* 17 November 1997.

53. Preston, "Telecom Revolución"; Anthony DePalma, "Telmex Gains in Attempt to Buy Cable-System Stake," *New York Times,* 22 June 1995; Peter Truell, "Citibank's Records Examined as Part of Mexican Inquiry," *New York Times,* 30 March 1996; and Laura M. Holson, "Shuttle Diplomacy Leads to New Corporate Marriage," *New York Times,* 12 May 1998.

54. Dolan, Johnson, and Millman, "The Billionaires"; and "Anheuser-Busch to Boost Stake in Modelo," *Houston Chronicle,* 15 November 1996.

55. For the data see *Proceso,* 3 May 1998; Wray, "The Drug War," 70, 73, 87–88, 90–95, 106, 114, 121, 123, and 133; *La Jornada,* 17 April 1998; and Barbara Larkin, Assistant Secretary, Legislative Affairs, Department of State, Washington, D.C., to Senator Patrick Leahy, Wahington D.C., in *Chiapas95,* 3 March 1998. For the information on the training of Asian, South American, and Central American troops, see *The Prism* (Chapel Hill, n.d.), available at Archive, *Chiapas95,* Harry Cleaver website, Department of Economics, University of Texas, Austin.

56. *Proceso,* January 1998.

57. Carlos Marin, "Plan del Ejercito en Chiapas, desde 1994," *Proceso,* no. 1105; and Darrin Wood, "Los GAFE: ¿Anti-narcos o anti-Marcos?," *Nuevo Amanecer Press,* 6 January 1998.

58. Darrin Wood, "Clinton's Interference in Mexico," *Nuevo Amanecer Press,* 28 December 1997; and Hart, interview with American instructors, American embassy, Mexico City, July 1971. Also *Nuevo Amanecer Press,* 28 January 1997; and *La Jornada,* 26 December 1997.

59. Matt Moffett, Craig Torres, and Dianne Solis, "Show of Force," *Wall Street Journal,* 3 September 1996.

60. *Mexpaz,* bulletin 101, 13 January 1996; *Mexpaz,* bulletin 142, 1 October 1997; and Larkin to Leahy, *Chiapas95,* 3 March 1998.

61. Reuters, 10 January 1997.

62. Resident information provided by Timothy Charles Brown, a Mexican researcher with the Hoover Institution. For the data on tourists, see Christo-

pher Reynolds, "Lack of Data Makes It Hard to Assess Threat of Crime," *The News,* 21 November 1998.

63. John Summa, "Markets and Manipulation," *Global Media,* December 1994; and DePalma, "Mexican Attitudes Shift."

64. Brendan M. Case, "Casting Big Nets for Latin American Channel Surfers," *New York Times,* 5 August 1996.

65. Ibid.

66. Larry Rohter, "Growing Latin Market Creates New Battleground of Cable TV," *New York Times,* 12 May 1997; and DePalma, "U.S. and Mexico Reach Accord."

67. Paul Lewis, "Jean Gerard, 58, Reagan Envoy Who Led U.S. to Leave UNESCO," *New York Times,* 6 August 1996.

68. *Nuevo Amanecer,* in *Chiapas95,* 6 June 1998.

69. Gustav Niebur, "A Ceremony in Mexico City Shows Growth in Mormonism," *New York Times,* 11 December 1994; and Ruiz, *On the Rim of Mexico,* 124. For the Mormons at Cuauhtémoc, see Hart, interview with Lilia Rubio, 3 November 1997, Mexico City.

70. Alan R. Myerson, "Tejano Star Sets Out to Bridge Music and Nations," *New York Times,* 1 January 1996.

71. Albert Sgambati, "New Jersey–Aztec Phenomenon," *The News,* 9 July 1997.

72. Edward Said, *Culture and Imperialism* (New York: Vintage, 1994), xvii.

CONCLUSION. IMPERIAL AMERICA

1. Interview with Guadalupe San Miguel, December 2000, Houston. San Miguel, an authority on Mexican-American affairs, provided the data. For immigration data see *1997 Immigration and Naturalization Service Yearbook* (Washington, D.C.: U.S. Government Printing Office, 1999), p. 21, table C.

2. For more on the American dream, see O'Brien, *The Revolutionary Mission;* and Emily Rosenberg, *Spreading the American Dream: American Economic and Cultural Expansion, 1890–1945* (New York: Hill and Wang, 1982). The best work on American Protestantism in Latin America is Andrew Chesnut, *Born Again in Brazil: The Pentecostal Boom and the Pathogens of Poverty* (New Brunswick: Rutgers University Press, 1997).

Bibliography

LIST OF SOURCES CITED

Archivo General de la Nación, Mexico City
    Ramo de Gobernacion, Tranquilidad Publica
    Ramo de Tierras
    Ramo Ferrocarriles
    Ramo Junta Protectora de las Clases Menesterosas
Archivo General del Estado, Monterrey, Nuevo León
    Ramo de Notarias
Archivo General del Estado, Saltillo, Coahuila
    Ramo de Notarias
Archivo Historico de la Secretaria de la Reforma Agraria, Durango, Durango, Mexico
Archivo Historica de la Secretaria de la Reforma Agraria, Guerrero, Chilpancingo, Guerrero, Mexico
Archivo Historico de la Secretaria de la Reforma Agraria, Mexico City
    Ramo Terrenos Nacionales
    Sección Composicion
    Sección Diversos
Archivo Historico de la Secretaria de la Reforma Agraria, Oaxaca, Oaxaca, Mexico
Archivo Historico de la Secretaria de la Reforma Agraria, San Luis Potosí, San Luis Potosí, Mexico
Archivo Historico de la Secretaria de Transportes y Comunicaciones, Mexico City
Archivo Historico del Tribunal Superior del Distrito y Territorios Federales, Mexico City
    Ramo de Haciendas

Ramo de Pueblos
Ramo de Terrenos

Archivo Historico, Seis de Enero de 1915, de la Secretaria de la Reforma Agraria, Mexico City
Ramo Comunal
Ramo Ejidal

Archivo Judicial del Tribunal Superior de Justícia del Distrito y Territorios Federales, Mexico City

Baker Library, Harvard University School of Business, Cambridge
Henry W. Peabody Papers

Banco de México, Mexico City
Archivo Historico de Matías Romero

Bancroft Library Rare Books and Manuscripts Room, University of California, Berkeley
Bancroft Interviews
Charles Whitehead Letter regarding the Mexican National Debt
Collis P. Huntington Papers (microfilm)
Pamphlet Box of Materials on United States and Mexican Claims
Placido Vega Papers

Barker Texas History Collection, University of Texas, Austin
Edward M. House Papers
James B. Wells Papers
James Stephen Hogg Papers
Jean B. La Coste Papers
John Salmon Ford Papers
Pioneers in Texas Oil, Oral History Library
San Roman Papers
Steven F. Powers Papers
T. W. House Papers
William Clifford Hogg Papers

Butler Library, Rare Books and Manuscript Library, Columbia University, New York
Edgar Turlington Papers
Frank Tannenbaum Papers
Frank Vanderlip Papers
James Stillman Papers
W. R. Grace Papers

Centro de Información del Estado de Chihuahua, Chihuahua, Mexico
Batopilas Papers

El Paso Public Library, El Paso
Otis A. Aultman Collection
Southwestern Mining Collection

Hart Collection, Houston
    Batopilas Mining Company Papers, Twelve Letterbooks, 1898–1921,
    diverse records (2 ft.) from United States–Mexico claims commissions
Houghton Library, Rare Books and Manuscripts Room, Harvard University,
Cambridge
    Charles and James Stillman Letters, Letterbooks, Accounts, Bills,
    and Other Business Papers, 1850–1879
    James Stillman Diaries and Personal Accounts
Houston Metropolitan Research Center, Houston
    John Henry Kirby Papers
    Joseph S. Cullinan Papers
Howard-Tilton Memorial Library, Tulane University, Tulane
    Minor Family Papers
    Townsend-Stanton Family Papers
Huntington Library, San Marino, California
    Albert Bacon Fall Collection
John E. Connor Museum, Texas A&M University, Kingsville, Texas
    James L. Allhands Papers
Library of Congress, Washington, D.C.
    Edward Lee Plumb Papers
    Geography and Map Division
    Josephus Daniels Papers
    Thomas Watt Gregory Papers
Library of the University of Texas, El Paso
    John H. McNeely Papers
Mandeville Collection, University of California, San Diego
    Topolobampo Papers
Manuscripts Collection, University of Arizona Library, Tucson
    Richardson Construction Company Papers
Marvin Scudder Collection, The Thomas J. Watson Library of Business
    and Economics, Columbia University, New York
    American Chicle Company
    Anaconda Copper Company
    Batopilas Consolidated Mining Company
    Boston Mexican Petroleum Company
    Cananea Consolidated Copper Company (including subsidiaries)
    Candelaria Gold and Silver (San Dimas, Durango)
    Cieneguita Copper Company (Sonora)
    Guanajuato Power and Electric Company
    Guanajuato Reduction and Mines Company (Chase Bank, Empire Trust)
    Guggenheim Exploration Company

Intercontinental Petroleum
Intercontinental Rubber Company (Baruch, Aldrich, et al.)
International Petroleum Company
Louisiana and Texas Railroad and Steamship Company (Morgan)
Mexican Central Railway (Old Colony Trust as trustee)
Mexican Electric Company
Mexican Industrial Railway Company (Mexico City Belt Railroad)
Mexican International Corporation (major New York banks)
Mexican Investment Company
Mexican Milling and Transportation Company (Guanajuato Mines)
Mexican National Railway Company
Mexican Panuco Oil Company
Mexican Petroleum Company
Mexican Producing and Refining Company
Mexican Seaboard Company
Mexican Sulphur Company (a division of American Sulphur)
Mexican Telephone and Telegraph Company
Mexican Utilities Company (Guanajuato)
Mexico Northwestern Railway Company (and subsidiaries)
Mexico-Ohio Oil Company (Coahuila)
Moctezuma Copper Company (Phelps Dodge)
Monterrey and Mexican Gulf Coast Railway (Mexican Pacific
    Railway)
Monterrey Iron and Steel Company (Salinas, Garza, et al.)
National Railways of Mexico
New York–Mexican Oil Company
Pacific Mail Steamship Company
Penn-Mex Fuel Oil Company
Sinaloa Silver Mining Company
Tampico Harbor Company
Tehuantepec Inter-Ocean Railroad Company
U.S. and Mexico Trust Company (Kansas City, Mexico, and Orient Railroad)
Waters Pierce Oil Company

Morgan Library, New York
    The Morgan Bank Syndicate Books

National Archives and Records Administration, Washington, D.C.
    Department of State Decimal Files, Series 312, 412, 512, 612, 712, and 812,
        Records Group 59
    Department of State Purport Lists for the Decimal File, 812.10–812.345/17,
        1910–1929, Records Group 59
    Dispatches Received by the Department of State from U.S. Consuls,
        1826–1906
    U.S. Adjutant General, Mexican Intervention, Collection Number
        2149991, Records Group 92

U.S. Adjutant General, Villa's Revolution, Collection Number 2212358,
    Records Group 92
Nettie Lee Benson Latin American Collection, University of Texas, Austin
    Corralitos Hacienda Papers
    Graham M. Ker Papers
    Lazaro de la Garza Papers
    Northwestern Railroad Collection
    Robert S. Towne Papers
    Sherman Kile Papers
    William F. Buckley Sr. Papers
New York Historical Society, New York
    Charles F. de Loosey Papers
    Francis Jay Herron Papers
    Gideon Welles Papers
    James Beekman Papers
New York Public Library, New York
    Auguste Belmont Papers
    Brown Brothers and Company
    Candelaria Gold and Silver Mining Company Papers
    Edith O'Shaughnessy Papers
    Levi P. Morton Papers
    Mexican National Railway Company Collection
    Mexico Mining Papers
    Moses Taylor Papers
    Phelps Dodge and Company
Registro Publica, Chihuahua
    Notarias Publicos
Registro Publico, Ciudad Victoria, Tamaulipas
    Registro de la Propiedad
Registro Publico, Durango
    Archivo Historico de la Propiedad y el Comercio
    Notarias Publicos
Rio Grande Valley Historical Collection, Pan-American University, Edinburg,
Texas
    American Rio Grande Land and Irrigation Company Papers
    Shary Collection
Rutherford B. Hayes Presidential Center, Spiegel Grove, Ohio
    Hayes Collection
Sherman Library, Corona del Mar, California
    Otto F. Brant Papers
Special Collections, University of California, Los Angeles
    William Starke Rosecrans Papers
Tom Hale Papers, Houston

Universidad Iberoamericana, Mexico City
    Colección Manuel González
    Colección Porfirio Díaz
Universidad Nacional Autónoma de México, Mexico City
Washington National Records Center, College Park, Maryland
    Military Government of Veracruz, Records Group 141
    Office of the Quartermaster General, Army Transport Service General File,
        1914–1940 (Declassified), Records Group 92
    United States and Mexican Claims Commissions, Records Group 76
    Records of the American Mexican Claims Commission, 1936–1947

        American Mexican Claims Commission Decisions
        Approved Agrarian Claims (Declassified)
        Approved Agrarian Claims, Extended (Declassified)
        Approved Cattle Claims, 1933–1947
        Approved New Agrarian Claims, 1939–1947 (Declassified)
        Deferred Miscellaneous Claims Approved after 1935 (Declassified)
        List of Plantations in the Isthmus of Tehauntepec, Entry 152
    Records of the General Claims Commission, United States and Mexico,
        Created under the Claims Convention of 4 July 1868

        Case Files for United States Claimants, 1869–1876, Entry 41
        Index to Case Files for United States Claimants, Entry 43
        Petitions Filed with the Commission, 1872–1873
        Report on Progress of the Commission, Entry 51
    Records of the Special Claims Commission, United States and Mexico,
        Created under the Claims Convention of 10 September 1923

        Agrarian Claims (U.S. Section)
        Approved Agrarian Claims, 1923–1937 (Declassified)
        Awarded Claims, 1924–1938, Entry 189
        Case Files for United States Claimants, 1924–1936, Entry 125 and 184
Woodson Research Center, Rice University, Houston
    Walter B. Sharp Papers
Yale University, Sterling Library, New Haven
    Edward Mandel House Papers
    John Lind Papers

Memoirs

Ford, John Salmon. *Rip Ford's Texas.* Austin: University of Texas Press, 1963.
McCaughan, John Sheppard. *Personal Recollections.* N.p., n.d.

Interviews

American instructors. American embassy, Mexico City, July 1971.
Archer, Lois. Pacific Palisades, 8 January 1984. (Secondary source.)

Avelar, Manuel. Durango, 25 July 1992.

Benson, Nettie Lee. Austin, 1978–1988.

Bluth, Oliver Scott (local historian). Casas Grandes Viejo, Chihuahua, 23 February 1984.

Brown, Lyle. Morelia, 8 December 1997.

Garcia Rodriguez, Manuel (supervisor of Servicios Portuarios). Veracruz, 17 August 1983.

Gibson, Charles. Dallas, 29 December 1978.

Hale, Tom. Houston, 8 March 1998. (Secondary source.)

Houck, Harvey. Houston, 8 March 1998.

Hugetz, Ed. Houston, 16 April 1988.

Hughes, James B., Jr. Deep River Armory, Houston, 3 August 1982. (Secondary source.)

King, John O. Houston, 3 September 1993. (Secondary source.)

Marshall, Billy, III (owner, Hacienda de Corralitos). Corralitos, Chihuahua, 23 February 1984.

Michener, James. Austin, July 1885.

Niemeyer, Victor. Austin, 1985–1996.

Rubio, Lilia. Mexico City, 3 November 1997.

Salazar Perez, Antonio. Veracruz, 28 July 1983. (Secondary source.)

Zuñiga, Jesús Luis. Guadalajara, 11 December 1997.

Newspapers, Magazines, and Websites

Barron's

Brownsville Herald

Chiapas95 (Austin)

Commercial and Financial Chronicle (New York)

Corpus Christi Gazette

Counterpunch (Washington, D.C.)

Diario Oficial (Mexico City)

El Paso Herald

El Paso Lone Star

El Financiero (Mexico City)

Forbes

Galveston Weekly News

Houston Chronicle

La Jornada (Mexico City)

Los Angeles Times

NACLA Reports (New York)

The News (Mexico City)

New York Times

Nuevo Amanecer Press

Omaha Daily News

Omaha World Herald

Proceso (Mexico City)
San Antonio Herald
San Antonio Press
La Tierra de México (Mexico City)
The Two Republics (Mexico City)
Wall Street Journal

SECONDARY SOURCES

Books

Aguilar Camin, Hector. *La revolución nomada: Sonora y la revolución mexicana.* Mexico City: Siglo XXI, 1977.
Allhands, James L. *Gringo Builders.* Dallas: privately published, 1931.
———. *Railroads to the Rio Salado.* Houston: Anson Jones Press, 1960.
Anders, Evan. *Boss Rule in South Texas: The Progressive Era.* Austin: University of Texas Press, 1982.
Anderson, Rodney D. *Outcasts in Their Own Land: Mexican Industrial Workers 1906–1911.* DeKalb: Northern Illinois University Press, 1976.
Andrews, Gregg. *Shoulder to Shoulder? The American Federation of Labor, the United States, and the Mexican Revolution, 1910–1924.* Berkeley: University of California Press, 1991.
Anglo American Directory of Mexico. Mexico City: Excelsior, 1911.
Araiza, Luis. *Historia del movimiento obrero mexicana.* 5 vols. Mexico City: n.p., 1964–1966.
Ashby, Joe C. *Organized Labor and the Mexican Revolution under Cárdenas.* Chapel Hill: University of North Carolina Press, 1967.
Bailey, David. *Viva Cristo Rey! The Cristero Rebellion and the Church-State Conflict in Mexico.* Austin: University of Texas Press, 1974.
Baklanoff, Eric N. *Expropriation of U.S. Investments in Cuba, Mexico, and Chile.* New York: Praeger, 1975.
Baldwin, Deborah J. *Protestants and the Mexican Revolution: Missionaries, Ministers and Social Change.* Urbana: University of Illinois Press, 1990.
Barber, Amherst Willoughby, ed. *The benevolent raid of Lew Wallace; how Mexico was saved in 1864; the Monroe Doctrine in action; testimony of a survivor, private Justus Brooks.* Washington, D.C.: D. C. R. Beresford, 1914.
Barry, Tom. *The Great Divide: The Challenge of U.S.—Mexico Relations in the 1990s.* New York: Grove/Atlantic Monthly Press, 1994.
Baruch, Bernard. *My Own Story.* New York: Henry Holt and Co., 1957.
Basse, F., and Robert H. Hord. *To the Public: A Brief Description of the Title to the Lands upon which the City of Brownsville is Situated.* Brownsville: n.p., n.d.
Bazant, Jan. *Historia de la deuda exterior de México (1823–1946).* Mexico City: El Colegio de México, 1946.
Beezley, William H. *Insurgent Governor: Abraham González and the Mexican Revolution in Chihuahua.* Lincoln: University of Nebraska Press, 1973.

———. *Judas at the Jockey Club and Other Episodes of Porfirian Mexico*. Lincoln: University of Nebraska Press, 1987.

Bemis, Samuel Flagg. *The Latin American Policy of the United States*. New York: Harcourt, Brace and World, 1943.

Benjamin, Thomas, and William McNellie, eds. *Other Mexicos: Essays on Regional Mexican History, 1876–1911*. Albuquerque: University of New Mexico Press, 1984.

Bernstein, Marvin. *The Mexican Mining Industry, 1890–1950*. Albany: State University of New York Press, 1964.

Bjarkman, Peter C. *Baseball with a Latin Beat*. Jefferson, N.C.: McFarland & Company, Inc., 1994.

Blaisdell, Lowell. *The Desert Revolution: Baja California, 1911*. Madison: University of Wisconsin Press, 1962.

Bosch Garcia, Carlos. *La base de la politica exterior estadounidense*. Mexico City: Universidad Autonoma Nacional de México, 1969.

Britton, John A. *Revolution and Ideology: Images of the Mexican Revolution in the United States*. Lexington, University of Kentucky Press, 1995.

Broehl, Wayne G., Jr. *Cargill: Trading the World's Grain*. Hanover, N.H.: The University Press of New England, 1998.

Brown, Jonathan C. *Oil and Revolution in Mexico*. Berkeley: University of California Press, 1993.

Bryant, Keith L., Jr. *Arthur E. Stillwell—Promoter with a Hunch*. Nashville: Vanderbilt University Press, 1971.

Buckley, Priscilla, et al. *WFB: An Appreciation*. New York: private printing, 1979.

Buendia, Manuel. *La CIA en México*. Mexico City: Ediciones Oceano, 1983.

Bulnes, Francisco. *The Whole Truth About Mexico; the Mexican Revolution and President Wilson's Part Therein, as seen by a Cientifico*. New York: M. Bulnes Book Company, 1916.

Bunn, Robert W. *American Foreign Investments*. New York: B. W. Hubsch and the Viking Press, 1926.

Burr, Anna R. *The Portrait of a Banker: James Stillman 1850–1918*. New York: Duffield Press, 1927.

Butterfield, Carlos. *The United States and Mexican Mail Steamship Line and Statistics of Mexico*. New York: J. A. Hasbrouck and Company, 1859.

Calderón, Francisco R. *La republica restaurada: La vida económica*. Vol. 1 of *Historia moderna de México*, ed. Daniel Cosio Villegas. Mexico City: Editorial Hermes, 1965.

Calero, Manuel. *The Mexican policy of President Woodrow Wilson as it appears to a Mexican*. New York: Smith and Thomson, 1916.

Callahan, James M. *American Foreign Policy in Mexican Relations*. New York: The Macmillan Company, 1932.

Calvert, Peter. *The Mexican Revolution 1910–1914: The Diplomacy of Anglo-American Conflict*. Cambridge: Cambridge University Press, 1968.

Carosso, Vincent P. *The Morgans: Private International Bankers, 1854–1913*. Cambridge: Harvard University Press, 1987.

Carr, Barry. *El movimiento obrero y la politica en México, 1910–1929.* Mexico City: SepSetentas, 1976.

Carreno, Alberto Maria. *La diplomacia extraordinaria entre Mexico y los Estados Unidos, 1749–1947.* Mexico City: Editorial Jus, 1961.

Castenada, Jorge. *México y el orden internacional.* Mexico City: El Colegio de México, 1956.

Cecena, José Luis. *México en la orbita imperial: Las empresas transnacionales.* Mexico City: Ediciones El Caballito, 1979.

Cerutti, Mario. *Burguesia y capitalismo en Monterrey 1850–1910.* Mexico City: Claves Latinoamericanas, 1983.

Cerutti, Mario, and Juan Ignacio Barragan. *Juan F. Brittingham y la industria en México, 1859–1940.* Monterrey: Urbis Internacional, 1993.

Chapman, James Gresham. *La construcción del ferrocarril Mexicano (1857–1880).* Mexico City: SepSetentas, 1975.

Chernow, Ron. *The Death of the Banker.* New York: Vintage, 1997.

———. *The House of Morgan: An American Banking Dynasty and the Rise of Modern Finance.* New York: Atlantic Monthly Press, 1990.

Chesnut, Andrew. *Born Again in Brazil: The Pentacostal Boom and the Pathogens of Poverty.* New Brunswick: Rutgers University Press, 1997.

Clark, James A., with Weldon Hart. *The Tactful Texan: A Biography of Governor William Hobby.* New York: Random House, 1958.

Clendenen, Clarence C. *The United States and Pancho Villa: A Study in Unconventional Diplomacy.* Ithaca: Cornell University Press, 1961.

Cleveland, Harold van B., and Thomas F. Huertas. *Citibank, 1812–1970.* Cambridge: Harvard University Press, 1985.

Clews, Henry. *Twenty-eight Years in Wall Street.* New York: Irving, 1888.

Cline, Howard. *The United States and Mexico.* Cambridge: Cambridge University Press, 1958.

Coatsworth, John H. *Growth against Development: The Economic Impact of Railroads in Porfirian Mexico.* DeKalb: Northern Illinois University, 1981.

Cockcroft, James D. *Intellectual Precursors of the Mexican Revolution.* Austin: University of Texas Press, 1968.

———. *Latinos in Beisbol.* New York: Franklin Watts, 1996.

Coerver, Don M. *The Porfirian Interregnum: The Presidency of Manuel González of Mexico, 1880–1884.* Fort Worth: Texas Christian University Press, 1979.

Cordoba, Arnaldo. *La ideologia de la Revolución Mexicana.* 2d ed. Mexico City: Ediciones Era, 1973.

Corey, Lewis. *The House of Morgan.* New York: Grosset and Dunlap, 1930.

Cosio Villegas, Daniel. *La promocion de las relaciones comerciales entre México y los Estados Unidos de America.* Mexico City: Banco Nacional de Comercio Exterior, 1961.

Coxe, Richard Smith. *Review of the relations between the United States and Mexico and of the claims of citizens of the United States against Mexico.* New York: Wilson and Company, 1846.

Creel, George. *The People Next Door.* New York: John Day, 1926.

Crespo, Horacio, and Sabine Manigat, eds. *"Oro blanco" y capitalismo.* Cuernavaca: Centro de Estudios Historicos de Morelos, 1989.

Cronon, Edmund David. *Josephus Daniels in Mexico.* Madison: University of Wisconsin Press, 1960.

Cue Canovas, Agustin. *Los Estados Unidos y el Mexico olvidado.* New York: Arno Press, 1970.

———. *Juárez, los Estados Unidos y Europa: El tratado de McLane-Ocampo.* Mexico City: Grijalbo, 1970.

Curtis, George Ticknor. *International Arbitrations and Awards.* Washington, D.C.: R. H. Darly, 1885.

Dabdoub, Claudio. *Historia del Valle del Yaqui.* Mexico City: Libreria Manuel Porrua, 1949.

Daniels, Josephus. *Shirt-Sleeve Diplomat.* Westport: Greenwood Press, 1973.

Davids, Jules. *American Political and Economic Penetration of Mexico, 1877–1920.* New York: Arno Press, 1976.

de Leon, Arnaldo. *They Called Them Greasers: Anglo Attitudes toward Mexicans in Texas, 1821–1900.* Austin: University of Texas Press, 1983.

Denny, Ludwell. *We Fight for Oil.* Westport, Conn.: Hyperion Press, 1976.

Desvernine, Raoul. *Claims against Mexico; a brief study of the international law applicable to claims of citizens of the United States and other countries for losses sustained in Mexico during the revolutions of the last decade.* New York: private printing, 1921.

Díaz Dufoo, Carlos. *Mexico y los capitales extranjeras.* Mexico City: La viuda de C. Bouret, 1918.

Díaz Soto y Gama, Antonio. *La revolución agraria del sur y Emiliano Zapata su caudillo.* Mexico City: private printing, 1961.

Didapp, Juan Pedro. *Los Estados Unidos y nuestros condiciones internos.* Mexico City: Tipografia El Republicano, 1913.

Directory of Directors of New York, 1910. New York: The Audit Company of New York, 1910.

d'Olwer, Luis Nicolau, et al. *El Porfiriato:La vida economica.* Vols. 7–8 of *Historia moderna de México*, ed. Daniel Cosio Villegas. Mexico City: Editorial Hermes, 1965.

Douglas, James. *The United States and Mexico.* New York: American Association for International Conciliation, 1910.

Dulles, John W. F. *Yesterday in Mexico: A Chronicle of the Revolution, 1919–1936.* Austin: University of Texas Press, 1961.

Dunn, Frederick Sherwood. *The Diplomatic Protection of Americans in Mexico.* New York: Columbia University Press, 1933.

Eagleton, T. *¿Por donde entro el beisol a Mexico?* Saltillo: n.p., 1990.

Engelbourg, Saul, and Leonard Bushkoff. *The Man Who Found the Money: John Stewart Kennedy and the Financing of the Western Railroads.* East Lansing: Michigan State University Press, 1996.

Evans, Rosalie. *The Rosalie Evans Letters from Mexico.* Chicago: The Bobbs Merill Company, 1926.

Fajnzylber, Fernando, and Trinidad Martínez Tarrago. *Las empresas transnacionales; expansion a nivel mundial y proyección en la industria mexicana.* Mexico City: Fondo de Cultura Economica, 1976.

Falcon, Romana. *Revolución y caciquismo. San Luis Potosí, 1910–1938.* Mexico City: El Colegio de México, 1984.

Fernández MacGregor, Genaro. *El Istmo de Tehuantepec y los Estados Unidos.* Mexico City: Editorial Elede, 1954.

Forbes, John Douglas. *J. P. Morgan Jr.* Charlottesville: University of Virginia Press, 1981.

Foster, John Watson. *Diplomatic Memoirs.* Boston: Houghton, Mifflin Company, 1909.

———. *In regard to the Candalaria Mine. Supplemental Brief for the Government of Mexico.* Washington D.C.: Beresford, 1905(?).

———. *Las memorias diplomaticas de Mr. Foster sobre Mexico.* Mexico City: Secretaria de Relaciones Exteriores, 1929.

———. *Trade with Mexico: Correspondence between the Manufacturers Association of the Northwest, Chicago and the Hon. John W. Foster, Minister Plenipotentiary of the U.S. to Mexico.* Chicago, 1878.

Frias, Heriberto. *Tomochic.* Mexico City: Valades y Cia., 1906.

Fuentes Díaz, Vicente. *El problema ferrocarrilero de México.* Mexico City: Edicion del autor, 1951.

Fuentes Mares, José. *Juarez, los Estados Unidos y Europa.* Barcelona: Editorial Grijalbo, 1983.

Gallegos, José Ignacio (Cronista de la Ciudad de Durango). *Compendio de historia de Durango, 1563–1910.* N.p.: Biblioteca de la Camara de Durango, n.d.

García Mundo, Octavio. *El movimiento inquilinario de Veracruz.* Mexico City: SepSetentas, 1976.

Geerligs, H. C. Prinsen. *The World's Cane Sugar Industry, Past and Present.* Manchester: Norman Rodger, 1912.

Getty, J. Paul. *As I See It.* Englewood Cliffs: Prentice-Hall, 1976.

Gilderhus, Mark T. *Diplomacy and Revolution: U.S.–Mexican Relations under Wilson and Carranza.* Tucson: University of Arizona Press, 1977.

Gilly, Adolfo. *La revolución interrumpida.* Mexico City: Ediciones El Caballito, 1971.

Gómez Serrano, Jesús. *Aguascalientes: Imperio de los Guggenheim.* Mexico City: Colección SepSetentas, 1982.

Gorsuch, Robert B. *The Mexican Southern Railway to Be Completed under a Charter from the Mexican Government through the States of Veracruz and Oaxaca.* New York: Hosford and Sons, 1881.

Grayson, George W. *Oil and Mexican Foreign Policy.* Pittsburgh: University of Pittsburgh Press, 1988.

Green, Rosario. *El endeudamiento publico externo de México: 1940 –1973.* Mexico City: El Colegio de México, 1976.

Gregg, Robert Danforth. *The Influence of Border Troubles on Relations between the United States and Mexico, 1876–1910.* Baltimore: Johns Hopkins Press, 1937.

Grieb, Kenneth. *The United States and Huerta.* Lincoln: University of Nebraska Press, 1969.

Guerrero Yoacham, Cristian. *Las conferencias del Niagara Falls: La mediación de Argentina, Brasil y Chile en el conflicto entre Estados Unidos y Mexico en 1914.* Santiago de Chile: Editorial Andres Bello, 1966.

Haber, Stephen H. *Industry and Underdevelopment: The Industrialization of Mexico, 1890–1940.* Stanford: Stanford University Press, 1989.

Hackett, Charles Wilson. *The Mexican Revolution and the United States, 1910–1926.* Boston: World Peace Foundation, 1926.

Haley, Edward P. *Revolution and Intervention: The Diplomacy of Taft and Wilson with Mexico, 1910–1917.* Cambridge: MIT Press, 1970.

Hall, Linda. *Alvaro Obregón: Power and Revolution in Mexico, 1911–1920.* College Station: Texas A&M University Press, 1981.

———. *Oil, Banks, and Politics: The United States and Postrevolutionary Mexico.* Austin: University of Texas Press, 1995.

Hanna, Alfred Jackson, and Kathryn Abbey Hanna. *Napoleon III and Mexico: American Triumph over Monarchy.* Chapel Hill: University of North Carolina Press, 1971.

Hart, John Mason. *Anarchism and the Mexican Working Class, 1860–1931.* Austin: University of Texas Press, 1978.

———. *Revolutionary Mexico: The Coming and Process of the Mexican Revolution.* Berkeley: University of California Press, 1987.

Hatch, Nellie Spilsbury. *Colonia Juárez: An Intimate Account of a Mormon Village.* Salt Lake City: Deseret Book Company, 1954.

Hayes, Rutherford Birchard. *The Diary of a President, 1875–1881. Being the Diary Continuously Kept by Rutherford B. Hayes from His Nomination, through the Disputed Election of 1876 and to the End of his Presidency.* Ed. T. Harry Williams. New York: David McKay Co., 1964.

———. *Mexican border troubles: Message from the President of the United States; in answer to a resolution of the House of Representatives, transmitting reports from the Secretaries of State and of War in reference to Mexican border troubles.* Washington, D.C.: Government Printing Office, 1877.

Herr, Robert Woodmansee. *"¿Quien Vive?": An American Family in the Mexican Revolution.* Wilmington: Scholarly Resources, forthcoming.

Herr, Robert Woodmansee, with Richard Herr. *An American Family in the Mexican Revolution.* Wilmington: Scholarly Resources, 1999.

Higgins, J. Foster. *A History of the Kansas City, Mexico, and Orient Railroad.* New York: Railroad and Locomotive History Society, 1956.

Hill, Larry. *Emissaries to a Revolution: Woodrow Wilson's Executive Agents in Mexico.* Baton Rouge: Louisiana State University Press, 1973.

Hinkle, Stacy C. *Wings and Saddles: The Air and Cavalry Punitive Expedition of 1919.* El Paso: Texas Western Press, 1967.

Hoffman, Abraham. *An Oklahoma Tragedy: The Shooting of the Mexican Students, 1931.* El Paso: Texas Western Press, 1987.

Holden, Robert H. *Mexico and the Survey of Public Lands: The Management of Modernization, 1876–1911.* DeKalb: Northern Illinois Press, 1994.

Horsman, Reginald. *Race and Manifest Destiny: The Origins of American Racial Anglo-Saxonism.* Cambridge: Harvard University Press, 1981.

Hoyt, Edwin P., Jr. *The House of Morgan.* New York: Dodd, Mead & Co., 1966.

Hu-DeHart, Evelyn. *Yaqui Resistance and Survival: The Struggle for Land and Autonomy, 1821–1910.* Madison: University of Wisconsin Press, 1984.

———. *The Yaquis: A Cultural History.* Tucson: University of Arizona Press, 1980.

Huitron, Jacinto. *Origenes e historia del movimiento obrero en México.* Mexico City: Editores Mexicanos Unidos, 1975.

Inman, Samuel Guy. *Intervention in Mexico.* New York: Association Press, 1919.

Jackson, Stanley. *J. P. Morgan.* New York: Stein and Day, 1983.

Johnson, Annie R. *Heartbeats of Colonia Díaz.* Mesa, Arizona: By the Author, 1972.

Joseph, Gilbert. *Revolution from Without: Yucatán, Mexico, and the United States, 1880–1924.* New York: Cambridge University Press, 1982.

Joseph, Gilbert, and Alan Wells et al. *Yucatán y la International Harvester.* Mérida: Maldonado, 1986.

Katz, Friedrich. *The Life and Times of Pancho Villa.* Stanford: Stanford University Press, 1998.

———. *The Secret War in Mexico: Europe, the United States and the Mexican Revolution.* Chicago: University of Chicago Press, 1981.

Kerr, John Leeds. *Destination Topolobampo: The Kansas City, Mexico, and Orient Railway.* San Marino: Golden West Books, 1968.

King, John O. *Joseph Steven Cullinan: A Study of Leadership in the Texas Petroleum Industry, 1857–1937.* Nashville: Vanderbilt University Press, 1970.

Klein, Alan M. *Baseball on the Border: A Tale of Two Laredos.* Princeton: Princeton University Press, 1997.

Knight, Alan. *U.S.–Mexican Relations, 1910–1940: An Interpretation.* San Diego: Center for U.S.-Mexican Studies, University of California, San Diego, 1987.

Kohl, Clayton Charles. *Claims as a Cause of the Mexican War.* New York: New York University Press, 1914.

La Botz, Dan. *Edward L. Doheny: Petroleum, Power, and Politics in the United States and Mexico.* New York: Praeger, 1991.

Langley, Lester D. *Mexico and the United States: The Fragile Relationship.* Boston: Twayne Publishers, 1991.

Lea, Tom. *The King Ranch.* 2 vols. Boston: Little, Brown, 1957.

Leal, Juan Felipe. *Agupaciones y burocracias sindicales en México, 1906–1938.* Mexico City: Terra Nova, 1995.

Liss, Sheldon B. *Century of Disagreement: The Chamizal Conflict, 1864–1964.* Seattle: University of Washington Press, 1967.

López Aparicio, Alfonso. *El movimiento obrero en México.* Mexico City: Editorial Jus, 1958.

Lytle, Joseph. *The History of the Sonoran Railroad, 1880–1882.* N.p., n.d.

Madero, Francisco. *La sucesion presidencial.* San Pedro, Coahuila: El Partido Nacional Democratico, 1908.

Marcosson, Isaac F. *Anaconda.* New York: Dodd, Mead & Company, 1957.

Marichal, Carlos. *A Century of Debt Crises in Latin America.* Princeton: Princeton University Press, 1989.

Martin, Percy F. *Mexico's Treasure House (Guanajuato): An Illustrated and Descriptive Account of the Mines.* New York: Cheltenham Press, 1906.

Maxfield, Sylvia. *Governing Capital: International Finance and Mexican Politics.* Ithaca: Cornell University Press, 1990.

McBride, Robert H., ed. *Mexico and the United States.* Englewood Cliffs: Prentice-Hall, 1981.

Melville, Roberto. *Crecimiento y rebelion: El desarrollo economico de las haciendas azucareras en Morelos (1880–1910).* Mexico City: Nueva Imagen, 1979.

Meyer, Jean. *La Cristiada.* 3 vols. Mexico City: Siglo XXI, 1973.

Meyer, Lorenzo. *The Mexican Revolution and the Anglo-Saxon Powers: The End of Confrontation and the Beginning of Negotiation.* La Jolla: Center for U.S.-Mexico Studies, University of California, San Diego, 1985.

———. *México y los Estados Unidos en el conflicto petrolero (1917–1942).* Mexico City: El Colegio de México, 1972.

Meyer, Lorenzo, and Josefina Zoraida Vázquez. *México frente a Estados Unidos: Un ensayo historico, 1776–1980.* Mexico City: El Colegio de México, 1982.

Meyer, Michael. *Huerta: A Political Portrait.* Lincoln: University of Nebraska Press, 1972.

———. *Mexican Rebel: Pascual Orozco and the Mexican Revolution, 1910–1915.* Lincoln: University of Nebraska Press, 1967.

Miller, Russell. *The House of Getty.* London: Michael Joseph, 1985.

Monroy, Guadalupe. *Archivo historico de Matías Romero: Catalogo descriptivo, correspondencia recibida,1837–1884.* 2 vols. Mexico City: Banco de México, 1965 and 1970.

Montejano, David. *Anglos and Mexicans in the Making of Texas, 1836–1986.* Austin: University of Texas Press, 1987.

Mosk, Sanford. *Industrial Revolution in Mexico.* Berkeley: University of California Press, 1954.

Niblo, Stephen R. *War, Diplomacy, and Development: The United States and Mexico, 1938–1954.* Wilmington: Scholarly Resources, 1995.

Niemeyer, E. Victor. *Revolution at Querétaro: The Mexican Constitutional Convention of 1916–1917.* Austin: University of Texas Press, 1974.

O'Brien, Thomas F. *The Century of U.S. Capitalism in Latin America.* Albuquerque: University of New Mexico Press, 1999.

———. *The Revolutionary Mission: American Enterprise in Latin America, 1900–1945.* Cambridge: Cambridge University Press, 1996.

Ochoa Reyes, Arnulfo. *Historia del Estado de Durango*. Durango: Editorial Patria, 1934.

O'Conner, Harvey. *The Guggenheims: The Making of an American Dynasty*. New York: Arno Press, 1976.

Olliff, Donathon. *Reforma Mexico and the United States: A Search for Alternatives to Annexation, 1854–1861*. Tuscaloosa: University of Alabama, 1981.

Olvera Miranda, Ramon. *12 anos de liga mexicana en Jalisco*. Guadalajara: n.p., 1995.

O'Shaughnessy, Edith. *A Diplomat's Wife in Mexico*. New York: Harper, 1916.

Osterheld, Theodore William. *The Mexican National Debt as of January 1st, 1918*. New York: n.p., 1918.

Palomares Pena, Noe G. *Propietarios norteamericanos y reforma agrarian en Chihuahua, 1917–1942*. Ciudad Juárez: Universidad Autonoma de Ciudad Juárez, 1991.

Pan American Petroleum and Transport Company. *Mexican Petroleum*. New York: Pan American Petroleum and Transport Company, 1922.

Pastor, Robert A. *Integration with Mexico*. New York: Twentieth Century Fund Press, 1993.

Paz, María Emilia. *Strategy, Security, and Spies: Mexico and the U.S. as Allies in World War II*. University Park: Pennsylvania State University Press, 1997.

Perry, Laurens Ballard. *Juárez and Díaz: Machine Politics in Mexico*. DeKalb: Northern Illinois University Press, 1978.

Person, Harlow Stafford. *Mexican Oil, Symbol of Recent Trends in International Relations*. New York: Harper and Brothers, 1942.

Pinera Ramirez, David. *American and English Influence on the Early Development of Ensenada, Baja California, Mexico*. San Diego: San Diego State University, 1995.

Pletcher, David M. *Rails, Mines, and Progress: Seven American Promoters in Mexico, 1867–1911*. Ithaca: Cornell University Press, 1958.

Price, John A. *Tijuana: Urbanization in a Border Culture*. Notre Dame: University of Notre Dame Press, 1973.

Public Opinion in the United States on the Annexation of Mexico. N.p., 1892.

Purcell, Susan Kaufman, ed. *Mexico–United States Relations*. New York: Academy of Political Science, 1981.

Quirk, Robert E. *An Affair of Honor: Woodrow Wilson and the Occupation of Veracruz*. Louisville: University of Kentucky Press, 1962.

———. *The Mexican Revolution, 1914–1915: The Convention of Aguascalientes*. New York: Citadel Press, 1963.

Raat, W. Dirk. *Ambivalent Vistas: Mexico and the United States*. Athens: University of Georgia Press, 1992.

Rankin, Melinda. *Twenty Years among the Mexicans*. Cincinnati: Chase and Hall, 1875.

Reed, S. G. *A History of the Land Grants and Other Aids to the Texas Railroads by the State of Texas*. Kingsport, Tenn.: Kingsport Press, 1942.

————. *A History of the Texas Railroads.* Houston: St. Clair Publishing Company, 1941.

Reina, Leticia. *Las rebeliones campesinas en México (1819–1906).* Mexico City: Siglo XXI, 1980.

Reyes Heroles, Jesús. *El liberalismo Mexicano.* 3 vols. Mexico City: Fondo de Cultura Economica, 1974.

Reyes Retana, Sergio, et al. *Historia del azucar en México.* 2 vols. Mexico City: Fondo de Cultura Economica, 1988.

Richardson, Rupert. *Colonel Edward M. House: The Texas Years.* Abilene: Hardin Simmons University Press, 1964.

Richmond, Douglas. *La frontera: Mexico–Estados Unidos durante la epoca revolucionaria, 1910–1920.* Saltillo: Consejo Editorial del Estado, 1996.

————. *Venustiano Carranza's Nationalist Struggle, 1893–1920.* Lincoln: University of Nebraska Press, 1983.

Ridley, Jasper. *Maximilian and Juárez.* New York: Ticknor and Fields, 1992.

Rippy, J. Fred. *The United States and Mexico.* New York: F. S. Crofts and Company, 1931.

Robbins, William G. *Colony and Empire: The Capitalist Transformation of the American West.* Lawrence: University of Kansas Press, 1994.

Roett, Riordan, ed. *The Challenge of Institutional Reform in Mexico.* Boulder: Lynne Rienner, 1995.

————. *Mexico y Estados Unidos: el manejo de la relación.* Mexico City: Siglo XI Editores, 1989.

Rojas Coria, Rosendo. *Tratado de cooperativismo.* Mexico City: Fondo de Cultura Economica, 1952.

Romero, Matías. *Correspondencia de la legación mexicana durante la intervención extranjera, 1860–1868.* Mexico City: n.p., n.d.

————. *Mexico and the United States: A Study of Subjects Affecting Their Political, Commercial, and Social Relations, with a View to Their Promotion.* New York: G. P. Putnam, 1898.

Romney, Thomas Cottam. *The Mormon Colonies in Mexico.* Salt Lake City: The Deseret Book Company, 1938.

Romney, Thomas Cottam, Richard Neering, and Arturo Gandara. *Mexico's Petroleum and U.S. Policy Implications for the 1980's.* Santa Monica: Rand Corporation, 1980.

Rosenberg, Emily. *Spreading the American Dream: American Economic and Cultural Expansion, 1890–1945.* New York: Hill and Wang, 1982.

Rosenzweig, Fernando, et al. *El Porfiriato: La vida economica.* Vol. 6 of *Historia moderna de México,* ed. Daniel Cosio Villegas. Mexico City: Editorial Hermes, 1965.

Rouaiz, Pastor. *Geografia del Estado de Durango.* Tacubaya: Taller Grafica de la Secretaria de Agricultura y Fomento, 1929.

Ruck, Rob. *The Tropic of Baseball: Baseball in the Dominican Republic.* London: Meckler, 1990.

Ruiz, Ramon Eduardo. *On the Rim of Mexico: Encounters of the Rich and Poor.* Boulder: Westview, 1998.

———. *The People of Sonora and the Yankee Capitalists.* Tucson: University of Arizona Press, 1988.

Saenz, Aaron. *La politica internacional de la Revolución: Estudios y documentos.* Mexico City: Fondo de Cultura Economica, 1961.

Said, Edward. *Culture and Imperialism.* New York: Vintage, 1994.

Salas, Miguel Tinker. *In the Shadow of Eagles: Sonora and the Transformation of the Border during the Porfiriato.* Berkeley: University of California Press, 1997.

Schmitt, Karl M. *Mexico and the United States 1821–1973: Conflict and Co-existence.* New York: John Wiley and Sons, 1974.

Schoonover, Thomas D. *Dollars over Dominion: The Triumph of Liberalism in Mexican–United States Relations, 1861–1867.* Baton Rouge: Louisiana State University Press, 1978.

———. *The Mexican Lobby: Matías Romero in Washington.* Lexington: University Press of Kentucky, 1986.

Sepulveda, Cesar. *Las relaciones diplomaticas entre México y los Estados Unidos en el siglo XX.* Monterrey: n.p., 1953.

Sepulveda Amor, Bernardo, and Antonio Chumacero. *La inversion extranjera en México.* Mexico City: Fondo de Cultura Economica, 1973.

Sepulveda Amor, Bernardo, Olga Pellicer de Brody, and Lorenzo Meyer, *Las empresas transnacionales en México.* Mexico City: El Colegio de México, 1974.

Shaiken, Harley. *Mexico in the Global Economy: High Technology and Work Organization in Export Industries.* La Jolla: Center for U.S.–Mexican Studies, University of California, San Diego, 1990.

Shepherd, Grant. *Magnate de plata (Batopilas).* Chihuahua: Centro Librero La Prensa, 1994. The translation is *The Silver Magnate: Fifty Years in a Mexican Silver Mine.* New York: E. P. Dutton & Co., 1938.

Sheridan, William H. *Personal Memoirs.* 2 vols. New York: Charles Webster and Company, 1888.

Sinclair, Andrew. *Corsair: The Life of J. Pierpont Morgan.* New York: Little, Brown, 1981.

Sinkin, Richard. *The Mexican Reform, 1855–1876: A Study in Liberal Nation-Building.* Austin: University of Texas Press, 1979.

Slotkin, Richard. *Regeneration through Violence: The Mythology of the American Frontier, 1600–1860.* Middletown: Wesleyan University Press, 1973.

Smith, Arthur D. Howden. *Mr. House of Texas.* New York and London: Funk and Wagnalls, 1940.

Smith, Arthur K., Jr., *Mexico and the Cuban Revolution: Foreign Policy Making in Mexico under President Adolfo López Mateos (1958–1964).* Ithaca: Cornell University Press, 1970.

Smith, Clint E. *The Disappearing Border: Mexico–United States Relations to the 1990s.* Stanford: Stanford Alumni Association, 1992.

Smith, Peter H. *Talons of the Eagle: Dynamics of U.S.–Latin American Relations.* New York: Oxford University Press, 1996.

Smith, Robert Freeman. *The United States and Revolutionary Nationalism in Mexico, 1916–1932.* Chicago: University of Chicago Press, 1972.

Speare, Charles F. *The Merged Roads of Mexico: A New Idea in State Control of Railroads.* New York: Mail and Express Company, 1909.

Stevens, John Austin. *The Valley of the Rio Grande, Its Topography and Resources.* New York: William C. Bryant, 1864.

Stillman, Chauncey Devereux. *Charles Stillman 1810–1875.* New York: Chauncey Devereux Stillman, 1956.

Sturm, Herman. *The Republic of Mexico and Its American Creditors. The Unfulfilled obligations of the Mexican Republic to citizens of the United States, from whom it obtained material aid, on credit—the nature and extent of that aid.* Indianapolis: Douglas and Conner, 1869.

Teitelbaum, Louis M. *Woodrow Wilson and the Mexican Revolution.* New York: Exposition Press, 1967.

Tello, Carlos, and Clark Reynolds, eds. *Las relaciones México–Estados Unidos.* Mexico City: Fondo de Cultura Economica, 1981.

Tello, Manuel. *México: Una posición internacional.* Mexico City: Editorial de J. Moritz, 1972.

Throup, Cathryn L., ed. *The United States and Mexico: Face to Face with New Technology.* New Brunswick: Transaction Books, 1987.

Tinker Salas, Miguel. *In the Shadow of the Eagles: Sonora and the Transformation of the Border during the Porfiriato.* Berkeley: University of California Press, 1997.

Tomasek, Robert Dennis. *Colorado River Salinity and New River Sanitation: Environmental Issues in U.S.–Mexican relations.* Hanover, N.H.: Universities Field Staff International, 1982.

———. *United States–Mexican Relations: The Blowout of the Mexican Oil Well Ixtoc I.* Hanover: Wheelock House, 1981.

Tomkins, Frank. *Chasing Villa: The Story behind the Story of Pershing's Expedition into Mexico.* Harrisburg: The Military Service Publishing Company, 1934.

Trujillo Herrera, Rafael. *Adolfo de la Huerta y los tratados de Bucareli: Con un capitulo adicional acerca el presidente de los E.E.U.U. Warren Gamaliel Harding.* Mexico City: M. Porrua, 1966.

Tullis, F. LaMond. *Mormons in Mexico: The Dynamics of Faith and Culture.* Ogden: Utah State University Press, 1987.

Turlington, Edgar. *Mexico and Her Foreign Creditors.* New York: Columbia University Press, 1930.

Turner, John Kenneth. *Barbarous Mexico.* Austin: University of Texas Press, 1969.

Ulloa, Berta. *La revolución intervenida: Relaciones diplomaticas entre México y Estados Unidos (1910–1914).* Mexico City: El Colegio de México, 1976.

Utton, Albert E., ed. *Pollution and International Boundaries: United States–Mexican Environmental Problems.* Albuquerque: University of New Mexico Press, 1973.

Vanderwood, Paul. *The Power of God against the Guns of Government: Religious Upheaval in Mexico at the Turn of the Nineteenth Century.* Stanford: Stanford University Press, 1998.

Walling, William English. *The Mexican Question: Mexico and Mexican–American Relations under Calles and Obregón.* New York: Robins Press, 1927.

Wasserman, Mark. *Capitalists, Caciques, and Revolution: The Native Elites and Foreign Enterprise in Chihuahua, Mexico, 1854–1911.* Chapel Hill: University of North Carolina Press, 1984.

Watkins, Lew. *Landman: Under Old Spanish Law.* Nashville: Parthenon Press, 1962.

Webster, Arthur. *Woodrow Wilson y México: Un caso de intervención.* Mexico City: Ediciones de Andrea, 1964.

Wells, Alan. *Yucatán's Gilded Age: Haciendas, Henequen, and International Harvester, 1860–1915.* Albuquerque: University of New Mexico Press, 1985.

Wheeler, George. *Pierpont Morgan and Friends.* Englewood Cliffs, Prentice-Hall, 1973.

White, Benton R. *The Forgotten Cattle King.* College Station: Texas A&M University Press, 1986.

Wilkie, James. *The Mexican Revolution: Federal Expenditure and Social Change since 1910.* Berkeley: The University of California Press, 1967.

Williams, William Appleman. *The Tragedy of American Diplomacy.* New York: Dell, 1962.

Wilson, Henry Land. *Diplomatic Episodes in Mexico, Belgium, and Chile.* Garden City: Doubleday, Page and Company, 1927.

Winegardner, Mark. *The Veracruz Blues.* New York: Viking, 1996.

Winkler, John Kennedy. *The First Billion: The Stillmans and the National City Bank.* New York: Vanguard Press, 1934.

Womack, John, Jr. *Zapata and the Mexican Revolution.* Vintage: New York, 1968.

Zorrilla, Luis G. *Casos de México en el arbitraje internacional.* Mexico City: n.p., 1947.

———. *Historia de las relaciones entre México y los Estados Unidos de America, 1800–1958.* Mexico City: Editorial Porrua, 1965.

Articles and Chapters

Alger, William E. "Mazatlan." *Daily Consular and Trade Reports,* no. 265, 11 November 1911, 746–748.

Anderson, Martin Edwin. "Civil-Military Relations and Internal Security in Mexico: The Undone Reform." In *The Challenge of Institutional Reform in Mexico.* Ed. Riordan Roett. Boulder: Lynne Rienner, 1995.

Anderson, Sara, and John Cavanaugh. "NAFTA's Unhappy Anniversary." *The New York Times,* 7 February 1995.

Anderson, Sara, John Cavanagh, and David Ranney. "NAFTA: Trinational Fiasco." *The Nation,* 15–22 July 1996.

Andrews, Edmund L. "Minister of Objection Nettles Washington." *The New York Times,* 21 May 1997.

Atlas, Riva D., and Tim Weiner. "Citigroup to Buy Mexican Bank in a Deal Valued at $12.5 Billion." *The New York Times,* 18 May 2001.

Beachy, Debra. "Mexico Selling Rail Line." *Houston Chronicle,* 10 August 1996.

Bennet, James. "Mexican Shock for U.S. Concerns." *The New York Times,* 23 December 1994.

Berbusse, Edward J., S.J., "General Rosecrans' Forthright Diplomacy with Juarez's Mexico, 1868–1869." *The Americas* 36, no. 4 (1980): 499–514.

Blaisdell, Lowell L. "Henry Lane Wilson and the Overthrow of Madero." *Southwestern Social Science Quarterly* 45 (1962): 136–155.

Bloch, Avital H., and Servando Ortoll, " '¡Viva Mexico! ¡Mueran los yanquis!': The Guadalajara Riots of 1910." In *Riots in the Cities, Popular Politics and the Urban Poor in Latin America, 1765–1910.* Ed. Silvia M. Arrom and Servando Ortoll. Wilmington: Scholarly Resources, 1996.

Bonney, William L. "Commerce of Central Mexico." *Daily Consular and Trade Reports,* no. 265 (1911): 737–752.

———. "Decree Prohibiting Exportation of Food Products from the State." *Daily Consular and Trade Reports,* no. 238 (1914): 181–182.

———. "New Labor Decree in Mexico." *Daily Consular and Trade Reports,* no. 238 (1914): 171–180.

Bradsher, Keith. "Obscure Global Bank Moves into the Glare." *The New York Times,* 1 September 1995.

Branch, H. N. "The Mexican Constitution of 1917 Compared with the Constitution of 1857." Supplement of the *Annals of the American Academy of Political and Social Science.* Philadelphia: American Academy of Political and Social Sciences, 1917.

Bretherton, Harold G. "Aguascalientes." *Daily Consular and Trade Reports,* no. 265 (1911): 750–751.

Broyles, William, Jr. "The Last Empire." *Texas Monthly,* October 1980, 150–173 and 234–278.

Bustamante, Rios. "As Guilty as Hell!: Mexican Copper Miners and Community in Arizona, 1920–1950." In *Border Crossings: Mexican and Mexican American Workers.* Ed. John Mason Hart. Wilmington: Scholarly Resources, 1998.

Canada, William W. "Commerce of Southern Mexico." *Daily Consular and Trade Reports,* no. 250 (1911): 417–437.

Case, Brendan M. "Casting Big Nets for Latin American Channel Surfers." *The New York Times,* 5 August 1996.

Chimerine, Lawrence. "Mexico Bailout Needed U.S. Strings Attached." *The New York Times,* 1 September 1995.

Coatsworth, John H. "Railroads and the Concentration of Land Ownership in the Early Porfiriato." *Hispanic American Historical Review* 54 (1974): 48–71 and 382–386.

Cockburn, Alexander. "Al Gore, Green Groups and Narco-Traffickers." *The Nation*, 12 August 1996.

Cornelius, Wayne A. "Designing Social Policy for Mexico's Liberalized Economy: From Social Services and Infrastructure to Job Creation." In *The Challenge of Institutional Reform in Mexico*. Ed. Riordan Roett (Boulder: Lynne Rienner, 1995).

Cosio Villegas, Daniel. "La aventura de Don Matias." *Historia Mexicana* 8 (1958): 35–59.

———. "Border Troubles in Mexico—U.S. Relations." *Southwestern Historical Quarterly* 72, no. 1 (1965): 34–39.

Cossio Silva, Luis. "La agricultura." In *El Porfiriato: La vida economica*. Vols. 7–8 of *Historia moderna de México*, ed. Daniel Cosio Villegas. Mexico City: Editorial Hermes, 1965.

Cruz Miramontes, Rodolfo. "La doctrina Harmon, el tratado de agua de 1944 y algunos problemas derivados de su aplicación (aguas del Río Bravo)." *Foro Internacional* 7, no. 1 (1966): 49–120.

Cunningham, Edwin S. "Production of Indian Corn in South Africa." Daily Consular and Trade Reports, no. 116 (1911): 643.

De la Garma, Felipe. "Resumen de los egresos efectuados por el gobierno federal desde el ano de 1876 hasta 1936." *Revista de Hacienda*, no.3 (1937): 3–19.

DePalma, Anthony. "After the Fall: Two Faces of Mexico's Economy." *The New York Times*, 16 July 1995.

———. "An American REIT Will Invest in Mexico." *The New York Times*, 7 April 1995.

———. "Avantel of Mexico Entering Long Distance." *The New York Times*, 12 August 1996.

———. "Casualty of the Peso: Investor Confidence." *The New York Times*, 27 December 1994.

———. "Dollar Duress." *The New York Times*, 22 February 1995.

———."Economics Lesson in a Border Town: Why That Asian TV Has a 'Made in Mexico' Label." *New York Times*, 23 May 1996.

———. "Hicks, Muse and Travelers in Mexico Deal." *The New York Times*, 9 August 1996.

———. "MCI Wins Mexican Long-Distance License." *The New York Times*, 7 September 1995.

———. "Mexican Attitudes Shift in Flood of U.S. Goods." *New York Times*, 22 November 1994.

———. "Mexican Banking's New Scorecard." *The New York Times*, 19 December 1994.

———. "Mexican Telephone Shares Drop Sharply." *The New York Times*, 11 November 1994.

———. "Mexico's Banks: A Weak Link in the Rescue Plan." *The New York Times*, 9 February 1995.

————. "Mexico's Garage Sale." *The New York Times,* 2 June 1995.

————. "Mexico's Leader, Breaking Silence, Outlines a Rescue." *The New York Times,* 30 December 1994.

————. "Mexico to Get 2nd Half of Its I.M.F. Aid Package." 1 July 1995, *The New York Times.*

————. "Mexico Tries to Restrict Some Foreign Investments." *The New York Times,* 5 April 1996.

————. "New Ethics in Mexico." *The New York Times,* 10 September 1994.

————. "Some Mexican Bonds Go Unsold." *The New York Times,* 25 January 1995.

————. "Telmex Gains in Attempt to Buy Cable-System Stake." *The New York Times,* 22 June 1995.

————. "U.S. Aid Plan Is Hardly a Cure All." *The New York Times,* 23 February 1995.

————. "U.S. and Mexico Reach Accord over Satellite TV Transmission." *The New York Times,* 9 November 1996.

————. "The White House Moves to Increase U.S. Aid for Mexico." *The New York Times,* 12 January 1995.

DePalma, Anthony, with Peter Truell. "A Mexican Mover and Shaker and How His Millions Moved." *The New York Times,* 5 June 1996.

Didion, Joan. "California." *New York Review of Books,* 21 October 1993.

Diesenouse, Susan. "Financial Advisors to the Rich Set a Conservative Course for '95." *The New York Times,* 31 December 1994.

Dillon, Sam. "Abuses Reported in Mexico at American-Owned Plant." *The New York Times,* 5 August 1998.

————. "Foreign Business to Put $6.3 Billion in Mexico." *The New York Times,* 5 December 1996.

————. "Mexican Traffickers Recruiting Killers in the U.S." *The New York Times,* 4 December 1997.

————. "Mexico Detains U.S. Brothers, Linking Them to Gunrunning." *The New York Times,* 14 January 1998.

————. "Mexico Drops Its Effort to Sell Some Oil Plants." *The New York Times,* 14 October 1996.

————. "Mexico's Lifeblood on the Auction Block." *The New York Times,* 4 November 1995.

————. "A Twenty-Year G.M. Parts Migration to Mexico." *The New York Times,* 25 June 1998.

————. "U.S. Drug Agents Want Mexico to Ease 'Rules of the Game.'" *New York Times,* 16 March 1997.

————. "With Drugs and Gangs Rife, Mexican Governor Resigns." *The New York Times,* 13 May 1998.

Dolan, Kerry A., Stephen S. Johnson, and Joel Millman. "The Billionaires; The Americas." *Forbes,* 17 July 1995.

d'Olwer, Nicolau. "Las inversiones extranjeras." In *El Porfiriato: La vida* económica. Vol. 2 of *Historia moderna de México*, ed. Daniel Cosio Villegas. Mexico City: Editorial Hermes, 1965.

Durgin, Hillary. "U.S. Natural Gas Firms Eye Mexico." *Houston Chronicle*, 30 May 1995.

Eaton, William J. "Forgotten War: Yanks in Russia." *Los Angeles Times*, 10 March 1987.

Edwards, Thomas. "Ciudad Juarez." *Daily Consular and Trade Reports*, no. 256 (1911): 559–560.

Ellsworth, Luther T. "Ciudad Porfirio Díaz." *Daily Consular and Trade Reports*, no. 256 (1911): 550–553 and no. 15 (1913): 309–310.

Feldstein, Mark. "Death on the Border." Impact, Cable News Network, 18 May 1997.

Figueroa, Hector. "In the Name of Fashion: Exploitation in the Garment Industry." *NACLA Reports*, January-February 1996.

Flaherty, Francis. "Foraging for Stocks with Life in Mexico." *The New York Times*, 24 December 1994.

Frank, Bertrand. "Apparel Workers Lose in World Trade Pact." *New York Times*, 24 November 1994.

Freeman, Charles. "Mexican Cotton Crop." *Daily Consular and Trade Reports*, no. 109 (1910): 528.

Friedland, Jonathan. "Citibank Buys Confia of Mexico." *The Wall Street Journal*, 12 May 1998.

Friedman, Thomas L. "The Coffin's Free." *The New York Times*, 13 December 1995.

———. "The Critics Were Wrong." *The New York Times*, 25 September 1996.

———. "Parent of Mexico's Banamex Improves Operating Results Despite Loan Woes." *The Wall Street Journal*, 26 January 1996.

Garret, Alonzo B. "Heavy American Exports to Mexico. " *Daily Consular and Trade Reports*, no. 107 (1910): 504.

———. "Nuevo Laredo." *Daily Consular and Trade Reports*, no. 256 (1911): 547–548 and no. 15 (1913): 310–311.

Gereffi, Gary, and Lynn Hempel. "Latin America in the Global Economy." *NACLA Reports*, January-February 1996.

Gerth, Jeff, and Elaine Sciolino. "I.M.F. Head: He Speaks, and Money Talks." *The New York Times*, 2 April 1996 and 30 January 1995.

Gilpin, Kenneth N. "Investors Weigh a Market's Safety." *The New York Times*, 23 December 1994.

Godoy Dardano, Felix E. "Transferencia de nuevas tecnologias: La electrificación del alumbrado en las principales ciudades de México (1880–1910)." *Siglo XIX* 5, no. 15 (1996): 39–51.

Golden, Tim. "The Citibank Connection: Real Money, Shadow Banks." *The New York Times*, 27 February 2001.

———. "To Help Keep Mexico Stable, U.S. Soft-Pedaled Drug War." *The New York Times*, July 1995.

————. "U.S. Report Says Salinas's Banker Ignored Safeguards." *The New York Times*, 4 December 1998.

Gracida, Juan José. "La decada de los 70 y la transición al capitalismo en Sonora." *Siglo XIX* 4, no. 11 (1995): 45–59.

Grieb, Kenneth. "Standard Oil and the Financing of the Mexican Revolution." *California Historical Quarterly* 49 (1971): 59–71.

Grindle, Merilee S. "Reforming Land Tenure in Mexico: Peasants, the Market, and the State." In *The Challenge of Institutional Reform in Mexico*. Ed. Riordan Roett. Boulder: Lynne Rienner, 1995.

Hart, John M. "Agrarian Precursors of the Mexican Revolution: The Development of an Ideology." *The Americas* 29 (1972): 131–150.

Henderson, Peter N. V. "Woodrow Wilson, Victoriano Huerta, and the Recognition Issue in Mexico." *The Americas* 41 (1984): 151–176.

Henwood, Doug. "The Free Flow of Money." *NACLA Reports*, January-February, 1996.

————. "Investing Abroad." *The New York Times*, 28 August 1995.

Holson, Laura M. "Shuttle Diplomacy Leads to New Corporate Marriage." *The New York Times*, 12 May 1998.

Ibrahim, Youssef M. "Genetic Soybeans Alarm Europe." *The New York Times*, 7 November 1996.

Kearney, Milo, and John Kearney. "A Historical Sketch of the Baptist Church in Brownsville and Matamoros." In *Studies in Brownsville and Matamoros History*. Ed. Milo Kearney, Anthony Knopp, and Antonio Zavaleta. Brownsville: University of Texas at Brownsville, 1995.

Kennan, George F. "Policy Planning Study 23, Department of State, February 24, 1948." In *Foreign Relations of the United States*. Washington, D.C.: Department of State, 1948.

Klein, Alan M. "Baseball Wars: The Mexican Baseball League and Nationalism in 1946." *Studies in Latin American Popular Culture* 13 (1994): 33–56.

Lauff, Marcelo Abramo. "Las luchas de los trabajadores ferrovarios: 1870–1908." In *Las luchas populares en México en el siglo XIX*. Ed. Leticia Reina. Mexico City: Casa Chata, 1983.

Lewis, Paul. "Bailout Plan for Mexico Wins Praise." *The New York Times*, 29 December 1994.

————. "Jean Gerard, 58, Reagan Envoy Who Led U.S. to Leave UNESCO." *The New York Times*, 6 August 1996.

————. "Peso Bounces Back, and Mexican Stocks Are Sent Soaring." *The New York Times*, 1 February 1995.

Lyons, Patrick J. "Mexico's Ripple Effects: Subtle Risks for Americans." *The New York Times*, 1 February 1995.

Mack, Toni, with Jose Aguayo. "The Education of Jesús Reyes." *Forbes*, 24 March 1997.

Marichal, Carlos. "The Vicious Cycles of Mexican Debt." *NACLA Reports*, November-December, 1997.

Marin, Carlos. "Plan del Ejercito en Chiapas, desde 1994." *Proceso,* no. 1105.

Meredith, Robyn. "The Brave New World of General Motors." *The New York Times,* 26 October 1997.

Miller, Clarence A. "Commerce of Northern Mexico." *Daily Consular and Trade Reports,* no. 15 (1913): 305–324.

———. "Import Trade of Tampico." *Daily Consular and Trade Reports,* no. 299 (1911): 1484.

———. "Mexican Importations of Grain." *Daily Consular and Trade Reports,* no. 98 (1910): 359.

Miller, Luther S. "Mexico's Hot: Come on Down." *Railway Age 6,* no. 4 (1999), at www.railwayage.com/jun99/inside.html.

Miller, Robert Ryan. "Matías Romero: Mexican Minister to the United States during the Juárez-Maximilian Era." *Hispanic American Historical Review* 45, no. 2 (1965): 228–245.

Millman, Joel. "High Tech Jobs Transfer to Mexico with Surprising Speed." *The Wall Street Journal,* 9 April 1998.

———. "Mexico's TMM Plans to Buy Shipper, but Spending Binge Rattles Investors." *The Wall Street Journal,* 17 January 1997.

Moffett, Matt, Craig Torres, and Dianne Solis. "Show of Force." *The Wall Street Journal,* 3 September 1996.

Mumme, Stephen P. "The North American Commission for Environmental Cooperation and the United States–Mexico Border Region: The Case of Air and Water." In *Transboundary Resources Report.* Albuquerque: International Transboundary Resources Center, 1995.

Myerson, Alan R. "Big Labor's Strategic Raid in Mexico." *The New York Times,* 12 September 1994.

———. "Borderline Working Class." *The New York Times,* 8 May 1997.

———. "Out of a Crisis, an Opportunity." *The New York Times,* 26 September 1995.

———. "Peso's Plunge May Cost Thousands of U.S. Jobs." *The New York Times,* 30 January 1995.

———. "Reich Supports Mex on Union Organizing." *The New York Times,* 13 October 1994.

———. "Strategies on Mexico Cast Aside." *The New York Times,* 14 February 1995.

———. "Tejano Star Sets Out to Bridge Music and Nations." *The New York Times,* 1 January 1996.

———. "U.S. Companies Competing to Be First in Gas to Mexico." *The New York Times,* 7 December 1995.

Niebur, Gustav. "A Ceremony in Mexico City Shows Growth in Mormonism." *The New York Times,* 11 December 1994.

O'Brien, Timothy L. "Prince of the Citi." *The New York Times,* 7 May 1998.

Oppenheimer, Andres, and Christopher Marquis. "FBI Helping Mexico Screen Agents." *Miami Herald,* 7 May 1997.

Passell, Peter. "A Mexican Payoff." *The New York Times,* 12 October 1995.

Pletcher, David. "The Fall of Silver in Mexico, 1876–1910, and Its Effect on American Investments." *Journal of Economic History* 18 (1958): 33–55.

———. "México, campo de inversiones norteamericanoas 1867–1880." *Historia Mexicana* 2, no. 4 (1953): 564–574.

———. "Mexico Opens the Door to American Capital, 1877–1880." *The Americas* 16 (1959): 1–14.

Porter, Katherine Ann. "La Conquistadora." In *The Collected Essays and Occasional Writings of Katherine Ann Porter*. New York: Delacorte Press, 1970.

Preston, Julia. "For Citibank, a Problem Plum." *The New York Times*, 21 November 1997.

———. "Mexican Fights Swiss for Honor and Millions." *The New York Times*, 30 December 1997.

———. "Mexican Peso Fall Leads to Auto-Sales Standstill." *The New York Times*, 10 August 1995.

———. "Mexicans Belittle Drug-Money Sting." *The New York Times*, 20 May 1998.

———. "Mexico Says It Plans More Privatizations." *The New York Times*, 7 December 1996.

———. "New Era of Phone Competition in Mexico." *The New York Times*, 13 August 1996.

———. "Scandal Spurs Bell Atlantic Shift in Mexico." *The New York Times*, 27 November 1996.

———. "Swiss to Seize Salinas Funds, Tying Money to Drug Trade." *The New York Times*, 4 April 1997.

———. "A Telecom Revolución in Mexico." *The New York Times*, 14 November 1996.

Purdum, Todd S. "Clinton Pushes Hard on Plan for Mexican Aid." *The New York Times*, 31 January 1995.

Ramirez Cabanas C., Joaquin. "Los ingresos federales de México durante los anos de 1876 a 1930." *Revista de Hacienda*, no. 2 (1938): 7–25.

Ravelo, Ricardo. "Laguna Verde es un gran negocio para algunos y no les importa el peligro; puede haber una catástrofe." *Proceso*, 21 July 1996.

Reding, Andrew. "Narco-Politics in Mexico." *The Nation*, 10 July 1995.

Reynolds, Christopher. "Lack of Data Makes It Hard to Assess Threat of Crime." *The News*, 21 November 1998.

Rohter, Larry. "Growing Latin Market Creates New Battleground of Cable TV." *The New York Times*, 12 May 1997.

Rosenzweig, Fernando. "El desarrollo economico de México de 1877 a 1911." *Trimestre Economico* 32 (1965): 405.

———. "Las exportaciones mexicanas de 1877 a 1911." *Historia Mexicana* 9, no. 3 (1960): 394–413.

———. "Las exportaciones mexicanas de 1877 a 1911." *Trimestre Economico* 37 (1960): 537.

Ross, John. "Boise in Guerrero." *Sierra*, November-December 1996.

———. "Treasure of the Costa Grande." *Sierra*, July-August 1996.

Salgado, Alicia. "Suma 157 mil 548 mdd la deuda externa total." *El Financiero*, 14 May 1997.

Salpukas, Agis. "Two Utilities in California Merge to Fight Competition." *The New York Times*, 15 October 1996.

Samstad, James G., and Ruth Berins Collier. "Mexican Labor and Structural Reform." In *The Challenge of Institutional Reform in Mexico*. Ed. Riordan Roett. Boulder: Lynne Rienner, 1995.

Sanger, David E. "Accord's Dark Side." *The New York Times*, 4 January 1995.

———. "Clinton Offers $20 Billion to Mexico for Peso Rescue; Action Sidesteps Congress." *The New York Times*, 1 February 1995.

———. "G.A.O. Study Cites Benefit of Mexican Bailout." *The New York Times*, 24 February 1996.

———. "Mexico Says It Will Repay $7 Billion to the U.S." *The New York Times*, 26 July 1996.

———. "An Old Wall Street Pro's Voice in the Campaign." *The New York Times*, 22 September 1996.

Sgambati, Albert. "New Jersey–Aztec Phenomenon." *The News*, 9 July 1997.

Shanklin, Arnold. "Commercial Conditions in Mexico." *Daily Consular and Trade Reports*, no. 252 (1911): 469–473.

Silverstein, Ken, and Alexander Cockburn. "Who Broke Mexico?: The Killers and the Killing." *The Nation*, 6 March 1996.

Smith, A. Donaldson. "Short Corn Crop in Central Mexico, Aguascalientes." *Daily Consular and Trade Reports*, no. 121 (1910).

Summa, John. "Markets and Manipulation." *Global Media*, December 1994.

Taylor, Lawrence D. "The Great Adventure: Mercenaries in the Mexican Revolution, 1910–1915." *The Americas* 43 (1986): 25–45.

Tedford, Deborah. "Cousin Tells Jurors of Murders Ordered by a Reputed Drug Lord." *Houston Chronicle*, 4 October 1996.

Todd, Walker F. "Dollar Drain." *The Nation*, 10 July 1995.

Torres, Craig. "Bell Atlantic Bucks Mexico's Gatekeepers." *The Wall Street Journal*, 17 November 1997.

———. "Sudden Targets: Foreigners Snap Up Mexican Companies; Impact Is Enormous." *The Wall Street Journal*, 30 September 1997.

Torres, Craig, and Laurie Hays. "Alleged Launderer Moved Millions Despite Scrutiny by U.S., Mexico." *The Wall Street Journal*, 1 April 1997.

Truell, Peter. "Big Investor Relations Task: Selling Mexico to Wall St." *The New York Times*, 15 March 1995.

———. "Citibank's Records Examined as Part of Mexican Inquiry." *The New York Times*, 30 March 1996.

———. "In Case Tied to Mexico, a Citibank Witness Is Called a Liar." *The New York Times*, 4 December 1996.

Tutino, John. "Agrarian Social Change and Peasant Rebellion in Nineteenth-Century Mexico: The Case of Chalco." In *Riot, Rebellion, and Revolution: Rural Social Conflict in Mexico*. Ed. Friedrich Katz. Princeton: Princeton University Press, 1988.

Uchutelle, Louis. "Pemex's Barrier to Its Grand Plans." *The New York Times*, 4 March 1993.

———. "U.S. Losses in Mexico Assessed." *The New York Times*, 26 December 1994.

Van Natta, Don, Jr. "U.S. Indicts Twenty-six Mexican Bankers in Laundering of Drug Funds." *The New York Times*, 19 May 1998.

Velazquez, Marco Antonio, et al. "Guayule; reencuentro en el desierto." In *La realización de la Conferencia Internacional sobre Guayule*. N.p.: Gobierno de Coahuila, n.d.

Wasserman, Mark. "Chihuahua: Family Power, Foreign Enterprise, and National Control." In *Other Mexicos: Essays on Regional Mexican History, 1876–1911*. Eds. Thomas Benjamin and William McNellie. Albuquerque: University of New Mexico Press, 1984.

———. "Oligarquia e intereses extranjeros en Chihuahua durante el Porfiriato." *Historia Mexicana* 22, no. 3 (1973).

Wood, Darrin. "Campus Mexico." *Chiapas95*, 20 March 1998.

———. "Clinton's Interference in Mexico." *Nuevo Amanecer Press*, 28 December 1997.

———. "Los GAFE: ¿Anti-narcos o anti-Marcos?" *Nuevo Amanecer Press*, 6 January 1998.

Unpublished Works

Caulfield, Norman. "Mexican Labor and the State in the Twentieth Century: Conflict and Accommodation." Ph.D. diss., University of Houston, 1990.

Corbett, Barbara. "The Political Economy of the Alcabala: Taxation and Dependency in Mexico's Restored Republic, 1867–72." Unpublished ms., Princeton University, 1987.

Cott, Kenneth. "Porfirian Investment Policies 1876–1910." Ph.D. diss., University of New Mexico, 1979.

Dussaud, Claude Philippe. "Agrarian Politics, Violence, and the Struggle for Social Control in Puebla from 1918 to 1927; The Case of Rosalie Evans." M.A. thesis, University of Virginia, 1990.

Ford, John Salmon. "Memoirs." BTHC.

Gomez Quinones, Juan. "Social Change and Intellectual Discontent: The Growth of Mexican Nationalism, 1890–1911." Ph.D diss., University of California, Los Angeles, 1972.

Gonzalez Quiroga, Miguel A., "La Puerta de México: Los Comerciantes Texanos y el Noreste Mexicano, 1850–1880." N.d., n.p. HC.

Graf, L. E. "The Economic History of the Rio Grande Valley 1820–1875." Ph.D. diss., Harvard University, 1942.

Hanson, Randall S. "A Day of Ideals: Catholic Social Action in the Age of the Mexican Revolution, 1867–1929." Ph.D. diss., Indiana University, 1994.

Hart, Lisa June. "Shepherd's Castle: Documentation of a Gothic Revival House in a Mexican Silver Mining Town." M.A. thesis, University of Texas, Austin, 1988.

Hart, Paul Brian. "Peasants into Workers: The Social Transformation of More-los, 1865–1910." Ph.D. diss., University of California, San Diego, 1997.

Kuecker, Glenn. "A Desert in a Tropical Wilderness: The Porfirian Project in Northwestern Veracruz." Ph.D. diss., Rutgers University, 1998.

Luan-Miller, Patricia Dolores. "U.S. Direct Investment in Mexico, 1876–1978: An Historical, Theoretical and Empirical Analysis." Ph.D. diss., University of Texas at Austin, 1980.

Nafari, Akbar. "U.S. Multinational Corporations in Mexican Manufacturing: A Study of Development and Balance-of-Payments Impacts." Ph.D. diss., Indiana University, 1978.

O'Horo, Thomas Kevin. "American Foreign Investments and Foreign Policy: The Railroad Experience, 1865–1898." Ph.D. diss., Rutgers University, 1976.

Resendez Arreola, Salvador. "Inversiones norteamericanas en México y sus consecuencias economicas." Thesis, Universidad Nacional Autónoma de México, 1953.

Saka, Mark Saad. "Peasant Nationalism and Social Unrest in Mexican Huasteca, 1848–1884." Ph.D. diss., University of Houston, 1995.

Santoro, Carmela Elvira. "United States and Mexican Relations during World War II." Ph.D. diss., Syracuse University, 1967.

Schell, William, Jr. "Integral Outsiders, Mexico City's American Colony (1876–1911): Society and Political Economy in Porfirian Mexico." Ph.D. diss., University of North Carolina, Durham, 1992.

Smith, Elizabeth. "Against the Grain: Nettie Lee Benson and Higher Education." Unpublished ms, University of Houston, 1995.

Tunon Pablos, Julia. "Mujeres de luz y sombra en el cine mexicano: La contrucción masculina de una imagen (1939–1952)." Doctoral thesis, Universidad Nacional Autónoma de México, 1992.

Villareal, Mario Treviño. San Carlos de Vallecillo, real de minas, 1766–1821. Monterrey: Archivo General del Estado de Nuevo Leon, 1987.

Walker, David. " 'Una Gran Familia': The Social Topography of Cuencame, Durango, Mexico, 1890–1930." Unpublished manuscript.

Wray, John Stefan. "The Drug War and Information Warfare in Mexico." M.A. thesis, University of Texas, Austin, 1997.

Documents

Acosta, Francis J. The Acosta Directory of the English Speaking Residents of the Republic of Mexico for 1910. Mexico City: F. J. Acosta, 1910.

Anglo American Directory of Mexico, 1946–. Mexico City: Excelsior, 1946–.

Los archivos regionales y el trabajo en equipo. Durango: Universidad Juárez del Estado de Durango, 1989.

Claims of Citizens of the U.S. on Mexico: Message from the President of the United States. Washington, D.C.: Department of State, 1842.

Committee on Appropriations. Relief of American Citizens in Mexico: Hearing *before the Subcommittee on the House Committee on Appropriations.* Washington, D.C.: Government Printing Office, 1916.

Correspondencia de la Legación Mexicana en Washington durante la Intervención Extranjera, 1860–1868. Colección de documentos para formar la historia de la Intervención. 7 vols. Mexico City: Imprenta del Gobierno, 1870.

Correspondencia Diplomatica Relativa a las Invasiones del Territorio Mexicano por Fuerzas de los Estados Unidos, 1873–1877. Mexico City: Imprenta Ignacio Cumplido, 1878.

Daily Consular and Trade Reports, Bureau of Manufactures, Department of Commerce and Labor, Washington, D.C.

Diario de los Debates del Congreso Constituyente, Tomos 1 and 2, Mexico City, 1922.

Diplomatic and Consular Reports, Numbered File 1906–1910.

Exposición de la secretaria de hacienda de los Estados Unidos Mexicanos de 15 de enero de 1879 sobre la condición actual de México. Mexico City: Imprenta del Gobierno, 1879.

Fall Committee Reports, Investigation of Mexican Affairs: Preliminary Reports and Surveys, 66th Congress, 2d session. Washington, D.C.: Government Printing Office, 1921.

In the Matter of the Claim of the Tehuantepec Ship Canal and Mexican and Pacific Railroad Company. New York: Evening Post, 1869.

Malloy, William M. *Treaties, Conventions, International Acts, Protocols, and Agreements between the United States of America and Other Powers, 1776–1909.* 2 vols. Senate document, 61st Congress, 2d session, no. 357. Washington, D.C., 1910.

"New Directions in United States–Mexican Transboundary Environmental Management: A Critique of Current Proposals." Reprint from the *Natural Resources Journal,* n.d.

Partnerships for Global Ecosystem Management: Science, Economics, and Law. Proceedings of the Fifth International Conference on Environmentally Sustainable Development, October 1997. Washington, D.C.: World Bank, 1999.

Pilcher, Jeffrey. "The Rockefeller Foundation and Mexico's National Cuisine." Research report from The Rockefeller Foundation, 1996.

Reclamaciones Internacionales de México y contra México sometidos a Arbitraje. Mexico City: Imprenta Francisco Díaz de León, 1873.

Robles Gil, Alberto (Secretario de Fomento). *Memoria de fomento, 1911–1912.* Mexico City: Imprenta del Gobierno, 1912.

Senate Select Committee on Mexican Claims. *Memoranda of four claims against Mexico.* Washington, D.C.: Buell and Blanchard, 1853.

Statistical Abstract of the United States. Washington, D.C.: U.S. Census Bureau, 1999.

United States and Mexican Claims Commission. *Benjamin Weil contra México.* Washington, D.C.(?): n.p., 1877.

———. *Claims on the Part of Citizens of the United States and Mexico under* the *Convention of July 4, 1868, between the United States and Mexico.* Washington, D.C.: n.p., 1877.

———. *Collection of Claims against Mexican Government brought by individual American Citizens.* Washington, D.C.(?): n.p., 18??

———. *Memoirs of Claimants.* Washington, D.C.(?): n.p., n.d.

World Bank. *World Bank Development Report.* Washington, D.C.: World Bank, 1997.

Index

Compositor:	Integrated Composition Systems, Inc.
Text:	10/13 Aldus
Display:	Aldus
Printer and Binder:	Edwards Brothers, Inc.